D1276429

CHARLES DREKMEIER

KINGSHIP
AND COMMUNITY
IN EARLY INDIA

STANFORD UNIVERSITY PRESS

STANFORD, CALIFORNIA

1962

915.4
D771k

Stanford University Press
Stanford, California

© 1962 by the Board of Trustees of the
Leland Stanford Junior University

All rights reserved

Library of Congress Catalog Card Number: 62-9565

Printed in the United States of America

ERRATA

p. 106, line 4. Line should read "authority free of the interference of priests. They strengthened the"

p. 129, line 2. Line should read "age of imperial expansion
dating from the rise of Magadha and extending"

p. 137, line 7. For *"mātsya-nyāna"* read *"mātsya-nyāya"*

p. 153, note *k*, line 1. For "Sankya" read "Sankhya"

p. 158, note *q*. For "369f." read "167f."

p. 192, last line of text. For "third" read "fourth"

p. 346, line 3. For "Taylor" read "Tylor"; for "436" read
"439"

Drekmeier, *Kingship and Community
in Early India*

For my parents

METHODIST COLLEGE LIBRARY
Fayetteville, N. C.   34117

METHODIST COLLEGE LIBRARY
Fayetteville, N. C.

PREFACE

I suppose that the reasons one gives for writing a book rarely do justice to the assortment of personal enthusiasms and prejudices, convictions and compulsions that surely enter into such an undertaking. Candor perhaps serves no more than the therapeutic needs of authors, but in the case of this book I feel impelled to say more than the usual things about the importance of a concern with the issues of political philosophy, a concern that was the germ of my own interest in Indian concepts of government, law, and society. I must admit, however, that this study has not led me into professional Indological pursuits, and I can make no claim to the easy familiarity with the ancient languages that some readers will insist is the only valid passport to the India of the Vedic warrior, the Buddhist monk, and the introspective emperor. This book is intended not primarily for specialists in the field of early Indian thought, but for the increasing number of persons whose attention has been drawn to the emerging nations of our world and whose curiosity has nourished the desire to know something about backgrounds, and for those students of political theory and the history of political ideas who wish to understand more about the nature of myth or about what happened at the other end of human time— or who believe (as I do) that political theory shades imperceptibly into what is sometimes described as political sociology and who would respond to the kind of treatment I have here attempted. I should like to think that the contemporary interest in the formal and historical sociology of Max Weber (who, in the words of Raymond Aron, both separated and united politics and science) will not only direct more thought to the study of the forms that the myth of authority may assume and reawaken a sensitivity to the importance of history in the study of social values and institutions, but will inspire a literature of humane scholarship that veers away from the self-conscious absorption in who and what we are as social scientists, while preserving the status of theory—both descriptive and prescriptive.

I am aware that many will argue, with considerable justification, that most political theorists are really historians. On this point I believe it will be sufficient to suggest that political theory is one of several marches of political science where the discipline merges with other areas of learning ; the problem is not that political theorists are historians or philosophers but that they often disregard the contributions that the behavioral sciences are able to make to their field and take the sort of defensive posture that can only invite the aggression of those weary of the usual preoccupations of political philosophers. As for history, I think it can be argued that in revealing the limitations of any single system of political and social speculation, in making us mindful of the changing role of philosophic ideas and deepening our perception of the relation of ideas to economic interests and social institutions (as well as the relation of ideas to one another), and in alerting us to the shortcomings of those techniques of social science which disguise or discount the dynamic nature of social phenomena, the study of history is unavoidable in the analysis of ideas and ideologies. In our search for new answers we sometimes forget the old questions, or fail to see alternative ways of posing the questions. A knowledge of other ages, like a knowledge of other cultures, takes us far enough outside our own time and place to provide the necessary perspective on ourselves, while simultaneously returning us to the perennial problems of social order and to fundamental principles that are easily obscured by the immediacy and urgency of events.

This book concentrates on the values that legitimized or disguised the use of power in ancient India, the manner in which these values were symbolized, the various attitudes toward political life and the different ways of thinking about questions of justice and freedom, the methods employed by those in positions of authority in resolving conflict and creating consensus, the ways action was explained and made consistent with religious values and the requirements of society, the concept of community itself and what man conceived his relation to his fellow men to be, and the effect of organization on political ideals. Essentially this is the story of the ancient heroic ideal, and of the norms of conduct that replaced it. A major problem in an investigation of this kind is the reconstruction of popular culture as well as the proper interpretation of the records left to us by the more articulate stratum of society. In this study I have enlisted the aid of psychology and the social sciences in an attempt to indicate something about the nonrational and symbolic experience of a civilization emerging from a tribal culture and experimenting with several forms of social coordination. This approach may not find favor with Sanskritists and Indologists; but taking heart from such studies as those of E. R. Dodds and F. M. Cornford (writing of Homeric and classical cultures) and, to cite only the most recent, the Cambridge ethnographer Edmund Leach ("Pulleyar and the Lord Buddha," *Psychoanalysis and Psychoanalytic Review*, Vol. 49, No. 2), I am prepared to support the contention of Professor Dodds that if we would get beyond the mere description of events and external behavior we must use what light is available to us, and that a diffused or unsteady light is superior to none at all.

It may appear that on occasion I have dodged technical problems or offered too generous a choice of interpretations, or even swept an inopportune question under the nearest palm leaf. In defense I can only say that I have tried to keep the text as free of involutions and arbitrariness as is within my power and consistent with the aims of the book.

There is an extensive technical literature dealing at least obliquely with the documents and phases of Indian social and intellectual history that concern us here, but much of it presupposes a sophisticated knowledge of Vedic and Hindu culture. Unfortunately this literature is not always readily available in Europe and America, though the notes and footnotes to the present volume should introduce the reader to a sufficient number of secondary sources to enable him to pursue further any problem that is of particular interest to him. Basham, Renou, and others have provided general studies of Indian religion and civilization that may be consulted for a more complete picture of the context in which political and social ideas developed. Indian religion is an exceedingly complex subject, but one that cannot be avoided in a work of this sort. I know that there are readers who will take issue with certain characterizations (particularly in this area) that may seem casual or misleading, or perhaps not sufficiently abreast of current scholarship (my reference to "renascent" Brahmanism may be a case in point). Here I ask only that it be kept in mind that my intention has been to provide no more than a backdrop for the more strictly social commentary and that the terms I have used must sometimes be understood in accordance with this purpose. I trust that my departure from standard orthography will make this book more appealing to the general reader, and that I have not lost ground thus gained by employing too much of the private language of the less modest social sciences.

The impression of a mindless, jewel-bedecked despotism colors the picture of the ancient East in many Western minds. This book is intended to correct that image. Historians have generally discounted the political fertility of the Orient and turned to the Greek city-state for the origins of speculation on government and public life. But there are probably few today who would say with Gibbon that "all Oriental history is one unceasing round of valor, greatness, degeneracy and decay." For we are discovering that the subject is neither that romantic, nor that futile.

This study grew out of a project designed to interest the Fulbright Selection Board in sending me to India, a country that has long fascinated me. I wish to thank those who made possible a year of study in India, and to express my appreciation to the many Indian scholars and friends who were helpful in steering me down the right paths in that first stage of research. A version of this study was submitted as a dissertation to Harvard University several years ago and was read by my major professors, Carl J. Friedrich and Talcott Parsons, as well as by Daniel H. H. Ingalls of the Department of Sanskrit and Indian Studies, and I thank them here for their assistance. I wish also to acknowledge my debts to teachers who, though not involved in this book, have provided me with a standard of teaching and scholarship: Professors Merle Curti and Hans Gerth of the University of Wisconsin; Professors Robert MacIver, Harry Carman, and the late Franz Neumann of Columbia; Professors Louis Hartz and David Owen of Harvard and Professor A. P. D'Entrèves. Miss Elaine Lasky escorted this manuscript through the press with agility and a gentle toleration of its author's vagaries. Finally, there is my wife Margot, who suffered (not always in silence) for many long hours over typewriter, footnotes, and index cards, but who could always be relied on for the heartening word that arms against despair.

C. D.

Palo Alto, California
August 1962

ACKNOWLEDGMENTS

I acknowledge with thanks permission granted by the following copyright holders to quote from the following sources: The Bangalore Press, publishers of *Hindu Polity* by K. P. Jayaswal; Robert N. Bellah, author of "Some Suggestions for the Systematic Study of Religion" (unpublished ms. 1955); S. K. Belvalkar, coauthor (with R. D. Ranade), *History of Indian Philosophy* (Vol. II); The Bollingen Foundation, publishers of *The Myth of the Eternal Return* by Mircea Eliade, and *Philosophies of India* by Heinrich Zimmer; George Braziller, Inc., publishers of *Symbolism in Religion and Literature*, edited by Rollo May; Oliver Cromwell Cox, author of *Caste, Class and Race*; Doubleday and Company, Inc., publishers of *Mythologies of the Ancient World*, edited by Samuel N. Kramer, for permission to quote from "Mythology of India" by W. Norman Brown; Edward Arnold, Ltd., publishers of *From Religion to Philosophy* by F. M. Cornford; The Free Press of Glencoe, Inc., publishers of *Man and the Sacred* by Roger Caillois; George Allen and Unwin, Ltd., publishers of *The Essentials of Indian Philosophy* by M. Hiriyanna, *The Hindu View of Life* by S. Radhakrishnan, and Radhakrishnan's edition of *The Bhagavadgītā*; Harper and Brothers, publishers of *Tomorrow and Tomorrow and Tomorrow* by Aldous Huxley, and *The Soul of India* by Amaury de Riencourt; Little, Brown and Company, publishers of *Politics and Vision* by Sheldon S. Wolin; Motilal Banarsidass (Delhi), publishers of *Aspects of Political Ideas and Institutions in Ancient India* by R. S. Sharma; Oxford University Press, publishers of *African Political Systems*, edited by Meyer Fortes and E. E. Evans-Pritchard; Philosophical Library, publishers of *Hinduism and Buddhism* by Ananda Coomaraswamy; Popular Book Depot (Bombay), publishers of *Introduction to the Study of Indian History* by D. D. Kosambi; University of California Press, publishers of *The Greeks and the Irrational* by E. R. Dodds; The University of Chicago Press, publishers of *Meaning in History* by Karl Löwith.

CONTENTS

KINGSHIP AND COMMUNITY
IN EARLY INDIA

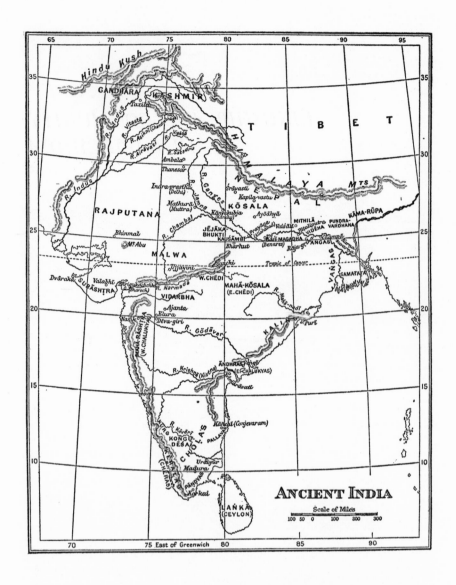

ANCIENT INDIA

Scale of Miles
100 50 0   100   200   300

1 ⋊ THE STUDY OF INDIAN POLITY

At different stages in its development, Christianity had challenged the forces of traditionalism from a perspective that transcended history. But by the seventeenth century, with the voyages of discovery and exploration, a new Archimedean point from which human societies could be judged, a perspective within history itself, had emerged. Toward the end of the century, a number of European intellectuals undertook to remind their fellow citizens that Europe had no monopoly on the truth. The reading public was introduced to the idea of culture, of worlds within the world. For a time the wise Egyptian captured popular interest; then attention turned to Persia as Chardin recounted his travels in that exotic land and Montesquieu viewed the institutions of his time through Persian eyes. The European imagination was fired in turn by Siam, China, the dignity of the Arab, and the nobility of the savage.

Accounts of strange lands and peoples were an effective device for holding a mirror to the social and political conditions in the states of Western Europe. In fact, they were more successful as critiques of European institutions and traditions than they were in revealing the nature of Oriental and primitive societies. It was often difficult to recognize where the descriptions left off and the utopias began.

This fascination with the exotic gradually gave way to the allures of science and progress and the vision of a society that would distribute its benefits more widely. By the nineteenth century, when the Orient was again contrasted with Europe—this time with a Europe moving toward enlightenment and prosperity—Asia no longer held the advantage. Peoples once admired for their sanity and sophistication were now held up as examples of decadence. The non-European world, the nonscientific world, had no lessons worth the listening. To Macaulay the whole literature of India was not worth a shelf of European books.

But some of Macaulay's contemporaries, scholars and artists under the spell of romanticism and idealist philosophy, were beginning to question the wisdom of his view. German romanticism had revealed what Mircea Eliade calls "the charm of the primordial image"; and, with the development of comparative philology and the discovery of the common origin of Greek and Sanskrit, Hegel was moved to remark that a world had been discovered. Before the century was over, a more systematic approach to the symbolism of mythology and the emergence of disciplines of objective social and cultural analysis gave a new respectability to Indic studies.

A knowledge of primitive cultures and ancient civilizations is of particular value in focusing our attention on the significance of myth in giving purpose and meaning to life, in explaining the fact of death and catastrophe, and in holding groups of men together. Myth tells men how they are to live in order to achieve the goals of their lives, and it tells them what their relationship to other men is to be. In the pages that follow, we shall encounter several forms of this myth of authority, ideas that had been elaborated in India by the third century B.C.

We find ourselves today in a world of newly independent nations, many of them little more than communities of clans and tribes. Even for the most communal of these societies custom is no longer able to provide a sufficient guide to conduct, and new types of regulation must replace the weakened voices of tradition and habit. In these infant states processes are at work that resemble those which concern us in this study.

A principal obstacle in an undertaking of this kind is the scarcity of materials necessary to establish the relationship of changes in social and economic organization to changes in the belief system. Consequently, monographs are often limited to descriptions of the sequence of beliefs— as though one idea simply gave birth to another. The decline of tribal culture and the emergence of an agricultural economy clearly influenced the evolution of political forms; but generally speaking, changes in modes of production and technology exerted less influence on political thought than did religious ideas, and far less than comparable social changes have exerted on modern political thought. It has been argued, in a well-known study of primitive political systems, that "the material interests that actuate individuals or groups in an African society operate in the frame of a body of interconnected moral and legal norms the order and stability of which is maintained by the political organization."[1] This statement is as appropriate to ancient India as it is to tribal Africa. It suggests the importance of the normative context in which social action takes place, but, as we shall see, it disguises certain problems.

The approach of social theorists such as Max Weber and Talcott Parsons, who recognize the power of social norms in regulating conduct, is often more valid in the study of ancient ideas and values than is the sociological model that stresses the direct power relationship and describes society simply in terms of coercion of some men by others. Karl Wittfogel has given us a study of the centralized, despotic government—which he sees as the all-important fact of Oriental "hydraulic" social systems.[2] In these states there are no other centers of power capable of challenging the bureaucracy. Coercion models, such as Wittfogel's, reveal very little about the interrelationships of social institutions and discount the role of consensus in holding a society together, but their greater attention to sources

---

[1] Numbered notes (primarily source citations) will be found at the back of the book, on pages 321–39.

of conflict may (as in the Marxian theory) indicate more about the dynamic processes at work in society than theories that stress values and integration.

Although few religions can equal Brahmanism in providing a rationale for gross social inequities, social institutions in ancient India did not function without producing antagonisms. The norms of society are not a seamless web; there may be serious incongruities between the directing values of a culture and the institutional forms these values take. The concept of a sacred order of things does not necessarily preclude a sense of the duality of politics and ethics. And although we tend to assume a high degree of cohesion in a ruling class, there is often dissension within the ranks of elite groups. Power is not always integrative nor does it always serve collective goals, and power is not always power over others in the struggle for scarce values. To understand power only in this last sense is to make Wittfogel's mistake, namely, to overlook the dependence of the ruler on different groups and institutions within the community.[3] But to deny the fact that power may become an end in itself would be to deny the subject of this study. Neither a consensus nor a coercion theory is sufficient in itself. The work of Max Weber (himself a student of Oriental cultures) suggests possibilities for relating the two images of society.

Weber did not seek to refute Marx, but only to demonstrate that although economic factors may indeed be the single most powerful conditioning element in society, taken alone they were not sufficient to explain why a society should organize productive relationships in certain ways. To Marx's question "Why does the history of the East *appear* as a history of religions?"[4] Weber might have answered that the appearance is not to be discounted, that a knowledge of Asian societies presupposes an appreciation of the coordinating function of religion. But religious belief could take a variety of forms and, for Weber, these differences were related to the class situation of those who create or receive the particular belief. Although the socio-economic order influences the ethic, religion was not seen as a class ideology.[5] And class itself was now defined in terms of life-style and sentiments of honor. The Marxian argument has been modified in many respects, but Weber's basic approach retains many similarities to historical materialism—particularly in the significance he attaches to class interest. The expression of these interests is always influenced by the cultural values of the individual. Weber believed that the one thing we can be certain of is that men *do* hold ethical and cultural values. He is, however, more convinced of the inner logic of the Indian belief system than the facts warrant. And he often leaves one wishing for further clarification of the conditions most conducive to the emergence of the charismatic ideas that are central to his argument.

Weber's sociological point of departure is the conviction that the social scientist must concern himself with the subjective meaning of actions. ("Meaning," as he understands it, is the consciously perceived relation between means and ends.) Behavior, particularly *inter*action of people, must be understood not merely in terms of its social function, but also in terms of the significance the actor attaches to his actions and to the way these actions are organized into institutions. What are the norms of the society, the values that integrate and legitimate actions, organize interests and provide the basis of an interpretation of the world, and establish alternative modes of conduct? These values must be understood if we are to establish standards of reasonable behavior.

Wilhelm Dilthey had argued that if we are to understand, we must enter the spiritual world of those we seek to know; we must grasp the fundamental psychological structure to which the symbols of a culture are related. No such task is attempted here. We seek only to suggest certain broad limits of ancient Indian thought—and always, necessarily, that of the more articulate aristocratic culture. What can we really know of the humble soul worshiping at the shrine of Shiva, let alone of the world-view of a Vedic warrior? We shall confront types of experience that are foreign to anything we have known. The structure as well as the categories of thought are in some measure dependent on their social context.

Even if this insight were possible, it would verify nothing. Nor would it be enough to try to determine the intentions of the actor without also determining the nature of the social structure and the way social relationships affect behavior. Nonetheless, knowledge inevitably must draw on whatever experiences of our own are apposite.[6] We can never completely escape the method of empathetic understanding if we wish to do more than observe the externals of action.[7] This fact must not be permitted to lend support to the old argument that history is concerned with unique events. No less than the scientist, the historian relies on general concepts in which events are related in patterns. We usually are not completely conscious of these regularities implied in our explanations.

In examining any Oriental subject, we of necessity find ourselves working within the conceptual framework of our own culture. In some cases it may be instructive to turn to the West for examples, to suggest a parallel, or to point a moral. The images and constructions we use will fit only imperfectly. For even the concept of the state (as we know it) has no exact counterpart in Indian political development. And the political function is not always readily distinguished from other social functions.[8]

Although the polity of ancient India provides many striking contrasts with the political structures of the West, it has its familiar aspects as well. There is, in fact, the danger that we may recognize too much; that we may perversely read the present into the past or equate ideas that are only superficially alike. Excellent scholars have succumbed to this temptation; an instance is Sir Henry Maine's treatment of Hindu jurisprudence. Without appreciation of these dangers, comparison of Indian and European political and legal institutions and values can be more misleading than illuminating.

An unfortunate feature of a good deal of the interpretation of Hindu political thought has been the willingness of Indian scholars, trained in Western history, to force an equation of Hindu and Western theoretical concepts. Often a certain similarity does exist, but the Western concept is allowed to shape the Indian situation. A case in point is the idea of the divine right of kings : the Hindu monarch never dreamed of such sweeping immunities as those claimed by the Stuart kings.

Some recent scholars have apparently been motivated by the desire to find in Indian political history a democratic tradition that could be exploited for purposes of nation-building. Of these attempts to discover modern ideals in the theory and structure of an ancient polity, Professor Nilakanta Sastri has remarked :

> To import the associations of democracy to the interpretation of early Indian records, because some of them happen to mention elections and ballot, is unconsciously to raise fresh obstacles in the way of a correct understanding of the atmosphere surrounding the working of these and other institutions in ancient India. By stressing the committee-system, the elections to the committees, and the employment of ballot in the elections, and then almost ignoring the whole complex of notions associated with caste, custom and religion which dominated social life in those times, one may find it easy to paint the picture of a society in which people cared much for political rights and representative institutions and regulated their daily conduct almost entirely on secular and rational considerations. But it seems hardly worth while to make the attempt; for the doubtful satisfaction that may be derived from claiming modern wisdom for our ancestors is purchased at the cost of any chance of our knowing them as they were.[9]

A final problem arises from the paucity of historical documentation, especially for the Vedic period. There is nothing comparable in detail to the early Anglo-Saxon charters and laws. Statements from ancient Hindu treatises can rarely be taken as simple declarations of historical facts, and the use of such materials accordingly requires much caution if we are not to be as wide of the mark as a historian would be who sought to re-create the English political scene on the basis of the *Policraticus* or the *Oceana*. But considerable ingenuity has gone into textual analysis and into comparison and substantiation based on epigraphical and other sources, slim as such evidence is. Since we are concerned primarily with political thought, the sacred texts are of course suggestive in ways they often cannot be in strict political history.

The few authentic works on law and polity that we have point to the existence of a great literature as yet unearthed. The central treatise, the *Arthashastra (Arthaśāstra)* of Kauṭalya, was not discovered until the early years of this century, and there is still no final agreement on its authorship or the date of its composition. Kautalya may not have been India's greatest political mind, but he is at least accessible and his peers— if any—are not. The *Shukranitisara (Śukranītisāra)*, which caused considerable excitement at the time of its discovery, is possibly a nineteenth-century forgery. Dependable material on Tamil polity takes us no further into the past than the closing years of the pre-Christian era, although southern political institutions probably antedate those of the north. Finally, most of our sources are compilations of earlier writings; none of the *puranas (purāṇas)*, epics, or law books are available in their original form, and it is likely that the *Arthashastra* also contains later interpolations.

Our study focuses on the ideas and doctrines that influenced the governing elites. We could wish to know more about their popular acceptance, but we cannot. Our emphasis will in any event be on theoretical considerations. These ideas will be examined in their institutional context. And here we have the record that coins, inscriptions, and occasional foreign commentary (particularly Greek and Chinese) contribute. Mauryan administrative systems will receive the greater attention that the relative wealth of such records allows and the importance of these structures demands.

A central theme of Indian political speculation is the relationship between brahman legitimation and kshatriya authority.[a] We shall attempt to show, by referring to the sacred literature and secular arthashastra texts, how this relationship was interpreted by brahman authorities, as well as how power was actually exercised. Ancient Indian political thought emerged in the context of the most conservative large-scale society history has witnessed, a society Max Weber pictured as the one logically consistent expression of the organic conception of community. Hindu social theory, as he observes, "furnished no principles for an ethical universalism which would raise general demands for life in the world." We find instead "a metaphysically and cosmologically substructured technology of the means to achieve salvation from this world."[10]

And yet, despite this dominance of religion, ancient India did produce a sizable body of political literature. It is almost wholly brahman. Political ideas in the West have frequently come from new classes asserting their claim to a more equitable share of social opportunity; in India, by contrast, the impetus to political thought was almost invariably conservative. When heterodoxy attempted to replace the detailed prescriptions and proscriptions of human conduct with general ethical principles or mystical withdrawal, or when kings sought to make political authority self-legitimating, the brahmans were forced into the ideological arena. As interpreters of the sacred code by which social roles and institutions were justified, the brahmans were forced to rationalize their privileged position. When their qualifications were contested by Buddhism and other heterodoxies, the brahman priests were pressed into a closer alliance with the political authority and the state became, in effect, the guarantor of religion. For with the possibility of new bases of legitimation the brahmans were confronted with the alternatives of making concessions to the king or losing their status.

In the evolution of Brahmanic authority, we witness first the priests' attempt to transform the Vedic sacrifice into a theological system beyond the reach of ordinary men. For centuries the brahman was successful in securing his power by his magical control of the ritual. Then came the era of the great heterodox systems, whose challenge impelled the broadening

---

[a] I have chosen not to capitalize the names of the major social groupings, in order to avoid confusions resulting from the several uses of the word brahman. (*Vide* pp. 80ff. below.) The brahmans (*brāhmaṇas*) were the repository of religious authority; the kshatriya (*kṣatriya*) nobility was the guardian of the secular power.

of Brahmanism into a way of life more closely related to the everyday needs of the people. In this exoteric form, renascent Brahmanism (Hinduism) was able to preserve its authoritative role. But Brahmanism had never actually been confronted with an ideology that admitted the wisdom, or even the possibility, of changing the world.

Despite the popularization of Brahmanism, it remained unchanged in one important aspect: the value attached to rigorous training of the mind and spirit through asceticism and meditation. This discipline makes demands on men that only a few can meet; its goal is an experience that is not directly communicable and which, because it teaches that the truth cannot be found in the things of this world, can never be achieved through direct empirical knowledge. Such awareness demarcates the religious life of the virtuoso from that of the mass of men. Although the gnosis of Buddhism was not the same as the abstruse technical knowledge of the brahman priest who officiated at the sacrifice, the mystical devaluation of the temporal and material continued to be the means of salvation.

Buddhism introduced into Indian religious speculation a rational ethic which, because of its logical clarity and consistency, contained at least the potential for effecting change in the social structure. But the Buddhist conception of Nirvana is fundamentally a turning from the world, a liberation from the suffering the world imposes. This goal could be attained without any significant alteration of social institutions; it called only for withdrawal and renunciation. And though capacity had replaced birth as the prerequisite of this training, the rigorous discipline of mind and body limited the mystical experience to the few.

In the Brahmanic revival of the last centuries of the pre-Christian era performance of caste roles was made the qualifying condition for the mystic gnosis. The moment of salvation through union with the impersonal and diffuse supernatural power must usually have seemed remote to the Hindu, but this does not justify Weber's argument that the masses were left in undisturbed magical bondage and that techniques of self-discipline lay removed from their interests and practical behavior.[11] Such an argument overlooks the many forms of religious expression and discipline that find justification within the system. Weber argues further that practical ethical and economic questions were of little interest to the Asian intelligentsia; this, too, must be qualified. There is an impressive body of Sanskrit literature devoted to such considerations, and of course the ruling elite and the priests could not afford to ignore immediate problems of government. Even in the brahman sources expediency appears in surprisingly modern garb as the basis of policy.

In European theory the political has traditionally been viewed as that which is shared by the people as a whole; society is commonly understood as an arena of competing interests seeking to influence the formation of public policy. In ancient India, the political was thought to be the province of one particular segment of society—a society broken into castes, for whom the idea of political competition would have been unthinkable. Indian political philosophy is preoccupied with the problem of order; it is a philosophy of caution, a warning against the unfortunate consequences of any disturbance of tradition and the institutions in which it was embodied. Often this warning involves more than denouncing heterodoxy or championing the established order. It may offer positive recommendations for action to safeguard the customary patterns of human affairs and aid men in the attainment of security and salvation. Or it may prescribe what amounts to an alternative to social life—a turning from the realm of sense experience to that of pure contemplation.

Fundamental to Indian religion is the concept of *dharma*. The word derives from *dhri* (*dhṛ*), to hold, to maintain, to treasure. By the time of the ritual texts known as the Brahmanas (*Brāhmaṇas*), dharma had replaced the earlier Vedic term *rita* (*ṛta*), which means "setting in motion" and refers to the principle of the universe that established the patterns and processes that regulate all things.*b* The conception of dharma includes a theory of the place of power in the cosmic order, and this in turn introduces the all-important role of the sacrifice—the bond between man and the gods.

> Forces of expansion and release were present, however, tendencies conducive to the ordered arrangement and setting in motion of the parts of the universe, but their activity was insufficient to overcome inertia. There was a deadlock until power was generated of heaven and earth. . . . The parts of the cosmos were now put into order or harmony and set in motion, to run like a machine. All, however, remained subject to power. Continued harmonious operation of the cosmic machine depended upon the performance of the sacrifice by men and gods in collaboration, each strengthening the other.[12]

In this same period dharma seems to have acquired two interpretations, related but distinguishable. It came to imply virtue, the moral duty, and it came to refer to the performance of caste function, the social duty.*c* These two meanings persist in later literature.

Dharma defies exact rendering in English; it has been compared to everything from Aristotle's "efficient cause" to Godwin's "political justice." All things have a dharma—the principle of their being and their harmony with truth. It is the eternal and necessary moral law, the code of righteousness; the term is used to denote both truth and righteous conduct.*d* The point has been made[13] that the dilemma of determinism versus free will, instinct versus reason, nature versus man, becomes meaningless when the same concept is used for both the totality of rules and duties and for truth, for both the natural and the moral. In short, dharma stands for

---

b The term *rita* is closely related to the Persian *asha,* and it would appear probable that the concept has its historical source in the age before the separation of Indian and Iranian peoples. The Brahmanas are discussed in Chapter 3.

c P. V. Kane ([208], I, pp. 1f.) demonstrates how the term went through a gradual evolution in meaning until, by the Upanishads, it had come to signify "the privileges, duties and obligations of a man, his standard of conduct as a member of the Aryan community, as a member of one of the castes, as a person in a particular stage of life."

d On the variety of meanings in the *Rigveda* alone, *vide Rigveda* III, 17.1; VII, 89.5; X, 56.3.

a manner of life, the whole duty of man in relation to the general moral, material, and intellectual purposes of life.

Dharma was frequently interpreted as that which possessed the authority of the Vedas or the commentaries on the Vedas, and it had its example in the virtuous conduct of those who knew the Vedas. Later the idea developed that when dharma fades it is made known anew by the appearance of inspired persons (*avatāras*). Some non-Indian religious systems, such as Christianity (*Khrista-dharma*), are considered tribal dharmas. Every study of dharma is complicated by the varying senses in which the word is used. Because it is taken to mean custom, obligation, sacred law, justice, and the norm of conduct—and is thus a category of theology, of ethics, and of law—the state in promoting dharma becomes a justice-dispensing and duty-enforcing institution as well as the guarantor of religion.[14]

The dharma of an individual, swadharma (*svadharma*), may recall the Platonic theory of justice[15] or Aristotle's definition of nature: "What each thing is when at its best, that we call its nature." It concerns essential function or purpose. The accomplishment of one's duty is an individual's highest achievement: in the famous words of the *Bhagavad Gītā*, "One's own duty, though imperfectly performed, is superior to another's duty ably accomplished."[16]

The preservation of dharma was the major obligation of the state. This is why Hindu political theory was essentially static, and this is also why any treatment of the subject will seem to flow into economics, sociology, epistemology, and metaphysics. Religious and political ideas are often juxtaposed. The gods, for example, were frequently credited with the authorship of ideas on government—a practice that indicates not only a desire for the prestige of traditional and divine personages, but also the very gradual evolution of ideas, the loss (through oral communication) of definite knowledge, and presumably in some cases the desire for anonymity. Life was a prelude to a greater experience, and most Hindu political thought, at least before the *Arthashastra,* bears a resemblance in general tone to Western medieval political theory.

Dharma expresses individual caste obligations, and the state, in committing itself to the maintenance of dharma, is thus only indirectly concerned with the achievement of a unifying common purpose. Essentially, as with the economic concept of the "invisible hand," the pursuit of the individual's interest is seen as resulting in the greater good of the community.[e] Differentiating as it does between the inherent worth of individuals, dharma precludes that equality in civil rights essential to a spirit of citizen participation, and tends to exalt the status quo.

One critic has remarked:

The conception of dharma has been taken to sanctify the existing social order with all the iniquity that is implied in the hierarchical arrange-

---

[e] Because the castes were governed by their own customs as well as by sacred law, there were frequent opportunities for laws to be at variance with one another. In instances of such conflicts and confusions, the king or the brahman was considered to be the appropriate arbiter (depending on the nature of the conflict).

ment. . . . Instead of making an attempt to actualize the ideal and translate the ideal in institutional terms, the actual has been idealized. Such an attitude makes inevitably for conservatism and kills the spirit of critical examination. There is to be no analysis of the very foundations of the social order. By connecting the state with dharma, the distinction between the actual and the ideal is ignored: and the state is placed beyond the range of criticism.[17]

Rangaswami Aiyangar provides a more generous, somewhat Aristotelian, analysis: "Innate quality and potentiality are related; so dharma is taken to be the mean between the ideal and the possible. . . . Whatever is enjoined by authority or the inward promptings of conscience is dharma and comes within the scope of Dharmashastra."[1] As a working definition in these pages, we shall content ourselves with Edgerton's more neutral interpretation. "Dharma is propriety, socially approved conduct, in relation to one's fellow men or to other living beings (animals or superhuman powers). Law, social usage, morality, and most of what we ordinarily mean by religion, all fall under this head."[18]

Law is thus ultimately god-given and removed from popular interpretation and appeal. The priests were its custodians; their exclusive access to the sacred learning of the past and their role as teachers consolidated this control. Dharma stood above the king, and his failure to preserve it must accordingly have disastrous consequences. Such neglect or misconduct called for the king and his ministers to make compensation and do penance. The ruler who abused the power of sanction and coercion (*danda*) was warned that he might find himself its first victim. Power must be employed impartially (impartially, that is, with reference to caste dharma) and in accord with higher law; failure to enforce the code would transfer guilt to the ruler, and the violation of dharma in some texts appears to justify revolt against authority. Danda was a two-edged sword.

It is the function of danda to ensure compliance with dharma; though dharma depends on danda, dharma is the higher power. Hindu political thought never escapes from this dilemma of royal power and priestly authority.[19] The *rajadharma,* the dharma of the king, exists as guarantor of the whole social structure. Danda is thus the means, dharma the end. The political power must ensure each man the broad opportunity to fulfill the conditions of his swadharma without interference. In the writings on dharma—the Dharmasutras and Dharmashastras—the dharma of the king is treated as the capstone of the dharma of other social groups. But in this emphasis on the role of punishment in maintaining order, some statements of the interdependence of dharma and danda come dangerously close to identifying the legal and the moral, to assuming (at least for the lower strata of society) that moral behavior is possible only through coercion and conformity. In this view there can be no real moral choice on the part of the masses, and fear of punishment replaces positive allegiance to dharma.

The *Mahābhārata* and the *Manusmriti* declare that society is regu-

---

[1] Rangaswami Aiyangar [349], pp. 25f. Dharmashastra refers to the brahmanical legal literature, the interpretation of the dharmic code.

lated by the ability of the king to punish. "It is danda that rules the subjects, it is danda that protects all. It is danda that keeps awake and guards the people when they sleep." And because there can be no dharma without the coercive power, "the learned style danda itself as dharma."[20] Behind the concept lies the belief that evil is inherent in man, that only the fear of danda makes men righteous. This view postulates a state of nature (*māt-syanyāya*) not essentially different from that of Hobbes and Spinoza, in which a strong authority is required to impose restraints on the natural appetites of the people. The state without sanctions is no state at all. The alternative to danda is the law of the jungle—or, to use the image beloved of brahman theorists, of the sea : the strong would devour the weak "like fishes in water."

Of the two major parts of this book, the first is primarily concerned with religion and philosophy, the second with social and political theory. Chapters 3 and 4 are devoted to a discussion of Brahmanism. Chapter 5 treats of caste and its justification; Chapters 6 and 7 deal, respectively, with the heterodox reaction to brahman myth and with the renascent Brahmanism, or Hinduism, which survives to our own day. This analysis enables us to discern both the bases of early Indian political authority and the nature of the dualism that pervaded the symbolism and structure of the social thought of the time.

Chapters 8 and 9 introduce the social thought of the *Mahabharata* and distinguish the theory of action of the *Gita* from that of Kautalya, the brahman architect of the imperial state. The description in Chapter 10 of the two great empires of ancient India is followed by a discussion of Kautalya's *Arthashastra* in Chapters 11 and 12. This part concludes with a commentary on minor secular treatises and the canonical law books.

The literature on polity is usually termed arthashastra or nitishastra. Arthashastra has a broader significance than most of the political terms employed by Hindu writers and comprehends both politics and economics (*daṇḍanīti* and *vārttā*) : material gain is its subject. It is one of the thirty-two "sciences" of the Hindus, and is conceived as a distinct branch of learning, coordinate with those others (*dharma, kāma, mokṣa*) that deal with the central purposes of man. In later writings, usually termed *nīti,* political advantage challenges the earlier concern with moral right. *Daṇ-ḍanīti* is translated as rules of government. The concept implies that fear of retribution is the real basis of order, and it represents a shift in emphasis from the more positive view (i.e., *rājadharma*) that the use of power is validated only by the welfare of the community. Government is frequently characterized specifically as the science of sanction and coercion, that is, of danda, the guardian of order.

The concluding chapters, Chapters 14 through 16, provide a topical treatment of the more important political ideas and institutions of early India, and a discussion of the concept of authority. With the spread of the Sultanate through northern India in the thirteenth century and the decline of political commentary in Indian philosophy, the analysis ends.

2 ✻ VEDIC CIVILIZATION

MYTH AND SACRIFICE

In the ancient Aryan clans there appears to have evolved a Veda, a body of myths and ceremonies, now impossible to reconstruct but undoubtedly the creation of court singers. These poets exalted the warriors on whom they depended for their livelihood, and were expected to induce the support of the gods, on whom the hero, in turn, depended for success.

The Vedic hymns (*saṃhitās*) that have survived have a common source in the religion that developed in the Upper Indus or in the eastern reaches of the Punjab. The *Rigveda* (*Ṛgveda*), oldest of the four major collections of hymns that constitute the Vedic literature and the earliest historical record of the Indo-Aryans, can be dated on linguistic evidence from at least the eleventh or twelfth century B.C., and perhaps from as early as the fifteenth. It has come down to us as a compilation of 1,017 hymns. These ancient stories and family traditions exist in what is probably very close to their original literary form, although the recension we have may be as recent as the sixth century B.C. This form reflects the need for easy comprehension and memorization, since for centuries they were transmitted orally. It might be supposed that this would provide ample opportunity for alteration of the hymns, but we may surmise that great care was taken to preserve the exact meter and phrase, for failure to render a proper accent or nuance of thought could destroy the efficacy of the verse and even imperil its teller.

It has been suggested that the hymns are poetic preliminaries used to introduce the Vedic rituals, and that the ones that have survived are those selected in verse competitions.[1] Their inspiration belongs to different periods of Vedic history, and the diversity is considerable. We should not be surprised to find that the beliefs expressed in the books of the *Rigveda* are sometimes inconsistent with one another. These texts reveal on the whole a sensitivity to nature, a belief in the magical and the occult, an optimistic outlook, and a sense of man's significance. There is almost nothing that would hint at the path of ascetic withdrawal in later religious thought.

Of the other collections, the *Atharvaveda*, although later than the *Sāmaveda* or *Yajurveda,* is more important for an understanding of early Indian history. Describing in detail the popular beliefs of the time, it

deals with spells and incantations and suggests the ways in which the
Aryan ritual was modified by the incorporation of the religious belief of
the aboriginal peoples.

We know little of the procedures of worship in early Vedic times. Two
cults apparently existed among the Vedic clans (*āryas*) : the popular cult,
with elements derived from the indigenous culture and comparable in some
respects to later Hinduism ; and the esoteric ceremonial cult, presided over
by a priesthood. The earliest Aryan priests, who administered the fire sacrifice (*atharvan*), were not brahmans. Nor were the aryas hierocracies
as such, since the priests were in the service of a warrior elite. Vedism in
its formal sense was not a religion of the masses.

The warfare that accompanied the Aryan invasion increased the importance of the sacrifice. The assistance of the gods was essential to victory, and thus the prestige and power of those able to invoke the gods
through sacrifice grew—often to the point where they were regarded as
superior to the gods themselves. The Aryans tended to look on the active
cooperation of the gods as fair exchange for gifts offered and rituals performed. There is a frankly materialistic cast to the Vedic sacrifice.[2]

There is no lack of system in either the domestic or the public rites of
the Vedic ceremonial. Over a period of centuries the sacrifice became
highly specialized and complicated, sometimes taking many months to
execute. A sacrifice that in the earlier Vedic period required at most five
or six priests had become by the Brahmanic age a remarkably elaborate
and expensive ceremonial requiring a host of officiating priests. Those
who actually performed the sacrifice were supervised by the brahman, who
made certain that the service was conducted in orthodox fashion. Technique had become all-important. The sacrifice was an attempt to impose
an order on the whole universe ; every detail of the ritual was charged with
cosmic significance. The *Atharvaveda* points to the increasing importance
of magic in the public rituals.

The symbolism of the *Rigveda* is often bewildering, but a central theme
is the creation and evolution of the world, with Varuna, the all-knowing
deity of eternal order, leading men from the age of chaos. Varuna shares
the cosmic stage with the virile Indra, who personified the heroic virtues
of the warrior aristocracy. The role of Indra gained in prominence until
this swaggering lord of the thunderbolt challenged the position of Varuna
himself.

The Vedas do not contain an explicit ethic. The gods to whom the
sacrifice was dedicated were representations of natural phenomena rather
than guardians of morality. The awesome Varuna was dreaded chiefly
because he would not forgive departures from the traditional forms of
worship. Perhaps because of the growing need for social controls as Aryan
society became more settled in the later Vedic period, Varuna acquired an
increasingly severe aspect, instilling for the first time a sense of sin and
insufficiency in the worshiper. But the *Rigveda* gives us a picture of
heaven as a place of "everlasting lustre," an "eternal, undecaying world"

where there is "food and full delight."[3] The soul[a] thus survives death and
may even have been conceived as reunited with the body. Purgatory has
little significance in the theology of the Veda. Punishment was imposed
by the gods in this world, although in the later hymns we do find references
to the bottomless darkness.

The *Rigveda* confronts us with a Homeric world of warrior-gods—
ancient heroes and tribal chieftains who took on supernatural powers as
the stories of their battles expanded in the telling. Indra, we may assume,
is one of these early heroes. He was closely associated with the soma cult,[b]
and embodied the attributes of several lesser deities. He stood as a challenge to the demonic forces, natural and supernatural. Contentious and
amoral though he was, given to drink and braggadocio, it was Indra who
led the Aryans to victory and assured the coming of the rain.

> "He killed the dragon [Vritra, the demon, who kept the vital elements
> imprisoned], set free the waters, and split open the mountainside. . . .
> You won the cows, O brave one, you won soma ; you released the seven
> rivers, so they should flow. . . . Indra, who wields the thunderbolt
> in his hand, is the lord of what moves and what remains in rest, of what
> is peaceful and what is horned. He alone rules the tribes as their king ;
> he encloses them as does a rim [enclose] the spokes."[4]

As the Aryan chief rode into battle at the head of a coterie of knights,
so Indra, god of the storm and lord of war, led his battalion of warrior
heroes, or Maruts, in their chariots across the skies.[c] But powerful as the
hold of Indra on the popular imagination was, the setting of Vedic mythology tended to shift more and more to the exaltation of the sacred fire
(Agni) and the sacrificial liquor.

The major concern of the priestly books, the venerable *Rigveda,* the
Samaveda, and the *Yajurveda,* is not so much with the problems of birth
and destiny that preoccupy the more familiar later writings, as with sacrifice and liturgy.[5] The French Sanskritist Bergaigne maintained that Vedic
liturgy should be interpreted as an attempt to reproduce the cosmic order so
as to assure the effective functioning of human society. The Veda must
therefore be understood in essentially symbolic terms. The world is con-

---

[a] Described as breath or the principle of energy or mind. (*Rigveda* I, 113.16; I,
140.8; VIII, 100.5; X, 15.1; X, 50.)

[b] Soma, which was consumed at the sacrifice, was an inebriating drink capable of
producing hallucinations. It is thought to have been a drug rather than a product of
fermentation. The *Rigveda* provides a guide to the mechanics of the soma ritual. It
describes the preparation of the sacred liquor in detail, but lacks any exegesis of the
liturgy of which the ceremony was a part.

Like the wine of Western religious tradition, soma could not fulfill the religious
function until the brahman priest had brought about its transubstantiation. The revelations and supernatural powers it induced were called Brahman.

[c] Yet the Vedic religion cannot accurately be characterized as polytheistic or
pantheistic. We can find, for example in the Hymn of Creation—in the last and most
speculative of the ten books of the *Rigveda*—suggestions of an ultimate cosmic principle, an impersonal force that lies behind creation: "That One Thing, breathless,
breathed by its own nature : apart from it was nothing whatsoever. . . . The gods
are later than this world's creation." And there are references elsewhere in the
Rigveda to the great Procreator, to whom even the gods do homage.

ceived as being at once profane and sacred; the social order and the ritual order are two manifestations of the same process. Knowledge is the comprehension of the complex system of classifications of which the world is composed;[6] the sacrifice, which represents the correspondences between the sacred and profane orders, attempts a ritual reproduction of the divine plan. The sacrifice accordingly provides a key to an understanding of social institutions, for the categories of belief mirror the categories of social organization. Unfortunately, however, the formularies of the priesthood border on the cryptic. This approach to the Vedic liturgy has led modern students to point out that the speculations of the Upanishads are logical culminations of the early texts; they describe different methods for achieving the same purposes.

The lack of any highly developed historical sense places ancient India among those civilizations possessing what has been called the cosmological style of symbolization. Such a characterization would of course exclude very few early peoples. Ancient man did not distinguish clearly between human society and nature. His knowledge of his environment was direct and emotional, and a will was attributed to all phenomena and every act. Man could not remain passive in such a world; the ritual was his instrument, his weapon. Through the ritual he participated directly in the eternal struggle against the demonic forces.[7]

In the elaborate cosmology that developed, the political order came to be interpreted as analogous to the cosmos, its creation a repetition of the divine creation of the cosmic system. In effect, the political order is understood cosmologically, and the cosmic is apprehended in terms that are essentially political.[8] The regime of the gods was itself the result of a profound conflict. The deities are no less subject to this fundamental opposition of *rita* and anarchy than is man. Their individual personalities reflect this struggle and complicate the attempt to characterize a god with any degree of consistency. In one sense this opposition, which provides a framework for the moral ideas of the Vedas, is the dilemma of power and authority. We shall return to this theme in the pages that follow.

In the India of the *Rigveda* the relationship of the king and his fellow warriors to the gods is more direct than it is in the later hymns and the Brahmanas. In the later literature the king is compared with Prajāpati, the deity (or principle) of creation. In the sacrifice the role of the king is identified with that of the god. "He, the Rajanya [king] is the visible representative of Prajapati: hence while being one, he rules over many."[9] The Brahmanas tell us that it was Prajapati who created Indra king of the gods.[10]

As in the Mesopotamian myth, where Hammurabi conceives of himself as the steward of Marduk as well as the earthly cognate of the god, the need for mediation between the social and cosmic realm has complicated the simple equation of the two orders. The sacrifice acts as a bridge, and the role and position of the king in the sacrifice is not necessarily the function he performed in his other capacities as ruler. In India the cosmological conception of the relationship between man and the gods was originally closer to the intimate intercourse that Homer depicts in the late Mycenaean civilization. But by the late Vedic period the anthropomorphic gods of the heroic age had been eclipsed by the more imposing, often aloof, deities of the Brahmanas. Eventually the impersonal cosmic principle *Brahman* came to dominate religious speculation, introducing a greater metaphysical depth and a concept of the human soul striving for attunement with the undisturbed cosmic order.

The germ of this complex idea may be found in Vedism, the name given to the early stage of Indian religion. Some Indian scholars, Ananda Coomaraswamy among them, have sought to explain Vedic mythology in terms of the psychic struggle. The eternal beginning, an idea that holds the cosmological view in bondage, is depicted as the endless serpent. Man is the dragon-slayer, demanding his freedom from the "psycho-physical prison."

> This "adversary" is, of course, none but our self. . . . Thus He in whom we were imprisoned is now our prisoner; as our Inner Man he is submerged in and hidden by our Outer Man. It is now his turn to become the Dragon-Slayer; and in this war of the God with the Titan, now fought within you, where we are "at war with ourselves," his victory and resurrection will be also ours, *if* we have known Who we are. It is now for him to drink us dry, for us to be his wine (i.e., the Eucharistic meal). . . . The death of the victim is also its birth. . . . Expiation is provided in the Sacrifice, where by the Sacrificer's surrender of himself and the building up again of the dismembered deity, whole and complete, the multiple selves are reduced to their single principle. There is thus an incessant multiplication of the inexhaustible One and unification of the indefinitely Many. Such are the beginnings and endings of worlds and of individual beings.[11]

Such an interpretation, though perhaps oversophisticated, is probably closer to the truth than those histories of religion that dispense with the Vedic religion as "primitive," or as without significance in the evolution of Indian thought. Animism and nature-worship have their place in the Aryan religion, but their importance has been too much emphasized. There is a life-affirming quality in earlier Vedic belief, particularly in the popular cult, which is in marked contrast to later religious orientations.

By the eighth century B.C., the Vedas were interpreted as direct revelation, and in the succeeding centuries a series of explanatory texts, the Brahmanas, were appended to the hymns as elaborations on Vedic ritual. These ritual manuals, as they became increasingly recondite, were mystifying to all but initiates. The rituals themselves had become a highly formalized religion, characterized by a complex ceremonialism with excessive attention to the details of performance. As religion came to be tied to a technical expertise, the priests strengthened their position, isolating themselves from social controls. This stage in the shaping of Indian culture, roughly 800–500 B.C., is known as the Brahmanic epoch. By the end of this period the Aryan invaders who had brought Vedism to India had extended their hegemony over the whole of the Gangetic plain. They had advanced to an agricultural economy based in part on irrigation, the institution of property was established, and the silver coins dating from this era attest to an extensive trade.

ARYAN SOCIAL ORGANIZATION

The political evolution of India is sometimes described in terms of four stages: the relatively simple Aryan community, the period of transition to monarchy, the flowering of the great imperial monarchies, and the period of decline and disintegration. In the rest of this chapter our concern will be with the first of these stages, and particularly with the tribal origins of kingship.

Modern scholarship is generally agreed that the Aryan invasion occurred in the middle centuries of the second millennium B.C. The Indus culture of Harappā and Mohenjodaro perished around this time.[d] Whereas the Indus civilization left an abundance of remains and no written record to speak of, early Aryan society left few artifacts but a sizable literature. The earliest samhitas reflect the initial phases of the Aryan invasion; the later hymns provide evidence of a more stable society deeper in the Gangetic plain. There is mention of the five rivers, the Himalayas, and the beasts of that region. Recent studies of this country indicate that the lands connecting India and the Middle East were much more fertile than they are now, and supported thriving communities until aridity checked their development in the first centuries of the Christian era. A theory that the Aryan eastern advance followed the Himalayan foothills rather than the Ganges, with its jungle undergrowth and forbidding swamp, has gained currency recently.

As the invaders from the Afghan passes spread across the plains of northwest India, they subjected the indigenous peoples. During the eastward movement of the Aryans (around the beginning of the first millennium B.C.), the name for these people, *dāsa*, came to mean "helot." Originally there was a decided color variation between the Aryan community and the dark-skinned native population, who may have been Dravidian peoples.[e] It is of some significance that the word for caste (*varna*) is also the Sanskrit word for color.[f]

---

[d] Gordon [158] dates Mohenjodaro from c. 2600 B.C., the decline of Harappan culture in the period 1800–1500, and the Aryan invasions in the four and a half centuries after c. 1750.

[e] There is at least the possibility that the peoples encountered by the invading Aryans belonged to the prehistoric Harappa culture of the Indus Valley. (*Vide* Piggott [320]; R. E. M. Wheeler, *Ancient India*, No. 3, 1947, pp. 81ff.; Kosambi [218] is also sympathetic to the theory.) This ancient civilization flourished at the probable time of the first Indo-European incursions and its members had many of the characteristics of those described in the *Rigveda* as dasas. They were a partly proto-Australoid people, living in well-fortified cities. Indra, the Vedic god, is pictured as the fort-destroyer, although we may question whether the fortresses were those of humans. Wheeler modifies his thesis in a more recent work, *Early India and Pakistan to Ashoka* [426]. Several scholars have argued that the Indus culture may have effectively assimilated the invader and provided the general direction of Aryan civilization; but evidence allows no more than a brave hypothesis.

[f] The Indian class structure will be discussed in Chapter 5 below; in this later, more detailed examination, it will be seen that this meaning requires qualification.

When we speak of this Aryan advance into the Gangetic country, we mean not simply the migration of certain peoples, but the extension of a way of life defined as Aryan. In accepting Aryan modes of organization and certain basic values, the native population became "Aryanized." The invaders were a cultural rather than a racial group, whose cultural identity was established by about 3000 B.C. Their early home seems to have been a temperate grassland of contrasting seasons, perhaps the land north and east of the Caspian Sea. These Indo-Europeans evidently had a religion without idol or temple; worship of their deities, sky-gods, was conducted by the head of the family.[g] In the south Russian steppes they may have been primitive agriculturists, but the Aryans described in the Vedic texts were primarily a pastoral people, occupied with herds and flocks, as well as a grain crop, and loosely organized into clans and tribes. The cow was their means of exchange and measure of value. They were a beef-eating, beer-drinking people, who tanned hides, cultivated barley, wove cloth, and were capable of fashioning metal weapons and tools. An increasingly important element of Aryan culture was plow cultivation, which made possible an economic surplus and hence the expansion of civilization. By the sixth century B.C. a settled agricultural village economy had replaced the semi-nomadic pastoral life of the early Aryans.

The *grāma,* which later came to mean village, was at first simply a collection of related families. This was the smallest political unit, the basic element of the social structure. Most villages had a *grāmaṇī,* or headman,[h] and a number were self-governing. The tribes were apparently subdivided into groups called *viśas,* which may have been fighting units.[i] The family itself, we learn from the Vedas, was consanguineous, patriarchal, patrilinear, and generally monogamous.

Jana and *janapada* refer to the people, "the subjects," and to district, tribal locality, and country as well. *Paura-janapada* may be the term for tribal free cities. Conjecture plays a large role in the translation of these Vedic terms into modern equivalents. Among the Aryans the tribe, or jana, was the highest level of political organization. From the Vedic texts we know of early tribal amalgamations such as those of the Pūrus and Bharatas, who formed the Kuru group, and the Turvaśas and Krivis, who became the Pañcālas.

Guilds of woodworkers, weavers, weapon-makers, hunters, and other craft and professional groups are mentioned in the Vedas. The existence of separate groups that organized education and economic life, as well as

---

[g] Around 1380 B.C. the Hittite ruler Subiluliuma and Mattiuaza of Mitanni (an Indo-European people on the northwestern frontier of Mesopotamia) entered into a treaty in which the Mitannian invoked gods whose names are those of the Vedic deities Mitra, Varuna, and Indra. This suggests a mythology common to Mitanni and the Vedic culture.

[h] The gramani, the "giver of gifts," seems to have been the individual who patronized the priests and the poor. But this is obviously an incomplete characterization. *Vide* pp. 47ff. below.

[i] There is some doubt about the precise meaning of vish (*viś*). It probably corresponds to the Roman curia, a grouping of families, and we can think of it as related to the clan. It is sometimes used in the Vedas to mean the common people as a whole.

religious, military, and political activities, suggests a crude pluralism. A sharp cultural division also existed between native and invader. The first of the Vedas contrasts the dasas (or dasyus) with the Aryans, but by the time of the *Atharvaveda* the distinction is between Aryan and shudra (*śūdra*). The shudras, it was once thought, were indigenous tribal groups who became slaves and serfs of the Aryans. But we can no longer say with certainty whether the shudras ever really became slaves; if they did not, this would distinguish them from the early dasas, who were drawn into servitude. The fact that the shudras were sometimes assigned a role in the sacrifice seems to indicate that they were not outside the Aryan community. It may be more accurate to view them as private workers—domestic servants, agricultural laborers, and artisans.

The *Rigveda* samhitas frequently refer to *Brahma, Kṣatra,* and *Viś* as three divisions in society. The last of these may be taken to mean the common people. Caste was still in the formative process, and the four traditional classes are not specifically mentioned in the *Rigveda* until the Purusha hymn of the relatively late tenth book. In this myth (X, 90.11f.) the four orders—now named *Brahmāṇa, Rājanya, Vaiśya,* and *Śūdra*—are said to have originated respectively from the mouth,[j] arms, thighs, and feet of the Creator. One would surmise that status in society is meant to be inferred from these parts of the anatomy, but the *Puruṣasūkta* does not directly indicate this. Several Vedic hymns refer to functional groupings of the population.[12] This division of the Aryans into farmers and artisans, warriors, and priests is similar to that of the early Persians. Aryan expansion must certainly have demanded great organizational efficiency and functional specialization, and must also have emphasized the need for the conservation of tradition as the encounter with a different set of customs threatened Aryan culture.

The powerful patriarch of the joint family was undoubtedly the precursor of the king.[k] Communities of families looked to the head of the senior joint family as the final authority in matters affecting their common welfare. The elders of the community probably selected the leaders in battle. With the advent of peace, the chief among these warriors would be retained in authority—perhaps to supervise the distribution of the spoils of war, or to assume responsibility for preparedness against attack and the organization of future campaigns. (When the gods chose a leader from among themselves, the *Rigveda* tells us, it was to ensure victory.) The most important incentive to the development of a strong central authority was the hostility of the indigenous population.

The *Atharvaveda* provides an account of the king's inauguration, describing his selection and the intense rivalry involved, and hinting at the importance of popular support.[13] The *rājasūya* sacrifice[14] seems to indi-

---

[j] *Mukha* means both "mouth" and "chief."

[k] The Hindu political tradition was essentially monarchical. Republican institutions were important, however, and will be discussed in Chapter 15. The republic was usually oligarchical and probably differed less from the monarchical polity, which was also dominated by an influential aristocracy, than Indian historians generally suggest.

cate that the king's "election" was conditional upon his success in the chariot race or the diceplay. In the coronation ceremony the right to govern was formally invested in the king. We are led to conclude that the people elected the king unanimously,[15] but the meaning of "people," "elect," and "unanimously" can only be guessed at. Few scholars consider this an election in the modern sense of the term. It is possible that in the early Vedic period the leader of the vish was chosen by the people and called king, but that in later times certain influential members of the community decided who would be king and the others concurred in the decision. Although there is no actual evidence that the monarchy was usually elective in Vedic times, there are many indications that the ruler was dependent on the support of the aristocracy. And, as Jayaswal observed, there was considerable popular participation in the appointment of the king.[16] Even if Vedic kings were accepted rather than chosen by the people, there is at least the suggestion of a greater power once enjoyed by the people.[l]

There is almost nothing in the Vedas to suggest the divine *nature* of the king, and his dependence on popular support tends to rule out any claim to divine right. Several students of Hindu religious theory have assumed that popular election conferred sacred authority on the king, but this cannot be concluded from the texts. In the Vedas the king is at most likened to Indra. The election hymn urges the king: "Stand steadfast here like Indra, and hold the kingship [kingdom?] in thy grasp. This man has Indra established and made secure by the power of oblation."[17] In the *Rigveda*[18] King Trasadasyu is referred to as a demigod, "like Indra." And according to the later Brahmanas[19] the sacrifice (the *rāja-sūya*, which could be performed only by a powerful king, and the *aśvamedha* sacrifice) enabled the performer to become a god, to acquire the vitality of Indra; but the potency seemingly derives from the sacrifice or from Indra, not from the king. It is not hereditary divinity that we find in the hymns, but rather an analogy with the gods. Divinity is not mentioned where we would expect to find it, in the hymns of creation. There is more evidence in the Vedas that the gods became kings than that the kings became gods.

As the king ascends the throne, the four quarters—East, South, West, and North, corresponding to the four orders of society—swear allegiance and promise to support and protect him. "Stand thou fixed, not unsteady; let all the people want thee; let not thy kingdom fall away . . . Vanquish firmly the enemy, crush him under you; [be] all quarters like-minded and let the gathering [*samiti*] here suit thee."[20] Authority would seem to come from the people ("king-makers, charioteers, workers of metal"), who present the king with the sacred jewel that is the token of royal power.

---

[l] Likewise in medieval Europe the monarchical principle had not made the king completely independent of the popular will. We find coronation oaths which, in one breath, locate the authority of the crown in inheritance, in consent, and in divine will. Germanic kings in the Middle Ages could claim at best only a "throneworthiness"; the right of succession was no foregone conclusion, and the ceremonial expression of the popular basis of kingship never entirely vanished.

On the throne was spread a tiger skin, symbol of the king's omnipotence.[21] One of the coronation sacrifices (*vājapeya*) included a chariot race in which the king was victor. This may be a reference to the time when military superiority, as tested in the chariot race, was the basis of kingship. In the ceremony the king was elevated to the status of *saṃrāṭ,* pre-eminent among all rulers.[22]

The position of the king was strengthened by the warfare of the Vedic period. As the military organization, the nucleus of government, grew in influence and defined its sphere of action more broadly, the associations representing the different interests and functions of the community were more closely integrated with the "state" and deprived of the autonomy they had once possessed.

The *Rigveda* tells us very little about the peacetime functions of the king. We do know that he not only was the worldly equivalent of Indra, warlord and chief of the gods, but also represented Varuna, whose position in the hierarchy of gods was as exalted as Indra's.[m] The king thus served as judge[23] and guarantor of the established order. The dharma of all men depended on the rajadharma, the fulfillment of these royal duties. At the same time dharmic law fixed the relationship of the ruling and subject classes, legitimating the supremacy of the kshatriya nobility.

In the earliest samhitas, we find reference to the king's obligation not only to protect his subjects, but to increase their welfare and prosperity. We may infer from the Vedas that the ideal polity was based on the pursuit of the virtuous life, the diverting of men and women from paths of sinful thought and action. To this end the state should further the spiritual and material well-being of the people. Perhaps the real intent of such passages in the brahman literature was to exalt the priests and justify their claim to privileged status. In the *Rigveda,* the brahman frequently appears to be of less importance than the rajanya (kshatriya) ; the performance of the tribal sacrifice had not yet become the exclusive property of the brahman. But in the later Vedic literature, the priest has clearly taken his place at the head of society. In this age before society was frozen into caste strata the position of the warriors and priests was in some measure based on talent and achievement as well as on ascribed status; but the rise of the brahman class clearly derived primarily from the increasing emphasis on religion in the Aryan conception of order.

Kingship was not a divine institution and the Vedic king differed from most other ancient kings in that he performed no priestly functions. Moreover, since law (or dharma) was theoretically beyond the reach of men, the king was confined on pain of supernatural reprisal to administra-

[m] In the *Rigveda,* dharma, or rita as it was then called, refers in most instances to religious ordinances and rites (e.g., V, 26.6; VIII, 43.24), although in other passages the term seemingly refers to fixed principles of conduct (e.g., V, 63.7; VII, 89.5). Order is secured through the ritual. Instead of attributing the binding force of custom to man's nature, the early Aryans ascribed the preservation of custom to the god Varuna. It was Varuna who was responsible for ensuring the order of the universe, and it was this same order that governed men. The breaking of custom invoked Varuna's wrath on the miscreant. It was only a matter of time before Varuna appeared as creator of the law.

tive decrees consonant with the religious and social code that governed the community. But there were controls on the misuse of royal power other than fear of Varuna's wrath. There was the possibility that a discontented populace might align itself with a rival prince. In cases of conflict between the king and the assembly, it is likely that the will of the latter prevailed. The authority of the assembly (probably an aristocratic group), the role of the people in the coronation ceremony, and their power to banish the king point to a degree of popular control in the Vedic age that was never equaled in later times.

Perhaps the most effective restraint of all on the exercise of the king's power were the claims of other members of the aristocracy. In the almost constant warfare of the time the ruler was dependent on his fellow members of the warrior class. He occasionally had to compel the homage of the more powerful members of the community, and it appears that gifts (the major source of revenue) were not always freely contributed.[24] All in all, many a king appears to have been little more than the head of an assembly of his peers. Some states evidently were ruled by two kings, in some cases governing jointly, in others dividing jurisdiction and consulting on major matters only.

As early as the Vedic period there seems to have been a distinction between criminal and civil law, but the *Rigveda* reveals little about the civil or criminal jurisdiction of the king. The explanation is probably that the king was not yet powerful enough to take on more than the supervision of private revenge (wergild). Criminal justice was largely the province of those who were wronged. There are no references in the Vedic literature to judicial agencies; all that can be said is that village councils evidently had the power of arbitration.

Vedic states were small in size. It is doubtful that differences in the titles of their rulers (e.g., *saṃrāṭ* or *mahārāja*) indicate much variation in the extent of dominion, since these terms refer to the number of victories, rather than the area of conquest, credited to a ruler. By the later Vedic period the territorial state had replaced the tribal state of the early Aryans. Although the language of the sacrifice suggests domains of majestic proportions, there were no great kingdoms or empires during this time. The rajasuya ritual is more the wish for empire than the symbol of actual imperial powers.[25] The ancient and vainglorious ashvamedha sacrifice, by which the king demonstrated that it was in his power to graze a horse wherever the animal should wander, suggests an age when the limit of the territory to which a tribal leader could lay claim was the grazing area of his herds.[n]

[n] The crucial significance of the sacrifice in Vedic society has raised a question concerning the proper interpretation of role and status in this early period. Hocart has warned against confusing ritual function with social function. It may be true that in many instances the hymns provide only a description of roles performed in the sacrifice, but we are probably justified in assuming that symbolization moves in two directions and that existing Vedic social relationships and functions are read back into the supernatural and mirrored in the ritual that maintains the order of things. On occasion, however, references to struggles with the indigenous population or with the powers of evil (which the dasas may be taken to represent) may indicate only the

Warfare became a more serious, expensive, and formal matter than it had been in the initial stages of the Aryan invasion; but with the development of dharmic doctrine, methods of fighting were influenced by more humane ideals of conduct—especially where Aryan fought Aryan. This code of conduct may also have contributed to the development of diplomacy. The envoy begins his career in this age.

The jewel ceremony confirmed a number of high functionaries in their positions: the *purohita* (high priest), the queen, the commander-in-chief, the treasurer, the tax collector, and the chamberlain. In later times caste dictated who could occupy these offices. The most important administrative officials of the Vedic period were the commander, the treasurer, the tax collector, and the village headman (gramani). At this time the military administration, at least at the higher levels, was generally separate from civil administration, though the gramani may have been charged with military duties at the village level. The army was composed of divisions of militia and cavalry, with a department of diplomacy under the *sūta*.

Several kings may have shared the services of the same priest, the purohita. There is some evidence that his office was hereditary, but it is not conclusive. The purohita's power was limited to matters of religion. He did not preside as a judge in courts of justice. As tutor to the prince and companion to the king, he might, however, make his opinion count in nonreligious matters. In addition, in the late Vedic age a board of at least ten brahmans advised the king on complex legal and administrative matters.

The primitive forms of Vedic witchcraft are concealed by an intricate philosophical system and epic poetry, but ritual practices suggest that ancient India was not without its own type of sorcery, which played a part in the unfolding of the theory of kingship. As the king became increasingly dependent on rite and magic, the power of the priests expanded and that of the people diminished. The decline and eventual demise of the Vedic council is very likely associated with the growth of brahman influence. He who controlled the sacrifice, upon which legitimacy and power depended, was destined to become more important than the tribal assembly.

The *Atharvaveda* indicates that the assembly at one time wielded substantial political power. It was on various occasions responsible for the appointment and the impeachment of the king, and for interregnum rule. After the king had been approved by the people (or their representatives) he consulted the assembly, which may have been composed of the people in special congregation or simply of the elders and other influential persons.[26] We know very little about the actual functions and operation of the *sabhā* and *samiti*. In Zimmer's analysis, the sabha was the assembly of the village, serving both political and social functions, and the samiti was the chief assembly that met in the capital and acted on matters of

---

enactment of this conflict in the sacrifice. The martial spirit of *Rigveda* VI, 75, is not that of an actual battle song but rather that of a magical incantation designed to secure victory.

interest to the whole state.[27] Other scholars (e.g., Macdonell and Hillebrandt) regard the functions of the two bodies as essentially the same.[o]
Strictly speaking, the *Atharvaveda* suggests little more than that the
samiti was generally an aristocratic body, and that the smooth exercise
of the king's power depended on its acquiescence.

Although the king's presence in the samiti is alluded to in the *Rigveda*,
the significance of his attendance cannot be determined. He may have
commanded the assembly; he may have deliberated with its members.
More likely, it was his duty to guide discussion to decision and agreement.
The Vedas make an earnest plea for concord between the king and the
representatives of the people: "The place is common, common the assembly, common the mind, so be their thoughts united."[28] The powers of the
assembly were evidently primarily regulative. Usually it was an accepting
rather than an initiating group. As administrative procedure became increasingly complex and the position of the monarch was strengthened, the
influence of the assemblies declined and that of the ministers grew. The
samiti fades from sight in the later Vedic age, to emerge again in the
early Upanishadic literature—with the king and priests in attendance.

The other assembly, the sabha ("a body of men shining together"),
was perhaps a group of distinguished persons called together to advise the
samiti or the king. It appears to have been a much more exclusive body
than the samiti, composed of men of high birth and competence. Very
possibly it evolved from a popular assembly into a council advising the king.
Often the sabha was under the guidance of the purohita, and a semi-reli-
gious atmosphere seems to have prevailed at its meetings. It is not certain
whether the organization had judicial functions.[29]

Of an even more mysterious and religious character was the *vidatha,*
a sacrificial organization whose patron was Indra and whose members
probably included women.[p] There is little indication of class differentiations in the vidatha. Some scholars are of the opinion that it served as
an agency for the distribution of produce, but they can only speculate on
its services in this capacity. There is less doubt about its having served as
a war council and as a religious body.[30] Other assemblies (*sada, pariṣad*)
had more broadly defined religious and social purposes, but are not as
important in a political analysis.

In the Vedic age land was considered the property of the community.
This does not mean that the individual occupier was without rights, but
rather that disposal of the land was a social concern. By the end of the
Vedic period, however, the distinction between private and crown properties had presumably become clear. The commentaries on the Vedas, *Manu*
excepted, contradict the right of the king to interfere with private lands,
save for nonpayment of taxes. Land was occupied by joint families, and in
dividing it, preference was usually shown to the eldest son. Women en-

---

[o] *Atharvaveda* VII, 12.1, and VX, 9, may, however, be taken to indicate that the
two were different bodies and probably different in purpose.

[p] *Rigveda*, I, 167.3; X, 85.26; *Atharvaveda* XIV, 1.21; XIII, 3.24. The presence of women, and the apparent egalitarian and communal character of the vidatha,
suggest that it might have been the remote ancestor of the Buddhist saṅgha (*vide*
pp 53ff. below).

joyed no right of inheritance. References to land "grants" refer to the granting of revenue rights rather than absolute title.

In earliest times, the king met expenses primarily through income from royal holdings, bounty, and donations inspired by religious motive. The meager references in the *Rigveda* suggest that the habit of paying taxes was not yet established.[31] The gods are asked to compel the subjects of the king to make contributions (*bali*) to the ruler in order to ensure the stability of his reign.[32] In the later Vedic polity warfare became more elaborate and costly, forays against indigenous tribes giving way to serious campaigns, often against other Aryan peoples. The king, who by this time had ensconced himself and his courtiers in a fortified town, now had a more or less definite territory to defend. The army and the court, with its idle nobles given to expensive amusements, could be maintained only by increasing and formalizing the burden of taxes. Voluntary gifts and the king's personal resources were no longer adequate sources of revenue.

In conclusion, we may say that early Indian kingship was broadly contractual, conceived of as a trust, subject to popular approval, and, most important, subject to higher law and certain other restraints, normative and practical. It was basically a secular institution.

In the period we turn to next, often referred to as the Brahmanic epoch, the priests assumed broad social power and used it to their own ends. At the height of brahman ascendancy, as we shall see, the state sometimes appeared to be little more than an adjunct of a social order that exalted the priest and his prerogatives. But before turning our attention to the ornate mysteries of that age of religiosity, it is worth pausing on a wonderful hymn, of the fourth book of the *Atharvaveda*,[33] intended to ensure the king's well-being. It expresses the heroic vigor of the great morning of Indian culture.

> Increase, O Indra, this Kshatriya for me; make thou this man sole chief of the clans [viś]; unman all his enemies; make them subject to him in the contests for pre-eminence.
>
> Portion thou this man in village, in horses, in kine; unportion that man who is his enemy; let this man be the summit of authorities [kshatra]; O Indra, make every foe subject to him.
>
> Let this man be riches-lord of riches; let this man be people-lord of people; in him, O Indra, put great splendors; destitute of splendor make thou his foe.
>
> For him, O heaven-and-earth, milk ye much that is pleasant, like two milch kine that yield the hot draught, may this king be dear to Indra, dear to kine, herbs, cattle.
>
> I join thee Indra who gives superiority, by whom men conquer, are not conquered; who shall make thee sole chief of people [jana], also uppermost of kings descended from Manu.
>
> Superior (art) thou, inferior thy rivals, whosoever, O king, are thine opposing foes; sole chief, having Indra as companion, having conquered, bring thou in the enjoyments of them that play the foe.
>
> Of lion-aspect, do thou devour all the clans [viś]; of tiger-aspect, do thou beat down the foes; sole chief, having Indra as companion, having conquered, seize thou on the enjoyments of them that play the foe.

3 × RELIGION AND SOCIETY

FLAMEN BRAHMAN

Religious systems employ a variety of techniques for establishing the relationship between man and the supernatural. When men believe that the supernatural can be comprehended and adapted to by means of certain formalized manipulative actions, we speak of these actions as *ritual* actions. When the supernatural is viewed as itself capable of deliberate action, and men seek to influence this divine will and obtain a favorable dispensation by prayer or sacrifice, we call this response *supplication*. Ritual and supplication commonly involve the participation of professionals who serve as intermediaries between man and his gods. The growth of a religious elite may result in a reaction to priestly controls that emphasizes direct communication with the deity and the responsibility of the individual for his own salvation. Such movements often employ a third technique, *contemplation*, a mystical "understanding" of the cosmic order—which is conceived as diffuse and impersonal.[1]

Where the belief system presupposes a deity or deities possessing will and design, the protest movement will usually establish a different type of relationship to the supernatural. The old liturgy is replaced by an ethic that may be aggressive and conversionist or resigned and aloof. The social status of the members of the sect and the possibilities available for modifying social institutions (to narrow the gap between values and opportunities for attaining them) will also affect the form of the protest. If the divine power is understood neither as objective law nor as a mystical unifying force, there may emerge the relationship conditioned by grace found in Christian Protestantism.[2]

In analyzing the evolution of Indian religion from Vedism to the heterodox sects, it is important to point out that the deities of Brahmanism are manifestations of an objective power, rather than the individuated personalities of the Vedic pantheon. Control thus takes a variety of forms —including contemplation, later to become central to mysticism.

We have remarked on the attempts during the Vedic period to reproduce the sacred, to achieve certain goals—such as victory in battle—by performing the necessary symbolic actions of the ritual. "Thus did the gods; thus men do."[3] The Brahmanic ritual aims at reconstructing the original unity of things; the world is created anew with each sacrifice.[a] Magic gained increasing prominence in the sacred rite.[b]

The ritual provides a means of acting out and thus reducing strains and frustrations produced by the uncertainties and rationally inexplicable occurrences of life. And, on the social level, it consolidates the values of the community, reminding individuals of shared purposes, and representing in simple, dramatic form the essentials of social and religious relationships.

But this latent cohesive function was severely curtailed by the Brahmanic sociological theory, which defined the appropriate expectations for the different members of society, legitimizing differentiated social roles and establishing a hierarchy of these roles. Because the order of society was considered to be a reflection of the supernatural order, there was little questioning of the institutionalized values. The radical turning away from the objects and relationships of this world is a later development. And even when mystical contemplation becomes a major religious orientation, there is no complete rejection of sensual experience. There is rather the view that deception lies in what men think about the nature and importance of sense experience. Though living in the world and a part of it, men must strive to prevent such involvement from dominating the deepest part of themselves.

Before such an attitude could develop, it was necessary for the concept of salvation to gain ascendancy in religious thought. It is likely that soteriology had been present in Vedic religion, but only with the gradual appearance of the ideas of *karma* and *saṃsāra* in the late Vedic (Brahmanic) period, does salvation become a conspicuous part of Indian belief. In the first centuries of the Aryan migration, salvation was presumably a group salvation.[c] The primary function of religion was the preservation of the Aryan culture in the face of a hostile native population. Later, when the integration of the dasas with the Aryan community became a major concern of the Aryans and rigidities within the class structure had greatly reduced social mobility, salvation became more a personal problem, the ultimate consequence of the faithful performance of social duty.

This new concern for individual salvation, and the distinctive relation of salvation to a stratified society, resulted in an emphasis on less immediate, non-empirical goals. The "religious" aspect of ritual now became

---

[a] Eliade ([116], pp. 78f.) remarks, "With every sacrifice the Brahman reactualizes the archetypical cosmogonic act." Cf. Riencourt [365], p. 25: "All Brahmanic sacrifices re-enact the Creation of the World, but in reverse, and re-establish the primordial unity of all things."

[b] Which is to say that the purposes of the ritual became more direct, specific, and empirical.

[c] Cf. Cornford ([72], p. 161) on the importance of the group in ancient Greek belief. "In a temporal sense of continuity, the life of the group, being a common life which transcends every individual, is immortal, which, to the Greek, means 'divine.'"

more important: the manipulative element of magic remained, but supplication assumed increasing significance. This sacrificial religion would
seem to be the necessary intermediate stage between primitive ritual and
the *vita contemplativa*.

There was certain to be a reaction to a philosophy that held the idea
that salvation was all-important and, at the same time, that only the proper
performance of religious rites could bring salvation, while the largest part
of the community—the shudras and vaishyas—either was prevented from
such performance or was severely restricted in its opportunities. Caste
could be preserved as the basis of the social order only if salvation were
made dependent on the fulfillment of the obligations of station, as eventually
came to be the case, or if salvation were related directly to the virtuous
life. In the latter case, salvation could be attained outside the caste system;
but, as in Buddhism, caste retained its position as the principle of social
organization.

Brahmanism is, then, more than a system of ceremonial. It includes
a particular type of social integration—one of the most completely rationalized in all of human history. Religion had become the province of an intellectual minority, the brahman priests, who controlled the means of salvation. Inspired in part at least by the need for a codification of Vedic rite and
a systematic statement of sacrificial obligation that could buttress Aryan
ceremonial and custom, the priests produced a body of doctrine and formulae that rivals any in the history of religion. The manifest purpose of
the sacrifice was to provide a thank offering and render assistance to the
gods and, more important, to induce their favor and obtain supernatural
power for the sacrificer. But the almost endless refinement of the dogma
and practice of the sacrifice shielded what was by this time a very real
instrument of social control and a definite vested interest.[a]

Two extremely influential and corollary ideas assume a central position
in Indian intellectual history at this time: karma and transmigration. The
idea of retribution for sins in the form of a cycle of births and deaths is
first found in the *Shatapatha Brahmana* (*Śatapatha Brāhmaṇa*). Every
soul, according to this belief, has existed from eternity and journeys
through a series of rebirths until it has earned eternal bliss. Each thought
and action has indelible effects on the destiny of the soul, determining
one's position in the status system. Birth is never simple accident: the
individual is born into the social environment most appropriate to the
spiritual development of the soul.

Thus birth into a particular caste is the consequence of one's own
action; the lower castes are denied even the satisfactions of resentment,
since responsibility for his position remains with the individual soul.
Metempsychosis and karma were the intellectual rationale for the hier-

---

a "The Brahmans were the first social group in the world to make metaphysical
reality, conceived philosophically, as contrasted with the 'gods' or 'god,' conceived in
terms of the daimonic universe, the supreme support of their social ascendancy."
(Turner [413], p. 395.)

archical ordering of men in society. In the light of these doctrines the individual could not reconcile religious interest with social reform. Any challenge to the social order must necessarily contradict the sacred scheme of things. The sanction for traditionalism, as Weber remarks, was as complete as any contrived by the mind of man.

By the seventh and sixth centuries B.C., the valley of the Ganges was populated by Aryan[e] and non-Aryan tribes, the more primitive not yet exposed to brahman ritual. Exploitation of the shudra had begun and the rudiments of stratification were visible. The vanquished dasas were included in the Aryan social structure, usually as shudras, the fourth and lowest of the caste orders, although they were forbidden to participate in the sacrifice. The three higher castes, collectively known as aryās, had come to be considered "twice-born," which meant that their members were eligible for rebirth through ceremonial initiation. Eventually that portion of the native population not incorporated into the shudra stratum (and outside the caste order altogether) appears in the literature as the *niṣāda,* a group with which the Aryans had some intercourse, and the incorrigible *pukkasa* and *caṇḍāla,* who were held in contempt. This social system, based on complex occupational, status, and religious differentiations, still influences Indian life. The status and defining features of the brahmans have undergone less modification than those of the other groups, whose functional and status significance has been altered through the years.

The growing intricacy of religious rite and the dire results that such errors as mispronunciation were thought to have, contributed to the development of the sciences of phonetics, etymology, and grammar.[f] In exercising exclusive control over religion, the brahman priests and scholars were also able to direct education. And although the king was not usually a member of the brahman class, the priests—as the repository of traditional and sacred knowledge and successors to the mythical seer, or rishi (*ṛṣi*) of antiquity—were able to make the full force of their strategic position felt in public affairs and government. In India cultural integration developed apart from political coordination. Later Indian history suggests that a society may be so strongly unified by religion that governmental regulation plays a relatively minor role. This integration was all the more remarkable in that it was accomplished without the formal organization of a "church." The relation between the brahman and the household he served took the place of congregation and parish.[4]

However, it should not be assumed that the brahmans constituted an affluent class. The years of discipline and Vedic study that consolidated the priests as a religious group (despite their heterogeneity in other respects) impaired their ability to earn a livelihood. And in the eastern valleys it appears that the supply of brahmans had begun to outrun the

---

[e] Which need mean no more than that they spoke an Aryan language or practiced Aryan forms of food production.

[f] These specialized areas of knowledge appear around the eighth century B.C.; probably politics emerged as a separate discipline sometime in the succeeding century.

demand for ritual services. Their own impoverishment often encouraged a sympathy for the poor.[5]

The destruction of tribal culture was a logical outcome, if not the conscious goal, of brahman ideology. For the brahman was sometimes without tribal status or, at best, enjoyed only an anomalous place in the traditional social organization. His marginal position made it possible for him to associate with all tribes, with whoever needed his services.[g]

D. D. Kosambi, like Weber before him, considers the incorporation of tribal elements into the dominant culture to be the major and fundamental fact of ancient Indian history.[6] The brahman took the lead in articulating and nourishing this culture and in infusing into it a principle of organization that could provide the basis of a society larger than the tribal community based on kinship ties. Because the close association of Brahmanism and caste encourages us to see this conception of society in terms of the divisive elements implicit in it, its unity is often overlooked. When the proper modes of worship had been established and the despised asura (demonic) rites eliminated from Aryan religion, the ritual lost much of its former rationale. Now the *integrative* role of the sacrifice in maintaining the community takes on new importance.

In considering society as system, we must deal with at least two functional requirements of that system: it must adapt to the larger environment in which it exists and modify that environment in accordance with requirements of security and sustenance, and, second, it must effectively integrate the units of society to maintain the society's smooth and proper functioning. An emphasis in the adaptive, or assertive, direction related to the attainment of specific goals of the system produces a strain in the integrative, or cohesive, area. Certain processes of adjustment are necessary to cope with the tensions created and maintain social equilibrium.[h]

The eastward movement of Aryan culture into hostile country called for an emphasis on the adaptive-assertive resources of the tribal society and the encouragement of heroic virtues. The warrior was the desired social type. Brahmanism (and later heterodoxy) lessened the strains produced by the need for constant military preparedness. Not only the ceremonial, but, at a later date, even caste (though ultimately destructive of the sense of unity), probably served a positive integrative role in social life. The units of the system, defined now in essentially functional terms, did not compete for the same rewards in the same areas; that is, integrative strain was reduced by rigid specialization—and the goal-object emphasized was of a transcendent nature.

---

[g] Each of the seven major brahman clans was supposedly descended from an ancient sage, whose name became that of the *gotra*. Actually there is indication of the infusion of non-Aryan elements in the early priesthood. Some scholars have undertaken to explain certain features of brahman history in terms of a merging of the matrilineal with the patriarchal culture.

[h] Integrative mechanisms include normative controls and supportive relationships of institutions that are concerned with anxiety reduction, the maintenance of behavior patterns, the definition of the "situation," and so on. For an analysis of functional imperatives, *vide* Parsons *et al.* [319], chap. 5.

On this transitional period, the later Vedic age, one history of philosophy comments:

> It formed the meeting point of two conflicting cultures, a fusion of them, involving considerable inner and outer re-adjustment. . . . It was a time when older gods were appearing in a newer light; when there was in evidence in every walk of life the need for forming newer basic ideas; when the old had to be preserved and made stronger by the incorporation of the new. Indra, as Oldenberg observes, had long laid down his bolt, as there were no longer for him any fresh iron citadels and the dark Dragons to be smashed. But the gods of the period, and the human legislators who arrogated to themselves the power of the gods, had to face the still more difficult task of social and religious reconstruction. And for one successful attempt to reconstruct there must have been made many a previous attempt along similar lines that failed. . . . We must not lose sight of the important conservative work of the [brahmans].[7]

THE POLITICAL THOUGHT OF THE SACRED TEXTS

The Brāhmaṇas, ritual texts of the Vedas,[i] are our primary source of information for the late Vedic period and the centuries preceding the Buddhist reform. By the time of the Brahmanas, caste relationships were clearly fixed, although caste development was not yet complete. The Vedic religion had undergone certain transformations and the sacrifice had assumed a central role in explaining a universe now envisaged as an organic and harmonious whole. The position of the priests as intermediaries between man and god was solidly established. The vitality and naive optimism of the Vedic age had succumbed to a more restrained *Weltanschauung*: life was seen as a constant struggle. The gods themselves are sapped of their vigor; they have lost the essence of their individuality and are little more than functionaries of the sacrifice. Prajapati, the lord of creation, now exalted above the other gods and in a position of paramount authority, is himself drained of vitality by the exhausting round of sacrifices—which is his very *raison d'être*. He represents all that is not expressed in the persons of the other gods: he is the harmonizing Sacrifice. As that principle which defies description, the undefined and indefinable Prajapati is a link between earlier Indian religion and the Upanishads, between the Vedic pantheon and the impersonal cosmic principle of mysticism.[j]

Of the two classes exercising power, the brahmans had the higher authority and were independent of the king. Mitra, who represented the priesthood, at one time stood apart from Varuna. That is, mind was conceived to be independent of will. But, just as will relies on intelligence,

---

[i] The *Aitareya Brāhmaṇa* is a text of the *Rigveda*, the *Pañcaviṃśa* of the *Sāmaveda;* the *Śatapatha Brāhmaṇa* is the exegetic part of the *White Yajurveda.*

[j] The progressive henotheism of the *Rigveda* can be seen in such passages as I, 164.46; III, 54.8; VIII, 58.2—references to the One who is all. "The belief in many gods of the early hymns now becomes more or less definite monotheism. . . . [The tendency] aims at the discovery, not of one god who is above other gods, but of the common power that works behind them all or, as we might otherwise put it, the principle immanent in all of them." (Hiriyanna [175], p. 14.)

regnum could not exist without *sacerdotium*. When, at the invitation of Varuna, sacerdotium united with temporal authority, Varuna succeeded where before he had failed. It was Mitra who ensured success, and hence was declared to be supreme. It followed that the brahman was not subject to the temporal authority, but brahman cooperation with the political class would aid the realization of the aims of both.

A passage in the very early *Brihadaranyaka Upanishad* (*Bṛhadāraṇyaka Upaniṣad*)[k] which forms the conclusion to the *Shatapatha Brahmana,* states that in the beginning only the Brahma existed, but that he created in turn a superior form, the Kshatra: "There is nothing higher than Kshatra . . . [But] Brahmanhood [*Brahma*] is the source of Kshatrahood. Therefore, even if the king attains supremacy, he rests finally upon Brahmanhood as his own source. So whoever injures him [i.e., a brahman] attacks his own source."[8] We see in the *Shatapatha Brahmana* that Mitravaruna is called the "counsel and the power." Mitra, the *sacerdotium* (Brahma), is the counsel, and Varuna, the *regnum* (Kshatra), the power.[l] "And the priesthood is the conceiver, and the noble is the doer. . . . So are the two united."[9] The priest, who officiates at the sacrifice, is identified with Agni, the sacred fire that mediates between heaven and earth. The interdependence of priest and king, who is patron of the sacrifice, implies a corresponding interdependence of kshatriya and priestly gods (Agnisoma, Indragni). Fertility depends on the uniting of the two—Mitra inseminates Varuna.[10]

Although the brahman is almost always seen as superior to the kshatriya and the spiritual power dominant over the temporal (as we would expect in texts of brahman composition), there are occasional qualifications that ought to be mentioned. Brahma and Kshatra are sometimes declared to be equal in authority, and there are even rare hints that the kshatriya ruling power has ascendancy over the brahmans.[11] This seeming contradiction may be caused in part by the complexities in the relationship of the two authorities. Western experience indicates that as a religion is institutionalized, it may either merge with the secular (political) structure, compromising spiritual values, or it may become segregated from the state.[12] But the peculiarities of the Indian situation complicate such an analysis and we are forced to conclude that such alternatives do not exist in the case of Brahmanism.

The differentiation of Brahma and Kshatra and the question of which constituted the higher authority does, however, have a parallel in European history—the Gelasian theory of the "two swords," first stated in the fifth

---

[k] The *āraṇyakas,* or "forest texts," which were appended to the theological treatises, were perhaps the earliest departures from ritualistic learning. They were intended to guide the brahman who, in his later years, turned to the quiet of the forest for meditation.

[l] Cf. Coomaraswamy [70], pp. 6f. "The Vedic 'dual' divinities imply, for the most part at least, a biunity [syzygy] of conjoint principles, active and passive in mutual relationship or both active in relation to things externally administered. . . . Mitravarunau is not an aggregate or mere composition of an essence and a nature, but the one Mixta Persona of both." Coomaraswamy suggests the similarity with Christian doctrine, in which "essence and nature, being and existence, mercy and majesty are one in God."

century. The dispute implicit in the Gelasian doctrine came to a head when, in the eleventh century, the Church claimed exemptions from the controls of the secular power. This would mean that the king could not impose the obligations of vassalage on his bishops. From here it was only a step to the argument, elaborated in the twelfth century, that secular rulers received their authority from the Church. The brahmans formed no corporate body as such and thus lacked the strength of the hierarchically organized medieval Church; but, through the *purohita* (the royal chaplain) the spiritual authority was able to exercise considerable political influence. The kshatriya rulers would not have been likely to claim, as did the theorists of the medieval European imperial power, that the authority of the priests did not extend beyond things spiritual. But the arguments of the late thirteenth-century European canonists in extending *plenitudo potestatis* over the temporal did have their equivalent in the Brahmanical literature. The purohita shared the governing function with the king. According to the *Aitareya Brahmana* the purohita is "half the self" of the king. The sacrifice of the king is not accepted by the gods if the king has no purohita.[13] The situation tended to prevent irresponsible tyranny on the one hand, and thoroughgoing theocracy on the other.

Presumably the first king appointed by the Aryans was not named as a judge, but as a general—the judicial powers accruing as the result of practical necessity. The *Shatapatha Brahmana* (V, 3.3.9) relates the passing of law enforcement power from Varuna to the king. The wielder of danda becomes *dharmapati,* lord of the law. A ceremony in which the king is touched with a symbol of justice is performed to ensure that the king will not look upon his position as being above dharma. The development of the concept of an immutable eternal law is probably the result of the brahman search for a means of getting around the executive power (danda), upon which they relied for the preservation of dharma. The priests were charged with upholding dharmic law and order, but without sanctions this prerogative could be meaningless. Because the brahman class was believed to be the immediate outgrowth of the fundamental creative principle responsible for the arrangement of society, its members found it practicable to declare law, or dharma, the bequest of the Creator. The will of the Creator is embodied in the priestly caste, which possesses a special intuitive wisdom as well as the technical knowledge required by the sacrifice. Indeed, those brahmans familiar with sacred lore are human gods.[14] Thus a very simple and effective guarantee of judicial hegemony was established.

The first suggestion of an attempt to explain the origins of government occurs in the *Aitareya Brahmana.* The gods, defeated by the demons (who were enemies of the sacrifice), attribute the disaster to the fact that they had no king. They then agree to make Soma their king.[15] Kingship is accordingly explained as a response to military need. The gods, at first disunited, came to realize that victory over the titans (*asuras*) could be theirs only if they yielded to Indra and granted him their collective powers. The theory has certain striking similarities to certain forms of the European governmental contract. It may be that the passages are significant only for the procedure of the rajasuya sacrifice. Considering the highly symbolic nature of sacrifice, however, it is not unreasonable to make this comparison with European postulates of an indissoluble covenant as the source of sovereign power.

The theory of divine origin appears at this time, but always it is the office of the king rather than his person that is exalted. The king is not exempt from traditional kshatriya obligations; at best he is "god-like." But as political authority became associated with divine sanction, the king became less dependent on the support of his people. The *Shatapatha Brahmana* says that the king is capable only of right. Although in its original form the coronation ceremony was inconsistent with the idea of dynasty, evidence of the increasing significance of heredity as the basis of kingship can be found in the Brahmana literature.[16] The more exalted the position of the king, the more it followed that preference in succession should be awarded to the crown prince as heir to this eminence. The priest was, of course, still very much in the foreground. In the coronation rite the prince was elevated to the status of brahman (without absorbing brahman attributes). Then he ascended the throne, was anointed, and the investiture began. The proclamation of the king by the priests was necessary if the king was ever to exhibit his strength.[m]

The king's council as described at this time included a cortege of companions, queens, princes, and officers of state. They formed a primitive bureaucracy, the ancestor of the Kautalyan system. These courtiers, called *ratnins,* or "jewels," were supported by gifts from the king.

The increase in area governed by the king contributed to the decline and eventual disappearance of the popular assemblies during this period. The sabha became the private council of the king and, having lost the popular nature it may once have had, was little more than an instrument of the monarch. Neither of the ancient assemblies can have served as a political organization much after the fifth century B.C But the village headman had become an official, or attendant, of the king and was known as a nonroyal "king-maker."[17]

Not all of Aryan India was monarchical. The area of modern Delhi (and east and south) and the Ganges (Madhyadesha) had monarchical institutions, but the *Aitareya Brahmana* indicates that a significant portion

---

[m] Jayaswal ([199], pp. 210ff.) comments on the "businesslike and contractual nature" of the coronation vow. (The oath is found in *Aitareya Brahmana* VIII, 15.) The oath was taken before the officiating priest who, according to Jayaswal, represented the whole society. This assumption rests on the frail argument that (according to the *Aitareya Brahmana*) the oath was common to all constitutions, republican and monarchical alike. In the oath the prince is called upon to swear: "Between the night I am born and the night I die, whatever good I might have done, my heaven, my life and my progeny may I be deprived of, if I oppress you." But is the king pledged not to harm the community, or only the priesthood? It is almost impossible to answer this question; but Jayaswal's position would seem to be supported by an earlier verse in the *Aitareya Brahmana* (VII, 29) which describes the brahman as subordinate to the king. Yet, *per contra,* VIII, 9.6 appears to leave little doubt of brahman superiority. The problem comes down to whether the brahman could speak for the community; considering his somewhat ambiguous tribal status at this time, it seems questionable that he could.

of northern India was republican. According to Jayaswal, this was the finest hour for the Indian republics.

> For national prosperity the Uttara-Kurus became proverbial. For learning the Madras and the Kathas, for bravery the Kshudrakas and the Mālavas, for political wisdom and valiant independence the Vrishnis and Andhakas, for power the Vṛijis, and for the philosophy of light and equality, for the emancipation of the low, the Śākyas and their neighbors, stamp their indelible marks on national life and national literature of Aryan India during that period.[18]

Monarchy, however, was the typical form of government in this age. The king's powers and dignity were increased by the support of religious authority. This legitimation served, at the same time, to subordinate kingship to religion.

From roughly the seventh to the fourth century B.C., India was the scene of the formulation and spread of a remarkable number of doctrines, pantheist and materialist, atheist and rationalist. Many asserted the complete freedom of the human mind from religious doctrine and were outspoken in their criticism of the Vedas and the Brahmanical system—going so far as to call the Vedic teachers impostors.

With the development of a money economy in the sixth and fifth centuries (and the resultant phenomena of debt and mortgage foreclosure) and with the expansion of commerce after the rise of Persia, a new distribution of wealth and power took place in India. These changes affected the position of the privileged orders of Aryan society adversely; indeed they seemed to menace the very identity of certain groups. The priests, whose status was challenged by this double threat of prophetic movement and economic surplus, sought to reinforce religious distinctions and, in many parts of India, to attach themselves more firmly to the less sophisticated village masses. The sutra literature undoubtedly represents one attempt of Brahmanism to meet the challenge of new values and beliefs.

The first of the sutras, the Śrauta Sutras, were introduced to clarify the Brahmanas. Later came the Gṛhya Sutras, concerned with domestic religious rituals, and the Dharmasutras, dealing with the broad area of human conduct. The Dharmasutras probably date from around the sixth century B.C.; *Gautama* is one of the first.[n] The dates of the Dharmasutras are confused by the constant modification and reinterpretation of the texts during the period. It is likely that the *Baudhāyana* and *Āpastamba* collections belong to the fourth and third centuries B.C.

The sutras are condensed technical prose works consisting of brief rules that were to be committed to memory. In time they came to be laced with couplets of varying meter that summarized the substance of the law, and these metrical stanzas with their aphoristic style (understandably

---

[n] The term "dharmashastra" is sometimes used in references to the sutras. It is advisable to keep in mind the general distinction between these early texts and their later expanded form. *Vide* Chapter 13 below and Kane [208], especially pp. 8–46.

more appealing than the rules themselves) became the basis of the subsequent dharmashastra, or smriti (*smṛti*), literature. The sutras were intended to provide a kind of manual of ritualistic conduct, with obligations precisely defined for each situation. They fall far short of being systematic treatises on jurisprudence. Rules concerning ceremonials, class relationships, brahman immunities, caste commitments, and the like, outweighed references to what we should call justiciable law.[19] A social order, organic in nature and based on rules and duties that divide society horizontally and vertically, is clearly visible in the codes.

The individual is never sharply distinguished from the group; man has been completely subordinated to the concept of function. It was also recognized that the many interests and needs of man should dictate his membership in a number of groups.[o] In the regulation of social activities, economic associations of various kinds assume a new importance. There is an almost Roman willingness to recognize local custom and law as political authority comes to embrace larger and larger territories on this eve of the great age of imperialism.

In the sutras, as in the Brahmanas, the autonomy of the brahman caste is maintained and its supremacy upheld. The *Gautama Dharmasutra* takes as its point of departure the transcendent role of the priests; the *Baudhayana* mirrors traditional social concepts and provides a good introduction to orthodox thought. Authority is explained in the sutras as a means of satisfying basic social needs: power is granted to the king, who provides the negative function of protection, and to the priest, who fulfills the positive function of providing advice and interpreting the moral law. Unjust exercise of power on the part of the king, and failure to meet the obligations of rajadharma, will result in spiritual retribution if penance is not undertaken. Possibly the system of penance, as outlined, for example, in the *Gautama Dharmasutra,* was the forerunner of the modern idea of justice. The king must accept responsibility for the moral laxity of the community.

Divine sanction of the king's power dealt the crippling blow to the popular assembly as a check on his authority, and we hear little of the sabha and the samiti. By the time of the Dharmasutras the official counsel of the priest had become the condition of prosperity and justice. The office of the purohita was equal in importance to that of the king himself and was in a class apart from that of the king's other ministers. Also prominent were the tax collector, military commander, treasurer, royal storekeeper, surveyor, and judicial officers. A fairly elaborate program of judicial administration, with the king as the final tribunal, extended into the village level of organization. A body of elders or brahmans served as judges under the counsel of the purohita.

---

[o] The *Gautama Dharmasutra* delegated authority for the regulation of occupational groups to those groups themselves. Individual castes were to decide problems that did not involve other social classes. The authority of the king was limited to differences arising between caste groups.

There is evidence of the definite emergence of civil and criminal law at this time. The sources of law, as listed in Baudhayana, are the Vedas and their commentaries, custom, and the example of the sages. With the entrenchment of the brahman class, a change in the apportionment of punishment, as well as privilege, appears. The *Baudhayana Sutra* asks no greater fine for the murder of a shudra than for the killing of a frog or flamingo. Yet, according to Apastamba, one may not be unduly frugal with his slave or free laborer, though he deprive his son, his wife, and himself.[20] We find statements to the effect that the brahman should not be made to pay taxes, and his property could not be appropriated. In the sutras malfeasance must be expiated by penance for the sin implicit in the act, as well as by punishment imposed by the secular authority. The king must discipline those who failed to fulfill the duties of their respective orders.[21]

The *Apastamba* introduces a relativist approach to politics and morals; an act must be judged in the context of the circumstances of time and place.[p] The concept of the relativity of dharma, which allows deviation from prescribed obligations in times of duress indicates that self-preservation was recognized as the governing principle of life. This doctrine, as we shall see, was to become a major theme in the development of Indian political thought.

The *Baudhayana Dharmasutra* indicates that subjects of the king, like the vassals of medieval Europe, received protection from their lord in return for performing certain duties. This was the justification of the taxes imposed on the people. Gautama lists the percentages of various taxable commodities that were due the king: one-fifth of cattle, one-twentieth of merchandise, one-sixteenth of honey. The shudras should work one day each month for the king. Some—students, priests, the disabled—are exempted from taxes. Of the four ashramas, or life-stages, particular emphasis is given the duties of the householder.[22] Because he fulfilled the economic and procreative functions, he was an indispensable element of the social structure.

At this time, there appears to have been a disproportionate number of entrants into the ascetic orders—hence the need for harsh penalties to discourage those who would circumvent the system of ashramas. By the third and second centuries B.C., the brahman codifiers sought to ensure that admission to the renunciatory life be conditional on adequate preparation through learning and discipline.

With the systematization of usage and tradition in the sutras, the legitimacy of the royal power—formerly dependent on priestly proclamation—came to be based on the law codes. But this in itself did not mean that the king was becoming more independent of brahman controls. Actually the powers of the king were more rigidly defined. The very fact of the heretical movements, however, served to increase the dependence of the brahmans on the king. Since there was the possibility that competing

[p] But ethical considerations govern warfare and the code of honor is exact.

ethical and religious systems would be successful in eliciting the support of the king for their own purposes, the prestige and power of the king must have grown in this age.

THE SACRO-POLITICAL POWER

The concepts *Brahma* and *Kshatra,* as we have seen, occupy a fundamental position in Brahmanic symbolism. These terms, which we have briefly described as *sacerdotium* and *regnum,* first appear in association in *Rigveda* I, 157.2. We are reminded of the sacred-profane dichotomy that anthropologists often discover to be the base of primitive symbolism. The contrast of sky and earth is one of the most common ways of suggesting this distinction. The Omaha Indians of America, for example, were organized into two phratries,[q] the Sky-people and the Earth-people, each divided into hierarchically arranged clans and charged with functions appropriate to the symbolism. The *Rigveda*[23] tells of the world's beginnings, of Varuna who pressed the sky upward and spread the earth out broadly. The *Chāndogya Upanishad*[24] has it that what was originally non-being developed into the cosmic egg, which eventually split asunder; the silver shell became the earth, the golden shell the sky.[r]

Perhaps the pairing of concepts that represent either contrasts or the ends of a continuum is essential to conceptual analysis. At any rate, an understanding of the order of the universe seems to depend on such a pattern of complementary and antithetical domains of the holy and the unhallowed. This dichotomy is reflected in the social organization of the tribe. Where power is diffused, according to Roger Caillois, the clans are divided into two parts, generally equal in weight and prestige; where power is concentrated, the division involves the ruler and the ruled and the two parts are balanced in unequal and inverse weight and prestige, the one compensating for the other.[25] We might speculate that the first division characterizes the earliest history of the Aryans, when power was more or less equally distributed in the tribe. The invaders, like the Mitanni warriors who may well have been their nearest relations,[s] formed a military fraternity that governed an alien population. Later, as the subject population was absorbed into the community and the old warrior gana represented only one of several modes of social organization, the second type of division became more important.

[q] The phratries were exogamous tribal moieties.

[r] The idea of the two births of man (physical birth and birth through initiation) reflects the same distinction between the profane and the sacred and employs the same analogy—the laying of the egg is the first birth, the hatching out (of the worldly confines) may be compared to the second birth.

[s] The Mitannians were an Aryan people who had a prominent role in the political fortunes of the Near East in the first half of the second millennium B.C. By the end of the sixteenth century Mitanni was supreme in the area of the upper Euphrates— a strategic position commanding communications between Egypt, Babylon, and Anatolia. We possess accounts of Mitanni diplomatic relations, particularly with Egypt. Mitanni's demise came in the period 1350–1300 B.C., at the hands of her neighbors the Hittites and Assyrians.

Wikander remarks that the theory of Indo-European "tripartition" opposes to the two politico-social functions, those of sovereignty and force, a third function, whose mythical and ideological expressions are multiple. This "function" is described variously as the "people," the earth, fertility, and riches. "Moreover," he suggests, "this third function is distinguished from the first two or even opposed to them, dialectically, mythically, and in certain texts, historically."[26] Here, then, is the basic theoretical structure of the class system.

The moieties of primitive (and, we may suppose, of prehistoric) societies form an organic whole. "They possess and represent complementary properties that coincide and are opposed. Each assumes well-defined functions, shares a precise principle, and is permanently associated with a particular direction in space, with a season of the year, with a basic element of nature."[27] This dualism emphasizes the dynamic nature of society. The unity, as Caillois puts it, is "the result of the fecund rivalry of its two active poles." In the *Maitri Upanishad*[28] we read that half the year is sacred to Agni, half to Varuna. It is possible that the Mitra-Varuna dichotomy (later the Agni-Indra pairing), which appears to be the precursor of the concepts of Brahma and Kshatra, was reflected in a division of Aryan clans similar to that which characterizes extant tribal communities. There is evidence to suggest that the Indra-worshiping tribes divided into two rival factions—but none to suggest that these two groups had the complementary functions of the clan moieties. Actually they may represent two distinct types of Aryan stock. The Yadu group, we are told, arrived more recently than the tribes associated with the Bharatas. The latter, followers of the fire deity, Agni, were evidently forced to endure much from the more powerful Yadus and their associated tribes and clans, the Pūrus, Turvaśas, Vrichīvats, Anus, and Druhyus. (In the *Rigveda* the Yadus and Turvaśas are at one point referred to as dasas, although they cannot have belonged to this racial group.) But the tide was to turn. In a series of contests the Bharatas succeeded in establishing themselves as the major Aryan power—a pre-eminence to which the *Shatapatha Brahmana* attests. These intra-Aryan hostilities, although they must have encouraged new developments in cosmological symbolization, were soon to be overshadowed by the more dramatic struggle between these tribes on one hand and non-Aryans on the other. It may be that the tribal rivalry inspired the two types of kshatriya character, as represented by the heroes Arjuna and Bhīma in the *Mahābhārata*.[t] At least it must have strengthened the proclivity to think in dualities.

The totems of clan moieties are often animals of the same species, but of different colors; thus elements of harmony and disharmony are combined. Zimmer expresses the idea in broader philosophic terms: "throughout the universe the numerous mutually antagonistic elements cooperate by working against each other."[29] And this is especially true of the principles of authority—which came eventually to be the basis of legitimation

[t] *Vide* Chapter 8 below.

of the two ruling classes. It seems likely that the theory had its sociological origin in a distribution of function now almost impossible to reconstruct.

The categories of authority we customarily employ are based on the assumption that modern "secular" society is, in essence, dynamic, innovative, and preoccupied with problem-solving, whereas traditional or *Gemeinschaft* communities go on from day to day embedded in the crust of custom. But there are, of course, situations in which the so-called traditional society is confronted with challenges. These situations call for a flexible policy, careful calculation of dangers and disadvantages, and perhaps even suspension of the codes of proper conduct. Change may be rapid and sweeping—and the society will survive. This capacity to respond effectively to environmental challenge indicates an adaptability in the ideological superstructure, an allowance for the necessity of sin. Symbols of foundation are continually invoked. The concept of foundation implies the possibility of the "artificial" establishment of social aggregates. The heroic role is thus institutionalized: it is the assertive, transmoral role charged with the acquisition of gain and the protection of what has been acquired. And it is kept within bounds by its subservience to the higher spiritual power. The harmony of the two complementary powers, temporal and spiritual, Kshatra and Brahma, ensures the harmony of the world.[30] The relationship, like the moieties, is complementary. It is the Indian version of the Chinese principles yin and yang.[u]

The concepts, which we might describe as the assertive-adaptive and the integrative-cohesive, have an important place in the literature of political sociology. Here is the fox and the lion, the prophet-agitator and the priest-bureaucrat, the driving force and the adjusting force, Varuna and Mitra.

Georges Dumézil has worked out an elaborate analysis of Mitra and Varuna as the two major components of sovereignty, and has compared this division with symbolism employed in Rome and elsewhere in the ancient world.[31] Mitra[v] is mind; he represents the ideal values of the community and facilitates social ties. The analogue of this principle is Brahma, the conceiver. Varuna is will, the symbolic expression of the Kshatra principle. His name is derived from the word meaning "to cover": he was the protector of the moral order (rita). Varuna, the violent and unpredictable, is the great magician who is able to contend with the darker forces at work in the world.[32] "Mitra is the sovereign in his rational, clear, ordered, calm, benevolent, sacerdotal aspect; Varuna is the sovereign in his aggressive, somber, inspired, violent, terrible, warrior aspect."[33] Other peoples have known the two as Numa and Romulus. It is the ordered, the calm, the benevolent—as opposed to that mysterious potency which

---

[u] In Chinese symbolization the prince represents yang, the people are the opposite (feminine) principle. On the subject of these oppositions, *vide* Granet [160]. The Indian duality more nearly approximates the ancient Mesopotamian distinction between the great deity of the sky, Anu, who embodied the principle of authority, and Enlil, the storm, who represented power. The assembly was guided by Anu, but Enlil executed its decisions.

[v] The Greco-Iranian Mithras.

is always in an equivocal relationship to society. The two principles, mind and will, Brahma and Kshatra, were at first distinct although Varuna was never completely independent of Mitra. The kshatriya (as the theory developed) is thus dependent on the priest, although the brahman may function without the temporal power.[34] But in the basic scheme the two are homologous and complementary.

Mitra and Varuna were bound to the moral order. As Dumézil expresses the commitment, "they are less in rita than rita is in them."[35] We know that in societies where authority is strongly rooted in the supernatural and symbolization is preoccupied with correspondences between the realms of the sacred and the profane, "virtue consists in remaining *in the order,* keeping in one's *own* place, not leaving one's station, keeping to what is permitted, and not approaching what is forbidden. Having done this, one also keeps the universe ordered."[36] Plato, in his theory of justice, is only restating a time-honored precept. We know from Homer that above the gods of the Olympic pantheon there was a power, *moira,* older and more exalted than the deities themselves. This principle, the basis of order, limited the gods as it did man—apportioning to each his special function and status. At first, like rita, it was morally neutral. But implicit in the concept was an "ought" or a "must."[37] Moira held things together by keeping them apart. It originally meant "allotted portion or province," the status or appropriate area of activity that gave to god and man alike a determined position in the social order.[38] By remaining in one's own place, one also keeps the cosmos ordered.

So, too, in India "everything was put in order and set operating under rules devised for control, and different deities had separate departmental functions for supervising the operation. All this systematization and regulation was known as rita."[39] Rita, too, antedated the gods. Varuna was its protector.[w] And just as moira came to be dominated by the element of destiny in the concept, so rita, overwhelmed by karma, would be reduced to the principle of swadharma—the idea that everyone is born to his own place. Dharma "implies not only a universal law by which the cosmos is governed and sustained, but also particular laws, or inflections of 'the law,' which are natural to each special species or modification of existence."[40] To pursue the duty of another is to invite disaster; according to the Gita, "the dharma of another is fraught with peril."[41] Both moira and rita are charged with keeping all things in their rightful places. Both imply law, custom, and usage—power within a framework. Both were originally strongly spatial concepts.

In this conception of order the Varuna principle, which is related to Mitra as authority is to legitimacy, must have seemed in times of crisis

[w] This power is the cognate of an aspect of moira which appears to be an early manifestation of *nomos*—and in its most terrible form is Styx. Moira is the limiting and static side of the more positive and dynamic nomos. "The power which holds a certain field and is lawfully exercised within it is also the power which recoils in anger upon the invading power from beyond its frontiers. . . . Styx, the shuddering chill of taboo, is nothing but the recoil, or negative aspect, of [moira]." (Cornford, pp. 34f., 25.)

to strain at the limitations on its power. In guarding the order against hostile forces it may be necessary to take on characteristics not unlike those of the enemy. Authority is transformed into force or naked power. The gods become all too human; they themselves participate in the original sin.

Sin is defined in relation to rita, as the violation of the moral order.*[x]* Varuna's merciless punishments had not been seen as such an infringement, for the gods were by definition the symbolic expression of the order.[42] But the volitional attribute of Varuna offered a clue to the solution of the problem confronting a dynamic, aggressive society engaged in acts of expediency.

In India the amoral dimension of Kshatra found its fullest expression in the figure of Indra, who represents the warrior virtues, power as well as authority. Indra has the right to go above the sacred code when necessary for its protection. But purification and compensation are always required. This is one reason for the importance of the sacrifice in Aryan ideology. The right to transcend the code meant that Indra could spare as well as demolish,[43] for the divine law embodied a harsh justice that took little account of human weakness. This extension of the Kshatra function carries the adaptive-assertive imperative to its nonmoral conclusion, but it also humanizes the divine law and contains within itself an integrative factor. Indra represents the flexibility essential to viable government.

Mitra and Varuna symbolize the functions of coordination and control associated with the worshipful aspect of the sacrifice and with the brahman,*[y]* and the functions relating to the active use of power for collective purposes. The adaptive functional needs always threaten the integration of society—this is the sociological principle expressed in the symbol of Indra, the ambiguity latent in the kshatriya dharma. "The warrior is exposed by his nature to sin; in the name of his function and for the general good he is constrained to commit sins; but he quickly exceeds this limit and sins against the ideals of all the functional levels, including his own."*[z]* The Mitra-Varuna dichotomy is expanded to allow for this unavoidable fact of power. The spectrum of power now extends from power as a function of the system of social relationships, power within the organiza-

---

[x] Perhaps the history of this development of the idea of sin as departure from the moral pattern of things paralleled the metamorphosis of the Greek concept *ate*, which is at first not a personal quality but a momentary clouding of the understanding. Zeus was said to have taken away the normal capacity for judgment. And just as wine is considered to be responsible for this rashness (probably because of some daemonic property), so the drug soma is associated with this state of mind in the ancient Aryan culture. Though the individual would appear to be not responsible for his actions under such an "influence," he is nevertheless expected to make compensation. In the post-Homeric age *ate* has retained its irrational character but has come now to mean the penalty for rashness, the punishment for *hubris*.

[y] "The problem of control of political power is above all the problem of *integration*, of building the power of individuals and sub-collectivities into a coherent system of legitimized authority where power is fused with collective responsibility." (Parsons [316], p. 127.)

[z] Dumézil [101], p. 103; "Victory in the field demands of the warrior a violence which must afterwards be made to disappear, lest it injuriously affect internal order." (Jouvenel [207], p. 45, n.1; *vide* Dumézil, *Horace et les Curiaces* [Paris, 1942], on the need to reintegrate warriors in society.)

tional context resulting from the orderly mobilization of resources, to power as force, the employment of drastic means.

In the course of this development Indra, who was originally closely akin to Varuna, comes to be seen as opposed to the authority principle as *raison de corps* is opposed to legitimate power. And Varuna, as we would expect, takes unto himself qualities earlier associated with Mitra—until by the age of the heterodox philosophical systems he has become the representation of moral virtue and is linked to the concept of hereditary pollution. The distinction between Indra and those gods who, by definition, are incapable of sin may well have been encouraged by the priests—to place the mark of impurity forever on the brows of their rivals for power. In the *Mahabharata,* a brahmanic work, the royalty is always passive, but sovereign. The second function, that of the kshatriya, is depicted as active and subordinated.[44] King Yudhishthira is more brahman than Aryan in his attitudes, the chivalrous knight Arjuna is resigned to the fact of his sinful mission (he is what the priest would wish all warriors to be). The guileless Bhima remains to do the dirty work with Vedic gusto.

On the supernatural level the god of the aggressive and culture-creating people was being forced to make way for the gods of a culture-maintaining and settled people. The agricultural economy and the territorial polity emphasized the need for *rex,* for the integration of power and authority. The original dichotomy in the Aryan principle of order had indicated the means whereby the brahmans could insinuate themselves into positions of influence.[aa]

[aa] We shall return to these themes in Chapters 8 and 9 below, which deal with the *Mahabharata* and the ambiguous figure of Krishna.

4 × FROM SACRIFICE TO SELF-AWARENESS

THE SACRO-ECONOMIC POWER

Concrete acts acquire their meaning from norms and ritual representations which, in turn, find their justification in the general value commitments of society, values which—as Weber insists—ultimately involve nonrational choices. This meaning is essential to social and personality stability. We are concerned in this chapter with the changes that took place at the decisive level of meaning and value, the basis of legitimation. At first on the lower "institutional" level of the meaning system, these changes were concealed behind ritual actions and the more formal aspects of religious and tribal life.[a] But the widening gap between higher values and the forms of religious expression made Brahmanism increasingly vulnerable to attack by the new salvation religions.

We must not make the mistake of isolating these changes in the ideational realm from events taking place on the social and economic levels. The effect of actual modes of social organization on the way the universe is understood is never a simple outward projection of human relations. Substructure and superstructure interact in an intricate and often ambiguous fashion. Anthropologists have studied primitive peoples who interpret natural phenomena in terms of relationships deriving from the kinship system or other social patterns. Nature is in fact seen as a continuation of human society. Yet in such cultures and in the more advanced civilizations that have not developed the "historical" frame of reference, the cosmic order tends to be viewed as the model after which social life and organization are patterned.[b]

In their symbolization of cosmic forces, the Vedic gods of the Aryan

---

[a] When the *major* commitment is to the lower of the two value levels, the other (the "reasons why") may be varied without great threat of social disorganization. *Vide* Bellah [26]. This is the process of "rationalization."

[b] *Vide* p. 15 above. Much of this chapter owes its approach to the Durkheim school of positivistic organicism. The commitment of the Parisian group to the idea that categories of belief mirror the forms of social organization (*vide* Durkheim's *Elementary Forms of the Religious Life* [105] and his essay, with Mauss, in *L'Année sociologique*, VI, 1901–2, on primitive modes of classification), as well as to such concepts as the group soul, has been criticized by social scientists since the time these ideas were enthusiastically accepted by intellectual historians like Cornford and Marcel Granet (*vide* the latter's *La Pensée chinoise* [160]). Durkheim's preoccupation with the individual's group orientation and with collective values, his reluctance

peoples were sufficiently similar in character to the earliest Greek deities to allow us to speculate from time to time on the basis of our greater knowledge of classical civilization. Except for Indra, and possibly Agni for certain tribal groups, the Vedic deities were not actually daemon-gods embodying the group spirit. The poets had created their individual personalities, and they were pre-eminently gods of the warrior aristocracy. For this reason the relation of these gods to the worshiper was not one of direct communion, but depended upon the sacrifice—a contractual relationship, so to speak. What Cornford says of the Greek Olympians applies also to the gods of the Aryans: "God and worshipers do not form one solid group, but confront one another as a society or political unit and a power of Nature—between which only an external relation, of a contractual or commercial type, can subsist."[1] In the discussion that follows, we shall attempt to discover the meaning of the sacrificial fire in terms of what we have earlier distinguished as the adaptive and integrative needs of the tribal community.

The sacrifice is both a useful act and an obligation. It is often conceived in contractual terms, for the gods have need of men just as men must ensure the cooperation, or at least the noninterference, of supernatural forces. Ritual is understood sociologically as an elaboration of expressive and evaluative symbolism.[2] The manifest purpose of the sacrifice is either to gain the assistance of the gods or to placate them. Its apparent function is essentially instrumental; but at least as important are the immediate gratification it provides and the possibilities for acting out psychological needs. We shall be concerned here primarily with the ideology of the sacrifice: man's attempt to influence the sacred or the profane, to prevent the two from harming or even devastating one another as a result of improper contact.[3] The size and elaborate nature of these ceremonies in ancient India indicate that Aryan society was absorbed with these problems: the sacrifices described in the *Rigveda* are the lavish spectacles of the chieftains and the more affluent members of the nobility rather than the simpler rites of the domestic hearth so important in later times.

The Vedic sacrifice grew increasingly complex as royal ambitions swelled and priestly power entrenched itself. An illustration of the Vedic rite (one which has its roots in the remote chivalric age) is that described in the *Aitareya Brahmana* (VIII, 28) as "the dying round the holy fire"— a ritual that Zimmer considers "at once a document of metaphysics and a curious power-recipe."[4] It is essentially a curse on the king's enemies, and by the time of the late Vedic or Brahmanic epoch, it had become one of the magical means for reducing fellow princes to vassalage. Conducting the ritual was a demanding task, replete with intricacies and detailed formulae. The king

> will have to be quick to mutter his curses at precisely the correct instant if he is to cast his spells at the distant enemy with any hope of success.

to work out a social psychology (and his refusal, until late in life, to admit the importance of psychology at all), and his concern with function and process to the relative neglect of social structure necessitate a certain caution in the use of such a sociology of knowledge and action.

And with all this business of remaining on one's feet, not lying down while the enemy is sitting, and not going to sleep before the rival, the one practicing the charm must have had much the look of a neurotic caught by a strange obsession. Yet, obviously, all would be worth the trouble if the secret weapon got rid of the ring of enemies and opened to him, *yo evam veda,* the dominion of paramount royal rule.[5]

For sheer magnificence nothing could equal that greatest of all sacrifices, the ashvamedha or horse sacrifice. The release of a consecrated horse to pasture at will was regarded as an invitation to dispute the paramount authority of the king, whose power was represented by the band of young knights accompanying the horse and accepting whatever challenge their invasion might produce. The horse selected to wander the world for a year was always a prime specimen, for he symbolized the warrior class and the generative masculine force, as well as Prajapati, whose fertilizing power had created the world.[6] It was to Prajapati that the animal was sacrificed at the end of the year. (Originally the horse was offered to Indra, and before it was let loose to graze, a dog, symbolizing the demon, was killed under its feet—as Indra had killed Vritra, and as the king would vanquish his own enemies.) With the sacrifice of the horse the king announced his sovereignty.[c] This was the primary purpose of the rite, but it also served to ensure prosperity and fertility. Book XIV of the *Mahabharata* is devoted to a brahmanic account of the ashvamedha which, we are told, "on account of the very large quantity of gold that is required . . . has come to be called the sacrifice rich in gold."[7] King Yudhishthira is advised to make the recompense of the brahmans three times the usual gift, so that his merit would be tripled. The ashvamedha is also transformed into a kind of expiation, by which the king absolves himself of the sin he acquired in killing his cousins in the Bharata war.[d]

This sacrifice seems more like a great festival, or at least an ostentatious display of wealth. We read that:

> intoxicated and carefree men and women giving themselves up to joy were there; the sounds of drums and the blare of conches echoed across the fields. It was a spectacle that gladdened the heart. "Give that which is desired!"—"Eat what you want!"—Such were the words that were repeatedly heard both day and night. This sacrifice was like a great feast, full of joyous and contented men. Finally, after wealth had been showered in torrents, Yudhishthira and his brothers were purged of all sin and he entered his capital.[8]

If such a "sacrifice" could purge Yudhishthira of his sins, we might question whether the usual interpretation of the sacrifice is entirely adequate. We know, of course, that implicit in the destruction of wealth on certain

---

[c] The imperial sacrifice lapsed under the Mauryas, but was revived by the Shungas. There is record of Samudra Gupta and Kumara Gupta I having performed the ashvamedha, but after the second Gupta dynasty the practice became rare. The Cholas, in the eleventh century, appear to have been the last to sacrifice the horse as the symbol of their suzerainty.

[d] *Vide* Chapter 8, part 1, below.

occasions is the belief that the sacrificer will be repaid. And, later, when the agricultural harvest became all-important, the prosperity of the following harvest was ensured by the reckless dispensing of the grain. "Fertility is born of excess. . . . In a sort of wager with destiny, ruinous consequences are courted in the attempt to be the one who will give away the most, so that destiny is obliged to return with compound interest what it has received. . . . Economy, accumulation, and moderation define the rhythm of profane life, while prodigality and excess define the rhythm of the festival."[9] The periodic festival-sacrifice intervenes to revitalize the world when, with the coming of winter, it appears to be losing its fertility.

From anthropological studies of the American Indian and Melanesian societies we learn of a socio-economic ritual institution known as the potlatch[e]—an exchange of goods that is a moral as well as an economic transaction. The potlatch, originally a feast given with the expectation of return, is in its most general sense a ceremony involving the distribution of gifts. Those who distribute food and gifts are entitled to reciprocation from those who receive. Because the rite is a communion as well as a competition, it has both integrative and divisive aspects. The banquet or gift distribution is a kind of conspicuous display of the host's wealth. It is a squandering match, a direct challenge to those who are now obligated to repay with equal munificence or else endure a loss of prestige and power in the clan or tribe. The potlatch is considered an important step in the process of individualization, in the assertion of personal power.[f]

The gods were bound by the sacrificial gifts of men, just as the guests at the potlatch were obligated to repay with the same liberality. The expensive and awesome Vedic ritual lacks some of the features of the potlatch; but in the conspicuous consumption of wealth and the central role of the gift, it seems to be a related institution. The great gambling match between Yudhishthira and Duryodhana in the *Mahabharata*,[g] whereby the former lost his entire kingdom, his four brothers, and their joint wife Draupadi, induced Mauss to comment that one does not stop "at the purely sumptuous destruction of accumulated wealth in order to eclipse a rival chief (who may be a close relative). We are here confronted with total prestation in the sense that the whole clan, through the intermediacy of the chiefs, makes contracts involving all its members and everything it possesses."[10] The game of dice in such ceremonies as the *ratnahavīṃṣa* (a ritual probably belonging to the later Vedic period) may be a symbolic remnant of the ancient potlatch.

Held believes that the deference shown the king by the brahmans in the rajasuya sacrifice ("Therefore there is nothing higher than Kshatra"[11]) is in effect an acknowledgment of the king's superiority in the potlatch.[12]

---

[e] From the Chinook *patshatl,* meaning "gift" or "giving."

[f] *Vide* Davy [91], especially pp. 234ff.: "*Potlatch* is not the substitute for heredity, but its complement, and, we may add, its corrective. In society it is promotion by election in contrast to promotion by birth. It promotes the new men whom wealth favors." The author is careful to insist that the potlatch also expresses collective relations—although it is always directed by the chief of the clan.

[g] II, 12; *vide* p. 133 below.

In the *Mahabharata* (I, 78ff.) there is the story of a king's daughter who boasts to a brahman girl that she is the daughter of a man who gives but does not accept. (But of course the king himself is astute enough to admit that all his wealth in fact belongs to the brahman.) The potlatch must have posed a problem for the brahmans who, since they were on the receiving end of the relationship, placed themselves under obligation to the king and the nobles. It was probably assumed that the brahman's position was comparable to that of the gods, who possessed a higher power that must constantly be courted by men. At any rate, the emphasis the potlatch placed on wealth would introduce confusions into questions of status, as the story of the king's daughter suggests.

There is the danger that we may be dealing with early ritual institutions after the manner of Procrustes. After all, every sacrifice is an act of abnegation—since the sacrifiant[h] deprives himself and makes a gift-offering. And sensitivity to honor is a characteristic of all military aristocracies. Honor must always be publicly acknowledged, and we should expect this ideal to pervade all aspects of social life. Such ritual actions as the stealing of cows from fellow clan members, followed by the return of at least as many cattle as were originally taken,[13] cannot be explained simply in terms of an aristocratic code or the usual ritual exegesis. The rites of the *Black Yajus* include a sham contest in which the king overpowers a kshatriya with his bow. "The whole ceremony," according to Professor Sharma, "means defeating the relative in the cow raid and then reinstating the vanquished in his position by doing him an act of grace."[14] These rites indicate the important latent integrative function of the ritual. It is the symbolic expression of the focusing of authority in one member of the clan as well as an appeasement gesture and an attempt to ease the strain produced by the struggle for power.

It is almost impossible to make any general statement about the relation of wealth to political power in the ancient Aryan tribal community, a culture in which there appears to have been at least some sharing of the wealth. The *Rigveda* describes a sacrificer in his chariot as "first in rank and wealthy, munificent and lauded in assemblies."[15] In a cattle-raiding group, wealth in cattle would be regarded as direct evidence of prowess, and we might expect that the techniques used to deprive the indigenous population of its property would become symbolic of power and reappear in the symbolic expression of an individual's authority over his clansmen. And in a predatory society of the early Aryan type the potlatch would probably take the form of the sacrifice—in which the wealth of the clan is expended for the purpose of obligating the gods to assist its members in future forays against the dasas. The competition among clan members for leadership (which was not originally a simple question of inheritance, but presupposed certain magico-religious powers) would tend to encourage the entry of technicians of magic into the inner circle of power. This was

---

[h] The one who benefits from the sacrifice—as distinguished from the officiating priest.

especially true when it was believed that power had to be restored or re-juvenated periodically through the sacrifice.

Wealth is, of course, never enough in itself. It must be consecrated through the initiation; the economic factor becomes sacralized. This supremacy of the sacred over the profane is increasingly stressed—until no amount of profane wealth can provide access to authority. The "sacred" has become the monopoly of the brahmans. And the kshatriyas are willing to support such an arrogation of power. For with the development of new economic forms the ideology prevents the more opulent vaishya mercantile class from becoming a threat to the ruling group and may even be used to justify appropriation of their wealth.

The potlatch concept may be helpful in determining what is meant by early references to the "election" of the king. The processes by which the individual establishes his authority over the gana or clan will, however, probably not be the same as those by which he acquires power over larger political units. The passage in the *Taittiriya Samhita* (II, 3.1) which states that by the partial performance of a sacrifice the king attains the people (*viś*), whereas full performance ensures the kingdom (*rāṣtra*) as well, may indicate an awareness of the growing distinction between the tribal polity and the territorial state.[16] We might surmise that the ruler first gains suzerainty over his own clan or tribe and then, as the leader of the ruling tribe, over the tribal complex that is in the process of consolidation as a "state." In the course of this development from intra- and inter-tribal power contests to the great ashvamedha horse sacrifice, the expression of true sovereignty, the sacrifice assumes a variety of forms and meanings. Always, however, the "sacralizing" of wealth has a role of central significance in achieving the purposes of the sacrifiant.

With the emergence of royal authority, the king assumes as one of his major duties the representation of the tribe at the sacrifice. The fertility and welfare of the community as well as the king's own magical potency are ensured by the public ritual. As protector of his people, the king is charged with pacifying the gods and obtaining their support in campaigns against the enemies of the tribe. But the king and the kshatriyas have a special interest in the sacrifice, for their morally ambiguous social role necessitates their ritual purification. Here perhaps is the seed of the guilt that has its historic culmination in the Buddha—a psychological phenomenon that the brahmans will use to full advantage.

The kshatriya traditionally has two roles: the protection of the people in battle and the acquisition of wealth. In the sacred texts we often find the latter emphasized. The inherent sin in the kshatriya dharma empha-sized the need for the sacrifice as a necessary antidote—and the sacrifice, in turn, fostered the emphasis on wealth. In the *Santiparva*[17] (of the *Mahabharata*) we read that wealth was created for the celebration of the sacrifice, that all wealth should be devoted to the sacrifice, and that it is improper to spend wealth on enjoyment. The idea that instead of being hoarded, wealth ought to find its way into gifts for the brahmans becomes evident. Wealth cannot be used to win the favor of the gods without the intervention of the priests. The brahmans had maneuvered themselves into a strategic position.[i]

Before we turn to the role of the priest in the sacrifice and the theory of the gift as revealed in the ancient sources, it is worth noting how simply idealism is fused with materialism in the concept of the food that feeds the sacrificial fire. The attention to food in Indian religious theory indicates that philosophy is rooted in some basic realities of life. "If one should not eat for ten days, even though he might live, yet verily he becomes a non-seer, a non-hearer, a non-thinker, a non-perceiver, a non-doer, a non-understander. But on the entrance of food he becomes a seer, he becomes a hearer [etc.]. Reverence Food."[18]

In Upanishad and brahmanic epic alike we find this theme. "From food, verily, creatures are produced . . . food is the chief of beings."[19] "The course of the world and the intellectual faculties have all been fixed on food. . . . It is food that keeps up the wide universe."[20] It is not simply a case of food being the sublime energy of the sacrifice. The symbolism of food in the sacrifice itself expresses the majestic and terrible cycle of life. Food produces food; "It both is eaten and eats things."[21] The growing emphasis on commensal restrictions is very likely related to the belief that food is mana, giving strength and vitality to the eater, and hence containing some mysterious power. Food announces itself in the *Black Yajurveda* as "the first-born of the divine essence." "Before the gods sprang into existence, I was. I am the navel of immortality. Whoever bestows me on others—thereby keeps me to himself. I am Food. I feed on food and on its feeder."[22] Food (*annam*) is the manifestation of the supreme principle that governs the universe. The concept contributed to the monism of the Upanishads, although in the earliest of them, the *Brihadaranyaka,* it is said that food must be supplemented by life.[23] In later Upanishads it is held that food *is* life.[24]

Food produces food. The cycle is without end. "The offering fitly cast in fire arises up unto the sun. From out the sun, rain is produced; from rain, food; living creatures thence."[25] And in the world of beasts and men: "Beings here are born for food, when born they live by food, on deceasing they enter into food."[26] The idea of food as the constant entity, the synthesis of matter and force that changes only its external form, is at bottom the expression of a *Weltanschauung* that pictures the world as a struggle for survival in which some forms live on others, which in turn

---

[i] In his study of Indian religion, which he hoped would help substantiate the thesis put forth in *The Protestant Ethic and the Spirit of Capitalism* [424], Weber did not discern the role of the potlatch in determining status relationships. For the anxious Calvinist, wealth was taken as a sign of God's blessing; for the kshatriya, wealth also served as an indication of the favor of the gods. But unlike the frugal and industrious Calvinist, the Indian nobles transformed wealth into power by squandering it in the sacrifice and the potlatch. Accounting for the failure of capitalism to take deep root in India, Weber emphasized the importance in Indian belief of mystical renunciation of the world, the devaluing of material things. In the formative years of Indian civilization, the lavish dissipation of wealth may have been as significant a factor in discouraging a capitalist culture as the ascetic disregard of wealth.

have fed on yet weaker creatures.[j] It is actually not a great leap from this materialism, which views the changing forms of life as only the outer symbolization of a fundamental and irreducible principle, and the philosophy that stresses the immortality of the soul in contrast to the impermanence of the body. We may even expect to find comparisons of the soul with food.

Zimmer[27] explains a line from the *Taittiriya Brahmana* ("By keeping his food to himself he becomes guilty when eating it") by suggesting that the individual "will not wish to break the circuit by hoarding the substance to himself. And by the same token, anyone keeping food withdraws himself from the animating passage of the life-force which supports the remainder of the universe. . . . When he eats, he eats his own death."[k] In the ascetic reaction to the sacrifice, nothing (or almost nothing) is kept for the self. But at the same time the individual is withdrawn from economically productive activity—a withdrawal for which the ascetic disciplines and cults are criticized in later orthodox literature.

The acquisition of wealth and the strengthening of the cycle are often linked with the stories of heroes in Indian mythology (as in the legends of every people). Indra released the waters and sent them "flowing for man's good"; he won the cows. Skanda, a non-Aryan deity (the son of Shiva), is gold itself: "gold is the powerful energy of the god of fire and was born with Kartikeya [Skanda]."[28] Rāma is thought to have been originally a vegetation deity who, if his wife Sītā ("furrow") represents the fecund earth, may be taken to symbolize the fertilizing rain. In both Skanda and Rama we can detect a combining of non-Aryan fertility and Aryan sky gods.

Wealth, say the brahmans, is made to be given away. Vain would be wealth if the brahman did not exist to receive it. Yudhishthira is told "to celebrate a great sacrifice with enough presents of all sorts and a sufficient quantity of the earth's produce. If you do not perform that sacrifice, O king, then the sins of this kingdom will visit you."[29] The presents are meant for the brahmans. One of the obligations of brahman dharma is to receive gifts. *Danadharma,* the law of the gift, seems to apply only to the brahman class. The priests reciprocate by ritually absolving sin. "Gift of gold, gift of kine, and gift of earth,—these are considered as sin-cleaning. They rescue the giver from his evil deeds. O king, always make such gifts to the righteous. Forsooth, gifts rescue the giver from all his sins."[30] When it is said that the kshatriya should either give away the earth in gift or renounce his life in battle,[31] it is meant that these are the only means the warrior has of purging his soul of iniquity. The brahmans' ability to demand gifts from others, based not on their own gifts but rather on the performance of a "service," is a striking modification of the potlatch prin-

---

[j] *Vide* pp. 11, 137: *matsyanyaya.*

[k] Mauss has commented ([260], p. 56) that "it is in the nature of food to be shared; to fail to give others a part is 'to kill its essence,' to destroy it for oneself and for others. Such is the interpretation, at once materialistic and idealistic, that Brahmanism gave to charity and hospitality."

ciple. The obligation in receiving the gift remained. For the brahman, the major obligation was purity—and he refused to accept the gift under certain conditions. The sin of the giver is transferred with the gift, and precautions must be taken.[32]

The gift to the brahman appears to have taken the place of the sacrifice in many situations. Indeed, according to a brahman text, "by making an act of giving, you [Yudhishthira] should consider yourself as performing a sacrifice." By supporting the brahmans the king gains higher merit than if he performed the rajasuya or horse sacrifice.[33] And once the gift is acquired by the priest it is taboo. The brahman's property destroys him who takes it—and will doom the second and even the third generation of the transgressor.[34] It should be remarked that in redirecting wealth from the extravagances of the sacrifice back to society (even though the brahmans usually intended this wealth for themselves) the priests performed a positive social function. And in fairness it must be said that at least a few of the brahmans realized that they could not insist on the inability of wealth to satisfy the true needs of man (in language of an almost Buddhistic ring), while accumulating property themselves. In that great statement of brahman prerogatives, the *Anuśasanaparva,* we read that "much wealth, when possessed by a brahman, becomes a source of evil to him. Constant association with riches and prosperity is sure to fill him with pride and cause him to be stupefied. . . . [Then] virtue and duties are sure to suffer destruction."[l] But perhaps this warning is intended to set the stage for the admonition that follows—this time addressed to the king —warning against the oppressive amassing of riches at the expense of the poor and the helpless.[m]

THE DUSK OF THE GODS

Many primitive societies actually possess two distinct types of structure. In addition to the clan or tribe with its often markedly egalitarian relationships, there exists (though sometimes for only a part of the year) a smaller association which is ordered hierarchically, and which allows an alternative to traditional ascriptive forms of authority.[n] In this organization, which we shall call the confraternity, the selection process is more apt to be based on achievement. The confraternity establishes a criterion

---

[l] *Mahabharata* XIII; the verses cited are 61.19f. Scattered references in the work to the sacredness of the cow, the four castes, and so on, indicate that the *Anuśasanaparva,* like the other books of the epic, exists in a relatively late recension. Much of the material (and the social life it reflects) is, however, of ancient date.

[m] The law of the gift is not systematically developed. It consists essentially of such maxims as: one protects himself from certain unsavory or dangerous types by making gifts to them (*Mahabharata* XIII, 59.13f.); one acquires different rewards by making gifts under certain conjunctions of the planets and stars; one may give what remains after necessary expenses for the food and clothing of his family have been met (*Brihaspati Dharmashastra* XV, 3; *Narada Dharmashastra* IV, 6). On the subject of gifts, and particularly gifts to brahmans, *vide* the *Anuśasanaparva* 9.11f., 20.37f., 59.5ff., 61–69, 71, 73, 76f., 84, 124, 138.

[n] It is most likely to assume prominence during the winter season when religious activity is most important—for the fertility of the earth must be regained.

of eligibility; power and prestige are linked to the possession of magical abilities. Members of the confraternity undergo a series of initiations that introduce the novice into a "second life" as a member of the sacred community. Historically the right to this ceremony seems usually to have been purchased: admission to the exclusive association was dependent in most cases on wealth. The confraternity and the potlatch thus have an affinity.

This organization of initiates tends to assume increasing political prominence. According to Georges Davy, it takes over the political function of the clan "just at the moment when the transformations of totemism and kinship are rendering obsolete the conceptions of communal authority diffused throughout the totemic clan, and are demanding a structure adapted to making power individual and hierarchic." The confraternity is "the incubator of individualization for sovereignty."[35]

From what we know of early Aryan society and its spread from the mountain passes of northwest India into the jungles of the lower Gangetic valley, some such transformation of authority must have taken place, although the attempt to find any collectivity among Vedic political institutions that very precisely resembles the confraternity goes unrewarded. The Vedic gana was probably an armed organization of the whole people, its only official the leader, or ganapati. The highly mobile gana was essentially a cattle-raiding operation. Its members seem to have shared equally in the spoils and the produce. A distinction between noble and non-noble ganas may already have existed in the early centuries of the Aryan invasion.

Also based on a system of communal sharing was the mysterious vidatha, which, in the earlier Vedic period, was more important than either the sabha or samiti (organizations likely to be products of a more mature society and more complex political structure). The general business of the community was carried on in the vidatha, and the distribution of produce appears to have been one of its functions. A strong collectivist sentiment dominated the gathering (at which women were often present) and one is tempted to see in the vidatha the ancestor of the sangha. As such, it is far from the confraternity, although it fulfilled some of the functions of the potlatch. The gana and vidatha antedate the time when classes were differentiated to the extent that they were in the later Vedic period— although in the very early hymns we learn of the distinction between the kshatriya nobility and the people.

In Held's opinion[36] the sabha was originally a secret society or "club" that belonged exclusively to the kshatriyas. These were the initiates who were admitted to the sacred meeting ground, the place of the ceremonial. In the *Mahabharata* the sabha represented the ritual world, and it was here that the potlatch and initiation took place. Held considered the two ritual activities to be the consummations of the social and religious life of the tribe, associated, respectively, with the Kauravas and the Pāṇḍavas.[o] The

---

[o] *Vide* Chapter 8, part 1, below. This relating of the two complementary functions to the two peoples would seem to be stretching the point. The Pandavas spon-

sabha may also refer to the building in which the kshatriya initiates met. It was the scene of the dice game that figures so significantly in the epic. Gambling was far more than a game of chance. The dice were thought to deliver the divine verdict. "Indeed, we may . . . say that for the human mind the ideas of happiness, luck and fate seem to lie very close to the realm of the sacred," Huizinga remarks.[37]

It is conceivable that the sabha once performed the function of the confraternity. But the sabha and the vidatha are not the only inner societies that may have figured in the shaping of power into authority. There was also the parishad, an organization as obscure as the vidatha. The term *parisada* is used in the *Rigveda*[38] to mean companions or associates. The early parishad was linked to Shiva and his son Skanda—a suggestion that it was not originally an Aryan institution.[p] It was at first a tribal military assembly, probably not of major political significance. Later its patron appears to have been Agni, and the parishad took on a definite religious cast. The *Baudhayana Dharmasutra*[39] holds that those without *mantra* and *vrāta* (sacred guidance and oath) "cannot shine in the parishad." According to the grammarian Pāṇini, members had to have high qualifications to be eligible for what was by the age of the Upanishads a small and exclusive body exercising social, political, and academic functions. The parishad had become an academic body and a council of the king.[q] Eventually, in its final stages of development, the organization came to be dominated by the priests—almost to the exclusion of representatives of other social classes.

It is impossible to say whether the parishad, or perhaps some other institution, introduced a new type of power structure into Aryan society. We can only postulate that something of this sort happened, and that non-Aryan elements must have contributed to the "enchantment" of authority. The original diffusion of power in the Aryan cattle-raising tribes was adequate to the needs of a simple nomadic life. The insecurities of such a life and the social problems confronted by the early tribe were not so complex that they could not be handled by the tribal chieftains and elders. Changing conditions, and particularly the widespread development of settled peasant life, modified the social cohesion that had been a major source of strength in the former community. The older forms of social integration were no

---

sored some elaborate feasts and conspicuous displays of wealth, and certainly two warring groups cannot be considered phratries in the strict sense. What Held evidently has in mind is the idea that the Kauravas excelled at the potlatch and were victorious in feast and gaming rivalries, whereas the Pandavas, under the aegis of Krishna, the divine initiate, were invincible in battle.

[p] Another such suggestion is the fact that there is no horse in the catalogue of totems.

[q] "A passage from a later Brahmana suggests that the *parisad* was a royal assembly, in which members evinced anxiety for securing victory over their opponent in debate. In the reference one party declares: 'I am a supporter of the king and you are a supporter of the kingless state,' which implies that it was not without tough fight that the champions of the kingless state gave way to those of monarchy. Perhaps it indicates the process by which the king was gaining his foothold in the early *parisad* with the help of his supporters." (Sharma [389], p. 95.) For a lengthier discussion of the parishad, *vide* Sharma [389], chap. 7.

longer appropriate to the social purposes of the tribe. The great battle in the *Mahabharata* may represent the struggle among clan leaders for supremacy, a struggle that more typically was expressed in less destructive competitions. The great ceremonies later associated with the king's investment with authority probably re-enact these contests.

We might surmise that in this contention for power the need for a basis of legitimation beyond the traditional kshatradharma, as well as the need to canalize competition in the interest of social order and harmony, made the sacrifice itself an instrument in the struggle for authority. Authority was symbolized by the individual who represented the tribe at the ritual, for the sacrifice was the ultimate source of tribal strength. The measure of heroic stature may have been the wealth a man could bring to the sacrifice—a variation of the primitive potlatch.

Another possibility is that as these tribes settled into a less nomadic life and social arrangements became more intricate, inner societies along the lines of the confraternity developed as a basis for allocating positions of responsibility in the society. Such groups may have developed first among those whose task it was to prepare the sacrifice—and from this "professional" organization the concepts and mystique we associate with Brahmanism emerged. If such was the case, we might conjecture that the confraternity represented influences from outside Aryan society, or even that it included magicians and priests from the non-Aryan peoples.

But it is more likely that the tribal priests who antedated the brahmans and who were not always distinguished from the kshatriya warriors[r] developed some such secret organization as a preparation for sacrificial purity or as a means of directing community wealth into the sacrifice. Or the kshatriya nobility itself, with the occult assistance of the priests, may have developed the device of the confraternity to safeguard its traditional prerogatives against the challenge of commercial wealth and non-Aryan culture. It should be clear that the confraternity limits social mobility as well as provides a new basis of power and status.

In the competition among the kshatriya lords themselves, we would expect the power of the priests to be augmented—as individual members of the nobility sought to advance or ensure their claims by enlisting the aid of the gods. The recurring statement in the brahmanic literature that the king is dependent on the brahman and owes his power to the priest may have a very real basis in fact.

Then, too, in the context of the total society, the Aryan community itself may be seen as a confraternity based on initiation. In the first birth man enters society, but if also born into the Aryan clan, he is qualified for a second birth, this time into the magical society dominated by the brahman. With the advent of the hereditary monarchy and the varna social structure with the priest at its pinnacle, status is again based on birth;

[r] The specialization of roles, like the development of free exchange relationships, is a feature of the structural elaboration of society. One is usually impressed by the absence of definite judicial organization in the early clan—as true for ancient Israel as for India. The same person frequently discharged political, religious, and judicial duties.

the ascriptive society is re-established. The irony of this interlude is that the basis of the sacred hierarchical structure was initially an instrument for surmounting the limitations of a system in which power was diffused throughout the tribal nobility. In later history the two types of control system continue to coexist within the hierarchically ordered bureaucratic state devised by the Mauryas and in the hierarchic structure of dharmic duty on the one hand, and, on the other, within the individual castes and in the villages, where power remained far more diffuse.

We reiterate that the model of the confraternity is only an attempt to suggest how the change in the structure of power might possibly have come about—as well as to explain seeming contradictions in the Vedic literature as to the different sources of the king's authority. We are, in the last analysis, always forced to make what we can of such frail hints as that in the *Brihadaranyaka Upanishad,* which tells of a young brahman going to the parishad of the Pañchalas, being cross-examined by a kshatriya noble, and discovering that there are mysteries that have not been revealed to the brahmans.[8]

We shall next consider the brahman's role in the sacrifice. This key position in the life of the community is the root of brahman power.

The most characteristic element of the sacred is its dangerous and proscribing property. Intermediaries are needed to make possible communication between the realms of the sacred and the profane, since the forces unleashed in the contact between the two spheres are so powerful that they might otherwise destroy each other. When we speak of the sacrifice we are speaking of these intermediaries—the sacrificial offering (the food and the gift) and the officiating priest. The sacrifice confers a sacred quality on the offering, which does not necessarily have this quality originally. The sacrificial presentation may represent a spirit in need of liberation—not simply a totemic animal.[40] The animal sacrificed may represent a repository of society's sins, impurities, and insufficiencies.[t]

Like the sacrificial gift, the brahman stands between god and sacrificer—functioning as a kind of lightning rod to protect the patron of the sacrifice from the potency of the sacred, and protecting the latter from an equally disastrous overdose of the profane. Without the priest, the sacrifiant would risk destruction—like the unfortunate who put out his hand to steady the ark of the covenant. The brahman must have found it to his advantage to emphasize the difficulties and dangers inherent in establishing a liaison between the two worlds. For by appearing to possess a special nature that immunized him against the deleterious effects of mana, he was able to establish himself in a strategic position in society. This special

---

[8] *Vide* p. 64, note [ee].

[t] The sacrifice of the cow persisted throughout the better part of the Vedic period. We find no attack on the practice until the *Atharvaveda,* a work which reveals many non-Aryan influences. The origins of the cult of cow worship are obscure. Although the cow was of foremost significance in the Indo-Iranian goddess cult, it is not depicted as a totemic animal in the remains of the Harappa civilization—in which the bull was regarded as sacred. The cow appears not to have been exalted until the emergence of the agricultural economy.

nature distinguished him from the other members of the tribal community, and it may have been that he was actually imported from outside Aryan society—as some scholars have suggested.

The brahman's unique ability is itself an extension of the supernatural potency; except in extraordinary circumstances, he did not need special consecration, for he was already nearly divine. Or perhaps it would be more accurate to say that he possessed the requisite purity to "pass from the world of men into the world of the gods."[41] Those responsible for the administration of the sacrifice must be pure: for the impure and the profane the approach of the divinity is terrible.[u] The holiness of the brahman was such that indeed, as Paul Masson-Oursel remarks, "there is no danger that [the gods of Brahmanism] will accept the rites and then refuse to hear the prayer; they can be guided by mechanical practice of the cult. They are subservient, if not to men in general, at least to the consecrated technicians, the Brahmans, and men cannot by any means be said to be at their mercy."[42]

The power to manipulate the gods must have seemed to be superior to the gods themselves. It is reasonable to assume that this magical skill would influence the very conception of the gods. And it is not surprising to find that where Brahman appears in the later Vedic literature as a mysterious and impersonal force it is not appreciably different from the mana of simpler religions.[v] The brahmans had in fact projected their own potency into the sphere of the gods. Prajapati ultimately emerges as a principle higher than the gods themselves. Among the gods, Varuna, the magician and protector of the cosmic order, best lends himself to this more generalized concept of the supernatural—and Varuna begins to appear as a stern, omniscient deity, whose insistence on purity extended beyond ritual propriety into the ethical sphere.

Some students of Indian religion have held that the monistic principle usually associated with the Upanishads had long been dominant in Brahmanism. Zimmer contends that "Brahmanical thinking was centered, from the beginning, around the paradox of the simultaneous antagonism-yet-identity of the manifest forces and forms of the phenomenal world, the goal being to know and actually to control the hidden power behind, within, and precedent to all things, as their hidden sources."[43] The gods symbolized the dynamic processes of the phenomenal world, but beyond and above them—representing the dialectical synthesis—was the very principle of Creation. The increasing abstractness and aloofness of such conceptions as Prajapati may even be seen as portraying the cosmic mimesis of the brahman's own isolation from the world around him. For the more man is imbued with the religious, the more he becomes enmeshed in interdictions that segregate him from society.

Prajapati originally sacrificed himself to produce the world. At every

---

[u] Cf. Exodus XIX, 10ff.; Numbers XI, 18ff.

[v] Oldenberg ([309], pp. 35ff.) considered mana a supernatural potency as opposed to the ritual formula (Brahman). Only later did Brahman come to approximate the Melanesian concept of mana, and then only in a limited sense; for mana has definite animistic connotations. But cf. Söderblom [399].

sacrifice the priest is Prajapati: "the sacrificer is the god Prajapati at his own sacrifice."[44] Prajapati returned from death to life. This second birth, the sacrificial initiation, is the true birth. The second birth was a birth out of the ascriptive Aryan clan. Hence it is no less than a new principle of legitimation. Also associated with the brahman were the gods who assisted in the sacrifice. Agni, like the priest himself, was an intermediary between the profane and the sacred. He was the messenger of the gods, carrying to them and sharing with them the offerings he consumed as the sacrificial fire.[45] Agni was believed to have been born of rita, and for this reason he was closely related to Varuna, the awesome guardian of order— a function Agni actually seems to assume when he seeks to return to rita.[46]

Agni is the eater of food,[w] whereas soma symbolizes the food itself.[47] Soma is the repository of all the nourishing and fertilizing principles of nature. At the same time it is the food of the gods and the intoxicating drink of man, symbol of the immortality of the one and of the fleeting life of the other.[48] But soma, the narcotic drink, brought exhilaration and at least the momentary sense of immortality. It united the imbiber with the gods: "we have become immortal, we have entered into the light, we have known the gods."[49] Here are the first vague hints of a concern for salvation. In time soma, the instrument, became confused with the divine life itself. And Soma became king of the brahmans.

When in late Vedic ceremonies such as the *devasūhavīṃṣi* it is announced that the king is the ruler of the people, but that Soma is the king of the brahmans, we might as readily assume that the brahmans were not actually members of the tribe as conclude that the brahmans are simply exempting themselves from the controls that govern the rest of the community. The language of the ritual is of interest: "This man, O ye people, is your king, Soma is the king of us Brahmanas! He thereby causes everything here to be food for it [the king]; the Brahmana alone he excepts; therefore the Brahmana is not to be fed upon, for he has Soma for his king."[50] The food metaphor is frequently employed to describe the ruler's relationship to his subjects; for example, the king eats the vaishyas.[x] In the commentary on the Buddhist *Digha Nikaya*,[51] the *rājā-bhoggam* is defined as the domain or "meal" acquired by the king. We know too that in ancient Assyria the word "gift" was used to designate the regular taxes long after these payments had become compulsory. Likewise in India the word *bali* at first referred to a voluntary contribution or gift, and later

---

[w] "In his divine personification, Agni rises into cosmic significance as a pervading energy sustaining the world, but he never loses his physical and sacrificial character." (James [198], p. 275.) In ancient Persia the sacred fire of the sacrifice was restored in Mazdean rite after the death of Zarathustra, and survives in the fire temples of the Pārsīs, a group who emigrated to India more than a thousand years ago and settled in the area around Bombay. The deity associated with the fire retained a strong moral quality that the Aryan Agni never achieved.

[x] "It seems, then, that the chief is the living synthesis of all the energies, all the capacities, and all the rights which are latent and diffuse in the group. To prove that the king really absorbs everything—religion, force, property—in himself, the Baganda [an African tribal group], to take but one example, represent him after his accession as 'eating the country.'" (Moret and Davy [280], p. 113n.)

came to mean the tax. Originally the chieftain or tribal leader received offerings from his people in return for his sacrificial efforts in behalf of the group—as well as to feed the fires. The man who sponsored the sacrifice devoured not for himself but for the sacrifice. When the brahman came to be the necessary intermediary in the performance of the ceremony, it would follow that the leader or king could not "eat" the priests.

At first the sacrifice involved simply the attempt to influence the actions of the gods by giving gifts. But in time, as the ritual grew more elaborate and fraught with danger if not properly performed, the sacrifiant (perhaps even before the priest) began to acquire special power or supernatural ability by virtue of his contact with the sacred, indirect though it might be.*ᵛ* It was in his interest to make the most of such a claim, since it would remove him from the competition for power. (The next step would naturally be the insistence on the hereditary nature of such power.) The leader or king, although he exercises divine power, is not yet divine. The position of the brahman as minister plenipotentiary between the mundane and the divine is the most important factor in delaying this development. But the practical advantages of this "mana" were many. For now the offerings brought to the king could be viewed as payment for the exercise of the mysterious power on which the economic and political good fortune of the tribe depended. Or it could be argued that mana depended on such gifts. The crux of the matter is that their voluntary character was diminishing. The gift had become the tribute and the tax.

Returning now to the concept of a fundamental cosmic principle that is "earlier than the gods" (an idea that becomes important in Indian cosmology in the late Vedic epoch with the ascendancy of the brahmans), we must note that this monism of Brahmanism provides a symbolic reorganization of the world. While relating the temporal and spiritual powers, the principle in fact exalted the authority of the priest. This development in the ancient myth reflects the growing integrative needs of Aryan society; it is comparable in a sense to the David berith (covenant) of ancient Israel, which provided for the effective regulation of social life when the nomadic phase of Hebrew civilization was over and which legitimized the structure of power—as distinguished from the Aryan sacrifice and the Sinai (Mosaic) berith, which established the original bond between the tribal collectivity and the sacred.

We have earlier referred to the *Rigveda* (X, 90) hymn of the cosmic man, from whose various parts have come sun and moon, Indra and Agni (fire), wind and air, sky and earth. In the *Atharvaveda*[52] the sky is interpreted as the head of Brahma, the sun and moon his eyes, and so forth. Similar constructions may be found in the *Brihadaranyaka Upanishad*

ᵛ Cf. H. E. Barnes and Howard Becker, *Social Thought from Lore to Science* (Washington, D.C., 1952), p. 23: "The concept of mana as a mysterious power akin to a potent fluid or quality that can be poured into the designated person or object, together with its implication of negative power or taboo, has influenced preliterate social thought in many ways, but particularly in notions of leadership, kingship, and so forth." The possession of such characteristics as endurance, agility, or strength attests to the leader's mana.

(I, 2), the *Taittiriya Upanishad* (I, 7), and the *Aitareya Upanishad* (I).
At death the aspects of man return to the elements: "Let thine eye go
to the sun, thy breath to the wind."[53] This segmenting process is carried
much further in the *Chandogya Upanishad*.[54] Brahma, we are told, was
divided into sixteen parts: east, west, south, north; earth, atmosphere,
sky, ocean; fire, sun, moon, lightning; breath, eye, ear, mind. In an earlier
verse[55] Brahma is described in terms of his four quarters (speech, breath,
eye, ear), which correspond with the gods Agni, Vayu, and Āditya, and
"the quarters of heaven." There are a number of correspondences between
cosmological phenomena and human anatomy, between the macrocosm
and the microcosm as it were.

This same conception is found in the *Brihadaranyaka Upanishad*
where, according to the sage Yajñavalkya, after all the parts—voice,
breath, eye, mind, hearing, body, hairs, blood, semen, the soul itself—
have gone into fire, wind, sun, and so forth, all that remains is karma.
" 'This is not for us two [to speak of] in public.' The two went away and
deliberated. What they said was karma (action). What they praised was
karma. Verily, one becomes good by good action, bad by bad action."[56]
The attempt to achieve control by disciplining mind and body is related
to the general identification of the cosmic elements with the faculties and
organs of the body. Zimmer remarks that in the later Vedic age "an extraordinary period of speculative research opened, in which the secret
identity of the faculties and forces of the human body with specific powers
of the outer world was exhaustively studied, from every possible angle, as
a basis for a total reinterpretation of human nature."[57]

The consequence of the imagery of the cosmic person was to subvert
the power of the older deities quietly, but effectively, and to pave the way
for a more abstract and moral characterization of the universe. In the
Kena Upanishad we find that Indra, Vayu,[z] and Agni have learned that
their power is dependent on Brahma and that this very knowledge has
given them a superiority over the other deities.[58] Perhaps it would be
better to say that the gods themselves were becoming symbolizations of
the more profound forces at work in the cosmos, useful devices for probing
the complexities of metaphysics.

But before this development could take place the social constellation
of the tribal organization (which was reflected in the pantheon) had to
undergo certain changes, which were to prove to be the first phases of
new and radical patterns of integration. Most important of course was
the consolidation of power, which in the tribal polity had been broadly

[z] Wikander believes that in very early Aryan India the authority of Indra was
shared with Vayu, the wind. We cannot here go into Wikander's arguments (*vide*
Chapter 8 below), but it is of interest that in the *Aitareya Brahmana* (VIII, 28) and
in the *Kauśītaki Upanishad* the wind is represented as the highest divinity: "All
these divinities, verily, having entered into the wind, perish not when they die in the
wind; therefrom indeed they come forth again." The following verse of the *Kaushitaki* proclaims that man's powers are revertible into breath; the wind-breath analogy
is obviously important here. The emphasis on the breath as superior among the bodily
functions, on the breathing spirit, a motif of the Upanishads, introduces us to the
world of Yoga.

distributed among the kshatriya nobility. This focusing of authority in the king and the high priest made power appear more abstract. The prerogative of the secular or spiritual leader tends to expand beyond traditional boundaries. The limitations on mana depend ultimately on the luck and ingenuity of its possessor. (The excesses of arbitrariness were to a considerable extent avoided by the division of this potency between the representatives of two groups that were conceived as complementary—a phenomenon that many Indian scholars are fond of evaluating as a type of constitutionalism.)

The cosmic order, depersonalized now and absorbing into itself all but the final consequences of man's actions, was experiencing a transformation that would reduce the universal rita to a rule of particular law based on social role. The new emphasis on Prajapati, the world-creating principle that appears also as the personification of the life-force, redirected attention from theogony to cosmogony and has some of the effect of the Greek concept of moira in that it tends to divide the pantheon according to a higher principle. Unlike moira, Prajapati created the world order by an act of will. It is a moral order incorporating justice and propriety. It is worth remarking that the early philosophers of Greece viewed nature as a moral order: nature embodies a truth. This idea is fundamental to all Greek speculation.

The brahmans, in focusing their religion less on the old Vedic gods and increasingly on more abstract principles, accomplish what Cornford describes Anaximander as achieving in his elimination of the Olympians from his scheme of things. The effect is that "he restores the more ancient reign of *Moira*. The primary order is still said to be 'according to what is ordained'; it is still a moral order in which Justice prevails; but the will of the personal God has disappeared, and its place is partly taken by a natural cause, the eternal motion."[59] The "cause" is perhaps not so natural for the brahmans, but the consequence of the transition from the god-influencing Vedic sacrifice to the new religions is similar. There are occasional indications in the Upanishads that a new "scientific" outlook is about to emerge. But we look in vain for an equivalent of that philosophical criticism which originated in Ionian Asia Minor.[aa] The clash between the ancient religion of Greece and the new learning of such as Anaximander, Democritus, and Anaxagoras, which was to provide the philosophical impetus for Western thought, had no real counterpart in India. As Zimmer puts it:

> The sun could not be both a divine, anthropomorphic being named Helios and a glowing sphere of incandescent matter; one had to settle for one view or the other. When a philosopher's focus, on the other

[aa] The statement in the *Brihadaranyaka Upanishad* (V, 5.1) to the effect that in the beginning the world was water recalls Thales' opinion that the "world-stuff" is water. (*Vide* also V, 1: Brahma is ether; as with Anaximenes the basic element is air.) But more characteristic is the thesis that originally there was only "non-being" —although some verses (cf. *Chandogya Upanishad* VI, 2.1) question the logic of creating Being from Non-being, or—the ultimate in abstraction—as in *Rigveda* X, 129.1f.: "There was then neither being nor non-being."

METHODIST COLLEGE LIBRARY
Fayetteville, N. C.   34117

hand (as was the case in India), is on a mystery the counterpart of which in the established theology is but a metaphysical, anonymous conception, well above and beyond the anthropomorphized powers, and revered simply as the indescribable fountainhead of the cosmos (an *ens entis* with which the polytheistic, more concrete, popular ritual cannot be directly concerned), then there can be neither an occasion nor a possibility for any outright theological-philosophical collision.[60]

BEYOND THE EGO

What consequences can we expect such changes to have for the individual? In very general terms we can say that where the old tribal patterns are modified by contact with foreign culture, by new modes of production, by warfare, and the like, man loses the security provided by the prescribed relationships that once dominated his life, and he experiences, in the deeper recesses of his psyche, a need to find a basis of meaning that transcends the flux and uncertainty that seem to characterize his world. In this turning to a level of meaning beyond the norms and symbolic actions that once provided the rationale for conduct, the ritual (with its close ideological connection to the tribe) lost much of its older cultural significance. The ancient cosmological symbolization was threatened by the new and individualistic salvation religions. Among the possibilities open to the individual, if the universe can no longer be seen as governed by a deity (or deities) who intervenes directly in human affairs, is to establish a ground of being by which he is linked to the "world soul" and through mystic insight acquires knowledge of the true meaning of life. Custom and taboo, rite and social duty, then become unnecessary and even inappropriate to his final purposes.

This is not to suggest an inevitable withdrawal into the mystical gnosis. Ritual itself takes on new meanings. Where a culture is made self-conscious and defensive by the proximity of different values and institutions, it will often seek to protect itself by basing legitimation of norms governing conduct on the possession of inherent qualities that are considered of symbolic importance. Knowledge of the sources of sacred tradition begins to take the place of achievement in what is, in effect, a regression to the ascriptive organization of society. Cultural differences have, for all practical purposes, created several communities.[bb] "Aryan" acquires an in-

---

[bb] Parsons' description of the universalistic-ascription type of social system cannot be entirely appropriate to a society that eventually became so rigidly stratified, one that came to rest in the limbo between universalistic-ascription and particularistic-ascription (depending on the level from which it is viewed). Of the latter type, which gains in importance as caste organization absorbs more of the regulative functions, Parsons comments ([316], p. 198): "Some integration beyond the local community both in power and in cultural terms is nearly inevitable. Such larger integrative and ecological structures tend, therefore, to be accepted as part of the given situation of life, and to have positive functions when order is threatened, but otherwise to be taken for granted. There is not the same incentive to use such structures as the political in order actively to organize a system, they are there first as given facts, second as insurance against instability." From the perspective of the individual member of such a society (by the late Brahmanic period), caste shared the political function with the state and must have seemed far more important.

creasingly exclusionist significance and comes to represent an ideal. It now becomes the duty of those in positions of authority to make sure that all the members of society either live up to that ideal (or a particular version of it), or, in the case of the non-Aryans, fulfill functions that, by their nature, would defile the members of the twice-born community. Thus the culture seeks to remove its institutions from foreign influences and preserve what is distinctive to it. And that which is considered distinctive becomes the basis of authority.

The salvation religions, caste, and the state (the subjects we shall deal with in the chapters that follow) are all answers to what might be termed "the tribal trauma." It is difficult to disentangle cause and effect in the great social and cultural alterations and transformations of the eighth to sixth centuries B.C. As was earlier remarked, it is a case of interacting forces, of developments that feed on and fertilize one another. That which is effect becomes cause. The tribal collective consciousness[cc] was lost as the old unity was challenged by new political and economic developments. New religious forms and practices might be seen as attempts to find a substitute for this lost reservoir of psychic strength. Caste ideology is related to the decline in the primitive and formerly dominant belief that the group has absolute supremacy over the individual. The tribe was confronted with a world too complex to be regulated by simple kinship relationships.

As a settled agricultural economy replaced the older, more nomadic life, religion reflects the greater concern for fertility and weather. Cyclical seasonal changes and their effect on vegetation reinforce the conception of periodic re-creation. This alteration of the symbolic system not only served the purposes of economic and social control, but also answered the popular need for the emotional experience of religion. The sacrifice had once served this purpose, as well as ritually renewing the bond of union that cemented the tribal community.[dd] Later, when new political forms replaced the tribe, and caste ideology had matured, the orgiastic cults of the old popular religion were introduced into Brahmanism to supplement its integrative power and broaden its base.

We would expect that with the breakup of community solidarity, the older, essentially impersonal "group soul" would be transformed into a concept of an individual soul or self that survived the body in which it was enclosed. Cornford believes that the hero (like the king, who is the embodiment of the collective power and luck of the community) is a transitional phenomenon, "a bridge from the daemon of a group to the individual soul."[61] The soul appears first as the social authority residing in the person of the king or hero or paterfamilias, a power that existed before and will continue to exist in his successor. This power is immortal because it is in fact a superindividual phenomenon. It is the collective con-

---

[cc] Durkheim's term to describe the beliefs and sentiments common to the members of the same society. *Vide* his *Division of Labor in Society* (New York, 1933), p. 46.

[dd] "The mysterious action of magical power only works within the field of a certain group of things, which are 'akin.' Our suggestion is that the notions of *mana, wakonda,* etc., were at first representations of the bond of 'kinship' uniting a social group—a supposed vehicle of sympathetic interaction." (Cornford [72], p. 86.)

sciousness personified—and, as such, becomes confused with the personality of the leader. At one time it was probably true that only such charismatic figures possessed "souls." If we are to believe the *Chandogya Upanishad,*[ee] the doctrine of metempsychosis was originally unknown to the brahmans, but had long been the possession of the ruling class, the kshatriyas. We might hypothesize that as rulers the kshatriyas were the embodiment of the tribal "spirit." In this sense they possessed what the brahmans, of ambiguous pedigree, could not have—a soul that transcended the life of the body. It remained for the brahmans to appropriate for themselves such a soul, the essence of community status. This they accomplished by encouraging developments that would culminate in a new principle of legitimation.

In time, and certainly by the century of the Buddha and Mahāvīra, there had developed a sense of separation and even isolation from the common life. This sense of estrangement is reflected in man's view of the self as a battlefield of "higher" and "lower" elements—the body-soul dualism that is the basis of the psychological structure of guilt. The self (or soul) had become one of many similar souls, no longer simply a part of the *conscience collective*. Borrowing from a parallel development in ancient Greece, we might say that the communal cult had surrendered to the individual soul of Orphism. The tribal religion, which on the highest ideological level found expression in the sacrifice, had given way to new salvation religions and disciplines of ego-modification. Communion and reunion were replaced by experiences reflecting the new "freedom" of the individual. For most this was an unwanted freedom, and it was no doubt felt as a frightening loneliness.

What anthropologists have called the "shame culture" is a characteristic of that stage in the evolution of a civilization when the individual experiences with emotional intensity the collective consciousness of the group to which he belongs. Later, with the development of the sense of a distinction between the self and the social environment, guilt and questions of morality make their appearance. The individual begins to sense the constraining aspect of social relationships.

Indian speculation, at this time of tribal disintegration, tended toward a preoccupation with man's isolation and vulnerability—conditions which, it was often maintained, were the product of his own incorrigibility. Perhaps it is only a short step from such a sentiment to a need for purification

---

[ee] V, 3 (cf. *Brihadaranyaka Upanishad* VI, 2); "Śvetaketu Āruṇeya attended an assembly of the Pañcālas. The Pravāhana Jaibali said to him: 'Young man, has your father instructed you?' 'He has indeed, sir.' 'Do you know unto what creatures go forth hence?' 'No, sir.' 'Do you know how they return again?' 'No, sir.' . . . Distressed, he then went to his father's place. Then he said to him: 'Verily, indeed, without having instructed me, you, sir, said: "I have instructed you." Five questions a fellow of the princely class (*rājanyabandhu*) has asked me. I was not able to explain even one of them.' Then [the father] said: 'As you have told them to me here, I do not know even one of them. If I had known them, how would I not have told them to you?' Then [the father] went to the king's place. [The king promised the brahman any wish; before imparting the desired knowledge, he remarked:] 'This knowledge has never yet come to Brahmans before you; and therefore in all the worlds has the rule belonged to the Kshatriya only.'"

by the rigorous pursuit of duty or devotion. There is, as we have seen, no sharp break between the older cosmological and the new soteriological theory. There is no very distinct dividing line between the Brahmanas and the Upanishads. It is more that the concept of correspondence loses its relevance as the individual seeks absorption in the objective principle that rules creation. Some treatises, such as the *Brihadaranyaka,* that are placed among the Upanishads might as easily be included with the Brahmanas, and likewise there are Brahmanas that could as properly be numbered among the Upanishads. But in the Upanishads, the infinite bliss of the superphenomenal Brahman (Prajapati) is contrasted with the world of imperfection—the home of frustration and distress. It is not so much a pessimistic theory as a disenchantment. In both the sacrifice and Upanishadic metaphysics the goal is the uniting of man and god. The difference between the two is that the latter (like the salvation religions) dispenses with the intermediary.

Regardless of the apparent chaos and impermanence of the world, there is, behind all diversity and change, a constant factor. We have earlier remarked on the cyclical theory of life as "food," an elemental substance which, although it changes its outward shape (in the forms of living organisms), is constant. The cycle of nature is viewed, as it was in Plato's *Phaedo,* as a balancing and repaying process. As such it assumes a moral character. But such a conception is not particularly congenial to the aspiring and idealist mentality. Imperishable matter would eventually be replaced by loftier concepts in the philosophic movements—a more optimistic theory than that which held that man was only matter to feed an impersonal dialectical process. Even in the oldest Upanishads we discover that the soul pervades all things: that there is but one soul. "Whoever worships another divinity [than his self], thinking 'He is one and I another,' he knows not."[62] To know this *ātman* is to unlock the mystery of the universe. Thus is the individual released from samsara, the cycle of transmigration.*ff*

The ancient Aryan principle of *performance,* the assertion of the self over the environment, with its concomitant ideology of mastery and power, succumbs to the principle of *learning.* Instead of ego as modifier of the external situation, ego seeks its own modification. Knowledge is no longer so concerned with the expedient relation of means and ends; it has become the basis of the transformation of the self. The aim of life is awareness of the unity of being that underlies all difference and change. Achievement is replaced as an ideal by "attunement." The intermediate stage in this development is *karma-marga,* the way of ritual action, which includes both the sacrifice and the performance of caste duty. And when the order of the world is thought to be ensured through the taboo of caste, there is no longer the need for the great rejuvenating and ordering act of the community sacrifice. The dharma-restoring avatar, reincarnation of the god, comes to take the place of the communal rite. It is *he* who acts.

ff In the Upanishads the theory that the soul is reborn in another body after death is not a subject for despair, although cf. *Chandogya Upanishad* V, 10.7.

But in the mystical gnosis the components of the sacrifice are reduced to one; it is the role of the priest, rather than the sacrifice, which has become irrelevant. The heterodox religions, such as Buddhism, in eliminating the intervening element in the sacred-secular encounter, announced the possibility that all men might acquire the magical Brahman that had previously belonged only to the priestly class. And now this mystique had become of more than instrumental value. It is salvation itself. If the Buddha sought to offer men directly to the sacred power, it was because death in the sacred was man's highest goal. The sacrifice had reached its fullest expression in this offering up of the body in order to free the ego, which becomes one with Brahman. In this sacrifice the body itself is the offering.

It is worth noting that Zoroaster's campaign against the haoma (soma) and the animal sacrifice involved the idea that he, Zoroaster, brought his own body and thought as a sacrificial offering.[63] In the *Maitri Upanishad* (VI, 10), the ascetic is described as a performer of the sacrifice to the Soul (Atman). In sacrificial terms man becomes both food and the feeder. When unity with the universal Being has been achieved, man attains perfect bliss. According to a marvelous Upanishadic verse,[64] he who knows this unity, "on departing from this world, proceeding on to that self which consists of food, proceeding on to that self which consists of breath, proceeding on to that self which consists of mind, proceeding on to that self which consists of understanding, proceeding on to that self which consists of bliss, goes up and down these worlds, eating what he desires, assuming what form he desires. He sits singing this chant:

Oh, wonderful! Oh, wonderful! Oh, wonderful!
I am food! I am food! I am food!
I am a food-eater! I am a food-eater! I am a food-eater!
I am a fame-maker [*śloka-kṛt*]! I am a fame-maker! I am a fame-maker!
I am the first-born of the world-order [*ṛta*],
Earlier than the gods, in the navel of immortality!
Who gives me away, he indeed has aided me!
I, who am food, eat the eater of food!
I have overcome the whole world!"[99]

To compensate for the lost community of his fellows, the mystic seeks to tie himself to all nature—to extend society to include all that exists. The individual atman seeks to merge itself with that which infuses all, with Brahman, the universal—to create a new "community" of the universe itself. The attempt to identify the essence of the individual with the great impersonal principle of the universe is the attempt to restore the older submersion of man in a power that engulfs him so completely that his

---

[99] This rapture of union with the infinite distinguishes Upanishadic philosophy from ego-restructuring Buddhism. In the verses from the *Maitri Upanishad* just cited, we read: "Thus the Manifest is food, and the Unmanifest is food. The enjoyer thereof is without qualities. [But] from the fact of his enjoying it is evident that he possesses consciousness."

capacity to sense its compulsion is extinguished. It is the external power that resided in the tribe and clan and that demanded absolute obedience of its members. However, the alienation that resulted from the erosion of the older political and social institutions made possible new perceptions of the self and the external world. Nature took on a different significance for man. No sooner had nature appeared as phenomena independent of the purposes and meaning of man than it was denied as illusion. No sooner had the self appeared as an independent agency than the search for the release from the prison of personality began.

The contrast between Olympian morality and mystical morality suggested by Cornford provides a clue to the cognate development from Vedism and Brahmanism to the new religions.[65] Basically the distinction is between the static and the geometrical: on one hand everything is seen possessing its own area of activity, limited by boundaries not to be transgressed, and on the other, there is the path of righteousness, a right way of doing and living. The moira that dominates the first became linked to individual experience and to discipline, which leads ultimately to salvation. This combination of the old and the new would seem to be basic not only to the new salvation religions but also to the awesome scheme of purification and stratification that dominated Indian life.

It is often said that ritualistic magic yielded to philosophy in the age of the Upanishads. It is probably closer to the truth to say that this magic, *karma-marga,* increasingly took the form of caste obligation in the elaborate system of correspondences linking the human with the cosmic.[hh] The sacrifice had been supplemented as a control mechanism by esoteric knowledge of an abstract philosophical nature (as distinguished from brahman technical "skill"), and by proper performance of caste duty. In orthodox theory, qualification for this knowledge came to depend on the fulfillment of class obligation. And this metaphysical knowledge had already been elevated above practical ethics in the Upanishads. Love and affection are important in that they represent the individual self reaching out for the all-embracing Soul that is the true reality.[66] This depreciation of moral distinctions undoubtedly also helped to prepare the way for an order of rigid social differentiation.[ii]

In the caste and transmigration theories that emerge at this time life itself becomes an initiation, a *rite de passage* to a higher phase of existence to which the soul passes if man fulfills the duties of the prescribed roles he is called upon to play. Just as dharma blends nature and justice, so caste relates the nature of man to a place in the social order commensurate with justice. The simple performance of the duties involved in one's own dharma endows one with a kind of magical potency. But man's sense of

[hh] The belief that the righteous (or sinful) behavior of the king infects the whole universe (the king is "the maker of his age") is as much a holdover of the old magical correspondence as it is the idea that rajadharma is the support of the whole dharmic system—in that the king possesses the sanction of danda.

[ii] Sometimes knowledge as well as deeds is thought to influence social station in the next existence. *Vide Kaushitaki Upanishad* I, 2.

power is never allowed to become stronger than his sense of his fate or responsibility.

Every profession and craft has its own tutelary divinity who incorporates the special skills of the occupation.

> Each of these, representing the principle and sum total of a certain highly specialized department of knowledge and skill, is a jealous and exclusive god and master. The human creature called by birth to the deity's service is to dedicate all of his powers and devotion to worship; the slightest failure can entail disaster. . . . From the very first breath of life, the individual's energies are mastered, trained into channels, and co-ordinated to the general work of the superindividual who is the holy society itself.[67]

In understanding caste it is important to try to see the different groupings as sources of strength and security for their individual members and, in terms of the satisfactions they provided, as not dissimilar to the older tribal collectivities they had come to replace. We too often think in modern terms of the individual versus the group—terms which are not appropriate to the time we are studying. Although caste restrictions tended to break the community apart along functional lines, there remained the need for the individual to lose himself in the common life through ritualistic union with the "daemon" of the profession or locality in which he lived. The popular religions that contributed so much to the character of Hinduism are important in social analysis in that they preserved the communal element of religious experience and often served as a basis of communication above caste division.

As long as the tribe remained the dominant form of social life, the negative and limiting side of the *conscience collective* (and the taboo of mana) could keep the individual in his proper place within the social system. When this ancient "nemesis," or fate, combined with the emergent sense of individual impotence and guilt,[jj] which had sharpened man's need for an explanation of his human condition, it lost its collective implications. Linked with the new concept of the individual soul, it began to take on the qualities we identify with karma. In the earlier ideology, a man shared responsibility for the actions of his kinsmen. (This hereditary pollution seems to have been associated with Varuna, who punished the individual for the sins of his fathers as well as for his own transgressions.)

The fact that the brahman was able to substitute new types of social integration for the older tribal variety, perpetuating quasi-individualistic doctrine, may explain factors that are almost unique to the Indian situation. We have not answered the question why social divisions should have attained the rigidities that made India the model *par excellence* of a caste society. We turn now to this problem and the attempts that have been made to deal with it.

[jj] There always was an element of guilt in the sacrifice—which was, among other things, an attempt to "buy off" the anger of the gods. This feeling was evidently especially acute in the case of Varuna, the purest of the gods, who hated sin and whose eye missed no transgression. *Vide* Chapter 9 below.

5 × THE GREAT WALL OF INDIA

SOCIETY RESTRUCTURED

"Democracy," writes Dr. Radhakrishnan, "is so interpreted as to justify not only the very legitimate aspiration to bring about a more equitable distribution of wealth, but also the increasing tendency for a levelling down of all talent. . . . [But] within the framework of democracy we shall have an aristocracy of direction. It is not true that all men are born equal in every way, and everyone is equally fit to govern the country or till the ground. The functional diversities of workers cannot be suppressed."[1] Certainly the recognition of distinctions is not inconsistent with democratic theory, particularly if these distinctions are understood as essential to the attainment of the common good. And all societies, regardless of commitment, must instill in the appropriate persons the willingness to fill certain positions and to perform the functions associated with them. In the modern world, however, the functional classification of mankind is defensible only if each individual is granted the opportunity to choose the life that can assist him in realizing the potential of his personality.

Although stratification is universal and essential to organized social activity, societies may vary greatly in degree of social mobility, in cohesiveness among members of a particular group, in value assigned to different gradations, and so forth.[2] To those reared in the liberal tradition, caste would seem to strike at the very basis of individuality. Caste did, in fact, produce a kind of pluralism and diversity—characteristics that we have learned to associate with the social structure of a liberal state. But in India such pluralism could not encourage individuality because of the complete identification of the person with his social role.[a]

The very word caste brings to mind the traditional social structure of India, but it is at least arguable whether caste accurately describes the sociological configuration of ancient India. Class restrictions had not completely hardened even in Gupta times. The *Mahabharata* often differentiates between the poor and the wealthy within the same caste, and Hopkins remarks of the society described in the epic that the social difference between the prosperous farmer and the poorer member of the same caste was far greater than that between the latter and the wealthy

---

[a] When we speak of pluralism today we assume the possibility of plural group affiliations for each individual—not simply the existence of multiple associations.

man's slave in all but religious privileges.[3] The Sanskrit word *varna,* often translated as caste, is more properly understood as color or "class." Ancient Indian sources only rarely refer to *jāti,* a concept that more closely approximates caste as we use the term.[b] In this chapter we shall be concerned with the four traditional classes or status groups of society, and although the word caste will be used, it must be remembered that the rigidities implicit in the term are more characteristic of a comparatively late period, when castes developed within the ancient varnas.[c]

The distinction between social function and religious values is always obscure. Salvation could not be achieved until social obligations had been met in this life and in the earlier existences of the soul. But if we are to comprehend the triumph of caste in the ordering of social life, we must understand that purity, rather than righteousness or mystical knowledge, had become the way to salvation. In the seventh and sixth centuries B.C. social changes threatened the traditional allotment of functions, and it became imperative that the system be provided with a definitive rationale. In the doctrine of the Brahmanical texts social life is organized to facilitate the fulfillment of spiritual ends. This theory was preoccupied with duty rather than with the rights of the individual.[4] There is no suggestion of an equality of rights among men, except for the right to the performance of those social roles upon which spiritual liberation depended. Questions of right were absorbed into the theology of salvation instead of remaining as security against the intrusions of society. Each social unit had its characteristic function; obligations were essentially those of the caste to which a man belonged and the stage of the life cycle in which he found himself (*varṇa-āśrama-dharma*).

Whereas democratic theory has rested on confidence in the conditioning power of environment and education, in India the concept of karma, the belief that character is stamped by the deeds of the earlier lives of the soul, could only discourage hopes for social melioration by alteration of the social and natural environment. The individual was predestined to a social station, and only by the diligent performance of ritual duty—largely the obligations of caste—could he hope for an eventual improvement in status, rebirth into a higher stratum of society. For the orthodox there was nothing accidental about birth into a particular class. There was no logical basis for social protest. Here was as convincing an answer to Job as has been devised. Caste was maintained by the promise of a future release from the cycle of birth, death, and rebirth—and negatively by those agencies empowered to enforce the performance of duty.[5] A man need not wait until the next life for punishment.

---

[b] *Jati* is a broad and inclusive term and can refer to a variety of types of common descent; it was more localized than the varna. In the complete tabulation undertaken by the Indian Census in 1901 there existed 2,378 major jatis, and these were in turn divided into subcastes of their own. There are sectarian castes, occupational castes (including those formed by change of occupation), tribal (or racial) castes, and those composed of the offspring of mixed marriages.

[c] It should be remarked that there is not even complete agreement that caste developed out of the four varnas.

Although the emphasis of Hindu psychology is on the inheritance of the consequences of past thoughts and actions, environment is important in that man must not be hindered in the fulfillment of his obligations. Each caste must live in a manner consistent with its function. This function is the reflection of man's nature, and only as his nature is modified should his social role change. Conduct was considered to be determined by three aspects of consciousness: thought, action, and desire. In each of the three "twice-born" castes (whose members were born again through initiation into Aryan society and investment with the sacred thread) one of these qualities was dominant. The brahman represented the contemplative attribute, the kshatriya was distinguished by his energy, and the vaishya was thought to be inherently impulsive. These three attributes can be related to the *trivarga,* the trinity of dharma, artha, and kama—the branches of Indian philosophy which relate, respectively, to man's need for spiritual, material, and sexual satisfactions.[d]

The dharmic ideal was expressed not only in this arrangement of social life, but also in the four phases of life which, like the four varnas, were intended to promote the realization of the trivarga. These life stages (ashramas) included the early years of preparation and discipline, followed by the period of married life and householding. The *brahmacārin* and *gṛhastha* stages of student and householder represented obligations that must be met before one could enter the ascetic stages of *vānaprastha* and *sannyāsin,* the withdrawal from the demands and distractions of social life for further preparation and service, and liberation through self-knowledge. In the first stages of his life man is dependent on society, but, as he comes to realize his true ends, he escapes this dependence. The brahman was expected to experience all four of the ashramas. The kshatriyas were to fulfill the demands of only the first three, and the vaishyas those of the first two.[e]

Reflecting differences in ability and temperament, such a varna-ashrama structure might be expected to promote efficiency in the pursuit of occupational goals. This justification of class hierarchy is occasionally reiterated by present-day scholars[6] who consider character the determining factor in explanations of caste organization. This analysis is, however, more Aristotelian than Indian. There may have been an element of truth in the argument if only the initial stages of caste development are considered, but it is ritual and its relation to class purity that is the real basis of stratification. Scattered throughout the ancient texts are indica-

[d] Often the three are joined by a fourth aim of life, moksha (*mokṣa*), liberation or deliverance, which is actually more a fulfillment of the others, particularly of dharma.

[e] The ideal of brahmacharya is expressed as early as the *Atharvaveda* (XI, 5). Regarding the life stages, cf. *Manu* VI, 87ff. and *Gautama Dharmasutra* III and IV. *Vide* pp. 5–51 of the Bühler edition of the *Apastamba Dharmasutra* for an elaborate discussion of studentship and the technicalities of Vedic study (e.g., "In the case of an eclipse of the sun or of the moon, of an earthquake, of a whirlwind, of the fall of a meteor, or of a fire [in the village] . . . the recitation of all the sacred sciences must be interrupted from that hour until the same hour next day." I, 3.30). Motwani's *Manu* [282] provides a general introduction to the varna-ashrama theory, but the author becomes at times almost spellbound by its symmetry.

tions that the effective realization of a man's swadharma depends on the development of those qualities that characterize the varna to which he belongs. These passages are sufficient to challenge the hypothesis that character or talent remained the theoretical basis of caste.

According to the traditional theory, one social group is to be concerned with the life of the spirit and the advancement of culture, another with the protection and administration of society, a third and fourth with the production of economic goods and services. The contribution of each group was important to the well-being of the whole. Such a structure, based on a priesthood, a military and governing class, a third estate, and peasant class, has not been uncommon in the world's history. But in India the classification of functions had religious and social ramifications that went far beyond anything known in the West.

When tradition and law support the rigid and continuing separation of social classes we may speak of a caste society. The French sociologist Bouglé considers hierarchy, hereditary specialization, and "repulsion" primary elements in any definition of caste.[7] A society possesses a caste system if it is divided into many specialized groups which are graded in status and mutually opposed, and which do not tolerate mixture of blood or change in vocation. A Hindu caste does not necessarily embrace all those who pursue the activity from which it derives its name, and different occupations may be included in a caste. But there are only a limited number of pursuits that will not defile the individual and bring loss of caste. In determining a person's caste the most important facts to be considered are where and what he eats, and whom he has married. There are exceptions, but usually those who may eat together are also permitted to intermarry. Impurity is not the result of personal association alone, but it may be the consequence of contact with certain objects. Caste provides one of the rare instances of several groups living in close proximity with one another and yet having little direct physical contact.

In India class regulations remained relatively fluid until permanent settlement was established. Among anthropologists and Indologists there is no agreement on the role of the Aryan immigration in the development of caste. Some have argued that the caste system antedates the arrival of the Aryans. Hutton and Oldham, for example, entertain the possibility of a type of caste system existing in a matrilineal society in the south before Brahmanism penetrated the area. Several of the more widely held or persuasive theories that attempt to explain the origin of caste will be presented in the following pages.

Megasthenes, a Greek at the Mauryan court (late fourth century B.C.), provides the first account of caste that we have. He lists seven castes, which may be rearranged to resemble the classical four, and mentions restrictions on marriage and on changes in profession.[1] The disparity

----

1 We know that Herodotus described seven social classes in the Egypt of his time. This may have induced Megasthenes to find the same number.

between the traditional four orders of Indian society and the seven-class system described by Megasthenes is the difference between the traditional culture of the Aryans and the increasingly abstract bureaucratic pattern of political life sponsored by the Mauryans. Megasthenes distinguishes the fighting men from the bureaucrats, whom he further classifies as superintendents and policy makers.[9] The *Manusmriti* delineates the four basic varnas but suggests a great number of subcastes to which are assigned the offspring of unions that cross class lines.[8] The relatively late *Shukranitisara* sees the actual number of castes as unlimited.[9]

There is a general consensus among modern scholars that the brahmans were the first class to become a caste. The exaltation of the priestly function appears to have been the consequence of a long struggle with the ruling nobility. By the later Vedic (Brahmanic) period the brahmans and those who shared authority with them, the kshatriyas, were defined according to social role, but the rest of society remained heterogeneous. Status, in this earliest stage of caste development, must certainly have been the major factor in stratification, although brahman ideology insists on the close relation of station and social contribution. By the time of the dharmasutra texts, the position of the two lower castes had deteriorated considerably, and the vaishyas and shudras had become almost indistinguishable. It is very possible that even in this later period these social divisions were status groups rather than economic classes or castes in any strict sense.[10]

At one time caste was commonly interpreted as the deliberate device of the priesthood to divide and control the people. But the popular acceptance of so complex and penetrating a social organization would certainly presuppose the previous existence of many of its features. Caste was not the result of brahman design alone, but the combination of a variety of factors rarely, if ever, found in combination elsewhere.

Although the Vedas do not directly indicate that caste existed in more than embryonic form, by the end of the Vedic period the institution had become stereotyped, and it was fairly prevalent by the time of the Buddha. The *Purushasukta* is a late hymn, not representative of the *Rigveda,* and it is only in this hymn that the word shudra appears. It heralds the distinction between Aryan and Shudra found in the Brahmanas, a distinction earlier drawn between the Arya and Dasa. Although the Aryans thought of themselves as culturally different from the indigenous population, it does not follow that they thought of themselves as culturally superior. We are unjustified in reading modern racial consciousness into this distinction.[11] The civilization the Indo-Europeans found on their arrival may indeed have been much more highly developed than that which the Aryans themselves possessed. One widely accepted explanation of the evolution of the caste system bases the division of function on organizational requirements that emerged in the *Drang nach Osten* of the Aryans. Conquest demanded further centralization of power; lesser tribal rulers

---

[9] Indeed, certain administrative occupations did begin to rigidify into castes at this time—such as the *kāyasthas* (the clerks and scribes).

were forced to substitute military position for direct political authority and other classes to exchange economic services for military protection.

In the initial phases of caste development the struggle for authority between the kshatriya nobility and the brahmans provided the fundamental antagonism. The *Shantiparva* (the twelfth book of the *Mahabharata*) tells us that once the people suffered greatly from the dissensions of the two groups. The brahmans had as yet no monopoly on priestly functions. But in time, as the liturgy became more and more complicated (perhaps to discourage those not of brahman birth from attempting to master the gnosis and ritual) and the memorizing of intricate formulae and techniques, which were communicated only by word of mouth, absorbed the better part of a man's life, the brahmans were able to secure control of the sacrifice. This function was then proclaimed as the most important of all human callings. It was not long before even the gods were declared to be subject to the power of incantation. When the ruling class—those possessing political and military power—ultimately acquiesced in this interpretation of things, brahman ascendancy and the status hierarchy were established. However, it was still possible in the late Vedic period for a family to experience an upward or downward change in caste position in the space of several generations.[12]

Western students of Indian social structure have generally neglected the importance of taboo and mana, of primitive belief and later Brahmanical and Hindu religious conceptions, in their hypotheses on caste and its development. Many Indian writers, on the other hand, give too much weight to philosophical principles which are more apt to be justifications than explanations and which, in any case, are appropriate only for certain stages of caste history.

Hutton observes that there are remote areas in India where there has never been contact with the outer world, where the religions associated with India have never penetrated, and where caste, as we know it, does not exist.[13] Yet in such areas as that of the Naga tribes of Manipur there are villages existing as independent administrative units with specialized economic functions. One will produce pottery but has no smiths, and in another a different trade will be localized. When a village people is forced to migrate to another settlement, its traditional occupations are often prohibited. The craft is considered taboo and its practice is thought to affect adversely the productivity of the land.[h] But the general taboos on marriage among different peoples or on commensality—which are central characteristics of caste—do not exist. There is, however, a belief in the magical effect of food, and certain foods are peculiar to certain clan ceremonials. Hutton believes that when peoples practicing different economic pursuits live close to one another, the consequences of suspect crafts and occupations are rendered less harmful by the forbidding of close personal relationships. The different vocation is tolerated, but another taboo re-

---

[h] Hutton [189] suggests that this might be taken as an offense to the ancestral spirits—or that the imported mana would counteract that on which the host village was dependent.

places the prohibition of the craft. Contact with the strangers and their food is dangerous. In the process of its preparation, food may be infected by the mana of the cook.

Hutton asserts that all this is not meant to suggest that the Aryan immigrants did not play an important role in the development of caste. "On the contrary, it is urged emphatically that the Indian caste system is the natural result of the interaction of a number of geographical, social, political, religious and economic factors not elsewhere found in conjunction."[14] And certainly the Indo-Europeans had their own ideas of magic. More important was the hierarchy of class they brought with them and imposed on a society already rent by prohibitions.[i]

Held's thesis, which if explored in detail would take us far afield, is that Indian social evolution may be explained if we posit a patrilineal relationship intersected by a latent matrilineal system. Each person belonged to two clans and was allowed to marry within the patrilineal clan of the mother, but forbidden to marry within the matrilineal clan of the mother.[15] Held conjectures that status superiority may have been based on the exchange of women: the clan to which women are given would be higher than that which serves as supply. The latter clan is, in turn, superior to the clan that furnishes its wives—and, eventually, we reach the point in the series of exchanges where the first clan (superior to the second) is the supplier of another clan, and thus of inferior status.[16] The question of the transition to caste endogamy remains, but Held claims that this status differentiation is the root of a tendency in the direction of endogamy. The cooperation that once characterized the relationship begins to diminish and take on new forms. In the circulative marriage system, the point may be reached where one clan refuses to continue the tradition of giving women to another, though it still accepts women from lower clans.

Held speculates that the exogamous matrilineal elements were transformed into exclusive patrilineal groupings, taking on a tribal character.[17] Racial differences were of minor importance, although cultural differences may have encouraged the tendency toward endogamy. The relationships that emerge in the circulating connubial system (each clan being "male" or "female" to another) provide Held with what he takes to be the analogy that inspired the ambiguity of the Indian classification system. Symbolism may be said to reflect the tribal subdivision into two phratries of contrasting function.[18] The relationship cannot be simply described as one of conflict, for it represents a dynamic interaction that can as often be seen as cooperation. The analogy of male and female comes to mind and, indeed, the relation is commonly conceived in these terms. The tribal phratries (or moieties) are as man and woman.

Several theories of the origins of caste are based on pre-Aryan hereditary vocations—with an endogamous marriage pattern introduced to ensure that occupational secrets were kept within the group.[19] Magic and

---

[i] Although the structure resembled the social organization of the ancient Persians, we have no evidence that it was not a product of Gangetic expansion.

religion aided the development of exclusive occupational groupings, and
the Aryan invasion buttressed these tendencies by introducing a racial
factor. Nesfield insisted that occupation must be taken as the sole basis
of caste.[20] Its beginnings were quite independent of religion. Blunt[21] and
Dahlmann follow this interpretation, the latter arguing that the three
major orders—priest, noble, "bourgeois"—could be found in every community that had made any advance at all. From these he postulated that
smaller groups based on occupational and kinship ties gradually formed,
and, in turn, caste took shape—the corporation being the intermediate and
essential stage.[22] But Dahlmann's explanation of caste as petrified guild
is inadequate, since, as Bouglé points out, it cannot account for the hereditary transmission of occupation.

Senart, in answering Nesfield and those emphasizing occupational
specialization as the crucial factor in the emergence of caste, contended
that they had ignored the obvious fact that men might practice the same
occupation but belong to different castes. The truth that lies in the occupational theory is simply that there are professions which a member of a
caste cannot practice without losing status. Hocart[23] and most recent
writers on the subject follow Senart in questioning the conclusion that a
man was always predestined to an occupation by heredity because of the
obvious association of caste with profession or trade. Even in that monument of orthodoxy, the *Manusmriti,* we find that the brahman was permitted to find his livelihood in agriculture and trade if he could not support
himself by his traditional vocation.[24] Ancient Sanskrit literature provides
examples of offices held by individuals not formally entitled to them. We
know that on more than one occasion a low caste man ascended the throne
—not always by forcing his way. The *Rigveda* speaks of men who bear
the rank of king though not of the noble class.[25] Men did cross caste
and occupational barriers. Positions must be filled when families die out
or when a person or a class becomes degraded. Groups themselves can
rise in the prestige system. And there are departures from the rules of
caste.

Senart emphasizes the practices of family worship in the primitive
community and considers commensality crucial in the elaboration of
caste.[26] And Held,[27] commenting on Russell's statement that "in early
times a sacrifice was the occasion for every important gathering or fes-
tivity, as is shown both in Indian history and legend,"[28] has argued that
the food communion, which became central in the delineation of caste,
must be traced to early attempts to give expression to the kinship solidarity of the clan.[*] The distribution of function and the hierarchical ordering of castes, according to Held, has its prototype in the clan rather than
in the tribe. But the crucial problem of clan exogamy persists—and it
was the parallel of caste and tribal endogamy, more than any other single
factor, that led Senart to the conclusion that the roots of caste were to be
found in the tribe. Senart's hypothesis fails to account for the hierarchic

[*] Vide Durkheim [105], p. 427, on the importance of reunions and assemblies in
reaffirming collective sentiments.

structure of the castes, but he at least avoids the problems raised by those who explain the origin of caste simply in terms of economic function or race. If racial feeling existed in early India, we still would want to know why it should have produced a caste structure when this has not necessarily been its consequence in other social contexts.

The term for the orders into which society was broken is more literally translated as "color," and a racial theory of caste origin has, for this reason, proved irresistible to many scholars. This theory has been combined with the view that aristocracy was the consequence of military conquest. The connotations of the word varna seemed apparent enough and little attention was given to indications in the sacred texts that the significance of color might be symbolic. "Those who adduce the racial theory of caste," argues Cox, "always assume that there were at first two castes, the Aryans and the Dravidians, conquerors and conquered, white and black. Their discussion of the relationship between these two peoples is always deductive and inferential, based upon the type of race relations with which we are now familiar among whites and peoples of color."[29] The *Rigveda* does not use the word varna in reference to the four orders of society; it is applied rather to the Aryan people as a whole in order to differentiate them from the darker (in some sense) indigenous population. By the time of the Brahmanas, the classes are described as varnas. Varna would appear to have retained both its distinguishing connotation and its reference to color. The latter was evidently persistent enough to encourage the assignment of a color to each social class. If these colors are taken to refer to skin tone, then ancient India was indeed bizarre.

It is as logical to suppose that the color of the original inhabitants acquired significance for the Aryan invaders because of theological associations of black with the powers of darkness as it is to assume that their color marked them as inferior. Varna may very well connote gradations from light to dark in the sense of forces of light and darkness, distinguishing those who represent deva (light god) from those who are the creatures of asura (dark god).[30] Hocart comments that "the connection of quarter, color, social division, season and element is . . . not peculiarly brahmanic, or even Indian, nor is it purely academical. . . . Medieval Ferrara was divided into four wards and four suburbs, each with its colors and banners."[31]

The sacred texts are preoccupied with symbolic significance, and the sacrifice can be understood only in these terms. Each caste is associated with an appropriate compass direction: the west, the dimension of the shudras, was the symbol of night and death.[k] The *Vishnu Dharmashastra* states that those things acquired by the mode of livelihood of a caste are

[k] Kautalya (*Arthashastra* II, 4, p. 58) describes the city: "On the eastern side, merchants trading in scents, garlands, grains and liquids, together with expert artisans and the people of Kshatriya caste shall have their habitations. . . . To the south, the superintendents of the city, of commerce, of manufactories, and of the army as well as those who trade in cooked rice, liquor, and flesh, besides prostitutes, musicians, and the people of Vaishya caste shall live." To the west are the shudras, and to the north the brahmans.

called, by members of the caste, "white."[32] That which is acquired by a
caste two or more degrees below their own is called "black." Color is not
only symbolic, but relative. And the fact that Krishna, avatar of Vishnu,
is usually depicted as blue in color, and Rama is also described as being of
dark skin, indicates that white may not always have been the preferred
color among the ancient Indians. Here and there in the literature, one
discovers passages that suggest that color refers to the sacrificial offering:
the vaishya, who gives rice, is born "white."

Hocart presents the thesis, highly speculative but worth considering,
that castes are groups to which different aspects and offices of the ritual
are assigned. The theory is based largely on recent evidence and rests
primarily on observations which were made in Ceylon—but which, he
believes, are appropriate for the mainland as well. He notes that in the
Mahabharata the king is the major actor in the state sacrifice, and in this
he represents the god Indra. (The king, who, like the rising sun, dominates the darkness, is frequently compared with the "ruddy" Indra. The
red hue of the kshatriyas is perhaps the color of the gods they represent.)
The ruler is distinguished from the priest in that he furnishes the offering
but does not officiate at the sacrifice. Patronage of the sacrifice appears
in the earlier texts to be the primary function of the king. This may of
course be merely from the vantage point of the brahman authors of the
literature. In the sacrifice, the king, in the role of Indra, restages the
struggles between the gods and the demons (or giants) in which Indra
by rite and magic vanquishes the powers of darkness. The royal functions,
as described in the Vedas, may be no more than the roles of the sacrifice.

Contact with decay and disease and anything associated with death
would threaten the capacity of the twice-born to perform the ceremonials
(which were ceremonials of life), and so there must be those who, not
being created with the gods, can accomplish the necessary but defiling
tasks of society. Hocart suggests, and the point is persuasive, that "crafts
and rites are not strictly distinguishable, and the Sanskrit word karma—
'deed,' 'work'—expresses both. The craftsman is actually the man who
has the ear of the deity presiding over some particular activity. Heredity
is an important, though not the only, qualification for this relation to the
deity."[33] Rank in the three higher castes was dependent not only on birth,
but on initiation: man is born anew from the sacrifice.[34] Descent and
sacrifice are the bases of caste, the former a qualification not always sufficient—a son of a princely house, for instance, was not always elevated
to the rank of noble. In the Brahmanical literature there are passages
indicating that initiation may have been considerably more important than
birth in determining caste.[35] Human birth is as nothing when compared
with the sacrifice—which is "the other self" of the gods. Upon taking the
vow, the sacrificer "becomes, as it were, non-human."[36] At the moment
of the sacrificial act, the initiate is consumed by the daemon of the initiatory
rite, and is reborn from this spirit: "That which is my body is in thee;
and that which is thy body is in me."[37]

It seems to be true that in many instances, as tribes were assimilated
into the caste system, status in the tribe qualified its possessor for similar

rank in the caste. Tribal priests may even have become brahmans. Workers at certain crafts were incorporated into the appropriate caste strata. The names of some of the so-called mixed castes suggest that they were actually tribal groups. Each of these groups was assigned a particular task, and was thus absorbed into the system. Whether or not such absorption was extensively practiced, it may at least be seen as a refutation of theories of caste origin that stress the importance of racial purity. We might expect that affiliation with the Aryan community by peoples outside the system was very often stimulated by the desire of their ruling groups for religious legitimation. In return for the right to conduct the sacrifice (which strengthened their own authority), the Aryan priests invented pedigrees for the tribal leaders.[38] For most of the members of the tribe or clan such integration meant taking on the burdens and degradation of an impure caste, with the right to certain work opportunities as perhaps the only advantage obtained in return. This minimum of economic security plus the often appreciable autonomy allowed these tribal peoples in their religious and social life may not have seemed a bad bargain.

"Guest peoples," as Weber terms those expropriated from their own lands and reduced to economic dependence on their conquerors, existed throughout the Aryan settlements.[39] These people lived on the fringes of the villages and commonly possessed their own jurisdictional organizations. They had pariah status when the occupations assigned them precluded intermarriage and commensalism. And in every village there were guest workers in indispensable but ritually unsanctioned occupations who were considered so impure that their very presence infected those of more elevated position with whom they came into contact. Their caste designation was usually the old tribal name.

Outsiders were usually accommodated by the Aryan system as members of an association. When there is little class mobility ethnic groups and class can coincide, as they did in ancient India. The many castes with place names suggest that after amalgamation into larger social units different peoples were allowed to retain considerable administrative control over their own affairs. This must also, in time, have contributed to the development of caste custom.[40] The reception of tribes into castes and the dangers that migration posed for ritual purity served to modify the older castes. Then, too, schisms occasionally resulted as different attitudes toward ritual duty developed within the caste; there were unavoidable variations in work methods and even departures from traditional occupations. Property distinctions encouraged status distinctions, and forbidden cohabitation altered caste and led to the formation of subcastes. Ingalls has suggested that one explanation for the proliferation of castes in India might be the complete dependence on monsoon rains and the disastrous consequences that occur when large areas are deprived of the necessary rainfall.[41] Great regions may be desolated and their reclamation may depend on having entrepreneurs with sufficient capital to import tribesmen into the abandoned areas to rework the land. Soon there would be a profusion of different tribesmen and at length the reclaimed district is organized by caste strata. Kosambi has suggested that Indian history be looked upon as the steady fusion of tribal elements into a "general society."[42] From such a point of view caste must be understood as an equilibrating institution of remarkable potency.

THE STATIONS AND THEIR DUTIES

The Brahmans. Brahman refers to a function—the propagation of learning—rather than to an individual in a particular category. The word originally meant prayer, devotion, or, in the later hymns, magical potency. It probably had its source in the root *brih,* to grow. In the Upanishads Brahman came to represent the eternal principle as it is realized in the universe, that which comprehends all. It is often combined with *ātman,* the essence of the self, and the identification of the two is the central teaching of the later texts.[l] Those who were considered the personification of this principle or function—gods in human form, as they were sometimes called—possessed the right to study the scriptures, to perform the sacrifice, to pursue the ascetic life, and to receive gifts.

The exalted position of the brahman (*brāhmaṇa*) is indirectly revealed in the statements of Vasishtha to the effect that the brahman alone is called upon to live in close accordance with the sacred law and discharge the debts incumbent on man. The other castes must live by the teachings of the brahman. A Hindu caste may dispense with the brahman as priest and even, as seems to have happened on rare occasions, may reject his judgment on matters of liturgy. But the brahman was the referent whereby rank position was determined. Distinctions were based on relative ritual purity. The two highest castes monopolized duties that required ritual purity—such as the preparation of food and the performance of sacrifice.

There is no indication that membership in the brahman class was originally confined to offspring of brahmans. At first knowledge and conduct, rather than birth, may have been the determining factors. A number of passages in the texts record the conversion of kshatriyas and even vaishyas to brahman rank. At this time priests took wives from other social classes, although marriage with the non-Aryan was not approved. By the later Vedic period the brahmans and kshatriyas seem to have been with few exceptions endogamous. Infrequently brahmans took kshatriya females as wives.

The responsibilities of high office are always stressed in Hindu thought, and rigorous discipline is demanded of those in influential and estimable positions.[m] The brahman, as we have noted, was generally expected to fulfill the requirements of all four ashramas. And because the Indian value system emphasizes nonmaterial achievement, prestige and honor belong to the man who puts his ability in the service of goals higher than his

---

[l] In some of the early literature Brahma (masculine) is represented as the primary deity, the Creator. On the concept Brahman *vide* Belvalkar and Ranade [27], pp. 346–54; Chatterjee and Datta [60], pp. 49–54; Hiriyanna [175], p. 21.

[m] "In order to be respected by the lower classes, the ideology of the ruling class must be practiced seriously by the upper classes themselves with a certain limit of obvious hardship." (Kosambi [218], p. 127.)

own interests. Brahman authority was buttressed by ideals that have had a long history in the Occident as well as in the East. These values exalt the authority of teacher and sage, of those who keep the ancestral tradition and have overcome the dictates of the lower self. But though the extensive privileges and immunities of the brahman are justified on the basis of the demanding social role of the priest and its critical importance to the community, we find several of the law codifiers holding that the brahman had only to pursue Vedic studies to be considered faithful to his obligation.

Gautama declares that it is the duty of all varnas to serve their superiors; the brahman accordingly inherited the services of the lower orders of Aryan society. And, as a consequence of his scholarly abilities and his control of the sacrifice, he had preference in the award of many high offices. His lands were exempted from tax and were rarely, if ever, forfeited to the king. The rate of interest charged on loans to a brahman was a nominal sum. Certain services were to be provided for him without charge. In cases of malfeasance, punishment of the brahman took the mildest forms. No matter what the crime, he was seldom subject to corporal punishment. If, for religious purposes, he stole from the shudra or from vaishyas and kshatriyas who had been negligent in their ritual duties, this was not to be regarded as a crime, in the opinion of some commentators. But attacks on the brahman's own property were considered among the most heinous of sins, and any threat to his life was regarded as a menace to the very foundations of social order. Often, where villages were granted to brahmans, a semi-feudal relationship seems to have been established between the priests and their peasant tenants; and though the brahman lords could demand only the traditional taxes, they had the right to forced labor (at least from the later seventh century A.D.).

These advantages of the priesthood may be an indication of the significance the community attached to the brahman function. There is less doubt that they attest to the importance the brahman authors and compilers assigned to their own social role and prerogatives. The advent of non-Brahmanical religions constituted a challenge to the traditional position and social privilege of the priests, but no great modification of their status resulted. They showed themselves capable of meeting that challenge and consolidating their control — without the support of an organized church.

The Kshatriyas. The concept *Kshatra,* as used in the Veda, means rule or ruler. It does not refer to a unit in the class structure. But whereas Brahman retained its abstract form, Kshatra became a more specific concept.

The kshatriyas (*kṣatriyas*) were those who filled the governing and military roles in Aryan society.[n] Kings who were not of kshatriya lineage appear to have sought legitimation by forging kshatriya descent or, in

[n] Although the martial tradition was closely linked to the kshatriya class, and war was the kshatriya function *par excellence,* all groups of society participated in military operations. Sometimes the military role was distinguished from the political function and the knight referred to as *rājanya,* the prince as *rājaputra.* But these

post-Buddhist India, by exploiting the myth of divinity. Brahmans who became rulers were, in later times, occasionally known as *brahmakshatris,* although there are instances in which no attempt was made to invent kshatriya status. Members of the lower castes who assumed the throne might, by ritual purification, gain status as kshatriyas. The very fact of governing was often enough to qualify the ruler as a kshatriya. The *Mahabharata* tells us that when a hostile army threatens the security of the people, when the royal troops are defeated in battle, the leadership of any strong man—even vaishya or shudra—is legitimate. "He that is a shore in a shoreless place, he that is a boat in a boatless place, whether he be a slave or whatever he be, is worthy of honor. . . . He that protects the good and drives evil away should be made king."[43] This suggests the lack of a common kshatriya origin, which accounts in part for the fact that kshatriya consciousness never developed the communal feeling that we find in the brahmans.

One can only speculate on the nature of the early relationship between brahman and kshatriya. That considerable tension should have developed between the two groups in the struggle for social supremacy seems almost a foregone conclusion. It is difficult to know how to evaluate such legends as the story of Paraśurāma who, singlehandedly, either nullified the kshatriya strength or wiped out the entire class of warriors. The great brahman beat the kshatriyas not with sacred rite and magical incantation, but on their own terms. The purpose of this brahman legend is clearly to show that wronging the priests would not go unavenged; but why is the ensuing age of brahman supremacy depicted as one of great chaos in which the lower orders of society, once the power of the kshatriya had been destroyed, violated the dharmic order and threatened the security of the brahmans?[44] The answer may be that this description is intended as an argument for the necessity of a ruling class that could take full responsibility for protecting and administering the realm, leaving the priest secure in the pursuit of his higher spiritual ends. It was the duty of the ruler to ensure certain minimum standards of well-being and to present the brahman with gifts of land and money.[45]

The brahmanic authority was to be regarded as superior, although more properly the two authorities must be understood as complementary. The *Brihadaranyaka Upanishad,* so often taken as a statement of kshatriya supremacy, actually identifies Brahma(n) as the source of Kshatra.[46] The king's attack on the brahman is thus an attack on his own source. The brahman is placed below the kshatriya at the sacrifice, the latter representing the "excellent form . . . such as Indra and Varuna" begotten by the original One, Brahman, out of itself.[o] Even after the creation of

terms can be misleading. In the Vedic period, for instance, *rajan* or *rājanya* included the whole nobility.

[o] Cf. *Gautama Dharmasutra* XI: "The king is master of all, with the exception of brahmans. . . . All, excepting brahmans, shall worship him who is seated on a higher seat [while they themselves sit on a] lower [one]. The [brahmans] shall also honor him."

the four varnas the world does not prosper, and it is necessary to conceive yet another element—dharma, which is the true ruler of the world. And of course the interpretation of this sacred law is the province of the brahmans.

To illustrate the royal prerogative Hocart relates the Tamil story of a king who wished to reward the expertise of his barber (who had shaved the king without waking him).[47] When asked what boon he wished, the barber replied that he wanted to be made a brahman. The brahmans were ordered to accept him as one of themselves within a few days, on penalty of forfeiting their grants of land. The distraught priests appealed to the court jester for help and he proceeded to so ridicule the idea of a barber's becoming a brahman that the king withdrew his demand. In this and like incidents it was not the king's prerogative but only the fitness of seeking a change in status and position that was called into question.[p] Apparently, in some instances, the South Indian king was able to award privileges of caste.

Passages in the Vedic literature that seem to point to an elective monarchy[48] must be taken to refer to popular acclamation of individuals who possessed (in Weber's terms) personal or gentile charisma—or (to use Durkheim's expression) who represented the collective consciousness. Charisma, in the Hindu social system, adheres to sib members and hence provides certain restraints on appointments to office.[49] This charisma had its source in dharmic authority, and when the nobility sought to mortify the brahmans by championing heterodox religious movements, which had been inspired by kshatriyas and which offered vehicles for the reassertion of kshatriyan pre-eminence, it was only to discover that the salvation religions were not capable of supplying legitimation comparable to that which the older symbolization had provided.

As the tribal organization became less appropriate to the new demands for social integration, the kshatriyas became more and more dependent on the brahman to vindicate the ruling authority. For dharma could no longer be interpreted simply in terms of kinship patterns. But the heterodox challenge to Brahmanism contributed to a general liberalizing of official appointments; we know, for example, that a number of shudras were employed in the service of Magadha. And with the rise of the new salvation religions the brahman monopoly on the literature of ancient India is at last broken. It is now possible to turn to Buddhist or Jaina texts for the kshatriya side of the argument.

Regardless of its acceptability to the brahmans, no government which did not provide protection (*daṇḍaniti*) and secure order could claim to be legitimate. The responsibilities of government did not end with security: the king and his ministers must promote ethical discernment (*trayī*) and the production of wealth (*vārttā*). But these goals are not always compatible. Security or opportunity for aggrandizement may dictate the subordination of moral law to the interests of the state. This problem of *ratio*

---

[p] Of relevance here is the ancient identification of the "good" with the "good for" (or fitness) that is most clearly seen in Greek thought. (*Vide* Arendt [8], p. 202.)

status is resolved by the intricate hierarchy of duties, the insulating character of caste, and the concept of swadharma. Although the texts suggest a
great range of governmental functions, we find on closer inspection that
these functions are not the exclusive province of the kshatriya class.

The characteristic obligations of the kshatriyas are punishment and
the conduct of hostilities. The world is such that order can be maintained
only by the threat of violence against those who would use violence. Where
the moral ambiguity of action would threaten the authority of others, the
kshatriya is required to do whatever is necessary to preserve stability and
sacred tradition.[q]

The kshatriya function is most clearly expressed in the relationships
of the state to other sovereign entities—relationships generally unclouded
by normative considerations. But the political sphere also includes functional requirements of an integrative nature. The control of internal
affairs was never the exclusive prerogative of the warrior nobility. These
legal functions—the enforcement of norms (ensuring what might be called
the system of expectations) and resolution of conflicting interests—involved the castes, corporations, and agencies specifically concerned with
the interpretation and administration of the dharma. Here, of course, the
brahmans were of crucial importance. The ultimate *executive* authority
rested with the kshatriyas, who wield the rod of danda.

The "facilitating" function of welfare and planning was usually broadly
shared with caste and local organizations; the "educative" function, which
the modern liberal state is reluctant to admit as a proper governmental
responsibility (though it may serve as a justification for legal institutions
and processes), was a brahman prerogative—usurped, as we shall see, by
Ashoka in his efforts to construct the ethical state.

The kshatriya ideal that dominated the centuries of the anabasis—
personal honor and military valor—was tamed with the establishment of
the territorial state. Protection and regulation became the major responsibilities of the governing nobility. The relative importance of aggressive
warfare declined. Armed combat could no longer be undertaken casually
as though it were a game; the stakes were too high. The demand was now
for specialists in the techniques of coordination and adaptation, and the
influence of the minister began to challenge the traditional status of the
knight. The needs of the settled community were bringing the brahman
more directly into political activity; he was often the person best qualified
for the deliberative, advisory, and supervisory roles of the emergent state
—duties that were not incongruent with the priestly swadharma. The
growing importance of law as an instrument of social control and adjustment established the brahman as arbiter in the affairs of men, as well as
intermediary between the human and the divine.

The history of the rise of Magadha to a position of supremacy in the
Ganges valley is also the account of the centralization of power in the

---

[q] The brahman rationale is similar to the argument of certain medieval papal
theorists that the temporal sword existed to perform those necessary tasks that were
beneath the dignity of the Church.

state. Agencies of the governing elite took unto themselves offices and
powers that had formerly been reserved to the various corporations of
society and to religious functionaries. These usurpations find their fullest
expression in the regime of the Mauryan emperor Ashoka, when the
vigor of countervailing institutions was at its nadir. By the last centuries
of the pre-Christian era, the kshatriya function had become more than
the defense of the community. The role had become political, in that
secular authorities, with bureaucratic instrumentalities at their disposal,
regarded themselves as charged with the mobilization of social resources
(including public support) for the achievement of common purposes. This
increasing rationalization of political activity is reflected, for example, in
the more utilitarian approach to the justification of punishment. Penalties
can no longer be understood simply as vengeance wreaked by an offended
conscience collective. Restitution begins to supplement retribution, and
social policy comes to be based on consideration of the consequences for
society of such official acts as punishment.

The Vaishyas and the Shudras. Although the three twice-born castes
were originally set off from the shudras, by the time of the law books the
major distinction is between the ruling classes, on the one hand, and the
vaishyas and shudras, on the other. The vaishya (*vaiśya*) class included
the agriculturists, cattle-raisers, traders, and artisans—members of professions that soon evolved into distinct subdivisions. Farming and herd-
ing were considered the representative work of the people.[50] Vaishya and
shudra (*śudra*) actually shared many occupations and were frequently
grouped together in matters of inheritance, form of marriage, the proper
greeting to be extended to them, and so forth. The vaishya was regarded
as a freeman, but he in fact possessed little security for his personal rights.
He was burdened with payments such as the *bali* contribution to the king
(or nobles),[r] and with encroachments on his property. That the vaishya,
responsible for the satisfaction of the economic needs of the community,
was recognized as the foundation of the state and its prosperity is indicated by the occasional references to the king as "lord of the vaishyas."
This may be interpreted to mean simply that the ruler was king of the
people, but we know that when asceticism became a popular form of religious expression the vaishya function and the grihastha ashrama acquired a prestige more in line with its true social significance.

The shudra may be described as a serf without security of tenure.[s]
In the time of the Brahmanas, when the position of the priestly class was
unassailable and its ritual monopoly secure, the shudra was not permitted
to practice austerities,[t] or to recite or even listen to the Vedic hymns—
let alone to perform sacrifices. His penalty for repeating the Veda was
to have his tongue cut out. He could not be present in the halls of sacri-

----

[r] Originally the bali was probably an offering to a god, and voluntary in nature.
The *Atharvaveda* (III, 4.3) suggests that the bali was already a compulsory payment
in later Vedic times. *Vide* p. 58 above.

[s] And, it seems safe to conclude, without the right of wergild compensation.

[t] It is asserted in the *Ramayana* that Rama killed a shudra for as much.

ficial ceremony and hence his marriage was no sacrament. The *Pancha-vimsha* and *Shatapatha Brahmana* describe the shudra as the servant of the other classes, and Manu holds that he was created expressly for the service of the brahman.[51] The shudra had no protection from the whim of the twice-born castes and no absolute claim to his property; for all practical purposes he was beyond the pale of justice. Nor had he even a claim to human dignity: he must content himself with the discarded food and clothing of others. The law books, or smritis, declare that he could never be released from the condition of servitude to others, for this was his natural state.[52] Indeed the shudra is like a child and unable to accept responsibilities.

But it may at least be said that the Indian economy was never dependent on slavery as was classical Greece.[u] Slavery probably did not have the same connotation that it had in Greece, and the treatment of slaves was no doubt more humane than it was in most societies where slavery existed. The *Yajñavalkyasmriti*[53] holds that a man may be reduced to slavery only with his consent. Narada, though he does not go as far as Yajñavalkya, discusses ceremonies for emancipating slaves.[54] The law books are not of one voice on the general subject of slavery, but they do suggest that by the time of the Guptas the institution was on the wane and the shudras gaining in rights. It is probably inaccurate to characterize the shudras, or even any significant portion of them, as slaves.[v] Their status in some instances may have been similar to that of the serf, in others it did not differ appreciably from that of the vaishya.[w] It was generally in the state's interest to prevent the expansion of slavery. Slavery would have aided the development of an economic system less congenial to state control of commodity production. The Mauryan state, eyeing the extensive tax yield of the village settlements, encouraged a policy more conducive to the development of a peasant or serf population.

Shudra revolt was rare, since their fragmentation into subcastes and the variety of shudra functions and occupations tended to weaken class cohesion. In the smriti literature we note the beginnings of the distinction between "clean" and "unclean" shudras. The former might be allowed to requisition the services of the brahman—although of course Vedic formulae could not be employed and hence the religious significance of the ritual was greatly curtailed. And there is the occasional grudging admission

[u] This fact impressed the Greek ambassador Megasthenes, who is quoted by Arrian (*Indika*, 10) as observing that "all the Indians are free and not one of them is a slave." Evidently what Indians would have viewed as bondage did not seem to qualify as slavery in the eyes of the Greek. Megasthenes' statement may indicate more about his attitude toward the institution of slavery in Greece than it tells us about actual conditions in India.

[v] For references to slavery in the ancient texts, *vide Rigveda* VII, 19.36; VIII, 56.3; X, 344; *Aitareya Brahmana* XXXIX, 8; *Brihadaranyaka Upanishad* IV, 4.23; *Arthashastra* III, 13ff.; *Mahabharata* II, 52.45 and 65f.; III, 272.11; V, 33.68; VII, 57.5ff.; VIII, 45.40; XIII, 45.18 and 23; *Manu* VII, 96; VIII, 412ff.; IX, 179; XI, 59ff.; *Yajñavalkya* II, 182ff.; III, 236. For a summary of positions taken in these treatises, *vide* Ghoshal, "Ancient Indian Slavery," in [143].

[w] *Vide* p. 19 above. Certainly by the seventh century A.D. the bulk of the shudras had become peasants.

that the shudra had a potential capacity for virtuous living. It is a matter of time. We must also qualify the statement that the shudra was without political rights. There are exceptions, although the sacred texts have little to say on the subject. Some shudras held high court offices and would have to be described as retainers enjoying status not without honor. Certain shudra families probably had a hereditary right to the office of steward or royal charioteer.

The Dharmasutras deny that unions of lower caste men with women of higher position can be considered marriages in the true sense. These hypogamous unions were unacceptable, the children resulting from them being without benefit of the sacred law.[x] When brahman woman joined with shudra male, the progeny must be considered chandala, the most contemptible of men.[y] Hypergamous marriage (the husband being of higher status) was considered less despicable and, in certain situations, seems not to have been questioned. Baudhayana considers the child of a kshatriya woman by a brahman to be a brahman and that of a vaishya woman by a kshatriya to belong to the caste of his father. This is likely to have been the common practice in the earlier stages of caste development. Marriages of males with females of the caste immediately below were by no means unusual, nor was there generally a loss of status for the child. But as the social gulf between the higher and the lower classes widened, sexual relations with a vaishya woman were discouraged by the codifiers. The social status of the father was no longer granted to children of unions between males of the vaishya caste and shudras. Shudra women, according to Vasishtha, were meant for the pleasure of the other castes, and we know that women of the lowest order were taken as mistresses by men of higher rank.

The problem of economic relations among the castes was solved by the principle of ritual cleanliness in caste occupation. "The Veda declares that the hand of an artisan is always pure," says Baudhayana.[55] Where intercourse among the various social classes was necessary, a rationale could be found. But class privilege was the rule. Rates of interest, for example, varied with the caste of the debtor: typically 2% for the brahman, 5% for the shudra for the same period of time. Whether the brahman killed a shudra or a dog, the penance expected of him was the same. The brahman host was to feed his brahman guests before the kshatriya guests; vaishya and shudra guests (it is difficult to conceive of the latter situation) must eat with the servants. But the brahman, in what must be one of the

---

[x] The exceptions being the *sūtas,* products of such a brahman-kshatriya marriage (*vide,* e.g., *Yajñavalkya* I, 93), and *magadhas,* offspring of kshatriya females and vaishya males. Neither were regarded as impure.

[y] Hutton ([189], pp. 129, 132) believes that the reason for assigning the offspring of the union of a shudra man and a brahman woman to so degraded a place may possibly be explained by the confronting of an indigenous matrilineal tradition by a patrilineal invading people. The child of a matrilineal father and a patrilineal mother would have status and kinship on neither side and find himself in a highly anomalous position. Where the two systems meet, the matrilineal usually gives way to the patrilineal. Perhaps, as the change took place after the migration, there also occurred a tendency toward a substitution of male for female deities.

earliest statements of *noblesse oblige,* is counseled to "use kindness."[56]
The authors of the smriti literature sometimes go so far as to require that
a brahman live on cow's urine for a certain period of time as penance for
drinking water from a well used by outcaste peoples, or even water from
a flowing stream. It would not be difficult to go to considerable length
on the subject of relations among different castes, but these examples
should be sufficient to illustrate the inequities of the system—at least as
judged by the standards of a later day.

The individual was called upon to accept his appointed place in the
social structure without questioning that order and the values upon which
it was based. But within the limits of his designated duty the ancient
Indian moved with some freedom in pursuing caste goals and seeking the
level of his ability. In respect to its own affairs, each caste enjoyed a high
degree of autonomy. Intra-caste difficulties were resolved by the caste
council or by caste-administered ordeals. If a caste could not reach a
decision by deliberation, there would be an appeal to the king. Unless
such a request invited the king's intervention, his jurisdiction was confined to conflicts *between* castes. According to the Dharmashastras the
king was charged with seeing that men observed the rules of their caste.[57]
But this was a very general and largely indirect responsibility; the duty
properly belonged to the caste organization. The king must avoid enforcing laws that were contrary in any way to caste function. A person was
normally free to accept the ritual and belief of any religion as long as they
did not interfere with the performance of his caste duties.

It is appropriate, in concluding this chapter, to suggest that the lot of
the lower caste Hindu may not have been as desperate as has perhaps been
implied. Kroeber notes that "the Hindu does not feel caste a burden as
the individualistic occidental might. To him it seems both natural and
desirable, its deliberate breach unnatural, perverse, and unforgivable.
Whatever his caste, the Hindu is proud of it as Westerners are proud of
their nationality. It gives him a sense of solidarity, and he does not seek
to escape it."[58] Bouglé believed that the respect for the regime of castes
is the patriotism of the Hindus.[z] And a contemporary Indian historian,
Kosambi, though generally sympathetic to Marxian analysis, is willing
to admit that an institution responsible for social stagnation and injustice
at least reduced the need for violence and was able to avoid the large-scale
chattel slavery that was so important in the productive relations of Greece
and Rome.[59] Then, too, the tolerance of differences, which observers have
found so appealing in Indian culture, is related to the formalized social
structure that is taken by Indians to be the expression of these differences.

---

[z] We might wonder how (if caste theory be taken seriously) the humble class
position of a man could be a source of pride—considering that it was to be taken
as testimony of the sins of the earlier existences of his soul.

6 ⋆ THE RESPONSE TO ORTHODOXY

In seeking to dramatize the critical importance of the millennium before Christ, Karl Jaspers has called this age of prophecy and philosophy "the axial period."[1] It was a time of remarkable spiritual exploration and development in many parts of the civilized world. One of the major causes of breaks with traditionalism, according to Weber, is the growth of a class of prophets who seek to impose an ethical ideal upon society. Representing what he called charismatic authority,[a] these prophets justify the ethic in terms of older values that have been perverted or weakened in the process of institutionalization. This ethical or emissary prophecy is associated with the belief that the things of this world are susceptible to control in the interest of the religious idea—a belief that is basic to asceticism. The world is viewed as evil. This evil may be fought within the individual soul, or the struggle may involve control of both the self and the external environment. Implicit in emissary prophecy is the conception of a transcendental personal God, and it is as agent of the divine will that the prophet seeks to establish religious ideals.

India, far from being isolated from the intellectual currents of the time and the movements they inspired, assumed a central role in religious innovation and the elaboration of values. The seventh and sixth centuries B.C. had been marked by profound alterations in the traditional social structure and by growing discontent with the formalized religion of the sacrifice. The brahmanic system was insufficiently flexible to answer completely the changing needs of the people and in particular the demands of rising groups in society. But in the Orient, in Asia beyond the lands of Semitic culture, pantheistic cosmology prevented the rise of the type of prophecy with which we are most familiar in the West. Man could only seek to live in harmony with the universe; at best he could challenge the traditional modes of achieving that harmony.

In India asceticism (in the narrower sense that Weber uses the term) was a less significant form of religious expression than mysticism—the

---

[a] Charisma is more exactly defined not as a type of authority but as the ultimate source of all authority. It is the essence of leadership, that which transcends the routine, the extraordinary quality in terms of which an order is accepted as rightful. It is related to mana and to Brahman, the magical potency discussed in earlier chapters. (Weber did not always distinguish clearly between authority and legitimacy.) Charisma resides originally in the person of the leader and is stabilized by being transformed into either traditional or legal authority. *Vide* Chapter 16 below.

devaluation of and indifference to worldly phenomena.[b] Whether or not we accept the distinction between asceticism and mysticism, the fact remains that in the later Brahmanic age, for reasons which are far from clear, the aims of asceticism were less often the achievement of magical power for purposes of gaining relatively immediate advantages, and increasingly a regimen for developing psychic abilities. The private and popular religions had never directly challenged the sacrifice in the sense and to the degree that the mystical experience constituted a threat to the public rite. Mysticism meant that the brahman priest could be bypassed in the effort to attain salvation. Discipline was no longer confined to the arduous tasks of Vedic scholarship and ritual performance, but was increasingly directed toward the attainment of a higher "consciousness" through contemplation. The mystical experience is also a challenge to the life that finds security in fixed social roles, a life in which perception and experience are limited to traditional modes and become stereotyped. Although mystical prophecy took a form other than the crusade or jeremiad, the mystical ideal posed certain difficulties for the maintenance of a stable social order. However, the conception of an impersonal order of the universe impeded social criticism inspired by the wish to transplant the kingdom of God to earth. Instead of emissary prophecy we find "exemplary" prophecy; the prophet wished only to show men by his example and his teaching the proper path to salvation. "Mysticism intends a state of 'possession,' not action, and the individual is not a tool but a 'vessel' of the divine."[2]

The intellectual movement which concerns us here and which must be included among the three or four most momentous in the history of civilization, began in the seventh century B.C. as an attempt to shift the religious emphasis away from sacrifice and ritual toward spiritual insight, away from the collective experience to an individual and private concern with salvation. This is the general intent of the more than 250 Upanishads, which begin with the later Brahmanas and continue into the Christian era. For the most part they are records, transmitted by memory, of local schools of religious thought. They were meant to form the concluding portions of the Vedas—usually the *Atharvaveda*—and hence are sometimes referred to as *Vedānta* (*Veda anta*: "end of the Veda"). Scholars generally agree that the Upanishads are actually addenda to the Brahmanas, their purpose being to provide for the speculative needs of students and ascetics

---

[b] Mysticism is often described as a way of viewing the universe in which the individuality is seen as unreal and the unity as the real—as contrasted, for example, with the humanist emphasis on the individuality as the real, or at least as the *more* real. The former world view produces the sense of oneness with other persons; in cultures dominated by humanistic values, the sense of uniqueness and distinctiveness develops. Where the *relationship* between the individual and the unity is conceived as real (insofar as it is an eternal relationship) and cohesion emphasized, we find yet a third *Weltansicht. Vide* B. K. Malik in P. A. Schilpp (ed.), *The Philosophy of Sarvepalli Radhakrishnan* (New York, 1952) and Weber's discussion of the distinction between the organic social ethic and other, more consistent, resolutions of the tension between religion and the world of power relationships (note 2, this chapter); *vide* also pp. 122f. below.

and to satisfy the yearning for an Absolute, a desire rendered more acute by the turbulence and change of the time. As such they represent a stage in the evolution of Indian belief from the religion of the functional deities of the Aryan communities to the universalist salvation religions—a development which, while it cannot be understood apart from political and economic changes, heightened the perception of a fundamental antagonism between religion and the coercive institutions that organize social activities and relationships. There is no sharp break and today the tendency is to play down the contrasts between Upanishadic thought and the theology of the Brahmanas. "It can be safely asserted that amongst the new ideas occurring in the Upanishads there is hardly one that is not implicit in, and logically deducible from, the ideas present in the different portions of the Brahmanas. Thus the continuity of tradition was maintained; and this circumstance was given an outward expression inasmuch as the Brahmanas, the Aranyakas, and the Upanishads were made to constitute parts of one whole revealed text."[3]

But it can be said that in form the later works were more philosophical than the orthodox literature had been; in imagery they were more poetic, in content more pantheistic. The central theme of the Upanishads is the existence of Brahman, the great impersonal world soul that exists in all things.[c] Pious works and sacrifice were not in themselves sufficient to afford escape from the cycle of birth; knowledge alone, acquired through meditation, transforms the individual, raising him to union with the eternal One. *Mīmāṃsā,* or reflection, is emphasized, and it is this more than anything else that sets the Upanishads apart from the Aryan and brahman literature. The correspondences of human and divine do not take the Vedic ceremonial form (indeed the gods have primarily an allegorical function), but become internalized and abstract.

Perception must be directed inward, away from the exterior world, for true comprehension comes through self-knowledge. The core of the self lies beyond the organic functions. Ultimately Brahman and the atman of the individual are one: introspective knowledge of atman leads man to the true wisdom that is immortality. And if the individual soul is identical with that of the universe, it follows that it is identical with that of every other man. To harm others, then, is to harm oneself. It is a humbling and an exalting philosophy. According to the *Śvetāśvatara Upanishad,* "the individual soul is a portion of the Absolute not greater than the hundredth section of the fine hair-tip; but it has *potentiality* to attain the Infinite."[4] Now each member of society is equal to every other in that all participate in the divine and each has a right to salvation if true to himself.

If man is to achieve a true knowledge of the One, the permanent tranquility and bliss of Brahman-atman, he must transcend the vanity and triviality of mortal life, the world of illusion.[d] The only desire admitted is the wish to flee the exhausting captivity of transmigration. The doctrine

---

[c] *Vide* p. 80 above.

[d] And yet sensory experience is not completely devalued. Salvation is dependent on the discovery of worldly pleasure—and then its rejection.

of metempsychosis appeared in the *Shatapatha Brahmana*[5] and received its first complete statement in the *Brihadaranyaka Upanishad.*[6] Although the tone of the Upanishads was not despondent,[e] the belief in the unreality of the phenomenal world leads to a pessimistic outlook. And this leaves us with the question of why this doctrine, this devaluation of mundane experience, came to be so widely accepted by an expanding culture in which more men were enjoying more of the good things of life than before.

One possible answer is that the disintegration of the old tribal bonds and the emergence of new political forms and new bases of wealth produced a sense of social and status insecurity. The anxiety resulting from the weakening of ethnic ties may have encouraged the internalizing of authority—the search for norms within the self that could be understood as indications of the moral order of the universe. With the increasing emphasis on individual expression and responsibility, it would be less feasible to understand misfortune as punishment for wrongs committed by others, and the individual had to seek new explanations for the suffering and injustice he encountered. A satisfactory answer to this question could be found in a theory of transmigration of the soul. Such an answer could explain the unjustified prosperity of the wicked (who would pay later) as well as the misery of the righteous (who were being punished for the sins of their former existences).

It has been suggested, with some caution, that the increased freedom from the time-honored obligations to the father in ancient Greece may have induced tensions that were resolved as the authority of the father was internalized.[7] With the gradual development of the belief that the individual had rights against his father and the concomitant intensifying of Oedipal desires, feelings of guilt were stimulated to the point where they were projected onto the heavenly paterfamilias. Thus the punishing conscience was born. These developments were further encouraged by religious movements originating outside classical culture, and they culminated in the pessimism of the great Hellenistic philosophies of withdrawal, which contrasted the private "garden" of experience with the old ideal of the public life. As in India, these systems flowered during an age of new and imposing administrative structures and a rapidly expanding commerce. Religion, no longer tied to the state cult, had come to play a more immediate and intimate role in men's lives as, in contrast, the world became increasingly complex and social relations more abstract.

Contemporary with this spiritual ferment that began toward the end of the archaic age and lasted into the Hellenistic period, and contemporary with the great age of prophecy in Israel, there appeared in the later Upanishadic epoch a great diversity of philosophic schools. By the time of the

---

[e] Brahman and atman are described as *ānandamaya*, "consisting of joy." And what vitality there is in such verses as these from the *Chandogya Upanishad*, XIX:

   Now, what was born therefrom is yonder sun. When it was born, shouts and hurrahs, all beings and all desires rose up toward it. Therefore at its rising and at its every return shouts and hurrahs, all beings and all desires rise up toward it.

   He who, knowing it thus, reverences the sun as Brahma—the prospect is that pleasant shouts will come unto him and delight him—yea, delight him!

Buddha there existed the better part of a hundred distinguishable doctrines, and they ran the gamut from extreme idealism to bald materialism, cynicism, and nihilism. There was, indeed, something for every temperament and inclination. But regardless of the theory or the discipline—whether Sāṅkhya-yoga, Buddhism, or Vedanta—the subjective condition and ends are similar: all are concerned with the recovery of a state of pure Being. Whereas the Indo-Aryans were in all probability the authors (or at least the importers) of ritual and metaphysics, the reactions against the abstract and formal, against ritualism and stylized speculation, and the drift toward immediacy of religious experience, are considered by many modern Indologists and students of mysticism[8] to be expressions of an earlier tradition that had never been completely submerged by the Aryan and Brahmanical culture.[f]

It is important to examine these new religious movements against the background of the tribal culture in which they were conceived, and particularly in the context of sacrificial observances that sometimes were of a markedly destructive nature. Some of these tribes, especially in the eastern regions, were only partially Aryanized. The Buddha himself was probably not of the old Aryan stock, and perhaps must be understood as opposing not only Brahmanism but many of the broader Aryan ideals as well. At the risk of making too much of the parallel, we might compare the early tribal community with the aristocratic polities of the Homeric age. The king was typically *primus inter pares,* and there was often a kind of popular assembly attended by armsbearing freemen. These tribal chieftains frequently appear to have been elected by their fellow nobles; rarely did they exercise absolute power. The lineage principle in these tribal organizations took the place of political allegiance, and territory generally corresponded to kinship ties.[g]

By the sixth century B.C. the ideal of tribal "community" in which all shared in a system of mutual services had succumbed to a scheme of exploitation in which the lower classes were made to serve the interests of the upper orders of society. Increasing demands on the food supply led to the substitution of an agrarian economy for the pastoral. These changes pointed up the inadequacies of the old aristocratic values, sharpened the awareness of the inequities of the social structure, and altered the role of power. Power became less an instrumental value (viewed from the perspective of the collectivity as a whole) and, increasingly, an end in itself, the basis of a hierarchy of privilege. As the sacrifice becomes the ideology of the ruling class, the function of the ritual is transformed to a justification

---

[f] On several stamp-seals of the Harappa period we see seated figures in the position of Yogic meditation. "One can only suppose that the practice of Yoga must already have been developed and associated with the concept of a heightened state of consciousness, not only worthy of worship but also capable of quelling and fascinating the animal world—like the music of Orpheus in the later tradition of the Greeks." (Campbell [53], pp. 435, 234.) Cf. W. Norman Brown [47], p. 44.

[g] In modern Africa, there are societies (the Nuer, Tallensi, Logoli) where kinship ties have an important role in political organization, although political relations are not coterminous with kinship organization. Cf. Fortes and Evans-Pritchard [125], pp. 6f. Regarding ancient Indian tribal associations *vide* [228, 229, 230].

of the distribution of power and the appropriation of the economic surplus by the priests and the nobility.

We shall concentrate our attention on the most important response to the religiosity of Brahmanism, the movement initiated by the Buddha toward the end of the sixth century. Like the Protestant Reformation two thousand years later, Buddhism stressed the personal aspect of religion, but Buddhism, as we shall see, was in many respects a more egalitarian movement than early Protestantism. It has been interpreted as a challenge by the second of the two power-sharing castes, the kshatriyas, to the brahman claim of monopoly on admission to the ascetic orders, an attempt to recover the status the kshatriyas were losing. Were Buddha and Mahāvīra, promulgator of Jainism, primarily motivated by a desire to reassert the ancient rights of the kshatriyas in an age that had witnessed the humbling of the warrior and noble class by the priests? Or are we to believe that in northeastern India Brahmanism had either been rejected or had failed to gain a foothold, and that the kshatriyas continued to enjoy the higher status?[9] In an earlier incarnation, according to legend, the Buddha decided to be reborn a kshatriya rather than a brahman inasmuch as the former caste was the more exalted.

What we know of early Buddhism comes from the Pali scriptures, preserved for centuries by memory in India and Ceylon and finally written down in the dialect of Ceylon.[h] The Pali literature dates from the third century before Christ, and extends into the sixth century A.D.[i] The canon actually provides few details regarding the genealogy of the Buddha. Buddha, which means "enlightened," is a name adopted by the religious leader himself. His dates are the subject of controversy: scholars now usually accept c. 560–480 B.C., although in Burma, Thailand, and Ceylon the years 623–543 B.C. are taken. The Buddha, Siddhārtha Gautama,[j] was born of a kshatriya people, the Śākyans, settled in the Himalayas in or near what is now Nepal.[k] Whether or not they were actual descendents of Indo-Europeans, their language and way of life were essentially Aryan. And though the tribal basis of Shakyan polity was still apparent at the time of Gautama's birth, a territorial state had begun to emerge.

Rhys Davids many years ago concluded that the Shakyas had a republican constitution with a clan assembly,[10] and this interpretation has been

---

[h] Pali is a dialect related to Sanskrit, but simpler in structure.

[i] According to tradition the *Jātakas* (popular legends) were taken by Ashoka's missionary, Mahinda, to Ceylon in the third century B.C., translated from Pali into Sinhalese, and, eight centuries later, back into Pali. The original recording of Buddhist sermons—the form that Buddhist literature usually takes—probably did not occur until the first century B.C. The most important of the collections of canonical writings is the *Pali Canon* with its three parts (*Tripitaka*) : the *Vinaya*, or Book of Discipline; the discourses of the *Sutta Piṭaka* arranged in five *Nikāyas*, the fifth of which contains the birth-stories or *Jātakas* ; and the *Abhidhamma*, containing religious philosophy. There is additional literature in Sanskrit. The Mahāyāna canon is voluminous and still growing.

[j] He was named Siddhartha; Gautama (or, in Pali, Gotama) is the clan name.

[k] Mahāvīra was the son of the chief of a clan associated with the oligarchical republican tribe of the Lichchhavis.

popular with students of Buddhist history. Evidence entitles us to say little more than that the chief of the Shakyan tribe was elected from among the more important families of the community. A number of Jataka stories[11] appear to support the theory that the Shakyas were collectively sovereign, but the Jataka legends were transcribed at a date too late to allow their use as an authoritative source. In Buddhist accounts the father of the Buddha is often described as "raja," leading scholars to speculate that the title was possessed by all the members of the ruling aristocracy or that the father (Śuddhodana by name) was possibly the equivalent of the Roman consul.[1] We know, however, of several passages where the father is mentioned without title,[12] and we must allow for the natural inclination of dedicated disciples to elevate the social status of their teacher.

Today there is a tendency to admit the possibility of a hereditary monarch (not the Buddha's father) who shared power with a group of nobles. This might explain, as Professor Ghoshal suggests, why the Shakyas are omitted from lists of typical sanghas and ganas. It has been argued that the patriarchs of the tribe wielded what was basically a moral authority over their respective clans—an authority different from that of the king.[13] And it may be that we are confronted here with a transitional stage in the development of authority, a stage characteristic of the transition from tribal polity to territorial state. The emergence of the new political form and the accompanying economic changes, which had far-reaching effects on the social system, and perhaps even on the personality structure itself, necessitated certain alterations in social controls. Buddhism may be seen as a combination of the older moral authority of the clan chief (which belonged to an age less dependent on overt political controls) with elements of the tribal assembly (in the Buddhist sangha) and pre-Aryan religious techniques.

Buddhist neglect of the ritual and the Vedic myth, like the Sophist disregard for the traditional concerns of Greek education, contributed to the disintegration of the old order. Both, in effect, challenged the traditional polytheism of the aristocratic culture of the tribes and poleis, questioning the myths and values on which that culture rested. But the new doctrines and disciplines of India, Buddhism among them, were not reform philosophies intent on social change; they offered, rather, an alternative way of life, introspective and world-renouncing. Nor were they designed to lubricate the social mechanism and inspire allegiance to collective purposes or to the ruling elite. Buddhism, however, may have had the latent function of preparing the way for the reorganization of society into the abstract political realm of the Mauryan kings. And the day would come when the salvation religion was employed as an ideological underpinning for the empire and as a means of transforming a society composed of militant tribal groups.

By the sixth century, when the vigorous young states of Magadha and Kosala were competing for suzerainty in the Gangetic basin (at this time

---

[1] The word raja was often used to denote distinction of various kinds.

still a land of thick forests), many of the features we have come to associate with the emergent European nation-state are revealed. The fighting
force had been freed of broad community controls and its allegiance was
to the king alone. The king himself had become practically independent
of tribal election. With the growth of a trading class that identified its
interests with those of the monarch, new sources of revenue became available. And now the king had allies in his struggle with the nobility and the
older tribal institutions. The development and expansion of agencies for
the collection of taxes and the administration of the realm required a
corps of bureaucratic officials who were to become a major element in the
political process.

It is necessary to make these remarks if we are to account for the
success of heterodox religion. The early adherents of Buddhism were
drawn from the urban patrician class, and included a number of kshatriyas
and even brahmans. Max Weber believed that the concern of Buddhism
for matters of decorum and etiquette at least partially explained its appeal
to members of the upper classes.[14] But it was the rising urban commercial
class, using heterodox doctrines to oppose kshatriya violence and arbitrariness, that became the most significant champion of Buddhism. The development of an agricultural economy produced a peasant class whose
interests would also be opposed to the persistent feuding of the tribes and
clans. The increasing demands for cattle and other animals to feed the
sacrificial fires amounted, Kosambi suggests, to an onerous tax on the
farming class.[15] The merchants and other rising economic groups supported the sects because although the monks were sustained by the lay
community, it was a cheaper religion than Brahmanism—at least before
the time of the great monastic establishments.

The anti-materialism of the sects and the principle of communal ownership of property in the sangha might lead us to question the appeal
Buddhism held for the producing and trading classes, but the religion
recognized the importance of the lay member and gave him a dignity he
had never had under the old alliance of the priests and the aristocracy. And
the ideals of Buddhism were more compatible with the orderly society
upon which the fortunes of these groups depended. The egalitarian element
of Buddhism won converts from among those who had endured the dis-
crimination of the system rationalized by Brahmanism (although Buddhism never sought to destroy the caste structure). And heterodoxy had
its appeal for the unarticulated anti-Aryan sentiments of certain segments
of the population.

At first Buddhism, Jainism, and Brahmanism existed together without serious conflict. Spiritual guidance might be provided by the Buddhist
monk, while the brahman priest directed the domestic ritual. The great
age of the Buddhist ethic was the third century B.C., when it enjoyed the
patronage of the enlightened emperor Ashoka. It might be said that the
fortunes of Buddhism roughly paralleled those of the state of Magadha.
The images associated with the religion acquired a grandeur comparable
to the imperial majesty of the Mauryan state. But its roots failed to go
deep into Indian life; it left behind only shrines to be visited by devout

pilgrims from other lands of Asia, where its fate was not so calamitous. It was perhaps too austere a religion for a people accustomed to an elaborate ceremonial. In its initial form it demanded a stern morality, which later was somewhat softened in certain branches of the faith. Nirvāṇa—the abolition of lust, anger, and ignorance—was too negatively conceived and lacked the imaginative appeal and romance of the popular cults.[m] The most important reason for its decline was the counterreformation of a revitalized Brahmanism. The brahmans attempted to incorporate as much of the new systems as was consonant with their own superior social position. The Upanishads were reinterpreted to make them consistent with theistic belief, and the authority of the ancient texts and customs was invoked.

The impact of the Buddha on the broader cultural forces of India has generally been exaggerated. It is true that Buddhism served to rejuvenate and purify older creeds, but these belief systems could not have recovered so quickly and so completely had they not been more firmly entrenched in the culture than many accounts of the Buddhist centuries would lead us to suppose. Despite the spread of Buddhist ideals and discipline, the need for religious rites of certain kinds remained and society continued to be stratified. The position of the brahmans was actually modified very little. And Buddhism, as it assumed the proportions of a great religion, became increasingly expensive, with large monastic orders to be maintained and a sizable sector of the population engaged in economically unproductive activities. Whatever the explanation, within several generations after Ashoka Maurya and the end of official concession and protection, the priests had regained what ground they had lost. Buddhism went into eclipse in the early centuries of the Christian era, and in the three hundred years c. A.D. 100–400, neo-Brahmanism, with a greater emotional vigor and introspective emphasis than had characterized the old orthodoxy, gained for itself new converts. It is this revitalized religion that has come to be called Hinduism.

THE PATH OF BUDDHISM

The ancient Vedic mythology was dominated by heroic extravagance and the virile affirmation of life; in the later brahman texts kshatriya activism is justified insofar as it contributes to the maintenance of the varna system. The ideal of heroic leadership appears in the orthodox

---

[m] This is not to imply that Buddhism did nothing to broaden its appeal. The visitor to the great stūpa at Sānchī is likely to be startled by the voluptuous female figure adorning the area below the bottom architrave on one side of the famous east gate. This *yakshī,* or tree spirit, a fertility symbol, would seem to be out of place in a Buddhist shrine. The nymph (one of whose sisters now graces the Boston Museum of Fine Arts) is a representative of an early nature cult which the Buddhists, evidently incapable of uprooting it, ultimately accepted. "Although their presence confirms acceptance by the Buddhist Church, their provocative charms seem almost symbolic of that world of illusion that the worshiper leaves behind when he enters the sacred precinct. . . . In the frankness of their erotic statement the Sānchī yakshīs are a perfect illustration of the union of spiritual and sensual metaphor that runs like a thread through all religious art in India." (Rowland [370], pp. 57f.)

religious literature only as a means of revivifying the traditional dharmic
order: the hero, a deity incarnate, steps forth to preserve the sacred tradition. It is of interest that when a protest philosophy does appear, sponsored in the case of Buddhism and Jainism by members of the kshatriya
class, it takes the form of a rejection of active mastery of the external
world. The Buddha was himself, as we have seen, a prominent member
of an important tribe, not a deracinated young intellectual driven by turn
of fortune to find compensations in the spiritual realm.

If we are to understand this protest, we must go beyond the types of
analysis employed in interpreting European intellectual history. We may
find it difficult to comprehend completely the Oriental belief that knowledge is power; we are too inclined to use the expression only in a figura-
tive sense. In the East, wisdom was traditionally the means of attaining
supernatural power and stature. The magical qualities of this power
require that the student be carefully trained if he is to use it properly.
Even in the secular and materialist *Arthashastra* of Kautalya, the idea
has central importance. This wisdom (which we might call charismatic)
was the preserve of certain families, the most valued inheritance a son
could have. The political significance of this potency was considerable.
Zimmer compares it to the secret weapon of the modern era. It had to be
carefully guarded, for it was the basis of brahman pre-eminence, and was
crucial to Aryan hegemony. The conquered dasa was therefore denied
access to this knowledge. Such was the power of gnosis, even in systems
of thought that were not founded on the Vedas. A vigorous discipline,
amounting to virtual rebirth, was the prerequisite for admission to the
inner circle of virtuosi.[16]

The teaching of the Buddha, as is so often true of reform movements,
aimed at restoring the purity of the ancient way. The older truths must
be reaffirmed. It was not enough to be born a brahman or to content
oneself with external forms. The Buddha would have men return to the
sentiment of the *Rigveda*: "Neither by action nor by sacrifices can He
be reached." Goodness must be judged according to the motive behind
the act. Karma is accordingly related to moral action, whereas in Brahmanism karma was based on the performance of ritual. But the ultimate
achievement of Nirvana can be neither an ethical nor a psychological state,
because liberation is from "alter" as well as ego. Both good and evil—
in fact, all social norms that relate men—cease to have meaning. Weber
is undoubtedly correct in his opinion that the universal compassion of
Buddhism is not the expression of active brotherliness.[17] Buddhism advocated a detachment from the world of men, a retreat from intense involvement in social relationships.

In early Buddhism we do not find the sentimentality that pervades
later accounts of the Buddha and his message. The emphasis of the doctrine is on knowledge—a type of recollection in which previously known
forms are recovered, similar in some respects to the epistemology we find
in Socrates and Plato. Like Socrates the Buddha turned from speculation
about the universe to concentrate his efforts on rediscovering the spiritual

world. Both were critical of the dogmatism of the older philosophy; both implied a rejection of the prevailing morality of social constraint. As with Plato, the Buddha's pursuit of knowledge takes on a religious significance; the world of sensual experience cannot provide the true basis for that knowledge. The very story of the life of Gautama is the story of the search for truth.[n] In comprehending this truth, the Absolute, man must overcome the intellect itself, for it is the very nature of the mind to distinguish, to perceive opposites, and intellect impedes the ultimate insight into the One.

Buddhist doctrine may be classified neatly into a series of premises, a happy contrast to the tortuous byways of Hinduism. The second of the three parts of the Pali canon contains a collection of the Buddha's sermons, basic to which is the idea of the four noble truths: pain and suffering are universal, the cause of pain is desire, suffering can be cured by the elimination of craving, and the way to eliminate pain is by following the eightfold way.[o] This eightfold path is a prescription of doctrine, ethics, and mental discipline: right views, right intentions, right speech, right action, right livelihood, right effort, right mindfulness, and right concentration.[18] It may take several lives before the seeker is prepared to enter the realm of Nirvana. As in the Upanishads, worldly accomplishment is deemed irrelevant to the true values to be found through the discipline of mind and body. Compared with the joys of spiritual insight all other satisfactions are ephemeral.

In the doctrine there is no such thing as the individual soul. This feature of Buddhism as well as the concept of group karma may attest to the strong influence of tribal ideology on the shaping of Buddhist doctrine.

---

[n] In the twenty-ninth year of his final mortal appearance he renounced his worldly fortunes and, forsaking wife and child, he departed the royal city for a life of wandering, meditation, and extreme asceticism. After six years he became convinced that truth is to be found neither through indulgence nor through self-mutilation, and began to advocate the doctrine of *dhamma*, the middle path. At the age of thirty-five he attained enlightenment under a bo-tree (sacred wild fig) at Gaya, in the modern province of Bihar. We are told that although the Buddha was at first reticent, the gods prevailed upon him to set in motion the Wheel of Law, and he began his teaching at Benares. The Buddha spent fifty years preaching in the Gangetic plain, "opening the gateway of immortality to all." He appeared not as the unreserved social critic, but as the author of a way to salvation available to all men regardless of social rank. Men could, through their own diligence, find the path of deliverance as he himself had found the way. This was his parting message to all mankind.

The Buddha never called on supernatural authority; he never claimed to be himself more than mortal. Knowledge and effort were the key to righteousness. To his great disciple he said, "And whosoever, Ananda, either now or after I am dead, shall be a lamp unto themselves, and a refuge unto themselves, shall betake themselves to no external refuge, but holding fast to the Truth as their lamp . . . shall not look for refuge to anyone besides themselves—it is they . . . who shall reach the very topmost height! But they must be anxious to learn."

[o] It has been suggested that the form in which the four truths are expressed is derived from the medical practice of the time—which divided medical science according to disease, its cause, the nature of health, and treatment leading to health. What impresses us is the mode of thought which ties human action to natural causes. In this we are reminded of Thucydides who, if C. N. Cochrane (*Thucydides and the Science of History* [London, 1929]) is right, adapted the principles of Hippocratic medicine to the interpretation of events.

Being consists of five components: body, feeling, perception, the mental elements, and consciousness. As desire ceases to dominate his life, these qualities will dissolve in man. The process is stimulated by a type of concentration that has a similarity to Yoga. The mind evolves through different stages of absorption; consciousness moves from the subjective to the objective as it moves, in philosophical Hinduism, toward union with Brahman. Individuality has its basis and motivation in craving, and men desire because they are unaware that the things desired can never, in reality, be possessed. Nirvana (Pali: *Nibbana*) itself can only be negatively described: it does not mean to annihilate, but literally "to extinguish"—to extinguish desire, to extinguish the cause and effect of rebirth, to gain a superconsciousness.

This reaction to the controls of the priests, with its stress on the personal aspect of religious experience which opened the way of salvation to all men, is of such a remarkable and psychologically intricate nature that we might well turn at this point to the theory of psychoanalysis for what light it may cast on the dynamics of the mental processes involved.*p*

From one point of view the Buddhist reform may be understood as an attempt to clear religion of restraints beyond those necessary for human intercourse. But no new political organizations were substituted for the old, nor was there any redistribution of social power. We find instead the internalizing of repressive authority, the systematic endeavor to subordinate the expression of the instinctual to what Freud has termed the reality principle.*q*

In terms of individual psychology the religious systems (both primitive and Brahmanical) that Buddhism reacted against allowed, to varying degrees, the direction of aggression outward toward the gods and fetishes —rather than turning it inward to stimulate the development of a strict super-ego. Brahmanism and Hinduism provided rich substitute gratifications in fantasy and the acting out of anxiety and emotion. Unlike the monotheistic religion with its all-seeing and all-powerful God, the author

---

p It is always hazardous to impose psychological categories developed in Western urban and industrialized society on experience belonging to a different time and culture. Professor Dodds, who has himself used Freudian theory most effectively in illuminating the intellectual life and popular culture of ancient Greece, has remarked most sensibly that "the evolution of a culture is too complex a thing to be explained without residue in terms of any simple formula, whether economic or psychological, begotten of Marx or begotten of Freud. We must resist the temptation to simplify what is not simple. And, secondly, to explain origins is not to explain away values." (Dodds [98], p. 49.) With this warning in mind, we turn to psychoanalysis as Dilthey would have us look to the artist—that we might see with a new eye and achieve new insights.

q It is of course true that many religions "have been able to effect absolute renunciation of pleasure in this life by means of the promise of compensation in a future life. . . . A momentary pleasure, uncertain in its results, is given up, but only in order to gain in the new way an assured pleasure coming later." (Freud, "The Two Principles in Mental Functioning," *Collected Papers* (London, 1953), IV, 18. This response to external reality is often advocated as a necessary condition of the mastery of the environment, and as a means of channeling energy away from aggressive and sexual activities and into the necessary economic tasks of society. Scarcity perpetuates the struggle between pleasure and the reality principle and demands instinctual repression. Cf. Freud, *General Introduction to Psychoanalysis* (Garden City, N. Y., 1943), p. 243.

of the supreme ethical principles that guide human relationships, Buddhism lacked a dramatic symbolization of authority. It was not primarily an ethical system; the social element was subordinate to its major purposes, the dissolution of the ego and the release it brings. Buddhism not only prescribed the relinquishing of sensual pleasures, which feed desire and are the ultimate cause of suffering, but aimed at the very reorganization of personality. It sought to do more than provide the happiness stressed in those religions more familiar to us, the happiness that comes with inhibiting the aim of love from the particular object that affords genital gratification. It sought to transform erotic love into friendship and brotherhood. But loving may well increase one's vulnerability to suffering and anguish.[r] Repression of the so-called "life instincts" was taught by the Buddha as the means of avoiding this vulnerability and preventing harm to the individual. There is not the same concern for loving one's neighbor that we find in Western religions, where the superego (or conscience) is strengthened in order to prevent ego's harm to alter.

In summary, then, the repressive order of society is not opposed, although it is transcended through the destruction of man's ties with the external world. True freedom, seen in this light, comes with the breaking up of the ego, which is subject to time, and the attainment of a state beyond pain and desire. Consciousness is no longer rooted in the separation of the self from the object-world. Through proper discipline objects come to be experienced from "within," and consciousness is freed from ego entanglements. Ego development may be necessary to self-preservation in early stages of life. But when the self has been defined in the process of interaction with the world, the point is reached where man must reverse a development that threatens to result in isolation and alienation. He must direct his energies toward achieving an infinite relationship with all that is the living cosmos.

In the opening pages of *Civilization and Its Discontents,* Freud mentions the comment of a reader who regretted Freud's failure to appreciate the "sensation of eternity," the ultimate source of religious sentiment. Freud remarks that he cannot discover this "oceanic" feeling in himself, but this does not prevent his attempting an explanation of the phenomenon. He accounts for this subjective experience as a vestigial ego-feeling that survives the age before the individual learns to distinguish himself from the rest of the world.[19] Nirvana, like the Freudian "death wish," is the attempt to regain the narcissistic maternal unity that existed before the ego separated subject and object (or, it might be added, to recover the *conscience collective* of the tribal community—a *Gemeinschaft* world in which the individual ego was submerged in kinship ties). This separation is the cause of desire, which can be overcome only by returning to the earlier state. For Freud, the death instinct is the organism's inherent tendency to reinstate a pre-existing, almost inanimate state, rather than an actual yearning for death.[20] It is the wish for the peace of the inorganic world, for freedom from all excitation. Nirvana is such a state: with the

---

[r] "We are never so defenseless against suffering as when we love." (Freud [131], p. 38.)

elimination of desire, the ego is no longer conscious of itself. In fact, with the fusion of id energies and super-ego, the relating and reconciling ego loses its purpose.

And yet ego processes appear to be very important to Buddhism. Actually, in this *participation mystique,* Buddhism sets out to awaken the faculty of intuition that resides in all men: "Look inward . . . thou art Buddha." There is no insistence on faith, a savior, or subtle doctrinal formulations. Enlightenment is everything, and the power of mind is central. Personality is "consciousness"—integrating and ever-changing as it moves toward enlightenment. And since consciousness is continuously being altered, how is it possible to exalt the idea of personality? Consciousness makes possible the acquisition of knowledge, and its very evolution brings the modification of the self. Atman (or self) is not a permanent quality of man; there is no individual immortal soul.[21]

Nirvana is not an unconscious state, but, as we have said, a super-consciousness that surpasses reason. It is an amoral state—there is no longer anything "that ought or ought not to be done." "Liberation [is] as much from the notion of 'others' as it is from the notion of 'self.' "[22] Nirvana, or harmony with the universe, annihilates the distinction "between life and release-from-life."[23]

The preoccupation of modern Western civilization with individual man, his uniqueness and his competitive relationship to others, impedes the development of an "oceanic" sentiment that puts the *unity* foremost. The Western ego experiences life as something to be overcome. Man must struggle and transform, and not be himself transformed. Performance, rather than learning, is accentuated in that the modification of the environment must be greater than that of the organism as a result of the inter-relation of the two. Aggression and competition become ennobled as social virtues, although for purposes of social cohesion brotherly love and charity continue to be stressed. Of the types of man that Freud describes,[24] "active" man (the type of personality represented by the kshatriya warrior of the vigorous Vedic age) tends to be valued in the West. Active man is contrasted with "narcissistic" man, who seeks "essential gratifications in the inner workings of his own soul." "Erotic" man is feared in all cultures, for, in his quest for close emotional relationships, he constitutes a threat to the larger group.[s]

There is, however, a second possible interpretation of Buddhist psychology and technique that transcends these Freudian categories. The id-

---

[s] The reason for this constitutes the theme of *Civilization and Its Discontents* [131]. Western intellectuals have often challenged the wisdom, virtue, or aesthetics of a value system that exalts active mastery of the environment. Sometimes, as in the case of Schopenhauer, Buddhist theory has been the inspiration for this criticism. "Instead of the restless striving and effort, instead of the constant transition from wish to fruition, and from joy to sorrow, instead of the never-satisfied and never-dying hope which constitutes the life of the man who wills, we shall see that peace which is above all reason, that perfect calm of the spirit, that deep rest, that inviolable confidence and serenity, the mere reflection of which in the countenance, as Raphael and Correggio have represented it, is an entire and certain gospel; only knowledge remains, the will has vanished." (*The World as Will and Idea* [New York, 1961], p. 421.) This quietism received a famous answer from Nietzsche (*Twilight of the Idols*), who pushed the image of active man to its logical and transmoral conclusions.

orientation of the Freudian school would discount the positive aspects of ego functioning that may accompany the mystical experience. The discussion that follows more nearly approximates the approach of the "ego-psychologists" than that of traditional psychoanalysis.[t] I shall take the view that Buddhism is essentially a means of coping with demands of the instinctual life in a time when the direct expression of these needs was increasingly inhibited by the needs of social organization. The solution lay in the ability to surmount the separation between the unconscious and conscious regions of the mind.

We must start by asking what is meant by loss of self, and determine to what extent the transformation of personality involves a renunciation of the world. The Upanishadic suggestion that consciousness itself is never overcome was mentioned earlier. Consciousness is consciousness of something other than itself—it implies a world independent of and prior to one's knowledge. When the Buddha speaks of transcending consciousness he appears to mean that this separation between reflexive consciousness and the external world, which is also the root of "self-consciousness," has been eliminated. We might say that he sought a prereflexive consciousness.[25] The immediacy of this relation between the self and the other reduces the feeling of separateness between the two, and with it those affects of self-consciousness rooted in a form of anxiety or conflict. Mystic "selflessness" is that " 'normal' unselfconsciousness characteristic of experience which is primarily non-anxious and motivated by neutralized drives functioning within the non-conflictful portions of the ego."[26] He who achieves enlightenment, we are told, knows neither sensation of struggle nor submission. Energy is liberated from the repressive process and the individual comes alive in the sense that the ego functions are freed from anxiety. This transcendence of the intrapsychic conflict of the dissociated personality makes possible the ultimate development of the self.

Such expression is impeded by both the structure of the personality and the environment in which man lives. But the two are treated as one problem. The illusory world of the neurotic is *māyā,* and with the emancipation of the ego that illusory aspect of the environment, which is the object of insatiable craving, comes to be seen as of little significance to man. This is the true "rebirth." Man is born anew as he attains a harmonious integration of instinctual drives, goals, and norms governing his conduct, as well as a realistic sense of the environment in which he must operate. With this integration he arrives at a proper comprehension of the self, free of the obsession with the self that anxiety produces. And in this sense he is also emancipated from the cycle of birth and death. The psychically unified ego ceases to fear death—which is so often the preoccupation of those who are unable to live autonomous and productive lives.

It is perhaps not surprising that such a psychology should have developed in the aristocracy. It was in this group that ego development and problems of conflict and anxiety were combined with the capacity to articulate a systematic philosophy and the opportunity to be heard. The

---

[t] In this approach I am particularly indebted to an essay by Herbert Fingarette, "The Ego and Mystic Selflessness" [124].

Buddha was himself something of an organizational innovator in his design for a community that would make possible the realization of the contemplative life. It is true, of course, that the monks relied on the local populace for the satisfaction of many of their basic needs, but work was not disparaged. The Buddha rejected extreme forms of asceticism and thought of himself as the proponent of a moderate way. In short, Buddhism was not the complete withdrawal from life and the concerns of the world that it is sometimes made out to be.

It is misleading to reduce the question to whether Buddhism makes man an object or an actor. If the problem were posed in this way, we would overlook the real contribution of Buddhism. From a psychological point of view, the Buddha sought to free man from the anxiety that accompanies the actions of alienated men. The action of the liberated man is not the kshatriya action motivated by the desire to master, nor is it action intent on appropriation (which may itself transform man into the object of his possessions). It is action that avoids the reification of either the actor or other men. Alienation is overcome when the individual succeeds in discovering himself in objects external to him. With this sense of oneness with the universe, the ego gains the self-sufficiency of pure substance without surrendering consciousness.

Implicit in the Brahmanical texts and in the Dharmasutras had been the idea of the divine origin of the universe and the human community. Though not itself a social philosophy, Buddhism, with its greater attention to ethical considerations and the role of human volition in determining social arrangements, opened new possibilities for political speculation. In the dialogues of the Buddha such factors as greed, lust, and vanity become the basis for change in the societal order.

The Buddhist view of social evolution postulates an idyllic, Edenesque state of nature in the beginning.[27] Gradual moral decline at length underscored the differences that divide men, and social institutions were introduced to cope with the problems that arose. Lust led to property, and property in turn encouraged the four evils of theft, censure, dishonesty, and violence. Man's very corporeality is considered the consequence of his fall from perfection. One day men found themselves no longer able to dance on air; the dream-world was succeeded by the world as we know it—a world concerned with time and space, sex and family, property and subsistence, social distinctions and the myriad of controls that we today believe to be necessary to community life. The story has a familiar ending: to establish order the greatest among men was named king and received in return a portion of the produce.

"When first propounded," writes Kosambi of the concept of Nirvana, "it was a negation, a return of the individual to the signless, undifferentiated state. . . . The memory of a classless, undifferentiated society remained as the legend of a golden age when the good earth spontaneously produced ample food without labor because men had neither property or greed."[28] It would seem that such a philosophy looks back to the ancient communal values of the tribe, instead of being the ideology of the new productive system (as Kosambi elsewhere suggests). It is not uncommon for men, in protecting themselves against disillusion, to put their Utopia in the past. A Utopia of this sort has a weak critical potential and generally constitutes no threat to the established order. But the goal of Buddhism was to regain the Arcadia of infinite peace. This could be accomplished by means of strict intellectual discipline, the clearing away of the impediments that prevent our understanding of the Absolute.[u]

The Buddhist doctrine shares much with certain theories of psychoanalysis. Freud never postulated an idyllic natural state like the golden age that haunts Buddhist cosmogony. Before men united in civil societies, they were governed by the rule of the strong. But there *is* a golden age in the life of man. "The memory of gratification is at the origin of all thinking, and the impulse to recapture past gratification is the hidden driving power behind the process of thought."[29] The quest (explicit in Buddhism, innate in man according to the psychoanalyst) is for this golden age before the organism had distinguished itself from its surroundings. The memory of gratification becomes a weapon against a world of alienation.[v] Buddhism (like Platonism) made a sharp distinction between the world of the senses, the external reality that gives meaning to "active" man, and the world of mind. Salvation depends on supersensory experience, which in turn demands the quiet of the forest. From the point of view of the state, such a philosophy constituted a menace only if it threatened to make the ascetic life too desirable.

The changes that were at this time seriously modifying the old tribal patterns of life were largely a response to increasing demands on the food supply. With the coming of an agricultural economy, there came also the promise of economic surplus—the production of goods and services in excess of what was needed for survival. This is the condition of civilization: the possibility of supporting a culture-creating class of professionals. It may have seemed to many in the sixth and fifth centuries that instead of yearning for a golden yesterday, men might confidently anticipate a bountiful age yet to come. The Ganges valley in the seventh century was the home of a nascent capitalism as well. These new sources of wealth were to make possible the fulfillment of imperial ambitions. Empire had not been economically feasible until this development. The territorial state, intent on its own aggrandizement, sought to buttress its power and centralized institutional structure with new ideological supports.

Where was the world religion that could support the splendor of em-

---

[u] On the possibility of the soul to recover what it has learned in the other world (*anamnesis*), cf. Plato, *Meno*, 81c.

[v] Though historically the reality principle develops as a consequence of Ananke (the struggle for survival necessitated by scarcity), the Biblical Eden story makes Ananke the punishment for man's partaking of the tree of the knowledge of good and evil. Man must share God's "reason"—that is, the reality principle must dominate his life. Perhaps because of the broad implication of the word "knowledge" (including carnal knowledge), the distinction between the pleasure and reality principles is not made clear in the myth. The gratification of instinctual needs was suppressed because of "abuse" in a golden age when abundance, instead of allowing for freer expression, ought to have made it unnecessary for man to seek knowledge of any kind.

pire? It appears that until the heterodox faiths succeeded in attracting too large a segment of the community away from economically productive pursuits, they served this function at least indirectly, and left the governing thority to another, the campaign to shatter the tribal polity would have hand of the ruling elite (not always kshatriya at this time) against the brahmans. Without the internalization of controls which the new religions encouraged, and which eased the transition from one type of external authority to another, the campaign to shatter the tribal polity would have been accompanied by greater reliance on arbitrary force. The sects, though determinedly free of this-worldly commitments, provided an alternative to the sacrificial cult—which had served for many centuries to justify the concentration of power in the hands of the old tribal oligarchies. Ironically, as we shall see, a subtle "totalitarian" threat was contained in the attempt to wed Buddhism to the purposes the ancient cosmological religion had served.

Before we turn to the more specific aspects of heterodox social thought, several observations regarding the concept of transmigration are in order. Our central problem has been to explain the appeal of a philosophy that emphasized the fact of human suffering—at a time when it appeared that the standard of living was beginning to rise. Do we encounter here what Gilbert Murray, writing of another culture, called "a failure of nerve"?[w] It is possible that this was the case, for many of the social agencies upon which men depended for support were losing their traditional functions.

The advent of a settled agricultural economy and the changes that accompanied and resulted from this development had produced a situation in which, as Robert Merton puts it, the most expedient procedures for reaching cultural goals are preferable to institutionally prescribed conduct, although these procedures may lack legitimacy.[30] With the waning of tribal values and institutions (caste was not sufficiently advanced at this time to take its place as an instrument of social control and cultural integration), and with the appearance of new forms of economic production and political organization, the individual must have begun to sense a loneliness and impotence he had not known in the traditional society that was being left behind. We do not mean to imply that this change was experienced on a conscious level. The process was slow; there is no moment when occupational role became sharply differentiated from kinship role. But before roles, expectations, and controls were effectively integrated, the sharpened sense of guilt—which, if we are right in our speculation, accompanied the relaxing of clan and tribal authorities—may very well have produced a tormenting uneasiness. It remained for the new salvation religions to turn this estrangement to positive ends.

Men will not rest until the cause and, especially, the meaning of suffering are found. Then, somehow, misery becomes bearable. Usually a

---

[w] "It is a rise of asceticism, of mysticism, in a sense of pessimism; a loss of self-confidence, of hope in this life and of faith in normal human effort. . . . There is an intensifying of certain spiritual emotions; an increase of sensitiveness, a failure of nerve." (Murray [289], p. 119.)

rationale is discovered, such as the doctrine of karma, which not only explains suffering but may even give it a positive value.[31] The concept of inherited pollution was older than that of reincarnation; the uniting of the two ideas was to become one of the most decisive events in the history of Indian culture. (Although a similar religious development was taking place in ancient Greece, it did not have the same consequences.) The techniques employed for overcoming transmigration may in many respects be compared with Orphic purification—which was thought to redeem the soul from the round of rebirth. All that tied man to the realm of sense experience must be surmounted.

In Greece, Orphism and other mystery cults accounted for the misfortunes of the virtuous and held out the promise of eventual compensation.[32] These other-worldly religions had a broader appeal than the public cults. They offered the masses a hope and a freedom. But toward the end of the archaic age and contemporary with the period in which Buddhist ideas were formulated, the popular group orgiastic rites were evidently no longer able to satisfy the religious needs of many members of the community. These persons found fulfillment in the private shamanistic experience.[*] Pythagoras was one of them; he believed if not in transmigration as such, at least that the soul could have a former life. Much of his inspiration was undoubtedly Orphic; he appears to build on a foundation of Orphic religion. And Pythagoras, like Buddha, founded a spiritual order, which (like the Buddhist sangha) was notable for granting women a status unique in the classical world.[y]

We shall return to the subject of shamanism in the next chapter, when we consider Yoga; what concerns us here is the private religious experience intended to transport the devotee by leading the way to ecstatic release of tension (shamanism) or personality reorganization. Individuality was a hindrance to be overcome. Yet salvation had become an individual matter. The *collective* orgiastic experience was rejected not in the interest of the private gnosis as such. With the distintegration of the tribal "group consciousness," the group was no more than an aggregate of souls destined to be born again and again, unless a way was found to circumvent transmigration.

Professor Dodds, in commenting on the parallel development in Greece, remarks that "it was only when rebirth was attributed to *all* human souls that it became a burden instead of a privilege, and was used to explain the inequalities of our earthly portion and to show that, in the words of a

---

[*] Shamanism may have been introduced into Hellenic culture with the extension of Greek commerce and colonization into the regions of the Black Sea.

[y] Cornford ([721], p. 176) believes that because Orphic and Pythagorean belief and Persian religion may be regarded as expressions of the same view of life, we are justified in using one to interpret the other. Persia may indeed prove to be the major link between Greek and Indian ideas, but we cannot now say, if similarities of Iranian and Indian religion are indeed significant, which direction of influence was the more important. On possible Iranian influences *vide*, e.g., Jean Przyluski, "La Théorie des Guṇa," *Bulletin of the School of Oriental Studies* (London), VI, 1; J. J. Modi, *Asiatic Papers,* III; Albert Grünwedel, *Alt-Kutscha,* 1920, I, 54ff.; Bloomfield [38], pp. 125ff.; Joseph Campbell [53], pp. 434ff.; Thapar [407], pp. 126ff.

Pythagorean poet, man's sufferings are self-incurred."[33] In India this doctrine, karma, the belief that one's lot in this life is the reward of the deeds of former lives, antedated Buddhism by no more than a century. But by the time of the Buddha it had captured the popular imagination and was rapidly becoming central to most schools of Indian philosophy and religion and fundamental to the ideology of caste.[z] Those in positions of power might be expected to champion a theory that made man himself, rather than society, morally responsible for whatever station he had achieved.[aa]

If man alone is accountable for his own fortune, it means at least that he is freed of the consequences of the sins of his father. The collective fortune of the tribe, ensured by the sacrifice, afforded psychological comforts that probably outweighed its disadvantages for the individual. Now that heroic age was fading and Aryan civilization was permeated with elements of the indigenous culture. These new ideas of the after-life had their source, for the most part, in this non-Aryan culture—or were the result of the encounter between the two cultures. And as Aryanism moved eastward, contacts with primitive totemism probably stimulated a dread of totemistic consequences of actions; this may also have been instrumental in winning converts to such religions as Buddhism.

It is too much to assume that originally the principle of karma was without appeal. Some men may have seen it as representing a kind of immortality; for others it perhaps held out the hope that modest as their status might be, they could anticipate the possibility of a better place in society. Professor Basham[34] believes that the almost universal acceptance of the doctrine is evidence of the appeal of samsara, but that the intellectual did not share this sanguine attitude.[bb]

HETERODOX SOCIAL THOUGHT

Buddhist thought does not offer much in the way of a systematic contribution to political theory, and the reason should by now be apparent. The value of secular studies was discounted; mental and spiritual discipline

[z] For the major distinctions between Buddhist and Brahmanical theories of transmigration, *vide* La Vallée Poussin, "Buddhism," in Garratt [136]. The Buddhist conception of transmigration is anticipated by the *Brihadaranyaka Upanishad* III, 2.13. It is there stated that only karma, the effect of work, survives man.

[aa] Individual responsibility continues in Western society to be an effective conservative ideology. But the logic of liberalism would seem to dictate that if men are to be held individually accountable, they must be granted a corresponding amount of power. The fact of the matter is that as man emerges as an "individual" free to express the uniqueness of his personality, he becomes more dependent on those others who supply his wants and (in this sense) free him for his own purposes. His fortune becomes intermeshed with the destinies of men who are not even known to him. Indian theory, as we have seen, sought to prevent this entanglement of fortunes wherever possible—perhaps to keep the moral record straight.

[bb] Varma [416] argues that Buddhism "was from the beginning characterized by a missionary orientation" and, in order to lure the people from their pleasures and apathy, it exaggerated the fact of suffering. This interpretation oversimplifies the motive for Buddhist missionary zeal, and Varma exaggerates the optimism of philosophical movements contemporary with Buddhism. His catalogue of psychological explanations for Buddhist "pessimism" does not include the emotional consequences of social change.

was stressed. Reform of earthly life was not a major concern of the sects, for peace and fulfillment were to be gained through a detachment from the affairs of the world. But in what speculation there is, induction and reason are more important because less can be explained as the result of divine intervention. More scope is given to human nature and ability. And Buddhist literature is more inflexibly moralistic, disavowing brahmanic tendencies to put other considerations first.

What is most striking is the brahman's loss of prestige. We are told that deeds, and not family, make the spiritual aristocracy. Both the Buddha and his Jaina counterpart, Mahavira, denied the supreme authority of the Vedas as well. Jainism represents a much more ardent critique of the sacrifice than Buddhism, which chose rather to ignore the brahman ceremonials. The Buddhists simply regarded the rite as irrelevant. But the Jainas went further toward the acceptance of caste ideology. (There was even the attempt to manufacture brahman origin for Mahavira.) Caste privilege was attacked by the Buddha, and though the institution was not yet fully developed, it was implicitly recognized as a powerful force too important to overlook. Fick quotes the *Kannakathāla Sutta* to the effect that the kshatriyas and brahmans take precedence over the other castes as far as visible signs of respect are concerned. Caste was recognized, but "just as the great rivers such as the Gangā, the Yamunā . . . when they pour their waters into the vast ocean, lose their names and origins and become the great ocean, so do the four castes when they pass, according to the doctrines and prescriptions of those who have attained perfection, from home to homelessness, lose their names and origins."[35] Caste became unimportant for spiritual salvation. The Buddhist justification of caste in terms of social function rather than by way of organic analogy avoided the implications of the Brahmanical theory, which assumed the divine origin of caste. The theory of the retrograde evolution of the world was expounded as an answer to the brahman claim of supremacy by virtue of birth from the mouth of Purusha. The special immunities of the upper classes are to be taken away.[cc]

In attacking the role and superior social position of the priests, who had constituted a primary check on royal despotism, Buddhism indirectly assisted the destruction of the old balance of power. The growth of Buddhism and the rise of absolutism are features of the same age, and it would not be too wide of the mark to suggest that the new religion contributed to this political development in much the same way that Luther aided the interests of the German princes. Later, under Ashoka, Buddhism served as a means of pacifying and integrating the peoples of the new empire.

We have already noted the Buddhist theory that civil society originated in the moral decay of man. Government, which grew out of the need for order, was rooted in a secular compact.[dd] Despite the references in the

---

[cc] The Buddhist Aśvaghoṣa censures caste inasmuch as human beings are "in respect of joy and sorrow, love, insight, manners and ways, death, fear and life, all equal." (*Vajrasūcī*, quoted in Beni Prasad [323], pp. 218f.)

[dd] There is an inference in the *Digha Nikaya* (III, 93) that the social contract is between the kshatriyas as a group and the rest of society.

Jatakas to elections held to choose a new monarch, with all the citizens in the capital city evidently participating in the voting, the Buddhist doctrine was not elaborated to justify the idea of popular sovereignty and to limit the power of the king in this respect. There are also references to the deposition of a king by the people, but we are not free to infer that the Buddha contemplated anything more than the typical oligarchy of his time. The king is looked upon as a functionary to be paid by his subjects for services rendered. Usually taxes were one-sixth of the paddy produce; they should be levied in accordance with the dhamma.[36] The most important function of the king, as we should expect, is protection. He is *mahāsammata* (chosen by the multitude), *khattiya* (kshatriya: lord of the fields), *rājā* (he who gratifies in accord with dhamma). This is the true origin of the social hierarchy. But it is always virtue and knowledge that determine superiority. King Milinda (Menander) is told, for instance, that the king is defined not only by his function (ruling and guiding the world), but by his righteousness, which makes his subjects rejoice and brings success to his ventures.

As in the brahmanic literature, punishment is a duty of the king, but it no longer has the central role that had been assigned to danda in earlier political speculation. The sacred principle is to be upheld in more positive ways; the use of coercive power is to be avoided if at all possible. The Buddhist conception of dhamma connotes the supreme principle of righteousness. It is closer to Western concepts of virtue than is the Brahmanical dharma, which has a more legal tone and is tied to the maintenance of class prerogatives. Dharma must be sufficiently flexible to allow the king to justify actions necessary to the preservation of order, even though these actions are not themselves compatible with ethical standards. Although Buddhist political thought also considers the primary purpose of the state to be the safeguarding of order, this order tends to be understood in more purely moral terms and the dhamma must be the standard for all the king's activities. This is far from a philosophy of stern justice. A king who rules without compassion is unworthy of his title. The state is also charged with the protection of the people against economic privation, and with their instruction in the life of the spirit and the mind. Hence it encompasses a variety of welfare functions. These responsibilities emphasize the need for the highest moral character on the part of the ruler.

The qualities of the king, as described in the canons, can be compared with those set forth in the arthashastra texts: discipline, wisdom, alertness, enterprise, benevolence.[ee] It is important also that the king have sufficient material resources, and high birth and a well-trained army are sometimes mentioned. The *dhammiko dhammarājā,* the idealy righteous king, is the possessor of the Seven Mystic Treasures: Wheel, Elephant, Horse, Woman, Jewel, General, and Minister. These are the symbols of the wisdom, vigor, and rank of the monarch. *Manta, ussaha,* and *pabhu,* the three powers, afford him the satisfactions of supremacy and prosperity;

[ee] *Vide* Chapters 11 and 12 below.

they are the legacy of the virtuous, selfless life. The first of the treasures, the Wheel, represents the principle of justice, and appears only to the king who rules scrupulously by the principles of dhamma.[37]

The Jataka stories do not present the "kshatriya science" (*khatta-dhamma,* roughly equivalent to arthashastra) in a very good light.[38] According to the stories, khattadhamma justifies unlimited selfishness and the killing of one's parents or siblings. Politics is opposed to salvation and practically irreconcilable with ethical conduct. Yet the importance of the ruler is emphasized in terms that recall the brahmanic characterization of the king as refuge of his people. The problem is resolved in the concept of righteousness as the true ruler. Virtue has its utilitarian justification: The king stands to gain if he allows himself to be governed by ethical precepts. The king's gentleness and piety may cost him his realm, but he will gain it back in time.[39] In the *Buddhacarita,* however, it is admitted that an unbridgeable gulf may separate politics, which is based on punishment, from salvation, which depends on quietude. In this later work, the Buddha is made to remark that royal power is the abode of delusion and that it rests on oppression.[40] But the author of the *Buddhacarita* extols the regime of the good king Śuddhodana.[†] The *Jātakamālā* of Āryasūra repeats this antithesis of ethics and politics, but, like the former work, seems to be of two minds on the subject.

Subsequent Buddhist literature, such as the Mahāyāna *Suvarṇapra-bhāsa-sūtra,* tends to equate the king with the gods. Sometimes he is declared to be a deity in human form. The earlier Pali canonical works had rooted authority in righteousness and in the contract in which protection was given in exchange for the agricultural tax. The attempt to relate righteousness to a status that transcends that of mere mortals indicates the need for a more complete theory. Yet the king is called on to sacrifice himself if righteousness so demands. Though the king be like the gods, he enjoys no exemptions. Famine, war, and pestilence lay low the land if the king is unjust and dissolute in his conduct. But righteousness and the punishment of the wicked bring fame to him and prosperity to the country. Virtue brings happiness to the people and must be protected at all cost. The people it is said, are always quick to discern and follow the example of the king.

The student-*guru* (teacher) relationship was considered to be the fundamental social relationship. Where the purpose is to impart the experience of enlightenment rather than knowledge *per se,* the relation of master and student takes on an intensity that assumes religious proportions.[41] This devotion to the guru is found in Brahmanism and can hardly be called a distinguishing feature of heterodoxy. But Buddhism offers much more in the theory and technique of organization than Brahmanism. It is probable that the Buddhist religious fraternities reflected the organizational experi-

---

[†] The *Saundarānanda* refers to king Śuddhodana's use of the five traditional expedients in dealing with his enemies: conciliation, creation of dissension, bribery, force, and restraint.

ence of economic and social groups at this time. Many scholars believe that the Buddhist order was patterned after the polity of a contemporary republican tribe, perhaps the Vrijjis. The concept of a group karma (*dhatu*), which is found in Buddhist thought along with that of the individual karma, would be expected to make for a more vivid sense of community. It also suggests the tribal legacy.

By far the most important Buddhist organization is the *sangha,* based, we are told, on companionship, mutual assistance, and compassion. The Buddha held that men ought to help one another to achieve Buddhahood —an idea that finds its most complete expression in the later Mahayana interpretation. Buddha was himself a leader of one of these communities and, from what we know, it was evidently a very democratic group, admitting women to membership. The coordination of social and missionary work, the preservation of Buddhist tradition and dhamma, and the supervision of discipline came to be the function of the sangha. With its basis in this monastic system, Buddhism was obviously a much more highly organized religion than the older sacrificial cult or, for that matter, than early Hinduism.

Resolutions of the sangha, in order to carry, had to be announced three times and have the consent of all present. Only on rare occasions was the majority principle employed. All monks belonging to the sangha were expected to be present at assemblies. If he was unable to attend, a monk must be represented by proxy. Each member could discuss propositions freely as they came up. The ballot seems to have been used from time to time. Such democratic procedure often characterizes religious orders in their infancies. But not always is there the attempt to preserve through formalized processes the egalitarian quality of the sect. The only distinction recognized in the order was seniority. As early as the first Buddhist council it was decided that the favored disciple, Ananda, should not be the successor of the great teacher, but that (as a necessary concession to organizational needs) the seniority principle should be instituted. When basic differences developed over matters of policy, the question was referred to the appropriate committee and modifications were agreed upon. When the committee could not provide a satisfactory solution, the proposal was returned to the assembly and then a majority vote was allowed to decide—unless proper procedure had not been followed, sacred law had been contradicted, a serious schism seemed likely to result, or the case had not been sufficiently argued.

The *Vinaya Pitaka* is a compilation of rules governing the conduct of the monastic order. These regulations and pronouncements are embroidered with traditional lore intended to explain the purposes of the law of the sangha. The precepts of the Buddha were declared to be the pattern and guide for all subsequent law. And though it was a self-governing democratic body, the sangha had no power to prescribe new laws that contradicted the teachings of the founder.

The individual member of the Buddhist corporation seems to have been completely merged in the organization and to have enjoyed a minimum of personal freedom. Frequent bathing, the possession of silk rugs or more than one bowl, or overindulgence in sweets, were considered extravagances and offenses against the group. Property was communally owned. Buddhism had an ethic for the sangha and a less demanding code for the lay members of the community. Caste regulations were included among the rules governing the behavior of the laity, but in the monastic order itself caste was disregarded. The monks and nuns were considered contributors of the gift of wisdom; the secular believers, on the other hand, were responsible for the gift of provision. There was thus a recognized role for the lay members. But though their function was regarded as highly important, lay members were excluded from the bimonthly meetings.

The individual sanghas were not welded into a larger structure; they remained relatively isolated local religious communities. Although the Buddhists expected every favor and protection from the state, they countenanced no restriction or interference from central authority. Ajātaśatru, king of Magadha, is reported to have assured Buddhist ascetics that the First Council could be held without compromising spiritual values, since, as he said, the authority of the sangha is religious, whereas the king's power is secular. The ruler was but the servant and agency of dhamma. But the isolation and the increasing opulence of the monastic orders made them highly vulnerable to attack by rulers hostile to the faith or jealous of the wealth of the community. Affluent Buddhist merchants or landowners bestowed generous gifts on the monasteries, and the orders were often the owners of extensive and lucrative landholdings. Although the individual monks were committed to a life of poverty—their possessions limited to robe, bowl, and such necessary articles as toothbrush and needle—the order itself was not restricted in the amount of wealth it could receive. Many monasteries, as they grew rich on the donations of the faithful, gave up the traditional practice of begging food from door to door in the village each morning.

Emphasis on equality in the sangha is generally interpreted as partiality to democracy, just as later Christian egalitarianism has been construed as constituting a social ideal. There seems, however, little proof that the Buddha had a goal more specific than the welfare, especially the spiritual welfare, of the people. Outlining the prerequisites for communal well-being, the Buddha takes his inspiration from the prosperous republican state. He advocated a government by clan elders, frequent assemblies, and a type of constitutional restraint on the exercise of power.[gg] He warned against the great danger to which the republic was especially vulnerable, the problem of internal dissension.[hh] Perhaps his sensitivity to this peril explains his insistence on unanimity in the sangha.

[gg] During this period there were no regular assemblies of the whole people, but the Jatakas do refer to popular gatherings held for a variety of reasons, meeting from time to time and representing large segments of the population.

[hh] The Buddha's seven techniques for maintaining the security of republican states may be found in Rhys Davids [361], pp. 79ff.

The Jainas have an explanation for the origin of social institutions similar to that which we find in Buddhist legend. History was conceived in terms of a series of cycles from the joyous to the wretched condition. We are told that men were originally golden-hued and a thousand yards tall, and kalpa trees provided abundantly for their needs. In the later stages of this evolution, when men had to struggle to keep alive, when evil entered the world and caste devolved upon man, the institutions of protection and punishment and all the accoutrements of civilization were introduced by the last of the great patriarchal lords, the last of the series of heroes who guided men in the transition from one epoch to another.[ii] Like Buddhism, the Jaina faith does not look to a Creator, and it too is quasi-secular in its political ideas. This line of Jaina theory makes social institutions the result of creative acts on the part of great patriarchs.[42] Another theory, closer to the more democratic compact of Buddhist philosophy, holds that the king is selected by men alarmed by the disorder around them.

Jainism teaches detachment, but differs from the *Gita* and philosophies of indifference to worldly concerns in that it is atheistic and its asceticism is extreme—often involving mortification of the body. But though the sect condemns the active pursuit and enjoyment of wealth, it does not limit the amount that may be acquired. Property was not in itself considered harmful. Wealth, which was not to be used for self-indulgence, was transformed into investment capital. Ritual prohibitions against killing and traveling encouraged resident trade and banking, and the reputation of the Jainas for integrity in business relationships increased their economic power. It is more than likely that the sect was instrumental in financing the expansionist ambitions of Indian rulers. And the Jainas, a group small enough to control without difficulty, did not constitute a threat to the prince. Though committed to nonviolence, the Jaina sages rarely call on the king to renounce war as an instrument of policy.

We would expect that the theory of the patriarchal act of creation would modify somewhat the attitude toward kingship exhibited in a number of Buddhist texts and stories; but we read that *rājya* (sovereignty) should be avoided by wise men, since it is by nature evil and cannot bring happiness. The Jaina literature reveals the same suspicion of the king's role and of arthashastra principles that we find in the early Buddhist works. The victories that matter are those over the self. But the attitude of later Jaina writers toward politics varies from the demand for total avoidance of political activity to its acceptance as an instrument for punishing departures from morality. Somadeva,[jj] a tenth-century scholar, believed (as did St. Thomas) that the state was a natural institution and that political activity was an essential part of life. "All subjects are dependent on the king," he wrote; "those without a lord cannot fulfill their desires."[43] War is justifiable only if alternatives are impractical or unsuccessful. If sugar can accomplish your ends, says Somadeva, why use poison?

[ii] It may be (as some scholars suggest) that the father role of the patriarchs fostered the essentially educational function of government in Jaina theory.
[jj] *Vide* pp. 220f. below.

Influential in the politics of the Chaulukya kings of the twelfth century was the Jaina monk Hemachandra (*Hemacandra*). He leaves a demanding model of a worthy king, but from what we know of his patron, King Kumārapāla, he may very well have lived up to it. The king is to avoid hunting, drink, gambling, and prostitutes, and he is to maintain a rigorous diet, bestow his wealth on others—and encourage all men to do likewise.[44] Somaprabha, who lived several generations later than Hemachandra, advises against any connection with politics, for it is inevitably tainted with sin. The service of the king may seem sweet, but true bliss comes only to him who dedicates himself to the search for righteousness.

The most pessimistic school of all was that of Gosāla, a one-time disciple of Mahavira and later the leader (though not the founder) of the Ājīvika sect. Gosala argued that all action was ineffective, and he went so far as to say that human effort and strength did not really exist at all. Men could only resign themselves to the unavoidable 8,400,000 cycles of existence. Fatalism could not go much farther than this.[kk]

[kk] The cult survived until the fourteenth century, but few records remain to enlighten us about the exact nature of its intricate philosophy.

7 ⁂ ASPECTS OF GOD

The broad categories of religious speculation have been examined in earlier chapters; it remains for us now to complete this spiritual landscape of ancient India with a discussion of Hinduism, that remarkably resilient way of life that survives into our own time. This chapter provides a brief sketch of the conception the Hindu has of the world around him, the supernatural forces at work in the cosmos, and the purpose of his life. We can no more comprehend the social thought of India without a knowledge of religious values than we can comprehend the social and political ideas of the thousand years between Augustine and Gerson without knowing the main features of the religious beliefs and institutions that molded these ideas.

Chronological problems are unavoidable in a discussion of this kind and it will be necessary, from time to time, to depart from a strict historical presentation. The great flowering of Hinduism is not until well after the collapse of Mauryan rule, toward the close of the pre-Christian era. But because the epic literature, one of the major sources of Indian political thought, is Hinduist in tenor, it seems appropriate to treat Hindu religious experience at this point. It is true that in their extant form the epics are later than the period that saw the consolidation of empire, but they are of interest to us for what they reveal of the old heroic culture and tribal political order. The essentials of the Rama myth, for example, probably existed as early as the fifth century B.C., but the Rama of the *Ramayana,* an incarnation of Vishnu, also represents ideas that are later accretions. As we shall presently see, the inspiration for much of the epic literature is legend of very ancient vintage.

Hinduism is a farrago of beliefs and customs. In addition to rituals and doctrines of traditional Brahmanism and many elements of the old popular cults, it incorporates norms that appear to reflect the influence of heterodox ethics and asceticism. However, we are on safer ground if we stress their common heritage in accounting for similarities between Hinduism and Buddhism. Both are legatees of the great spiritual ferment of the seventh century. But Hinduism has absorbed more than the monistic idealism of the Upanishads, and there are cults within Hinduism that are totally devoid of the cool detachment and discipline that we associate with the teaching of the Buddha. Hinduism is the great synthesis; where other religions select and discard, Hinduism includes.[1] Too often descriptions emphasize one facet of Hinduism to the exclusion or disadvantage of others, and thus distort the picture of this complex array of forms and myths and styles of life. No religion (if Hinduism may be called a religion) is more protean, more resistant to description.

The Hindu belief that God may be discovered in many ways leads to a tolerance all too rare in the religious experience of the world. This toleration is rooted in the assumption that religious conceptions are not either true or false, but are significant in varying degrees. Such sufferance must not be mistaken for indifference; it is simply the belief that each individual and group must come to the truth in its own way, through its own traditions and its own gods. And yet not all revelations are considered equally sublime.

The intricacy of symbolization, which is so exciting and so bewildering to the outsider, has been a feature of Indian religious expression almost from the beginning. It is due largely to what might be called "polytheistic pantheism." We have suggested earlier that the worship of many gods is not necessarily incompatible with the worship of the neuter One.[a] In the *Rigveda* we read that "they call him many who is really one."[2] The acceptance of metempsychosis, or transmigration, the acknowledgment of the Veda as authoritative, and the belief that the Absolute may be experienced are also characteristics of Hinduism.

The religions of the Orient, with the exceptions of Shinto and Islam, are not theistic as we understand the term. The God of the Semitic creeds has a determinate character, which the Absolute of most Asian religions lacks. The impersonal force, the Brahman of Hinduism, defies definition; it is ineffable. We may more easily say what the divine is *not*. The Absolute is often identified with the totality of the universe, but it must be taken to mean that which is changeless—the ultimate reality. If, as in Buddhism and the more philosophical reaches of Hinduism, the Absolute may be realized by all through discipline and immediate aesthetic engagement, then, of course, it cannot be the god of a particular locality or a chosen group.

The rarity of great and permanent Hindu empires with centralized direction of political and religious activity hindered the consolidation of a state religion on the order of those that appeared in the Near East at this time. Hinduism itself is distinguished by its lack of organization; there is no prescribed priestly training and there are no congregations as such. The religion is as amorphous as the social system is structured and ornate. Although under Ashoka Buddhism was made the official religion, it failed to capture the emotional support of the great mass of the people, and probably, in that stage of development, lacked the components necessary for a state cult of the type we associate with the ancient world. After the Guptas, most dynasties accepted Hinduism in one form or another. Today the religion is strongest in the more remote sections of India; where

[a] Max Müller has used the term "henotheism" to indicate the worship of a sacred principle through attributes represented in various deities.

foreign contact has been marked, it has been diluted by Islam or Christianity. But despite modifications, Hinduism remains the great energy of Indian life, and caste the basic institution. Today industrialization, education, legislation, urbanization, and travel are altering the traditional social patterns—but less, perhaps, than might be supposed.[3] The belief in the many lives of the soul is too deeply enshrined. The strength of Hinduism lies in its capacity to enfold diverse traditions and beliefs.

Behind the surface complexity of Hinduism there is a cosmology no more elaborate than the "great chain of being" concept that figured prominently in European thought as late as the seventeenth and eighteenth centuries. All human and animal life, and even the deities themselves, are ultimately part of a single monumental system, a grand design in which all creatures are related through time and space. Man need not, however, resign himself to the human condition. All men could strive to surpass their earthly state; all could seek out the path. Karma is not determinism in the strict sense; it is the essence, the inherent destiny, of all things. Man determines his destiny by his actions. His character and position in life are bequeathed by the thoughts and actions of previous existences. "The cards in the game of life are given to us. We do not select them. They are traced to our past Karma, but we can call as we please, lead what suit we will, and as we play, we gain or lose. And there is freedom."[4] It is true, of course, that habit and custom govern much of our conduct, and little in human action is the product of deliberate choice. It might even be said that freedom depends on the direction and supports that the patterns of our lives provide. In Gandhi's words, "the free will we enjoy is less than that of a passenger on a crowded deck."[5]

The Hindu believes that we are guided by a spiritual and ethical necessity, and that sin is actually the betrayal of our nature. There is no fatalistic assigning of the future to the whim of the gods. If fate exists at all, it is the consequence of man's own action. And there are means for escaping the cycle. Among them is Yoga, which is considered one of the more effective techniques for hastening the process of self-comprehension and for achieving liberation. Liberation may be a state of enlightenment that is union with the divine principle or with a personal god, or it may be a state of nothingness.

In most parts of India, Hinduism has its basis in devotion to either Vishnu or Shiva (*Viṣṇu, Śiva*)—or auxiliary figures associated with these deities. It is likely that when confronted with the challenge of Buddhism and other philosophical systems, the brahmans became increasingly receptive to those popular religious movements that could be adapted to their interests. Presumably the two major gods of Hinduism have their principal source in the cults incorporated into Brahmanism at this time.[b] The roots

---

[b] By the Gupta age Vishnu (representing the principle of preservation), Shiva (destruction), and Brahma (creation) were fused into the *Trimūrti*, God worshiped in three aspects. The complexity of the symbolism prevented wide acceptance of this triune concept, however, and generally devotion continued to concentrate on one of the three.

of the Shiva myth are to be found in the old Vedic god Rudra and in the religious practices of the dasas; hence the cult is a combination of Aryan and non-Aryan components, and elements of demon-worship and animism. Despite his questionable pedigree, Shiva came to be the preferred god of the brahmans, and has a wide following—particularly in South India. Since the priests of the cult of the Mother Goddess, which attracts many followers in modern India, are not brahmans, the extra-Aryan origins of important branches of Shaivite worship would seem to be confirmed.[c]

In many respects Shiva corresponds to the Greek god Dionysus. He is the symbol of destruction, but destruction in order to build anew.[d] The mysteries of the reproduction of life are associated with Shiva, who is usually worshiped in the form of his symbol, the *lingam* (male organ), or through his consort, who is also a syncretic deity capable of assuming a variety of forms. The sexual element is most important in Tantrism, where, in the technique sometimes described as the path of the left, liberation is achieved through the breaking down of the components of the ego —ultimately ritualized in the sexual act. But the sexual function is not seen as specialized and temporary; it is recognized as the force that rules the whole organism. Aggression is fused with sexuality, rather than turned inward as the energy behind conscience. The erotic symbolism may be understood in terms of the selflessness of the perfect lover, who forgets the distinction between self and other: "as a man when in the embrace of a beloved wife knows nothing within or without."[6]

Tantrism attributes a major significance to the female deity. It constituted a Dionysian answer to the older quiescent "Apollonian" modes of reintegration, employing nature as an aid to fulfillment and the reconciliation of dualisms.[7] Its robustness contrasts markedly with the more detached and intellectual systems of Upanishadic inspiration.[e] And Tantrism welcomed men and women of all classes if they were spiritually prepared for initiation. Shiva, like Dionysus, had the broader appeal of the god who was not himself part of an official state cult. But Tantrism never became a doctrine of social reform.[f]

[c] The Mother Goddess is usually the consort of Shiva, known in her benevolent form as Pārvatī. For a brief discussion of this aspect of popular religion and of the *śakti* (Shaivite potency personified in his wife), *vide* W. Norman Brown [49], pp. 309ff.

[d] "He that is richest in the fullness of life, the Dionysian god and man, can afford not only the sight of the terrible and the questionable, but even the terrible deed and any luxury of destruction, decomposition, and negation; in his case, what is evil, senseless, and ugly seems, as it were, permissible, as it seems permissible, in nature, because of an excess of procreating, restoring powers which can yet turn every desert into luxurious farm land." (Nietzsche, *Twilight of the Idols*, "Nietzsche contra Wagner.")

[e] But note that in the Upanishads the sexual act is viewed as a type of sacrifice: "Woman, verily, O Gautama, is a sacrificial fire. In this case the sexual organ is the fuel; when one invites, the smoke; the vulva, the flame; when one inserts, the coals; the sexual pleasure, the sparks. In this fire the gods offer semen. From this oblation arises the fetus." (*Chandogya Upanishad* V, 8.)

[f] What Dodds says of the mystery religion applies equally well to the parallel development in India: "If I understand early Dionysiac ritual aright, its social function was essentially cathartic, in the psychological sense: it purged the individual of those

There is also the way of the meditating Shiva, the lord of the yogin and the greatest of the ascetics. On Mount Kailāsa he sits, absorbed in mystic contemplation. The two paths may seem to be extremes, yet both may free man from the human state. We shall turn presently to a consideration of the spiritual discipline known as Yoga.

In the early part of the ninth century A.D., a Shaivite brahman, Shankara (*Śaṅkara*), intent on restating the Vedic texts and working them into a consistent body of thought, developed the most profound set of moral premises in Hinduism. Shankara is widely regarded as the foremost Hindu philosopher, and through the influence of his teaching Vedanta became the major philosophical system in Hinduism. The reforms of Shankara amounted to an overlay of Buddhist principle and practice; he saw the grandeur of Buddhism in its ethical ideals, its freedom from superstition, and its ecclesiastical organization, and undertook to strengthen Hinduism by introducing these virtues into the religion. Salvation was to be achieved through meditation of Brahman, the impersonal world soul, which the Upanishads had linked with the individual soul. Shankara's synthesis, his emphasis on the spirit, has been seen as introducing into Hinduism a somewhat puritanical note. It is difficult to say whether the system represents an ultimate victory of Buddhism, or was indeed its *coup de grâce*.

Vishnu would seem to us a more sympathetic figure than the often turbulent and always somewhat disquieting Shiva. But what Vishnu gains by his more amiable visage, he loses to the singular fascination possessed by the dancing (or brooding) god of Kailasa. However, this ground would seem to be more than regained by Vishnu's capacity to appear in the form of ten major incarnations (*avatāras*). Of particular appeal are numbers seven and eight, Rama (kshatriya prince, great warrior and savior, *Kulturträger*) and Krishna (prankster, lover, hero). The last historical appearance of Vishnu was as Buddha, but theologians are not agreed on the reason for this incarnation.[9]

The religious movement known as *bhakti,* which sought to personalize the divine force, is closely associated with Vaishnavism because of the latter's tendency toward expression through avatars; it never gained a comparable foothold in Shaivism. In contrasting man with the incarnate God, bhakti modified the older monism. But like Tantrism it imbued

---

infectious irrational impulses which, when dammed up, had given rise, as they have done in other cultures, to outbreaks of dancing mania and similar manifestation of collective hysteria; it relieved them by providing them with a ritual outlet. If that is so, Dionysus was in the Archaic Age as much a social necessity as Apollo; each ministered in his own way to the anxieties characteristic of a guilt-culture. Apollo promised security: 'Understand your station as man; do as the Father tells you; and you will be safe tomorrow.' Dionysus offered freedom: 'Forget the difference, and you will find the identity . . .' His joys were accessible to all [and he] was at all periods a god of the people." (Dodds [98], p. 76.)

[9] Christ is sometimes included among the avatars of Vishnu; the possibility that Christianity might be absorbed into Hinduism in this fashion was once a cause of great alarm among Christian missionaries. Even the legend of Adam and Eve has found a place for itself (*Bhaviṣyottara Purāṇa*).

Hinduism with new vitality and appeal. God was portrayed as having qualities more meaningful to man than the nebulous abstraction that was the neuter Brahman, and this accounts in large degree for the increasing popularity of Vaishnavism in the eleventh and twelfth centuries. Except in southern India, a stronghold of Shaivite brahmans, this form of Hinduism has been in ascendance since that time.[h] Bhakti, like the movement launched by Shankara, depends more on psychological attitude than on ritual, but its appeal is probably wider in that it requires of its adherents no metaphysical preparation. And yet it satisfies the same wish for the concrete and intimate experience that we find in the more esoteric yogic technique. Krishna, in the *Gita,* recommends bhakti as a simple but reliable way to God. If man possesses a loving heart, he will succeed.

Indian religion is rendered somewhat baroque by the mixture of elements of different sects, traditions, and systems. The external ornamentation of the Tanjore temple is Vaishnavite; everything inside is Shaiva. An avatar of Vishnu may be worshiped in public and the consort of Shiva in private. Disputes occur between rival Vaishnavite groups, between devotees of Shiva and those who follow Vishnu. But each admits the existence of the other's deities and the record of coexistence could well be emulated in the West. The basic relativity of Indian thought and the reluctance to propound dogmas demanding close adherence to a prescribed body of principles have made possible a profusion of sects. Each has its peculiar philosophical point of departure, and each attempts to buttress its position with proofs of its ancient heritage. Although little is known of the early history of the sects, there has been a historical tendency for them to cluster around either of the two central deities, and the division allows a valid basis for classification. Most of the later sectarian movements (such as Sikhism) derive from Vaishnavism.

A few Vedic gods—such as Indra, Varuna, Agni, and Sūrya—survive in modern Hinduism, but their role is of secondary importance. Tribal and local gods, related in various ways to Shiva and Vishnu, have taken their place. This may not always be apparent from the commentaries of contemporary Hindu writers, who sometimes lead their readers to the conclusion that Hinduism is founded on the veneration of a highly abstract Absolute. In the less sophisticated lower social groups religious experience tends to become absorbed in personal gods who are more likely to represent forces of nature, even the grossest fertility concept, than they are to personify metaphysical principles. The Hindu peasant may express his religious commitment through a variety of morning ablutions, the circumambulation of a cow, a polite gesture to the village deity, and the mumbling of Krishna's name (or that of Rama); he may take part in a festival that has only indirect religious significance; one day he may visit a sacred river or a shrine. He is expected to be of service to the brahman whenever possible. He will perform a variety of birth, marriage, and death rites, and—

___

[h] The Vaishnavite sects, especially in South India, did not have the unified monastic organization established by Shankara for the Shaivite movement. This worked to its disadvantage and prevented its success from being even more pronounced.

of greatest importance—he will adhere to the strict observance of caste law and duty. Certain rivers have magical powers, and to die at the waters of the Ganges is believed by most to be one of the surest means of salvation.

By the epoch of the Gupta monarchs, beginning in the fourth century A.D., Indian religion had become overladen with orgiastic mysticism and sympathetic magic, animism, and a proliferation of gods. From time to time there were attempts to purify—such as the movement led by Shankara. Often it will be argued that outward forms are not essential to reverence, and that the proper method of devotion is ardent meditation. But in truth there are many paths to emancipation, many forms that liberation will take, and many answers given to the multitude of questions that surround the imposing theory of transmigration. As one Indian scholar has remarked:

> To those intent on work, there is Karma-yoga, the path of fulfilling the ordained duties and performing such meritorious acts as have been prescribed by scriptures. To those who are of an emotional nature, whose heart is not satisfied with impersonal acts or principles of ethical conduct and in whom there is an inner cry for hugging a supreme personality to whom it could pour forth its love and homage, there is the path of devotion, Bhakti-yoga. And to those of the highest class who can revel only in the Abstract, there is the path of knowledge, Jnana-yoga, and the goal of realizing the one impersonal Absolute Brahman, which is the essence of Being, Light and Bliss, *Sat, Chit* and *Ananda.* Truly cultivated, these are not mutually conflicting, but different paths to one ultimate goal.[8]

Many critics of Hinduism have regarded the confusion of morality with the performance of family and caste duty (the accomplishment of ritual acts rather than good deeds) as the most regrettable aspect of the religion. Too often the finer qualities of devotion are lost in cow worship, fakir excess, and caste functions. Too often social injustices are treated with indifference and even condoned. Yet Hinduism has brought satisfaction to even the most miserable peasant. It has answered the popular need for a more concrete and accessible religious experience.

THE TRANSCENDENTAL MIND

"Knowledge," according to one student of the mystical experience, "is acquired when we succeed in fitting a new experience into the system of concepts based upon our old experiences. Understanding comes when we liberate ourselves from the old and so make possible a direct, unmediated contact with the new, the mystery, moment by moment, of our existence. . . . Understanding is not conceptual, and therefore cannot be passed on."[9] The distinction is intended to point up basic differences in the Oriental and European approaches to and appraisals of the cognitive process. As a recent writer has commented, the Westerner moves from thought to thought, concept to concept, whereas the Indian more typically advances from subjective condition to subjective condition.[i] The Westerner seeks to dominate nature, the Chinese to immerse himself in nature, and the Indian to escape it altogether.[10]

In the Upanishads mystic comprehension (gnosis) was considered to be the way to salvation. That which makes possible the comprehension of the universe is good. Desire and earthly ties impede this discovery of the immortal and hence are to be avoided.[11] Awareness had become the means for escaping the cycle of birth, death, and rebirth; in unity with the Universal is liberation. To be freed from himself, man must renounce his old identities; he must cease to think in terms of "I." In short, he must cease to *be* himself and, renouncing pleasure (which is the substance of the world's restlessness), he finds his true identity—with Brahman, the eternal and comprehensive, the unmoved Mover, Creation and the Cause. Then, death ceases to have any significance. The anxious ego has already ceased to be.

In the West the dominant tendency has been to view man and nature as a manifestation of God, His creation. But in India it was different. Sensory impressions hinder man's knowledge of the life divine. Shankara did not maintain that life and experience were without value for man, since if he is to benefit from renunciation, he must first have learned the lessons that the worldly pilgrimage provides. But the most important of these lessons is that the universe revealed to us through our senses is only illusion, maya. Because historical particulars continually perish, man can realize himself only outside the historical process—by transcending time, which holds the ego captive.[j] Reality is the eternal, the changeless.

This ideal of the *vita contemplativa,* of knowledge attainable only through retreat from worldly activities, replaced the ancient aristocratic ideal of the active, life-affirming man. The essence of the new philosophy was *samādhi,* a trance-like state of contemplation, intense mental application that in its full realization destroys the boundary between subjective and objective. It was an ethic of nonaction, although such statements as "Kshatrahood deserts him who knows Kshatrahood in aught else than the soul"[12] permitted the ascetic theory to be modified in the interest of fulfilling caste duties.

Eliade, in the introduction to his study of Yoga, remarks that the central concern of Indian thought is the "conditioning" and "deconditioning"

---

[i] Northrop analyzes the difference between the type of knowledge (Huxley's "understanding") that can be gained only through experience, and thought that can be expressed in logically developed formal treatises and understood with only an indirect personal experience, focusing as it does on particulars abstracted from the entirety. The East stressed oneness, continuity, the all-embracing, and because logical inference and theoretical representation are considered subjective (and therefore unreal or at least highly relative), has lagged in the development of science. Northrop argues that the West neglects the religious import of immediate primary experience, and that therefore each outlook has something to offer the other.

[j] "*This* world is rejected, *this* life depreciated, because it is known that *something else* exists, beyond becoming, beyond temporality, beyond suffering. In religious terms it could almost be said that India rejects the *profane* cosmos and *profane* life, because it thirsts for a *sacred* world and a *sacred* mode of being." (Eliade [117], p. 10.)

of man.[13] Indian philosophy differs strikingly from European thought in the emphasis it places on the latter. Yoga, the general name for a vast assortment of techniques employed in this liberation, represented a reaction against metaphysics and ritual—though it, too, is a patterning and systematizing of life. Yoga is a discipline directed toward the achievement of the same kind of concrete and personal experience that is found in the popular devotion known as bhakti. "We always find some form of Yoga," writes Eliade, "whenever the goal is *experience of the sacred* or the attainment of a perfect *self-mastery,* which is itself the first step toward the magical mastery of the world."[14]

Leading to the same ends as Yoga, similar to it in many ways, and closely associated with it, was the Sankhya (*Sāṅkhya*) system. Zimmer describes the two as aspects of a single discipline.[k] Radhakrishnan remarks that "the Sāṁkhya method involves the renunciation of works and the Yoga insists on their performance in the right spirit. They are at bottom the same but the Yoga way comes more naturally to us. The two ways are not inconsistent. In Sāṁkhya, jñāna or insight is emphasized. In Yoga, volitional effort is stressed. In the one, we know the Self by thinking away the alien elements; in the other, we will them away."[15]

The atheistic Sankhya shares a number of features with Buddhism, such as the belief in the "constant becoming" of the world and a conception of life as suffering.[l] The origin of the system is the subject of much controversy. Like Yoga it is very old, and outside the Vedic tradition. There have been several schools of doctrine but with the refinement of Sankhya theory it became possible to outline the basic presuppositions of the belief. Matter and spirit were considered to be derived from a single substance, *prakriti,* which was composed of three qualities (*guṇas*), interdependent, and yet counteracting. They are *sattva* (that which is pure, the contemplative power), *rajas* (that which is active), and *tamas* (that which is resistant to alteration, inertia). Prakriti possesses a spontaneous dynamism that manifests itself in evolutionary processes. There is also the concept of awareness, *purusha* (*puruṣa*), sometimes called the life-monad. The concept implies purpose in nature; because transformations of nature seek the realization of pure spirit, purusha may be understood as a final cause. Prakriti is the substance through which it works and the two exist in combination, acting together until the spirit is liberated from physical nature. The function of Yoga is to eradicate rajas and tamas, leaving only sattva, which reflects purusha without perversion or distortion. Such de-

k "Sāṅkhya provides a basic theoretical exposition of human nature, enumerating and defining its elements, analyzing their manner of coöperation in the state of bondage (*bandha*), and describing their state of disentanglement or separation in release (*mokṣa*), while Yoga treats specifically of the dynamics of the process of the disentanglement, and outlines practical techniques for gaining release, or 'isolation-integration' (*kaivalya*)." (Zimmer [441], p. 280.)

l Sankhya, in its theory of the creation of the universe, pictures a deterioration from perfection, eventual dissolution followed by re-creation, and the cycle continues —a conception approximating heterodox belief. *Vide* Eliade [117], pp. 377–81 for a discussion of the relation between Sankhya and Buddhism, and pp. 367ff. for a bibliography on Sankhya.

conditioning and emancipation come with the removal, through discipline, of all that hinders true perception. Purusha will then be seen as distinct from prakriti. It is this comprehension that is the instrument of escape. Sankhya is not dependent on revelation that comes from without.[16]

This variety of asceticism, which finds its fullest expression in Yoga, has its roots in the aboriginal tradition, rather than the Indo-European. It "represents a living fossil, a modality of archaic spirituality that has survived nowhere else."[17] It antedates the introduction of shamanism, and though it possesses many unique aspects, it shares with shamanism certain symbolisms and practices: "They meet in 'emergence from time' and the abolition of history. . . . But while the shaman can obtain this spontaneity only through his ecstasy . . . the true yogin . . . enjoys this unconditioned situation continuously—i.e., he has succeeded in definitively abolishing time and history."[18] Yoga and shamanism represent, respectively, the techniques of samadhi and ecstasy—absorption in contrast to an overpowering rapture. Yoga may be an expression of pre-Aryan belief, but reincarnation is most probably not an idea indigenous to India. Nor did it arrive with the invaders. It made its appearance at about the same time that it came to Greece, and Central Asian shamanism appears to have been the source of both.[19]

Aristotle, concerned as he was with the conception of form struggling to realize itself in all matter, possessed a sharp sense of historical development and was one of the first to distinguish historical and physical time. Historical time is cumulative and progressive; the past preserves itself in future stages—but they are never the same as what has been before. Historical time, the milieu of emissary prophecy, stands in contrast to the cyclical conception of time. For the archaic Greeks "everything moves in recurrences, like the eternal recurrence of sunrise and sunset, of summer and winter, of generation and corruption."[20] Whatever was to come would not be essentially different from what had been.[m]

The Greek temporal sense was far more positive than the view of time associated with Indian asceticism, which tended to emphasize decay over growth and to question the reality of the external world.[n] In fact, the attempt was made to eradicate what little there was of the temporal per-

---

[m] The images rooted in the periodic conception of time have had their champions in the West. Nietzsche is the most famous of those who demanded that Being should not be sacrificed to Becoming. In discussing the theory and psychology of the eternal return, Eliade has remarked that archaic man "is free to be no longer what he was, free to annul his own history through periodic abolition of time and collective regeneration. This freedom in respect to his own history—which, for the modern, is not only irreversible but constitutes human existence—cannot be claimed by the man who wills to be historical. We know that the archaic and traditional societies granted freedom each year to begin a new, a 'pure' existence, with virgin possibilities." (Eliade [116], p. 157.) This kind of argument has been reinforced in recent years by several attempts to employ Freudian concepts of the nature of repression, gratification, and the like, for purposes of evaluating freedom and happiness in modern industrial societies. It has been suggested, for example, that guilt has increased to the point where expiation in annual ceremonies is no longer possible; it is cumulative guilt that produces cumulative time. (Norman O. Brown, [46], p. 278.)

[n] The concept of the periodic creation and destruction of the world appears first in *Atharvaveda* X, 8.39f.

ception, to replace the cyclical alteration with the subjective equilibrium
of anesthetized man. Indian thought is driven "to sublimate space into
the Infinite . . . rather than time into Eternity. Its goal is, psychologically, the boundless rather than the timeless, since there is no inward feeling for the time dimension at all."[21] With the triumph of the caste principle, the spatial appears to have vanquished the temporal. Life, the diary
of suffering, can be transcended only outside time; the things of this world
must be put aside. The great cycles of time, the smallest unit of which was
one thousand to four thousand years, could only have the effect of destroying time.[o] And what are these units when measured against the life of
Brahma, which was considered to be from 30 billion years to 700,000 billion years? Such a conception dwarfs man so completely as to make the
relationships of man in time quite meaningless.[22] The endless birth, destruction, and rebirth of universes, staggering to the imagination and
shattering to the spirit, must have provided a powerful impulse to a view
of life that would discount as illusory the world of sense experience. Deliverance would have to depend on spiritual transcendence of time and
mastery of the unconscious.

The function of memory is less emphasized in Yoga than in Buddhism,
although the capacity to recollect former lives is deemed important.[p] The
unconscious, to be controlled, must be made manifest, and memory is one
of several techniques for revealing the recesses of personality. "Thus one
reaches the paradoxical moment beyond which time did not exist because
nothing was yet manifested. The meaning and end of this yogic technique,
which consists in unrolling time in reverse, are perfectly clear. Through
it the practitioner obtains the true superknowledge, for he not only succeeds in re-cognizing all his former lives, but he reaches the very 'beginning of the world.' "[23] It might be said that remembrance transports us
back to that moment when reality and the pre-ego of narcissism were not
differentiated. Memory may become a weapon against a world of alienation. And it may, as in Platonic theory, be a safeguard against the illusion
of "reality." In clearing away impediments to recollection of the true
principle, we find a method similar to the role of free-association in psychoanalysis—the patient inquiry that educates the emotions. In this process
time may be vanquished and the past regained, a past devoid of tension. As
this relief from excitation is approximated (or, put positively, as the state
of gratification is reached) the distinction between life and death diminishes, the distinction between pleasure principle and Nirvana fades.[24]
Yoga teaches how to escape the world, how to find release from the prisons
of time and personality.

---

[o] The ages that compose a cycle of time are named for throws in the dice game.
The original age of perfection is represented by the winning four pips—a number
that symbolizes completeness. According to some sources, in the present age (the
Kali Yuga), only one quarter of the dharma remains and the epoch lasts only a
quarter as long as the original (Krita) yuga. The yugas may be likened to (and
perhaps had their inspiration in) the Avestan world-ages, which divided time into
four periods of three thousand years each.

[p] Krishna says in the *Gita* (IV, 5) that he knows all his lives.

It is interesting to note that although Rousseau exalted the classical ideal of the citizen, there runs through his writings a theme that would seem to subvert his major thesis and to link him with the mystical tradition. For Rousseau, the self is larger than the confines of society (and of sense experience). In solitary contemplation, which heightens man's sensibilities and allows him to escape the constraints of time, the individual "loses himself with a delicious intoxication in the immensity of that beautiful system with which he feels identified. Then all particular objects escape him; he sees and feels nothing except in the whole of things."[25] Such a feeling, intensifying as it does the sense of pure existence, is no self-denying yogic trance; it is the attempt to confront nature directly as men once did—but the experience is richer, more clearly articulated, because man has risen above his original natural state. Society seems to find its highest justification in those men (Rousseau would include himself) who take flight from reality in imagination and meditation. And there is no insistence that the philosopher return from the blinding light of Truth to teach his fellow men. The idea would seem to be an attempt to provide a haven from society, but, as Leo Strauss points out, it was more than that: "It was the ideal basis for an appeal from society to something indefinite and undefinable, to an ultimate sanctity of the individual as individual, unredeemed and unjustified."[26]

In Western thought the individual is thus so often protected, and his value preserved, by reference to an undefined and undefinable freedom. In classical Hindu thought, contemplation and the escape from time did not have as their goal the sensitizing of the individual to the fact of his existence. For Rousseau, freedom is always essentially an affirmation; for the Hindu a "liberation," the negation of error. Contemplation is, for Rousseau, always an active experience; it is the meditation of the artist, acutely aware of his historic individuality. P. Masson-Oursel[27] suggests that the Indian idea of liberation does not take on a positive nature until the later Buddhism of the Greater Vehicle, which teaches the importance of re-employing energies released from their former enslavement of egoism and desire.[q] The purpose is to create a true and active freedom based on the discipline that allows full unfolding of potential.

The ancient ritual of the tribal communities had had the effect, Eliade suggests, of cleansing man's relation with the world around him, of wiping the slate clean, so to speak. The gods were believed to be directly manipulated by the sacrifice. Now, in the epoch of the salvation religions, man's supreme realization had come to be seen in terms of identity with the sublime principle of the universe. And this principle was itself drained of

---

[q] We have argued above (p. 103) that such a freeing of ego functions may have been the original intent of the Buddha. We must of course be wary of employing naturalistic theories, which assume an autonomous center of energy (although the concept of *rajas* would seem to indicate a belief in such an energy source), and we must avoid identifying the mystical experience with modern "authoritarian" attempts to escape an unwanted self. Such feelings as the desire for revenge will not take the same destructive forms in a society of fixed social ranks. *Vide* Max Scheler, *Ressentiment,* transl. by W. Holdheim, Glencoe (Ill.), 1961, pp. 50f.

the positive, assertive Eros. Instead of emphasizing a higher form of psychic life that is of value in itself, religious theory remained centered on the idea of a universal world-soul. Man can free himself from his environment because he can transform the organic world into objects. And he can objectify only to the extent that he frees himself from the affects and drives that immerse him (like the animal) in the world. But the free play of spirit is not the goal. The mystic seeks to reimmerse himself in the universal One. By repressing his vital drives he seeks to overcome the consciousness of his own self as object. The world then ceases to appear as resistance.[28]

Whereas formerly man purified himself and influenced the gods *through the act* (of ritual), he was now counseled either to avoid the act or to surmount the distinction of subject and object that shapes responses to the world. But the dancing figure of Shiva and the loving god Krishna were moving to the center of Indian religious life. The rigorous discipline of the yogic practitioner is representative of only a small, though influential, fraction of the community. Most of the people have chosen less demanding paths, such as bhakti, and have made do with the purely receptive vision when intense mental application was beyond their capacity. In the bhakti religions, we encounter the revelation that radiates from grace, an idea more familiar to the European. God comes to man who, in his helpless state, can qualify himself only through belief and his own humility. In God's benevolence there is not the caprice or miracle that so often is found in Western conceptions of grace.

Basic to the Indian mentality is an imagination that combines with a metaphysical inclination to press the search for unity and to magnify concepts into terms of the infinite and universal.[r] It would not be too far from the truth to say that for the typical Hindu the universe and the life it supports are viewed as a comprehensive whole, each part contributing in its own way to the harmonious working of the totality. God is not the same as the universe, although he permeates the world: "the world is in God and not God in the world." There may be varying degrees of divinity in this world, but nothing is undivine. Though the sentiment may not be easily articulated, the Hindu believes that greater regard for the particular over the universal ends in self-love. And he knows that through the performance of the functions of his station in life he may ultimately find his true fulfillment.

---

[r] Beni Prasad comments that the Hindu intellect appears at its best in synthesis. "It is seldom at home in analysis and induction. It achieves its triumphs in declaration rather than in dissection. On the other hand, Indian thinking is remarkably clear and tends to run an idea to its extreme logical consequences. It gains in fulness but it underestimates the complexities of life." (Prasad [323], p. 2.)

8 ✗ THE *SHANTIPARVA*
AND THE LOGIC OF DANDA

INDRA'S SIN

The period most fertile in the formulation of political ideas was the age, asceticism and the mystical gnosis, metempsychosis, and the belief into the early centuries of the Christian epoch. By the beginning of this age, asceticism and the mystical gnosis, metempsychosis, and the belief in avatars of the gods had been incorporated into Indian religion. The Upanishads were instrumental in guiding Hinduism away from dualism and giving it a primarily monistic theological form. In addition to the great philosophical systems of the age, there developed a new and in some instances almost secular, literature, which included the two great heroic epics—the *Rāmāyana* and *Mahābhārata*,[a] the *Arthaśāstra* of Kautalya, and the law books of Manu, Yājñavalkya, Nārada, and Brihaspati. Some of these works—especially the *Mahabharata*—reflect institutions and ideals of earlier periods of Indian history as well as conditions of the time in which they were written, compiled, or revised. In the centuries encompassed by this literature, political units had grown to a considerable size, and their earlier tribal character had all but disappeared. The Aryans had settled as far east as modern Bengal, and as far south as the Andhra country.

The epics are, in part, attempts to popularize Vedic religion and metaphysics. However, it is clear that significant portions of the *Mahabharata* were influenced by Sankhya doctrine—perhaps the most important philosophical influence on the development of early Hinduism—before the epic was revised to conform with Vedānta. But the Sankhya of the *Mahabharata* may never have been entirely that of the philosophers. In its classical form the system was atheistic and rationalist, but it was very closely associated with theistic Yoga in many respects, including basic technique. Yoga incorporates a God far superior in power to the purusha (pure spirit) of Sankhya. Though contradictory to the central philosophical conceptions of Sankhya, the concept of God appeared in the

[a] The *Mahabharata* reaches its philosophical culmination in the *Bhagavad Gītā*, which appears in Section VI of the sixth book (*Bhiṣmaparva*).

course of the development of the system. This God figured as but one of the purushas, and was therefore not conceived as designer of the universe. It might be said that God represented the highest excellence—an example for man and an object for his devotion. And he was seen as sympathetic to men: if they would place their trust in him, he could be relied upon to help them attain spiritual release.[1]

In Sankhya, man himself is responsible for the working out of his destiny. But God's ways are sometimes mysterious, and social actions have no particular relation to salvation. Weber has remarked that, in its religious theory, the *Mahabharata* leaves us with the question of Job:

> King Yudhischthira of the Epic in his blameless misfortune discusses with his spouse the reign of God. The woman comes to the conclusion that the great God only plays with men according to his whims. A genuine solution is as little found here as in Job: one should not say such things, for by the grace of God the good receive immortality and, above all, without this belief the people would not practice virtue. This has quite a different ring from the philosophy of the Upanishads which knows nothing of such a world regime by a personal God.[2]

This new concept of faith, the need for devotion to a redemptive agent, figures prominently in the *Bhagavad Gītā*. Right action pertains to caste obligation. Action must be performed without thought of gain; the actor who remains detached is freed from the guilt that might accrue from his actions.[3] The poem is primarily concerned with the swadharma of the warrior noble, whose role could not be reconciled with ascetic withdrawal. It is probably valid to say that Sankhya did not encourage an ethic for the conduct of worldly affairs. From a social point of view it was necessary that its gnostic mysticism be modified by caste considerations. Conduct was regulated by caste prescriptions and prohibitions, detailed and particularistic regulations sanctified by the older religion.

Nevertheless, in the epic, the discipline of concentration and meditation has begun to replace the earlier emphasis on sacrifice, though clearly it is understood that not all men are qualified to pursue this technique. The relationship of myth and ritual was no longer as direct as it had once been; liturgical attempts at "correspondence" had declined in significance. Caste distinctions were fully admitted, and the worst of crimes was to challenge the caste order. Some new gods appear, among them Kama, god of love, and Kubera, god of riches. However, although the popularization of Brahmanism and the influence of new religious and philosophical systems did appreciably change the nature of belief and worship, the debt of Hinduism to non-Aryan spiritual elements should not be taken to imply a break with the older hieratic religion.

Sankhya doctrine and the emphasis on yogic practice in effect replaced the professional gnosis of Brahmanism; instead of the comprehension of the holy, the goal becomes the attainment of a miraculous ability. There was never a complete departure from the older brahman conception of the magical quality of gnosis. Yogic technique could not be judged heterodox. The position of the brahman was not questioned, nor were ritual duties as such disparaged. But in fact, salvation conceived in Sankhya or Yoga terms constituted a serious threat to the authority of the sacred writings and allowed no substantial role for ritual—except as a preparation for gnostic knowledge. The brahmans could not condone such devaluation of Vedic rite. It was the Vedanta system, with its stress on the value of social and ritual duties in the attainment of the higher wisdom, and its relation (as the name suggests) to the Vedic samhitas, that was to prove more congenial to the priestly group. The impersonal principle of Brahman, which had come to take the place of the older Prajapati in esoteric thought, made too many demands on the imagination to permit any wide appeal. Brahma at length emerged as a personal deity not appreciably different from Prajapati who, in the Vedic age, stood supreme over the frequently capricious gods of the pantheon.

The bulk of the *Mahabharata,* the "fifth Veda," is a collection of legends of the northwest, and especially the Punjab—India's holy land. The *Ramayana* contains the stories of the northeastern kingdoms. But here the legends were rewritten by one man, the poet Vālmīki, who played a role analogous to that of Homer. The *Ramayana* contributes little to political theory, though it does dwell on the need for government and the misery and misfortune that result from its absence.[b] The work recounts the exploits of one of the incarnations of Vishnu, the indefatigable hero Rama, who is depicted as bringing civilization to the benighted aborigines.[c] Macdonell believed that *Ramayana* II–IV antedate the *Mahabharata* in its epic form. And there is little doubt that the first and last of the seven books of the narrative are later in composition than the others. But because the Rama legend presumably relates to the Aryan invasion of South India, we are probably not justified in concluding that it is an earlier work than the *Mahabharata* on the grounds that the setting of the latter seems to indicate that Aryan civilization had extended over a broader area and the culture had become less homogeneous than that described in the *Ramayana*. It can be said, however, that in their final form the *Mahabharata* and the *Ramayana* were approximately contemporaneous.

Such incarnations as Rama and Krishna provide a means for relating the worship of specific and manifold forms with monotheism—a monotheism that in itself eludes precise definition. It is the function of the avatar to rescue dharma in times of stress and disorder. The concept of the avatar introduces into Indian thought a type of leadership that deviates from traditional authority based on ascription and committed to the established institutions and values of the community. When the basis of the social order is threatened, the hero emerges to restore authority through his charismatic power.

The *Mahabharata*[d] is frequently more secular than religious in tone;

[b] The anarchic state of nature is described in detail in *Ramayana* II, 69, but the discussion differs little from that in *Mahabharata* XII, 67.

[c] For a brief account of the Rama myth, *vide* W. Norman Brown [49], pp. 291ff.

[d] The Great Poem (or War) of the Descendants of Bharata. The work exists in two recensions, known as the "Northern" and the "Southern" versions, the latter of which is the longer. A critical edition is being prepared by the Bhandarkar Oriental Research Institute in Poona. It will be based on all the extant manuscripts of the work.

the work had its origin in lays composed to commemorate the deeds of a great warrior and may have been connected in some way with the royal sacrifice. Many of the incidents go far back into the remote Vedic period. Transition from one story to another is often confused and awkward. These lays were later worked over by the priests, who expanded the meaning of the ballads, linked them together with prose narration, and interpolated treatises on ethical and theological problems. The major brahman modifications and additions probably date from about the second and first centuries B.C. A considerable part of the rajadharma portion of the *Shantiparva,* which shares so much with the dharmashastra texts, belongs to the first centuries A.D. Many of the peoples mentioned could not have been known to the Indians before this time. And some of the practices referred to in the epic suggest certain quasi-feudal institutions of Gupta times. But a large portion of the epic predates the apotheosis of the knight Arjuna, which would make it earlier than the time of the grammarian Pāṇini, who lived in the fourth century B.C. The mythology of the *Mahabharata* may in some respects be more ancient than the *Rigveda* itself.[e]

The great conflict at the heart of the epic, arising from a dynastic controversy in the Kuru tribe and involving Pāṇḍava and Kaurava cousins,[f] probably took place in the tenth or ninth centuries B.C., although popular tradition has located it as early as 3102, the beginning of the Kali-yuga. All India supposedly participated in the battle, which stormed for eighteen days on the plain of Kurukṣetra, in the vicinity of modern Delhi. Bhīṣma, the senior statesman of the Kurus, destined to die within half a year from wounds acquired in battle, grants the combatants his parting words of wisdom on law and polity and the more abstract problems of philosophy and ethics. These words, and those recounting the rivalries of the two noble houses and the adventures of Yudhishthira (*Yudhiṣṭhira*), add up to a narrative bulk eight times the size of the *Iliad* and *Odyssey* combined. In the *Bhagavad Gita,* Krishna, avatar of Vishnu and charioteer of the warrior-prince Arjuna, seeks to convince the kshatriya of the need to fulfill his caste duty. Arjuna, who had lost conviction in his motives for fighting, returns to the battle confident of the importance of upholding dharma. This rationale has sometimes been interpreted as a criticism of Buddhist pacifism. Its significance is still debated.

Hopkins many years ago concluded that the original narrative core of the epic is impossible to isolate from the later mythical and moralistic accretions,[4] and few present-day students of the *Mahabharata* would question this judgment. Several years before Hopkins' commentary on the epic, Dahlmann argued that the work must be analyzed in terms of both narrative and didactic components, but he concluded that the story of the great battle had been made the vehicle of a moral lesson by a diaskeuast

---

[e] For a guide to the elaborate and confusing array of epic deities and mythologies, *vide* Hopkins [181].

[f] It is worth noting that the word for foe (*bhrātṛvya*) means, etymologically, cousin, son of the father's brother.

sometime in the later Brahmanic period—and went so far as to suggest that the engagement between the Kauravas and Pandavas may never have taken place.[5] Fifty years earlier, Holtzmann had advanced the theory that at first the Kauravas were the representation of virtue, and that traces of this earlier moral superiority remain,[g] giving the epic a tone of moral ambiguity.[6] It is not only this ambivalence that has confused scholars—the very figure of Krishna alternates between saintliness and deception. Held rejects the solution, popular among students of the *Mahabharata,* that evidences of Krishna worship are later interpolations, and insists that the dual character of Krishna must provide the point of departure for a proper interpretation of the work.[7] This ambiguity is most evident in the relationship of the two combatants. Employing the analogy of the phratry relationship (but without equating the two peoples with the tribal moieties), Held claims that the Pandavas and Kauravas exist in a state of "hostile friendship"[h]—an association that creates the tension on which the ritual life of the tribe depends.[8]

Held would have it that the Kauravas and Pandavas are specialists in the ritual functions of the potlatch and of the initiation, respectively. The primary instance of the potlatch and the gaming competition often associated with it is to be found in the second book of the *Mahabharata,* in which the splendor of the Pandava's sabha and the magnificence of the food and gifts are described. After the festivities, Duryodhana, the son of the Kuru king and cousin of the Pandavas, experiences a series of humiliations and swears vengeance. The Kauravas counter with a sabha of their own and build a pavilion that glows with countless precious stones. Here was an opulence and extravagance that had never before been known. At the potlatch Yudhishthira was challenged to a game of dice. Gambling was Yudhishthira's fatal flaw, and his ruin was rapid and complete. Stripped of their wealth and their realm, he and his brothers and their common wife, Draupadī, were banished for thirteen years—after which time they were to receive back their kingdom.

For the initiatory rite, the ritual that reveals the sacred to men, we must turn to the *Bhagavad Gita.* On the eve of the great battle between the Pandavas and the forces of Duryodhana, which followed the refusal of Duryodhana to honor the settlement whereby Yudhishthira and his brothers would recover their rights, Krishna instructs the initiate Arjuna in the ways of knowing God and the obligations of the varnashrama-dharma. We shall turn presently to this divine counsel.

Several scholars have attempted to solve a problem that has long fascinated Indologists.[9] The five Pandava brothers share a wife—and yet we know that among the Aryans polyandrous relationships were rare. Wikander has reached the conclusion that the five sons of Pāṇḍu[i] were

---

[g] The Kauravas, for example, can be conquered only by means of fraud.

[h] "From whatever angle we may view the relation between the two parties, it is ever that selfsame wavering between the extremes of friendship and enmity which we perceive." (Held [171], p. 298.)

[i] The younger brother of the blind Kuru king Dhṛtarāṣṭra.

actually not his sons, but children of the gods. Three of them, Yudhishthira, Bhima, and Arjuna, were sired by Dharma (a later name for Mitra), Vayu, and Indra, respectively. Their mother was Pandu's wife Kunti. Pandu's other wife, Madrī, conceived the twins Nakula and Sahadeva by the Vedic twin deities known as the Aśvins. Nakula and Yudhishthira, therefore, have no blood relationship. According to this thesis, Yudhish-thira represents the sovereign authority of Mitra, and Bhima and Arjuna are the great warriors who symbolize the two types of kshatriya character. Although Indra is depicted as intemperate and boastful, he is mildness itself when compared with the vigorous Vayu. The hero who represents the latter type is, in Dumézil's words, "a human beast," a lusty adventurer, a trifle stupid but free of malice. His fellow warrior, Arjuna, the son of Indra, stands for the true chivalric spirit; he is civilized and ordered in his ways, knowledgeable in the use of arms, and sociable. The twins, like the helpful Aśvins, exist to serve their "brothers"; they personify the vaishya virtues.

Their wife, Draupadi, appears to be the human counterpart of the Vedic goddess Sarasvatī (or Vāc), who serves to synthesize the three functions. This, then, could explain a marriage arrangement that was surely atypical. Though we know that at one time Mitra was associated with the Brahma and Varuna with the Kshatra principle, the equating of Yudishthira with the brahman ideal poses difficulties, since so much of the epic is devoted to teaching him the proper conduct of a *king* and since Draupadi herself is critical of him for his anti-kshatriya attitudes.[10] It is of course impossible to construct a consistent theory on the basis of a text that has been reworked time and again and that in its extant form reveals a heavy brahman influence. The brahmans, intent on making the world safe for orthodoxy, must describe the kind of rule most compatible with sacred law and most congenial to their interests. In certain of the episodes in the great epic, Krishna appears to have been appropriated by the priests and made the vehicle of their arguments. But he also represents values that had begun to threaten the integrity of Vedic culture. The revised docu-ment may be understood as an attempt to buttress brahman authority against the threat of alien beliefs. We may assume that secular ideals were still fairly uniform throughout society and that, as in the last years of the eleventh century when the clergy of Europe began to adapt the *chanson de geste* to its own ends, the heroic epic was a means of influencing the humbler strata of society.

Insofar as Yudhishthira would make political and military considera-tions secondary to the ethical and religious, he may be viewed as the em-bodiment of the spiritual principle—which, according to the brahmans, must be the true sovereign power. The mythology probably goes back to the time of the original atharvan priests, an age before the brahmans had

---

j It is significant that the lower orders of society are not considered blood brothers of the ruling classes, and that even the three who represent the brahman and kshatriya groups are only stepbrothers.

achieved an authoritative position in the social hierarchy. We might even surmise that the two kshatriya types (Vayu and Indra) were the most vivid expression of the distinction that became the symbolic basis of the later Brahma-Kshatra duality. Possibly the original Mitra-Varuna dichotomy was restated to preserve the early kshatriya dual character (which may have symbolized the two main Aryan groups), and Mitra appropriated by the rising brahman class. Eventually the twofold principle of sovereignty would be restored.

More revealing for the study of political thought is the dual character of Lord Krishna himself. Krishna, who appears in the epic as a tribal god, was probably an actual person. In the stories that surround him (which may well represent different traditions) he is portrayed as the divine herdsman and great lover and as the clever consultant to his cousin warriors in their campaigns. Krishna was closely associated with the kshatriya nobility, and his role as avatar, protector of the dharma, would necessarily involve him in kshatriya functions. We should expect Krishna, as an expression of divinity, to personify righteousness as well as honor. We are not prepared, therefore, to find him described as a trickster, a master at deception, a wily fox. The explanation goes beyond Huizinga's contention that in archaic culture, departures from the rules of the game were not regarded in the same way that we would regard them today.[11]

In ancient civilizations order and tradition were sanctified. Mitra, as we have seen, represents stability and symmetry. But Mitra, though supreme, is dependent on Varuna, and Varuna stands for the active, assertive quality that we have contrasted with the cohesive. Here is the essence of the ambiguity: the sacred is clearly distinguished from the lower political order, and yet the indispensable role of protection and regulation, and even of violence, in preserving dharma is recognized. We might speak of the kshatriya or political function as a "sanctioned sin." Arjuna sees clearly (in the *Gita*) the evils of war; it is the divine Krishna who reminds him of the kshatriya obligation to fight. The kshatradharma maintains the order of things, just as the avatar comes forth to restore the sacred order when dharma is threatened. This "sinfulness" inherent in the kshatriya duty (because order demands its very opposite, violence) makes the warrior dependent on the brahman for absolution. This is not a grudging admission of the political function. The brahmans are themselves too convinced of the tendency to anarchy that results when the governing power is weakened.

The idea of the political as sinful (albeit a necessary evil) is not unique to India. It can be seen in the warning of the high priest Samuel; in the moral ambiguity surrounding David, who went so far as to disregard the very ritual taboos by which the warrior role was purified—but who succeeded in reconciling the covenant between God and Israel with the authority of his own house.[12] In Platonic theory it can be seen in the qualitative difference between change *per se* and the "change" that establishes an order based on the Good (an idea that may have its source in the ancient

Greek concept of the Great Legislator[k]). And Plato hoped to eliminate most of what we would consider the political, once this order was established.

Public policy may have to deviate at times from accepted values and standards of conduct. It is not simply that expedience serves the private purposes of those in power. Far more important is the need to reconcile conflicting claims with one another and with social norms. The Romans sought to meet this difficulty by rooting authority in the act of foundation itself—the charismatic and peculiarly political act that creates community. With Christianity the concept of revealed Truth reappears, but the Roman emphasis on tradition shaped the Christian theory of temporal authority. In medieval philosophy, before the Aristotelianism of St. Thomas, government was closely linked to man's capacity for sin: political institutions were at once the punishment and remedy for sin, and the consequence of man's imperfection. And finally, at the beginning of the modern era, we find Machiavelli insisting that morality can exist only in a context that is itself not created by morality, and counseling the leader to learn "how not to be good" if he would know the ultimate secret of political life. The violent act of Romulus is justified by its results, and the Roman myth of foundation receives a new significance in Machiavelli's argument that society is ever being founded anew. Authority struggles to free itself from tradition.[18]

Krishna and the kshatriya noble represent the inevitable tension between the action that social justice and social order require and the very principles upon which this order is structured. The dilemma, which haunts the political and gives it the semblance of amorality, is first expressed in the figure of Indra, the boisterous god of the Aryans, whose sins are carefully chronicled in the brahman texts. In this chapter and the next, we shall deal with the attempt to tame Indra and the heroic ideal of action he represents, the recognition of the reality and necessity of power, and the search for a principle of legitimacy that could provide the basis for distinguishing force from authority.

The *Shantiparva* is the major source of political commentary in the *Mahabharata*. The subject of this didactic collection of folk-wisdom, the twelfth book of the epic, is *nīti*—the science of worldly pursuit. In it the king's responsibilities are enumerated and the broader questions of caste obligations, right conduct, and ethics of government are discussed. We are told repeatedly that in the state which has no king, the natural order of the universe is disrupted and destroyed. Therefore, when kshatriya power declines and the social order is threatened, members of any class may take action to prevent lawlessness, for anarchy is to be avoided at any cost.

[k] "From the great deeds attributed to a Draco, Solon, Lycurgus, and Cleisthenes, there was drawn the towering figure of the law-giver, suddenly intruding to save the disintegrating life of the *polis* and to re-establish it on a fresh foundation." (Wolin [434], p. 53.) The statement could as accurately describe Krishna—except that the avatar gives new inspiration to old forms.

The state of nature, as Bhishma describes it to Yudhishthira, was first a condition of righteousness and bliss.[14] Dharma kept everything in its proper place and there was no need of danda.[1] Decadence, taking the form of anti-social personality traits that developed gradually in man, at last made necessary the restraining power of the king. The shadow of greed and lust fell over the peaceful scene and a disorder, comparable to Hobbes' state of nature, resulted.[15] This condition of anarchy is *mātsya-nyāna,* the "law of the fishes" (i.e., no law). It is a metaphorical description of lawlessness employed frequently in the literature of Hindu polity. In these verses it is the gods—not the people—who appeal to Brahma in the time of chaos. The dandaniti[m] composed by Brahma was ineffective without an executive power to enforce the sacred laws. Vishnu was therefore appointed to this office by the gods and, entering the body of Prithu, who had made a compact with the people and sworn to uphold brahman immunities, he became king.[n] Hence the king was seen as the heir of Vishnu, a product of the divine energy, and his legitimacy was derived from his divine ordination.

It appears that we are really more justified in considering this a contract between the king and the brahmans, and a unilateral contract at that: the king promises to protect and respect the brahmans and to grant them privileges. This view of the origin of kingship is almost certainly a later addition to the *Shantiparva,* and it has been contrasted with the ideas that appear in chapters 67 and 68 of the *Shantiparva.*

The intent of both portions is to exalt the authority of the ruler. Very little is said of restrictions on this authority. The crucial importance of danda in combating the evils of anarchy is stressed. Without the king, who wields the rod of punishment, "men cannot enjoy their wealth and wives." And for this reason, "an intelligent man should protect as his own what belongs to the king. . . . The king is the heart of his people; he is their great refuge; he is their glory; and he is their greatest happiness. Those men, O king, who are attached to the king, can conquer both this and the next world."[16] Here the state of nature seems to be from the

---

[1] Jayaswal held that this condition was once the ideal—that men believed that dharma could and should rule without danda. The term for this positive state of nature he took to be *arājaka.* And he went so far as to claim that such a political experiment may have taken place, though it must have been confined to small political units. ([199], pp. 86f.) This idea has been criticized by Ghoshal ([146]; [144], p. 213, n.3), who goes back to the texts themselves to prove that *arājaka,* the ruler-less state, was far from a Tolstoyan ideal. Jayaswal admits the cynical view of the *Mahabharata* which makes arājaka synonymous with matsyanyaya (survival of the strong). Part of the difficulty is that Jayaswal draws attention to *Shantiparva* 59.14 ("All men used to protect one another piously") without noting that the spirit of this verse is quite distinct from the tenor of *Shantiparva* 67.17f. In view of clan and family regulation (what we might call "traditional" authority), a political unit without a central government is not an impossibility. But Ghoshal is right in stating that Jayaswal's theory of early Indian idealism does not do justice to the facts.

[m] The *Mahabharata* uses the term dandaniti to designate the science of constraint or, more broadly, of government.

[n] The first mention of Prithu (*Pṛthu*) as the original anointed king appears in the *Shatapatha Brahmana.* Prithu was not the first king, but seventh in line. Experience under his predecessors had been so unfortunate that he was constrained to take a coronation oath before ascending to his office.

beginning a state of anarchy, a situation radically different from the golden age of Buddhist theory. "If there were no king on Earth for holding the rod of punishment, the strong would then have oppressed the weak after the manner of fishes in the water. We have heard that men, in days of yore, in consequence of anarchy, were ruined, devouring one another like stronger fishes devouring the weaker ones in the water."[17] In these passages kingship is not the result of a bilateral agreement between the people and one of their own; it is the creation of divine will, and in the agreement, if we may call it such, the people make extravagant promises to the (reluctant) king designated by Brahma. One verse[18] does refer to the "election" of the king, but in no modern sense of the word does election play a part in the theory of the origin of the coercive authority of the state.

According to the *Shantiparva* ("The Book of Peace"), what men want most—or at least what is most necessary—is order; and "when the science of politics (chastisement) is neglected, the Vedas and all virtues decline."[19] The king who possesses the rod of chastisement, says Arjuna, "sways all subjects and protects them. The rod of chastisement is awake when all else is under sleep. For this, the wise have designated the rod of punishment as righteousness itself. . . . If punishment were done away with in this world, creatures would soon be destroyed."[20] The theory is postulated on the same assumption of man's natural wickedness that we find in earlier writings. Danda is that which sustains righteousness. We are provided with a vivid image of the "god" chastisement. "In form he looks like a blazing fire. His complexion is dark like that of the petals of the blue lotus. He is equipped with four teeth, has four arms and eight legs and many eyes. His ears are pointed like shafts and his hair stands erect. He has matted locks and two tongues. His face has the hue of copper and he is clad in a lion's skin."[21]

The ruler who fails to protect his subjects is compared in the *Shantiparva* to the barren wife, the dry cow, and the bull that bears no burden.[22] A king was theoretically unable to take refuge in the particular nature of the age in which he lived as an excuse for failure to fulfill his duty as protector and upholder of dharma.[p] The *Mahabharata* declares, on the contrary, that the king is the maker of his age.[23] Dandaniti was conceived as the guarantor of the proper functioning of the universe. This concept, expressed more positively as rajadharma,[q] the royal duty, is the keystone of the arch of duties, the duty upon which all others depend, the securer of property and the guardian of the family.

But in times of emergency it may be necessary to depart from the customary precepts of dharma. We read that duties may be based on truth (*satya*), on reasoning (*upapatti*), on good custom (*sādhrācāra* or

[p] Hinduism divides time into *kalpas*, which are further divided into *mahāyugas*, which, in turn, consist of four ages. According to the *Mahabharata* (III, 12, 826) and *Manu* (I, 69) a mahayuga lasts 12,000 years. A thousand mahayugas make a kalpa, which is equal to one day in the life of Brahma. It is our bad fortune to be living in an age of evil which follows an idyllic period that existed some five thousand years ago.

[q] The study of polity was first designated *rajadharma* and, as the word suggests, referred more specifically to principles of royal conduct.

sadācāra), and on expediency (*upāya*.[24] The recommendations of the sage Bharadvāja, who expounds a program of expediency, are meant to apply only in crisis situations when dharma can be preserved only by extreme measures.[25] If possible, the king must avoid using the "wily wisdom." Although the ruthless techniques employed at critical times were not to govern the conduct of the state in normal times, we must remember that the "normal" situation for this society was a condition approaching what we would today call cold war. Stability depended on diplomatic arrangements that shifted as the loci of power shifted, and that were based on the calculation of advantage, the wily wisdom.

As Bhishma explains it, the kshatriya dharma is beyond good and evil. Rama declares at one point that he is renouncing the kshatradharma, which masks sin as righteousness and invites hypocrisy.[26] The "sinfulness of Indra" is the theme of *Shantiparva* 97: Yudhishthira expounds on the iniquity inherent in the king's duty. But the guru Bhishma answers that the stain of sins incurred in battle leaves the hero with his very blood.[27] It is the kshatriya duty to die in battle. In the faithful and selfless accomplishment of the rajadharma, sin is unavoidable. (It is the premise of Buddhism, without the conclusion.) "I do not see any creature in this world," announces Arjuna, "that supports life without doing any active injury to others. Animals live upon animals, the stronger upon the weaker. . . . There is no act that is entirely pure."[28]

In *Shantiparva* 64–66 we find a great paean to the kshatriya dharma— that upon which all else depends. But several chapters earlier the dying Bhishma conceded (if the commentator Nīlakantha is correct) that the kshatriya role must always be understood as inferior to the duties of the brahman—inasmuch as the principle of action is subordinate to that of renunciation. If renunciation is the essence of the Brahma, then it would not do to have the knights coveting for themselves that which was the *raison d'être* of the priests. "Wise men, therefore, do not praise Renunciation as the duty of a Kshatriya. On the other hand, the clear-sighted think that the adoption of such a life (by a kshatriya) involves even the loss of virtue."[29] Bhishma rebukes Yudhishthira for wishing to turn to the forest in order to find spiritual merit and avoid the performance of the morally ambiguous duties prescribed by his noble status. Yudhishthira's brothers and his wife condemn renunciation as dereliction of kshatriya duty,[30] and the theme of devotion to one's dharma reverberates throughout the books of the massive work.[r]

THE PRINCIPLES OF SOUND POLITY

The admonition to avoid war when possible, and to engage in hostilities only when attempts at peaceful settlement have failed,[31] may tell us more about the ideals of those responsible for the later recension than about the

---

[r] Note especially the remarks of Nakula: "O king, the person who in sacrifices gives away his fairly acquired wealth to those Brahmanas who are well conversant with the Vedas, and contracts his soul, is, O monarch, regarded as the true renouncer. . . . A person becomes a true renouncer by casting off internal and external attachments, and not simply by leaving home for the forest." (*Shantiparva* 12.7f. and 12.35.)

kshatriya nobles apotheosized in combat. When war was inevitable, the kshatriya had no choice but to dedicate himself to the preservation of the state and the dharma, and to fight in accordance with the code governing hostilities. The moral law forbade the use of weapons against those not actively engaged in battle (such as peasants and craftsmen), or those who retire from the fray, who are unarmed or disabled, or who plead for mercy. Camp-followers and sleeping soldiers are also protected. A warrior could contend only with another who was similarly armed (e.g., charioteer against charioteer), and he must not use poisoned weapons. He must always give due notice of his intention to strike.[32] The narrative itself provides a lively picture of the Hindu warrior in battle. At the height of the conflict he seems to have used anything he could get his hands on: iron clubs, spits, swords, knives, darts, arrows, wheels, axes, iron balls, staves, cow-horns, mortars, lances, and even uprooted trees. Anything from molasses and snakes to plowshares and chariot planks might be employed. And when such ammunition was exhausted, there were always dirt, stones, fists, and teeth.[33]

The constant warfare of the centuries preceding the consolidation of the great empires severely modified the ethics of diplomacy and made survival justification in itself for all manner of actions. However, the epics advise against a militaristic and garrison state, and indicate that the Hindu monarchy was essentially civil. Yet the ritual-sacrifice itself, the *brahmaṇah parimara* (the "dying around the magic power") and the ashvamedha (a virtual invitation to hostilities) produced what Zimmer has called a "magic arthaśastra" which makes futile the attempt to disentangle political expedience and religious practices. These practices contributed to an age of internecine war so terrible that the nobler kshatriya was sorely tempted to renounce the world and find peace and fulfillment in the forests. The soul-searching of Yudhishthira and Arjuna culminates in the teachings of Buddha and Ashoka. The unhappy turn in the fortunes of the brahmans during the regime of the emperor Ashoka may provide a clue to the insistence by later redactors on the faithful performance of traditional duties and the importance of the sacrifice—on which brahman supremacy traditionally depended.

The ancient canon of morality could be laid aside on the theory that without the state to ensure its existence the code would be meaningless. This dilemma produces moral flexibility as well as cynicism: "There is no act that is wholly meritorious, nor any that is wholly wicked."[34] "Sin, O king, sometimes assumes the form of virtue, and virtue sometimes assumes the form of sin."[35] Bhishma, in the *Shantiparva*, enunciates the doctrine that might makes right; elsewhere right is defined as "that which a strong man understands to be right."[36]

When the king is counseled to eschew war if at all possible, the intent of such advice is not necessarily that the king should avoid conquering, but that he should acquire "victories" without battles.[37] The king is urged to tempt his enemy into ways of self-indulgence, to encourage him to deplete his resources in expensive sacrifices and to rely on religion and fate rather than on his own efforts.[38] The formula for diplomacy involves deception, appeasement of the powerful and suppression of the weak, hypocrisy, bribery, economic exhaustion, soothing reassurance and lightning on-slaught, ruthlessness, vigilance and secrecy, and readiness to risk and to sacrifice. But, if feasible, victory should be gained without hostilities.

The king must be always alert to detect the peculiar vulnerabilities of his foes. In order to discern these weaknesses, he should employ spies. In times of peace the spy served to detect conspiracies and antisocial actions. In no corner of the kingdom could the king be completely certain of the loyalty of his subjects. Virtue is the cornerstone of the king's legiti-macy, but vigilance guards his authority. And shrewdness supplements caution: "Carry your enemy on your shoulder," the king is advised, "until you have got from him what you want, then throw him off, shatter-ing him like an earthen jar against a rock."[39] To fail to do so is to run the risk of the mother crab who is consumed by her offspring. It is always dangerous to conclude peace with an enemy.[40] The king is advised to fear that which merits fear. Uncritical trust is an invitation to disaster. The king must be sweet in speech, yet always on guard.

As we have seen, the *Shantiparva* is one long argument for the vested interest of the community in the welfare of the king.[41] This is surely the reason for the lurid picture of the state of nature presented in chapter 67. But the king should merit loyalty: he must have conquered pride, lust, and weakness—replacing them with righteousness, vigor, and wisdom. "The king should first conquer himself and then try to subdue his enemies. How can a king who has not been able to conquer his own self be able to conquer his enemies?"[42] Birth, military skill, and courage are mentioned as the chief attributes of royal office. Bhishma exhorts the king to be both mild and strict (without becoming oppressive) in order to preserve re-spect. It will be to his advantage to assume a variety of forms, as the occa-sion demands.[43] Yet the king must be man enough to endure unpopularity in the greater interest of the state. "He is the best of kings who is wise, who is liberal, who is ready to take advantage of the short-comings of foes, who has an agreeable countenance, who is conversant with what is good and what is bad for each of the four orders of his subjects, who is prompt in action, who has anger under control, who is not vindictive, who is high-minded."[44]

The coronation oath of the Kurus limited royal authority to the pro-tection of the people, the maintenance of custom, and punishment, and made the king subject to the laws of the realm. Failure to carry out re-sponsibilities was as grave a misuse of authority as the unlawful use of power. The absence of the superstitious and the mystical in the Hindu coronation oath has often been remarked upon. Prithu is addressed di-rectly and asked to swear to

> accomplish all those tasks in which righteousness ever resides! Dis-regarding what is dear and what not so, look upon all creatures with an equal eye. Cast off at a distance lust and wrath and covetousness and honor, and, always observing the dictates of righteousness, do thou

punish with thy own hands the man, whoever he may be, that deviates from the path of duty! Do thou also swear that thou wouldst, in thought, word, and deed, always maintain the religion inculcated on earth by the Vedas! Do thou further swear that thou wouldst fearlessly maintain the duties laid down in the Vedas with the aid of chastisement, and that thou wouldst never act with caprice![45]

And then we come to what is perhaps the root of the matter: "O powerful one, know that Brahmanas are exempt from punishment, and promise further that you would protect the world from an intermixture of castes."[46]

The *Shantiparva,* if conceiving the king as at all divine, locates divinity in the office rather than in the personality of the king. Heredity and primogeniture determined royal succession in epic polity, though the formality of nomination was preserved.[47] Some scholars interpret the succession of Rama's younger brother, Bharata, to the throne as the result not of a promise of King Daśaratha to his wife (as is sometimes argued) but of Rama's willing resignation. It is an instance of self-sacrifice to save his father's honor rather than of injustice to Rama. The king could not legally contradict the custom of regal succession. Rama had no disabilities that could disqualify him from office, as Dhritarashtra and Devapi had.

A kind of contract relationship existed, in theory, between the ruler and the governed. Taxes were considered the king's remuneration for protecting and furthering the interests of his people. In taxing his people the king must be like the subtle leech and the gentle cowherd, extracting the necessary revenue with mildness and care, and without destroying initiative.

That avaricious king, who foolishly oppresses his subjects by levying taxes not sanctioned by scriptures, is said to wrong his own self. As a person wanting milk never gets any by cutting off the udders of a cow, similarly a kingdom, assailed by improper taxes, never gives any profit to the king. He who treats a milch cow with kindness, always obtains milk from it. Likewise the king, who rules his kingdom by proper means, gets much fruits from it.[48]

Therefore, the king should try to convince his subjects of the need for the tax: "Pointing out to them the necessity of repairing his forts and of meeting the expense of his establishment and other heads, striking them with the fear of foreign invasion, and pointing to them the necessity that exists for protecting them and enabling them to ensure the means of living in peace, the king should impose taxes upon the Vaishyas of his kingdom."[49]

The king was advised to consider the selling price of a merchant's goods and the distance these goods traveled before taxing them. The customary tax on the produce of the land was one-sixth (though it often varied considerably), and the king is occasionally referred to as *shadbhagin,* "he who gets one-sixth."[50]

Despite the liberality recommended in the tax policy, the king is told to keep his treasury full.[51] Wealth is a necessity, and the king need only take his cue from the people, who "make as much as they can."[s]

The state may take the property of the wicked, for ownership is ultimately based on virtue.[52] But maintaining the security of property remains one of the fundamental duties of the state. In case of loss of property, such as that resulting from theft, the king is called on to make good the amount taken from his subjects. "That king, who, realizing his tribute of sixth, does not protect his kingdom, shares a fourth part of the sins of the kingdom."[53] The very fact of thievery indicates that the rajadharma is imperfectly realized. It is unlikely that the ruler took such extreme responsibility seriously. The concept is linked to the broad theory that all virtue and stability ultimately rest on political foundations.[t]

Commandments of the early heterodox religions not to steal or trespass on the possessions of others suggest the importance private property had begun to assume. In the *Mahabharata* property is conceived as the creation of the state.[54] The argument is that with the emergence of civil society, property—in the sense of title—comes into existence. A distinction is made between *bhoga* (possession) and *mamatva* (ownership).

Certain circumstances justified the subjects in deposing and killing the king. The people, according to the *Anusasanaparva,* should take up arms and slay the king who fails to protect them or who attempts to take their wealth or to level class distinctions.[55] Force is prescribed to oppose the unlawful use of force. And the king who failed to protect his people should be abandoned—like those other undesirables, the vixen wife, the leaky boat, the barber desiring the forest and the cowherd the village, the teacher who does not instruct, and the priest who is ignorant of scripture.[56]

The king is not to destroy the special customs of families, corporations, and defeated nations, unless the welfare of the state makes it imperative to

[s] On the importance of wealth, *vide Shantiparva* 8.16f.

[t] Heinrich Zimmer [439] retells a popular Indian tale known as "The Twenty-five Stories of the Specter in the Corpse." There are five Sanskrit versions of this story of king Vikramāditya, who is believed to have lived around the first century B.C. It involves a series of enigmatic situations, one of which concerns a prince and his friend, the son of the chancellor of the prince's father, who one day discover a beautiful girl bathing with her companions in a lake situated in another kingdom. A liaison is arranged between the prince and the girl through signals interpreted by the chancellor's son. The girl, later fearing that her amours will be betrayed, determines to poison the prince's friend. But he, anticipating such a plan, disguises himself as an ascetic and, to teach her a lesson, causes the girl to be condemned as a witch responsible for the death of the infant prince of the kingdom in which she lives. The girl is left to die in the jungle outside the town, and as soon as she is abandoned, the two young men carry her off to their kingdom and she of course marries the prince. But grief-stricken and disgraced, her own elderly parents soon die. Who, asks the spirit in the corpse, was guilty of these deaths? The answer—which is considered to be correct—is that love excuses all as far as maid and prince are concerned. The chancellor's son is cleared because he was always acting in the service of his master and, presumably, any act is justified if it is in line with duty. But the king of the girl's country is responsible for allowing such things to happen in his realm; he should be able to detect trickery and penetrate disguise. "Therefore, he is to be judged guilty of failure in his kingly duty, which was to be the all-seeing eye of his kingdom, the all-knowing protector and governor of his folk."

do so. On the contrary, he is obligated to preserve the traditional order of things, for custom is regarded as sacred. A passage in the epic that describes a prince, defeated in battle, worrying about what he will say to the priests and the heads of the corporations suggests that the ruler had to maintain the favor of influential members of society.[57]

The *Shantiparva* describes the creation of the castes from the mouth, arms, thighs, and feet of Brahma. The *Gita* also attempts to justify the varna structure, but its theory is more sophisticated. God, it is argued in the *Gita,* assigned duties to men according to their inherent abilities. If man would but carry out the functions proper to his social position, he would ensure his salvation. All this is by now familiar and will be considered again in the following chapter. But there appears at this time the idea that different social functions are equally valuable in the attainment of individual salvation. The theory undoubtedly represents the influence of other religious systems, such as Buddhism, which had a notable impact on the society of the time. Although the epic in its present form is a brahmanic work, it is sometimes critical of the excesses of Brahmanism; Krishnaite influences are in evidence from time to time. The priest, despite the brahman manipulation of the text, is still clearly far from the king's master.

The later redactors leave no doubt in our minds as to what they thought the priest's power should be. Just as fire has no effect on water, so the kshatriya can have no power over the brahman. The ruler without his brahman adviser is like an elephant without its driver.[58] The kshatriyas are exhorted to work in close cooperation with the brahmans, but it is evident that the priests exercise little direct political power. The arguments and tales worked into the older narrative are frequently in dramatic contradiction to the main story. However, the influence of the brahmans is clearly increasing.[u] The epic reveals a general willingness to allow tribal units to preserve the integrity of their cultures, yet it was thought essential to work out some *modus operandi* between these groups and Brahmanism: the priests were expected to guide the major ceremonies, administer the necessary sacraments, and modify those beliefs which were flagrantly in opposition to brahman theory.[59]

In the *Shantiparva* we find mention of legislative council in which, according to Hopkins, the commercial class enjoys almost twice the representation of the two upper classes.[v] But the passage Hopkins relied upon is not in the critical edition of the *Shantiparva.* It does appear, however, that all the castes were represented and though the shudras had only a negligible position in the higher councils, their presence points to a recognition of the need for their loyalty and their opinion on matters of policy. Nine members of the council were to be chosen to confer with the king, and, of these, four were to be selected for his immediate circle of advisers. Three or four councilors were considered the ideal number,

---

[u] Hopkins ([184], p. 162) believed that the brahman's power originated in the secret council, where his rhetorical and logical skill outshone that of the nobles and he awed the king with his religious authority.

[v] Hopkins [184] refers to twenty-one vaishyas on a council of thirty-six; cf. *Shantiparva* 85.6ff.

since fewer might lead to a combination of ministers contrary to the interests of the country, and more would tend to diminish efficiency. Only the man who has sublimated his senses is fit for such offices.

> Such persons as are endued with modesty, self-control, truth, sincerity, and courage to say the proper thing, should be your law-makers. . . . Those who are of good birth and good behavior, who can interpret all signs and gestures, who are shorn of cruelty, who know the requirements of place and time, who always seek the well-being of their master in all works, should be appointed as ministers by the king in all his affairs.[60]

It appears that members of the mantri-parishad (the large council) were consulted individually on urgent matters. The inner council was, however, regularly consulted on general affairs. The king is advised to respect his ministers, for it was unlikely that he would be wise enough to be able to forgo counsel on complex issues. The first indication of complete secrecy in the councils dates from this time. In the *Ramayana*, the king's ministers are referred to as *amātyas*; they are usually eight in number, and are possibly a hereditary class. The position of the brahman is generally more secure in the *Ramayana*. Hopkins held that the *Mahabharata* reflected three stages in conciliar development. In the older legends there is still evidence of the power of the people, but it is limited to civil affairs. The popular assembly gave way to that of the nobility—which probably originated in the war council and continued to be more concerned with military matters. Finally, in the late didactic parts of the epic (not part of the story itself), the priests assume the prerogative, insisting on their right to advise the king on all questions in counsel protected by absolute secrecy.[61]

Sabha, by this time, referred to the king's court, or to any judicial, political, or festive gathering. Jayaswal makes a case for an administrative body, the *paura*, which was charged with the conduct of municipal affairs in the capital and consisted of an advisory council of leading citizens—apparently representing all social classes. The *janapada* served as a constitutional assembly for the rest of the state.[62] But paura probably refers to a resident of the city and not, as Jayaswal infers, to an assembly member. His interpretation of the janapada as an institutional form rests on the thinnest evidence, and though the king may have taken pains to determine the will of the people, it is doubtful that a formal constitutional check governed the king's activities. If the paura-janapada assemblies actually existed, there would certainly be more evidence in the records that have come down to us than the occasional references Jayaswal cites (e.g., the *Ramayana*[w]), which are decidedly ambiguous.[x] Popular ex-

---

[w] Paura-janapada is used in the plural in the *Ramayana* (II, 14.40 and 14.54) to refer to the citizens as such. The term is employed in *Manu* (VIII, 40) to refer to men of all castes.

[x] Professor Altekar [6], p. 108f., points out that the paura-janapada assemblies —if such existed—are not mentioned on a single one of the thousands of copper plate grants (going back to A.D. 500) which have been discovered, even though every possible authority is cited. No inscription or work on polity refers to such a popular assembly.

pression of opinion, in the *Mahabharata,* is extraconstitutional. The emphasis is less on assemblies and village elders than on royal courts and dancing girls. Everywhere but in the easternmost regions, public opinion continued as a force to be reckoned with, although there was a tendency, as government became more complex in its authority and function, for popular participation to become formalistic. There is still the suggestion that many monarchs felt compelled to strengthen their claim to the throne by eliciting the approval of their subjects, or at least the support of the more influential segment of the populace.

As for the administration of the realm, we are told that the king should think of his subjects as his own children. But he should show no mercy in the settlement of disputes. Charges and defenses in judicial suits must be heard by men distinguished for their wisdom and experience in the ways of the world. Honest and reliable men are to be appointed to supervise the mines, the ferries, the elephant corps, and the warehouses.[63] A headman must be selected for each village, a superintendent for each ten villages, and so forth.[64]

The *Mahabharata* indicates the existence of a number of states in the north and west where sovereignty seems to have rested with the people and monarchy was more form than fact (e.g., the Kurus of what is modern Sirhind).[y] Though concerned chiefly with the monarchical form of government, the epic does comment on republics (or clan-republics), and specifically on the need for unity and cooperation among them. Their main vulnerability is their tendency toward internal dissension. Bhishma's critique amounts to a commentary on the divisive effects of the combination of political equality and economic inequality.[z] Each man comes to covet the wealth of others. Another problem is the frequent need for secrecy—which the councils of these ganas cannot by their very nature maintain. The remedy is to concentrate power in the natural nobility of talent and character.[65]

The *Mahabharata* is a manifesto in behalf of the strong monarch. But the monarch does not rule arbitrarily: he must govern in accordance with the sacred authority represented by the brahmans, and he knows that "the eternal duties of kings are to make their subjects happy, to observe truth and to act sincerely."[66]

---

[y] The Pandava princes are reported to have been restored through popular pressure. It is worth remarking that the word *gaṇa* (cf. *Shantiparva* 107.6) seems to refer to self-governing communities rather than to guilds or corporations—or to an elite, as it is sometimes translated.

[z] Bhishma's caveat has been compared with Aristotle's warning regarding the "stasis" of Hellenic city-states.

9 ✕ THE TAMING
OF THE HEROIC IDEAL

What is action and what inaction?—as to this even the wise are bewildered. I will declare to thee what action is, knowing which thou shalt be delivered from evil.—BHAGAVAD GITA

THE DISINTERESTED ACT

The values and goals of a society tell us much about its institutions and the ways in which men relate to one another. In this study we are primarily concerned with three goals of ancient Indian society that provide a useful frame of reference for the analysis of Indian social thought and political philosophy. These are religious salvation (which may be achieved in a variety of ways), material gain, and the heroic act. Scientific, aesthetic, and humanistic considerations are relatively less important in shaping Hindu theory, and the ideal of knightly valor, although it was of major significance in the early phases of Indian history and shaped the norm of conduct for the kshatriya class, was to prove incapable of surviving the decline of the tribal polity.

Ancient India had no "citizen" ideal as such, but, as we have seen, one class in Aryan society, the kshatriyas, did have a tradition of political experience. The kshatradharma was basically a martial ideal, from which the concept of the rajanya as protector of the people developed. We turn now to the question of what happened to the old aristocratic values, which appear to be moribund by the beginning of the Christian era. There is no *Heldendämmerung,* only a paling and dwindling into irrelevance.

In his study of the *Mahabharata,* E. W. Hopkins comments:

One is too apt to dispose of the general Hindu as Max Müller does with the words: "To the Greek, existence is full of life and reality; to the Hindu, it is a dream and a delusion." . . . If we study the coarse, sensual, brutal, strife-loving, blood-hungry Hindu warrior; if we revert to the Vedic ancestor of this ferocious creature, and see what joy in life as life is portrayed in battle-hymn and cattle-hymn, we shall be ready to admit, I think, that through the whole history of the Hindu, from the early Vedic until the pseudo-Epic period, there reigned the feeling, in the larger class of the native inhabitants, that existence is full of life and reality.[1]

Our problem is that this lustier view of life can only be inferred from such sources as the epics, since the brahman editors and compilers were intent on shaping the narrative to their own purposes. The stark anatomy of the hero is discreetly clothed with moralisms; the crude ethos is tempered and muted.

It is sometimes argued that the victory of the Pandavas over the Kauravas in the great battle in the *Mahabharata* is to be interpreted as a pragmatic justification for employing methods of warfare (frequently with divine blessing) that had not yet been reconciled with the traditional code. For at the time of the composition of the epic the political struggle was entering a new phase, and in the work itself the ideals of the military aristocracy are contrasted with the new requirements of Realpolitik. Hopkins holds, and his argument is more convincing, that the moral and spiritual elements are, for the most part, an overlay, and that the bulk of later interpolations in the *Mahabharata*—the *Bhagavad Gita* among them —were intended to excuse the transgressions of ancient heroes who had become models of knightly honor and thus to bring them into conformity with brahman teachings regarding kshatriya duty and the proper behavior of a king. Later religious feeling, he contends, "was less simple and less pure than the earlier, but the later morality was higher and stricter than that of a former age."[2]

This subsequent ethical concern pervades the epic and is often strikingly at variance with the robust amorality of an earlier and less civilized culture. We are reminded of a similar development in ancient Greece— the transition from the heroic ideal of the Homeric nobility, when the esteem of one's peers was highly valued and honor was the major regulating principle, to the later classical period with its sense of man's impotence and its preoccupation with the dire consequences of hubris. The Aryan invaders were a vigorous, beef-eating, liquor-drinking lot— Indra of the tawny beard and powerful arm, cattle-raider and stormer of citadels, reduced to human proportions.[3] The verses of the *Rigveda* are the hymns of these victorious warriors. But the boasting, life-affirming hero of the Vedic and Homeric ages was to succumb to the god-fearing penitent. In the struggle for power among the gods themselves, the justice-dispensing Varuna and the awesome Rudra are clearly gaining ascendancy.

The persistence of tribal elements in the Indian myth makes the interpretation of legend and symbol difficult. The battle itself, by the time of the epic, must probably be seen as having ritualistic implications. Conflict is in the order of things—or at least is essential to the preservation of that order. This is as true of the sacred world of the gods and the ritual (which perhaps is better understood as a form of combat[4]) as it is of the world of men. It is for this reason that fighting comes to be considered the mission of one segment of the population. This conflict, which may have had early expression in phratry antagonism, assumes an increasingly elaborate symbolic form. Krishna, for example, and his brother Balarāma represent contrary characteristics. Krishna, the trickster, is black; Balarama, the benefactor, is white. But Krishna also embodies both qualities in himself.[5] This ambitendency would seem to be partially explained by the position Krishna occupies, intermediate between the gods and men.[a] He is at once the terrifying daemon of the initiation and the initiate.

The eponymous hero, Cornford remarks, "owes his position not merely to his really exceptional character and powers, but to the fact that there already exists a representation, personalized and daemonic, of that super-human *mana* which is recognized as embodied in his individuality. . . . His actual achievements blend with the other glorious acts of tribal history in a composite memory that defies analysis."[6] According to Cornford, this charismatic figure is essentially a *persona,* a representation of the collective genius. He establishes his own norm. For all his later sanctity, Krishna initially appears in legend as such an *Übermensch.* He is often represented as advocating action that would be hard to conceive as virtuous in any sense.

In the earlier portions of the *Mahabharata,* which reflect the Vedic aristocratic mores, the brave knight Arjuna, whose character is taken to represent the kshatriya ideal, slays the warrior Karna, who has been rendered helpless. In the hands of the priests, however, Indrāvaraja is made the true instigator of the act. Thus the hero is relieved of responsibility and the god is credited with occult reasons for his order.[7] Here, then, was an attempt to explain away the reprehensible.[b] The priests could not call men to a life of virtue and at the same time eulogize those for whom rules meant nothing.[8] The actions of the warriors and princes were governed by a norm, the "Aryan way," which knew no ethical injunction.[c]

No greater shame could befall the warrior than to take flight in the face of the enemy.[d] But he who dies in the field may anticipate heaven:

[a] "It is exactly this indeterminateness in his dealings with gods and men which constitutes one of the outstanding features of the culture-hero." (Josselin de Jong, "The Origin of the Divine Trickster," cited in Held [171], p. 175.)

[b] Cf. *Apastamba Dharmasutra* II, 6.13.8–10, where we find the passage: "Transgression of the law and violence are found amongst the ancient (sages). They committed no sin on account of the greatness of their lustre. A man of later times who seeing their (deeds) follows them, falls." Bühler (*Sacred Books of the East,* II, xviii) comments that "these utterances prove that Apastamba considered himself a child of the Kali Yuga, the age of sin, during which, according to Hindu notions, no rishis can be born."

[c] Of the Bantus of Kavirondo, an African tribe dependent, as were the Aryans, on cattle-raiding, it has been remarked that "the fact that the two ultimate motives in warfare were the raiding of cattle and the conquest of territory has a definite bearing upon the conduct of warfare, as it involves conflicting aims. While it lies in the interest of expansion to carry on aggression in a ruthless manner which drives the enemy away as far as possible, the aim of raiding cattle clearly requires the presence of enemy groups in the neighborhood. Owing to the necessity of balancing these two aims, warfare tended to be conducted with certain restrictions, above all with provisions for terminating a period of hostilities and with generally observed rules regarding the treatment of slain warriors and of women and children. Such 'rules of warfare' were more pronounced in the conduct of hostilities between the various Bantu groups than between Bantu and non-Bantu." (Fortes and Evans-Pritchard [125], p. 228.) Possibly it was to the economic advantage of the Aryan clans to impose similar limitations on the conduct of hostilities.

[d] We may surmise that, for all the talk about honor and duty, courage may also have been nourished by the fear of the consequences that awaited the deserter, who might even be put to the flame. (*Vide Shantiparva* 97.22.) In such a culture public humiliation can be a very dreadful thing.

"the path to heaven lies in fighting." The story of Vidulā, in which a cowardly son is reproved by his mother for not discharging his duties as a kshatriya, glorifies the heroic act and the "Aryan way."[9] We are reminded at once of Krishna's famous counsel to Arjuna in the *Bhagavad Gita,* but it is possible and even likely that remarkable and sweeping changes had occurred in the Indian belief system between the two stories.

In the Vedic period man could look forward to a happy postmortal existence in heaven if he lived an acceptable life. Such a prospect had ceased to exist for the ordinary Indian by the seventh and sixth centuries B.C. With the development of the doctrine of the soul's passage to another body at death (samsara), salvation came to be rooted in esoteric knowledge —a gnosis which made possible a kind of magical power over the ends sought by man. Eventually this magical element lost much of its former import, but knowledge remained the basis of control. Knowledge might be acquired in ways that eliminated even the activity of thought. And where philosophy took as its premise the contrariety of two principles, spirit and matter, the devaluation of the latter would devalue action, the traditional justification of the kshatriya. The heroic ideal yielded to the ideal of the wandering ascetic and the bodhisattva.[e] The term for hero (*vīra*) now comes to be applied to the saint rather than to the man of action.[10]

Responsibility for the change does not lie solely with Buddhism,[f] though this is an explanation popular among historians. The depreciation of the assertive and heroic is symptomatic of a general religiosity that pervaded Indian society—a phenomenon that was very probably related to the erosion of older communal ties. Now, in the society reconstituted along functional lines taken to represent degrees of purity, when Krishna advises the reluctant Arjuna to join his fellow warriors in battle he is justifying the tasks necessary for the preservation of the social order, although they may be morally tainted.

The hero of the epic is already a different person from the warrior of the *Rigveda.* The proud knight is not afraid to contend with the gods themselves; "to him they are unreal; to him even the new god is but a myth of fancy. . . . The knight's acts are his own; his reward is his own making; his sin is self-punished. Fate, or the embrace of Death; Duty, or to follow the paths of custom—these are his only moral obligation. His supernatural is understood too little to be true; or it is debased to incantation and witchcraft. The knight of our present poem stands on the border-

---

[e] A sociologist would describe this as the shift from performance to learning. In the former, the change in the situation exceeds that in the individual, whereas the learning experience can be said to produce a greater change in the individual than in the situation in which he operates.

[f] Professor Kosambi, for example, refuses to hold Buddhism responsible for the relative lack of what he calls the "poetry of prowess" in later Indian literature. Many Buddhist kings pursued militant policies. We might question whether Buddhism led to an externalization of inner conflict, as Kosambi suggests, and whether, if it did, it should have "made intercourse within a society smoother." ([220], p. xlv n.)

line between two faiths."[11] In the *Mahabharata* the impersonal force, *daivam,* had begun to replace the old Vedic deities in importance: "Fate I deem the highest thing; manliness is no avail."[12] This theme punctuates the epic, suggesting the new influences at work. However, the older, more positive approach to the world did not yield without a struggle, as the following lines from the *Shantiparva* indicate: "Do not fear the results of karma, rely on your strength . . . all things belong to the man who is strong."[13] Words like these are taken to anticipate the power philosophy of the *Arthashastra.* It would be as accurate to say that they look back to the "Aryan way."

The emphasis on punishment (danda) as that which ensures the constancy of the universe presupposes the projection into the supernatural realm of man's demand for justice. The gods had originally been viewed as jealous of their honor, resentful of any slight (as was the Vedic hero himself), but not preoccupied with considerations of justice. The emergent sense of justice, with its political manifestation in the concept of danda— which supported the social order as the sacrifice ensured the cosmic order —culminated in the idea of inherited guilt. The sins of this life are punished in the next. The sinful might prosper, but the reckoning would come. This doctrine serves the purposes of the eschatological aspects of the Semitic theologies. The beginnings of a sense of sin, with the concomitant heightening of sensations of guilt, may be observed in the increasing prominence of the mysterious Varuna, guardian of rita and the major ethical deity in the Vedic pantheon. The conception of Varuna is essentially theistic. Nothing could be concealed from him, and he could not be bribed by the sacrifice. He inspired dread and awe, which distinguished his power from that of other early Vedic gods.[g] He could even inflict punishment for the sins of the father. But though merciless in his loathing of sin, he was on occasion moved to compassion.

This developing awareness of human helplessness and utter dependence on an arbitrary power is noticeable also in the growing significance of the later Vedic god Rudra, who has much in common with Indra but lacks his more appealing qualities. The great wielder of the thunderbolt, who had been the example for the Aryan warrior, had never inspired the fear that Rudra was able to evoke. Rudra, like his early counterpart, was beyond good and evil. But whereas Indra shared many human weaknesses,[14] Rudra was a distant figure never entirely comprehensible to men. In the twilight of the Vedic age the gods had lost their humanity, and not until devotional religion introduced a more positive element into the mainstream of Indian belief did the divinities take on an attractiveness comparable to that of the early Vedic gods. Unlike the gods of the Greek epic, those of the *Mahabharata* do not comfort and assist the epic warrior. They are active in man's behalf only in the stories of the Vedic past that have

---

[g] *Vide Rigveda* VII, 89. Basham has compared the sense of humility and guilt that Varuna inspired with the sentiments expressed in the penitential psalms of the Old Testament. ([24], p. 237.)

been incorporated into the narrative. Krishna's intervention (in the *Gita*) is evidence of the impact of later devotional and theistic religious thought.[h]

Implicit in the epic is a debate over the ability of personal valor and prowess, the heroic quality (*vīrya*), to combat the force of destiny (*kāla*).[15] Those who take the determinist position hold that the hero is made by the age. If the times are not with him, the man of courage and virtue will be swept away. Man is impotent against fate. In discussing a problem of this kind it is always difficult to be sure that one is not reading too much of the modern world into the remote past. The ancient Indian, like the Greek knight of the Homeric age, may have distinguished action of a volitional nature from actions subject to a power beyond the actor—such as a divine agency or even the restraints of family and class relationships. In the Greek epic the hero experiences a strange infusion of energy (*menos*), fortifying his spirit and increasing his strength.[16] This energy appears to be of a somewhat vagrant nature, but to the ancients—the Aryan aristocracy as well as the Homeric heroes—it is the gift of the gods.[i] This intervention of the gods had diminished to relative insignificance by the time the main body of the *Mahabharata* was composed. But theistic developments and the eventual humanizing of the gods were to encourage a return to the concept of divine intervention. Although the god is generally regarded as aloof, avatars (extensions of the divine essence) appear on earth from time to time in moments of crisis. Krishna bestowed the superhuman power on the kshatriya Arjuna, just as the spirit of the Lord came to Samson in his hour of need. Thus does fatalism come to be modified. The Krishna story may well be an attempt to locate the source of kshatriya strength in moral and supernatural agencies, but religion had at this time evolved beyond the more primitive device of ritualistic control of the supernatural as exercised by the brahmans.

In India access to this mysterious potency had once been the province of the priests, who acted as link between the gods and man. But fate itself (daivam) seems to have been immune to prayer and spell, a force superior to the gods and one that defied personification. Attempts to circumvent the priestly power had to transcend the Vedic pantheon, which was so intimately connected with the sacrifice and the magical formulas of the brahmans. The impersonal daivam—Zimmer's "godly essence"—is encountered when the "comforting illusion of the magical tradition" has been thrown off.[17] Man apparently had no choice but to seek the transformation of the mundane self, neutralizing the power of destiny by becoming as one with the universe, the essence of which is daivam. The *Gita* and the doctrine of the personal god offer an alternative to this philosophy of resignation and renunciation.[j]

---

[h] Although often considered an Upanishad, the *Gita* differs from the Upanishads in that it is a revelation of a system of ethics by a god—rather than a mystery that the teacher transmits and comments upon.

[i] Theognis, Dorian elegist and champion of courage and discipline, bemoaned the fact that more depended on a man's daemon than on his character. Fortitude availed little if the daemon was inferior.

[j] Of the Hindu literature available to us, the *Bhagavad Gita* is without doubt the best known work. The title of the poem comes from Krishna's designation in the

The *Bhagavad Gita,* which is generally held to have attained its final form in the first or second century before Christ, is considered the first major attempt to bring together heterodox doctrine (based on the dichotomy of matter and spirit and the exalting of spirit through discipline) and the later Vedic concept of the transcendent eternal One.[k] Certain religious innovators of the time had begun to regard sin as a condition of will, challenging the older idea of inherited guilt, which was closely linked to brahman ritual purification. Motive and conscience take on new importance as the moral element threatens to replace the supernatural, and fear of magical pollution gives way to a sense of individual responsibility. This development, however, is not enough in itself to explain the poem, which has become the very cornerstone of Hinduism. Krishna calls for action prescribed by one's "calling," but unhampered by the sense of personal accountability. Bhishma's counsel to Yudhishthira is recalled in the words of the divine charioteer: "Verily the renunciation of any duty that ought to be done is not right."[18] Warfare, for Arjuna and the kshatriya caste he represents, is a sacred charge sanctioned by the order of things. Society functions properly only when each group fulfills its obligations. Those who allow themselves to be controlled by lust and hatred become the victims of their own action. "He who is free from self-sense, whose understanding is not sullied, though he slay these people, he slays not nor is he bound (by his actions)."[19] Action is called for, even though it brings death and destruction, and fatalistic withdrawal is rejected.[l] The spirit is not slain when the body dies.

This famous poem of the sixth book of the *Mahabharata* was perhaps

---

Bhāgavata religion as Śri Bhagavan. Krishna's message incorporates much of the Bhagavata creed. The name of the author of the work is lost to us, but many commentators believe that the *Gita* is an elaboration of the advice of an actual Krishna, as the similarity to the teaching of Ghora Angirasa, the teacher of Krishna, in the *Chandogya Upanishad,* suggests.

Readers of the poem are sometimes confused by Krishna's attempt to incite the warrior Arjuna to violent action. But Krishna is not defending war as such, and Arjuna is advised to fight always without passion or meanness. Life in this world must be accepted, but man must try to improve the world where possible—and he must understand that the concerns of this world are never more than a means to a higher end. It may be helpful to recall the story of Brahma's grandsons in the *Vishnu Bhāgavata* (VI, 5). The youths were instructed by their father, Daksha, in the life of action. But Narada taught the young men (15,000 in number) the path of renunciation as the preferable way of life. Daksha argued that the pursuit of earthly things must precede the life of the spirit. Men have obligations to the community and the race that must be fulfilled—the ashrama of the householder must come before that of the recluse. Sensory phenomena cannot be rejected as being of trivial importance until they are first discovered and understood. Dharma is of prime significance, but artha and kama must not be ignored.

[k] Cf. Zimmer [441], pp. 378ff.; scholars do not agree on whether the Sankya system or Vedantic monism is the dominant influence in the Bhagavata creed and in the *Gita.* Radhakrishnan describes the work as both metaphysics and ethics: "*brahmavidya* and *yogashastra,* the science of reality and the art of union with reality." (Radhakrishnan [327], p. 12.) It may be said that it provides a bridge between Hindu metaphysics and our study of political thought—which is, in the final analysis, concerned with the problem of action.

[l] Much of that attitude of mind that Max Weber considered the psychological (rather than logical) consequence of Calvinism is more or less explicit in the *Gita.* Although fundamentally a fatalist, Kautalya, the designer of the bureaucratic state, warns against defeatism and what we might call the psychology of determinism.

originally intended as an exhortation to the common soldier who lacked kshatriya motivation. The hesitation of the knight Arjuna, who has never before in the epic given any hint of such sensitivity, provides the occasion for a sermon on duty. Death, he is told, is preferable to defeat—or, put more strongly, the highest duty of the warrior is death in battle. This device was used by later philosophers to popularize Hindu theistic doctrine, and it was evidently acceptable to the brahmans because it provided a further justification of class differentiation and harnessed kshatriya dharma to religious conceptions. Such theistic sects as the Bhāgavatas, which directly influenced the *Gita,* did not break completely with orthodoxy, and it was not difficult to conceive of their deity as an emanation of the supreme principle of Brahmanism.

The *Gita* directs mystical experience away from contemplation and toward action, from esoteric knowledge to exoteric activity. And yet it is an exhortation against egoism, ambition, and greed, calling for the rejection of individuality as a value in itself and of the world as possession. Krishna asks that everything a man does be done as an offering to him.[20] The fruits of action are dedicated to God; they must therefore not be cherished by man. The philosophic poem thus offers an alternative to the world-renouncing ascetic ideal of the monk who severs his ties with everything that might distract him from his true ends. Worldly activity is valued in the *Gita* as long as it is not motivated by selfish desire. Motive was emphasized: man could find his salvation through disinterested action. It was not necessary to forsake the world in order to attain moksha. The *Bhagavad Gita* contends that man is in the world, though not of it.[m] "Out of attachment comes desire; from desire, fury and violent passion" and ultimately the ruin of man.[21] Living life in a mood of devotion to God, accepting but not attaching oneself to action leads finally to escape from karma. And so man is to accept and fulfill his duty without ever desiring that which does not have enduring worth. "Think of nothing but the act, never its fruits, and do not be seduced by inaction"—this is the message of Krishna.[22] In this anti-materialism the physical body itself, the very instrument of action, is discounted and devalued.

Caste gains in religious significance in such a philosophy, while, at the same time, the promise of salvation is offered to every man who leads a

---

[m] Hannah Arendt's discussion of Plato is of interest here because the predicament she claims existed for Plato is parallel in many respects to that of the *Gita.* "It is essential to remember that the element of rule, as reflected in our present concept of authority so tremendously influenced by Platonic thinking, can be traced to a conflict between philosophy and politics, but not to specifically political experiences. That is, experiences immediately derived from the realm of human affairs. One cannot understand Plato without bearing in mind both his repeated emphatic insistence on the philosophic irrelevance of this realm, which he always warned should not be taken too seriously, and the fact that he himself, in distinction to nearly all philosophers who came after him, still took human affairs so seriously that he changed the very center of his thought to make it applicable to politics. But the rule of the philosopher-king and the domination of human affairs by something outside its own realm are demanded precisely because, from the standpoint of philosophy as well as the philosopher, under no circumstances must they acquire a dignity of their own." ("What Was Authority?" in Friedrich [133], pp. 93f.)

life of detachment, pursuit of caste obligation, and devotion to God. Krishna holds out the hope of salvation even to the shudra who turns to him.[23] There is, however, some confusion in the poem as to whether deliverance can be attained in this life or only after death, and, if the latter, whether the soul must ascend the ladder of varna as the condition of salvation. Nor is it entirely clear whether man is sometimes or always the instrument of divine will, whether he is determined in his actions by his character, or free to choose the path of righteousness. Radhakrishnan interprets verse XVIII, 63 ("Thus has wisdom more secret than all secrets, been declared to thee by Me. Reflect on it fully and do as thou choosest") as meaning that Krishna is concerned that each man come to God by his own choice. Radhakrishnan compares this emphasis on man's freedom to decide for himself with the position of Duns Scotus: "since freedom of will is God's command, even God has no direct influence on man's decision. Man can cooperate with God's grace but he can also refrain from it."[24]

The attitude of enlightenment that marks the highest stage of self-realization may well reflect a doctrine older than the more "democratic" concept of devotion (bhakti), the love of the redeemer. Both knowledge and devotion are accepted means to salvation. Knowledge (jñāna) represents what Professor Sircar[25] refers to as the Absolutist view, and has as its goal absorption in the Absolute. Bhakti, the service of God and communion with him, is the Theist view. The appeal of the poem is both intellectual and emotional. But the combination makes for certain difficulties. The Supreme Being in the *Gita* is aloof and unconcerned (here the Absolutist view would seem to dominate the conception of God). Nevertheless Krishna describes himself as constantly active—and his action must inspire a similar activity in man ("there is nothing which I must get, and yet I labor forever"[26]). The Lord does not demand the immediate allegiance of all men, and he is tolerant of many ways of expressing worship. Each person, in fulfilling the prescribed social obligations of his varna in a spirit of equanimity, worships God.[27] Thus we find in the *Gita* an effective middle way between the passive, detached life (*nivṛtti*) and the energetic, worldly existence (*pravṛtti*).

The ideal of conduct recommended by Krishna could be described as asceticism of this world, and is comparable in some respects to the Calvinist ethic. Karma-yoga, the ethical principle at the root of the *Gita,* demands that the individual pursue his "calling,"[n] the vocation that has

---

[n] "It is well known that the Middle Ages conceived of society as an order fashioned by God in which every form of life, every estate, every profession, had its own ethico-religious ideal to which the individual had to adapt himself if he wished to be obedient to God. But it is only after Protestantism unequivocally condemned monasticism that this ideal passed into the foreground as a norm of life subordinate to none other." (Carlo Antoni, *From History to Sociology,* transl. Hayden White [Detroit, 1959], pp. 154f.) The condemnation of monasticism had its counterpart in the *Gita's* reaction to world-renouncing asceticism. A difference exists, of course, in that the calling is prescribed by the class into which one is born. Weber, in his study of Indian religion, does not attempt a comparison of the *Gita* with the Calvinist ethic, but inasmuch as he considers such religious movements as Buddhism to represent a variety

come to be understood as a kind of commission from God: "Be thou nought but my tool."[28] As in Calvinism, man's actions serve to glorify God. The *Gita* counsels man to act without becoming personally involved in the action; Calvinism, without consuming wealth in self-indulgence. Sensualism is condemned in both theologies, but the *Gita* goes beyond this to discourage any accumulation of wealth or power that would lead man away from his true interest. Man is to act without seeking success. Calvin says simply that "we will only follow such fortune as we may enjoy with innocence."[29] The cumulative effect of the Protestant doctrine and its theory of predestination as worked out by Calvin was to lead its adherents to find in worldly success the sign of salvation. This is a major distinction between the two systems of religious thought. In the doctrine of Krishna we do not find the uncertainty of salvation that contributed to the psychological consequences of Calvinism which so interested Weber.[o] In fact, it is the *certitudo salutis* that makes salvation possible. And, too, work has less value in and of itself in the *Gita*: Calvinism emphasizes the moral value of work, whereas in the Hindu poem it is work of moral value that is stressed. Like Calvinism, the teaching of the *Gita*—though influenced by the kshatriya ethos—is a rejection of much that we associate with the aristocratic way of life, such as indulgence, leisure, and the cultivation of mind for its own sake. But action is not to be directed toward specific goals in which the individual has a personal interest; it is anything but the expedient rationality of the bourgeois.

THE RATIONALIZED ACT

Although the territorial state represented a revolutionary departure from the tribal polity, the organizational model employed by the theorists of the new state (the authors of the arthashastra literature) borrowed images associated with the Aryan tribe—particularly the kshatriya ideal of the active man. But the kshatriya was always more the hero than the achiever, and in this sense the ideal of the selfless man depicted in the *Gita* is not a radical departure from the traditional figure of the knight. He is more political man than economic man. The Vedic hero, the man of action for its own sake, could never satisfy the requirements of the state, which, in this interlude between the simple and direct relationships of family,

---

of asceticism diametrically opposed to that of Calvinism, it is instructive to examine the teaching of the *Bhagavad Gita* (critical as it is of many fundamentals of Buddhist doctrine) in terms of the analysis Weber [424] employed in his discussion of the Calvinist mentality. The following comments differ from Weber's treatment of Calvinism in that they are necessarily confined to the content of the poem itself rather than to the effect of the doctrine on those who responded to its inspiration. Weber's analysis dealt not with Calvin's theology but with the mentality it helped to form.

[o] R. E. Hume ([187], p. 59 n.1) holds that the *Katha Upanishad* II, 20 and 23f. (cf. *Mundaka Upanishad* III, 2.3) and the *Svetāśvatara Upanishad* represent a foreshadowing of the strict Calvinist doctrine of election—a reaction to the typical Upanishadic doctrine of salvation through knowledge. Verse 20 (second valli) of the *Katha Upanishad* is one of the first expressions of the idea of grace (*prasāda*), though the conception appears in *Rigveda* X, 125.5. It might be mentioned that the *Katha* verse follows two which are identical with *Bhagavad Gita* II, 19f.

clan, and tribal leaders and the frozen pluralism of caste regulation, depended on a corps of administrative officials whose dominant loyalty would be to the state, but whose values would be more appropriate to its material interests. It may be said that the *Gita* and the philosophical currents it contains are an attempt to civilize the knight and turn his energies to the larger goals of the community. But it remained for such theorists as Kautalya to emphasize achievement and to declare that artha (material gain) was the fundamental principle of society.

In Vedic times warfare had been the sport of kings, the means of fulfilling the kshatriya duty and attaining glory and honor. The traditional literature on caste function continued to view war as its own justification, a positive good in itself and intrinsic to kshatriya dharma. By the age of empire (and implicit in the *Arthashastra* of Kautalya), war had ceased to be regarded as an aristocratic pastime having as its main objective military glory, and had come to be conceived as an instrument for strengthening the state and enriching its treasury. War is now serious business, not to be undertaken lightly and without weighing carefully the probabilities of success and defeat. The kshatriya ideal of honor in battle and the discounting (and even disparaging) of material profit were undoubtedly hindrances to empire-building. Traditionally the annexation of territory had not been approved, and conquest was not generally regarded as a means to power and wealth. The chakravartin (*cakravartin*) was regarded as the greatest of kings, the overlord, and not as the head of a comprehensive state controlled directly from the capital. This ancient ideal of *dharmavijaya*, "righteous conquest" or war motivated by considerations of glory rather than by material gain, is as old as the Vedas and has an important place in the *Mahabharata*. But this ideal was little esteemed by the ambitious architects and rulers of Magadha, the Gangetic state that was to become the core of the great Mauryan empire. Nor could the antimaterialism of heterodoxy and those sects whose beliefs eventually found expression in the *Gita* have been of political value to these statesmen except insofar as it represented a challenge to brahman power and encouraged a tractable population.

Kautalya retained the kshatriya ideal of action, but opposed the disinterested action idealized in religious theories that consider desire and acquisition responsible for the evils of the world.[p] Kautalya must be understood as attempting to liberate the heroic ideal from the debilitating influences of religion and from the older noble preoccupation with honor as the goal of action (which threatened to degenerate into idleness and superficiality as the knight's role became that of courtier). Although his image of man appears often to be close to the vaishya, Kautalya was not a champion of the lower orders of society. The *Arthashastra* quotes (for purposes of refutation) a statement to the effect that if one must choose between losing noble men or losing vulgar men, the latter is more serious

[p] *Arthashastra* I, 19 (p. 41): "Prosperity depends on effort . . . readiness is the king's vow." (The page references are to the second edition of the Shama Sastri translation [Mysore, 1923].) *Vide* pp. 196f. below.

in that it causes obstruction to work. No, Kautalya answers, "it is possible to recruit vulgar men since they form the majority of the people; for the sake of vulgar men nobles should not be allowed to perish; one in a thousand may or may not be a noble man; he it is who is possessed of excessive courage and wisdom and is the refuge of vulgar people."[30] Nobility, it would seem from this, is a quality of character rather than of birth, but the brahman minister was too committed to class ideology to have been convinced that noble virtues would often appear among the lower classes. If he was in truth Chandragupta's minister, the possibility of the low birth of his master[q] may account for the manner of expression. A number of passages from the *Mahabharata* state explicitly that the hero is made by the occasion and not simply born to the role. He who offers protection is king.

Kautalya, like Machiavelli (with whom he is frequently compared), combined a pessimistic view of man's nature with a belief that man can shape his own destiny if he is able to develop heroic stature and place the common good above private interest. In *The Prince,* Machiavelli speaks of a strange force, which he calls *fortuna*. He does not permit this force to justify pessimism and inaction. *Virtù* is, for him, the supreme value, and virtù—the ability to translate plans and ideas into practice—is man's response to fortuna. This courage and energy necessary for effective action are the essence of Kshatra, the distinguishing trait of the warrior and ruling caste in India. It is this quality that Kautalya saw as the antidote to the fatalism, passivity, and renunciation of the belief systems of his day. He, too, sees nature as fortuna (*śrī*) and life as the interplay between virtù and contingency. The rules of the battle (the image is extended to life itself) are those which the occasion dictates to the shrewd. Instead of action without regard for its results, we have action without regard for fate. Fatalism persists in Kautalya's world-view, but it is not resignation. This attitude is reflected in his somewhat cavalier regard for transcendent values. Man must supplement virtue with organization in order to preserve and extend the victories over fortuna and thus secure the social framework that moral virtues presuppose. In this Kautalya seems to agree that "the king is the maker of his age." The *Mahabharata* is often even more candid than Kautalya: "Right proceeds from might. . . . Right is itself devoid of command."[31]

The *Gita* admits that although man may act with detachment, without self-interest, and in faithful pursuance of duty, he can never be certain of the consequences of his actions nor even of the meaning of the act. He can never know what chain of action and reaction has been set in motion. (Hence philosophy throughout the ages has warned of the dangers of entanglement and advised man to be wary of the illusion of freedom.) Krishna, knowing that "all undertakings are enveloped by evil, as is fire by smoke," asks only that every act be of the nature of worship.[32] Kautalya is no less aware of the moral ambiguity of action. This ambiguity is

---

q Vide, pp. 369f. below.

especially apparent in the problem that the collectivity faces when it insists on its sovereignty yet judges the actions of the state by standards which exist for individual citizens who, by nature of their membership in the community, cannot claim such independence. Preoccupied as he was with a grand design for creating the basis of imperial power, Kautalya, the brahman counselor, could have no sympathy for a metaphysics such as Buddhism, which was interpreted as advocating nonaction and withdrawal as the condition for preserving the true freedom of man. (Ashoka, master of India, could afford to renounce war—but even so we have no record of Ashoka's disbanding his army.[r] And later kings who embraced Buddhism or Jainism did not reject war as an instrument of policy as Ashoka had done.)

Kautalya understood that disinterested action, such as that represented by the chivalric or Krishnaite ideal, could not build strong organizations, and that to renounce action altogether was to renounce the real world. His systematic theory in effect brings together the idealization of action, the concept of self-discipline (which had reached its fullest development in heterodoxy), the rajadharma tradition, a strong statement of the artha position ("on material gain depends the realization of dharma and desire"[33]), and the matsyanyaya[s] view of nature. What is new is the shaping of these concepts to the needs of the territorial state; the relating of economic, military, and religious models to the requirements of political institutions and political conduct; and the pervasive worldliness that tends to exalt the vaishya material function—merging the aristocratic ideal of action with the virtue of production, and even applying the fabrication image to political activity, as Plato and Machiavelli do.

Kautalya must have disregarded his fellow brahmans as those who must implement ideas and proceed by a "sense of the situation" reject those who remain in the pure world of images that need never entirely conform to reality. In Greek philosophy, however, contemplation and fabrication appear to have had an affinity that may be illustrated by Plato's craftsman who is guided by the "idea" of the object he creates—an idea that he imitates in the process of fabrication.[34] Contemplation is thus tied to the creative experience and the transformation of external reality; when applied to the political realm the image serves to justify the authority of the expert and to locate the source of authority in the supernatural. We might speculate that the great brahman, inspired with the idea of empire, ultimately reconciled his own traditional function with the requirements of state-building in a similar fashion. As Plato sought to preserve philosophy, so Kautalya knew that the brahmans, if they were to survive, must relate their roles more realistically to the complexities of political life.

It is worth recalling Professor Voegelin's suggestion that the abstract

---

[r] The Great Rock Edict no. 10 is evidence of the emperor's attempt to replace the ideal of valor with that of piety, which was considered to be attainable by all but was thought to be more difficult for those of high status to attain.

[s] The world belongs to the strong—literally, the law (*nyāya*) of the fishes (*mātsya*).

cosmic principle of China and the less complex symbolism it in fact made possible contributed to a conception of social order dependent not on the emperor alone (as Son of Heaven), but on councilors and bureaucrats as well.[35] Instead of being projected into the cosmic order, political events were confined to the area of human activity—which was conceived in terms of power and conflict, a model inappropriate to the impassive transcendent realm. If this hypothesis is valid, we might ask whether the triumph of the Mauryan secular administration in the later fourth and third centuries B.C. may not have had some philosophical relation to the emergence in Indian culture of a comparable cosmic principle several hundred years earlier. The conception of a soul or "self" seeking identification with the cosmic force left the ritualistic sacrifice far behind.

But the bureaucrat acquired a charismatic quality only toward the end of the Mauryan epoch, and then it was hardly comparable to that of the Confucian scholar. In India, it was rather a case of justifying material and secular ends as important in their own right, legitimate human pursuits that the increasing differentiation of the cosmic and human realms may have indirectly encouraged. And when salvation had become more distinctly a private affair, the state was allowed a freer scope for its activities than could have been the case in the age of brahman supremacy.

A clearly perceived tension between sacred and profane could produce either the spirit of world-renunciation and asceticism or the frank acceptance of the contrary demands of the two levels of existence. Other ancient Oriental empires were established before such a differentiation took place, and in India a vestige of the older amalgamation of the religious and the political survived in the concept of the chakravartin or *sarvābhauma,* the world emperor, whose role was analogous to that of the ruler of the cosmic order.[t] In the Christian era new invasions from the northwest tended to restore the older cosmological analogy—with new implications for the theory of the king's divinity.[u]

As organization (in the sense of arrangements entered into by men for the accomplishment of specific purposes) spreads into more and more areas of social life, we might expect that the "historical imagination" would begin to capture the minds of men. The sociological and philosophical are linked in the awareness of man's new capacity for controlling forces external to himself and achieving definite objectives through a hierarchical system of command and coordination—as compared to his former dependence on the magically induced correspondence of the political order with the natural order. The belief in the efficacy of united effort encouraged man to see new possibilities in his environment: the world need not be the same tomorrow as it is today. The cyclical view of time is thus tempered. Once the nobles became involved in actual state-

---

[t] Even here Achaemenid influence may have been more important than Indian tradition.

[u] After the Mauryan state collapsed, a hierarchical quasi-feudal structure took its place. Though we must exercise a certain caution in using the term "feudal," the titles of Kushan chieftains imply a relationship of lord and feudatory, and the existence of a collection of tributary political units.

making, molding a portion of the world to their purposes, the universe began to lend itself to human comprehension in ways that would not have appeared possible in the age when the power to transform was attributed to the gods alone. Thought loses its esoteric character and becomes instrumental to action.

The theory is complicated by the fact that there are two basic types of organization reflecting two goals that are present in varying degrees in every ordered collectivity. Where the attainment of a particular objective (the winning of a battle, the making of a decision, the production of a commodity, and so forth) is of major importance, a sense of the future emerges, a feeling of expectation and, commonly, of optimism. These are responses not generally associated with the cyclical view of time, based as it is on the concept of the eternal return. But where the organization is more concerned with its own survival and the maintenance of its equilibrium—goals which eclipse the express purposes that were its original justification, or which persist after those purposes have been achieved—we are confronted with a different situation.*v* This is the problem that Michels, believing such a transformation of means into ends to be the inevitable fate of all social organization, termed in its political aspect the "iron law of oligarchy."[36]

During the change from "instrumental" organization to that type in which integrative needs and mechanisms are given a higher priority than the mobilization of facilities to accomplish a specific purpose,*w* we may observe important modifications in the structure of authority. Authority is less likely to be based on rational knowledge, expert skill, or extraordinary power of some kind, than on the fact of incumbence in office. And as *dux* becomes *rex*, as the "representative" tribal organization gives way to the "punishment-centered" state,[37] the purposes of the ruling elite diverge from those of the other members of the collectivity. With this dissensus in ends, obedience comes to be stressed for its own sake. Formerly, values and shared purposes made possible noncoercive types of socialization and social control. In the later development, the integrative requirement of organization can no longer be ignored. There are now different purposes or claims to be related and reconciled. This amounts to saying that dharma must be supplemented with danda; punishment is necessary to bring the purposes of one part of the community into line with the purposes of the other.

The empires of ancient Persia that may have inspired Kautalya were

v "Whatever the plans of their creators, organizations, say the natural-system theorists, become ends in themselves and possess their own distinctive needs which have to be satisfied. Once established, organizations tend to generate new needs which constrain subsequent decisions and limit the manner in which the nominal group goals can be pursued." (Alvin Gouldner, "Organizational Analysis," in Merton [267], p. 405.

w It should be noted that some organizations have as their purpose the gratification that membership itself provides. Our concern here is not with associations of this type but with those organizations which, as Parsons expresses it, "produce an identifiable something which can be utilized in some way by another system." (*Vide* "A Sociological Approach to the Theory of Organizations," in [317].)

often extensively bureaucratized (as in the case of the Achaemenid state), but they functioned less as agencies for the realization of the collective purposes of the people than as "punishment-centered" bureaucracies intent largely on their own perpetuation and aggrandizement. In such a structure the empire comes to be seen as universal in the scope of its authority, and the king seeks to derive (tautologically) his authority from his own exalted position in society and its correspondence with that of the chief of the gods.[a] The cosmological style of symbolization finds its fullest expression. The conservative ideological implications of the cosmological-correspondence symbolization are generally congenial with the interests of the ruling groups.

This type of organization, which stresses the integrative elements necessary to the survival of the collectivity, is personified in the brahman, whose function is largely equilibrating and whose concern is the preservation of order. But the brahmans could offer little in the way of organizational concepts, and the priests did not represent a positive affirmation of worldly existence. Ironically it was a kshatriya who figured as the most influential force in the triumph of the spirit of quiescence and the sacralizing of experience, and who stood in a relationship to the brahmans as did the world-decrying prophet to the magisterial technician-priests. When a disciple of the Buddha, the emperor Ashoka, adopted the new religion as an appropriate basis for the organismic state, the importance of organization must have become apparent to the brahmans. And now as different religious ideals began to compete with the traditional ideology for the king's favor, the brahmans were forced into closer collaboration with the ruling clique—in what amounted to a return to the ancient partnership in the sacrifice of officiating brahman and sponsoring king.

The role of the brahman had become that of legitimating the royal power and harmonizing the diverse interests of social groups. Whereas the function of the sacrifice had been to ensure victory, the later collaboration of *regnum* and *sacerdotium* in Hindu culture guaranteed the caste division of rights and duties. Caste ultimately replaced the system of ministers, officials, and superintendents as the major regulating mechanism. This was the concluding phase of the evolution of control from the tribal struggles for hegemony and the competitive operations of incipient capitalism, later rationalized in the imperial bureaucracy and state controls over the economy, to a system that distributed social functions on the basis of birth into certain social stations. The state had become the punishment-wielding power, ensuring that the order remained "self-regulating." By the beginning of the Christian era, the shoots of capitalist enterprise had withered and all but died.

What remained of the more virile culture of the Vedic age was the idea of the exceptional man who is able to remake the world—the "historical man" who emerges to save the dharmic order from whatever decay

---

[a] In the post-Mauryan period of Indian history we actually find several instances of states in which the king functioned as the vicegerent of a god—who was conceived to be the true ruler.

may be at work in the structure. This is the avatar or chakravartin, who retires into legend once the cosmic order is re-established. Never was the point reached where a whole people came to be regarded as having a historical mission, as happened in ancient Israel.

Archaic man, as Eliade remarks, when "placed between accepting the historical condition on the one hand, and his reidentification with modes of nature on the other . . . would choose such a reidentification."[38] In the transition from the archaic to the cosmological, the modes of nature had perhaps become less "natural"; a society regulated mainly by kinship and tribal norms and the ideals of the heroic culture was eventually replaced, not by a rational administration designed to develop and coordinate the resources of society for the realization of collective goals, but by what we might call the "integrative" organization, which saw itself, if not as a replica of the cosmos as such, at least as the embodiment of the moral principle embedded in the cosmic order. It was the complete triumph of the organizational concept over the political. The state itself had paled into relative insignificance by the later Gupta period. The oligarchic tribal polity, that still flourished at the time of the Buddha, was a political structure in which a representative segment of the community participated in making decisions, and an appreciable number were treated as the social equals of those in positions of power. The new forms of integration, the territorial state and caste stratification, were hierarchical; no longer was there a place for the older political arrangements. Kautalya sought a centralized government by experts; caste represented a return to a traditionalist type of legitimation.[y]

All of this is relevant because of the central importance for our study of the centuries from the close of the Vedic period to the establishment of Magadha as the most powerful state in India. In this period the rudimentary forms and processes of capitalism made their appearance and there was a systematic attempt to build a rational bureaucracy for the purpose of unifying the Gangetic plain and, ultimately, all of Aryan India. The development of the organizational apparatus by the Mauryans and their ministers made possible a centralization of control that had never been known before. And the organization, when it succeeded in eliminating the contingencies of the world, left the hero without his stage.[z] Virtù is dependent on fortuna.

History also becomes irrelevant as men approach the organizational utopia. There remains only a need for the administration of things (as

[y] Unlike the Greeks, the Indians had difficulty seeing the state as a natural product, and so were also less likely to see it as an ideal. It is the system of social roles (the Purusha analogy, etc.) that was considered the reflection or worldly symbolization of the principle of order that governed the universe; the state was viewed primarily as an instrument of that transcendent principle of order and justice. Punishment is the very essence of the political function. We might surmise that the priests, who wished to prevent too close an identification of the political and the cosmic, encouraged such a conception of the province of government.

[z] Cf. Wolin [434], p. 423: "The special irony of the modern hero is that he struggles in a world where contingency has been routed by bureaucratized procedures and nothing remains for the hero to contend against."

Lenin put it). In the process men themselves tend to become things. Their actions are less the expression of their personality than the necessary responses to the requirements of the system. Achievement and performance have taken the place of the expressive symbolism of the act. Man stands apart from his own action—as though he had acquired the psychological consequences of the message of the *Gita* without the ethical content that justifies such alienation.

In India the heroic ideal revived from time to time, particularly under the Rajputs, who typified kshatriya values, and, in the seventeenth century, with the martial programs of the Marathas and Sikhs. But soteriology, class solidification, and the imperatives of polity had crippled the ancient ideal irreparably. In the imperial state, which we turn to now, there was no longer a place for the old heroic ideal apart from the purposes of the state.

10 ⁕ THE EMPIRES OF ANCIENT INDIA

THE RISE OF MAGADHA

The seventh century B.C. was notable not only for the appearance of new religions but also for the consolidation of political units into a number of independent kingdoms. There were at this time at least sixteen kingdoms in India north of the Vindhya range, but by the sixth century four Gangetic states had become the major actors in Indian politics: Kosala (the realm of the legendary figure Rama), Vatsa, Avanti, and, destined for greatness, Magadha. Magadha controlled strategic sectors of the major trade routes of northern India—via both land and water. And Magadha had access to the important iron deposits. These were the primary economic foundations of an expansion that culminated in the vast imperial system of the Mauryas. "In its own way," Kosambi has remarked, "it corresponds to the Roman Empire in Europe."[1] In this process of consolidation, popular institutions were gradually replaced by forms of government more amenable to the political integration of large areas.

Max Weber[2] and, more recently, several other scholars have remarked on a fact often overlooked in studies of ancient Indian history. Contemporary with the rise of powerful territorial states, and more than simple coincidence, was the appearance of capitalist enterprise. The Ganges provided a natural trade route, and wealthy nobles, beginning to move to urban centers to spend their rent, provided a market. The city, which had begun its development in the eighth and seventh centuries B.C., ceased to be primarily a fortress as opportunities for the accumulation of wealth through trade expanded. The king became increasingly dependent on the guilds, and the financial power of these craft and merchant associations qualifies them for comparison with those of medieval Europe. But the Indian guilds never developed an organization capable of resisting the state's efforts to meet expenses by means other than capitalistic tax farming. The new mercantile class, with its need for security of property and an orderly setting for business operations, could be expected to lend willing support to the autocracies of the Gangetic plain. And in return for financing the imperial ambitions of the prince, these merchants often gained important rights and privileges. Wealth made possible greater social mobility, and it was not uncommon for members of the lower orders of society to attain positions of prestige. We know that the Mauryan dynasty employed a considerable number of shudra officials.

The *purāṇas* (compendia of ancient legends and lore covering a wide variety of topics) do not provide a reliable account of the rise of Magadha, and the Sinhalese *Mahāvaṃsa,* a Buddhist text, is now usually taken as the basis for reconstructing the early history of the kingdom. In the time of the Buddha and the Persian emperor Cyrus, Magadha was ruled by the efficient and resolute Bimbisāra, a man distinguished for military prowess and administrative acumen, who knew what to do with territory after he had conquered it. Bimbisara reigned for fifty-two years before his death at the hand of his own son (eight years before the Buddha's own demise). Ajātaśatru, his son, succeeded in establishing hegemony over neighboring kingdoms and republics, incorporating, among other states, the once-powerful Kosala. By the fourth century B.C. Magadha—its capital now at Pāṭaliputra (modern Patna)—controlled the basin of the Ganges and the area as far north and west as Rajasthan and the Punjab. The foundations of imperial Magadha had been well laid by the Nanda rulers when the remarkable Chandragupta Maurya entered the scene.

Plutarch has written that "Androkottos himself, who was then but a youth, saw Alexander himself."[3] The discovery by the early Sanskritist Sir William Jones that "Androkottos" (sometimes "Sandrocottos") referred to Chandragupta is one of the great chronological anchors of Indian history. Alexander left the Punjab in 324 B.C., having dramatized the military weakness of the small states of northwestern India. It is difficult to reconstruct the ensuing campaign of Chandragupta against the Greek forces. Justin says simply that one Sandrocottos was responsible for liberating India after the death of Alexander. The Greek position had deteriorated, morale was low, and the conquered peoples proved difficult to govern. Chandragupta, already having proclaimed himself king, engaged his army in a series of battles with Greek forces that must have preoccupied him until Eudemus and his troops retired from the Punjab in 317, ending the threat of the Greek garrisons and leaving Chandragupta supreme in the northwest.

But he had managed during this time to march on Magadha, turning an almost certain disaster resulting from poor strategy into victory. Pataliputra was besieged, the Nanda ruler killed, and Chandragupta was anointed by his adroit brahman minister, Cāṇakya (or Kautalya), c. 321. The *Mudrārākṣasa,* a political play of the Gupta era, suggests that a palace revolution may have placed the Mauryas on the Nanda throne, and it is of course possible that some such intrigue may have been involved. The Mauryan ruler's position was finally secured by his triumph in 305 over the Greek king Seleucus, Alexander's successor in the eastern reaches of the empire, who sought to reclaim the area that had been lost. The Greek sources enlighten us little on this conflict, but they do state that Seleucus ceded extensive territories to the Indian leader in return for 500 war elephants—an exchange which indicates that Chandragupta had the upper hand. At the time Seleucus surrendered Afghanistan and Baluchistan, the Indian army is reported to have numbered 650,000 men, 30,000 cavalry, 9,000 elephants, and 8,000 chariots. Arrian maintains that these soldiers were paid so well that they supported themselves and their dependents with comparative ease. Even allowing for the usual exaggeration in these figures, the burden on the Mauryan treasury must certainly have been enormous.

Although the sources present us with a number of problems, we probably know more of Mauryan polity than of any other period before the rise of the Mogul dynasty. The administrative organization and regulations of Kautalya[a] are generally taken to be a description of the Mauryan system. However, the *Kautaliya* never purports to give an account of a specific polity. It is a theoretical work, and any attempt to deduce more than the broad outlines of the Mauryan administrative system from it must bear this in mind. Despite its formal structure it is a *shastram,* a philosophical study. Those who insist on a late date for the Kautalya *Arthashastra* are usually willing to concede that the work refers to conditions which, by the Mauryan epoch, had come to characterize Indian polity. The *Arthashastra* is supplemented by the observations of the Greek ambassador to the Mauryan court, Megasthenes, who exists for us only through citations in the subsequent writings of Diodorus, Strabo, the elder Pliny, Plutarch, Justin, and Arrian. In a recent article, R. C. Majumdar argues that the classical writers had little confidence in Megasthenes' veracity; his *Indika* was not highly regarded.[4] Arrian considered his descriptions generally unreliable: Megasthenes did not take pains to verify what he heard and frequently recorded quite fantastic things. It would appear that classical writers were not as influenced by the accounts of Megasthenes as Indologists have assumed. It must be remembered also that Megasthenes was presumably describing Magadhan institutions in terms that would be meaningful to his countrymen. His extravagant description of Magadha under Chandragupta may have been partially inspired by a desire to make of India an example for his fellow Greeks. India, a land of villages and country states, does not translate well into the vocabulary of the city-state, although some similarities are no doubt present. If this allowance is made, the differences between his account and Kautalya's are not significant. For the later Mauryan period the most reliable information comes from the imperial edicts—pillar and rock inscriptions—of the Emperor Ashoka (*Aśoka*). Perhaps the greater number of these inscriptions had no binding authority. They were essentially the idealistic pronouncements of a spiritual leader.

There is some question about the class origin of Chandragupta. The Punjabi king, Porus, is reported by Curtius to have told Alexander that the Nanda king ruling at this time was of low birth—a barber who had become the queen's lover and accomplice in the assassination of the former king. Mahāpadma, the founder of the dynasty (c. 364 B.C.), is described in the puranas as another Paraśurāma (the exterminator of the warrior

[a] The *Arthashastra* of Kautalya will be discussed in some detail in Chapters 11 and 12 below.

class). If we are to believe the Buddhist sources, the youngest of the nine Nanda brothers, and the last to rule, was begotten by a man of unknown origin, probably a shudra. Plutarch reports that Chandragupta referred to the base origin of his predecessor, which suggests his own higher status. Kautalya accepts him as a kshatriya, but it is likely that the role of king conferred kshatriyaship by this time. Foreign sources reveal nothing about Chandragupta's alleged humble origin, and there is little evidence to indicate that he himself was of the Nanda dynasty, as some have held. The theory that Chandragupta came from the lower orders runs counter to the puranas and the Buddhist literature. However, the -gupta suffix was most common among members of the vaishya class. Professor Mookerji believes that the clan name Moriya provides a more convincing explanation of the dynasty name Maurya than other theories (such as those which would derive the name from "Mura," suggesting humble birth).[5] This argument is based on Buddhist tradition, which holds that the emperor was the son of the chief of this clan.

By the time Chandragupta's son Bindusāra ascended the throne in the early years of the third century B.C., the empire of the Mauryas had reached vast proportions. It was divided and subdivided into provinces,[b] divisions, districts, and villages. Most large empires followed this administrative pattern. Members of the royal family often served as provincial governors: Ashoka, Chandragupta's grandson, served his apprenticeship in this capacity. In the absence of princes, military officers respected for their valor were appointed to these governorships. The talent for military leadership was a necessary qualification, since the governors were responsible for preserving order and protecting the marches of the empire. The provincial governors maintained their own courts and ministerial councils, and, owing to the difficulty of communication with the central government, autonomy tended to vary proportionately with distance from the imperial capital.

Megasthenes mentions three groups of officials: the *agronomoi*, district officials; *astynomoi*, town officials; and the War Office. The district officials superintended irrigation and surveying, hunting, agriculture, metallurgical and forest industries, mining, and road maintenance. The town officials were attached to six boards of five members each, which were charged with the care of foreigners, supervision of factories, registration of vital statistics, inspection of goods, collection of taxes, and regulation of certain marketing operations. The committee of the War Office dealt with affairs of the admiralty, transport and supply, the cavalry, the elephants, the chariots, and the infantry. A headman (*grāmaṇī* in the village, *gopa* in the town), guided by the panchayat of elders, supervised the affairs of the smallest administrative units. He was registrar, tax administrator, and general arbiter. Villages were classified according to the contribution they made to the central government: those supplying troops, those giving free labor, those providing produce instead of taxes, those paying in either grain or coin as they wished, those exempted.

[b] Avantiraṣṭra, Dakṣinapatha, Kalīnga, Prāchya, and Uttarāpatha are known to us today.

Mauryan administration seems to have involved two coordinate divisions of government: city and country. This division was continued into succeeding centuries.[6] At this time the cities of the realm, like other corporate entities, enjoyed a high degree of independence. The central government rarely interfered with the administration of local affairs, and Megasthenes hints that at least some of the cities had arrived at a democratic form of government.

Pataliputra, the capital city, was located at the point where the river Son joins the Ganges. It is described as a handsome city, more than nine miles in length, about one and a quarter miles broad, and surrounded by a moat sixty feet deep and two hundred yards wide. A timber palisade with sixty-four gates and 570 towers ran along the moat. It is possible that the audience hall at Pataliputra was modeled after a design used at Persepolis. The social and economic activities of the city were, for the most part, administered by the thirty-member council.

The king relied mainly on his chief minister (*mantri*) and on his purohita. Three or four councilors composed his immediate advisory cabinet, and there was a larger council, or mantri-parishad, charged with the execution of royal orders. The central government had eighteen departments headed by *tirthas*.[c] A committee of five superintended the operations of each department, and a number of inspecting officers served to coordinate the activities of all departments. There were also military and economic officials. As administration increased in complexity, the power of the ministers grew. By the later Mauryan era evidence of ministers' refusing to execute the orders of the king can be found.

Reconciling bureaucratic responsibility with autocratic control must have posed a major problem for the Mauryan ruler. The position of the minister may have been similar in some respects to that of the present-day Soviet bureaucrat confronted with the demand for efficient administration by a government reluctant to delegate the control over resources necessary for such efficiency because it fears the development of independent centers of power in the bureaucracy. As a consequence of such a dilemma the central government is burdened with the details of administration. Megasthenes reported that the Mauryan king was kept so busy that his daily rubdown with wooden rollers had to take place while he continued to hear cases in court. The ministers were appointed by the king, whose actions they advised in the interests of the people (at least in theory); they were usually chosen for their disposition to judge impartially and for those qualities of character that Hindu doctrine identified with the governing classes. There was no actual check on the executive power, although sacred law supposedly guided the policy of the king and he was expected to have the advice and approval of his ministers before acting. Chandragupta and his successors took on considerable legislative power, and the *Arthashastra* mirrors this new emphasis on the sovereign authority of the king's law.

The state described by Megasthenes and outlined in the *Arthashastra*

---

[c] It is not clear from evidence we have whether department heads were generally distinguished from ministers.

is a bureaucratic polity—perhaps a resurrection of the ancient Harappa administrative pattern. This power structure, centered in a great citadel within the walled city of Pataliputra, might be described as a mixed system of rational and bureaucratic relationships on the state level, with guild, tribal, and caste associations absorbing residual administrative functions. These associations were destined to increase in importance—until by Gupta times the situation had reversed and the state was all but reduced to military and diplomatic functions.

In referring to the Mauryan bureaucratic structure, we imply a distinctively political area of activity with its own characteristic roles and purposes, which can be differentiated from the institutions, organizations, and goals of economic, religious, and other sectors of society. Chandragupta had established himself as a relatively independent force in politics, possessing a new freedom from tribal, clan, and caste restrictions and able to develop and pursue his own ends through agencies which were not affiliated with and legitimated by other social groups, but which were committed rather to the king and the governing elite. The function of these organizations was to implement policy by mobilizing material resources and popular support.[d]

In addition to the struggle for power in the bureaucracy itself (particularly the attempt to prevent the growth of clusters of power within the hierarchy), there is of course the larger struggle between the political decision-making group and other foci of power within the community. Mauryan consolidation was aided by the failure of traditional institutions to integrate and stabilize society effectively and to cope with changes capable of disrupting equilibrium. The territorial expansion of the earlier Magadhan rulers and the Mauryas made available new sources of wealth and power, which also served to upset the established position of different groups in society. We have earlier indicated that members of the lower classes began to gain at least some measure of prosperity as economic advances created new demands for their services. By encouraging the organization of a money economy and the increase in the volume of international trade and contacts with the Hellenistic world, the Mauryan rulers hastened the decline of the isolation upon which the traditional society depends for the preservation of the customary and the sacred.[e] The shrewd

---

[d] We assume here that hierarchical patterns employed in the administration of large territories may take the form of (1) rational bureaucracy, characterized by the allocation to each post of rights and duties that are arranged in a definite chain of command with relationships assuming an impersonal and formal nature, or (2) charismatic bureaucracy, which is characterized less by loyalty to office than by loyalty to the person of the leader. Charismatic bureaucracy may be a totalitarian bureaucracy, which allocates functions and responsibilities frequently without requisite control of necessary facilities, or it may be patrimonial bureaucracy, which amounts to an extension of the ruler's household and introduces a paternal element into the relation of the leader to his subordinates. (Though the latter may acquire hereditary land grants, they remain more like bureaucratic officials than vassals.) Decentralized types of control (i.e., control over areas of limited size) include the household, dominated by the patriarch; the feudal relationship, based on a contract that stipulates rights and duties instead of the paternal relationship; *polis* democracy; and the tribal, caste, or village council of elders or influential members of the community.

[e] As early as the sixth century B.C. trade united Magadha with Persia. Silver coins attest to this development.

Kautalya may have seen the consequences of territorial expansion and concentration of political power, and may have sought to utilize these developments to strengthen the brahman position by encouraging the expansion of Aryan culture, curtailing the growing influence of heterodox religion (especially an alliance with the state), and providing an effective check on the kshatriya nobility. But the motives of the brahman minister we may only surmise.[f]

Raising money to finance the extensive undertakings of the state without inducing widespread popular discontent must have called for considerable ingenuity. The war with Seleucus made further demands on the resources of the state, and, if the *Arthashastra* does in fact date from this period, we can easily understand its preoccupation with the financial needs of the state. Chandragupta, as we have noted, maintained a vast army numbering hundreds of thousands of troops. The Greek ambassador remarked that the soldiers constituted a "class" second only to the agriculturists in size. They were salaried and equipped by the state, and when not fighting, which was their only duty, they "abandon themselves to enjoyment."[g]

Mauryan economic policy eventually had the effect of pushing production into the villages. As a part of the program to augment the wealth of the state, Chandragupta established many village communities, which appear to have been subject to extensive controls by the bureaucracy, although they often became virtually self-sufficient economic units.[h] The Mauryan king had the right of eminent domain over all the land in the kingdom. Evidently this right was so broadly interpreted in the Mauryan state that it suggested to Greek observers a parallel with Egypt, where the king owned the land. Export and import duties, excise and *octroi* taxes were often burdensome, but despite this and the fact that the Mauryan king did not encourage small private enterprise as such, commerce expanded and Megasthenes was able to comment enthusiastically on the prosperity of Magadha. With land taxes sometimes reaching a third of the yield, the coffers filled. The state operated the mines, supervised the forests, managed its own dairy, cotton, sugar, and oil industries, and controlled the manufacture and sale of liquor.

The government provided many public services, which included rural development programs and experimental farms for the improvement of

[f] In terms of basic forms of social organization it would appear that the tribal group represented a greater challenge than the bureaucratic state to the caste order. We might go so far as to say that though it brought with it a certain leveling of society, the Mauryan state in its struggle with the older tribal elements found that the alternative to the former horizontal divisions involved social controls that only the system of sanctified stratification could provide.

[g] Megasthenes records also that they had hired attendants to wait on them, so that evidently they were well paid. This may indicate that their loyalty was uncertain and that the king was forced to purchase their allegiance. Chandragupta's title to the throne rested on conquest, and suspicions about his origin may have threatened his legitimation.

[h] "The idiocy of village life was carefully fostered as a state economic measure; for the increased wealth which was hardly any use to the villager found its way into the hands of the state, which supplied him with cattle, tools, utensils, on its own terms and charged heavily for irrigation and any special service." (Kosambi [218], p. 219.)

crops and animals. The dharmic code dictated a charitable program, and the state provided for the less fortunate members of the community. Food was allotted to the hungry, and care given to orphans, the sick (animal as well as human), and the aged. Travelers and foreigners in distress were similarly provided for. Places of worship and entertainment were sponsored and subsidized by the government. The forests were made to yield scholarship as well as timber; the government set up learning "reservations," and was as assiduous in furthering education as in backing religion. The state also sought to protect the consumer from fraud and from unauthorized commodity prices. A series of judicial bodies, ranking from the village court, presided over by the headman, to the imperial court, administered the law. With the possible exception of the village court, these bodies differentiated between criminal and civil cases.

The Mauryan emperor, or his representatives, conducted periodic tours of outlying regions to renew contacts with the people as well as to inspect provincial administration. Megasthenes reports that the king relied on spies. There were apparently so many of these special agents that the Greek concluded that they constituted a separate class in the Mauryan state. It was their duty to relate to the king or the magistrates everything that transpired in the cities and army and countryside. Prostitutes were often employed in this way. The attention Kautalya devotes to the intelligence system may reflect the importance attached to spying activities in the Mauryan empire. The spies and the army may be said to have been the pillars of the Mauryan power, making possible the reasonably effective administration of a great territory in a time when transportation and communication systems were still primitive.[i]

Although slavery was recognized in Hindu theory, slaves were treated with more human consideration than was the case in most ancient states. Megasthenes claimed that the institution did not exist, which may indicate that by the time of the Mauryas many slaves were receiving their freedom and the worst evils of the system were being abolished.

THE REGIME OF ASHOKA MAURYA

Occasional shafts of light pierce the dense tangle of the Indian past and reveal the teaching of a religious virtuoso, the career of a monarch, the exploits of a hero. The reign of the emperor Ashoka in the third century B.C. left its monument in the form of inscriptions that remain to us today. These records make it possible for us to reconstruct the heyday of Mauryan power with some confidence. The empire of Ashoka, the last great Mauryan king, embraced all of India with the exception of the Tamil country at the southern extremity, stretching north to the Hindu Kush and Kashmir and Nepal.[j]

The chronicles of Ceylon, the *Dīpavaṃsa* and *Mahāvaṃsa,* probably

---

[i] We are not certain whether regular embassy posts were established. Ambassadors were often primarily envoys of good will, or were intent on specific missions, such as negotiating commercial or diplomatic treaties, or espionage.

[j] Kāmarūpa (modern Assam) seems to have remained outside the empire.

dating from the fourth and fifth centuries A.D., tell us something of the period of Ashoka's reign, although these Buddhist sources can hardly be considered disinterested commentaries. The chronicles state that Chandragupta ruled for twenty-four years, Bindusara for twenty-eight years followed by a four-year interregnum, and Ashoka for thirty-seven years. Ashoka was apparently not the crown prince, and the sources touching on his early reign indicate a struggle for power among the Mauryan princes—which would account for the four-year interval after the death of his father. He acceded to the throne of Magadha in 269 or the following year.

Buddhist texts imply that Ashoka was extremely wicked before his conversion to the faith, but we may assume that this characterization is intended to dramatize the change wrought by the emperor's acceptance of the teaching. Accounts of conversions to Christianity are not free of such exaggerations, and some Augustine scholars believe that the saint deliberately overstated his own youthful sins and indiscretions in order to emphasize the power of his new-found faith. The distress and destruction caused by the war with Kalinga, in which, we are told, "150,000 persons were deported, 100,000 were slain, and many times that number died,"[7] are reputed to have had a profound effect on the great emperor, causing him to renounce future armed conquest and to dedicate himself to imbuing the world with the Buddhist ethic and sacred duty. But we can be reasonably sure that Ashoka's desire to control the routes to southern India must have been an important motive for the war. And with the defeat of Kalinga, Ashoka overcame the last significant obstacle to the control of India. (The edicts point to generally amicable relations with the kingdoms of the south, and there appears to have been no need for their subjection.) For all his remorse, it is interesting to note that Ashoka did not confess these feelings in Kalinga itself. To do so would surely have been unwise. We may, however, speculate that in embracing Buddhism, Ashoka had determined on a faith capable of cementing the empire he and his grandfather had built.[8] It may well be that Ashoka was not the first of his line to show partiality to a nonorthodox sect. His father is said to have been influenced by the Ājīvikas,[k] and Chandragupta himself very possibly became a Jaina in his later years.

The Buddhist chronicles are surprisingly quiet regarding the Kalinga war. The Ceylon texts do not refer to it, although it is commonly assumed to have been the event that stimulated the famous conversion. A recent study of Ashoka concludes that the emperor's acceptance of Buddhism actually preceded the Kalinga campaign.[9] In the Brahmagiri Minor Rock Edict (c. 256), Ashoka remarks that he has been a lay Buddhist for more than two and a half years, but, he says, "for a year I did not make much progress." His conversion thus seems not to have been the dramatic transformation that we have come to expect in such situations. After a year of exposure to the heterodox teaching, Ashoka was able to announce that at

---

[k] An ascetic group somewhat like the Jainas in the discipline that guided their conduct (*vide* Basham [23]).

last he had drawn close to the Order. The Bhabra edict (which was most probably intended for the monks of the sangha rather than for the general population) further attests to his acceptance of the major elements of Buddhism. But the dhamma, the expression of this ethic, is more a concept of social responsibility than a purely religious ideal.[10] Ashoka evidently did not seek to identify dhamma as a Buddhist principle, but rather tried to emphasize the universalist content of the idea and its freedom from any specific doctrinal roots. Dhamma represents a civic ethic, something that would not, of course, be stressed in orthodox Buddhism.

The Mauryan ruler made it clear that he considered the welfare and happiness of the people his mission; to bring them contentment in this world and heaven in the next is the purpose expressed in the Rock Edicts.[l] We know that Ashoka provided for groves of shade trees along the major highways of the realm to accommodate merchants and other travelers.[m] In the sixth Rock Edict he says that no matter where he is "in the enclosed [female] apartments, in the inner chamber, in the royal ranch, on horseback or in pleasure orchards, the Reporters may report people's business to me. People's business I do at all places."

But it was not the comfort of this world that most concerned the great king. Ashoka took it upon himself to establish a code of ethics that amounted to a rejection of the sacrificial cult and the brutalities and inequities it justified. The military program of his grandfather was replaced with a policy of "righteousness": only through dharma could lasting conquests be made. "The sound of drum has become the sound of Dhamma."[11] This was the basis of the practice of nonviolence (*ahiṃsā*) advocated by the Mauryan emperor. A more skeptical assessment might suggest that expansion was no longer profitable. The costs of maintaining the empire were more than the income from the less fertile Deccan could bear.[n] And yet, despite its cost and despite Ashoka's rejection of aggressive war, there is no mention in the edicts of his reducing the size of the imperial army. Ashoka, for all his dedication to humanitarian ideals, gives no evidence of having relaxed the methods of punishment prescribed by earlier Mauryan kings. Nor did the principle of nonviolence lead him to abolish capital punishment.

In the ninth year of his reign he embraced Buddhism, which, of all

---

[l] Rock Edict VI: "For the welfare of the whole world is an esteemed duty with me. . . . There is no higher duty than the welfare of the whole world. And what little effort I make is in order that I may render some happy here and that they may gain heaven in the next world." Probably the *Singālovāda Suttanta* or similar Pali texts are the source of the moral rules laid down in Rock Edict VI.

[m] "On the roads have I planted the banyan trees. They will offer shade to man and beast. I have grown mango-orchards. I have caused wells to be dug at every eight koses; and I have had rest-houses [built]. I have made many watering sheds at different places for the enjoyment of man and beast. This [provision of] enjoyment, however, is, indeed, a trifle, because mankind has been blessed with many such blessings by the previous kings as by me." (Pillar Edict VII. *Vide* also Rock Edict II.)

[n] Professor Kosambi makes the point that between the regimes of Chandragupta and Ashoka the silver content of coins was diminished from three-quarters to less than a third—and this debasement continued.

religions, he saw as the most perfect embodiment of ahimsa. Under the patronage of the great emperor the Buddhist ethic spread beyond the confines of the peninsula; within several centuries most of southern Asia was exposed to the religion, and during the first five centuries of the Christian era central Asia and the Far East came under Buddhist influence.[o] But tolerance was the keystone of official policy under Ashoka. "The king, beloved of the Gods,[p] honors every form of religious faith, but considers no gift or honor so much as the increase of the substance of religion; whereof this is the root, to reverence one's own faith and never to revile that of others. Whoever acts differently injures his own religion while he wrongs another's."[12] All men should respect the doctrines professed by others, and, in the administration of the realm, the customary law of different peoples must be allowed to prevail. The ideal had a secularizing effect on society for it must have meant the end of many special concessions and immunities to the priests. It should be noted that Rock Edicts III and IV recommend respectful and generous behavior toward brahmans as well as toward heterodox ascetics. More often than not the brahmans are mentioned in the edicts before the Buddhist holy men. These inscriptions indicate that Ashoka was always careful to avoid antagonizing the priests directly. But Ashoka certainly did not share the deference to the sacrificial order that marked Kautalya's acceptance of varna.[q]

It is relevant to ask at this point what dhamma (dharma) may have meant for Ashoka. Surely there had been a decisive modification in the concept as it developed from the Vedic rita. Under brahman influence, dharma had become intimately linked with caste. And though caste continued to be recognized by the Buddhists as an institution fundamental to social order, it had lost its former significance for personal salvation.

Despite the declared intentions of Ashoka, it can be argued that the tradition of royal patronage of religion had its real beginning in his regime. Although he counseled tolerance and demanded that men be restrained in their speech regarding religious matters and that all sects be allowed to flourish, Ashoka was intent on encouraging certain types of conduct and he must have infringed on religious freedom when he condemned practices such as the killing of animals for sacrifice. His very sympathy toward heterodox groups, his active proselytizing and establishing of missions, held a danger to the traditional balance of power. The royal authority had become the protector of sacred law in a way that was new to India. Government had always been an instrument of religion, but less actively so. Now the king must concern himself directly with the common good, an

---

[o] Migration, political upheaval, the development of sects, the brahmanic revival, and the Muslim conquests all contributed to the destruction of Buddhism as the basis of a common Asian civilization, and drove the religion from India—where it survives only in monuments and shrines. But elements of the Buddhist faith were assimilated by Hinduism, and in this highly altered form it survives.

[p] *Devānampiya*, "beloved of the gods," is the title Ashoka took for himself.

[q] But *vide* Mookerji [272], Appendix III, for parallels between the Rock Edicts and the *Arthashastra*. A number of the reforms undertaken by the king would appear to be the realization of changes proposed by Kautalya, if we are correct in assuming the earlier date of the *Arthashastra*.

idea anticipated in the *Arthashastra* (if it is not, indeed, Ashokan experience that inspired the ideal commonwealth of Kautalya).

Ashoka's conversion to Buddhism ended the ability of the brahman ministers to check the royal power. When the state combined Brahma and Kshatra in its own authority it approached a self-legitimating caesaropapism. And now there existed the opportunity for religion to become the instrument of government—in a more insidious fashion than that devised by the author of the *Arthashastra*. The individual could accept official policy or oppose it, but there were no effective agencies of protest and social change. Before the advent of Buddhism, the inchoate caste system had at least served as an intermediary institution between the individual and the state. Freedom was still only the freedom to prepare oneself for salvation. And here the state justified its intervention, since its function was conceived in moral terms. The state recognized no sphere of life beyond the pale of state regulation, and Ashoka himself decided what constituted the good of the people.[r]

We may wonder what law Ashoka employed in dealing with those, such as Jainas and Buddhists, for whom the traditional caste-based codes would have been inappropriate or inadequate. What replaced Brahmanical law? We should, of course, assume that the emperor relied on the usage and custom of non-Brahmanical peoples. But this would still require a technique for adjusting disputes arising among persons of different religious commitments. The development of positive law must have been at least in part the consequence of the need for equitable administration of a people professing a variety of faiths. To a considerable extent the tradition of pluralism, which allowed different groups to regulate their activities in accord with their own laws and customs, could be extended to these peoples. But there were always problems of conflicting local laws, and the secular authority would have to arbitrate such problems. This pattern of development may have been similar in some respects to the evolution of the Roman *ius gentium*. There were ample opportunities for Ashoka to promulgate law, and the emperor did in fact issue orders that cannot be called in any sense the application of customary or sacred law. He had appropriated the legislative function, although in theory the rules he handed down were in accordance with sacred law.

The Buddhist king governed directly, announcing his policy in imperial edicts which, whether of a civil or ecclesiastical nature (no careful delineation was made), were communicated to the citizens by his viceroys and

---

[r] Émile Durkheim discusses the relationship between the state and the group life of society in these words: "In holding its constituent societies in check, [the state] prevents them from exerting the repressive influences over the individual that they would otherwise exert. So there is nothing inherently tyrannical about state intervention in the different fields of collective life; on the contrary, it has the object and the effect of alleviating tyrannies that do exist. . . . [But] if that collective force, the state, is to be the liberator of the individual, it has itself need of some counterbalance; it must be restrained by other collective forces . . . " (*Professional Ethics and Civic Morals* [Glencoe, Ill., 1958], pp. 62f.) *Vide*, e.g., Hegel, *Philosophy of Right*, pars. 302f.

governors. Thirty-three of these inscriptions remain.[s] These edicts, which mirror the ethical ideas of the early Buddhist canonists,[t] are concerned with dhamma and methods of disseminating these ethical principles. The edicts are similar in expression to those of Darius. With several exceptions in the northwest, the inscriptions are in Prakrit (popular dialects) and are written in the Brāhmī script, which is usually read from left to right. The use of Prakrit indicates that the edicts were meant to be accessible to all literate men. Most of the Minor Rock Edicts are concerned exclusively with Buddhism and Ashoka's relation to the Order,[u] and the Minor Pillar Edicts are devoted to Ashoka's religious activities.[v] The pillar edicts date from the twenty-seventh and twenty-eighth years of his reign. They are his last testament. The seventh edict, which summarizes his achievements, is followed by ten years of silence. If the emperor left further records, they have yet to be discovered.

The central government undertook to propagate dhamma; in the fourteenth year of his rule Ashoka established a corps of dhamma-mahāmattas (dharma-mahāmātras) to serve as religious supervisors as well as welfare agents.[w] The mahamatta seems to have had access to the homes of all members of society. In the first pillar edict (twenty-seventh regnal year) we learn that it was sometimes necessary for these officials to persuade men who wandered from the true path. But we are not enlightened as to the form this persuasion takes. The dhamma appears to be more narrowly defined by this time and to have taken on the nature of a comprehensive civil code.

The higher officials were ordered to tour at regular intervals in order to learn the wishes of the people as well as to instruct them in the moral

[s] Fourteen Rock Edicts, the minor Rock Edicts, seven Pillar Edicts, and the minor Pillar inscriptions. Not all of the pillars are in the places in which they were originally inscribed. Many of the inscriptions begin with the phrase "Devanam-priyo Piyadasi Raja evam aha," "Thus saith King Priyadarshin, beloved of the gods." Ashoka refers to himself as Priyadarshi.

[t] It is not often observed that the emphasis of the Ashokan inscriptions has shifted to a value more "positive" than Nirvana; we learn of a heavenly reward (*svarga*) for pious and dutiful behavior in this life. (Cf. Rock Edicts IV, IX, XIII; Zimmer [441], pp. 499f.)

[u] These include the Bhabra and Rummindei edicts.

[v] Evidently Ashoka did not consider himself head of the sangha. Had he, he would surely have played a more instrumental role in convening the Third Council at Pataliputra.

[w] In Rock Edict V he relates that "Dhamma-mahamattas were created by me when I had been consecrated thirteen years. They are employed among all sects; and [are concerned with] the establishment of Dhamma, promotion of Dhamma, and the welfare and happiness of those devoted to Dhamma." In Pillar Edict IV he says: "They will make themselves acquainted with what gives happiness or pain, and exhort the people of the provinces so that they will find happiness in this life and the next. . . . Certainly, just as [a person] feels confident after turning over his children to a competent nurse, [saying to himself] 'the nurse desires the welfare of my offspring,' so have I appointed the rajukas for the welfare and happiness of the country people. In order that they may perform their duties without fear, confidently and willingly, I give them independent authority in judgment [reward] and punishment. But uniformity in administration and punishment is desirable." Although the *missi dominici* of the Frankish kings (with whom the mahamattas are compared) were charged with the promotion of religion, their duties were far more secular than those of the mahamattas.

life.[13] It could be argued that the emissaries of dharma were less expensive representatives of the law than the usual officials and soldiers (and the spies necessary to watch their activities).[14] Ashoka himself was frequently on the move. This entrusting of government officials with moral as well as political functions has been cited as the most important single innovation in the political organization of Ashoka's regime.[15] Every few years a council of administrative officials met to consider methods of promoting justice and advancing the ethical concepts which, in the Buddhist Law of Piety, were conceived as the foundation of religion.

In addition to illuminating Ashoka's religious faith and his missionary activity, the edicts tell us something of his administrative system. Two of the Rock Edicts (III and VI) refer to the Ashokan council. The ministers had the right to debate the orders of the king and his departmental advisors.[x] This was meant to imply not that the authority of the king was limited, but rather that the advice of the council should be sought before the people were informed by local officials of administrative decisions.[y] Members of the parishad appear to have been free to express opinions contrary to the king's, and, in the later years of Ashoka's regime, to have successfully deterred or modified actions contemplated by the king. Parts of the empire (especially frontier areas) were governed by local rajas, but the governors and district officers (*rājūkas* and *prādeśikas*) were the important administrative figures. One of the edicts grants these officials sovereign jurisdiction in governing the provinces. They need not fear contradiction from the central authority. Here is the first suggestion of the diminishing power of the central government.

The Buddhist legends imply that Ashoka's control began to loosen toward the end of his regime, but there is little of a specific nature to suggest how or where this weakening came about. In its attempts to regulate life—first in the material sphere, under Chandragupta and his able minister, and later in the spiritual, under Ashoka—the state at length overextended itself. Difficulties of communication and finance and pressures from discontented or ambitious elements of the community were to prove too much for the Mauryan state. If Magadha had been able to produce leadership of comparable talent, these obstacles might have been overcome. But such ability is rare: Chandragupta and Ashoka were, respectively, India's greatest organizer and India's greatest king.[z]

Although the economic, military, and religious policies of the Mauryan

[x] The third Rock Edict indicates that Ashoka's council did little more than approve the policies of the king. But in the sixth Rock Edict the authority of the ministers is somewhat greater, though the council is rarely more than an advisory body.

[y] The size of Ashoka's privy council is not known, but his father's is said to have numbered five hundred members.

[z] Thapar ([407], pp. 194f.), relying on passages in the *Kunālasūtra,* a Kashmiri account, has suggested that on the death of Ashoka the empire was partitioned between Kunāla and Ashoka's grandson, Daśaratha. Kunala, who governed in the west, was very possibly Ashoka's son. If this theory is correct, Kunala could be expected to have had administrative difficulties that the eastern empire, governed from Pataliputra and based on the organization inherited from Ashoka, would not have experienced. But evidence for all this is far from conclusive.

rulers and their innovations in political organization did not appreciably transform the daily life of the humbler member of society, the effects of their administrations must surely have altered the traditional social structure. By traditional (or communal) society we mean one in which norms and goals are established by custom, and there is little capacity for change and invention. Ascribed status determines the political elite, and social groups are relatively free of domination by the central authority or by other groups, and are able to control many aspects of their members' lives. When the state itself asserts control over these groups, the structure begins to take on a totalitarian character. Without the technological devices available to modern totalitarian states, the state could not hope to alter the behavior of the individual to the degree possible today. But indirectly, by controlling the economy, introducing new classes into political life and excluding others, actively promoting particular religious ideals, administering sanctions efficiently in various areas of conduct, mobilizing for expansion, and the like, the Mauryan state was threatening the time-honored institutions and modifying customary social relationships.

We should not be surprised to learn of a reaction on the part of those groups whose position in society was dependent on the older patterns of conduct. Although there is little evidence of actual maltreatment of the brahmans, the priests lost much of their former influence on political policy and religious life. Some historians postulate a brahman uprising, and attribute the collapse of the empire to Ashoka's patronage of Buddhism and commitment to pacifism. The theory of a brahman uprising was possibly inspired by the fact that Puṣyamitra, who led the palace revolution (c. 184 B.C.) against the Mauryan king Brihadratha, ending a dynastic rule that had lasted for 137 years,[aa] was evidently a brahman.[bb] A less dramatic, but more realistic theory of the downfall of the Mauryas would have to emphasize the practical problems of administering a territory that included most of India—as well as the need to rely on officials who were often ambitious and of divided loyalty. An empire of these proportions depends on effective control at the center. This direction appears to have been lacking in the later years of the empire. The movement for local autonomy was encouraged by foreign invaders such as the Bactrian Greeks. In the court itself there were undoubtedly factional disputes and ministers eager to arrogate more power to themselves.

Pushyamitra, who organized the *coup d'état* that overthrew Brihadratha, held a high office under the king as commander-in-chief of the army. He established his own family, the Shungas (*Śuṅga*), on the throne of Magadha; they ruled, if tradition is correct, until Sīmuka, the first Sātavāhana king, vanquished the Shunga empire sometime around 72 B.C.

[aa] According to the puranas the Mauryas ruled for this period of time, the regimes of Chandragupta, Bindusara, and Ashoka accounting for eighty-five years. After Ashoka the dynastic chronicle becomes confused.

[bb] Most scholars consider Pushyamitra to have been a brahman, but though the family name suggests brahman lineage, we know that by this time members of the twice-born castes were taking the names of their priests—rather than the priests taking the name of the tribal chieftains, as had been the custom in Vedic times.

By this time Ujjayinī, the capital of the old kingdom of Avanti, had regained its prominence, and, with Magadha cut off from the ports of the west, it replaced Pataliputra as an economic and cultural center. In northern and western India foreign conquerors consolidated their positions. The Kushans (*Kuṣaṇa*) controlled almost all of this area in the first century A.D., shifting the political focus to Peshawar. The domain of the powerful Kushan king Kaniṣka, a patron of Buddhism, extended as far east as modern Bihar. But the Kushan power was already so decentralized as to justify the use of the term feudatory in describing the political structure. The successors of Kanishka ruled until the third century, when, with the victory of Shapur I, the northwest was brought under Persian influence. In the northwestern Deccan, the kingdom of the Satavahanas (*Āndhras*) was paramount for the first three centuries of the Christian era. In this unstable period between the empire of the Mauryas and that of the Guptas, the term matsyanyaya gained increasing currency. Lawlessness characterized large parts of India; it was indeed a "time of troubles" marked by pillaging invaders and almost constant struggle among the Indian states.

Small kingdoms as well as a number of republics had begun to reappear as early as the concluding years of Mauryan rule. It was not uncommon for the leadership of these republics to become hereditary, and for the rulers to take the title of maharaja. Of these republics, the Yaudheyas, in the southern Punjab, the Mālavas in what is now Rajasthan, and several others survived into the Gupta period—but not beyond the fourth century A.D. More often than not, kings followed the traditional advice to refrain from annexing conquered territory. The vanquished king, or a close relative, would be restored to the throne—the state becoming a feudatory. Or, when annexation did take place (as it did occasionally in the Gupta epoch), the former king might serve as a provincial officer.

These tributary states were independent in domestic and foreign policy, save for their duties of homage on ceremonial occasions and their obligations to assist their lords in time of war. The elaborate gradation of rank (ranging from king to "supreme king of kings"[cc]) reflected the relative position of these states in the political structure of the time. These grandiose titles appear to have been largely the contribution of invading tribes that descended on India during these centuries and all but exhausted kshatriya power.

Yet in this time of barbarian encounter and religious competition that followed the decline of Mauryan rule, the institution of kingship was strengthened. If the invaders were to be repulsed, the king must have full responsibility and the state must be effectively organized to take maximum advantage of its resources. And it was in the interest of religion to buttress the authority of the king. In the acute religious conflict that followed the

---

[cc] By Gupta times the title maharaja could no longer compete with such lofty descriptions of the monarch as "son of the gods." "Maharaja" had become the title for the rulers of modest feudatories—a hollow memory of the grandeur and potency the term once connoted.

break-up of the Ashokan empire, the states usually took a strong partisan position (most of them disposed to renascent Brahmanism) and the king was rewarded with a sanctification that had never been equaled in earlier Indian history. It is at this time that the divinity of kings really emerges: the innovations of Ashoka, the new interpretations of the royal function, and the introduction of Near Eastern and Greek concepts encouraged this development.

IMPERIAL ADMINISTRATION OF THE GUPTAS

The second century A.D. saw a reassertion of guild power, which Weber believed coincided with the new influx of money from the Roman Empire;[16] the availability of precious metals may have encouraged Indian kings to mint coins of their own. But between the second century and the early Gupta period the great urban centers had begun to decline. Archeologists tell us that by this time coins had become coarser and cruder and the fine pottery of an earlier age had disappeared. The Gupta rulers, Kumāra Gupta excepted, issued almost no copper coins. Trade was diminishing in importance and the money economy was declining. Officials were, with increasing frequency, paid in kind or by grants of revenues. The village had become the basic unit of the economy. Commodity production and purchasing power were reduced to a level that discouraged capitalistic development. When the costs of centralized administrative control became prohibitive the village assumed increasing political importance as well.[17] And the village, practically self-contained politically and economically, would remain the fundamental social entity until modern times. With the replacing of the city by the village in the Gupta epoch, commodity production was no longer equal to the rich cultural development that had earlier flowered under the Satavahana dynasty.

Records of a number of land grants to brahmans have survived. These gifts of land were intended by their donors as a kind of spiritual investment. By the fifth century A.D. the grants comprised control over revenue sources, including even the mines (which had long been considered the king's personal domain), as well as administrative control over the villages included in the land grants.[dd] The practice of granting land and administrative rights to the brahmans in the Gupta era was one of the factors leading to feudalizing of Indian society.[ee] During this period land appears to have been sold for religious purposes only, though we cannot be certain of this. There is evidence (if the *Arthashastra* can be considered evidence) that in Mauryan times there were land transactions for other reasons.[18] The descriptions of Gupta society provided by Chinese pilgrims in the fifth and seventh centuries A.D. indicate that the state did not keep registries

[dd] In the days of tribal organization, land was jointly held. By Gupta times the concept of private property was fully developed. Land in the new settlements sponsored by the state seems to have been frequently assigned for the life of the tenant cultivator on the condition that he perform his economic duties.

[ee] Administrative rights appear to have been first surrendered in grants made by a Satavahana ruler in the second century A.D. *Vide* Sharma [390], p. 297.

of households, which suggests, in turn, that the state was not directly involved in collecting taxes, but assigned this function to intermediaries. We have the statement of Fa-hsien that Gupta officials were granted land revenues.[19] The power of the guilds had long been challenged by princes jealous of their wealth and influence, and though there had been revivals of these mercantile associations, in the Gupta period they remained subordinate to the feudal barons, who controlled the village surplus and constituted the market for luxury goods.

This was the economic setting of the second of the great Indian empires. Again it was Magadha that succeeded in realizing the ancient ideal of the chakravartin. The Guptas and their allies, the Vākāṭakas, ruled most of central and northern India in the fourth and fifth centuries A.D. The second Gupta ruler (though the fourth of his house mentioned in the inscriptions), Samudra Gupta, who ruled for forty years in the fourth century, established a dominion that stretched from the Punjab to modern Assam in northeastern India and was centered in the old Mauryan capital. His son, Chandra Gupta II, who reigned until A.D. 415, extended Gupta sovereignty over almost all of northern India and the adjacent Deccan. It was he who consolidated the alliance with the powerful Vakatakas, who were paramount in west central India. Fa-hsien records that the government of the Guptas interfered little in the affairs of the people, and then always with a gentleness he found impressive. The Chinese pilgrim was able to report that travelers could journey from one end of India to the other without fear of violence. (How different was his experience from that of his countryman several centuries later whose movements were always in jeopardy!) By this time Hinduism was entrenched as the dominant form of religious expression, and the subsidence of warfare enabled the country to profit from the enlightened heterodox ethical systems that infused Hindu religion. Poets and dramatists who flourished in these regimes portrayed the refinement and splendor of Indian courtly life. Samudra Gupta himself was an intellect and musician of the first order. Toward the end of the rule of Kumāra Gupta I, son of Chandra Gupta II, India was again beset by invaders who, like the Greeks and Central Asians, poured over the mountains of the northwest into the fertile plains. Now an Iranian people (Hūṇas) appeared to herald the collapse of Gupta power.

Before we turn to the main features of Gupta polity, mention should be made of the sources of information available to us. In addition to fairly extensive numismatic evidence, we have the puranas, which tell us much about the history of the early Guptas. The *Nārada Dharmaśāstra* (in many ways reminiscent of the *Arthashastra* of Kautalya) and the *Bṛhaspati Dharmaśāstra* may both date from the fourth century. A number of inscriptions of the period are evidence that these codes (or smritis) greatly influenced the Gupta kings.[11] One of the most valuable of the sources available to us is the record left by the Chinese Buddhist pilgrim whose observations we have already noted. He spent fifteen years in India during the reign of Chandra Gupta II (three of them in the capital at Pataliputra).

---

[11] J. F. Fleet's monumental *Corpus Inscriptionum Indicarum*, III, 1888, is a catalog of inscriptions of the imperial and later Gupta periods.

The *Kāmandakīya* belongs to the fourth or fifth century A.D., and it is reasonable to ascribe it to the late fourth century when the empire of the Guptas had been consolidated. There is some speculation that the author may have been Śikhara, the minister of Chandra Gupta II; however, it is generally believed that its author was an academic theoretician removed from active participation in politics. In our brief examination of Gupta polity we shall depend in part on this treatise.[gg]

The *Pañcatantra,* a book of fables belonging to the late fifth or early sixth century and intended for the instruction of statesmen, is also in the arthashastra tradition and quotes frequently from the treatise of Kamandaka. The *Harṣacarita* of Bāṇa and the literature of India's laureate poet, Kālidāsa, belong to this era—the former (a biography of the emperor Harsha) to the seventh century, the twilight of the grand empire. Kalidasa has been located everywhere from the first century B.C. to the middle of the fifth century A.D. The problem of dating his works is complicated by the number of "Kalidasas" and "Vikramadityas" (with whom the poet was associated) that appear throughout historical references, but most historians now place this foremost of Sanskrit writers in the time of the Gupta monarchs Chandra Gupta II and Kumara Gupta I (375–455). The political passages in his *Raghuvaṁśam* would suggest this brilliant period of Gupta power.

Then there is the undistinguished *Kaumudīmahotsava,* a five-act drama of unknown authorship, which illumines the opening years of the dynasty. The *Devīcandraguptam,* which exists only in fragments, and the *Mudrā-rākṣasa* (both dramatic works) contribute to our picture of the Gupta court. The *Mudrarakshasa* is of particular interest in that ostensibly it refers to the establishment of the Mauryan empire through the efforts of Chandragupta Maurya and Kautalya, and emphasizes the importance of diplomacy and expediency. Although the setting is Mauryan, the events probably mirror conditions contemporaneous with its author, Viśākhadatta. The play is essentially a rationale of Kautalyan statecraft, which is put forth as a model for political negotiation. It illustrates the dictum that political ends justify the means of their accomplishment: Kautalyan opportunism definitely pays. (Portions of the play have been included in the Appendix.) Parallels in Mauryan and Gupta politics and the inspiration that Kautalya provided the later dynasty have often been remarked upon.

Evidence other than these literary sources must, however, be given more weight. The stone pillar of Samudra Gupta at Allahabad is the most important of the inscriptions that remain. It attests to the vastness of Gupta dominions. Even the king of Ceylon admitted the supremacy of the Gupta kings. The pillar, though it makes clear that primogeniture is the traditional basis of succession, indicates that the final decision lies with people and the ministers.[hh] Other inscriptions suggest that the eldest son was not always selected, qualification being a more important con-

---

[gg] The work is considered at greater length in Chapter 12 below.

[hh] Chandra Gupta, his father's choice, was passed over in favor of the eldest son, Rama Gupta, who was later removed by Chandra Gupta.

sideration. Popular opinion and law appear to have been honored to a degree almost unparalleled in Indian history. Authority was (in theory at least) confined to a prescribed area. The office rather than the king himself was revered; the Guptas appear not to have claimed supernatural authority. Again law and tradition, if the one could be separated from the other, were considered the supreme powers. The king could not modify or even interpret the law; at best he could stress one aspect of the code rather than another through the methods he chose to execute the law. The Gupta inscriptions are not edicts as were the notices of Ashoka. And though the inscriptions of Ashoka are certainly not injunctions, they had more legal significance than those of the Guptas.

Discipline of mind and body is stressed as strongly by Kamandaka as by Kautalya. Drink and sex could be enjoyed in moderation—but the other two corrupters, hunting and gambling, should be avoided altogether. Fa-hsien implies that men may have been aided in living up to these standards by the prohibition of both drink and the killing of animals. He saw no shops where meat[ii] or intoxicating drink was sold. Dikshitar remarks that this must have deprived the government of the considerable income the earlier Mauryas obtained from the tax on these commodities. As for the conduct of the king himself, we learn from Gupta sources that he must be impartial, not given to anger. He must be righteous in behavior, vigorous but controlled in his actions, cultivated in mind. His education should include practice in the use of weapons as well as the study of dandaniti and vartta (economics) and the Vedas. Because danger was always present, the king must take every precaution to safeguard his person.

The king submitted his plans to a council (parishad, or *mantri maṇḍalam*), which deliberated the proposals put to it. Discussion must take place in strictest privacy. At the head of the council was the *mantri mukhya,* the first minister, who acted in the king's behalf when the king was not present. The number of ministers was greater than that recommended by Kautalya, but probably did not exceed eight or nine. They were carefully selected; character, wisdom, and dedication to the service of the state were the main criteria. But records indicate that at least in many instances, office was hereditary. And we know that the ministers were almost invariably brahmans. There is little reason to believe that the king dared act without consultation, or that he could controvert the decision of a cabinet constituting the best minds in his kingdom. He might ask for further debate, but he was expected to approve the opinion of the council without further question. The council, on the other hand, must anticipate all contingencies. The king emerges as an approving and administering agent.

Moral guidance was provided by the purohita, who was charged with what a later age might call judicial review—interpreting the decisions of the parishad in the light of the sacred texts. Kamandaka also speaks of a war council, which possessed great power.[20] The nature of the assembly

---

[ii] Though there were butchers in the society depicted in the *Mudrarakshasa.*

must remain for the present in relative darkness. The sabha was a representative organization intended to give some kind of political significance to the wishes of the people. It evidently played a role in approving the choice of a king. We are told that the sabha forced the nomination of Rama Gupta,[21] but it was essentially a rubber stamp, initiating little or no policy.

The central duty of the king is still to hold other men to the performance of their own prescribed duties. Protection receives the same emphasis in the *Kamandakiya* as it did in the *Shantiparva* and the *Kautaliya*. The rod of danda must be wielded in accord with the offense and without prejudice.[22] Protection involves more than the punishment of disorderly men. The king must preserve his people from disease, flood, fire, and economic privation. He is charged with installing and maintaining irrigation and with taking those measures necessary to protect the health and economic prosperity of his subjects. Encouraging commerce and agricultural improvement and providing sanitation and medication are among his duties. The construction of shrines and temples came within this sphere of activity.

To meet expenses—the costs of military campaigns, the salaries of government employees, the upkeep of the palace, gifts to deserving institutions and individuals, and so forth—the Gupta kings depended primarily on the land tax, the customary sixth of the produce. The state had a monopoly on salt production, and first claim to other minerals. Fa-hsien refers specifically to the royal lands, and it is probable that these holdings were an important source of income througout the Gupta era, although the Mauryan designation for the demesnes (*sita*) had been abandoned. (Some 250 years later, another Chinese pilgrim, Hiuen Tsiang, listed four uses of income from crown lands : expenses incurred by the affairs of state and sacrificial gifts, subsidies for the officers of government, honorariums for men of merit and distinction, and charity.) The village rendered certain services and payments to the state directly, or to the army when it was nearby. Military conscription seems to have existed, although whether it extended beyond the kshatriya caste is a moot point.[jj] Associations of artisans, merchants, and bankers were taxed. And in emergency situations the king resorted to inflating the currency.

Final appeal in the execution of justice was to the king, but it is likely that he did little more than restate the position of the chief judge. It was the king's duty to appoint those who would administer the law. The law itself was a combination of sacred code, custom,[kk] and the opinion of the sages. The principle of equity supplemented ordinance and convention. And arbitration was allowed to determine certain cases involving no actual crime. Three great codifiers of the law lived during this time : Nārada, Brihaspati, and Kātyāyana. Their task was to relate earlier smritis (especially *Manu*) and arthashastra principles to the changing needs of the time. Distinction between civil and criminal law was more sharply drawn

[jj] Such characteristics of European feudalism as the granting of land in return for military service were not present in India—a reason for circumspection in describing social developments in post-Mauryan India as "feudal."

[kk] Local deviation from general convention was respected.

than it had earlier been. Judges seeking appointment had to meet rigorous requirements, but once in judicial office they were relatively free of state coercion. A series of appellate courts further protected the citizen. According to Narada, a case tried in the village assembly went to the city council, and one tried in the city court might be appealed to the king.[23]

Gupta administration was decentralized and, as patrimonial bureaucracy reached its logical conclusion in hereditary land grants, it reflected the quasi-feudal character of the economy. It comprised a network of self-governing tribes and tributary kingdoms, their chiefs often serving as representatives of the imperial power. The central authority was remarkably tolerant of local variation and evidently extended patronage equitably to Hindus, Buddhists, and Jainas. The empire was essentially rural in character, and official policy generally encouraged village settlement. District officers were usually appointed by the provincial governor. The emperor had *de jure* power to dismiss his officials, but there is little doubt that the tenure of these district officers rested in fact on their local strength. Such offices tended to become hereditary as did the ministries, and records attest to four or five generations' having held a commission.[u] The district officer consulted a council composed of prominent citizens (probably caste or guild leaders) before making important decisions. A Gupta inscription honoring the official who instigated the rebuilding of the Girnar dam in A.D. 455 provides a most attractive picture of one of these Gupta administrators.

> He caused distress to no man in the city, but he chastened the wicked. Even in this mean age he did not fail the trust of the people. He cherished the citizens as his own children and he put down crime. He delighted the inhabitants with gifts and honors and smiling conversation, and he increased their love with informal visits and friendly receptions.[24]

The towns were governed by an official (*purapala*) who may have been aided by a council. But the fundamental unit of administration was the village, and the Guptas allowed the village executive bodies the usual autonomy. The village headman was known as *grāmeyaka*. He, too, had a council, with which he generally worked closely. The district and village councils exercised the bulk of governmental functions, protective and developmental.[mm]

---

[u] Public servants were subject to a system of regulations that shares much with the civil service code of today. Included were a number of benefits such as vacations, pensions, sick leave, and incentive payments, which are described in terms often strikingly modern.

[mm] Ghoshal has criticized Majumdar's suggestion that the Indian political system be viewed during the millennium that began with the rise of Magadha as a checking and balancing of the popular, bureaucratic, and royal power. Majumdar (*Ancient India* [Banaras, 1952]) argued that by the fourth century A.D. the popular element in this tripartite division of power had all but disappeared as a viable political factor —the result of renascent Brahmanism which supported the social hierarchy and the monarchy. Ghoshal observes ("The Genius of Ancient Indian Polity," in [143]) that Gupta inscriptions point to the representation of various community interests on district governing boards, that a brahman-court coalition had existed before this time,

The later history of the Guptas is obscure, but historians are reasonably certain that the empire maintained a unity despite barbarian incursions and feudalization from within until the time of Budha Gupta, whose reign ended in 495. Gupta power survived in northern Bengal through the first half of the sixth century. There are a number of later "Gupta" princes who may or may not have been connected with the great line of Chandra and Samudra Gupta. The early sixth century saw the Hunas clearly in ascendance, but by mid-century the Chālukyas in the Deccan and the Maukharis of the Ganges basin had become the dominant powers in India. When Grahavarman, king of the latter people, died in A.D. 606 without an heir, the nobles, it is said, offered the throne to Harṣa (or Harshavardhana as he is sometimes called). The forty years of his reign were to revive the imperial glory of the Guptas and see Harsha, suzerain of an empire increasingly feudal in structure, recognized as supreme in northern India.

The reign of this king, who was reputed to be a vaishya, is relatively well documented. The court poet Bāṇa has left a narrative in the *Harṣa-carita* (which tells of the indefatigable energy of the king and his devotion to duty and justice), and the account of the Chinese pilgrim Hiuen Tsiang has survived. Harsha, we are told, was a great patron of learning, religion, and the arts. We have mentioned Hiuen Tsiang's description of how the king parceled out the revenue from royal lands with a portion for state-sponsored worship, another for gifts to the different sects, and a third to reward cultural achievement. The beliefs of the royal family are an indication of the religious eclecticism of the time. Prabhākara, father of Harsha, was a sun-worshiper; Harsha's brother was a devoted Buddhist of the Hīnayāna mode; Harsha is mentioned by Bana as a Shaivite, but later (under the influence of his Chinese guest) became sympathetic to Mahā-yāna Buddhism.[nn]

Harsha died leaving no heirs, and Indian political history sank once again into the chaos of warring dynasties. No one power was sufficiently strong to bring the princes of India under its control, nor were the princes to prove able to cooperate for their own defense against the rising Muslim menace. During the reign of Harsha, Kashmir was a major power in the north—its pre-eminence challenged only by Harsha's own authority. Sa-śāṅka, fervent anti-Buddhist and murderer of Harsha's older brother Rājyavardhana, ruled ancient Bengal and Assam and extended his authority as far west as Benares.[oo]

The topography of the Deccan early encouraged political fragmenta-tion. As Mahalingam has remarked,

---

and that there is a lack of any convincing evidence that the Guptas encouraged the interests of one group over those of another. The balanced constitution, if it ever existed, belonged to a much earlier period of history.

[nn] Hiuen Tsiang undoubtedly exaggerates Harsha's partiality for Buddhism. By this time Buddhism had lost its original purity; it was being absorbed into Hinduism, and Harsha's faith is probably best described as a mixture of the two faiths. *Vide* Bagchi [12], pp. 405ff.

[oo] Among the evils for which he is remembered is the burning of the sacred bodhi tree at Bodh Gaya, the scene of the Buddha's enlightenment.

The history of South India from the earliest times is largely the history of small kingdoms and principalities. There was no lordly imperialism or great empire with considerable concentration of power in the hands of one authority, except probably for short periods under distinguished rulers of some dynasty or other, as for instance under the imperial Colas or under some of the kings of Vijayanagar. In such periods, the acceptance of the overlordship of the suzerain authority was only personal. Further, the extension of the imperial control did not necessarily and always mean the complete removal of the older kingdoms and rulerships and the establishment of colonies or military governorships by the conqueror.[25]

It is sufficient for our purposes to note that southernmost Dravidian India was divided among the Pāṇḍyas, who governed the southern tip of the peninsula, the Cholas (*Cōḷas*) on the southeastern, or Coromandel coast, and the Cheras (*Cēras*) on the southwestern, or Malabar coast. Although imperial consolidation was not the typical political experience of the south, these monarchies have been described as almost Byzantine in their splendor and elaborate court ceremonial during the post-Gupta period.[26]

This magnificent courtly life must have entailed a substantial revenue. The Tamil kingdom spent an enormous amount of its wealth on irrigation. We know also that the encouragement of culture and religion constituted an important item of expenditure. The sources of revenue were approximately the same in the south as in northern India, the tax on the produce of the land being also a sixth of the yield.[27] The theory of the tax as payment for protection seems to have been as characteristic of the south as of the Aryan kingdoms.[28] The king is warned in similar terms of the dangers of onerous taxation. The Cholas had a more centralized and exacting administration than the other kingdoms of the Tamil country. The land was carefully classified for tax purposes and the bureaucracy was distinguished by fine gradations of rank. It appears that the Cholas were the only Indian state to develop a regular navy and make it an effective instrument of military policy.

In this historical account of the imperial systems of ancient India we have got considerably ahead of our analysis of the ideas that lie behind political organization and legal and social institutions, and the religious values that provided the foundation of authority. In the two chapters that follow we shall be dealing with the most important of the political texts that are known to us, the *Arthashastra* of Kautalya. Most scholars believe that the work belongs to the early Mauryan period or that it was based on the teaching of a sage or minister of that time.

11 ※ KAUTALYA AND THE ARTHASHASTRA SCHOOL, I

> To him who shone like a thunderbolt and before the stroke of the
> thunderbolt of whose witchcraft the rich mountain-like Nandas fell
> down, root and branch; who alone, with the power of diplomacy like
> Indra with his thunderbolt, bestowed the earth on Chandragupta,
> the moon among men; who churned the nectar of the science of
> polity from the ocean of political sciences—to him, the wise and
> Brahma-like Vishnugupta, we make salutation.
> —KAMANDAKA'S SALUTATION TO KAUTALYA[1]

AN INTRODUCTION TO THE ARTHASHASTRA

In early India politics was considered one of the three or four major
sciences. The school of Uśanas (Shukra) goes so far as to suggest that
artha is the only true science and that hence it takes precedence over the
sacred law.[a] Most political thought of the time assumed the existence of
a monarchical form of government, and politics was accordingly defined
as the science of kingship. The arthashastra texts were intended as a
political guide for the king and his ministers. Their scope is broad, embracing economic as well as political principles and including such subjects
as public administration, foreign policy, techniques of warfare, civil law,
and social structure. Their emphasis is on the need for sanctions capable
of preventing social disorder. Anarchy is considered the greatest catastrophe that can befall mankind.

Whereas the dharmashastras considered government and the political
process with reference to the ideals expressed in the Vedic canons, the
largely secular analysis of arthashastra treats this subject more objectively.
In the arthashastra literature the interests of the state, rather than the
king's personal fulfillment,[b] are of foremost importance. Dharmashastra
is of an essentially deductive nature; arthashastra, by contrast, introduces
inductive reasoning and a greater realism. But the allegation that arthashastra differs from dharmashastra in that it is not dependent on the Vedas
for validation must be rejected. To be sure, the authors of the arthashastras
enjoy a relative intellectual freedom, and their contribution lies in the

---

[a] "Literally, the word *artha* means 'thing, object, substance,' and comprises the
whole range of the tangible objects that can be possessed, enjoyed, and lost, and which
we require in daily life for the upkeep of a household, raising of a family, and discharge of religious duties, i.e., for the virtuous fulfillment of life's obligations." (Zimmer [441], p. 35.) The word is pronounced art-ha.

[b] The science of politics was, in the earlier stages of its history, known as *rajadharma*. The term was, in time, replaced by *dandaniti* and *arthashastra* and, eventually, by *rajanitishastra*, or simply *nitishastra*. *Vide* Jayaswal [199], pp. 5f.

separation of political speculation from theology. But this need not and should not be taken to imply a repudiation of orthodoxy.

Very possibly the arthashastra school was a reaction to the asceticism and despair of heterodoxy, an attempt to return men's thoughts to practical problems of social life. In the argument idealism tends to be subordinated to a philosophy of power politics and materialism. It has been suggested that the traditional belief that arthashastra is a science ancillary to the *Atharvaveda* is based on their similar view of the relation of means and ends; both have a concern with ends that overshadows attention to the methods employed.[2] Kautalya, for instance, in his reluctance to allow dharmashastra to modify the goal-orientation of the efficient political system, is led to extol positive law. His arguments must have appeared to justify a radical departure from tradition.

Kautalya refers to at least four different doctrinal schools,[c] and the names he mentions of early writers in the field agree with those we find in the *Mahabharata,* although the two works differ in conceptual scheme. It is apparent that arthashastra, in a simpler form, had existed since the fifth or even sixth century B.C. But the oldest formal treatise on government that remains is the *Kautaliya Arthashastra.* The manuscript, generally attributed to the minister of the first Mauryan emperor, Chandragupta, was discovered in the early years of this century at Trivandrum by R. Shama Sastri.[3] A number of early sources attested to the existence of the treatise; Bana, the bard of Harsha's court, knew of a work on polity by Kautalya, and Dandin[4] mentions the author of the *Arthashastra.*[d] Perhaps by their day the work had been lost. It remained hidden until our own time; the effect of its discovery on Indian scholarship was little short of revolutionary. (Since the ruling groups had an interest in limiting the

---

[c] Mānavāḥ, Bārhaspatyāḥ, Auśanasāḥ, Pārāśarāḥ; he alludes to more than a dozen authors. B. C. Law, "A Short Account of the Wandering Teachers at the Time of the Buddha," in the *Journal and Proceedings of the Asiatic Society of Bengal,* XIV, No. 7, 399ff., has listed the names of forty-one wandering scholars whom he considers to have provided the precedent for technical and systematic manuals such as the arthashastra and nitishastra literature. Brihaspati and Shukra were venerated as the founders of the science of arthashastra. Works of the former school have been published by F. W. Thomas (*Brihaspatisutra*), and a relatively late version of the Shukra teaching has been edited by G. Oppert (*Shukranitisara*). *Vide* Chapter 12 below.

[d] Dandin parodies the arthashastra teaching. (The names Vishnugupta and Chanakya are generally understood to refer to Kautalya.) A king is warned against rascals who promise much but can deliver little: they will say that, of the four royal studies, " 'theology, agriculture, metaphysics, are big and slow to show results. Leave them alone. Just study political science. Now Professor Vishnugupta has made a little epitome of this for the king—twenty-four thousand lines of poetry. Learn it by heart, apply it in detail; and it does what it promises.' 'Good,' says [the prince], and starts to study. He learns it (meanwhile growing old) and finds that book leading to other books. It can't be truly understood until the whole wordy mass is mastered. Well, suppose he does master it, later or sooner. The first result is that he no longer trusts anyone, even son or wife. Even for his own belly he must have just so much porridge, made of just so many grains of rice. For the cooking of just so much porridge, he must be given just so much firewood, correctly weighed and measured. "Having risen from table . . . he must spend the first eighth of the day in listening to a complete statement of receipts and disbursements. While he is listening, a double amount is stolen by the knavish bureaucrats who have the wit to multiply a thousandfold the forty tricks of peculation taught by Chanakya." (*The Ten Princes,* transl. Arthur Ryder [Chicago, Phoenix paperback, 1960], pp. 202f.)

circulation and preventing the popularization of the arthashastra treatises, it is not surprising that few of these works have survived.)

In the arthashastra manuscripts both the Kauṭilya and Kauṭalya spellings appear, and the latter occurs in inscriptions of the tenth and thirteenth centuries. "Kauṭalya," it has been widely argued, is the correct Sanskrit spelling of the name of its author. The Kautalyalogist Ganapati Sastri maintains that his manuscripts support this form. Those partial to the *Kautilya* spelling include among their arguments the hypothesis that the name derives from *kutila* ("crooked") and that *Kautalya* is an attempt to cover up that fact. But, inasmuch as this "crookedness" was employed against the infamous Nandas, the author might actually have delighted in the name. And in the *Mahabharata* Bhishma says to Yudhishthira that "both kinds of wisdom, the straight and the crooked, should be available to the king," and proceeds to elaborate the subtle "morality" (the "dharma of distress") occasioned by times of emergency.[5] This is simply the doctrine of *raison d'état,* the power philosophy. The word may not have had the pejorative sense it has today—although the epic in another place states that the man who strikes below the navel is "crooked and unAryan."[6] At any rate, the comparative edition of the Patan folios based on the palm-leaf fragments of the *Arthashastra* (dated on paleographic grounds c. the eleventh century A.D.), when published, will use *Kautalya* as the preferred spelling.

References in the *Kāmandakīya Nītisāra,* the *Daśakumāracarita,* and the *Pañchatantra* to "Vishnugupta" and "Chanakya" indicate that Kautalya had other aliases. The personal name of the author was most likely Vishnugupta, Chanakya the patronymic, and Kautalya (or Kautilya) the name by which he was generally known. Legend not only connects Kautalya with Chandragupta as the latter's chief minister, but associates the two as early as Chandragupta's meeting with Alexander during one of the Punjab campaigns. The brahmanic sources for this period, the puranas, credit Kautalya rather than his king with the overthrow of Nanda rule.[7] The *Mudrārākṣasa,* a drama of considerably later date, provides us with a similar picture of Kautalya as king-maker. But there is no mention of the Mauryan minister's having written a political treatise. It is of course possible that Kautalya compiled no more than a set of political aphorisms —and that he quoted these along with the maxims of other arthashastra writers, or that they formed the basis for an elaboration by a later scholar or statesman. Perhaps it is safest to say that the *Arthashastra* we possess includes additions and revisions by several later writers. "Vishnugupta" could be a redactor of a period as late as the fourth century A.D. rather than the minister of Chandragupta.

The social setting of the political commentary of the *Arthashastra* seems to antedate that of the early smritis. References to religion indicate the relatively recent appearance of Buddhism and Jainism,[e] and the persistence of Vedic ceremony. Lists of parallels in the accounts of Megas-

---

[e] Kosambi [221] argues that the language of the glossators shows them to be Buddhists and Jainas and that they would have had no reason to adopt a forgery of the third or fourth century A.D. as genuine.

thenes, the Greek ambassador to Chandragupta's court, and the *Artha-shastra* have been made.[8] Similar descriptions of tax collection and high-ways, the palace, the bureaucracy and its functions, manufactures, the army, and precautions to be taken by the king for his safety suggest not only that the Mauryan king and the author of the *Arthashastra* were con-temporaries, but that Kautalya is recommending much that he has already witnessed.

But these parallels are far from conclusive: indeed the later *Manu-smriti* is closer to Megasthenes than the *Kautaliya* is. The Greek observer mentions a navy and regulations for dealing with foreigners—references one would expect to find in the *Arthashastra*. Megasthenes also suggests a less developed revenue system and a simpler commercial life than we find in the Indian work. But Megasthenes' dependability has been ques-tioned; he is known to have had a vivid imagination and to have recorded much that he could not possibly have seen for himself. Further, he may not have understood the language of the Mauryan court very well.

Philological comparisons with Pāṇini, the great grammarian who is said to have lived c. 350 B.C., have supported an early date for the *Artha-shastra*. Vincent Smith, Jacobi, F. W. Thomas, Jayaswal, N. N. Law, J. F. Fleet, and Shama Sastri subscribe to the Mauryan date. But con-troversy over the date and authenticity of the *Arthashastra* is still active. Those who deny the association of its author with Chandragupta point out its reference to a small kingdom. Others argue that although the work does seem to reflect the needs of a small polity, the theory was meant to apply to monarchies of all sizes. Kautalya's treatment of the administra-tion of justice points to a sizable empire rather than to a state of limited proportions, and on one occasion he refers to the dominion that stretches from the Himalayas to the ocean.[9]

Those who ascribe a later date to the *Arthashastra* claim that the work may have been inspired by the teachings of the Mauryan minister, but that this does not necessarily mean that it dates from the late fourth century B.C. Their case is built on considerations of meter and language, the absence of reference to Chandragupta and to the royal title employed by the Mauryans, the silence of later works (puranas, Patañjali) regard-ing Kautalya's *Arthashastra,* and particularly Megasthenes' failure to mention Kautalya in his description of the Mauryan court. There is a reference in the treatise to China, although there is no evidence of contact between India and that country before the Han period, and in style and authorities cited the *Arthashastra* may be compared with the later work on erotics, the *Kāmasūtra.[f]* Jolly and Winternitz, who place the *Kautaliya* in the third century A.D., argue that the author was a theoretician and not a statesman. There is, in fact, little indication in the work that its creator led an active political life.

We know that the *Kautaliya* cannot have been more recent than the third century A.D., since authors of that period refer to it with admiration.

---

f On the other hand, there are those who stress stylistic similarities with the Brahmanas and the Upanishads.

And in no very convincing argument does it antedate 350 B.C. P. V. Kane's summary statement can be taken as representative of the most reliable scholarship on the subject. He writes that the work "has certainly an ancient atmosphere about it, . . . all that has so far been gathered from it agrees with the traditional date of 300 B.C. and no cogent arguments have been yet brought forward that would compel us to assign it a date later than the above by six centuries."[10]

Jacobi, in contradicting Hillebrandt's argument that the *Arthashastra* is the work of a school rather than a single author, cites the abundant criticism in the treatise of earlier works as evidence of a potent individuality. Kautalya attends to matters of practical administration, matters that would not generally absorb the deliberations of a school of political thought. The style of the *Arthashastra* is frequently similar to that of the bhashyas, which, in contrast to that of the sutras, is a style that suggests individual authorship. Jacobi claims that if the passages in the work which attest to the authorship of one man are removed, the metrical conclusions will be lost. And it was not unusual for writers to refer to themselves in the third person, as Kautalya does.

Certain of the provisions of the *Kautaliya* that are in agreement with the later law books are probably modifications made by commentators on the *Arthashastra,* but because the work undoubtedly refers to the Mauryan period—although the date of composition may be centuries after Chandragupta—we can accept it as throwing light on the politics of the time and on the great preceptor. Possibly the *Arthashastra* was written as a guide for the king of a modest realm who wished to become a great ruler. The Mauryas provided an example, and we may assume that whoever composed the text on statecraft had an extensive knowledge of Mauryan administrative and diplomatic procedures.

Kautalya is not seriously concerned with broad political speculation on the origin and nature of the state, and his originality is not to be found in the abstract theoretical realm. It is difficult to separate the myths he uses to justify techniques of government and methods of aggrandizement from the legitimate theoretical foundations. Radhakumud Mookerji suggests that in form the *Arthashastra* lies midway between the practical regulations of the Code of Hammurabi and the systematic theory of state and constitution in the political writings of Plato and Aristotle, combining the principles of government with a realistic consideration of the details of policy implementation and regulation. The treatise is, as its author explains, a compendium and summary of earlier arthashastra writings. Kautalya's main task was sifting and organizing this material, and resolving the ambiguities that characterized its disorderly state.

The fifteen books of the *Arthashastra* deal with the discipline of the prince, qualifications of the ministers, and duties of the king (Book 1); departments of government and general administration (2); civil law (3); criminal law (4); removal of dangers to the state, replenishment of the treasury (5); elements of kingship and policy (6 and 7); threats to the welfare of the state (8); military campaigns (9 and 10); corporations (11); theory of conquest (12 and 13); devices, magical and other, for advancing the interests of the state (14); general scheme of the study (15). Or, to classify further, Books 1, 6, and 8 relate to the theory of kingship; Books 2–5 to administration and law; and the remainder (7, 9–14) to war and diplomacy. A considerable portion of the *Arthashastra* is thus devoted to techniques for achieving universal sovereignty, a major theme of Hindu theory. Kautalya has seen to it that in the process no aspect of life should go unregulated.

Of the threefold ends of earthly life—dharma, artha, and kama (virtue, wealth, and enjoyment)—Kautalya assigns first importance to wealth and, anticipating the most outspoken of Western materialistic pronouncements, proclaims that the condition of righteousness is wealth.[11] In his hands the concept dandaniti is broadened to reflect this materialism. Arthashastra becomes "the art of Government with a view to public acquisition."[12] But although there is this emphasis on the material bases of the state, Kautalya, unlike many of his predecessors, defends the other branches of knowledge as useful in establishing security, the class basis of society, and discipline of mind. There is, in Indian philosophy, a hedonistic current that ridicules religion and ethics, but Kautalya is always aware of the instrumental value of religious rites and ethical norms in preserving the social structure.

The Vedas and later texts not properly part of the Vedas are considered sacred knowledge and hence sources of dharma.[g] In the same spirit, custom and tradition are accepted as bases of law. But Kautalya gives the king the final word in determining what shall have the sanction of law in governing social relations. Even custom is subject to the king's interpretation. Dharma, in this radical conception of law, is brought more directly within the province of the monarch. Yet statute law must be compatible with the Vedas and the social order defined therein. The king's discretion is limited by Kautalya's warning of the dangers involved in any radical departure from custom. In claiming the highest authority for the royal edict, Kautalya shares the company of only one or two writers on law and polity. This elevation of the king's role as lawmaker is not in the mainstream of Hindu politics.[h] Kautalya's theory of law may have been

---

[g] Kautalya goes so far as to include historical and administrative texts and even arthashastra literature in the category of "Vedas."

[h] There is the possibility that the bureaucratic structure elaborated by Kautalya and the importance he attaches to the royal edict may reflect the influence of Hellenistic governmental practice. The regard for positive law and for the purposes of the state as ends in themselves also suggests a comparison with the legalist (or realist) school of Chinese political thought which dominated the Ch'in state in the third century B.C., although it is extremely doubtful that the great brahman writer can have known anything of this philosophy. The *Book of Lord Shang*, supposedly the work of Wei Yang (died c. 338 B.C.), is in some ways a Chinese equivalent of the *Arthashastra*, although the latter does not have the same totalitarian implications, nor is it in substance a critique of the old order. The legalists, who took their inspiration from the *Book of Lord Shang*, set out to destroy hereditary class privilege and the feudal structure of China, and to challenge the traditional Confucian ideals and anything that was thought to detract from the strength of the state. In the place of the former

influenced by Buddhist jurists who attacked the concept of sacred law, and by the fact that Mauryan kings exercised the legislative function.[i] *Rājaśāsana*, the king's law, was held to be sovereign in any dispute. But although the philosophy of expedience dominates the *Kautaliya*, an occasional passage suggests an acceptance of higher law and a Brahmanical outlook.

In the initial book of the treatise Kautalya comments on the importance of each man's performing the duties of the station into which he was born.[13] He supports the social order associated with the brahmans and justified by the varnashrama theory as long as brahman religious practice and ideology do not get in the way of the interests of the state. Although Kautalya does not include the brahman purohita among the essential officers of the state, he nevertheless continues to award preferential treatment to the brahmans.[14] Kautalya championed the brahmanic social structure because he saw it as the best means of providing a balanced artha-dharma. It permitted a segment of the population to attain the spiritual life and provided for the more limited spiritual needs of the remainder of the population engaged in material production. Kautalya reminds us of Greek political thinkers in his conception of the polity as the framework within which the individual finds fulfillment and social institutions have their justification.

In the *saptaṅga* theory, an attempt to analyze and explain the political regime that replaced the tribal polity, Kautalya outlined the seven constituent elements of the sovereign state.[15] But it will be noted that the saptanga conception of the state is not actually an organic theory. The components are graded, and it is argued only that damage to one of the seven components of sovereignty might adversely affect the others. A true organic theory must await the later Gupta and post-Gupta age when internal dissension and external threat become a constant and serious menace to order. In *Manu* and in a late didactic portion of the *Shantiparva* the term *aṅga* is employed, and more is made of the analogy of the elements to the limbs of the body.[16]

These components of sovereignty and the general tenets of government and colonization presuppose the ability to keep the population from returning to older tribal loyalties. Kautalya's fear of insurrection and of attempts to re-establish the tribal associations led him to emphasize the integrative as well as the goal-attainment function of the specifically political agencies and to promote caste organization as an alternative to older patterns of coordination. At the same time he predicted that asceticism,[j] in transforming the people into a contemplative society, would undermine

---

values and institutions, these theorists and politicians advocated a rigid code of laws, a harsh discipline oriented toward service to the state, a Hobbesian psychology and naturalistic ethic, and a political policy based on expedience. *Vide* Dirk Bodde, *China's First Unifier* (Leiden, 1938) ; Moore [278], chap. 2.
[i] As the policy pronouncements of Ashoka's edicts indicate.
[j] The reference is evidently to Buddhism. He does, however, recognize that the adherents of heterodox faiths constitute a force to be reckoned with, and he places the "heretics" fairly high on the list of those whose affairs the king must be careful to attend to. (*Arthashastra*, I, 19, p. 41.)

the necessary material foundations of community life. His main criticism of such forms of religious expression is that they are not economically productive. Thinking in terms of the state and its ends, he values asceticism primarily for its usefulness in espionage and intelligence activities; he recommends, for example, that spies be disguised as monks. Before a man could embrace the ascetic life he must have provided for those dependent on him. Kautalya is concerned that religion not be allowed to exert too great a strain on society. Dharma, he insisted, must be realized through artha.

Buddhism had questioned the relevance of action to man's salvation— action, the very essence of the class to which the Buddha himself belonged. And Buddhism warned against the seductions of material things. Although in the early sixth century B.C. the philosopher Cārvāka had elaborated a materialist doctrine that rejected everything that could not be known through sense experience, and repudiated asceticism, ritual, mystic knowledge, and all conceptions of the supernatural, and although the school of arthashastra study was established by this time and capitalist enterprise had taken root, action in the "economic" sense of construction and acquisition had not yet developed as an ideal for the higher orders of Indian society. The traditional brahman roles were actually closer to instrumental activity than were those of the kshatriya class. The ritual had a utilitarian function, but the conditions and rules under which the ritual was performed had a symbolic rather than an intrinsic relationship to the sacred.[17] Ritual represents a need to take action—in this instance by the manipulation of symbols. "Thus ritual is the expression in action, as distinct from thought, of men's active attitudes toward the nonempirical aspects of reality."[18] It tends also to reconstruct life and the universe in mechanical and even materialistic terms.[k]

The kshatriya had traditionally found confirmation of himself in action *per se,* the direct relationship with other men, which found its fullest expression in warfare and governing. It was in the actual battle, rather than in the victory, that the warrior fulfilled his duty. This varna ideal may be contrasted with the function of the shudra, *animal laborans,* who existed to satisfy the basic biological requirements of the community and was expected to resign himself to the drudgery of producing that which is immediately consumed. And it differs also from that of the vaishya, who might be described as *homo faber,* the craftsman who creates the durable

[k] What Cornford says about the relationship of Olympianism and philosophy may have some relevance for the parallel development in India and may help explain why brahman ritualism, based as it was on the manipulation of the Vedic pantheon, could actually be a necessary step in the development of arthashastra ideology. "The type of philosophy to which an Olympian theology will give rise will be dominated by the conception of spatial externality, as *Moira* had dominated the Gods; and it will tend towards discontinuity and discreteness. Originating in an essentially polytheistic scheme, it will be pluralistic. It will also move steadily towards materialism, because, having no hold upon the notion of life as an inward and spontaneous principle, it will reduce life to mechanical motion, communicated by external shock from one body to another. It will level down the organic to the inorganic, and pulverise God and the Soul into material atoms." ([72], p. 123.)

artifact—that which gives permanence to the world and makes it human.[l] In seeking an explanation for the materialism and realism of the arthashastra school and for the *Kautaliya* in particular, one is tempted to find in the dharma of the vaishya class the model for economic action, which when extended to include the activities of building, maintaining, and augmenting the state, transformed kshatriya action, pure action, into material gain.[m]

We have noted in earlier chapters that the challenge of the heterodox systems to Brahmanism, the erosion of older communal ties, and the need to control tribes and other groups incorporated into the Mauryan imperial state encouraged experimentation with new forms of social integration. For Kautalya the problem is not action so much as organization, the preservation of a consistent pattern of human relationships and the creation of new sources of power. Although Brahmanism could offer no design for the necessary structure of authority, it did suggest the principle of authority based on function. At the same time the state envisaged by Kautalya required the expansion of the area of the political to include many offices which had historically been performed by the brahmans but which could no longer be left to religion—particularly in a time of religious debate. The administration of justice, economic regulation, and the maintenance of internal order were to be incorporated into the political sphere—which in earlier times had been more or less confined to offensive and defensive warfare and patronage of the sacrifice. The demands of order and effective integration forced the area of state activity far beyond the classical confines of kshatriya dharma.

It is possible that the *Arthashastra* was intended for a prince not himself a kshatriya, and that this may have influenced Kautalya's conception of the nature and scope of royal power. Or the brahman author of the treatise may have been moved by the interests of his own class to extend the direct political influence of the priests. But although he mentions that ministers should be born of high family (which may mean simply that they should be of Aryan birth),[19] he does not insist, as the *Manusmriti* does, that offices be restricted to members of the priestly class. Kautalya advises qualifying examinations supplemented by tests of character to ascertain loyalty, courage, and integrity.[n] The emphasis of the work is on the requirements of the state and public welfare, rather than the maintenance of positions of privilege. Kautalya was concerned with the development of an independent bureaucracy capable of providing the administrative structure for a stable empire spanning the length and breadth of the land. Such an organization was among the major accomplishments of ancient China, but, with several notable exceptions, Indian political history was to be marked with less success.

Bureaucratization invariably modifies the traditional social structure.

---

[l] I have here borrowed the distinctions employed by Hannah Arendt [8] in her study of the various modes of activity and their relation to political life.

[m] This problem was discussed in Chapter 9 above.

[n] There is no discussion of the techniques for recruiting lower officials.

We know that caste privilege, especially in the area of legal rights, existed in the empire of the Mauryas, but it is also apparent that a number of the grosser inequities had been reduced. The brahman no longer escaped with reproof or a token punishment for his crime. He continued to be favored in many regards, but was dealt with more severely in his transgressions. It is not known whether Megasthenes' division of the "philosophers" into Brachmanes and Sarmanes represents a distinction that the Indians themselves made, though Fick thinks it very likely that the orthodox brahmans were differentiated from those negligent in discipline and more secular in their way of life.[20] The tendency to relate punishment to the act rather than to the status of the offender indicates a departure from ascription. The law was often stern, and yet we are impressed with the greater justice of its administration. Kautalya recommends punishments significantly less harsh than those elaborated in the later smriti literature. On occasion he seems to speak out against cruel and inhuman punitive measures.

The author of the *Arthashastra* emerges as something of a champion of the shudras, espousing their rights as freeborn citizens, and going so far as to suggest that the sons of slaves should enjoy the status of Aryans. Kautalya, like the compilers of several of the law codices, sanctions mixed marriages in many cases. Generally, however, the tradition of the Vedas is accepted in the *Arthashastra,* and the king is charged with the preservation of custom and religion.[21] This deference to the Vedic canon is inspired at least partly by Kautalya's sensitivity to the power of superstition and religion over the minds of men. It is difficult to assess the sincerity of his belief in incantation, spells, and magic. Often superstition and magic are enlisted in the service of the state and perform a frankly political function. The state is not beyond exploiting the natural gullibility of the people. The need to fake miracles suggests the importance Kautalya attached to retaining the charismatic element of authority.

There is an oblique reference in the *Arthashastra* to the state of nature, but no actual theory of the origin of government is developed.[22] The passage is obviously official propaganda intended for use in justifying public policy and taxation, as well as in ensuring the loyalty of the masses and silencing "treacherous opponents of sovereignty." The monarchical state, which is the basis of Kautalya's political speculation, originates in the unwillingness of men to tolerate the evils of anarchy. The difference between the agreement with Prithu[23] and the compact Kautalya describes is sometimes compared to the difference between a social contract and a governmental contract that deals with definite arrangements between the king and his subjects. The contractual theory put forth in the *Arthashastra* is not meant to suggest limits to the royal authority. Kautalya rationalizes the king's authority in terms of service in return for grain and merchandise, but this contract is visited with spiritual sanctions and the office of the king is compared with the functions of the gods. It is likely that Kautalya looked on the state as an inevitable (and, in this sense, natural) device for ensuring the divinely ordained social order.

The theory of the state in the *Arthashastra* is actually little more than an analysis of the elements essential to the efficient operation of the political organization. Sovereignty is made to depend on seven properties. This is the saptanga theory, to which we have referred. At the head of Kautalya's list is the *svāmī,* or master, a term used instead of *rājā* (ruler) to designate the head of the state, perhaps in order to allow the theory to apply to republics as well as to the monarchical state. It is evident that Kautalya considers the svami, the sovereign power, the most important of the seven components. Despite the significance he attaches to the role of the sovereign, Kautalya contrasts his position with representatives of other schools of arthashastra, each of whom championed a different aspect of the saptanga,[24] in that he would give priority to whichever factor the times should dictate as being of most consequence. Kautalya is a pragmatist in his political approach. But he does commit himself to ranking the factors, for although there is no general agreement among arthashastra theorists as to the relative disadvantage resulting from the injury or destruction of the various elements in the sevenfold theory, Kautalya considers harm to king, official, and populace,[o] in this order, as the most serious misfortunes. Kautalya is no determinist in the sense of seeing social destiny as the toy of the gods. Because he believed in the ability of man to learn from his experience and to exercise his rational faculties, he devoted his treatise to the king as the architect of his time—not as the instrument of fortune.

The second element in the construct is the *amātya,* or administrative class; following Ghoshal,[25] we shall distinguish the administrative officials from the advisers or chief ministers (*mantrins*), whom Kautalya limits to three or four in number. It is probable that originally the amatya was the clansman of the king. By Mauryan times these nobles had become his officers, the foundation of the bureaucracy. These two crucial constituents, the ruler and the official class, are followed by the rural and fortified (or urban) areas, the revenue (or treasury), the standing army, and the permanent ally of the state.[26] Dharma is not included among the components of commonwealth. This list appears in the later treatises of Kamandaka and "Shukra," and in the *Manusmriti.* The theory, in which diplomacy is made an integral part of politics, is intended to show the necessary conditions for the effective functioning of the state. The king occupies a dominant and, in fact, sovereign position. Indeed, "state" and "king" are often used interchangeably. Kautalya's definition of sovereignty remains vague.

A primary source of the king's power is the devotion and allegiance of his people. The king is therefore advised to see no interest other than the interest of his subjects and to guard against their dissatisfaction. "In the happiness of his subjects lies his happiness; in their welfare his welfare."[27] The basis of prosperity is the good will of the people. Kautalya does not speak of the rights of the people against the king, but he does regard the king as the servant of the people. There is no defense of arbi-

---

[o] The people are not properly an element in the theory.

trariness, but Kautalya stops short of securing the rights of the citizen against the authority of the government, and, as in the theoretical outgrowths of Rousseau's ideas, the interest of the people must ultimately be identical with those of the state. Opposition to the king is seditious. The relation of king and subject is paternalistic. The state is obligated to protect the subject from transgressions on his rights by others.[28] And not only life and property, but reputation as well, are safeguarded. The concealment of a daughter's premarital experience would cost the father a heavy fine. And woe to the bridegroom who did not advertise his defects (presumably physical).[29]

POLITICS AND ETHICS

The reader often comes away from the *Arthashastra* with the impression that the work exhibits a complete indifference to ethical considerations. But, as we have seen, side by side with ethical ideal and injunction there exists in ancient Indian theory a willingness to allow ends to sanction the methods employed in reaching those ends. Such political expedience is found in the earliest arthashastra schools cited by Kautalya. We might expect that when, as in the arthashastra school, the principle pervading political analysis and giving unity to the structure of the argument is altered, statements once accepted as merely descriptive of certain situations will take on new implications—as the doctrine of the survival of the fittest comes to justify expediency when the goal of political activity shifts to its own preservation and aggrandizement. When the state's military position was precarious, or when its security was at stake, any means of striking at the enemy was warranted. At such times the chivalric code was a luxury the state could ill afford. Nor is this policy of expedience and reason of state (*kūṭayuddha*) limited to the specifically arthashastra teaching. The counsel of Bharadvaja in the *Mahabharata*[30] anticipates the dicta that later came to be known as Machiavellism. In (admittedly extreme) statements, it is argued that nothing should be allowed to frustrate the purposes of the king, and selfish ambition need be the only aim of policy.[p] Public interest has little place in this unblushing opportunism; the king need recognize no moral obligation—might and cunning are beyond such standards. "Right . . . leans on might as the creeper on the tree. Right is in the hands of the strong; nothing is impossible to the strong. Everything is pure that comes from the strong."[31]

The advice of the brahman minister Kanika is similar.[32] The warrior is told to be remorseless with his enemies, to speak softly but firmly, to be ever prepared and always alert, to trust no one, to employ all techniques that might further his purposes, to excite the fear of the timid, and to be guarded in his movements. The images of political life that appear from time to time in the *Mahabharata,* and especially in the *Shantiparva,* are of battlefield and jungle (matsyanyaya). "Without piercing the vitals of

---

[p] And such works as the *Manusmriti* and the *Shantiparva* hold that wars of aggression, if certain basic humanitarian rules are observed, are no less justifiable than wars to defend the kingdom.

others, without achieving the most difficult feats, and without slaying creatures like a fisherman [slaying fish], no person can obtain great prosperity. Without slaughter no man has been able to achieve fame or subjects in this world. Indra, himself, by the slaughter of Vritra, became the *great* Indra. . . . Animals live upon animals, the stronger upon the weaker. . . . This has been ordained by the gods."[33] And again: "A king desirous of prosperity should not scruple to slay son or brother or father or friend, if any of these seek to thwart his objects."[34] Here is something of the old amorality of the heroic age. In the early Dharmasutras as well, political theory does not rely entirely on the scriptures for its authority. And, as several Indian scholars have pointed out, even in major religious works we find the search for a rational basis of politics, for a separate science of government. In Buddhist commentary, however, politics is returned to its subordinate position.[q]

There can never be a thoroughgoing divorce of politics and ethics for Kautalya; he never denies that the ultimate purpose of the state is a moral purpose, the maintenance of dharma. This is not to say that the state has no justification of its own; and when morality does find a place in Kautalyan politics, expedience continues to be served. When Kautalya remarks that might and self-aggrandizement are more important than religion and morality, he means that moral principles must be subordinated to the interests of the state inasmuch as the moral order depends upon the continued existence of the state. Kautalya is not above employing moral concepts either as a guise or because of their efficiency in securing appropriate conduct. Religion must, from the point of view of society, be judged in terms of its capacity to produce order. But had this not always been implicit in the relationship of Brahma and Kshatra authorities? Traditionally it was the religious proficiency of the purohita that determined the success of the king. Now, of course, the point had been reached where the brahmans must look to the state for the security of their interests.

For the most part, unscrupulous tactics are recommended only against those who would subvert and destroy the order on which society rested.[35] Even in war, moral considerations may decide the outcome. In the *Arthashastra* war is no longer the sport of the kshatriya and legitimate in its own right. It has become an instrument of policy to be employed when all else has failed. Kautalya distinctly prefers means short of open conflict, but he is more concerned with the cost and the possibilities of defeat than with the moral and ethical aspects of the problem.

We have earlier remarked on the fact that dharma embraces both a

---

[q] The earlier discussion of the *Bhagavad Gita* pointed up the relativism in Indian thought, a relativism which is dictated by more than caste considerations and which extends to codes of conduct. This element, when it enters the realm of political philosophy, has proved more shocking to students than it has when it figures in religion and is characterized as "tolerance." The career of Lord Krishna, as it unfolds in the *Mahabharata*, exhibits what by other standards might be seen as the most flagrant abuses. (It is interesting that two of the major roles he assumes, those of lover and warrior, are areas of activity where we might ironically admit that "all is fair.") There is no shortage of evidence that for all the syncretism and devaluation of the world in Indian belief, the social divisions it sustained (directly or indirectly) impeded the development of a universal ethic.

natural and a moral order.[r] This fusion might in itself have encouraged
a naturalistic ethic. We must remember that the concept of swadharma
links moral good with the fulfillment of caste function. The obligations
of the king's personal dharma may necessitate certain acts which, of themselves, are not easily justified. Max Weber[36] remarks:

> The problem of a "political ethic" has never preoccupied Indian
> theory and in the absence of ethical universalism and natural right, it
> could hardly be otherwise. The dharma of the prince was to conduct
> war for the sake of pure power *per se*. . . . All political theory . . .
> went far beyond what was familiar and average practice for the
> *signores* of the early Italian Renaissance in these respects and was
> completely devoid of all "ideology" in our sense of the word.[s]

Danda itself provides at least a partial explanation for the Kautalyan doctrine of expediency. The principle represents a bridge between morality
and *raison d'état*. Danda was nemesis for the king who misused its power
as well as for subjects who offended against the moral order. "For punishment (daṇḍa), when awarded with due consideration, makes the people
devoted to righteousness and to works productive of wealth and enjoyment; while punishment, when ill-awarded under the influence of greed
and anger or owing to ignorance, excites fury even among hermits and
ascetics dwelling in forests, not to speak of householders."[37] But this
quality of the royal power was easily eclipsed by the tremendous authority
the coercive function assumed as guarantor of the dharmic system. The
Arthashastra provides ample evidence that Kautalya understood the true
significance of the two-edged sword of danda.

The fact remains, and it cannot be brushed aside, that in the first book
of the *Arthashastra* Kautalya remarks that "the sole aim of all the sciences
is nothing but restraint of the organs of sense. Whosoever is of perverted
disposition and ungoverned senses will soon perish, though possessed of
the whole earth bounded by the four quarters."[38] The sentiment appears
almost Buddhist in tone. A later excerpt may be taken as a fairly complete expression of the moral argument applied to political rule: "A wise
king can make even the poor and miserable elements of his sovereignty
happy and prosperous; but a wicked king will surely destroy the most
prosperous and loyal elements of his kingdom."[39] These statements are
no attempt to disguise the political realism of the work and soften the harsh
counsel to come. Kautalya here is very much the brahman minister, representative of the power essential to victory. For all his commitment to
a philosophy of opportunism and force, Kautalya would not have limited
might to mere physical mastery. Such may be the primary obligation of
warrior and even king, but the *ultimate* power is spiritual.

---

[r] Such a principle is not unique to India. In Greece and elsewhere in the ancient
world we encounter similar concepts which combine fate and justice and which, as
rules, ordain what must be as well as what ought to be.

[s] Elsewhere Weber, referring to the *Arthashastra*, says that "in contrast with
this document Machiavelli's *Principe* is harmless." ("Politics as a Vocation," in
Gerth and Mills [139], p. 124.)

It is the politically unrealistic exaltation of nonviolence and mystic self-trandscendence that Kautalya rejects. The world remains with us and must be conquered if the difficult task of conquering ourselves is to be successful. Self-mastery and world-mastery are interdependent. There is, however, the suggestion of a debt to the great philosophical systems of the "axial age." In the Buddhist tradition some men are already close to enlightenment at the time of their birth. They may choose to become either buddhas or chakravartins. The chakravartin, or world master,[t] must have achieved self-discipline; this is the condition of his success. The concept of a state spanning the length and breadth of the subcontinent under the rule of a chakravartin goes back at least to the tenth century B.C., but Buddhism gave the concept the special significance it has had for Indian history. The idea came to be understood as the hope that the sphere of interstate politics, the area of political activity subject only to the primitive law of survival, might be made more amenable to moral controls. Ashoka Maurya was the embodiment of this lofty principle.

Kautalya believed, no less than did the great emperor, that control of the senses is crucial to the king's effectiveness as a ruler. Indeed the principle that one should be able to rule oneself before attempting to rule others is a major premise of Indian philosophy, antedating its most famous and systematic statement in the *Republic* of Plato.

We have noted earlier the resolution of the dilemma of action in Krishna's counsel to the hesitant kshatriya knight. To act is not to commit evil if the act is performed in a spirit of detachment. Such a philosophy may have provided an adequate rationale for the traditional social role of the warrior class in the face of the new ethical and ascetic doctrines appearing at the end of the Vedic epoch, but for the emerging state there remained the practical problem of defense and material well-being. Action could not be disinterested if the state were to survive and prosper. Thus does the problem of *raison d'état* develop—before its appearance in the West.[u] The statesman, faced with conflicting demands and feeling called

---

[t] This concept (*cakravartin,* from *cakra,* wheel), which we have referred to on several occasions, was utilized by Buddhism to symbolize the universality of the Buddhist spiritual message. The wheel represents the Buddhist dharma. Although the emphasis on self-mastery reflects the influence of heterodoxy, it also has roots in the importance of discipline as the basis for proper fulfillment of caste function. The priests stood to secure their own positions and protect themselves by insisting on righteous behavior buttressed by restraint and obedience. In brahman hands the idea of self-mastery seems to have been fused with the older Vedic belief that power could be communicated from the supernatural sphere to man (the Greek concept of *menos*) : self-mastery was a source of increased strength.

[u] The dialogue that Thucydides (*History of the Peloponnesian War,* Book V, 84–116) represents as having taken place between the Athenians and the citizens of Melos is usually considered to be the first clear statement of the issue, but in classical Greece there was no distinct division between the ethics of national conduct and that of individuals, for man found his highest realization in the *polis* and could not rightly be considered apart from it. In India the separation was more sharply drawn, although Kautalya sought to relate state and society more closely, without destroying the regulative function of the caste order in the process. This ambiguity complicates any attempt to label his thinking "solidarian." It is true that he worked to clear away impediments to the efficient operation of the political process, but he cannot be accused of actively striving to eliminate agencies that served to mediate between the masses and the governing elite.

upon to compromise traditional ethical principles in the interest of the state, may find justification for his acts in the knowledge that he has put the general welfare first. The ruler who remained faithful to the Kautalyan teaching could have such consolation; for the author of the *Arthashastra* the welfare of the state meant ultimately the welfare of the people, and the well-being of his subjects must be rated higher than that of the king himself.

Kautalya is aware that power must always be allied with shrewdness and restraint if it is not to be self-destructive. It is the element of cunning or, more positively, the sense of the situation, that has earned the brahman writer a sinister reputation in the minds of many. In discussing the traits of character indispensable to the king, he mentions "non-fatalism"—quite possibly as a criticism of attitudes of mind encouraged by Buddhism but incompatible with political life. The king must possess qualities of energy, among which he lists valor, impetuosity, agility, and dexterity. Immediately the tone of the work is set when Kautalya calls on the ruler to utilize "the opportunities afforded by the proper place, time and personal energy; [demonstrate] skill in discriminating between conditions which require conclusion of a treaty and manifestation of valor [i.e., in determining when it is appropriate to pursue a policy of peace or war], letting off the enemies and curbing them, and waiting under the pretext of some mutual understanding and taking advantage of the enemies' weak points."[40]

The state has a strong interest in encouraging civil morality; hence the ruler, who is an example to his people, cannot in his own conduct repeatedly challenge the bases of this morality. The ruler of unrighteous character is unable to rely on the loyalty and support of his subjects. "Which enemy is to be marched against—a powerful enemy of wicked character or a powerless enemy of righteous character?" asks Kautalya. "The strong enemy of wicked character should be marched against, for when he is attacked, his subjects will not help him, but rather put him down or go to the side of the conqueror. But when the enemy of virtuous character is attacked, his subjects will help him or die with him. . . . Hence, no king should give room to such causes as would bring about impoverishment, greed or disaffection among his people. If, however, they appear, he should at once take remedial measures against them."[41]

Certainly it is as valid to judge a political thinker on the measure of what he sought to accomplish as it is to examine him in the context of later-day politics. Had not the Renaissance yielded Machiavelli, nor the nineteenth century Bismarck, if we were not sensitive to the arguments of reason of state, we would perhaps assess Kautalya in a kindlier light. Similarities in the theories of the Mauryan minister and Machiavelli have long preoccupied students of Hindu polity. (It has even been suggested that the Italian was inspired by the *Arthashastra*.) But the validity of such a comparison is limited. Whereas Kautalya emphasizes the personal character of the king, and indeed sees the prince's capacity for righteous deportment as basic to beneficial administration, recommending that where possible he be exemplary in his conduct, Machiavelli is primarily concerned that the prince be able to inspire the loyalty of his people. In the *Discorsi*, he warns against arbitrariness and the dangers inherent in disturbing existing laws, remarking that security is what men want most.[42] Private morality is valid only in the sphere of personal relations and not in politics, but the morality of the individual is closely linked with the interests and goals of the community. Machiavelli hoped that the state could elevate the man who, inspired by a public spirit, would rise above his natural weaknesses. Virtue thus became civic virtue, patriotism. Because righteousness as such is irrelevant to the realm of politics, men must learn "how not to be good."[43]

Kautalya's greater concern with the life of the community and its role in shaping the institution of government is due not to his greater respect for man's moral nature and capacity for virtuous conduct, but to his acceptance of caste organization and the general noninterference of the state in the fulfillment of personal duty. Dandaniti exists to aid the processes of control and socialization, which are essentially the province of caste and religious institutions. Machiavelli's state exists to restrain man from the worst excesses of his own character. For Kautalya, the caste system (though still not fully developed) assumed the major burden of this regulatory function.

In the *Discourses* Machiavelli is intent on reviving ancient virtue as the basis of political society. He, like other Renaissance humanists, turned to the past in an attempt to find the foundations of the virtù that had motivated men to deeds of glory. But where corruption is the rule, the only hope for stability and cohesion is the prince. Loyalty to the leader must take the place of public virtue. In Indian theory there exists a myth that the king was originally named to combat some imminent danger to the order or to cope with some great need. (Likewise does the avatar appear in moments of crisis to ensure the preservation of dharma.) The same concern for order and security inspires the *Arthashastra*, and the work is comparable to *The Prince* in its reliance on the *tyrannos* as the ultimate agent of stability and prosperity when the times are out of joint and social integration threatened. But where does Kautalya find *his* model of heroic virtù? The materialism of the arthashastra teaching must be supplemented with concepts and images of traditional Vedic belief.

With Kautalya we arrive at a new stage in the development of the principle of political authority. In Brahmanic theory the legitimation of power and the activities of the state had customarily been rooted in the ruler's duty of protection. The *Arthashastra* represents an important step in the direction of authority based on interests and concerns shared by all, authority which takes unto itself many functions previously reserved to institutions outside the state proper. But though caste appears to play a less important role in the treatise than in the law books or religious works (as we should expect), and though the state has entered into areas of regulation historically the prerogative of economic associations, tribes, or other social organizations, and has expanded its judicial and welfare activities, the primary intent was not to destroy the pluralism of Hindu society.

Kautalya opposes any decentralizing tendency that would weaken the control of the state over the economic life of the community; the state is directly concerned with the accumulation of wealth, upon which its overall strength depends. It is true that the state he pictures has a strong interest in the values and sentiments of the people, and he is not above using religion for the purposes of the state, but he advocates no program of systematic indoctrination of the sort carried out in the regime of Ashoka. Nor does the state seek to eliminate the independent group life of the community and detach the individual from his old moorings. It is more appropriate to suggest that state policy constituted a greater threat to the tyranny of the group over the individual than to the freedom of the individual to pursue his own purposes as defined by custom and religious tradition.

The first step in the direction of what we have come to call totalitarianism may have been taken, but a wide area of autonomy remained with the many associations that composed society. The state's control over the thought and movements of the people could not in any sense approximate the regimentation of the modern totalitarian state with an advanced technological and organizational apparatus at its disposal. What Kautalya has done is to assert the importance of state participation in economic matters —active entry into the productive process, control of prices, interest rates, and licensing, and even supervision of occupations. All of which must, of course, amount to a significant weakening of one aspect of caste authority.

Montesquieu postulated that the central feature of tyranny was its basis in the isolation of the ruler from his subjects and the subjects from one another.[44] Seen in these terms, the caste basis of Indian society served to fragment the population and insulate the masses against control by an elite. Caste, however, organized the people as well as divided them, creating groups along functional lines. Caste organization did represent a hindrance to the formulation of collective goals and, as such, constituted a challenge to the state-builder. Kautalya did not oppose the supporting and sustaining function of caste, as long as the general welfare was not prejudiced by narrow class interest. He advises the ruler, for example, to allow the people of a conquered territory to pursue their traditional way of life, retain their language, celebrate their festivals. And the king must not seek to cut himself off from the populace in splendid aloofness. He must actively seek their affection and be constantly alert to the main currents of opinion. Members of the community are encouraged, for their part, to think of themselves as subjects having in common a number of purposes that only the state can fulfill. Political authority, in the Kautalyan state, has become more differentiated from other forms of authority, and its scope has broadened immensely.

Kautalya was faced with the same need for political union in the face of disorder and external threat that confronted Machiavelli in northern Italy. In a sense, Mauryan India was itself in the throes of a renaissance, which would culminate in the enlightened rule of the emperor Ashoka. Belief stirred against belief, culture against culture; extensive discretionary powers were granted the ruler as the means for deterring disruptive forces, and authority was centralized as it had never been before.[v] The times called for flexibility, which in turn presupposed goal-directed collective activity. It is likely that with the increased gravity and expense of war the state would have found it more efficacious, when possible, to employ intrigue in meeting challenges to its authority.

Kautalya's opportunism—even if it does not represent the political position of the Mauryan preceptor—must also be seen in the context of brahman struggles with heterodox systems of thought. The very defense of brahman interests may have made the reappraisal of religious controls imperative. It was now to brahman advantage to seek the active cooperation of the state, to block any alignment of the state with heterodoxy, and to support the ambitions of political authority sympathetic to the brahmans. Perhaps it appeared to the brahman author of the *Arthashastra*, writing in a time of momentous change and declining power of old institutions, that the basis of the traditional code was forever lost, that matsyanyaya had become the characteristic of all relationships.

As Burckhardt has pointed out, Machiavelli viewed the state as a work of art—not as a product of nature working through man, or as part of the divine plan, but as the conscious creation of man, analogous to artistic fabrication. The *Arthashastra* can be characterized in the same terms. It is the art of government rather than a theory of the state that we find in the writings of the Florentine and the Hindu: both are preoccupied with techniques of achieving[w] supreme power, both are confronted with situations that make some degree of arbitrary government necessary. Both are concerned with the leader (*dux*), who establishes the authoritative role. Both (and this would follow) write from the vantage point of the ruler, and their treatises belong to the "mirror of princes" category of political literature.

The Machiavelli of *The Prince* is a political thinker engrossed with practical questions of the actual foundation of the state, the creation of a viable political order in the face of contention, timorousness, and debasement. The Machiavelli of the *Discourses* defends republican government as producing the most vigorous state once order has been established and secured. It is not inconceivable that, had Kautalya composed a "Discorsi" which assumed a condition of unity and strength, his emphasis would have shifted from *dux* to *rex*, the sovereign whose role is predetermined. We would have a work of the nature of the rajadharma literature, with all the safeguards against arbitrariness that the term implies. But there is little indication in the *Arthashastra* of any consuming interest in the development of a popular virtù, a mass public-spiritedness that could make possible a transition to republican institutions.

[v] Book V, chap. 11, of Aristotle's *Politics* (on methods of ensuring the stability of monarchies) suggests a number of rough parallels with Kautalya's advice to the ruler who would increase his power.

[w] Acquiring *and* maintaining power. Machiavelli discusses the problem of preserving power and order in the *Discourses*; the creation of order holds his attention in *The Prince*.

The approach to politics of Kautalya and Machiavelli has a definite empirical character, and their theories rest on a naturalistic ethic. The good tends frequently to be that which contributes to the satisfaction of universal needs and desires. Security is one of the most important of these needs; it is the wish for security that bridges the private and public spheres of activity. The major function of the state is the provision of stability and security. Because religion itself depends on order, the state is justified in employing religion as a means for achieving stability. The constancy of human nature makes it possible for man to learn from history, but history is viewed by Kautalya and Machiavelli as a storehouse of examples, rather than as a dynamic process.[a] Kautalya is sensitive to the economic aspects of power, whereas Machiavelli works with more purely political concepts. Though rich in political maxims intended for broad application, Kautalyan theory is strongly pragmatic and adaptive. There is room in the argument for the unforeseeable. Unfortunate the king who does not constantly gauge the temper of his people, who does not estimate carefully his chances for success before acting, who does not seek advice from the experienced and the astute. In attempting to systematize the study of politics as a science in its own right and to treat the subject objectively, both Kautalya and Machiavelli were pioneers.

Perhaps Machiavellism is a characteristic of the transition from traditional authority to legal-rational authority—a development that failed to complete itself in ancient India, possibly because of a change in the legitimation pattern which served the interests of the monarchy without fundamentally altering the "sacred" structure. But problems of administering a large territory and conflicts within the normative system forced the initial break with the older principles of legitimation.

[a] There is a tendency among Indian scholars to credit Kautalya with a keener historical sense than the *Arthashastra* in fact reveals—or than we should expect, considering the nature of the Indian belief system.

12 ⨯ KAUTALYA AND THE ARTHASHASTRA SCHOOL, II

Kautalya goes far beyond Machiavelli in his attention to the structure and processes of administration. He places great emphasis on the intellectual and moral discipline of the king, which is essential to the successful functioning of the state. The king must be continent, industrious, and alert—a man of refinement and sound judgment. If the king is vigorous, his subjects will be equally so.[1] Like Plato, Kautalya regards self-mastery as the beginning of wisdom; it is indispensable to the achievement of political purposes. But the training that Kautalya prescribes for the king does not approach the rigorous self-denial that Plato advocates for the class of guardians; Kautalya advises moderation rather than asceticism. The education of the prince should include arithmetic, the art of effective expression, the Vedic literature, and political economy—in addition to the techniques of self-control and the discipline of the senses.[2]

The king clearly occupies the central position in the theory of the *Arthashastra*, and Kautalya devotes four chapters to means by which the king could safeguard himself against the wiles of courtesan, prince, and minister. Court intrigue was common, and kings occasionally had reason to suspect those closest to them of subversion. Often the crown prince himself was not to be trusted—Magadha is reported to have been ruled in its earlier history by several parricides—and the king is advised to watch carefully the movements of even his son. The prince is likened to the crab, who devours his own parents.[3] Kautalya devises a series of complicated stratagems to test the loyalty of ministers, as well as to determine how and where they can best serve the state.[4] He recommends also that the palace be equipped with hollow columns, collapsible floors, secret passages, and other devices for the king's protection.

The king rarely enjoys an idle moment. His day is divided into eight parts.

> During the first one-eighth part of the day, he shall post watchmen and attend to the accounts of receipts and expenditure; during the second part, he shall look to the affairs of both citizens and country people; during the third, he shall not only bathe and dine, but also study; during the fourth, he shall not only receive revenue in gold, but also attend to the appointments of superintendents; during the fifth, he shall corre-

spond in writs with the assembly of his ministers, and receive the secret information gathered by his spies; during the sixth, he may engage himself in his favorite amusements or in self-deliberation; during the seventh, he shall superintend elephants, horses, chariots, and infantry; and during the eighth part, he shall consider various plans of military operations with his commander-in-chief.[5]

The night is similarly divided and includes the reception of secret emissaries, bathing and study, meditation on "the injunctions of sciences" and the day's duties, the consideration of administrative measures, and benediction from the priests.

Kautalya conceives of sovereignty not as a right but as an almost sacred obligation. The king is held responsible for the progress and prosperity of the times; he is "the creator of epochs." Kautalya's advice on commissioning spies to learn whether or not the conduct of the monarch is condoned indicates the importance of public opinion to the king. He appears to have in mind particularly the opinions of the leaders of tribal groups. He considers it better that a wrong action be taken than that public dissatisfaction be courted. Poverty and oppression incite the people to revolution; hence the king is told to identify his own welfare with that of his subjects. In discharging these duties of his office and advancing the welfare and security of the people, he fulfills his religious obligations.

Yet the king, no matter how accomplished, is physically incapable of assuming all the duties of government unto himself, and must therefore rely on ministers for assistance.[6] The king does not actually delegate authority; he seeks to lessen his burden but not his responsibility. Final decisions rest always with him, and he is not bound by the prevailing opinion of his cabinet—although he is generally expected to follow the advice of the majority of its members. Kautalya states that Manu (i.e., the ancient school of Manu) recommends that the council of ministers have twelve members, Brihaspati suggests sixteen members, and Ushanas (Shukra) twenty, but he himself characteristically holds that the number should be dictated by practical need.[7]

The council was to be composed of an inner and outer body. The first, informal in nature, was concerned with deliberation and policy-making, and the other was charged with carrying these decisions into action. Meetings of the royal council were usually held in strictest secrecy. Kautalya goes so far as to proscribe certain birds and animals from the council chambers for fear of their transmitting information of the proceedings. Although it is recommended that the king be to his purohita as the servant to his master, the priestly adviser does not have the eminence that he enjoys in the Dharmasutras. The purohita is included in the components of sovereignty only as one of the ministers. A quarter of the total income should be expended on these governmental servants: enough to "infuse in them the spirit of enthusiasm to work."[a]

---

[a] *Arthashastra* V, 3 (p. 297). The distinction between ministers and department heads is not entirely clear. Evidently the more important heads of departments were

Punishment, the guarantor of the social order, must always be in accord with the principles of justice, severe or mild as the offense requires.[8] And yet Kautalya is so zealous in his efforts to strengthen the position of the monarch that punishment for disaffection and official misconduct are out of all proportion to the offense committed. Caste position is not allowed to limit punishment for offenses against the state, and even those of exalted birth are subject to banishment. Kautalya demands decisive evidence for conviction, but advocates third-degree methods for attaining confessions.

The provisions for economic justice include injunctions against the confiscation of a man's total property and the attachment of production goods, the safeguarding of returns from labor and of women's property rights, and the limitation of creditor rights. There is also an elaborate set of provisions covering slavery, ownership and sale of property, and interest rates and debt. Guilds were to handle differences arising among their own members. But the nature of these economic regulations must certainly limit the traditional tolerance of local usage, the respect for the customary legal arrangements of the various groups and corporations existing within the state. The penal law, in addition to covering the usual categories of criminal activities, dealt with rights of and disputes among guilds and administrative authorities, and included provisions for the supervision of foreigners. Problems of distribution, measurements, and price and profit regulation all came under penal law.

Kautalya recommends immediate justice as well as equity. The defendant should be granted from three to seven days to file his defense. The administration of justice was to be decentralized to further speed decision. In the Mauryan era there were two classes of courts in addition to the village tribunals (which handled minor disputes). The *dharma-sthiya*[b] courts were concerned with civil matters—inheritance, debt, contract, boundary disputes, sales, and so forth. A case could be appealed as high as the royal courts. The courts dealing with penal law, *kantaka śodhana,*[c] tried political cases, including those concerned with the mal-

---

ministers. These officials are called *adhyākshas.* The second book of the *Artha-shastra* deals with the duties of government superintendents: the chamberlain (*sanni-dhātā*) "shall see to the construction of the treasure-house, trading-house, the store-house of grains, the storehouse of forest produce, the armory and the jail"; the collector-general, who was responsible for forts, mines, buildings and gardens, forests, herds, and roads; the superintendent of accounts; the commander in chief, who "shall be so capable as to order either advance or retreat." These appear to be the major administrative officials; their salaries were from twice to twelve times those received by lesser public servants. Kautalya devotes chapters to officials concerned with mining operations, the superintendent of the mint and the state goldsmith, supervisors of the storehouse and of forest products, commerce, weights and measures, tolls, and passports; there are those in charge of agriculture, weaving, and ships; superintendents of liquor and prostitutes, of the slaughterhouse and the armory, chariots and infantry, elephants, horses, and cows. And, finally, there is the officer responsible for the affairs of the capital city, who, among his other duties, "shall make a daily inspection of reservoirs of water, of roads, of the hidden passage for going out of the city, of forts, fort walls, and other defensive works." (*Arthashastra* II.)

[b] In addition to using dharma in its customary ethical and social sense, Kautalya on occasion employs the term to refer to civil law.

[c] Literally, the extirpation of thorns.

feasance of officials,[d] and other cases of an especially serious or difficult nature. Procedure was apt to be less ceremonious than in the civil courts, and the actions of judges in these courts were circumscribed.

The doctrine of *maṇḍala*, which refers to the sphere of influence in interstate relations, is thoroughly analyzed in the *Arthashastra*. Books 6–14 treat of these relationships, particularly with reference to the extension of empire; the major theme is the dependence of peace upon power. Foreign policy must be based on the careful assessment of the resources and support available to the state and to its enemies. The state must be always prepared; it exists in an alien world governed only by force. The intricate system of alliances in ancient India was based on the assumption that contiguous states are hostile. It followed that the state adjacent to one's own enemy was a natural ally. Approximate equality of military might must dictate a policy of neutrality, since neither power is capable of easily crushing the other—and when it is not certain that advantage will result from battle, war should be avoided. If it is superior in strength, the state should pursue a policy of aggression; comparative weakness calls for conciliation and the security of alliances, and the adoption of treacherous methods. This theory was originally an attempt to create a balance of power in a system of small states, some of which were always in an expansionist mood.[9]

The six alternative policies are agreement with pledges (i.e., peace), war, indifference or neutrality, "making preparations," alliance with another power, and making peace with one state while engaged in hostilities with another ("double policy").[10] The ideal of honorable conduct in war is a luxury that only the strong can afford. Even religion may be employed in the defense of the state. Kautalya recommends hollow idols in which spies or assassins may be hidden. The maintenance of order and the extension of empire justify any means. The philosophy of expedience is never more explicit than in the theory of interstate relations.

In outlining military campaigns Kautalya disregards the traditional humanitarian principles laid down to regulate the conduct of war. He marks out the area from the Himalayas to the seas (*Himavātsāmudrantāram Udichīnam*—a concept that recurs in the literature of ancient India) as the "natural sphere of imperialism." Six boards were charged with the conduct of warfare and the maintenance of the army, which was open to recruits from all castes.[11] After conquering a nation, the king must consolidate his position by cultivating the loyalty of the defeated people. Kautalya advises generous treatment of these subjects and respect for those customs and traditions that can be tolerated without jeopardizing the security of the state. The ambassador in the *Arthashastra*, like his modern

[d] Kautalya remarks at one point on the difficulty of detecting dishonesty among officials: "Just as fish moving under water cannot possibly be found out either as drinking or not drinking water, so government servants . . . cannot be found out [while] taking money [for themselves]." (*Arthashastra* II, 9, p. 77.) He suggests that departments should have more than one head as a safeguard against the embezzlement of public money as well as against the overconcentration of power in a single person.

counterpart, enjoyed immunities—although he was clearly a foreign agent commissioned to determine the defense position of his host country and the extent of its resources. For this reason it was necessary that the king keep close watch on the movements of foreign envoys.[12]

The elaborate intelligence system of the *Kautaliya*, which is indeed one of the distinguishing features of the work, is fundamental to Kautalyan foreign and domestic policy.[e] Spies were drawn from a number of social classes, assumed a variety of poses, and were assigned many different tasks. The agent was employed to test the loyalty of public officials, to gather information, to undertake secret missions, to prevent crime and sedition, to ascertain the tenor of public opinion, and to ensure the popularity of the regime by countering criticism and praising the king. Five classes of spies were under the authority of five different departments. In addition to these there were the women spies (beggars, nurses, cooks, prostitutes) and the "wandering" spies. The king must give a daily audience to the reports of these agents. Kautalya cautions against implicit reliance on the accounts of spies. However, if three sources not in contact with one another were in essential agreement, the king could have confidence in their accuracy. But if the reports were not consistent or if the information was considered insufficient, it appears that no action was to be taken. Contradiction in the reports was cause for reprehending the informants.[13]

The *Arthashastra*'s emphasis on fiscal matters may be explained by the great cost of maintaining an army that received cash payment and very likely accounted for more than half of the revenue expended. (Kautalya plotted to regain much of the money paid out by having pseudo-merchants, who were agents of the king, sell goods to the soldiers at twice the usual price during military operations.) The author of the treatise demonstrates great ingenuity in devising and justifying means for augmenting the wealth of the state, including state ownership of gambling houses and bordellos, and state control of the sale of liquor. This concern with the public coffers has caused many analysts of ancient Hindu administrative institutions to regard the state as solely a tax-collecting device. But if the brahman minister was engrossed in budgetary matters, it was because he considered the safety and unity of the state to be dependent on an adequate revenue.

Income was derived from government-owned mines and other properties, from excise taxes, tolls for transportation facilities, fees for use of land, import duties, sales and excess property taxes, compulsory contributions from the people, and income taxes from certain groups of the community (artists, seers, prostitutes). Kautalya suggests in addition to these sources a number of questionable techniques for acquiring wealth for the state. A man might be hidden in a tree to give it certain unusual properties and a collection taken to rid the tree of its evil spirit. Or admission would be charged to see a state-constructed multiheaded serpent. Agents of the king could induce trances and charge the victims to have

---

[e] There is at least the possibility that Kautalya borrowed the design for his espionage (and also administrative) organization from the empire that flourished for more than two centuries under the Achaemenid rulers of Persia.

the spell removed. The extent to which such means for parting the population from its money are to be condemned as unscrupulous has been debated. Those who would excuse the author of the *Arthashastra* point to the effectiveness of his schemes in equalizing taxation and to his recommendation that they be employed only in extreme situations.

Taxation policy in the *Arthashastra* and in the *Manusmriti* (as in the great body of theory culminating in the *Shukranitisara*) reflects the view that while the state has its right to the golden egg, the goose must be protected. Taxation should be gradual, increased only in times of emergency, and then only when rationalized to the people. It should be based on net profits instead of gross earnings, and an article should be taxed only once. Incentives in the form of moderate taxes should encourage production from marginal lands. Remission of taxes is recommended for a number of socially desirable endeavors.[14] Realizing that the incentive to produce will be reduced by excessive exactions, Kautalya urges that officers who collect more than the allotted tax be punished, and warns against oppressive assessments. In short, the king should be governed by a comprehension of what the traffic will bear. And yet, despite this sensitivity to the productive process, Kautalya's state was itself a gigantic enterprise and regarded the private trader as a competitor, an enemy of the public interest, the "thief who is not called thief."

Kautalya would assess the customary sixth of the produce of the land, though this proportion might, when necessary, be raised to a third.[f] Essential commodities, such as grain, inexpensive textiles, sugar, and oil, were to be taxed at one-twentieth of their value. The tax on other goods could be as high as twenty percent. Goods might not be sold at the place of their production, but had to be taken to a government agency, stamped, and, after sale, appraised for taxes. Attempts to evade this procedure brought the sternest penalty.[15] The customs duties recommended by Kautalya (and probably practiced by the Mauryans) amounted, for certain commodities, to a protective tariff—normally twenty percent. Usually, however, rates were calculated to allow a profit. In revenue policy emphasis was as often on indirect as on direct measures of taxation.

Kautalya claims for the king control of the forests and game, the wasteland, and the mineral and salt mines, and supervision of the production of spirits. The *gabelle* and the liquor tax were evidently important sources of revenue. Punishment for infringements in this area of the royal domain was particularly severe.[g] Few natural resources were beyond the royal authority.[h] Kautalya outlines a program of industrial and commercial

---

[f] Usually where irrigation was accomplished by pumping water from the rivers. Additional water rates must have made the tax onerous.

[g] On special occasions home-brew was sanctioned.

[h] By the later Brahmanic period a person could be dispossessed of his land only for failure to pay his land tax. And there is evidence from inscriptions to indicate that, at least by the Christian era, the landholder could dispense with his land in a number of ways without interference by the state. The several authorities who imply that all land is the property of the crown (cf. *Manu* VIII, 39) are not convincing. The Sanskrit commentator on the *Arthashastra* says (II, 24, p. 140) that the king

development and regulation. And the king should encourage agricultural production by directing the surplus population to the cultivation of undeveloped tracts of land. The author of the *Arthashastra* advocates (and it was probably a Mauryan practice) giving land to brahmans in order to extend tillage and settlement.[i]

Provision is made for emergency periods. Kautalya argues the need for a reserve stock of all essential commodities,[j] and in critical times the state could appropriate private food stocks. The degree of government control anticipates that of the modern welfare state. Famine relief programs are contemplated, and a scheme resembling public works projects was designed to provide employment for the needy. The king must guard his subjects against calamities caused by fire, flood, pestilence, famine, rats, tigers, serpents, and demons.[16]

The efficiency of the worker was to be encouraged by ample reward. Each laborer was entitled to a certain number of free days, and work on holidays justified extra pay. Kautalya's demand for the punishment of physicians whose patients died, in cases that were not previously reported to authorities, indicates that the professions did not escape state control. The role of the state in the economy was even more direct; the government was in business for itself as the owner of industries, land, and mines—the last a state monopoly. The attention Kautalya gives to the economy points to the importance of trade and mining—a consequence of the strategic location of Magadha. The Mauryan state controlled access to the iron and copper mines of Dhalbhum and Singhbhum.[17] It is significant, too, that those employed by the state received a cash wage.

The *Arthashastra*, like the later *Shukranitisara*, is essentially a handbook for the guidance of the governing group, a manual for the practical politician. For the most part Kautalya prescribes for specific needs and uses tested administrative procedures. His system is highly centralized; he recognizes the need for uniformity in administrative institutions, and he is careful to prevent the ambiguities that arise from divided sovereignty. The basic unit of administration is the province, or janapada, which included at least eight hundred villages of from one hundred to five hundred families. At the apex of local and provincial administration stood the collector general, who was charged with supervising the collection of revenue and maintaining order. Below him were the district and deputy

---

is owner of both water and land, and that the people cannot exercise ownership over these two things. But early in the same chapter Kautalya refers specifically to the crown lands, implying a special category of land. Kautalya remarks (VIII, 2) that in *vairājya* lands, which Jayaswal ([199], p. 83) believes are those without kings, the people do not distinguish "mine" and "thine." This seems to indicate that in the republican and older tribal communities private property did not exist, and that the appearance of the territorial state and the institution of property were roughly contemporaneous. This suggestion lends itself very well to a Marxian analysis of social institutions. For the argument that the king did indeed lay claim to the land of his domain, *vide* Ghoshal [143], p. 166.

[i] *Vide* Kosambi [218], pp. 291ff. Sharma ([390], p. 316) sees little evidence of this in the post-Mauryan epoch. In the Gupta period cultivated land was customarily granted to the brahmans.

[j] With the possible aim of modifying the effect of supply and demand on prices.

collectors assisted by village superintendents. Little attention is given to village institutions, but it seems that the village council was an autonomous body as far as the supervision of local affairs was concerned. The guilds, which were granted only a minimum of independence, were placed securely in the service of the state.

Kautalya, in short, traced the problems of the state to the shortcomings of internal administration, and not to the perversities of fate.

LATER TECHNICAL TREATISES ON POLITY

The *Nītisāra* of Kamandaka is usually placed in the Gupta period. Like the *Arthashastra*, it is concerned with the material lives of the people and the requirements of the state. The *Nitisara*, or *Kāmandakīya* as it is also called, contributes very little that is original, since it is, by its author's admission, a summary of the *Arthashastra* of Kautalya. Large parts of the work are scarcely more than abridgements of Kautalya's treatise. Kamandaka, however, neglects the subjects treated in four of the fifteen books of the *Arthashastra*, which contain materials equal in importance to that in the other eleven. These excluded portions deal with the administrative system and with civil and criminal law. Either the author of the *Nitisara* did not comprehend these more technical and less evocative passages, or he did not find them relevant or applicable to the needs of his time. Ramachandra Dikshitar believes that the work was written to meet the needs of monarchs too concerned with affairs of state to be able to read the *Kautaliya*.[18] The emphasis on foreign relations suggests the preoccupation of the period with preserving a balance of power and a stable political order. Two-thirds of the *Kamandakiya* relates to foreign policy and the conduct of war.

Carlo Formichi, in his *Salo Populi*,[19] finds common ground in the thinking of Kamandaka, Machiavelli, and Hobbes. The political conditions of the periods in which each wrote were similar. The three writers are in essential agreement on the principles basic to a theory of the state. Man is, for the most part, nonrational, sovereignty is by nature unrestricted, interstate relations are not governed by moral considerations, and the claims of the state come before those of religion. But their respective methodologies are those of the poet, the historian, and the philosopher.

The king, declares Kamandaka, is more necessary than the rain, for the failure of the rains can be survived, but the absence of the ruler cannot. Indeed, injury to the king is more calamitous than injury to the "state" (*rājya*) itself—for the king is the active agent who is able to remedy calamities that befall the state.[20] Kingship is magnified to all-embracing importance. Yet, in his discussion of the saptanga theory,[k] Kamandaka

---

[k] *Sharma* ([389], p. 28) believes that this departure from Kautalya's elevation of the svami, or king, above the other elements reflects a time when the royal power was no longer so important as an agency of social control and integration. But Kautalya also allowed that other elements of sovereignty might at times be more important than the king—and this waning of the practical significance of kingship might also account for the elaborate attempts to exalt the king that we find in the *Nitisara*.

never states that one of the elements is inherently more important or of greater merit than the others. Each component is complementary to the others and circumstances dictate their relative significance.[21] Nor is there any effort to buttress the king's position with analogies of divinity. The argument is rational: "A righteous king, protecting his subjects to the best of his resources and having the power of capturing hostile cities, should be held in as high regard as the Lord Prajapati [Brahman] himself."[22] The king must furnish protection and, in return, his subjects will yield taxes. Beyond this, Kamandaka has very little to say about the specific obligations of the king. But the author of the *Nitisara* stresses the need for discipline on the part of the king in words that recall the *Kautaliya*. How can a king hope to conquer the world if he cannot master himself? Self-indulgence is the trap that ensnares the elephant.[23]

The king can no more hope to control his subjects without punishment than a fisherman can hope to catch fish without a rod.[24] But punishment must be proportionate to the offense if the king is to be feared and yet respected. These measures must be countenanced by the sacred writings and by society; dharma itself is that which is approved by the enlightened members of the community.[25] "Thus, like rivers that flow through right courses, falling into the sea, all prosperity devolves—and never dwindles away—upon a king who, knowing the good and evil of the infliction of punishments and following the path chalked out in the Vedas, frames rules of conduct for his subjects."[26]

Kamandaka, like Kautalya, holds that fair means of fighting can be afforded only by the state that enjoys the most advantageous position. And again like Kautalya, he argues that no war should be undertaken where victory is uncertain.[27] In general he holds that if there is an alternative to actual warfare, hostilities must be avoided. When the confidence of the enemy is secured, or when he is off his guard, the king and his officers may strike in devious ways, creating dissension in the ranks of the enemy. Had not Indra himself slain the demon Vritra when a truce existed between the two? Kamandaka clothes his opportunism in moral principles and maintains that "the slaughter of foes by deceitful measures is not detrimental to one's righteousness."[28]

Tamil literature provides no systematic treatment of political principles, though the *Tirukkuṟaḷ* (*Kuṟaḷ*) of Tiruvaḷḷuvar, which has been claimed by all the religious sects of India, contains general references to the science of artha. All we know about Valluvar with any degree of certainty is that he was a native of Madura.[l] The work, which belongs to the fourth or fifth century A.D.,[m] owes much to Sanskrit studies, and par-

---

[l] He is supposed to have been a weaver by profession, but there is no real confirmation of this. There is not even complete agreement on whether the work is anti-Brahmanical or not. Its author was, according to legend, a pariah. Nilakanta Sastri ([300], p. 349) believes him to have been a learned Jaina divine.

[m] Dikshitar places the work in the first or second century B.C. For his argument see [342], pp. 132ff.

ticularly to the *Arthashastra*.ⁿ This political code of the Tamils may be based on Kamandaka's interpretation of Kautalya, but many scholars consider the *Kamandakiya* to be a slightly later work than the South Indian treatise.

In the Tamil, as in the Sanskrit literature, the three great purposes of life are taken as meaningful only in the context of one another; the 1330 stanzas of the *Kural*, the "Tamil Veda," are accordingly organized in three sections—righteousness, politics and wealth, and pleasure. The second portion of the *Kural* treats the political and economic as interdependent—for the pursuit of wealth depends on capable government, and the strength of the state is based on its wealth. On wealth dharma and kama depend.[29] Like Kautalya, the author of the *Kural* is not involved in highly speculative aspects of political theory, such as the nature of the state. And in policy considerations Tiruvalluvar is willing to place moral principle in the wake of expediency.

Perhaps one difference between the early arthashastra work of Kautalya and the later Tamil version is that the latter does not appear to be a part of the "mirror of princes" literature. It is hoped that both the common man and the prince can profit from the advice offered in the verses. The *Kural* echoes the emphasis of earlier writings on the importance of just rule. The prince is counseled to make his actions conform to the law, and the scepter, which brings victory to the prince, must lean to neither side.[30] Tyranny and anarchy are the twin curses of mankind. The protection of his subjects is the central responsibility of the king.[31] In return for this security the *Kural*, like the Sanskrit texts, awards the sixth part of the produce of the land to the ruler.ᵒ

The *Kural* follows Kautalya in the moral demands it makes on the king, restating the need for the king to be of noble deportment as well as noble birth. The prince must seek the guidance of the experienced and the wise; he must work with diligence and vigor to develop the wealth of the land and bring prosperity to his people. And he must be bold and firm in his purpose, continually guarding against weakness in his own person.[32] The prince must be accessible to the people and must tolerate the right of his subjects to reprove his actions. He must personally supervise the operation of government. The *Kural* does not make the same extravagant claims for the king that we find in the *Nitisara* of Kamandaka. However, in the *Maṇimēkhalai*, a Tamil epic poem, we are told that because the righteous rule of the king keeps the planets on their course, ensuring adequate rainfall, the king may "regard as his own the life of every living creature."[33]

"Judgment in the choice of projects and the means of their execution, and positiveness in the expression of opinion are the necessary qualities in the councilor," according to Valluvar. The minister must know the law, speak with eloquence, "see things in their right proportion"; he must persevere in the accomplishment of a project with attention to "the re-

ⁿ Note, for example, Chapters 74 and 75, which correspond closely to *Artha-shastra* II, 1, and II, 3, respectively.
ᵒ And it seems likely that this was the maximum rate.

sources in hand, the instrument, the nature of the action itself, the proper time, and the proper place for execution."[34] The ambassador is advised to be cool-headed, persuasive in speech and engaging in manner, learned, and loyal to the death.[35] We are not surprised to find that sovereignty requires the possession of an army, fortresses, resources, people (territory), allies, ministers. Having these, the king is "a lion among princes." In foreign policy the *Kural* is again reminiscent of Kautalya: "Strive not with the powerful, but against those that are weaker than thyself carry on wars without relaxing even for one moment."[36] There is the same reluctance to allow moral considerations to rule diplomatic conduct that characterized the *Arthashastra*. In order to judge the enemy's capabilities it is essential to calculate the resources required in an undertaking, to evaluate one's own sources of power and those of the ally as well as those of the foe. The proper timing of campaigns is of crucial importance as is patience (and even the willingness to retreat—as a fighting ram draws back before the attack). It is as necessary that the place be favorable as that the proper time be chosen.[37] "Glory is not for the unwatchful."[38]

The *Brihaspati Arthashastra* (also known as the *Bārhaspatya Sūtras*) was discovered even more recently than the *Kautaliya*. What we have consists of only six chapters—probably a small portion of the original.[p] Kautalya and the *Mahabharata* refer to an author on polity known as Brihaspati, but the passages noted do not appear in the extant treatise. Beni Prasad ascribes the work to the twelfth century A.D. if references to certain religious sects are not later interpolations. Stylistically it would appear to be earlier. It is a work of little originality and contributes almost nothing to our study. The policies and principles put forth in the *Brihaspati Arthashastra* are often in open contradiction to one another, the author at times arguing that the pursuit of wealth is all-important[39] and elsewhere holding that material ends must be subordinated to virtue.[40] Sometimes the work seems to be closer to the dharmashastra school than to the usual arthashastra position, e.g., in the occasional deprecation of the office of the king. But then we find that, like the school of Ushanas (Shukra), Brihaspati insists that politics is the only science with the right to call itself that.

The writer resembles Kautalya in the emphasis he places on the importance of punishment in preserving the social order. There is the same dependence on doctrines of material gain and even of naturalism. We find all the customary arthashastra policies of expedience—conciliation, bribery, the creation of dissension and of illusion, pretense of indifference, and killing—all, that is, except the use of magical devices. The need for discipline and ethical conduct is stressed, but the secular nature of the work prevents any rooting of morality in religion. Although Brihaspati advocates regular consultation with advisers, he cautions the king in the selec-

---

[p] The sutras should not be confused with the dharmashastra work attributed to the same authority.

tion of his councilors and demands constant wariness. The king and his ministers must be sensitive to the needs and opinion of the people; for if dharma is to have the force of law, it must conform to the popular will—and it is particularly urgent that it reflect the opinion of the learned.[41]

In this same broad classification of arthashastra and nitishastra works are the fables intended as a manual of instruction for young princes. The *Pañchatantra* (The Five Books) testifies in its opening verses to the great influence of the arthashastra school. What are vices in ordinary men, according to the unknown author, may be virtues in the prince. The standards that apply to the conduct of men are not those which govern the conduct of policy.[42] Here is the dictum of Kautalya and Machiavelli—that moral principles cannot themselves ensure the context in which they operate. The moral tone of the *Pañchatantra* may be suggested by the story of the lion who, suffering from acute hunger, is advised by a crow to kill and eat a camel to whom the lion had given protection.[43] For, says the crow, the sages have told us that such actions may be committed for the sake of self-preservation. The noble creature is unconvinced, and the crow continues his lecture: the individual may be sacrificed for the family, the family for the village, the village for the state—and for the self all the world may be sacrificed.[q]

Somadeva, a Jaina author living in the tenth century, probably in southern India, extols the state as the source of all satisfactions. But although government is essential to human fulfillment, the absence of government is better than government by fools and knaves. The prince must be instructed in the sacred writings and arthashastra. As king, he must be aware of his obligation to provide protection in order to ensure prosperity, and he is advised to take a daily oath to the effect that he is "protecting this cow which yields the milk of four oceans, whose calf is dharma, whose tail is enterprise, whose hoofs are varna and ashrama, whose ears are kama and artha, whose horns are diplomacy and valor, whose eyes are truth and purity, and whose face is law." Those who injure her shall not be endured.[44] In spite of the fact that the king rarely enjoys a more elevated status than in Somadeva's *Nītivākyāmṛta,* we find the familiar recommendation that he seek constant counsel with his ministers, from whose ranks foreigners as well as those of low character and those wanting in common sense are to be excluded. Somadeva proposes that control of policy be in the hands of civil authorities, and that the military be kept in a subordinate position. The policies of this civil state must consider what the people can bear without hardship and what will not be harmful to the economy.

Despite the Jainist commitment of its author, the *Nitivakyamrita* shows the influence of earlier political commentaries, especially the *Arthashastra*. Somadeva introduces no variation into the saptanga theory, the

---

[q] In assessing the literature of this period (the Guptas and their successors), it should be noted that the expedience and materialism of the arthashastra school are attacked in such classical Sanskrit works as Bana's *Kādambarī* and the epic *Śiśupālavadha* of Magha.

concept of danda, or the four sciences and their role in the education of the prince. Force should be used in internal regulation only as a last resort, but where prowess, intrigue, and authority are inadequate, Somadeva would permit the use of violent means. He follows Kautalya in limiting aggressive warfare to a situation in which the enemy is weaker. Where the two powers are of approximately equal strength, mutual destruction would result from war.[45] The arthashastra policy of harsh and remorseless conduct toward the enemy or potential enemy is advocated in Somadeva's tale, *Yaśastilaka* (IV).

Hemachandra, who lived several centuries after Somadeva, claims that his treatise is based on advice given by Mahavira himself to Bimbisara, king of Magadha. He is more willing than Somadeva to introduce the ethical standards of his religious faith into political life, but he does not hesitate to recommend severe punishment or the death penalty when the occasion justifies it. We may generalize that moral considerations are confined by the Jaina authors mainly to internal administration. These later Jaina works can be contrasted with the Buddhist canonical works, which demand the subordination of politics to ethics, and which hold in contempt the "kshatriya science."

THE SHUKRANITISARA—EPITAPH FOR ARTHASHASTRA

We come now to the last great comprehensive political study of the ancient Hindus, the *Sukranītisāra.*[r] *Nītisāra,* the designation of the political writings of Kamandaka and Shukra, suggests a very general treatment of the principles of sovereign authority. Though a smaller work than the *Arthashastra,* the *Shukraniti* is broader in scope. Its author, in fact, criticizes the more limited character of other shastras. In addition to defining and describing the duties and functions of the prince and ministers, diplomacy and the conduct of war, political and social institutions and customs, and the broad principles of statecraft, the manual provides a standard for human behavior. Shukra enlarges the concept nitishastra to include conduct on all levels, in all situations; it is as ethical as it is political in nature. In including a section on ethics (chap. 3), the *Shukranitisara* goes beyond the traditional province of earlier treatises—and yet it can be argued that insofar as the arthashastra theorists held that it is through fear of punishment that men become virtuous, they too had involved themselves in ethical questions.[46] And it was customary for these writers to declare that by enforcing the laws which support the social order, the king is indeed the maker of his age.[47] Other examples of statements bridging the political and ethical spheres come readily to mind. In this work attributed to Shukra, nitishastra emerges as the comprehensive and integrating science that the founders of modern sociology conceived their study to be. But Shukra's predecessors had prepared the way.

B. K. Sarkar remarks: "In Kamandaka and especially in Shukra we

---

[r] The authenticity of the work has recently been questioned: there is at least the possibility that the *Shukranitisara* may have been a nineteenth-century forgery by students working with Oppert in Madras. But evidence is not sufficient to allow us to dispense with an examination of the text.

have . . . not only the pedagogies of Plato, e.g., his *Statesman,* but also his ethics, the monograph on justice, viz., the *Republic,* as well as his treatise on political administration, the *Laws.*"[48] But the comparison, if it must be made, is with Botero or Bodin. Beni Prasad believes that as the relative liberalism of Buddhism declined and Brahmanism regained its position in Indian life, the secularism of arthashastra was modified and nitishastra was the result. The greater attention of the *Shukraniti* to the moral norms necessary for regulating conduct prevents the sharper distinction of politics and ethics, or the separation of public morality from private, that we find in the *Kautaliya.* A. K. Sen, in comparing Shukra's modification of the materialism and opportunism of the *Arthashastra* with Bodin's tempering of Machiavelli, is more to the point. Standards of conduct are suspended in war; any policy that is effective against the enemy may be employed.[49] Generally, however, Shukra stands for the superiority of ethics to politics. It is righteousness that in the last analysis legitimates the royal authority. A comparison with the Jaina texts would reveal many similarities between the author of the *Nitisara* and contemporary heterodox theory.

The *Shukraniti* was ostensibly composed by an anonymous medieval writer who credited the work to Shukracharya, a legendary figure, to give it credence and the authority of antiquity. The controversy that has long been waged over the *Shukraniti* is characteristic of the range of disagreement on the dates of political texts. Oppert, who discovered the treatise, places the work prior to the Christian era, while P. C. Ray has it as recent as the sixteenth century. Jayaswal placed the *Shukraniti* in the eighth century A.D., and others attribute it to the fourth. In dating the work different scholars have selected different passages for emphasis. Some have pointed to the description of the building of a firearm[50] as evidence of the late date of the treatise. But the date of the introduction of gunpowder into India is also disputed. The authors of the medieval digests of politics do not quote the *Nitisara* of Shukra, and for this reason among others, the tendency is to place the work somewhere in the period bounded by the ninth and thirteenth centuries A.D.

Despite his innovations, Shukra relies on Manu and Kautalya (via Kamandaka). Like Kautalya, he views the state as a means for preserving order and prosperity. Human existence is possible because the state affords protection. Probably the dearth of comment regarding the origins of state and government must be taken to mean that both Kautalya and Shukra considered the state as having existed in some form from earliest time—the product of human needs. Both are more interested in the actual mechanism of government, the organization of power, and the theory of empire. They approach their subject from the point of view of the ruler. Shukra elaborates the traditional seven components of sovereignty, and introduces an analogy with the various organs of the human body (king: head; minister: eye; army: mind; etc.).[51] This may not be sufficient to justify our calling the work an organic theory of the state, although the construction is certainly meant to suggest the intimate relationship of the factors and the work goes far beyond the model of the *Arthashastra* in the direction of an organic theory.

Both Kautalya and Shukra assign to the king a position of fundamental importance in the social system, and consequently both emphasize the importance for the king of moral discipline and a rigorous program of preparation for leadership. Shukra, like the author of the *Arthashastra,* prescribes for every waking moment of the king: his day included study, distributing prizes, making inventories, engaging in military maneuvers, and hearing reports and clarifications from ministers and spies. Once a year he was to inspect the domain. In advising that the monarch give personal attention to a variety of administrative details, Shukra (like Manu) implies a kingdom of limited size. The functions of the king are, foremost, punishment and protection, conquest, the performance of the sacrifice, the furthering of economic prosperity, cultural and religious advancement, and charity. The *Shukraniti* places less stress on the material aspects of polity than the *Kautaliya.* The king was personally responsible for balancing finances, correlating income and expenditure. He must administer law as set down in the shastras: there is no question that law must be rooted in dharma. Here we notice a deviation from the legal principle of the *Arthashastra.* For Kautalya the royal edict had supreme authority.

The king exercises power not only by virtue of his ability and worth,[8] but also because he represents the eight great deities who symbolize his eightfold duty.

> Like Indra, the sovereign is able to protect the wealth and possessions. As Vayu or Air is the spreader (and diffuser) of scents, so the prince is the generator (and cause) of good and evil actions. As the sun is the dispeller of darkness (and the creator of light) so the king is the founder of religion and destroyer of irreligion. As Yama is the god who punishes (human beings after death) so also the monarch is the punisher of offenses (in this world). Like Agni, the prince is the purifier and the enjoyer of all gifts. As Varuna, the god of water, sustains everything by supplying moisture, so also the king maintains everybody by his virtues and activities. As the god of wealth protects the jewels of the universe, so the king protects the treasure and possessions of the state.

To be radiant, like the full moon, the king must fulfill these duties.[52]

But the willful monarch who neglects the wishes of his councilors and subjects "is the cause of miseries (and) soon gets estranged from his kingdom and alienated from his subjects."[53] Although he sanctions the removal of an unjust or negligent king, Shukra, always the moderate, never acknowledges the popular right of tyrannicide. But when the king becomes intolerably wicked, the brahman is obligated to destroy him—even though this would involve the priest in violence.[54] And when the king becomes addicted to vice, the people are justified in going over to the enemy if the

---

[8] Shukra emphasizes the central importance of ability.

latter is both powerful and virtuous. "The subjects desert a king who is uncharitable, who insults men, who practices deceit and uses harsh words, and who is severe in punishments."[55] More powerful than the king is the unity of the many: "The rope that is made by a combination of many threads is strong enough to drag the lion."[56]

Shukra makes clear that it is the institution and not the person of the king that is divine. He asks if it is not true that "even the dog look(s) like a king, when it has ascended a royal chariot."[57] The author of the *Nitisara* attempts to relate the doctrine of the king's divine appointment with the older theory that based authority and the right to tax on the ability of the ruler to provide protection. Thus for Shukra the ruler is divinely endowed with authority for the purpose of protecting the people.[58] He is both the servant and the master of the people. Primogeniture dictated succession to the throne in Shukra's theory, but if the eldest son were mentally or physically incapacitated, the crown should pass to a younger brother. In later arthashastra works such as the *Nitisara* we find what Ghoshal describes as "a tendency towards progressive simplification of the qualification for kingship so as to make it pass from ceremonial consecration to a customary formula, and thence to sheer possession of the kingdom."[59]

Of major importance in the political thought of the *Shukraniti* are the ministers, who were to be consulted on all questions of polity. But only those ministers that the king feared and respected could be effective. Shukra argues that the power the king exercised in his own right was limited; administrative authority resided in the council, and without written documents, agreed upon and signed by the ministers, no official business could be carried on. The written document was, in fact, the sovereign authority. By the time of Shukra, eight ministers had come to be the standard size of the parishad.[t] With the exceptions of the minister of religion and the crown prince, the roster is not greatly different from modern cabinets. Most important were the *sumantra* (treasurer), the *mantrin* (foreign secretary), the *sachiva* (war minister), the *pradhāna* (premier), and the *yuvarāja* (crown prince). We cannot say for certain whether or not the royal chaplain played an important role at this time. Shukra also mentions the *pratinidhi* (deputy), the *prādvivāka* (justiciary), the *pandita* (superintendent of religious policy[u]), and the *amātya* (registrar for revenue purposes). The *Shukraniti* advises that ministers be transferred from one post to another every three or five years to prevent the concentration of authority for too long a time in one man.[60] The system of rotating ministers and the need for several ministers to approve a plan before its adoption meant that a proposal submitted by the minister of finance, for instance, would be scrutinized by those who had occupied the office at a previous date. Each minister should have the opportunity to study every administrative proposal. Shukra insists that recommendations made by the ministers be accepted by the king.

---

[t] As many as thirty-two ministers are mentioned in earlier writings.
[u] Comparable to the *dhamma-mahamatta*.

These ministers were to be chosen on the basis of character and accomplishment; circumstances of birth were of less importance. Shukra does, however, introduce caste considerations in assigning village offices. Whether or not a shudra could move with ease into occupations not allotted to his caste, we do know that the *Shukraniti* contemplates an order in which a vaishya could become a councilor or an army officer. Shukra goes further than other theorists in assigning economic and political functions on the basis of ability. It is not by birth that worth is measured, but by character, merit, and industry.[61] This does not mean that Shukra disregards caste duty. Happiness, he writes, depends on the fulfillment of duty. Caste distinctions are the product of virtue and deeds. Hence it is the duty of the king to enforce the caste order.

The *Shukraniti* provides a better description of the machinery of government than any work since the *Arthashastra.* The state pictured is more pronouncedly socialistic than that of Kautalya, and has a broad cultural mission—the fostering of learning and the arts, religion, and the virtues of respect, charity, and loyalty. The king's permission is needed, according to Shukra, before the subjects can engage in gambling, drinking, hunting, or the use of weapons; selling and buying cows, elephants, horses, camels, buffaloes, men, immovable property, silver, gold, jewels, intoxicants, poisons, and wine distillations; practicing medicine; drawing up deeds, accepting pledges, or advocating new rules; defaming castes; receiving unowned or lost goods; disclosing secrets of state; forsaking one's own religion; lying and perjuring, or forgery; realizing more than the fixed revenue; stealing; violence; and determining measurements.[62] Before a person could indulge in serious cursing, adultery, or discussion of the king's weaknesses, he must have obtained leave of the ruler. Shukra allows the state to banish undesirables, and, in his emphasis on the need for vigilance, advocates the disclosure to the authorities of any actions or expressions suggesting behavior of an unsocial or unpatriotic nature. The people must willingly cooperate with the state in all its functions. On the other hand, the *Shukraniti* provides for popular expression through such devices as the plebiscite. When the conduct of an officer is questioned by a hundred men, the king must attend to the people's wish. The government that allows its subjects neither too much nor too little power is the government that will enjoy the greatest success.[63]

Shukra believes land to be the source of all wealth, and, like the physiocrats, condemns commerce as essentially unproductive.[64] (Rarely is arthashastra literature hospitable to the merchant, although the latter's importance as a source of revenue is generally understood.) Taxation is justified on traditional grounds as payment for protection. Just as the cowherd must provide fresh grass if his cows are to provide an abundant yield, so must the king adjust the tax rate to encourage the production of wealth. No class or group is exempted from taxation, but taxes are graduated to ensure a basic standard of living.[65] Shukra recommends that the laborer be paid according to his contribution, and suggests a minimum wage and a number of compensations as safeguards against class uprisings. If the welfare of the state makes it necessary, the king may seize the property of his subjects.[66]

Social offenses were classified according to whether they were committed through action, association, or speech. Like the Jaina Somadeva, Shukra warns against punishment motivated by revenue needs or reasons other than the dispensing of justice. The courts initiated criminal proceedings, and in many of these cases there was no restriction on the qualifications of witnesses—although the professional pleader was usually not permitted. No trial should be held in secret, and punishment, when bestowed, must take local and guild practice into account. In his tolerance of local customs, Shukra accepts the relativity of moral concepts. Popular usage must always be respected.[67] Leniency must be shown certain peoples indulging in cousin marriage, flesh consumption, promiscuity, the drinking of wine (by women), and marriage with a brother's widow. "These people do not deserve penance or punishment for the practice of these customs."[68]

After the eleventh century there is little that is original in Indian political commentary; a number of general works on the broad topic of dharma provide casual treatments of polity. Among these are studies by Bhoja (of Dhārā), Caṇḍeśvara, and Mitramiśra.

13 ⋆ THE CODES OF DHARMASHASTRA

> Where justice is destroyed by injustice, or truth by falsehood, while
> the judges look on, there they shall also be destroyed. Justice, being
> violated, destroys; justice, being preserved, preserves; therefore
> justice must not be violated, lest violated justice should destroy
> us.—MANUSMRITI[1]

THE MAJOR HINDU LAW BOOKS

In the first centuries A.D. the prose dharmasutra texts were reworked
in verse form, and it may be that the difference between the Dharmasutras
and the dharmashastra literature is primarily one of style, although the
latter are distinguished also by a greater concentration on law. The Dharmashastras, of which *Manu, Yājñavalkya, Bṛhaspati,* and *Nārada* are the
most important for our purposes, are also referred to as smritis—a more
general classification that includes the epics and puranas as well as the law
books. These codes expand and systematize the social and religious regulations of the orthodox Brahmanic culture and are accepted as authentic
guides to law, custom, and duty. In his monumental *History of Dharmashastra,* P. V. Kane lists more than five thousand authors known to have
written dharmashastra treatises.[2] The major smritis belong to northern
India: *Manu* to the Gangetic plain, *Yajñavalkya* to the northeast, and
Narada to the Himalayas.

Through the centuries, as the Vedic hymns and ritual injunctions became more difficult to comprehend and to relate to current practice, and
as the smriti codes themselves were absorbed into the tradition (their
authors often acquiring a status as exalted as that of the Vedic poet-sages),
the ordinances achieved a stature comparable to that of the ancient hymns.
The first stage in this apotheosizing of the dharmashastras was the belief
that knowledge, to be complete, must include the study of the codes, or,
alternatively, that the support of the Veda was not essential for authoritative statements in certain areas of conduct. When the Vedas became inadequate for the regulation of large segments of social life, the smritis filled
this gap. Ultimately we find that in cases of conflict the smritis come to
represent an authority superior to that of the earlier tradition, though there
is a reluctance to discard the Veda openly without some justification.[a]

[a] Cf. Altekar [5], chap. 2. This short excellent study takes exception to the belief
that the normative structure of ancient Hindu society was firmly anchored in the Vedic
theological heritage. The author argues that in fact there existed a flexibility in choice
and interpretation of authorities which did not leave out of account reason, considerations of equity, and changes in custom. He holds that the Veda had ceased to be an
important influence on the development of Indian social thought as early as the sixth

No one escaped the jurisdiction of dharmashastra, and its province was the whole of life. But the smritis were to confront the same problem of adaptation to social need that earlier had enabled them to supplement and even replace the Veda. Closer to the everyday life of society, more sensitive to popular need and usage, were the authors of the digests. The smritis had become numerous and often prolix, and the convenient digest, a commentary on the law codes, was seized upon as a ready and simple guide to sacred law and custom. The authority of the commentary at times rivaled that of the smritis themselves. It, too, played its role in the evolution of Hindu law.

Although dharmashastra combines the practical with the hypothetical, and though the codifiers of the principles of dharmashastra may sometimes have administered the law, it is questionable whether or not any of the law codes were deliberately employed as regulations backed by coercive sanctions. How closely the smritis reflect the actual laws and rules of society cannot be determined from archeological records, but as commentaries on the Vedas and as a valid aspect of tradition in their own right they were accepted as authoritative in the administration of justice and the prescription of duty. It is not entirely accurate to say, as Sir Henry Maine does,[3] that the codes represent an ideal picture rather than a reflection of the political scene of the time.

The rules of the *Manusmriti* imply a small-scale polity, a village economy, and perhaps the beginnings of a kind of feudalism. The private laws of the various groups and associations that comprise the community play a more important role in the mosaic of petty principalities to which the code is meant to apply. In internal affairs the state is more the referee. But concern for social stability and prosperity induces the dharmashastra authors to elaborate rules of statecraft with Kautalyan candor; they are surpassed only by the author of the *Arthashastra* and the redactors of the *Mahabharata* in their ethical ambiguity. But unlike Kautalya, the smritis generally elevate sacred law, whether written or unwritten, above rational law and royal edict.[b]

It has been said that "differences between rules of Dharmashastra and Arthashastra are neither more numerous nor wider than those within each according to different writers."[4] Incongruities in emphasis and doctrine do exist and are often important. At the time the early smritis were compiled, the two schools were not yet clearly distinguished, and *Manu* and *Yajñavalkya* may be characterized as combinations of arthashastra and dharmashastra (as is the brahman recension of the *Mahabharata*). But they lean, as their designation suggests, to the latter. Yajñavalkya is suf-

---

century B.C., citing, for example, the fact that only once in the *Manusmriti* (IX, 20) is a Vedic authority introduced directly. This is not to say that the Vedas had ceased to be recognized as the supreme authority.

[b] Kautalya remarks that "whenever sacred law [shastra] is in conflict with rational law [*dharmanyāya*: king's law], then reason shall be held authoritative; for there the original text [on which the sacred law has been based] is not available." (*Arthashastra* III, 1, p. 185.) The *Naradasmriti* gives priority to royal ordinance as a basis of law, and is unique among the law books in this respect.

ficiently conscious of doctrinal differences between the two schools to insist that in case of conflict, dharmashastra must be held the final authority.[5] The codices contain references to civil and criminal law as well as to canonical law. In the *Manusmriti*, civil and commercial law are not yet separated from penal law, and it is not until the *Brihaspati Dharmashastra* that this distinction appears. Narada, Brihaspati, and Katyayana, who wrote at a somewhat later date, enlarge on provisions put forth in the *Manusmriti*. These works are preoccupied with legal considerations— Narada primarily with civil law. In their broad treatment of law and polity, there is actually little basic variation among the law books. But their legal codes are not always consistent in detail, and a number of glaring contradictions are apparent in the texts. In case of conflict between different law books, later authors frequently assert that the wisest members of society should choose the argument most beneficial to the community. As we might expect, this rule tended to elevate the more recent dharmashastra works to a position of great authority among the smriti writings, though they could never actually enjoy the same prestige as the lordly *Manu Dharmashastra*.

The literature on sacred law dates from the decline of Buddhism and the Brahmanical revival. The law books of Manu and Yajñavalkya and the later didactic portions of the *Mahabharata* may be taken to represent the post-Mauryan brahmanic renascence. *Manu* is the oldest and most widely known of the codes, and is generally considered the most authoritative work on Hindu law. Manu (from the root *man*) was the name of a divine law-giver, the founder of the social order in the *Rigveda*, "the father," the ancestor of man. "Man" and "thinker" are derived from the same root, and Manu is also the great instructor, the all-knowing. The name, which is most accurately translated as a title or a position (rather than as a proper noun), was taken by an author-compiler of legal principles. The founder of the arthashastra school, Brihaspati (whose work exists for us only through indirect references), was believed to have abstracted the portions dealing with the political art from the "Dandaniti," a colossal treatise attributed to Brahma and promulgated by Manu. Abridgments by Shiva, Indra, Brihaspati, and Kavi of the great pronouncement of Brahma on life, morals, and government reduced the original hundred thousand verses (so the story goes) to a more manageable number. It is this august tradition that is supposedly represented in the ordinances known to us as the *Manusmriti*.[c] A. B. Keith has compared the work to the great poem of Lucretius as an expression of a philosophy of life. But the two works have not much else in common.

The society portrayed in the *Manusmriti* is later in many respects than that pictured in the *Arthashastra*; hence the work must fall between the treatise ascribed to Kautalya and the *Shukranitisara*. This conclusion (not particularly brave, considering the expanse of time involved) is sug-

---

[c] Max Müller and A. Weber considered the work a recasting of the ancient *Manava Dharmashastra*. Most contemporary scholars are unwilling to accept this thesis—or even to find any convincing evidence that the Manava code actually existed.

gested by a comparison of the three works on the subjects of primogeniture, suicide, brahman immunities, *niyoga,*[d] the organization of gambling and prostitution, and the remarriage of widows. Shukra usually tends to follow Manu. The social conditions described in the epics are similar to those prevailing at the time the law book was compiled. Müller dates it later than the fourth century A.D. Bühler places it in the second century; Jolly concurs, and this seems the most reasonable date.[6] The *Yajñavalkya-smriti* is probably a century or two later; the work attributed to Narada may antedate *Manu,* but the smriti was extensively revised and little that would qualify it as the most ancient of the law treatises has survived this editing.

In defining sacred law, Manu would include, in addition to the sacred texts and sacred tradition, individual conscience and the example of the virtuous. Allowance must always be made for local custom, and past usage must be considered in settling legal disputes.[7] It should be noted that custom often is qualified as *sadācāra,* good custom; i.e., if it is to be authoritative, custom must be exemplified in the conduct of those who know the Veda and are selfless, just, and dispassionate in their actions. Sometimes, however, custom is defined as that which is accepted by society (and not simply by the more cultivated and pious minority). The implication may be that the custom of those not knowledgeable in the Vedas shall be authoritative for that group and its descendants.[8]

In the *Manusmriti* the king is divinely created and ordained to rule and to protect the people from a barbarous state of nature. Manu's views on the natural depravity of man[9] can be taken as fairly typical of the position of a great number of Hindu legal and political theorists. As in the arguments of Seneca and the Church Fathers, social institutions are themselves the consequence of human corruption.[e] Although Manu declares that the king is the product of divine components, the absolutism of the European divine right argument is not found in the conception. The king who is an oppressor must be destroyed by the very authority (the two-edged sword of danda) that inheres in his position. By defying dharma the king brings destruction on himself.[10] On the other hand, when the king fulfills the functions of his office, a subject's refusal to honor and obey him is indefensible. The king as a person is subordinate to dharma; in his function as preserver of sacred law he is coordinate with dharma. Jayaswal believes that the divine origin attributed to the king in the code is an attempt to justify absolutism in order to support a specific political

---

[d] The institution of substituting a proxy sire when a male is unable to produce offspring.

[e] Morality was always relative to the order, purity, and fertility of the world. Manu claims that in the ancient Krita age, austerities were the chief dharma. In the succeeding age, knowledge replaced austerities; in time knowledge was itself replaced by sacrifices, and in the present age the gift (to the brahman) is alone the basis of dharma. (I, 85f.) A similar analysis of decay can be found in the *Ramayana* (VII, 80.9f.): in the age of righteousness only the brahmans practiced austerities; in successive ages the dharma diminished by one quarter every time another caste came to practice austerities—until in the Kali age, the most unrighteous of all, even the shudras have invaded the traditional brahman function.

situation, the brahman rule of Pushyamitra,*f* that was contrary to recognized tradition.[11] But evidence is inconclusive, and brahman rule was probably not this unique.

The king embodies the virtues of eight deities and is likened to the gods in the functions he performs.[12] "The king should practice the glory and conduct of Indra (the storm god), of Arka (the sun), of Vaya (the wind), of Yama (here the god of the dead), of Varuna (here the god of punishment), of Chandra (the moon), of Agni (fire), and of Prithivi (the earth)."[13] His authority is derived from the supernatural origin of his person, the divine nature of his office, and the significance of his function in preserving social order. The *Mahabharata*, which claims that the god Vishnu actually entered the body of the king,[14] goes farther toward a theory of the king's divinity than anything we find in the Manusmriti.

Manu emphasizes the interdependence of the seven components of sovereignty. Each limb is peculiarly adapted to fulfilling a particular, necessary function, and it is difficult to say that one part is more important than another. The four main classes are said to have originated from the mouth, arms, thighs, and feet of the Creator,[15] but Manu diverges from the dharmasutra argument in making caste distinction the product of divine decree, and, only secondarily, of social necessity.*g* Brahman superiority is described and justified in the most extravagant terms. Even the gods depend on the brahmans. Though the prosperity of the community rests on the king, the king's welfare, in turn, depends on the brahman class— the spiritual power is the source of the temporal power. To anger the priests is to seek destruction. If either caste is to flourish, the brahmans and the kshatriyas must work together.[16]

Perhaps because at the time of Yajñavalkya the canonical smriti writings were less appropriate to the needs of India than were the teachings of the arthashastra school, we find the *Yajñavalkiya* influenced more by Kautalya than by contemporary dharmashastra theory. The date of the treatise is based on such evidence as the advanced astrological views of the work, its scope, and certain references to the Buddhists. It belongs to the Gupta epoch (around the fourth century A.D.), and is considered by many scholars to date from the same period as the *Kamandakiya Nitisara*. The smriti is composed of three books, which contain rules relating to the three major categories of Indian law: proper conduct (*achāra*), expiation (*prāyaschitta*), and criminal law (*vyavahāra*). Yajñavalkya borrows freely from earlier theorists, reducing their commentary to a compendium of political and legal thought.

In the *Yajñavalkyasmriti* the obligations of the king are somewhat greater than in the *Manusmriti*, the position of the brahmans equally

---

f Second century B.C.; *vide* p. 179 above.

g The *Manusmriti* takes up a theme mentioned earlier in the discussion of sutra literature. All orders are ultimately dependent on the householder. The grihastha is therefore the most excellent of the life-stages (III, 78). The fact that at this time Buddhism had served to swell the ranks of ascetics is of course relevant here. The *Vishnu Purana* (III, 11.5) remarks that for the householder, virtue is not opposed to either wealth or pleasure.

exalted. The author would allow popular usage to prevail when there is disagreement among the law codices; sacred law must be compromised when it is objectionable to all the people, and the king must respect the customs and laws of a country that comes under his control.[17] The king's edict is not law unless it complies with the basic norms governing the social order. Religious and secular law are clearly demarcated, and the emphasis has shifted from criminal to civil law. Though this smriti is one of the most systematic and comprehensive of the law books and its influence is second only to that of the *Manusmriti*, it makes only a small original theoretic contribution.[h]

Narada provides the first legal commentary that is not encumbered with moralization. The text is confined to the matter of law, almost ignoring precepts of religion and morality. Its author does, however, like Kautalya before him, base judicial procedure on the foundations of dharma, rational law, and royal decree. Narada considers the last of these to be legitimate in its own right. Perhaps the most authoritarian of Hindu writers, he demands that the king be obeyed whether right or wrong in his actions,[18] though he doubts that it is possible for the king to do wrong. The conception of danda and the duties of the king in the *Naradasmriti* does not vary appreciably from that of other commentaries. On this subject there is almost complete agreement in Hindu theory. By the time of the law books, punishment is linked with the preservation of the caste structure. The fear of punishment kept the lower classes producing for the privileged.[i]

THE LABYRINTH OF LEGAL THEORY

We turn now to the major substantive and procedural elements of ancient law. The Indian talent for cataloguing and refining is nowhere more fully expressed than in these Hindu codes. Manu suggests that cases should be divided into eighteen categories, ranging from illegal sale of land and nonpayment of taxes to domestic disputes and gambling.[19] Sometimes Manu permits a person to take the law into his own hands, as in the case of a creditor recovering his property. The *Brihaspatismriti*, a work of the sixth or seventh century, classifies thieves into overt and concealed types, according to their abilities and methods. There are a thousand varieties of theft. Each has its special punishment—hanging (highwaymen), the sacrifice of a nose (stealth of a cow), or burning in straw (kidnapping). Lawsuits are classified as those relating to injuries sustained, and those concerning conflict over wealth.

Brihaspati, like Manu and Yajñavalkya, holds that a person being tried

---

[h] Vesey-Fitzgerald believes that "although second in popular reverence to the *Manusmriti* on which it is based, it is more important; both because it represents a liberal recension of Manu and because it is the basis of most of the work of the succeeding period, especially of the *Mitakshara*." ("Law [Hindu]," *Encyclopedia of the Social Sciences.*) The *Mitākṣarā* of Vijñāneśvara, a work of the early twelfth century, provided the basis for the family law followed in most of India.

[i] Manu (VIII, 418) considers it especially important that the king compel the two lower castes to perform their social obligations.

in local courts for a crime should be judged by those who share his pro-fession. Acceptance of witnesses might transcend considerations of caste, although it was frequently held that a man could not give evidence against another of higher caste. Then, too, members of certain professions were not allowed to serve as witnesses, and large categories of persons, such as women, minors, government servants, those with physical defects or criminal records, were generally regarded as not eligible to present evi-dence in courts. Qualifications of good character, disinterestedness, and sound reason were required. Failure to give honest testimony negated all the good works that a shudra had accomplished since birth, and "head-long into utter darkness shall [such a] sinful person tumble into hell." But Manu goes on to advise giving false evidence if the truth will result in the death of a man.

When evidence and documentation were insufficient, or the judges unconvinced, there was recourse to the ordeal—usually by fire, by water, or by poison. The ordeals described in Brihaspati include trial by balance (if in the second weighing the accused is heavier, he is judged guilty), by fire (innocent if the heated iron ball fails to burn), by water (sub-mergence for as long as it takes to return a dart shot at the moment of submersion), by dharma and adharma (the accused is acquitted if he draws from a jar containing two leaves the one inscribed with the symbol of dharma).[20] The later law books admit the right of appeal to higher judi-cial bodies.[21]

Yajñavalkya warns against letting a crime go unpunished, regardless of the status of the wrongdoer, and punishment must be relative to the circumstances and the nature of the crime. Yet he also holds that punitive measures must conform strictly to the sacred writings.[j] Generally, in the law books, punishment increased in severity as social status diminished. A shudra could, in theory, be deprived of his life for an action which would cost a brahman only a small fine or a reprimand. In the *Manusmriti* the severest punishment for a brahman is banishment—and he is per-mitted to take his possessions with him. (Kautalya would drown the brahman guilty of high treason.) A shudra who shows contempt for a brahman should be punished, we are told, by having an iron spike, ten fingers long, thrust down his throat. Greater insult might result in his losing his tongue or having hot oil poured in his mouth and ears. But there is little indication that these harsh punishments were actually exe-cuted. They served primarily as a reminder of caste barriers and the exalted position of the brahmans. The smritis also suggest that a man's ability to comprehend his social duty should be considered in deciding his penalty. The *Katyayanasmriti*, in a remarkable passage,[22] doubles and quadruples for the kshatriya or brahman the penalty paid by the lowest caste for the same offense. But the brahman was rarely expected to pay this greater price.

---

[j] The commentators on these smritis make less of brahman privileges and im-munities, some of them arguing that they be dependent on the brahman's learning and character.

The most important types of punishment were torture, imprisonment, forced labor, and fines. If a man could not pay the fine imposed on him, he could be placed in bondage until his labor had compensated for his offense. Large portions of the arthashastra and legal literature are little more than compendia of fines and other penalties. The death penalty might take the form of impalement on spikes, hanging, decapitation, piercing by arrows, burning, bleeding until dead, or being pulled apart by teams of oxen. Capital punishment was not often employed by the Guptas, if we can accept the reports of the Chinese travelers.

We have mentioned the importance of custom as a component of the legal system. The dharmashastra literature and the general theory of Hindu law also reveal an occasional readiness to make law respond to the changing needs of the community. This awareness of the need to relate law and tradition to evolving social conditions is most apparent in the *Yajñavalkiya*. The consciousness of change and relativity is a feature of later brahmanic thought that distinguishes it from the proud claims of a thousand years earlier, when brahman power was at its zenith. The codes sometimes advise that a body of learned brahmans be commissioned to determine the needs of the people and assist the king in the administration of justice. Because the law books frequently recognize the customs of different groups in society, it can be said that they represent a definite step toward the accommodation of various religious creeds. Indeed the Gupta state, in contrast to the polities of the centuries that preceded its establishment as an imperial power, appears to have been relatively free of religious partisanship. But it is difficult to say how much the dharmashastras influenced Gupta policy—or whether the influence worked the other way, Gupta institutions stamping the later, more liberal codes.

A basic tenet of Hindu political and legal thought was the belief that the king should regard himself not as the creator of the law, but only as its guardian. We have already noted one exception to this principle among the authors of dharmashastra, and a further qualification remains to be added. From about the third century B.C., there seems to have developed a growing appreciation of the need to supplement tradition and the sacred texts with other, more tractable, means of regulating the community. In varying degrees, Mauryan kings had assumed a legislative function. The theory that emerged after the fact held that this departure from the original rajadharma must be carefully controlled and that the royal edict, *rājaśāsana,* must harmonize with customary and sacred law. Rajashasana is not properly king-made law, but is more in the nature of a commentary, an administrative edict, a codification, or an attempt to enlighten the public on the subject of dharma. Conformity with the sacred texts was imperative where religious practice was concerned. In secular legal usage, reason and equity might be considered as important as the smritis or the time-honored Vedic norm.

Gradually, with the recognition of a sphere of statutory law, a distinction between moral and positive law (and the sanctions of each) came to be understood. But such factors as the objectification of sacred law in the caste structure prevented a sharp delineation of the two that would allow the individual a freedom of moral choice and prevent the interference of the state in the realm of values. The state could best serve its function as protector of the law by not instituting legislation itself (presumably by not intervening in the normal channels of the judicial process), not hindering investigation, and not failing to punish a guilty party.[k] The judicial function was traditionally the province of the brahmans, and injunctions against intrusion on the prerogatives of the priesthood were intended in part to preserve a countervailing area of power as assurance against the state's assuming totalitarian controls.

In summary, we can say that in Hindu thought, law includes both the ethical conception of law,[l] to be discovered in conscience or in custom or in the model provided by the conduct of righteous men, and law established by legislation, which commands because it has the backing of the coercive state. "Created" law, for Narada and other authors, followed the debilitation of law as self-imposed duty. Basically, law was conceived as God-given, and as codified and interpreted by learned men versed in the Vedic tradition. In the event of dispute over the interpretation of the Veda, a parishad (or council) of up to ten brahman sages was to be convened. Thus, in the last analysis, Hindu law (like other systems) was what men agreed that it was. But consensus honors certain first principles which remain fairly constant, the consequence of man's aspiration, his need for consistency and for an explanation of the universe in which he lives. The realms of fact and value are not as discrete as many would suppose. Just as values are facts of man's existence, so facts become values as man is confronted with the need for choice. The principles of Hindu law, guides to choices consonant with the attainment of salvation and the preservation of order, took the form of such dicta as the doctrines that a contract must not transcend sacred law, and custom must have precedence over statute. These four categories—contractual obligation, the law of the shastras, customary law, and royal edict—were the fundamental elements of Hindu jurisprudence.

Judicial offices were almost always filled from the brahman class, since no man could be judged by one who was not at least his equal. And since the sin involved in the crime must also be judged, judges must be drawn from the guardians and interpreters of dharma. The tenure of judges depended on their effectiveness and conduct in handling cases. Wrong

---

[k] "The unrighteous punishment destroys the heaven, the glory and the worlds of the king. But the proper punishment procures him victory, glory and heaven. A brother even, or a son, anyone to whom *arghya* [respect] is due, a father-in-law or maternal uncle, as well, is not to go unpunished by the monarch if he falls away from his duty." (*Yajñavalkyasmriti* XIII, 357f.)

[l] With the important reservation noted earlier: Hindu law lacked the ethical universalism of the *ius naturale*. Law may not exist in the hearts of *all* men (as the Stoics would have it), but it can be found in the example of the sages and virtuous men. *Vide Manu* II, 1, and the dharmasutras of *Baudhayana* I, 1.1.4–6 and *Apastamba* I, 7.20.8.

decisions were said to transfer the sin involved to the judges themselves. Lawyers were appointed to argue civil cases, but in criminal cases the parties themselves usually presented their evidence before the jury. The law was administered in the district courts, and special canonical courts handled questions of dharmic law. The committees of elders that governed the castes were responsible for regulating caste affairs, and this involved the interpretation of customary law. The laws of the corporate organizations were left to the various associations that made up Hindu society. The earliest law court was likely the king's palace. By the time of the dharmashastras, complexities of judicial administration necessitated formal institutions of a more specialized nature. The king's courts became agencies for the adjudication of suits involving the criminal or civil law, which by their character lay beyond the jurisdiction of the lower courts. Although there is ample indication of a regular procedure for appeal from lower to higher courts, we have no way of knowing how this right was actually exercised.

The trials themselves were held in public. The theory of the jury goes back at least to Buddhist times, and probably has its origin in the council of elders. The *Chulla-vagga* (Book IV) lists certain qualities essential to the jurist, including impartiality and the possession of analytical ability. The law books usually insist that jurors be brahmans. The king or his judicial minister was to be assisted by a jury of from three to seven men knowledgeable in the sacred and customary law. The brahmans were, of course, the recognized authorities on sacred tradition, and actions in law and equity calling for interpretation of the sacred law must of necessity involve the priesthood. But if only an acquaintance with customary law was required, it was recommended that the jurors be of the same caste as the parties to the dispute.

Hindu jurisprudence was guided by the principle that judge and juror were to be as impartial as possible, and that the motive for the crime or injury, its nature, and the person committing it were to be taken into account. Manu, for example, considered contracts made by the intoxicated, by the deranged, by those wholly dependent on others or grievously diseased, or by unauthorized individuals to be invalid.[23] The fact remained that punishment, more often than not, was related to the caste of the offender. And yet we do find recommendations, notably in the *Brihaspatismriti* and, less emphatically, in the *Naradasmriti,* that penalty for theft or violence be apportioned according to the seriousness of the offense rather than on the basis of caste.[24] Unnecessary delay must be avoided in bringing a case to trial. The broadest publicity should be given to statutes and decrees, so that the legal consequences of actions would be known; the trial itself should be open to the people. The evidence of witnesses was generally held to be conclusive.

Every person (except possibly the shudra, who was considered by the most orthodox schools of law to have forfeited his claim to justice) possessed the right of judicial protection. Woman, although frequently the subject of paean in Indian literature, was regarded in legal theory as a dependent.[m] The woman's right to own certain types of personal property was upheld, and she was partner to her husband in the conduct of household affairs—for which at least a minimum of education was considered her due. As wife and mother she had considerable security, and, in particular situations, Kautalya and a few other authorities permit her recourse to legal action. But in status she was inferior to man (even under the more democratic principles of the Buddhist sangha), and her husband possessed the right to control her freedom. Any gesture on her part that might arouse suspicion of her fidelity could be severely punished. One indignity prescribed for such behavior was a public lashing at the hand of an outcaste.[n] There were few restrictions against aliens. Residence made the citizen and formed the basis of civic obligation. Rarely have so few encumbrances been placed on the foreigner.

The jurisdiction of the law was far-reaching, and penalties were often extreme. Certain theorists, for instance, recommend that one convicted of drinking intoxicating liquor be punished by being made to drink boiling water until death resulted. Loss of caste, penance, and expulsion were common punishments. What appears to be excessive punishment for misdemeanors of small import can be understood in terms of the theory of reincarnation and the effect of actions in this life on the character of future lives of the soul. Punishment and atonement might prevent jeopardy to lives yet to be lived. Usually Indian criminal law was based on the principle that punishment must not exceed the requirements of the community. But the ideals that the community represented called for a greater emphasis on harsh penalties, and on expiation, deterrence, and the education of the public than we would today require. We might expect the concepts of karma and samsara to have far-reaching effects on the concepts of personal character and responsibility, and that this would in turn influence the theory of reformation.

Something of the spirit of the ancient law can be inferred from the following scattered fragments of the *Brihaspatismriti,* a Gupta code which relies heavily on the *Manu Dharmashastra,* but which is generally less orthodox in nature.[o]

> In former ages men were strictly virtuous and devoid of mischievous propensities. Now that avarice and malice have taken possession of them, judicial proceedings have been established. [I, 1.]
>
> The king, his chosen representative (the chief judge), the judges,

---

[m] "Her father protects her in childhood, her husband protects her in her youth, her sons protect her in old age—a woman does not deserve [i.e., need] independence." (*Manu* IX, 3.)

[n] There are occasional indications that women held high political positions. Rarely did they rule, however. We find women serving as trustees for princes not yet of age, in some instances participating in important political decisions, and even serving as provincial governors.

[o] Note the list of parallels between the two works in Jolly's introduction to Brihaspati (*Sacred Books of the East,* XXXIII, pp. 271ff.).

the law (Smriti), the accountant and scribe, gold, fire, water,[p] and the king's own officer are ten members of legal procedure. [I, 4.]

Cultivators, artisans (such as carpenters or others), artists, money-lenders, companies (of tradesmen), dancers, persons wearing the token of a religious order (such as Pâsupatas), and robbers should adjust their disputes according to the rules of their own profession. [I, 26.]

(Meetings of) kindred, companies (of artisans), assemblies (of co-habitants), and chief judges, are declared to be resorts for the passing of a sentence, to whom he whose cause has been previously tried may appeal in succession. [I, 29.]

When any man injures (another), or when he refuses to give what he ought to give: such are the two principal motives for going to law. Their subdivisions are manifold. Lawsuits are of two kinds, according as they originate in (demands regarding) wealth or in injuries. Lawsuits originating in wealth are (divided again) into fourteen sorts; those originating in injuries are of four sorts. [II, 4f.]

No sentence should be passed merely according to the letter of the law. If a decision is arrived at without considering the circumstances of the case, violation of justice will be the result. [II, 12.]

He who refrains from killing an aggressor who abuses him aloud and is ready to murder him (because the aggressor) is a virtuous man (otherwise) and practices regularly the recitation of the Veda, obtains the same reward as for performing a horse-sacrifice.[q] The judgment in a doubtful matter is declared to be of four sorts, according as it is based on moral law, or on the issue of the case, or on custom, or on an edict from the king. [II, 17f.]

The time-honored institutions of each country, caste, and family should be preserved intact; otherwise the people would rise in rebellion; the subjects would become disaffected towards their rulers; and the army and treasure would be destroyed. [II, 28.]

He who, divesting himself of avarice, hatred, and other (evil propensities), passes sentences according to the dictates of law, obtains the same reward as for the performance of a sacrifice. [II, 42.]

Those acquainted with (the true nature of) a plaint declare that to be a (proper) plaint, which is free from the defects of a declaration, susceptible of proof, provided with good arguments, precise, and reasonable, brief in words, rich in contents, unambiguous, free from confusion, devoid of improper arguments, and capable of meeting opposite arguments; when a plaint of this description has been proffered by the plaintiff, the defendant should tender an answer conformable to such plaint. [III, 5ff.]

Let him remove superfluous statements and amplify incomplete ones, and let him write down (everything) on the floor, till the (whole) matter has been definitely stated. [III, 14.]

A charge founded on suspicion, (one founded on) fact, a petition regarding the recovery of a debt, and claiming a fresh trial of a cause previously tried: thus a plaint is represented as fourfold. [III, 17.]

---

[p] "Gold and fire serve the purpose of administering ordeals; water is required for persons suffering from thirst or hunger." (*Brihaspati* I, 7.)

[q] This is obviously the ticklish case of the brahman offender. On the subject of the brahman desperado (*ātatāyī*), *vide* Ghoshal [144], pp. 433ff.

When the defendant asks for a delay through (natural) timidity, or terror, or because his memory has been deranged, the delay shall be granted to him. [IV, 5.]

When the evidence is equally strong on both sides, and law and custom divided, in such a case a mutual reconciliation between the two parties through royal order is recommended. [V, 13.]

Evidence is declared to be twofold, human and divine. Each of these is again divided into a number of branches by sages declaring the essence of things. Human evidence is threefold, as it consists of witnesses, writings, and inference. [V, 17f.]

By the time of the Guptas, the administration of justice was markedly more humane and less apt to be prejudiced by wealth or descent than had formerly been the case. Fa-hsien observed the great happiness and freedom of the Indian and the absence of harsh punishment except in cases of sedition. His countryman Hiuen Tsiang, who traveled in India several centuries later, remarked of its people: "They are not deceitful or treacherous in their conduct, and are faithful to their oaths and promises. In their rules of government there is remarkable rectitude."[25] But either the contrast with contemporary China was striking or not all of Harsha's subjects in this later age were so law-abiding. The pilgrim was robbed twice by bandits and once narrowly escaped being sacrificed to Durga by pirates.

DHARMASHASTRA POLITY[r]

The king, the cabinet, and the civil service constituted the three executive branches of government as outlined in the smritis.[8] The monarch must personally supervise diplomacy, civil affairs, and the administration of finance and law. For him public life was as rigorous as it was for Kautalya's sovereign, and again the protection of the people was the prime justification of his rule.[26] Without the sanction of danda "all would be upside down." The king must learn the threefold wisdom of the Vedas: the art of policy, logic, self-knowledge.[27] He can maintain order only if he is able to control himself.[28] His morning was to be devoted to meditation, worship, study, matters involving legal decisions, and consultation with ministers, ambassadors, spies, and the commander in chief on civil, external, and military affairs. The remainder of the day was to be devoted to prayer and personal matters, inspection of military forces, deliberation with the secret service, and rest.[29] In addition to supervising the administrative machinery and ensuring the protection of the people, the king must safeguard his subjects against corrupt officials. When the king could not personally direct the functions of government, the purohita, the crown

[r] This section brings together much material that will by now be familiar to the reader. The smriti literature is a compilation of principles and precepts, many of which figured in earlier political and social writings.

[8] The dharmashastras suggest the attempt on the part of the brahmans not to undermine and destroy the bureaucracy, but to utilize it where possible for their own purposes. Such acceptance of the administrative framework with the objective of exploiting it is more often than not the aim of different groups with actual or potential power in ancient empires. *Vide* Eisenstadt [114], p. 24.

prince, or the premier served as his administrative agent. Though generally authoritarian, the *Manusmriti* warns against the misuse of punishment. Danda was a blade that cut both ways, and the king who swerved from his duty would be struck down.[30]

Manu recommends a cabinet of seven or eight ministers, who should be "hereditary, learned in the treatises, brave, skilled in the use of weapons, and well-descended."[t] Probably these ministers represented both the kshatriya and brahman castes, with the latter in the majority. Several of the smritis make cabinet posts the exclusive prerogative of the brahmans. Katyayana[31] suggests that the mind of the king is apt to go astray because, among other reasons, his position calls for the exercise of power—an early version of the thesis that power corrupts. Therefore, the brahman must remind the king of his duty. Because ministers were often required to be military leaders, we may assume that a good many ministers were not brahmans (though the priests were not absolutely forbidden to take part in hostilities). In this regard the writers on polity make caste less important than do the codifiers, and in such later treatises as the *Shukranitisara* and the *Nitivakyamrita* of Somadeva, ability, regardless of caste, is made the prime consideration. Administrative records left by several dynasties show that cabinet posts were, in fact, frequently hereditary.

It was the function of the ministers to deliberate matters of peace and war, wealth, protection, and the general condition of the kingdom; the king, having ascertained the opinion of each minister individually and then of the council as a whole, should only then proceed to make his decision.[32] Often consultation with the ministers would follow the king's early morning interview with the "people."[33] Such conferences should be held in strictest secrecy. Sacrifice now played a less important role, and this may be a reason for the purohita's substantial decline in power. Several historians believe that by the time of the later smritis the purohita may even have been excluded from the council.

To meet the problems of legal interpretation and legislation necessitated by the changing needs of the people, Manu advocates a parishad of from three to ten persons, with at least one member learned in each of the three Vedas (*Rigveda, Yajurveda,* and *Samaveda*). Capability, rather than number, of the legislators is emphasized in order to ensure prompt and considered action. The multitude is believed to be inadequately informed and not sufficiently intelligent to name its own legislative delegates. The assembly of ten included logicians and "representatives" of the first three social orders as well as Vedic scholars.[34] Although its function was properly interpretive, serving to reconcile the Vedas and their commentaries with the requirements of a changing society, this parishad comes close to being a formal legislative assembly.

In addition, a well-disciplined civil service would perform the duties of administration and tax collection. The king should make the honesty of these civil servants his personal responsibility. Manu advises occa-

---

t "Even an easy deed is difficult to be effected by one only, especially by one without a helper; still more a very prosperous kingdom [is hard to rule]." (*Manu* VII, 54f.)

sional inspection tours to investigate the administrative methods and the integrity of state officers (whom he rather cynically regards as mostly cheats and takers of the property of others),[35] and to determine the specific condition, opinion, and wishes of the people. Sometimes these tours were made by special inspectors, sometimes by the king himself. Spies were often employed to watch the activities of public servants.

In Manu's welfare state, prices are subject to governmental control,[u] and the state assumes responsibility for promoting cultural institutions and granting certain charities to those unfortunates unable to help themselves. The smritis recommend that the country be populated with traders, artisans, and peasants, since these economically productive classes provide the tax revenue on which the state depends. The tax is seen as the king's rightful due in return for the security he provides. In times of distress a king is entitled to as much as a fourth part of the wealth as revenue.[36] Manu exempts almost nothing from taxation. Those who live by their hands should give a day each month to the king.[37] Not only must the tax be flexible—heavy in times of prosperity and decreasing when the economy recedes—but it must be gently exacted: "as the leech, calf, and insect eat little by little (their) food, so yearly taxes are to be taken little by little from the kingdom by the king."[38] A sixth part of trees, meat, honey, and ghee may be taken, and one-twentieth of the cost price as the tax on marketed goods.[39] Taxes were to be taken on income (in kind), on imports and exports, on warehouses and highways, on mines and manufactures.[v]

Among those exempt were students and brahman sages, and such a concession constituted an indirect subsidy of learning and the arts. Women, children, and ascetics were also to be excused, but it is not likely that these exceptions were always recognized in actual practice. Although there is a suggestion that property is conceived as title resulting from the application of human effort,[w] Manu raises the problem of royal claim to the land and waters of the realm. But if such a claim was actually made, it was of a most general nature (perhaps of the order of eminent domain), and protection, not ownership, justified the sovereign authority of the monarch and his right to taxes.[40]

Several of the dharmashastras, especially the earlier works, mention guild assemblies, but deal primarily with their chief executives and qualifications for this office. The king was evidently able to discipline these officials and to criticize guild policy.[x] The corporations (or *śrenis*) had their own judicial organizations, as did the villages and families. The

---

[u] And so are interest rates: the brahman may be charged 24%, the kshatriya, vaishya, and shudra 36%, 48%, and 60%, respectively. (*Manu* VIII, 142.)

[v] The king "should make the traders pay taxes, after having considered the purchase and sale [of their goods], the journey [they have made], the food [and other expenses], and the means for security [they employ]. Having considered [the matter], let the king ever arrange the taxes in [his] kingdom, so that the king and the businessmen may get profit." (*Manu* VII, 127f.)

[w] "The field belongs to him who clears it for tillage—the deer to him who first injures it with an arrow." (*Manu* IX, 44.)

[x] "The families, castes, the shrenis, the ganas, and the janapadas who have deviated from their duty, should be disciplined and set in the right path." (*Yajñavalkya* XIII, 361.)

village judicial bodies were comparable to the later pañchayat. The defense of the village, formerly the province of the village headman, was left to the military cantonments, which were responsible for the protection of small clusters of villages.[41] We know that a gradual decentralization of power marked these times—a process that the terminology of the law books sometimes seeks to disguise. In the *Manusmriti* version of the saptanga theory, fort (or fortified area) and janapada are replaced by *pura* and *rashtra,* i.e., capital and kingdom.[42] *Janapada* had strong tribal connotations, and the term includes population as well as territory; *rashtra* refers to the territorial state.

The law books, in advocating aggression, were not as careful as modern propagandists to provide a moral or biological rationale, and we are disarmed by the frankness with which the codes recommend offense against weak and unsuspecting neighbors.[43] We must remember, however, that war was the profession of the kshatriyas, and that the priests, for their part, stood to gain by the "brahmanization" of new areas. These works, in contrast to the arthashastra literature, at least manifest a concern with the consequences of aggressive actions for the life hereafter. When a state is threatened, first recourse should be to methods short of war: bribery and gifts, attempts to disunite the enemy, mediation, and conciliation. But man could realize happiness and well-being only in a sovereign state. If the group was to live with honor, it could not tolerate vassalage. Manu holds in one place that no matter what the strength of the enemy, the king must not refrain from battle. It is his duty and that of his fellow kshatriyas to fight even if death on the battlefield is certain.[44] Elsewhere, however, Manu advises the king to avoid war where the outcome is uncertain[45]—an ancient arthashastra principle. Yajñavalkya holds that force must be resorted to after other expedients have failed.[46] But military action must conform to a higher code of conduct. Fairness, mercy, and forbearance should, when possible, govern hostilities. The technique of the power balance was understood[v] and alliances were considered among the most important of the state's assets.[47] Manu holds that peace depends on the ambassador, "for, verily, the ambassador alone unites." An envoy should have a psychologist's understanding of personality, and a facility for gaining confidence in order to discover the foreign king's ambitions.[48]

The smritis are somewhat equivocal on the subject of territorial conquest and annexation. The goal of diplomacy is rather to achieve a power balance that will ensure the security of the state.[49] (Kautalya would have been disdainful of a foreign policy that settled for "equilibrium" instead of aspiring for universal dominion.) After conquest, respect must be shown for that which the defeated holds sacred. Brihaspati considers disregard for local customs and institutions to be an invitation to rebellion,

---

[v] "A neighboring sovereign, the one next to him, and the one situated beyond the latter, [should be considered] as an enemy, a friend, and as a neutral power in due order. Thus the circle of neighboring powers (on all his four sides) should be considered in due order and should be treated with negotiation and the other means of diplomacy." (*Manu* XIII, 345.) This is the familiar mandala theory.

and he is joined by several major smriti schools in counseling respect for and protection of the traditions and regulations of a conquered country. The conservative Manu goes so far as to state that a conquered country should be governed by one of the native princes, rather than by a ruler imposed by the victorious power.

A note on the puranas. In many respects the major puranas are similar to the law books in both substance and form. Eighteen in number, they deal with the creation of the world; the great ages (*yugas*) through which it has passed, each with its characteristic dharma, reflecting the retrograde condition of man; the genealogies of gods, sages, and dynasties; and the transcendent goals most worthy of men. There is a strong monotheistic note in the books, supplemented by a rich infusion of Sankhya doctrine. The puranas ("ancient legends") had wide appeal and served as authoritative sources for popular Hindusim. They do not provide a dependable chronology and are frequently fantastic.

The literature cannot be dated with any hope of accuracy, but it is likely that the puranas developed in Vedic times as a special branch of the sacred literature and were learned by the priests along with the hymns. These early narratives were incorporated into the *Mahabharata*; those that survive today in the purana form evidently did not exist at the time of this compilation. Even before the inclusion of the first series of puranas in the *Mahabharata,* these legends extolling the kshatriyas had departed from brahman orthodoxy. In their present form the puranas fall between the early centuries of the Christian era and the seventh or eighth century A.D., although the stories that these works comprise belong to antiquity. After the decline of the Gupta empire, many of the collections greatly increased in size as the exploits of tribal gods and the genealogical lists of the many small kingdoms were included. Alterations continued for many centuries after the Gupta period, but the eighteen major puranas are presumably eighteen versions of a common source.[50]

Brihaddharma and *Vishnu,* and certain other of the puranas, postulate an age free of misery and corruption, followed by gradual decline. In the *Vayu Purana* (VIII), caste did not exist until Brahma assigned men to different social roles as their personalities and conduct dictated. Here again we encounter the legend of the evil king, Vena, and the restoration of order and prosperity with Prithu. The moral is the same: the need for punishment in preserving dharma. The tyrant Vena himself, the most despicable of rulers, must be tolerated—for he at least keeps the land from being overrun by outlaws. The alternative to the king is anarchy.[z] In the puranas, as in the smritis, the king's divinity is a metaphorical expression of the majesty of his office and is used to augment

[z] It is remotely possible that the account of the wicked king Vena (father of the great Prithu), which is a recurrent theme in the puranas, was inspired by the regime of the Buddhist king Ashoka. Vena, we are told (*Vishnu Purana* I, 13.11ff., *Bhāgavata Purana* IV, 13.16ff.), forbade sacrifices and religious gifts. But Vena set himself up as the object of worship and ordered that the sages obey him without question-

respect on the part of his subjects, although several passages approach an actual philosophy of divine right.[aa] The right of resistance is ignored in most of these texts, and respect for the king, regardless of his character, is advocated.

The king is advised to be neither mild nor harsh in dealing with his subjects, and to exert his authority to bring about their full spiritual and material development. The state described in the puranas has a broad cultural mission, and the king is the great moral example for his people. His office is justified only as he serves their interests and protects them from internal and external enemies. The king should never expect that this will be a life of ease and enjoyment; his lot is one of pain and toil. If, however, he fulfills his duty well, he earns a sixth part of the merit accumulated by his subjects.[51] The puranas counsel the king against making policy decisions without advice. The minister, according to the *Agni Purana,* should be consulted on measures of state; he is charged with ensuring the success of projects undertaken, providing for future contingencies, supervising finances, drafting civil and criminal laws, and, with the king, protecting the realm.[52] The *Agni Purana* accepts the traditional four bases of law: custom, scripture, the edicts of the king, and the example of the righteous.

---

ing his authority. When they could tolerate no more, the sages killed him—and from the dead king's arm emerged the exemplary king Prithu (from the negation of the negation).

   [aa] E.g., *Brihaddharma Purana* III, 3.7: "The gods take the form of kings when they visit the earth." The *Vishnu Purana* I, 13f., like *Manu* VII, 4f., maintains that a variety of gods reside in the person of the king. More typically the puranas suggest, as do most of the dharmashastra schools, that there is only a similarity of function between the king and the gods.

14 ⚹ THE AUTHORITY
OF THE KING

THE ORIGINS OF KINGSHIP[a]

Emergencies, especially war, demand a strong executive. Ancient Indian theory, like the Biblical account of Saul's ordination, holds that the institution of kingship originated as a response to hostile pressures. The Hindus, unlike the ancient Greeks, did not view political authority as the natural consequence of the interdependence of men. The state was rationalized in terms suggesting a compact, or was said to have been established through the intervention of the gods.[b] These ideas are inevitably linked with a justification of coercive institutions that differs from the Greek conception of the polis as the fulfillment of man. In Indian political thought, the sinful nature of man legitimates compulsion; the state is indeed the *sine qua non* of existence. Danda is the necessary result of man's fall and the instrument for ensuring sufficient order to make a decent life possible. But, at the same time, the state has the more positive function of providing the conditions of salvation. A parallel may be found in early medieval European theory—where social institutions were regarded as both the consequence of and the remedy for man's imperfection. Augustine makes justice dependent on the state, though justice can never be perfectly realized in the secular state.

In Western theory, the idea of compact can be traced to the Epicurean philosophers, but a crude formulation of the concept exists in the Indian political literature of a considerably earlier date. The first hint of the contractual theory appears in the *Aitareya Brahmana*,[1] but the idea is not extensively developed until the Buddhist literature.[c] The Hindu governmental contract, like the Buddhist, was in essence an exchange of taxes for protection, and the king's authority was limited by sacred law. The

---

[a] This and the following chapter are intended to provide topical analyses of certain important aspects of Indian political thought and institutions which do not lend themselves to the approach employed thus far.

[b] Kautalya, however, occupies a position intermediate between Greek and Hindu theories.

[c] The contract may have been both social and governmental. Several modern writers on Hindu theory believe that because a republican form of government existed *pro tem* until Brahma sent the community a king, the contract was actually a governmental contract. *Vide*, e.g., A. K. Sen [383], p. 42.

medieval author of the *Shukranitisara* goes so far as to describe the king as the salaried servant of the people.[2]

The theory of compact is not tied to a conception of the people as the ultimate source of authority. In fact, at least one source suggests that the compact is made "for inspiring confidence among all classes of the people,"[3] and the *Arthashastra* recommends, evidently as a kind of Platonic noble myth, that the contractual explanation of the king's origin be circulated among the people.[4] It is difficult to find instances of actual conditions placed on the exercise of royal power by the people—conditions which would normally accompany a contract. The coronation oath is a pledge of loyalty to dharma, and only indirectly is it a pledge to the people. The king vowed (to representatives of the spiritual authority) to confine his actions to the province assigned by dharma and to keep the spirit of the sacred law. The contract, unlike that postulated by Hobbes, imposes obligations on the king as well as on the people. Occasionally the texts mention the subjects' right to dethrone an unjust or irresponsible king, but such statements are rare. The most important check on the king was the fear of the misfortunes that were certain to result if he violated his charge.

The contract theory suggests a concern with what it is that authorizes one man to control others. "Authorize" implies that that which bestows the right to rule is outside the individual who exercises power. This right may reside in certain *procedures* by which a man is authorized (Weber's legal type), or in the possession of *status*, which automatically authorizes. Modern commentators on ancient Indian polity frequently see the contract as evidence of popular authority. These historians overlook the importance of status considerations—which provided the eligibility at the base of authorization. It was rarely a "pure" form of authority one way or the other. We have argued that brahman authority was legitimated by a combination of sacred tradition and merit. The royal power was based on a concept of authority that contained diverse elements. Some of the images employed to suggest analogies with other aspects of life (e.g., the father or the conquering hero) were themselves intended to justify the relationship of the king to his people—the need for some to command and others to obey.

But the vacuum left by the waning influence of tribal values could not be filled by analogies with what were often merely power relationships. The question of authority is phrased most tellingly by Yudhishthira in the *Shantiparva* (59.6ff.). The prince, far from claiming divinity for himself, asks why, "having hands and arms and neck like others, having an understanding and senses like those of others, . . . possessed of vital airs and bodies like other men, resembling others in birth and death, in fact, similar to others regarding all the attributes of men, why does one man, the king, govern the rest of the world consisting of many brave and intelligent persons?" The dying sage Bhishma answers by describing a world in which virtue had disappeared and men no longer protected one another, a human jungle so terrible that the gods themselves were overcome by fear. The passages of the text that follow suggest that the moral decline is both cause and effect of the loss of the Vedas.

The Grandfather of the universe, at the request of the gods, composed a learned treatise of a hundred thousand sections, which treated of dharma, artha, kama, and moksha. After a series of abridgements that reduced the monumental proportions of the work to a thousand chapters, Vishnu was asked to appoint a man who would be equal to the task of ruling other men. By an act of his own will, the god created a son, Virajas. It is important to stress that Virajas chose not to govern—having determined on a life of renunciation. And Virajas' son also preferred to practice austerities, as did *his* son. The brahman functions are obviously to be preferred to those of the kshatriya. At length Ananga consented to rule, and his reign was distinguished by his piety and competence. But his son succumbed to passion (there seems to be an increasing worldliness in the lineage) and his grandson was a thoroughly wicked man. The sages had no choice but to slay him.

From the arm of the dead Vena the brahmans drew forth Prithu, versed in the Veda and the science of punishment, who promptly called on the assembled gods and sages to advise him in his tasks. Prithu thus relied on the brahmans to delineate his authority. He was told to regard all men with impartiality—which meant that he should punish any man, whatever his caste, if he did not fulfill his duty. Several verses later (59.108) we read that he is to know that the brahman is exempt from punishment. The idea that the king is legitimated by the priests, whose knowledge links men with the sacred law as revealed in the Vedic hymns (which it is the king's first duty to protect), is implicit. The entry of the god Vishnu into the body of the king *followed* the king's performance of righteous acts. The account contains justifications of authority in terms of function, charisma, heredity, subordination to the brahmans, and finally, divinity itself.

Though references to the state of nature exist in almost all the major documents, it is doubtful whether they were meant to suggest an actual historical period. Often the state of nature appears to be no more than a logical deduction. In some instances, when its purpose is to justify a strong political authority, the concept closely resembles that of Hobbes and Spinoza; in other writings it approximates the more attractive Lockean condition of man before the institution of civil society. Narada claims that "when mortals were bent on doing their duty alone and [were] habitually veracious, there existed neither lawsuits, nor hatred, nor selfishness. The practice of duty having died out among mankind, lawsuits have been introduced; and the king has been appointed to decide lawsuits, because he has authority to punish."[5] We may wonder whether the smriti looks back to an idyllic state of nature such as we find in the Buddhist sources, or to the ancient tribal community of an age before property had become a fundamental institution of society.

The puranas remark that with the cultivation of the soil and the development of private property, contention and vice came into the world as men sought to appropriate more and more for themselves.[6] The Buddhist *Digha Nikaya* describes a golden age: the ethereal dominated the corporeal and men danced in the air.[7] Gradually the appetites manifested themselves and the social institutions necessary to their satisfaction evolved. Man became the slave of his passions, and it was now imperative that a leader be appointed to establish order. In return the "Great Elect" would receive a share of the people's grain. It is possible, however, that this is less a theory of the origin of the state than a further glorification of the Buddha, who is undoubtedly the leader referred to in the passages. This description of the state of nature and the subsequent fall from grace can be found in Hindu writings as well. Both the Buddhist and Brahmanical texts postulate the appearance of a savior who restores order.

The pre-political society pictured in the *Mahabharata*[8] has degenerated to the rule of fang and claw. After the fall from "absolute" dharma, men ceased to be guided by wisdom, justice, and righteousness. The world (as the epic puts it) had become the workshop of the devil. Property is precarious, honor and morality decline, men give themselves up to the excesses of their passions, sacrifices are not celebrated, the brahmans do not practice austerities, and castes can no longer be distinguished from one another. Coercion (danda) had become necessary to maintain order, to preserve virtue, and to hold men to the duties of their respective castes. Hence the function of the state is to maintain stability by employing danda : dharma cannot exist without danda in a world of imperfect men.

This degradation is never fully elaborated in the political treatises. The state of nature may be meant to do no more than dramatize the need for an authority to restrain the worst impulses of men. We are probably justified in seeing in the agreement that results not so much the attempt to institute controls over the monarch as the authorization of a strong, centralized kshatriya control. Misery and corruption would otherwise be the lot of the people.

The vice and selfishness that were thought to characterize man before civil society was established led to a glorification of the artifices of social life—all the conventions, values, and organizations that serve to guide men toward decency and dignity. The state, like caste and other institutions, is guarantor and moral agent. Men cannot live apart from the protection danda provides. "A legal rule without coercion," Ihering has commented, "is fire that does not burn, a light that does not shine."[9]

There remains a gulf between the constantly recurring idea that the people renumerate the king for services rendered to them, and an actual contract theory that bases government on the consent of the people and prescribes the sanctions that the people may take against an oppressor. In serving the community, the king seeks to fulfill the obligations of his rajadharma, and since dharma remains in theory the sovereign authority, it is really only implicitly and indirectly—through the acceptance of the framework of social duty by both parties—that a compact between the king and subjects exists. By the time of the smritis and the brahmanic reworking of the books of the *Mahabharata,* kingship had become hereditary. Election plays no role in either of the theories of the origin of civil society in the *Shantiparva.*

Though the king is described in Bhishma's story as being "not different from a god," elsewhere in the *Mahabharata* when the people are advised to abandon a king who is incompetent or who fails in his undertakings for other reasons, it is because he is no longer an "authority." It is the authorized function that is sacred; a bad king does not possess that which deserves reverence. The king, wielder of the rod of punishment that preserves the law, was himself restrained by this very power. Should he depart from his duty and take it upon himself to go against the precepts of dharma, he would be struck down by danda. This conception is reminiscent of the phenomenon of taboo, which haunts the pages of anthropological studies of primitive communities. Though there was no constitutional restraint on the Hindu king, the dharmic code itself must have served as a powerful check on his conduct in office. For the king, like the humblest of his subjects, could be reborn in a despised form.

But the code of conduct works both ways. Those who are charged with the preservation of order may be duty-bound to perform acts that are in themselves evil. Occasionally in the epics kshatriyas pause on the brink of battle to consider the moral implications of their acts. Yudhishthira, like Arjuna in the *Gita*, is sorely tempted to retreat to the forest and the life of an ascetic. Alas, this is not the kshatriya prerogative. The warrior carries with him the sin of Indra, that greatest of fighters. His fate is to die on the battlefield protecting the sacred order of things.

The constant reiteration of the need for coercion (danda) in the preservation of the dharmic order suggests a cynical view of human nature. In addition to the *Mahabharata*, the *Kautaliya* and the *Kamandakiya*, the *Manusmriti* and the *Shukranitisara* all attest to the natural depravity of man.[10] The suspicion of human nature that dominates Hindu thought can be summed up in the words of Manu: a guiltless man is hard to find.[11] A society without constraints is no society at all: men feed on one another as do the beasts of the jungle and the fish in the sea.[d] "When the law of punishment is kept in abeyance, it gives rise to the disorder implied in the proverb of the fishes; for in the absence of a magistrate, the strong will swallow the weak; but under his protection the weak resist the strong."[12] How individuals in the vicious state of matsyanyaya come together to work out their destinies is never revealed. But the same criticism may be leveled against certain of the European contract theories. Evidence of the pervasive fear of anarchy can be found in Hindu theory as late as the last centuries of the medieval period.[e]

[d] When asked how fishes live in the sea, a character in Shakespeare's *Pericles* (Act II, Scene I) answers that they live as men do on land—"the great ones eat up the little ones." Breughel's drawing of the big fish with the many little fish inside is well known, and Swift has a poem on the same theme. This image has been employed by European political writers, and was particularly popular in the seventeenth century. The simile was used by Boccalini in his *Ragguagli di Parnasso* (1612–13) and by Spinoza in the *Tractatus Theologico-politicus*, chap. 16.

[e] The *Laukika-Nyāya-Samgrāha* of Raghunātha, a compendium of legal maxims compiled in the fifteenth century, speaks of a "logic of the monsters." This adds to the struggle for survival in the condition of anarchy the concept of two opposing powers, equal in strength, neutralizing the efficacy of one another.

The scriptures are not in agreement on the beginnings of sacred law. One school makes dharma responsible for the state of supreme happiness that characterized earliest existence. Dharma thus precedes kingship. On the other hand, another theory postulates a pre-dharmic state of strife and misery. Though these two traditions differ—the former seeing Virajas as the first king, the latter tracing kingship to Manu—they agree that government is necessary.[f] The latter argument, which had the greater influence, tends toward a human and secular view of kingship. The other seeks to elevate the king to divine stature. But the Hindu king never enjoyed the immunities that accompanied the European concept of the divine right of kings.

Because appointment by the people and appointment by the gods would seem to be much the same thing in Hindu political thought, social contract and divine origin meet in a shadowy union. It cannot be argued that the king acquired sacred authority from popular election or that popular sentiment was an expression of divine will. The problem is one of the most complex that confronts us.

We know that early societies tended to attribute supernatural qualities to anything unusual or awesome in character. As a depositary of the special power that derives from the community, the king represented the impersonal group "spirit" and was to this extent extraordinary and the possessor of *mana*. It is this power that is sacred. Rational investigation into the nature of many political institutions and concepts was restricted by belief in their divine origins, but this does not mean that the political system was not often justified in rational terms. The gods were not necessarily as fearsome or exalted as the God of Western religions.[g]

We have noted that one of the traditions of the origin of the monarchical institution considers the king to be a product of the divine personality of Vishnu. The sixth in the succession of kings, a tyrant, was killed by the brahmans, and from his right arm emerged Prithu, who embodied the kingly virtues. Yet Prithu, of divine descent, must take an oath to uphold the customs and institutions of the people. Rather than "divine right," we must speak of "divine obligation"—the duty of the king to preserve the social order. Many passages that appear to glorify the king are in fact reminders of the duties implied in his office. The Vedas only touch on the subject of divinity, and in contexts that are not greatly revealing. Although the Vedic king did not claim divine origin, Trasadasyu, the Puru king, is referred to as a "demi-god" and as being *like* Indra.[18] But this is still a long way from a real ascription of divinity.

---

[f] We are reminded of the two versions of Saul's investiture. In the royalist argument it was held that God anointed the king directly; in the other tradition it was held that authority was granted by the priest Samuel, and that therefore the spiritual power is the higher.

[g] "It is difficult to say how seriously the Indians took this matter of royal divinity, and the point has been much argued. My own feeling is that they took it seriously enough, but that gods were not so awesome a thing as they may seem to us. . . . The Indians claimed their king to be an incarnation of gods, not of God." (Ingalls [191], pp. 41f.)

Those schooled in the Western tradition are apt to confuse the theory of divine origin with that of divine right. In Hindu political philosophy the two are distinct. Never was the Hindu king vested with divine right. Only when he is virtuous and self-restrained, only when he carries out his duties of providing protection for his people and attending to their welfare, is the king to be compared with the gods. According to the *Shantiparva*, in a crisis the king is that man who is able to fulfill the kshatriya function; if the ruler is incapable of governing, he should be abandoned as one would desert the leaky boat.[14]

The *Mahabharata*, the smritis, the puranas, and other texts refer to a functional similarity of the king to the gods. The sacrifice, as we have seen, infused the king with the vitality of Indra and made him like the gods.[15] In the sacrifice Indra may represent protection, Kuvera punishment, Vayu the diffusion of culture, and Varuna the economic function. As a consequence of the ritual the ruler became godlike, but this was not meant to imply that he became a god or even that his office necessarily received divine sanction.

The word *deva* is often translated by Western scholars as "god." Deva is used, however, to connote moral superiority rather than omnipotent divinity in the Judeo-Christian sense. It meant resplendent or awe-inspiring and was applied to that which possessed more than ordinary power. When the king is described in the ancient scriptures as *devata*, his importance to the community is extolled, and we are not justified in reading more into the term. The functions of the king, and not the king himself, are usually equated with the gods. The claim to godlike qualities comes from kingship—rather than kingship from divinity.[h] And if the king was often termed the guardian of dharma, this designation must not be taken to imply that he occupied a high religious office.[i] Sarkar has pointed out that the expression "the king is the maker of the age" is the exact opposite of the dictum that the king can do no wrong.

The concept of the king's quasi-divinity was never intended to justify irresponsible rule; it served as a means of promoting deference to authority. The *Naradasmriti* is the only political treatise in which an unrestricted absolutism can be found: a ruler must be obeyed irrespective of his worth and competence if the social order is to be preserved. And the somewhat ambiguous doctrine of the king's divinity in the *Manusmriti,*[j] in which the king is said to embody (the virtues of) eight deities, is not referred to in the *Yajñavalkyasmriti*, the Tamil works, or other treatises and commentaries in which we might expect to find it.[k] Medhātithi, the most important of Manu's expositors, is uneasy with the theory and seems to wish to de-emphasize it. The counsel of Bhishma is as representative of

---

[h] Though the institution of kingship was considered divine in origin, this does not mean that republics were viewed as contrary to the natural order of things.

[i] Though no exclusive "official" religion existed, and the brahmans were usually accepted as the spiritual authorities, there are occasional instances (the most notable being that of Ashoka) when the king took upon himself the role of religious leader.

[j] *Vide* pp. 230f. above; *Manu* VII, 4–8 (which appears to ascribe divinity to the king) must be contrasted with *Manu* VII, 27.

[k] It does, however, appear in the *Ramayana*.

Hindu theory. The sage observes that the king who fails to protect his subjects must be slain "like a mad dog." This is certainly more a warning to the king than it is a doctrine of tyrannicide, but it is sufficient to suggest that the king did not rule by divine right as defined by the Stuart kings. We never find the idea that the ruler is accountable only to God.

The brahmanic recovery depended on a strong royal authority, and the priesthood found itself having to encourage the development of the monarchical power—and even deifying at least the office of the king.[l] A number of foreign invaders, such as the Kushans, were led by rulers who styled themselves sons of devas,[m] and these provided a precedent for the exaltation of the monarch. Old analogies of king and god were embellished to imply that there was more than simply a comparison between the royal and the divine. The king was declared to be an aspect of Vishnu, to whom the god had granted his own luster.[n] This claim of the divinity of kings is associated with a period in which power was becoming increasingly decentralized, a time marked by the appearance of divisive forces. In England, by contrast, the idea of divine right accompanied the emergence of a strong political authority.[16]

In summary we may say that usually the concept of divinity was used metaphorically in ancient India to describe the functions of the royal office. Only the king who fulfilled his duties could claim divine stature; the deposition of unjust kings was encouraged, and their fate was described in terms that would give pause to the most indurated.[o] Peter Abelard's statement, "it is one thing to resist the tyranny of an evil king, and it is another to resist the just power that he has received from God," represents the general theoretical position taken by Hindu writers. In India (as in the European Middle Ages) divine right, at least in the period before the decline of Mauryan rule, must be located in the institution of kingship and not in the king himself.

THE LIMITS AND NATURE OF AUTHORITY

The substitution of artificial ties for the familial bonds of the tribal community stimulated an awareness of the distinction between authority and power. Authority introduces the idea of "right," the legitimate use

---

[l] It seems reasonable to assume that the later emphasis on the divine nature of the king was often an attempt to disguise the humble origins of the Dravidian (shudra) kings who were sponsored by brahmans to oppose Buddhist kshatriyas.

[m] Though most of the Kushan monarchs were Buddhists, they attempted to deify themselves.

[n] In South India there was less inclination to confer divinity on the ruler. Nor was the king generally regarded as a religious leader. The distinction between the spiritual and social well-being of the people never became so confused as it did in Vedic and Brahmanical polity.

[o] The bluntness of such language was made possible by the relative independence of the priests; but the brahmans were themselves too aware of the dangers of anarchy, too sensitive to their own privileged position, to advocate a popular uprising against the crown or even to champion the rights of the people against the secular power— as the medieval Church would do in goading the estates into stronger opposition to the monarch.

of power. Men may have the right to exercise power without being in a position to exercise it; or they may have the position without the right. But we use authority in a variety of ways. The brahman, because of his superior understanding of the Vedas, was an "authority"—much as a man who is respected for his knowledge in tactical matters and his successes in plotting military maneuvers may be accepted as an authority.

The capacity to inspire respect is undoubtedly a factor in the transformation of charisma into authority. Max Weber used the term charisma to describe certain distinctive personal attributes (virtue, courage, and the like) that are out of the ordinary and inspire deference. He considered charisma the ultimate source of authority—before it becomes located in status or rules. But Weber tells us little about the conditions and circumstances that encourage people to respond to the saint, the prophet, or the hero. It is not enough that the leader possess these attributes—even though they are combined with personal dynamism and a burning conviction of the rightness of his cause. We must know something of the age and the effect of institutional change on the personalities of those who are affected by the appeal of the charismatic figure.

In India the avatar, such as Rama or Krishna, appears when dharma has become weak. His mission is to restore the law, just as Christ had seen as his mission the rescuing of the spirit of the law from those who would stifle it in a rigid legalism. This suggests that charisma is not as distinct from tradition as Weber might seem to imply (though Weber does say that the prophet appeals to an older norm, the purity of which has been lost).[p] Changes in institutional forms that create inconsistencies in the normative structure would appear to be closely related to the emergence of charismatic leadership.

Weber's categories tend to blur the distinction between authority and legitimacy. This perhaps explains the difficulty that arises when charismatic power is described as a type of authority rather than as leadership. Legitimacy is the rightful ground of authority: the cultural foundation of authority. A person may have authority because of his success, because he has been named to an office by proper procedures of appointment, because he is able to command respect or devotion, or for any of a variety of reasons. Legitimacy is the final appeal of that authority. It is the ultimate limit of the reasoning process. Authority, in contrast, possesses a rational element; it is, according to Professor Friedrich, a quality of communication. Authoritative communication possesses "the potentiality of reasoned elaboration."[17] Reason is the process of appraising a command in terms of the values on which it professes to be based. Legitimacy refers to these values—values which are beyond the capacity for reasoned elaboration.

[p] "It is very misleading to *oppose* charisma to tradition. The point about it is not that it stands apart from established ways of doing things but that it stands to them in a very special relation." (Peter Winch, "Authority," *The Aristotelian Society*, Supplementary Volume XXXII, London, 1958, p. 238.) *Vide* Radhakrishnan [327], p. 152n. (on the "ancient yoga").

This line of argument stresses *what* is to be decided rather than *who* is to decide. But brahman theory often attempts to locate authority in status and to make a communication authoritative *because* it is commanded. In ancient India the search for a principle of authority necessitated the subduing of the capricious and amoral Vedic gods who were incapable of providing a basis of legitimation for more than the small aristocratic segment of society. In place of the all-too-human deities, scripture was emphasized as authoritative. Sacred tradition as revealed in the Vedic hymns became the foundation of authority. And when interpretation of the scriptures was made the exclusive prerogative of the priests, *legitimation* of the king's authority came to be associated with the brahmans. This development represents the triumph of *knowing* over acting. But knowledge in this instance was knowledge of tradition and not a rational or even intuitional knowledge. Ultimately the very fact of being born a brahman entitled a man to the privileges and respect associated with the order, for he was believed to have charismatic qualities that enabled him to serve as an intermediary between the sacred and mundane spheres of the universe.

Authority, of course, may be based on no more than the acceptance of rule-patterned behavior—activity expressed in social roles. We might distinguish between relatively formal rules and institutionalized authorities on the one hand, and, on the other, the learned responses and anticipations that are implicit in most actions and that guide conduct. In the latter instance there may be no "authorities" other than custom and popular usage.[q] Brahmanism, by means of the caste organization of society, extended its control into this area of experience so completely that criticism of the system was all but inconceivable. Authority in this respect is based less on the public claim on the individual than in the future claim that man, desiring salvation, has upon himself.

Though dharma encompasses justice as well as law, we must not assume that in the Brahmanical literature law necessarily implies justice or is meant to ensure more than order. The Buddhist writers are fairly consistent in maintaining that the state has authority only if that authority is righteous, but the law books (for example) take as their point of departure a conception of human nature that requires the artifice of legal sanctions if society is to have any stability at all. Kautalya holds that danda must be applied with justice if authority is to have the respect of the people—which amounts to saying that justice is what transforms power into "authority."[r] The unjust exercise of power can produce the same chaos and contention that the authors of the smritis and the didactic portions of the *Mahabharata* associated with the lack of government. Dharmashastra literature stresses the importance of virtue in those wielding danda,[s] rather

---

[q] I have devoted a chapter to Buddhism because Buddhism represented a radical attempt to reduce this rule-governed, role-organized area of life to a psychological minimum. As such, it may be seen as a remarkable attempt to free man from internalized authorities incompatible with his effective and harmonious functioning.

[r] In this sense the idealist position of the Buddhist theorists is justified.

[s] Bhishma, in the *Shantiparva*, would evidently see this as a contradiction in terms.

than insisting that danda always be the instrument of justice. According to Manu and Yajñavalkya, wisdom, perception, honesty, and the willingness to submit to canonical authority qualify a king to use his coercive power.[t] It is essential that danda be employed properly and appropriately—i.e., to buttress the caste hierarchy. It is not uncommon to find an author raising the king to the most exalted rank and testifying to his ceremonial purity, and then including him among those associated with butcheries and brothels. The explanation is that the king who fulfills the duties implicit in his office is worthy of worship. He who oppresses the people and avoids his duty is contemptible.[18]

As in the philosophy of Plato, we find several myths whose purpose is to legitimate coercive social authority. For the masses, the doctrines of karma and samsara provided the myth that justified social institutions and threw responsibility back on man himself. This ideology is augmented by a paternalistic conception of the king as well as by theories of the king's quasi-divinity. For the more sophisticated members of society (those who remain unconvinced by the Myth of Er), the basic myth was supplemented by a more rational theory, which made the right of governing conditional on the fulfillment of definite functions.

The word *praja* is translated as both subjects and children, suggesting a type of paternalism that often distinguished post-Vedic theory. In the second Kalinga edict, Ashoka remarks that his interest in his people is that of a father in his children.[19] But the designation of the ancient Hindu state as paternalistic has been criticized inasmuch as karma—the very breath of Hindu religion—postulates individual responsibility. A characteristic of paternalism is the belief that the people are unable to manage their own affairs. Yet the theorists of kingship and law did conceive of the king's authority as that of a father—probably less to emphasize the despotic aspect of the father's role than to symbolize his duty to sacrifice for the well-being of those dependent on his protection. In theory the monarch could know happiness only as his subjects prospered and realized themselves in the dharmic order. And he is continually reminded that his character must provide an example for his people.

The king's chief duty was, of course, to protect his subjects. But this involved more than law enforcement. By the fourth century B.C. there had been a notable increase in the welfare functions of the state in India. The king was obligated to promote education, religion, and the arts, charitable services, and agricultural and commercial development. If the sacred tradition was upheld, the country would prosper; this idea had the effect of making the king accountable for the general prosperity of the people as well as for their security. Use of the royal prerogative to advance the ruler's own ends was considered to be theft of the people's wealth—and was as grave an offense as failure to provide security. In truth, the king's obligations (in the brahmanic texts) appeared to outweigh any benefits accruing from his position. In meeting the responsibilities of his office,

---

[t] It follows that he is disqualified if he lacks virtue and knowledge and if he refuses to heed the advice of his ministers and the brahmans.

he must guard against provoking the people unnecessarily, and he must always take public opinion into account. He must stand above contending groups; his duty was to reconcile the diverse interests that struggled for advantage within the community. A factional system of politics was, for the most part, effectively avoided.

The Hindu state was, then, a civil rather than a military polity. Social institutions were valid insofar as they contributed to the well-being of the people in this world and in the next. It was the king's duty to rule in accordance with the paramount authority of sacred law and tradition, and the ruler was obligated to respect and encourage the various customs and rules of family, caste, and association, if they were consistent with the dharmic code and the preservation of order. The stated goal of the *Arthashastra* is the protection and welfare of the citizens. Their happiness must come before that of the king—indeed their prosperity and good will shall bring happiness to the king.

Rangaswami Aiyangar suggests that a number of similarities exist between arthashastra and nitishastra thought and the cameralist system that developed in Germany at the beginning of the modern era.[20] Both vest final temporal authority in the king, who, while accountable to the higher power that governs the world, is enjoined to view the promotion of the public welfare as the justification for the royal office. The interests of the king are the same as those of his subjects. In both the theories of cameralism and the Hindu state the life of the king is regulated with an attention to detail and moral discipline seldom equaled in political literature. Both demand the subordination of the self-interest of individual members of the community, from the king to the humblest citizen. And in neither is the king constrained by constitutional checks on his power.

Restraints on the king were not formal; they were the restrictions imposed by the obligation to uphold custom and sacred law and to fulfill the requirements of rajadharma. The implication of much of Indian theory is that when a king, as a result of incompetence or arbitrariness, failed to fulfill the duty of his office, he ceased to be a king. Yet the significance of the political function is always acknowledged and the need for discretionary powers is admitted. The ruler may be forced to depart from the law in order to preserve it. For this reason, rajadharma is often broadly defined. And the brahman theorist is accordingly inclined to see it as inherently sinful. But no ancient Indian writer seems to have regarded the state as an evil to be endured for want of an effective alternative.

The occasional justification of popular opposition must not be interpreted as a concern for the protection of civil rights. Nor must references to the welfare of the people be understood as in any way a concern for more than each man's right to pursue his own salvation. The Hindu view of life prevented setting man against society. The problem of individual rights as opposed to the right of the state does not arise in ancient Indian theory—except, possibly, with reference to brahman immunities. The question is rather one of mutual obligations. We must be wary of conclusions that the Western frame of reference could force upon us. Evidence suggests that the people were opposed not to authoritarian rule as such, but only to the misuse of royal power. The king was responsible to dharma —variously defined to include the system of social duties, good custom, the sacred (Vedic) tradition, the example of the virtuous.[u] It was the law, not his subjects, that punished the errant king.

When law and religion become as closely intertwined as they were in ancient India, the only practicable check on absolutism is the separation of *imperium* and *sacerdotium*. This was accomplished with no small effectiveness in the lodging of executive and "judicial"[v] authority in the kshatriya and brahman castes, respectively. In earlier theory, the purohita, as representative of the brahmans and the sacred law, was the crucial factor in the king's success. The brahman who administered the sacrifice was more than *l'éminence grise*; he was Mitra to the king's Varuna, Agni to his Indra. The king was subject to the superior authority of *sacerdotium*: the legitimacy principle of dharma. In theory, the Stuart kings were likewise subject to the spiritual authority of God, but they, unlike the Aryan and Hindu kings, were able to determine the nature of divine will.

If we seek a comparison with European experience, we must turn again to medieval theory (especially earlier medieval thought) with its separation of the ecclesiastical and the temporal power. Secular rulers, it was held, require the services of the priest if they are to gain life immortal, and the priests, in this world, are dependent on the state. The two powers, though closely related, were conceived as independent, and the obligation of the priests and bishops was considered the greater inasmuch as they must account to God for the actions of the ruler.[21] This argument led eventually to an assertion of the supremacy of the spiritual authority. In the Mauryan period the Buddhist king Ashoka succeeded in transcending the traditional dichotomy of authority. But by the end of the dynasty, with the waning of imperial power, the brahmans were able to renew their claims. However, it is doubtful whether the older balance was ever reestablished.

The texts at our disposal undoubtedly exaggerate the role of this countervailing spiritual authority of the keepers of the sacred law, but the power of the brahman is never to be discounted. References to the king often actually pertain to the king in council—and the brahman usually had access to the most important positions in the royal council. The king was

[u] The Germanic contribution to Western legal theory was the conception of law as the immemorial custom of the tribe. Isidore of Seville and Glanvill were later to bring together *lex* and *consuetudo*. It is this interpretation, rather than the absolutist theory of imperial Rome, that comes closest to the idea of dharma. Though Rome was his tutor and he granted the broadest powers to his prince, Machiavelli well knew that rulers must "learn that from the hour they first violate those laws, customs, and usages under which men have lived for a great while, they begin to weaken the foundations of their authority." (*Discourses*, Book III, chap. 5.) Kautalya, who is notable for having broadened the base of monarchical power, shares this respect for custom and the traditional modes of social control.

[v] The term is used advisedly and in the sense of St. Augustine's maxim: The duty of judges is not to judge the law, but to judge according to the law.

advised to surround himself with men who were wise and of unimpeachable character. His ministers must be consulted on matters of policy, and they were expected to have approved the decisions of the king before policies were executed. Never do the political commentaries lose sight of the need to unite power with wisdom as well as law and moral sanction.

The ministers sometimes exercised considerable power. We are told of occasions when the royal council decided questions of succession, and (usually in the regimes of weak kings) the council was known to have imposed checks on the power of the king. It is recorded that many kings paid high tribute to their advisers. The texts indicate that there were instances when the king had no right to veto the recommendations of the council, but we may question whether this limitation on the ruler's sovereignty was of great practical significance. The normal situation seems to have been one in which the judgment of the minister was highly respected and he, in turn, was unwavering in his loyalty to the king.[w] Rarely in the commentaries is the minister a mere figurehead, and the king is often warned of the dangers that ensue from failure to consult with his councilors or to heed their advice. But final responsibility for state action remained with the king. It was he who was answerable for the proper and efficient operation of the departments and agencies that administered the realm.

The crown prince was required to go through an extensive period of education and apprenticeship before he was judged competent to fulfill such posts as governor or general. Since restraints on royal authority were moral rather than constitutional and political, this preparation included rigorous character training and discipline. Such a check on despotism was considered the more effective in that it came from within the man. The conception of power as a sacred trust is certainly one of the most difficult lessons a man can master. The education of the prince aimed at nothing less than the production of a philosopher king. Moral duty was buttressed by a dread of the consequences of forsaking rajadharma. Even the secular Kautalya sounds this warning. Because the king is "the maker of his age," it would logically follow that the sinfulness that makes danda necessary is, in the final analysis, the sin of the king. This idea is explicit in the *Shukranitisara*.

This relatively late work and other Hindu treatises assert that the wise king will subordinate his own wish to the considered opinion of his subjects as well as that of his official advisers. More powerful than the king was the general will: the rope that pulls the lion is composed of many small threads. A number of times in the *Mahabharata* the king is made to justify his opinion or change his plans because of popular criticism.[x] The sacred texts provide several instances of actual popular election of kings. Rudradāmana, Śiśunāga, and Gopāla all acceded to the throne by election,

---

w It should be emphasized that loyalty of officials was to the king rather than to the state. The "state" as we know it did not exist.

x If the epics can be taken as an authority, referenda to gauge the current of public opinion were employed on several occasions.

and Harshavardhana was appointed by the ministers. There is also record of commoners having become kings. Gopala, the founder of the Bengali empire, was of humble origin.

Often in historical interpretation the acceptance of Vedic kings by their subjects is confused with active election. In later Vedic times the role of the people in the investiture ceremony became little more than a formality. But when the king's position was less secure, a high regard was shown for the wishes of the people. Even when a dynasty became firmly entrenched, the rituals recalled the "elective" origin of kingship. As in medieval England, the coronation oath was the *lex regia* and, as in England, it included promises to the people.[22] It served as an effective reminder of royal obligation. Bana tells us that the last of the Mauryas, Brihadratha, was deposed because of his failure to keep the oath. With one exception, no important Sanskrit theorist advocates unquestioning acquiescence on the part of the subjects. As early as the Vedic period, passive resistance (usually in the form of fasting) appears to have provided an occasional check on tyrannous power.

It is probable that the king was the proprietor of only the crown lands, but few scholars today would insist without qualification that individual private property in land was widely recognized.[23] Manu, as we have seen, was of two minds on the subject. All land and water belongs to the king— yet the land is for him who tills it.[y] We are perhaps involved in no more than a question of the king's right to tax or his right to control the disposal of land. It is unlikely that he possessed absolute title to the land. Because it was implicitly held that taxes were payment for protection,[24] theft was felt to justify an insurance payment equal to the value of the loss. The king's continued failure to provide adequate protection entitled a citizen to seek a new king. It is difficult to determine whether Kautalya's dictum that the king must forfeit thirty times the amount of the fine levied on a mistakenly or falsely convicted person[25] can be properly considered a constitutional check to protect the people, or an atonement to protect the king from divine retribution.[z] The practical effect was certainly to the people's advantage.

Under the ancient imperial system the home province was usually governed by the king and outlying districts were administered by viceroys. Restraints imposed on the people and interference in their activities tended to vary with the distance from the capital. The possibility of restless feudatories was undoubtedly a significant check on absolutism. Although the ancient Hindu monarchy can be called an autocracy, the fact remains that it was limited from below by a variety of forms of local self-government. (Village institutions will be considered presently.)

Although the king's authority was rooted in custom and canon, crises could justify a departure from custom and sacred tradition. Moreover,

---

[y] *Vide* p. 241 above. Manu also makes a case for the brahman's universal ownership, and restricts the king's property rights to protect his subjects.

[z] Manu states (VIII, 336) that the king must be fined a thousand coins for a deed that the ordinary man would be made to forfeit one coin as a penalty for committing.

different age-cycles have different standards of morality, and some authorities hold that the traditional injunctions and sacred teachings may be disregarded if they are in open contradiction to enlightened opinion. In the *Shantiparva* we find the argument that the kshatriya dharma removes the warrior and the ruler from the conventional moral restraints. This theory—that sin is the necessary consequence and violence the inevitable means of fulfilling the kshatriya duty—is a development of the "dharma of distress" into a kind of "original sin," which forever taints the aristocracy. It can be transcended only by performing the sacrifice and granting gifts to the brahman.

Authority always allows a certain initiative in the exercise of power. But this discretion is not to be used arbitrarily, and broad rules exist to govern the use of power beyond areas of the king's customary authority.[aa] By the fifth and fourth centuries B.C. the ancient tribal institutions had lost their ability to regulate society effectively. New modes of production, new types of social relationships, new salvation theologies were changing the old ways. Kautalya was the theorist who most clearly saw the need for expanded state activity to fill the ever-widening gaps left by the declining authority of tradition. The king needed greater freedom of movement if he was to provide security and the conditions of prosperity. The state was forced to take measures that frequently ran counter to the accepted moral standards of the community. But Kautalya well knew that such policies were all that could save society from collapse. He was led inevitably to a theory approximating the reason of state arguments of sixteenth-century Europe. But he sought to emphasize the fact that such actions were not irresponsible. Indeed it is the duty of the ruler to his subjects that compels him to take drastic steps to ensure their welfare. Survival and progress are recognized as bestowing authority. He who protects the people is the true kshatriya, we are told in the *Mahabharata*. Function, merit, and initiative had actually long been components of the traditional justification of power. They receive new emphasis in the Kautalyan model of the bureaucratic state and the theory of authority on which it was built. The author of the *Arthashastra* departs most radically from orthodoxy in his intimation that religion exists as a social ideology. And he threatens the base of authority when he attempts to utilize religious symbols fraudulently to accomplish the purposes of the state, for this is to transform authority into power.

Kautalya attempted to raise the royal decree to the status of true law and even to make the king's edict the supreme authority whenever it came into conflict with other types of law. Before Kautalya, two schools of arthashastra had already gone so far as to refuse a place in the catalogue of "sciences" to the Vedas. These arthashastra innovations influenced the smriti literature and appear there in a somewhat modified form—

[aa] This discretionary extension of authority will meet with less opposition insofar as the individual possesses the personal qualities that Weber associated with charisma. Initiative may in fact create new roles or expand the old roles associated with the office without the transformation of authoritative action into arbitrary action. Discretion lies between role-determined "authority" and role-determining "leadership."

though the *Naradasmriti* goes even further than the *Kautaliya* in making the king's edict authoritative.[26] Those theorists who acknowledge the place of statute law usually hold that the purpose of such ordinances must be the maintenance of dharmic law. Kautalya, in fact, limited the king's power to regulatory decrees.[27] And never in the ancient writings is the royal edict considered the only source of law.

Dharmashastra theorists, in justifying state action, usually worked with the more limited conception of government as a restraining force. About half of the *Manusmriti* is devoted to secular law, which was administered directly by the king and allowed him a considerable prerogative in rendering decisions in criminal and civil cases on the basis of sacred law, local tradition, and the example of the virtuous. But the need for royal enactment had become apparent to even the most orthodox writers. Though the typical dharmashastra treatise insists on congruity of the edict with sacred tradition, we can assume that despite such restrictions there remained a wide latitude for the king. He had to relate the traditional bases of judgment to the actual problems before him, choose among these authorities, and judge for himself where the recognized authorities were inadequate to the situation or dilemma with which he was confronted.

In Indian society, government was only one of a number of regulating and welfare agencies, and the tendency by the beginning of the Christian era was to leave social controls to caste institutions, local councils, and such, rather than to formal administrative mechanisms. In a caste society the individual is removed from the immediate impact of political authority.[bb] The activities of the state were again more commonly confined to those occasional ventures, of which war was the most important, that demanded coordination of social resources for the attainment of a specific goal.

Arbitrary rule need not be the consequence of absolutism. The subservience of the king to sacred law and customary practice, the emphasis on the responsibilities implied in power, the strategic position of the brahman group in a traditional society, and the practical problems of administration belie the popular assumption of the West that despotism characterized the political history of ancient India.

A sociological note on authority and legitimacy. When action is appraised with reference to the common values of society, we speak of legitimation.[28] Ancient India is often held to represent a traditional type of authority pattern, which Max Weber defines as authority not restricted to a clearly delineated political context.[29] In societies characterized by

---

[bb] "The daily lives of the people were governed by custom, Vedic laws, and the concept of one's own dharma. Participation by the individual in the politically organized pattern of relationships was small—only a small segment of his personality was affected by things which we could call political. Hence, even if the political authority would have had glaringly vicious features, these would not be apparent and therefore, while an absolutely rigid authoritarian rule would have been intolerable in small family groups . . . it could be tolerated in the context of the political universe which was remote and impersonal." (Varma [417], XXXVIII, part I, chap. I.)

traditional authority there is generally no clear differentiation of the political from the nonpolitical spheres of life. Émile Durkheim has noted two basic types of social solidarity: that which is the result of common beliefs and attitudes, and that which results from the complementary functional usefulness of the members of the community. Neither of Durkheim's categories is sufficient in itself to describe Hindu society because caste organization and the religious system that provided its legitimation have combined the two in a social organization that has had few parallels in human experience.

In India, the kshatriya order *was* distinguished from other functional groups. As those to whom political responsibility, with the power and authority it carried, was specifically assigned, the nobles were considered the instrument of dharma, a principle intimately associated with the general status hierarchy. Dharma was revealed in the sacred texts, in tradition, and in the exemplary life of the sage, and the priests were therefore in a position to legitimate the political authority. Woe to the king who misused the coercive power and disturbed the operation of the dharmic order.

We may say, more correctly, that the king had a regulatory power and that authority was closer to Weber's traditional type, with its hereditary charisma and sanctity of everyday routine, than to the type associated with functional differentiation. Institutionalized rights in the caste hierarchy were less important to the integration of the system than institutionalized obligations. Because the management of these obligations was almost always left to the castes themselves, and because dharma, in theory, allowed no possibility of legislative enactment, political regulation was defined in context. But political authority, as distinct from political regulation, was of a traditional nature; it was based on values that legitimated a status structure rather than on a system of rules and procedures that are the foundation of legal-rational authority.

15 ✻ POLICY AND
THE DIFFUSION OF POWER

THE PILLARS OF THE STATE

The ancient texts leave little doubt that power has its basis in the capacity of the state to mobilize men and resources in the service of its goals. In the final analysis, the strength of the state rested on the revenue and on the army. We turn now to the principles that guided taxation policy, military strategy, and diplomatic relations.

Financing the state. The doctrine of economic determinism was one of the earliest lessons of the prince. Several thousand years before Marx, Kautalya insisted that "in economics lies politics." "Economic considerations are the shelter of society," echoes Kamandaka. Before the rise of the Gangetic states the king had relied primarily on his own private resources to maintain his household and support what few political functions he exercised. But the territorial state could not develop the extensive bureaucratic and military apparatus it needed to consolidate its power until it had some effective system for procuring revenue. The same forces that contributed to the collapse of the tribal organization were to make possible the new political structure. With the developing market economy, a new source of income became available to the state and made possible a system of money payment.[a] By Mauryan times, the *bali,* which had originally been a voluntary offering from clansmen, had become a definite tax.

The state maintained the palace, the army, the police and the law courts, public works and irrigation projects, sanitation and medical facilities, and institutions of learning and worship, and it regulated and supported commerce.

Revenue for these purposes was derived from crown lands and from lands that became state property when they were forfeited or when there were no heirs, from state monopolies, such as forestry and mining, and from state-owned industry, such as distilling, the transportation of goods, and the manufacture of cloth, from tolls, fees, and water assessments, ceremonial offerings, tributes, fines and gifts. The more enterprising re-

[a] Yet Kautalya's attitude toward the merchant was not particularly sympathetic. He may have understood that the prosperity of the state was dependent in no small part on commerce, but he was suspicious of the growing power of the guilds, which could be seen as a potential threat to the state.

gimes made even the waste lands yield revenue by offering such induce-
ments as tax exemptions for a period of years to those who would cultivate
these lands.[1] But the most important source of revenue and the major
tax collected by the revenue officers was the land tax, which was usually
collected in kind, though sometimes in cash. The standard tax was one-
sixth of the produce. A man too poor to pay taxes to the state could donate
his labor for a day or two each month. Hiuen Tsiang, who visited the empire of Harsha (A.D. 629–645), notes that labor for the construction of
public works was not conscripted, but hired. Taxation may have been
used for more than meeting expenses: it is conceivable that it was occasionally employed to modify patterns of consumption.

One tenet of Hindu taxation was the importance of preserving incentive. Extraction must be as subtle and as painless as possible: "Milch
the cow, but don't bore the udder."[2] And revenue policy usually exempted
the means of production[b] from taxation; there were land and excise taxes,
customs, and assessments on property instead. New industry should be
fostered by whatever means were available to the state. Taxation should
be used to encourage rare or beneficial imports, and to discourage the
detrimental. (There is little evidence of protective tariffs as such, however.) The convenience of the taxpayer and his ability to pay, as well as
the source of his wealth, were taken into consideration. There seems to
have been an effort to make tax policy consistent from year to year, and
policy was remarkably indulgent.

References to fiscal oppression exist, but the people were often able
to prevail against excessive taxes, and they may in some instances have
stated the rates they would agree to pay. The king's commitment to his
subjects and the contractual form it took were at least a theoretical guarantee against exploitation. The Buddhist Jatakas, as well as a number of
important Brahmanical works, counsel the king against fines and taxes
that are too harsh. But there is often the accompanying warning against
overleniency, which also may be fatal. The revenue that the king collected
was, in a sense, his "wage"—but at the same time it was his royal prerogative, justified in terms of dharma.

In times of emergency the government is advised to couch its appeal
for loans in such gentle words as these:

> There is a grave danger facing us in all nakedness. The enemy wants
> to ruin us, but will in turn be ruined by your help. For your protection
> I require funds which are returnable after we have got over the danger.
> If, on the other hand, the enemy gets possession of this land he will
> deprive you of your property, and even of your wives and sons. To
> avert this you must co-operate by lending me a helping hand. But in
> this let there be no violation of the accepted canons of taxation. By
> your help again I shall be protected. What is the use of treasure, if it
> were not used in times of great crisis?[3]

This approach is far more admirable than that suggested by Kautalya

---

[b] Narrowly defined—land was certainly not included.

(V, 2), who recommends that secret agents of the king shame small contributors with their own lavish gifts, that pretexts be invented for seizing the property of heretics, that the superstitious be fleeced by means of staged spectacles, and that trumped-up charges be brought against critics of the state as justification for confiscating their property. But the king must be particularly cautious in such measures. It is recommended that the victims be limited to enemies of the state and the sinful.

Taxation of the brahmans was not uniform throughout India, and it varied according to whether the brahman pursued a life of poverty and religious or intellectual activity, or was engaged in material production or enjoyed a profitable official position. Though the vaishya caste shouldered the great bulk of taxation, only rarely was the brahman completely exempt. Nor were temples—many of which owned extensive tracts of land—excused from taxation. References to the vaishyas as the foundation on which the state was built indicate that their contribution did not go unappreciated.

Land taxes appear to have been related, in many cases, to the imperial designs of the state[c] and to the type and condition of the land,[d] the rate varying usually from one-sixth to one-tenth of the yield.[4] These taxes were almost always collected in kind, although there is evidence that toward the end of the period under study some payments were made in cash. In certain cases, failure of the subject to meet his taxes resulted in the state's eventually appropriating his lands, but this seems not to have been a common recourse until a later date.

Most of the land was evidently privately held, though small, individually owned tracts were not the rule. Little attention is given to the concept of property rights, and we find again and again (especially in the *Mahabharata*) the argument that property is dependent on the state for its existence. But this does not entitle us to say that the king owned the land. Sometimes the claims of the ruler were actually disallowed and possession by those who labored on the land and produced its fruits upheld. The *Shatapatha Brahmana*[5] contains the story of a king who was reproved by the earth for treating the land as his private property. References to the king's rights to the land are usually taken to mean his right to collect revenue from the land. We cannot assume that ownership had the meaning we attach to it today. And the problem is further complicated by the close identification of the king with the state—which makes it easy to overlook the distinction between the lands owned personally by the ruler and those he controlled by virtue of his office.[6] Nilakantha denies the right of the conquering king to more than the personal possessions of the vanquished king and his right to collect taxes.[7]

The revenue department consisted of the superintendents of the crown demesne, herds, and forests, and the officials charged with keeping records,

---

[c] For Kautalya's rationale, *vide Arthashastra* V, 2. Taxation in the Mauryan regime may have been as high as 25–33 percent of the yield.

[d] The richer land of the Gangetic basin was taxed more heavily than the less fertile soil of the hinterland.

developing lands, and collecting taxes. The bureaucratic complexity of such administration as that of the Cholas is reflected in tax policy: land was carefully surveyed, and that which was declared taxable was further classified according to use and fertility. In this southern kingdom a magistrate and an army official made regular inspections of the villages, auditing the accounts of the assemblies and determining the tax rate. Tamil inscriptions refer to license taxes, taxes on bazaars, excise taxes on necessary commodities such as salt, taxes on animals, on finished goods, on land (one-sixth of the produce), on water for irrigation, and on weights used in business transactions. The Chola subject appears to have been heavily taxed. In times of emergency, or when sizable public works projects made it necessary, the state might make additional financial demands on the people. Sometimes peasants left their villages to escape the tax burden; sometimes they refused to pay, and their villages were looted.

Not all public developments were the work of the state. Fa-hsien mentions that the hospitals of Gupta Pataliputra were often endowed by philanthropic private individuals. Gupta records mention an officer called *agraharita* who supervised the administration of grants to religious agencies and saw that the condition implicit in these gifts from the state or individuals were carried out. The government sought to encourage voluntary contributions by publicizing donations.[e]

Relations among states. It was in the administration of foreign policy and in war that the king was least restrained in his actions. Only in recent history has the doctrine of ahimsa, or nonviolence, been interpreted to include outlawing war. Although Ashoka renounced war in the name of the Buddhist ideal, he did not disband his army. The *Shantiparva,* the *Manusmriti,* and the *Kautaliya* insist that foreign relations must be dominated not by ethical considerations but by self-interest, even if this should involve attacking a friendly power.[8] In the actual conduct of international affairs, however, ancient Indian rulers were rarely as cold-blooded as Kautalya advised.

This expedience is sometimes justified by the view that rajadharma is as much the product of experience as of sacred tradition. The lesson experience teaches is usually dependent on the goal one seeks. One may learn, as the wily jackal learned, that " 'one should gain over the best by prostrating oneself before him, a brave enemy by setting up another against him, a mean person by a small gift, and an equal by one's own valor.' . . . Then [continues the *Pañchatantra*] he peacefully ate the elephant's flesh for a long time."[9] Here again a moral relativism clouds the attempt to relate dharma to political life. More palatable is the familiar dictum, voiced by these authors, that distress justifies much that is distasteful at other times. Today we have become increasingly aware of the dangers of allowing political issues to become moral issues. The zealous, moralistic attitude that reduces complexities to black and white terms may be far more dis-

[e] For Kautalya's discussion of tax policy and procedure, *vide* pp. 213ff. above.

astrous than an international policy based on self-interest. But the ancient Indian theorists were not content with such a rationale.

These writers on politics employed what often appears to approach an organic conception of the state—especially in the dharmashastra literature. Each element of sovereignty had its importance. Some were ranked higher than others, but the functioning of the state depended on the proper integration of the parts. Although the model is one of equilibration, the assumption was that conflict is the natural condition of the world. The war of all against all depicted in the *Shantiparva* may well have been inspired by interstate relationships—which then, as today, were in a condition approximating anarchy. A basic proposition of Hindu thought is the inherent unfriendliness and the potential enmity of foreign powers, and the consequent need for preparedness. Broadly speaking, a people is to be feared or disregarded in international politics according to its proximity to the state. The frontiers must be guarded with vigilance at all times. Needless to say, military expenditure consumed a major portion of the state's revenue. We know of the existence of standing armies as early as Mauryan times. From the most ancient arthashastra literature to the end of the age of Hindu supremacy when Krishnadeva Rāya, a late emperor of the Vijayanagar Empire,*f* warned of the need for security in all things, kings are advised to be wary of those near them, to be suspicious of all motives, and to purge the land of those suspected of being enemies of the state.

The primary concern of foreign policy when expansion was not feasible was usually the maintenance of a balance of power. The theory of international politics is based on an analysis of the possible participants in hostilities. These were the *vijigisu,* the ambitious, aggrandizing state; the *ari,* or enemy (an immediate neighbor of the vijigisu); the *madhyama* and *udasina,* which may be of potential assistance to either of the principal belligerents—the former being located closer to the adversaries and having, therefore, a more directly mediatory role. A complex *Geopolitik* further elaborates the allies of the central contestants and their secondary allies (i.e., the ally's ally): ally of the rearward ally, ally of the enemy's ally, and so forth. Thus diplomacy is constructed on the interrelationships within a group of twelve states, all neatly catalogued as to the ways they can affect the fortunes of the home state. This "sphere of influence" is termed *mandala.*[10] The mandala theory is based on the assumption that the king, by nature, aspires to conquest, and that the adjacent king is his enemy. The king's natural ally is the kingdom on the other side of this enemy—for the two are not in immediate competition and the other neighbor of the enemy would also stand to benefit from the weakening of the latter. Surround and conquer.

Though maintaining the balance of power was often the immediate goal of foreign policy, the long-range objective of universal sovereign

f Which lasted from A.D. 1336 to 1565.

jurisdiction[g] dominated Hindu writing before the smriti literature began to support a more moderate aim.[11] Peaceful coexistence is hard for the arthashastra theorists to imagine; this is as true of the later *Shukranitisara* as it is of the *Mahabharata*. One explanation for this concern with the idea of universal sovereignty is the lack of natural barriers in northern India—barriers capable of providing political boundaries and obstructing invasion. States elbowed their neighbors and conflict was practically inevitable. Northern India was comparable in this respect to the Italy of Machiavelli's time or to eastern Europe in the twentieth century.

The king must exhaust the possibilities of diplomacy, espionage, intrigue, any procedure short of war, before entering into military campaigns against the enemy. Sometimes kshatriya honor requires that the king and warrior nobles go to war, even though there is not the faintest chance of victory.[12] To be killed in battle was to fulfill the kshatradharma. Kautalya and certain other theorists obviously consider this attitude more sentimental than sagacious and discuss warfare in terms of profit rather than honor. Only if the opportunities for success are clearly apparent should the king involve himself in war. One school of arthashastra quoted by Kautalya tells the king to submit to a more powerful enemy "like a reed in water."[13] The enemy may be approached in six ways.[h] The four major techniques are conciliation, attack,[i] bribery, and sabotage (including the encouragement of dissension). In addition, there are "indifference" and deception.[14] The type of policy used depended on the strength of the aggressor in relation to that of the other state.

When all else failed and no choice but battle remained, war was often a struggle to the unconditional and desperate end. The texts recommend that hostilities be preceded by a formal declaration of war. With few exceptions the conduct of war was regulated by a code of honor, and treatment of the defeated was not necessarily harsh. Despite the philosophy of expedience that pervades the writing on the subject, moral standards that went far beyond those of the modern world usually characterized warfare in post-Vedic India.[15] Conquest of a state did not necessarily imply annexation. In India's early history such annexation was rare. And even in later periods it appears that as often as not, the victor was satisfied with acquiescence and tribute. Of the objectives of policy (usually described as the acquisition of an ally, of money, and of land), the acquisition of land is commonly considered the least important.[j] Autonomy was not greatly disturbed; the defeated king would be soon restored to power, or

[g] This military objective was limited to India; Samudra Gupta, who conquered the Mleccha (non-Indian) countries of Kashmir and Afghanistan, would not extend his authority beyond Bharatavarsha (India). The only world conquest was cultural: the expansion of the Buddhist faith. Though the great poetry of Kalidasa yields little that is of interest to us here, it is noteworthy that the concept of world empire recurs throughout his work.

[h] Actually seven, but *māyā* and *indrājala* are both trickery and misrepresentation. The latter seems to refer more to the actual conduct of hostilities.

[i] Manu (VII, 109) considered these two, sāman and danda, the chief means.

[j] Kautalya, who recognizes the purchasing power of land, is an exception to this. Cf. also *Shantiparva* 95.6.

possibly he or a member of his family would remain on the throne without any interruption of his authority. He was expected to pay homage to the conqueror, and, as feudatory, was subject to constant supervision.[k] Universal "sovereignty" need be no more than the recognition of the hegemony of the conquering state.

Patriotism as we know it did not exist. A man fought not for his homeland, but for his king and his personal honor. (The abstract loyalty of the patriot is also a comparatively recent phenomenon in the West.) The subjects of these Hindu monarchs knew that regardless of the outcome of hostilities, their local pattern of life would not be much altered.

LEVELS OF AUTHORITY

The primary duties of the state were to protect and promote dharma, to defend the community against enemies without and disorder within, and to coordinate and support the social agencies through which the individual realized his private and group purposes. Caste and the group-consciousness it stimulated tended to encourage the conception of the state as integrator and regulator of the various associations that made up society. It might be assumed that the Indian societal structure and the high value attributed to religious experience would transform the central political authority into a mere arbiter of corporate groups, mediating the differences that arose in the relations of various groups. This implies, however, a negative relationship to social collectivities that was not usually typical of early India. Caste and corporation relied on the state to maintain their laws and customs, but it was the function of the central authority to assist in keeping these groups within the bounds delineated by custom and, when possible, to encourage conditions that would contribute to their welfare as well as their security. In ancient theory a weak state is all but inconceivable.

The multiplicity of social organizations through which the individual realized his ends implied no restriction on the sovereignty of the state. The very concept of dharma dictated plural loyalties and a functionally organized society. The state, wielder of danda, was the guarantor of this order, for danda was the guardian of social life and the dharmic code. Obedience to the political authority was thus corollary with acceptance of the social order and the norms of conduct. Modern democratic pluralist thought, as represented by Figgis and Cole, and by Laski in his early writings, reflects a distrust of the state that was not present in ancient thought.

According to Kautalya, the ruler must fulfill a variety of functions: first, and of fundamental importance, he must protect his people—safeguarding the weak from the arbitrariness of the strong and the fraudulence of the unrighteous, as well as defending them against hostile enemies; he must secure justice through punishment and restitution; provide for the

---

[k] The conquered did not fare so well in the Tamil South. The monarch could expect death to follow his defeat, and the cities were pillaged and razed.

welfare of the aged, the infirm, and the needy; promote economic prosperity; encourage cultural contributions; and instruct the people in a sense of their respective social roles. The state rarely achieved the organizational competence to discharge all the functions envisaged by Kautalya. The primitive state of communications was a factor that even the author of the *Arthashastra* was unable to remedy.

The state was able to direct many constituent, juridical, and welfare activities without the oppression that so often accompanies ambitious undertakings, because many of these functions relied on instruments other than the central authority for their execution. Assembly, village council, guild, and religious authority were all partners in policy administration—and even, on occasion, policy formulation.

On the surface the administrative system itself in post-Mauryan times appears to have become a type of feudal-federal organization. Authority was diffused among conquered kingdoms, feudatories, villages, and corporations; alliance and delegation were the very essence of government. As noted in the preceding discussion, in the imperial age defeated kings were frequently returned to positions of authority and enjoyed a remarkable independence in administering the affairs of their subjects, relying on the victor primarily for the conduct of external affairs.[1] The vassal ruler owed allegiance to the paramount authority, but there existed no contractual basis of the relationship. The relation of lord and vassal was not like that usually associated with feudalism, nor did the manorial system develop; administrative officers seem not to have been paid for their services with grants of land. And if feudalism is to be considered a social as well as a political structure, it must be observed that ancient Indian society was organized in terms of a caste hierarchy. Ancient India, in Weber's opinion, was distinguished not by feudalism, but by tax-farming and military prebendalization.[16] The main objectives of the patrimonial bureaucratic organization were the procuring of weapons and supplies for the army, and tax collection—which was granted as a prebend in return for a fixed payment. (According to Weber, the tax farmers were the initial stage of the *zamindari* system.) In the periods of patrimonialism, the exclusive control of offices by nobles and priests was broken as the king introduced members of the lower castes into positions of power.

The hierarchy of political subordination might be continued through a system of vassalage. But distance encouraged these lords to grow bold, and in India the state was a great political amoeba with segments regularly breaking off at the frontiers to form new units. By the age of the Guptas, the political feudality had reached its most advanced stage. The various gradations of government are revealed in the array of titles employed in administration. Gupta land grants attest to the concession of political functions and economic rights to brahmans. It has been argued that by the

---

[1] Even in a newly acquired territory, if Kautalya's advice (Arthashastra XIII, 5) may be taken to reflect practice, the only customs that could be interfered with were those which were obviously harmful to the king's interests and those which went against righteousness (*adharmiṣṭha*).

time of Harshavardhana, feudatories supplied troops to the king.[m] There would seem to be no accounting for the size of the army as recorded by Hiuen Tsiang if such an establishment had to be maintained on the resources available to Harsha.

The tendency toward administrative decentralization, already apparent in the earlier Mauryan dynasty, was to culminate in the division of India into a collection of small powers—an invitation to the invader. And as in the case of the Greek city-states, he came. He came in the eighth century and stayed more than a thousand years as the dominant power. Although India was unable to achieve a stable and enduring political unity, she constructed an effective and viable cultural unity and survives where vast empires, possessing a political but not a cultural cohesion, have disappeared. This strength enabled India to absorb foreign invasion and await the day the lessons of Kautalya could be relearned.[n]

The village. The administration of large areas was possible in India because rural society was largely self-governing. It might even be said that it functioned separately from the state. Aloof from the political vicissitudes of the central government, and protected by strong traditions from the ravages of war, the villages were the storehouses of Indian culture.[17] Outside the capital the king was forced to reckon with the local councils and committees through which the wish of the people was expressed. Political decentralization was certainly the most significant practical check on monarchical power.

The ancient Indian village varied in size from around two hundred families to as many as eight hundred. Apart from the priest and a few craftsmen, there was usually little occupational specialization.[18] The village was the center of, or basis for, administration—the primary organizational unit. Each was in fact a small, self-sufficient republic, but for purposes of administration, villages were arranged in groups of ten, twenty, one hundred, and one thousand. Each headman (gramani) was responsible to his superior and was expected to report all important occurrences within his

[m] Sharma [390], p. 318. And *vide Harshacharita* VII (parts of which are reproduced in Basham [24], pp. 448f.) for a colorful description of Harsha's entourage striking camp.

[n] Evidence of feudal institutions (in a truer sense) is confined to Rajput and Muslim rule in a later period than that which concerns us here. But because the Rajput states of the late medieval period "preserved more of their antique structure than any other basic region of India" (as Daniel Thorner suggests: *vide* his essay in Coulborn [73]), the following observations are appropriate. Although it was true that obligations of vassals to their lords included military service and payments reminiscent of feudalism as it evolved in Europe, the essential relationship was that of tribal chieftain and blood kin rather than that of vassal and superior. Tenure, according to Lyall [240], was rooted in blood and birthright; to see land tenure as the basis of nobility is simply to reverse the actual justification of authority. Rajput authority was centered in a group of vassal chieftains and their king (or *rana*), to whom they rendered military service on demand and whose court they devotedly and regularly attended. The rana was assisted by a prime minister-treasurer; the *bakshi*, who served as liaison with the nobles; the chamberlain; and the *sahai*, a combination home and foreign minister. The division of the territory into eighty-four districts, each autonomous in the administration of civil affairs, was the basic political organization. Power was widely diffused.

bailiwick. The control exercised by the central and provincial governments over the village assembly and its committees was usually limited and of a very general nature. The headman might be called to the capital to account for village activities, or government inspectors, supervisors, and accountants might be sent to the villages. Local officials seem to have been responsible to the central authority primarily in matters of finance. Only rarely did the state intervene in village affairs. Certain regulations passed by the assembly needed the approval of the king, and, reciprocally, the king had to secure the sanction of the assembly before effecting any substantial change in the status of the village. In the Jataka stories, the village headman is sometimes represented as a petty tyrant and more than once villagers were forced to appear to the king for relief from oppression.[o]

The actual administrative work of the villages was performed by committees of the assembly, particularly the *pañchayat*,[p] the executive organization. There were age, character, and property requirements for membership in this council, but caste appears to have been of relatively minor importance. It seems to have been a common practice to forbid the reelection of council members during a period ranging from three to ten years after they had completed a one-year term of office. Membership in the assembly itself was normally governed directly by certain property qualifications and, indirectly, by the principle that all should have a chance at one time or another to participate in its deliberations. There is some evidence in the *Epigrafia Indica* that in parts of India all householders were members of the village assembly. At least all the more important family heads appear to have had the right to join the assembly. It was known by various names, all of which are translated as the "great men of the village."

But the village council was the important political organization. It was responsible for settling disputes, collecting land revenue, maintaining temples and supervising the use of waste lands.[q] It undertook such public works as the construction, administration, and repair of roads, reservoirs, hospitals, and accommodations for travelers. Measures were taken to alleviate famine. The general welfare of the village necessitated such functions as mortgaging public lands in times of economic distress and encouraging cultivation of marginal lands. The council served as banker and trustee, and it organized recreational and educational facilities. We would expect various village responsibilities to be divided among subcommittees, but there is little to indicate that this was the general pattern—except for the Tamil country. The headman and his council of from two to five advisers were accountable to the village assembly, and gave reports at its regular meetings. The majestic banyan tree, generous in its shade, sheltered these deliberations, and the tree has itself become a symbol of self-government.

---

[o] Cf. *Shukraniti* II, 343, where the headman is described as a father to the villagers.

[p] Literally, the "council of five."

[q] Maine's argument that communal land tenure was the general pattern of ownership in ancient India is no longer accepted.

The office of the village headman was usually hereditary. He seems generally not to have been a member of the brahman caste. The council could reprimand the gramani and insist on changes in policy and administrative procedure. As head of the village council, the gramani collected government taxes, kept the village records, directed the militia, and was responsible for the safety of the village. In return, he was exempted from taxes or paid in kind. In some of the larger villages certain of these functions might have been assigned to subordinate officials. The village accountant performed the necessary/secretarial duties and assisted with records. Though the headman and the council exercised judicial functions, the most serious cases were sent to the royal court—but the village court had unlimited authority over cases of civil law, settling disputes if lesser associations to which the disputants belonged were unable to do so. This judicial power was a deliberate delegation of power from the central government, not an informal assumption of authority.

Hindu writers probably tend to overemphasize the degree of cooperation that characterized community projects, but the sense of group feeling and pride in collective enterprise was, by modern standards, highly developed. The revenue collected in the village and allotted to local projects was, on occasion, augmented with assistance from the central government.[r] The village had a limited income of its own from special fines, levies, and grants. The temples, which often commanded considerable resources, made loans in return for certain privileges and concessions. Because of the important role the temple played in the social, intellectual, and economic, as well as the religious life of the citizen,[19] the village assemblies were often preoccupied with temple affairs. By the fourth century A.D., important members of the community, non-brahman as well as brahman, were sometimes represented in a district council—at least in southern India. The operation of this council and the extent of its jurisdiction is not known to us.

(A fundamental element in town government was a committee (*pañchakula*) representing all elements of the population.[8] Administration was expedited by an executive assisted by a secretariat. The *Mahabharata,* the *Kautaliya,* and the *Manusmriti* refer to the mayor of the city.[20] Individual participation in local administration was much more highly developed in the village than in the commercial centers of early India. Whereas the village approached autonomy in managing its own affairs, the city possessed no joint association representing the community as such. There were castes of traders and artisans, but they are not to be compared with the Western burgher stratum. Citizenship as a specific status was lacking in China and Japan as well as in India.[21] The taboos of the endogamous caste prevented the emergence of an effective urban status group. An urban commercial class might conceivably have developed to the point where it constituted a serious threat to the traditionalist system, but guild

---

[r] The central government would frequently allow the villages to retain for local use a small percentage of revenues collected.

[8] Records of these town councils pertain, for the most part, to the northwest states.

power was successfully challenged by the great patrimonial states—and the towns were never to emerge as independent corporate units as they did in the medieval West. In the ancient Oriental city we find nothing that resembles the city law of the classical and medieval periods of European history.

In South India, organs of local government developed beyond the less formal organizations of the north. In the Chola kingdom the village assumed great political importance.[t] The village assembly was the center of administration, directing commercial, financial, police, and maintenance activities such as the upkeep of irrigation ditches and local roadways. Most of the inscriptions found in southern India that refer to village assemblies indicate that the administration of justice was a major function of the assembly. The regulations and procedures governing the operation of the assembly were probably developed by the organization itself; each village had its individual constitution. The sabha could sell or lease land, commission public works, borrow from the temples, punish offenses, and tend the public morality.[22] Being an extensive landowner in its own right, the sabha was chiefly concerned with agricultural problems. Tamil records point to the final authority of the village pañchayat in the use and disposal of land. This jurisdiction was conferred on the local councils by the Chola kings. By about the tenth century, government supervision of the village had increased considerably.

Though qualifications for election to the assembly were usually not exacting, there do exist records that point to relatively strict conditions for membership in some village assemblies. A knowledge of the Vedas is mentioned as a prerequisite, but this may have been true only for brahman villages. Or it may have been that, as Nilakanta Sastri claims, the sabha, or assembly, was restricted to brahman villages. Chola villages could have several assemblies—for brahmans, for merchants, and for residents. Perhaps the sabha was the brahman assembly.

In the Chola kingdom, and possibly in central India as well, all, or most, of the residents qualified for election to the assembly.[u] Most of the actual administration was carried on through an executive board, or pañchayat, of the influential elders of the community. In earlier times this executive group acted primarily as a negative force, a check on the operations of the headman. By the Gupta period they had become formal councils. Appointment to the assembly of South Indian villages was apparently based on a combination of election and lot. An inscription discovered at Uttaramallur gives an account of the methods employed. The village was divided into thirty wards. Residents wrote the name of their choice on a ticket. Under the supervision of the priests a young boy drew from a pot

---

[t] "The most striking feature of Chola polity in this period was the unexampled vigor and efficiency of the functioning of autonomous rural institutions." (Nilakanta Sastri [299], p. 256.) But cf. A. Appadorai, *Economic Conditions in Southern India*, Madras, 1936, pp. 135ff., for the less widely-held view that most South Indian villages were governed much like those in the north.

[u] Some Chola records indicate that the village assembly may have had a property qualification: one and a quarter acres of land and a house.

a bundle of tickets, and from these tickets one was selected by another drawing. The individual appointed served for one year. The system of rotation had the effect of instructing a larger segment of the population in the problems of government. Even women participated in political affairs. Several Chola inscriptions indicate the wide use of the committee method of local administration. Re-election to the committee within a three-year period was forbidden in at least a few instances—probably to give more people an opportunity to hold office. The Ukkal inscriptions imply that in addition to the village corporations in the south there were also unions of villages. Many of the intervillage assemblies may have been convened for ad hoc purposes only.

The village, with the opportunities it provided for self-expression and self-government, has, more than any other institution, served to keep Hindu civilization alive despite political conditions hostile to that culture. "They seem to last where nothing else lasts," wrote Lord Metcalfe. "Dynasty after dynasty tumbles down; revolution succeeds revolution; Hindu, Pathan, Mughal, Mahratta, Sikh, English are all masters in turn; but the village communities remain the same."

CORPORATIONS

The guild. The importance of guild organization dates from the sixth and fifth centuries B.C. The guilds may originally have been confined to economic objectives, but by the early Mauryan period they had acquired broader social functions. Indeed these corporate groups appear to have embraced every sphere of human activity and to have exercised controls over noneconomic aspects of their members' lives. In this respect the guild resembled its medieval European counterpart; both exerted a closer regulation of human behavior than would be countenanced in the modern state. Expulsion from the guild could of course prevent an individual from practicing the trade or craft of his family.

Narada, who has heretofore been represented as the theorist of monarchical absolutism, goes so far as to say that the king must uphold even those prescriptions of the guilds which go against his and the community's best interests.[23] Other authorities are mindful of the guild's function as moneylender to the prince. Yajñavalkya assigns to the state the responsibility for ensuring that the guilds deal equitably with the people and that they do not gain "disproportionate" power or quarrel among themselves. Nor could a guild be organized without state approval. The state recognized the judicial rights of the guild over its members. Most of the Hindu theorists justified the intervention of the state in trying and punishing guild members when the guild itself was clearly unfair in its treatment. The question of compatibility between guild regulations and sacred law was generally left to the king, who exercised a type of judicial review, and whose authority was final.

In actual practice, the state seems to have interfered with the affairs of the corporations when their actions prejudiced the general welfare or when they disagreed among themselves. Although in ancient India the state intruded only infrequently in the affairs of the various associations that made up the community, with the accumulation of wealth and the development of commercial centers the state saw the guild as a challenge to its own power. An active conflict developed between the economic and political agencies as the state sought to control the corporations. Guild organization was, however, incapable of challenging state intervention. The state was ultimately triumphant in curbing the guilds, at the same time curtailing the opportunities for capitalist expansion—which would have had far-reaching consequences for subsequent Indian history.

The guilds could make compacts with other guilds or with private individuals, and these contracts were evidently guaranteed by the state. Assets and liabilities acquired by persons on guild business were the property and responsibility of the corporation. In addition to owning property, the guilds in the Gupta Empire and in Andhra acted as bankers and trustees—which implies, in turn, a considerable degree of organization and efficiency. Kautalya and other early writers imply that the guilds possessed military resources (which might be lent to the king) and certain of them may have relied on war as well as trade for their livelihood.[24] Law was enforced by private guild tribunals, as well as by those of caste and village. The guild courts, according to the *Shukraniti*,[25] would try cases not dealt with by the "families"; those cases that did not come before the guilds were to be tried by the appropriate assemblies.

The guild contributed to the maintenance of religious establishments and took upon itself services to the community other than the regulative and welfare functions it performed for its members. Majumdar's words may lean toward the extravagant, but his appraisal of the economic corporation is probably valid: "The guild in ancient India was . . . not merely the means for the development of arts and crafts, but through the autonomy and freedom accorded to it by the law of the land, it became a center of strength and an abode of liberal culture and progress, which truly made it a power and ornament of the society."[26]

Each of the corporations that composed ancient Indian society had its own tradition of law. Each combined the legislative,[v] executive, and judicial functions of government. These bodies were governed, typically, by boards of from two to five persons. Removal of an executive officer for misconduct need not always be sanctioned by the king, although it was necessary that he be consulted, and in cases of serious conflict between the parties concerned, the king could issue a verdict. But dismissal was generally the task of the guild assembly. Apprenticeship had much in common with Western guild practice. Merchants, craftsmen,[w] and even unskilled workers were organized into these associations, membership in which tended to become hereditary. Guilds of soldiers, musicians, farmers, arti-

---

[v] The legislative authority of the guilds has probably been made too much of. Professor Ghoshal believes that Bühler's loose rendering of the *Gautama Dharmasutra* (XI, 21) is responsible at least in part for this error.

[w] The Jatakas list eighteen traditional crafts.

sans, doctors, fishermen, and priests appear in the chronicles. Even high-waymen and beggars seem to have been organized. The political and economic strength of the people was due in large part to the effectiveness of these organizations.

The guild was, properly speaking, a merchant association, and was originally distinguished from the craft or vocational organization. The latter, known as shreni (*śreni*), was an occupational group found in villages and towns and organized for the pursuit of a common economic objective by its members. It may have been composed of persons of the same vocation but of different castes. Kautalya, however, suggests that this corporation was based at first on blood ties. In the *Arthashastra* "shreni" is used to denote a former tribal association that had become an occupational grouping. Kosambi[27] considers the shreni discussed by Kautalya to be an organization intermediate between tribe and caste—its members not yet absorbed into the caste hierarchy. Industry was highly localized: there were villages of carpenters and villages of iron-workers. It can be seen how political and economic functions became fused in these organizations. Probably this more pronounced political role is all that sets the shreni apart from the typical guild. In the epics these corporations are described as representative assemblies, and they acted as constitutional checks on the king. It is possible that members of the shreni also bore arms. By the third century B.C. these organizations of workers had become less influential than the merchant guilds dominated by wealthy families on whom the state had come to depend—as the Renaissance prince would later rely on the great banking houses. Village settlement was expanding, encouraging a lively trade in necessities. A luxury market had also emerged. And the state, beset with problems of administration, sometimes had no choice but to distribute among the guilds functions it had formerly reserved for itself.

The republic. There is a passage in the *Avadāna Śataka* in which merchants from north central India (Madhyadesha) are asked about the form of government in that part of India, and the merchants answer that "some provinces are under kings while others are ruled by ganas." Gana generally refers to corporation,[a] but in the *Shantiparva*[28] it appears to mean a republican community. Earlier scholars held that it meant tribe, but Jayaswal[29] and F. W. Thomas have ably controverted this view. Following Sharma,[30] I have accepted a position that diminishes the significance of the debate.

The Vedic gana we take to have been originally an armed organization whose purpose was probably cattle-raiding. Its only official was the leader, or ganapati. The egalitarian tribal association, of an age before brahman ideology consolidated society on the basis of varna distinctions, hereditary kingship, and costly sacrifice, was the inspiration for the post-Vedic gana.[31]

---

[a] Kautalya's use of the term *sangha* to denote corporations has been taken as proof that the *Arthashastra* antedates at least those portions of the *Mahabharata* which employ the later use of *gana* to refer to corporations. But the latter term is also used in the *Mahabharata*, at least in the *Shantiparva*, to mean republic.

The grammarian Panini equated gana with *sangha,* meaning "group," a collection of living beings. But sangha, in different contexts, may mean a collection of gods, men, or beasts. D. R. Bhandarkar,[32] working from the references to sangha in the *Arthashastra* (XI, 1), distinguished three types of group—the craft guild, the mercenary tribal band, and the *rāja-śabdopajīvin,* an organization whose members bear the title of king.[33] Actually Kautalya distinguishes only two kinds of organization. The first type refers to a group living by the "combined arts of war and peace." The second type is a political community in which the royal title is used to describe the executive head, although it is not a monarchy.[34] This would lend some support to the view that the gana was at one time the instrument for supervising communally owned property and distributing booty, becoming later the model for the republican constitutions of the oligarchic states that flourished toward the end of the Vedic period.

Buddhist descriptions of northeastern India, and the writings of Greek visitors (which pertain primarily to northwestern India), are the major sources relating to the ancient republics. But the discussion in the *Shantiparva* provides what is undoubtedly the best description we have. It assigns to the assembly of such polities the administration of financial, military, diplomatic, and legal affairs. Theorists who wrote after the gana had ceased to exist as an effective political device refer to the institution as an assembly, gana rule being contrasted with royal rule. But the references to the ganas in the *Mahabharata* are sufficient to claim a theory of republican government for the ancient Hindus. *Sangha* and *gana* are both broadly employed to refer to autonomous political corporations. Thomas, Fleet, N. N. Law, and others have concluded that autonomous tribe or self-governing community is a more adequate translation than simply tribe or clan.

Republics were, with few exceptions, confined to northern India. In the seventh century B.C., prior to the flowering of Magadhan imperialism, there were sixteen "great peoples," most of them monarchies, but among them a few republics.[y] There is no definite indication of republican constitutions before the eighth century B.C. The first period of republican government ends about 325 B.C. with the spread of Mauryan influence, and the second period, which began about 150 years later, was over by A.D. 325.

At least two references in the journals of the Greek observer Megasthenes refer to "democratic" governments in ancient India. The Greek envoy at Chandragupta's court mentions governments headed by magistrates "where the people are self-governed." Diodorus, Arrian, and Curtius also cite instances of kingless states. Arrian reports that an official class called superintendents reported to the magistrates in states where there were no kings. There is even the suggestion in these Greek reports that generals were sometimes elected rather than appointed. The descrip-

---

[y] Eight oligarchies are mentioned in the Buddhist literature.

tions that came out of the Alexandrian invasion tell of many republics, including one (the Yaudheya), aristocratic in nature, composed of 5,000 councilors. Almost all the peoples the Greeks encountered as they retreated possessed a republican form of government.[z] One state is described as a democracy (the Ambashthas), and another as having the same kind of constitution as Sparta.[aa] The *Mahabharata* tells us that the Andhakas and Vrishnis had a council presided over by a chairman and that "all" were allowed to voice their opinions. There were a number of chiefs, each with his coterie, and one of them was named commander of the army. Policy-making seems to have resided with these chiefs (or elders).

The citizen army of the ancient republics was far superior to the hired mercenaries of the monarchs, and it endowed the sanghas with an uncommon political strength. We know that the republics of northwestern India offered strong resistance to the forces of Alexander—attesting to the loyalty of their subjects. Kautalya remarks on their invulnerability when this inherent power is augmented by alliances among themselves. These leagues were common, though not always enduring.

Nonmonarchical forms of government tended to develop primarily on the fringes of the lands consolidated under Aryan rule. The Buddha was born in a part of India where republican government was the rule. Among these republics were the Mallas, Koliyas, and Vrijjis. The last of these, among the most famous of the republican states, was a confederation of eight clans. Panini even suggests the existence of upper and lower houses in some of these states. Republics in Sind and the Punjab existed into the fourth century B.C., bowed before Mauryan expansion, and emerged again with the decadence of the regime to flourish until the early centuries A.D. By the fourth century their power had faded.

The republics of India were about the size of the Greek city-states, averaging perhaps several thousand square miles. The need for quick action or for security often resulted in the delegation of power. Executive authority was usually vested in a council of elders, a cabinet, or an assembly. The Lichchhavis seem to have had an executive officer (*senāpati*) who held office for a certain term, governing in conjunction with an assembly that chose the senapati by free election. The constitution of the Vrijjis names a president, vice-president, and general.[bb] The small size of these states facilitated popular government where it would never have been practicable in a state of imperial dimensions. But probably only nobles were eligible for election to these offices. The power structure of nonmonarchical states can best be described as aristocratic.

The assembly was of considerable size: there are records of 5,000 and

[z] Porus was one of the few kings.

[aa] Diodorus records that Patala was governed by two hereditary kings and a council of elders. The real locus of power was most probably the latter. The arrangement may have been similar to that of Sparta—or perhaps the example of Sparta shaped the Greek image of Patala. (J. W. McCrindle, *Ancient India as Described in Classical Literature* [Westminster, 1901], p. 212.)

[bb] A Jataka reference adds the position of exchequer.

7,707 "rajas"—usually of the kshatriya caste. The prevalence of factions was the chief weakness of such states.[cc] When parties formed, their members sat in separate groups. Assemblies of republican states exercised relatively complete control over the executive council; council members, as well as officers of the military, were chosen by the central assembly. The executive group of these republics may have had as many as twenty or thirty members, or as few as four.[dd] The assembly controlled foreign relations, but the need for secrecy eventually shifted this control from the assembly to the executive. We are well aware that foreign policy deliberation is one of the more exasperating problems of democracy today.

One reason for the decline of republics by the end of the fourth century A.D. was the tendency for offices to become hereditary as they were in the monarchies that dominated the political picture at that time. Powerful families assumed positions of control and identified the state's interests with their own. Survival, in the face of imperial expansion, demanded the strengthening of government; and in time the Indian republics, for reasons that are not entirely known to us, became indistinguishable from the monarchies in their political structure. Those who exercised executive functions were, in fact, often referred to as kings. It can be argued that the distinction between monarchy and other types of government was never so great as is commonly supposed. Autocratic methods and oligarchic ruling groups appear to have been characteristic of political structures in the period preceding the rise of Magadha, and throughout their history republican states were almost always controlled by a small segment of the population.

The republican system had ceased to be an effective challenge to the principle of kingship long before the rise of the Mauryan empire. Monarchy had proven itself more fitted to the needs of the time, more capable of elaborate and efficient organization. The expansion of Magadha marked the nadir of the great bulk of republics, but with the collapse of the Mauryan empire the sanghas were quick to reappear. The Malavas, Arjunayanas, Yaudheyas, and Vrishnis are cases in point. Succeeding empires and the waves of invasion eventually proved too much for these political corporations, and from that time they ceased to exercise any influence. It has been suggested that the lack of any systematic theory of republican government is due to the diminishing prestige of republicanism by the fourth century B.C., when formal political speculation gets under way. Then, too, the nonmonarchical governments ruled by the kshatriya aristocracy were not favored by the caste that provided the bulk of the literature upon which we depend for our understanding of ancient Indian civilization.

[cc] The eleventh book of the *Arthashastra* is devoted to means of undermining tribal communities. Its author recommends *agents provocateurs* to sow the seeds of dissension, and there is at least one instance on record of the success of such tactics in breaking down the mutual confidence of tribal leaders. The Buddha was himself alert to the peculiar vulnerability of the tribal organization in this respect.
[dd] The Lichchhavis had a council of nine, the Malla state four.

With the destruction of the Pushyamitras by the Guptas, the last great republic was crushed. But the victory was Pyrrhic. The Gupta empire never recovered its former stature. And from this time on, Indian history crumbles into fragmentary sketches of great men without great epochs.[ee]

[ee] Several dynasties did in fact succeed in establishing themselves in the later period. In reviewing the major political systems of India after the achievement of empire under the Mauryas in the fourth and third centuries B.C., the list would include the Andhras in southern India (second century B.C. to third century A.D.) and the Pallavas (from the third to ninth centuries A.D.), the Gupta regime of the fourth century (in decline by the end of the sixth century), the earlier Chalukya dynasty of the western Deccan (which lasted for two centuries after its establishment in the middle of the sixth century), Harshavardhana's empire in northern India during the first half of the seventh century, the imperial states of the Gurjara-Pratiharas and Bengalis of the eighth through thirteenth centuries in the north and northeast. We have referred briefly to the empire of the Cholas, who succeeded the Pallavas, and to the feudality of the Rajputs in northwest India, beginning in the tenth century. In the high medieval period there existed the kingdoms of Kashmir and Vijayanagar. In the seventeenth century the Sikhs were a major power. In 1627, Shivaji founded the great Maratha Empire, which thrived for half a century. With the attempts of the Marathas and Sikhs in the seventeenth century to throw off the foreign power, political theory enjoyed a temporary revival as the need developed for a new rationale of the ruler's authority.

16 ⚹ CONCLUSIONS

The critical period of ancient Indian history was the age that spanned the Upanishads and the fullest development of Mauryan administration under Ashoka. In these formative years, roughly from the seventh to the middle of the third century B.C., the dimensions of Indian philosophical and social thought were established. All subsequent speculation was embellishment, the logical development of ideas, and the transformation of philosophy into ideology. Our study has attempted to indicate certain relationships between social organization, styles of thought, and prevailing ideas and values. Within these four centuries new modes of economic production evolved, which threatened the old tribal organization and made possible experimentation with new forms of social integration and, ultimately, the achievement of empire.

The connection between economic surplus and political systems capable of coordinating large territories has often been observed, but the tie between such institutional developments and the philosophical ideas and psychological states that seem to accompany them—namely awareness of the self, moral consciousness, and monotheistic religious conceptions—is still somewhat obscure. Among the most promising attempts to explain this connection are the psychologies that account for types of mental functioning in terms of the destruction of the original unity of emotional and intellectual processes. Expanding on the Hegelian distinctions of subject and object, Marx made the concept of *Entfremdung* central to his early social analysis, and today these youthful humanistic writings are considered by many to be among the most important in the body of Marxian literature.[1] In the foregoing chapters such concepts as alienation have been employed in the attempt to account for the psychological consequences of the deterioration of tribal culture with its strong ethnic ties and communal ownership of property. The details of that culture remain uncertain, and conjecture necessarily has a prominent role in our reconstruction of Vedic society. We glean what we can from the epics, the Buddhist records, and the like, and occasionally in the pages above the methods and theories of modern social science have been introduced in the effort to understand ancient Indian civilization.

But it is not only the need to fill historical lacunae that leads us to supplement the institutional approach and that of the history of ideas with a psychological-cultural method. Any analysis of the dynamics of social systems must concern itself with the motivational processes of human beings. The centuries that culminated in the imperial state of the Mauryas are of interest precisely because they were productive of so many ideals, life-styles, and elaborations of symbolism—the study of which calls for techniques that go beyond the traditional textual dissection and chronicling of institutions.[a] In a recent study of the nature of symbolism, a psychologist has remarked that man *"experiences himself as a self* in terms of symbols which arise from three levels at once; [symbols which have their source in] those archaic and archetypal depths within himself, symbols arising from the personal events of his psychological and bio-logical experience, and the general symbols and values which obtain in his culture."[2] We shall probably never know more than the barest par-ticulars of the symbolic experience of early Indian culture, and in the summation that follows we shall do no more than compare the most sig-nificant responses to a world that could no longer be interpreted and manipulated through the sacrifice, or understood as inexorably given.

Economic change and the incorporation of indigenous peoples into the Aryan community had rendered the traditional agencies of social in-tegration inadequate. When old values and institutions are challenged, old certainties are gone, and new social relationships demand new justifica-tions, men are faced with the need to articulate that which earlier could have been left unsaid. In such a time many men must have become acutely aware of differences between their own needs and purposes and those of the collectivity to which they belonged. Such questions as how to live with poise and integrity began to arise. The Buddha is the most famous of those who questioned the old ways, and the answer he proposed was in essence psychological. It involved a discipline that aimed at no less than the transcendence of the dichotomy of subject and object.

The two other solutions proposed at this time were basically organiza-tional—the bureaucratic state designed for the efficient mobilization of societal resources, and the more or less self-regulating society based on clearly-defined status groupings among which different social functions would be distributed. The first of these is best described in the *Artha-shastra* of Kautalya, in which society is politically organized to meet the

---

[a] In the last decade or two a school of political analysis, inspired by logical positivism, has taken upon itself the task of purifying the language of political dis-cussion. Obviously these attempts to point up the ambiguities of argument and clarify the terms we use should have a salutary effect on the development of political theory. If, however, we should become preoccupied with the fine points of definition to the exclusion of a concern with the ends of government (because we cannot get beyond the posing of the question), then the very life of political philosophy is threatened. It is an easy victory to bring the instruments of modern social inquiry to bear on the ideas of theorists who lived and wrote in ages less congenial to the critical spirit or who were sometimes contradictory because they saw farther than their fellows and lacked the means to express accurately their vision. But we may be the real losers if we deprive ourselves of the insights of a Plato or Rousseau because we insist on equating departures from consistency with deception, or epistemologies that differ from our own with fatuity. It is our responsibility to apply the refinements of methodology and the social sciences in searching out the intended or latent sense of the ideas that confront us. The discovery of meanings that might otherwise remain hidden to us is a nobler employment for our newer knowledge than its restriction to the essentially negative tasks of controverting and deriding.

security and welfare needs of its people. The adaptive requirements of the community are stressed in the theory, and politics as administration tends to replace politics as interaction.[b] Caste, on the other hand, emphasizes the integrative imperative of society. It is no less than a professionalizing of society, the freezing of actions in the mold of role. Historically, caste represented in part the attempt to preserve status based on birth from the threat of status based on wealth; but, in the *Bhagavad Gita* (which Radhakrishnan places in the fifth century B.C., though it is doubtful that it attained its present form until several centuries later), caste achieves its most sophisticated rationale as the social reflection of a philosophy of self-realization through the pursuit of inherited duty.

The earliest sources reveal a society dominated by a warrior aristocracy. The chieftain was *primus inter pares* and rarely acted simply on his own volition. Tribal religious beliefs were symbolized in the sacrifice, the manifest function of which was to sustain the universe, to win the favor of the gods and their support for the various objectives of the tribe. It also provided a mechanism of adjustment to social and psychological strains, and though Vedic man understood the sacrifice as a propitiation of the gods and the ceremonial reproduction of the cosmic order, he was in fact reading the social structure of the tribal community into his belief about the sky-gods he worshiped. The sacrifice thus served to maintain the pattern of social relationships under the guise of preserving the universe. But it did contain an important truth: our intentions toward the world are what constitute that world, the object of our consciousness. Man was not yet alienated from his gods—or rather he had not yet come to feel the need to project his feelings of estrangement upon them.

Probably only the very few who, because of their role in the performance of the sacrifice were looked upon as representing the tribal community, had any sense of individual distinctiveness. Vedic man was, for the most part, submerged in the group and in nature.[c] This is not to say that there was no active political life. Scattered references in the texts point to popular assemblies and tribal councils; power appears to have been dispersed among the members of the community to an extent that was

---

[b] "Every social process may be divided into a rationalized sphere consisting of settled and routinized procedures in dealing with situations that recur in an orderly fashion, and the 'irrational' by which it is surrounded." (Karl Mannheim, *Ideology and Utopia* [New York, 1949], p. 101. Mannheim sees the distinction as the difference between administration and "politics."

[c] The dominance of tradition in the communal society provides "a basis for self-relatedness, rather than a source of self-alienation. In the second place, adherence to tradition favors group-centered attitudes, rather than self-centered orientations. That is, the traditional man conforms in order to fulfill his obligations to the group, to avoid shame, whereas the [member of a mass society] conforms for the purpose of overcoming the diffuse *anxiety* which accompanies the lack of self-confidence." (William Kornhauser, *The Politics of Mass Society* [Glencoe, Ill., 1959], pp. 110f.) The variety of principles that organized ancient Indian society at different times discourages the use of broad characterizations like "communal" or "traditional" in describing Indian civilization without mention of such refinements as the distinction between the heroic "shame-culture" of the Vedic warrior and the penitential "guilt-culture" of the later Brahmanic age, or the distinction between types of cosmological symbolization (as suggested in Chapter 9 above).

rare in Indian history. The close identification of the individual with the social unit made possible such political life—as it had in the ancient polis before the internecine wars of the later fifth century and before the influence of the great teacher whom Hegel was to describe as the first "self-conscious" man. In this world where gods and men are still on familiar terms the historical manner of viewing the sequence of events was as yet unborn. Nature provided the model and, like nature, social life renewed itself with comforting regularity. But the process was not automatic. The sacrifice was of crucial significance in this periodic regeneration.[d]

The sacrificial rite served to exalt those who officiated and those who, in the name of the tribe, sponsored the increasingly elaborate ceremonies. Eventually, as these roles became stabilized in the offices of brahman and king, tension developed between the two authorities—the priesthood of the sun and the imperium of the moon as the problem was sometimes summarized in medieval European theory. Perhaps Buddhism must be explained as a reaction to brahman controls, but such an explanation seems less than adequate: we know that Brahmanism was not fully developed in the Himalayan foothills where the Shakyan people lived. We are equally justified in viewing Buddhism, in its original expression, as the search for a way of life that would make possible the reintegration of personality.

As long as instinctive responses to the environment had provided an adequate basis of social activity man had not even the experience of a "self." At best the Vedic warrior had seen himself revealed only in his failures to live up to the heroic ideal that had inspired the tribal community. But now, in the more complex social environment of the sixth century B.C., the instinctive and reflexive aspects of the self had diverged to a degree unknown in the lusty, combative Aryan culture of the Vedic era. Guilt and moral consciousness began to emerge as the basis of an internalized authority. In this "birth of tragedy" the self made its appearance as a burden to be suffered. The teaching of the Buddha can be understood as a technique for coping with the demands of the instinctual life (the free expression and satisfaction of which may no longer be tolerated by civil society)[e] by bridging the unconscious and conscious aspects of the mental processes. By removing the causes of personality dissociation, the Buddha

---

[d] Our definition of freedom does not exhaust the possible views of what constitutes freedom. We tend to convince ourselves that men can and do make history, and we differ from "archaic" man in that we see freedom as the relative independence from normative controls. The cyclical conception of time encourages the belief that man can annually begin life afresh. No small freedom this—and how far removed from the later ideology that placed man in bondage to his past, the deeds of his previous lives. When caste came to be the dominant social institution, based on the theory of karma, history was understood in terms of regressive cycles. Once men were virtuous, but as a consequence of a fall (which is never really explained), law and agencies of its enforcement became essential to social life. Theories that justify strong social controls put the golden age in the past. But Vedic man had faith in his capacity to manipulate the sentiments of the gods. He was master of his destiny. (It is instructive to compare the Oedipus of the heroic culture depicted in the *Iliad* with the tortured soul portrayed by Sophocles. *Vide* Dodds [98], p. 36.)

[e] I have in mind here a distinction between immediate discharge of tension in action and the social need to inhibit action. *Vide* Parsons, *et al.* [319], p. 82.

hoped to overcome the sense of alienation that had served to define the self. He saw the problem as rooted in man's seemingly inexhaustible cravings. It is desire that produces consciousness of the self; desire is the cause of alienation. And the sense of alienation is conquered only insofar as man succeeds in recognizing himself in objects exterior to his body. This recognition would be possible only when man emancipated himself from the wish to possess these objects as his own.

Employing the vocabulary of modern psychology, we might say that the Buddha sought anxiety-free ego functions by means of a technique which did not disregard the self but rather freed it for the realization of its purposes by eliminating the interpsychic conflict that impedes this pursuit. Conduct would cease to be the anxiety-generated action (as analyzed in psychoanalysis), or the alienated act motivated by the desire for the products of a system made possible by the worker's estrangement from himself (as analyzed by neo-Marxian theorists), or the action that seeks to establish the identity of the actor by making of the self a thing (as analyzed in existentialist writing). We are told that the Buddha rejected the extreme asceticism that was directed toward the destruction of the self, that he himself remained active in the world of men, and that he established a community in which men could live together amicably with only those few possessions absolutely necessary to survival and health. The sangha was an association of equals, which operated on the assumption that unanimous agreement on policy questions would be possible, given this reintegration of personality.

If truth is not readily apparent in phenomena as they are revealed to the senses, there must be present in man an active faculty capable of discovering truth. This view would seem to provide the basis for an epistemology compatible with a democratic political theory, but in Buddhism this comprehension demanded a rigorous training of the mind (which in turn presupposed leisure)—and this must have seemed to the average man as remote from practical possibility as the esoteric technical knowledge of the brahman. Democracy, for the larger community, would have to await the romantic identification of truth with the subjective feeling available to all men.

The Buddha sought a standard for the proper functioning of the organism—which might also have served as the basis for a critical evaluation of the society of the time (in contrast to the brahman theory of the sacrifice, which made of the cosmos a mirror reflecting the existing social order). But the philosophy and technique of the Buddha's teaching were never intended to inspire a movement of reform. The psychological ideal was itself a rejection of attempts to find security in an established identity that forces perception and experience into stereotypes and systems. The mystic sought a freedom from customary modes of understanding and action; the relationship with the environment must acquire a directness and an immediacy that diminished the distinction between self and other. Only in this sense is the self "destroyed." The Buddhist attack on the fixed identities established in the caste system, which substitutes ascription (the individual as object) for performance (the individual as actor), reflects this aspect of Buddhist philosophy.

Buddhism might also be understood as a challenge to the new, more abstract, political arrangements of the time (but not as a return to the more immediate political relationships of the tribal polity, i.e., to politics as the direct resolution of conflict—a form of interaction that was being replaced by the administrative systems necessary to the governing of large territories). The tribal organization had been "political" in something of the sense understood by the Greeks; it represented the common life of its members, even though actual political activity was confined to those who represented the familial groups that composed the tribes. Politics as the expression of that which is common to the members of a group implies by definition a certain homogeneity of culture. Never, of course, in the poleis, constructed as they were on a slave economy, did all men participate in these activities. The Aryan tribal collectivities were generally of an aristocratic nature, but those who participated in political life enjoyed a relative equality. What is important is that the *res publica,* insofar as it was capable of being distinguished from other aspects of tribal life, was viewed as the means for realizing those purposes shared by the whole community.

The Buddhist sangha was not an attempt to recapture a political life rendered obsolete by new modes of production and the organizational requirements of ever-expanding territorial units, the consolidation of royal power, and the incorporation of dasa peoples. Buddhism, though perhaps not the quiescent philosophy it is frequently made out to be, supplemented the *vita activa* with a new emphasis on contemplation.*ᶠ* In discounting the claims of caste and the state, it turned (as did the Hellenistic philosophies) to the private experience as the ultimate vehicle of fulfillment. The individual was reunited with the species by virtue of his humanity—that which is more fundamental than his membership in a specific group. The spiritual had come to replace the political as the highest expression of human purposes. "Compared with the attitude of quiet," as Arendt³ says of a similar development in European civilization, "all distinctions and articulations within the *vita activa* disappear."*ᵍ*

The second challenge to the heroic ideal provided an alternative to the communal polity in the form of hierarchical organization—empire based on the bureaucratic rationalizing of areas of conflict. As political

---

ᶠ Vide pp. 89f. above—Weber's distinction between the emissary phophecy (more familiar to the West) as typified by Jeremiah or Isaiah, and the exemplary prophecy of such teachers as Gautama Buddha.

ᵍ In the earlier discussion of Buddhism I have suggested certain parallels with modern psychological theories and techniques aimed at attaining an effective integration of personality. In a recent study of Freudian analysis, Philip Rieff remarks of psychoanalysis that "it undercuts the whole problem of the freedom of the individual in any society, emphasizing instead the theme of the anti-political individual seeking his self-perfection in a context as far from the communal as possible. All politics are corrupt, in the democratic community as well as in the totalitarian state. Since freedom is a psychic condition (residing essentially in the individual, not in him as a member of a group), the possibility of freedom exists in all societies." (*Freud: The Mind of the Moralist* [New York, 1959], p. 256.)

life became increasingly abstract, the need for political symbolization became more acute. We find new attention to questions of authority and
legitimacy, and political theory begins to take on a systematic and sophisticated form. One might almost say that with the failure of politics (in
the sense of face-to-face political relationships), political and moral philosophy flourish. Justifications and explanations are needed for the new social
relationships that appear, or these new forms are decried in the name
of traditional values—or the attempt is made to diminish the importance
of these institutions and relationships by encouraging self-sufficiency.

Just as the invasions of Alexander introduced the Greeks to the organizational techniques of the Persians, so may the intercourse between
Persia and India have served to familiarize Indians with large-scale political structures and administrative processes. Kautalya best represents this
application of rational thought to the problems of social organization. By
the time of the Buddha the Gangetic valley was divided among a number
of kingdoms, the most important of which was Magadha. Tribal elements
were still present in this transitional period before the establishment of a
central authority capable of effective control. It was still common for
power to be conceived in terms of what we would today call a scarcity (or
conflict) model, which sees power as essentially power over others rather
than as a resource for achieving the desired goals of the collectivity. Conflict in such societies tends to be resolved directly—either by violence or
in the more or less intimate political associations of clan and tribe. The
growth of political units and the consequent dilution of the kinship ties
that had characterized the earlier Aryan communities had produced what
Banfield, in another context, has referred to as "amoral familism."[h] Custom and the natural bonds of the tribal "nation" were no longer sufficient
to the needs of ordered life, and it remained for the kings of Magadha to
superimpose the artificial bonds of the state on a situation moving toward
anarchy. New types of law were required for resolving disputes, and the
royal edict came to be increasingly emphasized.

The remaining centers of tribal power, such as the kshatriya military
associations, constituted a threat to the emergent states, and a major concern of the monarch was to subvert those tribal institutions that remained
potentially capable of impeding the purposes of the state or dividing the
loyalties of the people.[i] One device for promoting ill will among the members of a tribal group was the use of agents to encourage the humbler seg-

---

[h] Speaking of modern Montegrano in southern Italy, Banfield remarks that "it
is tempting to compare the ethos of the Montegranesi with that of their very early
ancestors as described by Fustel de Coulanges in *The Ancient City*. The early Indo-
Europeans were amoral familists too, but their families consisted of thousands of
persons and the bonds within the family were immensely strong." (*The Moral Basis
of a Backward Society* [Glencoe, Ill., 1958, p. 164, n.2.})

[i] Often the kings lacked the legitimacy that kshatrahood provided and it was
necessary for them to establish a new basis of authority, itself a departure from
tribal values. From this time on, kings were "shudra-like" according to the puranas.
And at least a few of them *were* shudras. We might speculate that in some instances
the brahman was able to establish a position for himself by providing legitimation
for kings who did not possess kshatriya pedigree.

ment of society to insist on equality of treatment and status. Those of higher position (the descendants of the original Aryan tribes, or the kshatriya aristocracy) were to be dissuaded from intermarriage and eating at common able with those of lesser rank. Thus were caste values introduced as a competing mode of organization. The Magadhan ruler Ajatashatru systematically undertook to create dissension among the Lichchhavi tribesmen. The master agent in his employ was reputed to be a shrewd brahman minister. Pretending to be *persona non grata* in the Magadha court, he gained the confidence of the tribal nobles and began circulating stories of his own invention designed to create bad feeling among them. Ultimately he was successful in sabotaging the assembly of the republic. But the real menace to the tribal community was less Magadhan imperialism than the new modes of production that called for new agencies of control and sharpened consciousness of the class divisions underlying the old societies.

The great Mauryan minister Kautalya and, later, the emperor Ashoka, were at least indirectly concerned with expanding the categories of political speculation to meet the needs of empire and the realities of the age. Kautalya wished his king to represent the political unity of the people—a unity that transcended the particular interests and varying status of the different sectors of society.*ʲ* The person of the king is distinguished from that of his subjects not simply because the king represents the collective purposes of society (this is true also of the tribal leader) but because he *is* that which the diverse elements of society share. The new and positive functions of the king are reflected in such statements as "the king is maker of his age," which begin to appear in the brahman literature of the time. For the brahman, the state represented a means of ensuring his own social position. He had as much, if not more, to gain from the substitution of a caste hierarchy for aristocratic tribal values. In the older society his status had never been secure. From the vantage point of the state, caste made possible social integration along functional lines, thoroughly rationalized through the elaboration of the idea (already present in tribal society) of inherited guilt.

The "individualizing" of anxiety was the product of the changes we have mentioned in our discussion of the Buddha, but it is perhaps worth remarking on the beginnings of a sense of the distinction between the goals of society and those of the individual, which encouraged the development of the concept of the private individual—an idea that appears to have been related to the appearance of the bureaucratic state in other cultures as well. When kinship could no longer provide the basis of social regulation, legal institutions evolved to supplement the communal bonds of the tribe. Functional differentiation requires the recognition of private areas of interest legitimate in their own right—goals not necessarily those of the larger society. If these are to be effectively implemented, private sectors

---

ʲ "A multitude of men are made *one* person, when they are by one man, or one person, represented. . . . For it is the *unity* of the represer, not the *unity* of the represented, that maketh the person *one*." (Hobbes, *Leviathan*, Part I, chap. 16.)

must enjoy institutional rights. Such claims are, in effect, a restriction on the exercise of public authority.

We have thus far considered two efforts to cope with the problems of an age of great social change. The first took the form of an attempt to overcome the separation of the perceiving subject from the perceived object. But Kautalya's state, in its dependence on the hierarchical division of labor, must itself contribute to this feeling of alienation. New controls over the environment sharpened the distinction between physical necessity and necessity that is created by man. We may surmise that men began to conclude that remaking the world was within the realm of possibility. The ancient belief in the cyclical periodicity of time, the eternal return, was modified or displaced altogether by a sense of continuity and development approximating a historical attitude. Accumulated wealth and the military power and administrative efficiency it made possible could now be used for achieving ambitious, long-range political and social goals. The great man is, in fact, the great organizer. He creates the very conditions that make the hero obsolete, for he imposes an order that limits the unpredictable contingencies against which the hero struggles. The hero was made by his age; the organizer is the maker of his age. Men can now do things that earlier could be accomplished only by the gods.[k]

Possibly the most basic of all political problems concerns the extent to which conflict may be permitted in a society. It was the practical necessity to integrate different tribal, linguistic, and religious backgrounds that was the most immediate concern of Ashoka Maurya. Like the Romans confronted with the tasks of imperial administration, he was compelled to find a set of universalistic principles that could be the basis of governmental policy and social coordination. (When the state was consolidated, this coordination could be based on the functional differentiation of the Brahmanical caste theory.) For this reason Ashoka sought, in a sense, to combine the Buddhist ethic with the administrative system of Kautalya. He was not primarily concerned, as his grandfather had been, with the mobilization of power resources. Most of India acknowledged his suzerainty. Ashoka wished to establish what might be called an educative state—a state that would take an active role in inculcating certain ethical tenets in its subjects. The dangers implicit in this caesaropapism have been commented upon. The illustrious emperor probably understood that, as a jurist has put it, "transpersonalized power is economical of the use of force,"[4] and that Brahmanism was too closely linked to the caste structure to be able to inspire a sense of social responsibility and the common conviction capable of transforming power into authority by relating it to ethical principles. The ambitions of the imperial Guptas were more modest; the Gupta kings were generally content to see themselves as mediators of the various interests that composed society. The task of integration was left to the castes.

> [k] This rudimentary historical consciousness, which is suggested in the *Arthashastra* of Kautalya, would later disappear with the ascendance of the village economy, practically self-sufficient and mirroring the natural cycle. Only the occasional merchant with the need to keep accounts bothered himself with dates that went beyond the year itself.

Caste was the third response to what we have elsewhere called the tribal trauma. The most positive expression of the values basic to the caste structure is to be found in that bible of Hinduism, the *Bhagavad Gita*. In one sense the poem may be understood as an attempt to retain the purity of the act—to prevent the kshatriya heroic ideal from developing into a conception of egoistic man. Though it seems to teach that actions are not to be transformed into objects (the "fruits of action"), it does in fact fuse act and object in that what one does is related directly to what one is. A man who is a warrior by birth must find his fulfillment in the battle. The demands of duty are foremost. Part of the difficulty of interpretation lies in the fact that the *Gita* concentrates on kshatriya obligation and thus emphasizes the risks that are implicit in life (i.e., in the warrior's role). In action man becomes a "subject" rather than the object of someone else. Krishna, the "divine charioteer," is concerned with easing the conscience of a knight whose disgust at the seemingly pointless ravages of war causes him to hesitate on the eve of battle. But he is a kshatriya; his identity in this life is fixed. He is the object of his past. Conduct is made the expression of a preordained mode of life.

The changes in social organization, the increase in economic opportunities, the new conceptions of personal responsibility, and the like, would be expected to affect the manner in which that most basic of human problems, the problem of suffering, is articulated and evaluated. The unrighteous prosper: why should this be? Suffering found its explanation in the belief that no man is innocent, for if he were he would not exist as an earthly being. He carries the weight of the transgressions of his earlier lives, and his sinful actions in this life will be punished in the next. There was at least the cold comfort of knowing that the wicked could not escape punishment. And in the ancient tribal solidarities each man, though never so preoccupied with the question of sin, was made to bear the burden of the actions of *all* the members of the clan. The concepts of the individual and history had taken a peculiar turn to leave man answerable for actions committed in the earlier lives of the soul. And he was rendered powerless by the belief that social institutions existed as the only possible remedy for man's sin. It would appear that religious, philosophical, and ideological symbolization, complex and "total" as it was, allowed man no flexibility in self- and social-image, no opportunity to break out of the cultic pattern and create a symbolism detached, in part at least, from this mythical, religious, or historical reality, a symbolism that is the work of the free imagination and is capable of projecting new combinations of images.[1]

One historian of Indian social thought has remarked that "India has always displayed an emotional flow and vibration which, on the whole, militates against rigidity of discipline and organization. If in one or two spheres organization was attempted on a scale unknown in the West, there were whole departments of life that were left unorganized. Here culture

---

[1] Erich Kahler calls this "ascending symbolism" and distinguishes it from the symbolism that descends "from a prior and higher reality, a reality determining, and therefore superior to, its symbolic meaning." ("The Nature of the Symbol," in May [261].)

was embodied in institutions to a far lesser degree than in Europe. Social thought is more diffuse and less exact and systematic than in the West."[5] We find much the same assessment of Indian polity in the writings of Aurobindo, who maintained that it reflects the vigorous and natural communal life freely incorporated into the large political structures that had emerged by the fourth century B.C.

> This spontaneous principle of life was respected by the age of growing intellectual culture. The Indian thinkers on society, economics, and politics, Dharmashastra and Arthashastra, made it their business not to construct ideals and systems of society and government in the abstract intelligence, but to understand and regulate by the communal mind and life, and to develop, fix, and harmonize without destroying the original elements, and whatever new element or idea was needed was added or introduced as a superstructure or a modifying but not a revolutionary and destructive principle.

Accordingly, India has not been productive of experiments involving the overthrow of traditional social devices, and the great cornerstone of the modern West—the idea of progress—has not taken a similarly idealistic and social form. Change was conceived in terms of a gradual evolution of custom "conservative of the principle of settled order, of social and political precedent, of established framework and structure."[6]

These evaluations have been included to help balance the record; they represent interpretations not usually found in studies by Western writers. They have much to commend them and they point up the limitations of a strictly political analysis, but a description of the more positive aspects of Indian cultural life in terms of "emotional flow and vibration" must not be allowed to obscure the limitations imposed on expression by the caste system and the consequent stifling of opportunities for social advancement on the basis of talent and achievement. To say that culture finds its embodiment more commonly in other than institutional forms is to ignore, with slim justification, the pervasive influence of caste and to give too much emphasis to individual forms of religious expression and commitment. Law became a system of detailed status-differentiated prescriptions and prohibitions based on these differing capabilities. The legal code, which depended on the coercive power of the king for its enforcement, was rationalized as the safeguard of the moral order; it insured the hierarchy of social duties—duties which, if performed faithfully and effectively, ultimately qualified men for those disciplines leading to spiritual emancipation.

We look in vain for ethical universalism in "official" legal and social theory: Hindu monarchy was government under law in a certain sense, but this was not law as the Western tradition has come to know it. At the apex of the structure, enshrined in immunities and privileges protected by the law codes and by tradition, was the brahman. This authority, according to the theory, could not be considered an encroachment on the freedom of the other orders of society. For it is through the exercise of brahman authority that the individual is established in those modes of life that make possible his ultimate salvation—which is more highly valued than freedom as such.

Studies of African political organizations in transition from relatively homogeneous tribal organization to centralized administrative systems appear to indicate that economic and cultural heterogeneity (an increasingly prominent feature of Indian society in the period that has concerned us here) is frequently associated with a statelike form of political organization. Centralized authority provides a framework for the accommodation of diverse peoples, and if economic and cultural differences are considerable, a class system will usually result.[7] Where class is combined with an ideology that rationalizes completely the hierarchy of status, different groups may live in peaceful proximity without the need for a strong central authority to ensure order and arbitrate differences arising among them. For all the criticism of the system, implied and otherwise, it was caste and the village, rather than the political and administrative organization, that during most of India's history preserved the integrity of her culture and made possible the absorption of alien elements. A remarkable and, indeed, almost unmatched attribute of early Indian society was the toleration shown by the Hindu to diverse traditions and outlooks.[m] Most traditional societies have been characterized by an aversion to that which varied from the orthodox, and even in secular societies it is difficult to find greater powers of cultural absorption than India possessed. Such hospitality has been her strength as well as her undoing. Respect for and delight in differences are still the charm of India.

Rarely in Indian history was there a concentration of authority at the center; authority was located in caste custom, guild, religious tradition, the teaching and example of the sage, and the village council, as well as in provincial and central governments. Throughout Indian history, the basic unit of administration was the village. Hindu law exhibits great respect for local variance in custom and tradition, allowing a remarkable autonomy to the village and the corporation. This is the virtue that Aurobindo and others have justly emphasized. Intervention by the central government might be necessary when these organizations were unable to settle internal disputes or problems arising from contact with other associations. Communal self-government was, as a rule, successfully combined with political stability, and the structure flourished for a longer period than any other.

Two of the three responses to the disintegration of tribal values empha-

[m] This toleration is related to caste organization in interesting ways—one of which was noted by Alexis de Tocqueville in a manuscript on India that occupied him intermittently between 1840 and 1843. (The draft of the projected book, edited by André Jardin, will be included in the collection of Tocqueville's works and papers now being prepared for publication by J. P. Mayer and others.) In this study Tocqueville remarks that "Brahmanism is at the same time the most absorptive and the most tolerant religion. This is easily explained when one notes that it is a religion of privileges. . . . One belongs to it by right of birth; it is impossible to enter it unless one is born within it. So it is impossible to feel hatred towards those whom Brahma has left outside." The implication of this, as Mayer has noted (*Encounter,* May, 1962), is that proselytism and persecution are closely linked with religious conceptions of the common nature of all men and their equality before God.

sized types of coordination more appropriate to cultural heterogeneity and
large territories. One of these may be described as social. Integration is
based on social duty, rigidly defined and hierarchically arranged. A man is
born into a set of obligations; he knows his place in the total scheme of
things and will hold to his duties—for their performance is the key to his
salvation. The problem of conflict, for all practical purposes, is solved.
This type of authority Max Weber called "traditional."

The second answer was political. Bureaucratic organization—a corps
of officials with defined political roles, whose offices are arranged in a
clear chain of command—enables the state to take an active part in social
regulation. In such a system rules become basic. The assumption here is
that there must be an agency of special competence to resolve the conflicts that constantly arise in society. The state represents a more dynamic
organization than the caste structure; in essence it is a set of procedures for
dealing with problems, mobilizing resources, and formulating goals. It
may exist to ensure that each man is permitted to find his salvation in his
own way, it may dictate the form this salvation takes, or it may subordinate
individual purposes to those of the state itself. Coordination comes from
"outside" the community; the state may take whatever steps are necessary
to preserve society and regulate the groups that compose it. Weber termed
this type of authority "bureaucratic." The central concepts of bureaucratic
authority imply a distinction of the political from other social functions.
Of course political roles exist in "traditional" societies, but integration
is accomplished by religion and custom. Weber was thinking primarily in
terms of the rational bureaucracy of the modern state when he developed
this category. But there are other types of bureaucracy that we may mention in passing because they provide a transition to the third type of
authority, charisma, which we have earlier described as "leadership."
These charismatic bureaucracies may take patrimonial or totalitarian
forms. Loyalty is to the person of the leader as well as to the office. The
ruler is both *dux* and *rex*.

The third solution is psychological and spiritual. It may involve a
turning away from the world, as in Buddhism, for man cannot find his
salvation in the things of this world. Or it may seek to transform the
world in order to make it more amenable to that salvation. The former,
the more passive "learning" process, is the more common in the East.
In Western history prophecy took more active forms and has thus had
more significant implications for political life. But although it could be
argued that the Buddha has no place in a history of political thought, he is
in one sense very important. For this withdrawal from the political is
one of the first expressions of protest, and marks the birth of critical
philosophy. In the case of the Buddha and of Lao-tse in China[n] this protest
took the form of reducing life to its simplest statement, detaching oneself

[n] Though his conception of government was far more positive than that of the
brahmans who sponsored the caste theory, Confucius' teachings may be compared
with the brahman "solution" in that he emphasized standardized conduct: man must
do what is proper to his station. Kautalya has his counterpart, broadly speaking, in

from the world in order to attain union with the all-embracing, impersonal One.

This questioning of the legitimacy of the old order is often an attempt to return to an original purity that had existed before social institutions appeared or before they became corrupt. But the basis of legitimacy may be no more than the uncommon personal characteristics that are believed to qualify a man to lead or instruct. The prophet or savior "has set his personal charisma against [the traditional hierocratic powers of magicians or of priests] in order to break their power or force them to his service."[8] The word charisma means, literally, "gift of grace." It is, in fact, the source of *all* authority—rooted in that which is extraordinary, which is removed from institutional routine.

The ritual and initiation possess much that is charismatic; they lift men from the commonplace world and transport them to the sacred. It is this sacred element in tradition that gives it authority. Chance and the unpredictable may find a place among the traditions, as for example in the symbolic game of dice played between the king and his ministers, in which the sacred wager was the wealth of the humblest member of society.[9] The dice game, or any of a number of rituals, dramatizes the fact that charisma has become objectified and inhabits an office as well as the person who has inherited charisma. The role has been established. Authority refers to such established roles; leadership to the creating or expanding of roles. Charisma is the mysterious quality of leadership, the magnetism, heroism, or saintliness that inspires a following, the magical element that the brahman sought to institutionalize in the sacrifice, that the Mauryan monarchs hoped to locate in the office of the king, that Indra personified for the Vedic warrior and that the divine avatar represented for the Hindu believer. Our story is ultimately the story of this force—which is, at once, power and authority.[o]

*   *   *

In this study we have observed the extent to which religion, law in its several forms, and political speculation were interwoven and served to reinforce one another. Indeed, political and social thought can be comprehended only in the light of prevailing belief and religious practice. Analyses dealing exclusively with ideas—which most commonly are found in the brahman literature of mythology, ritual, and religious philosophy, or in manuals intended primarily for the instruction of the prince—cannot provide the impression of social life that is needed if we are to have more

---

the Chinese Realists (or Legalists, as they are usually called). In the classical world the same dimensions of authority may be found in Plato, in imperial Rome, and in the withdrawal philosophies of the Epicureans. But Greek experience also indicates that politics may be based on persuasion, just as the excesses of the Ch'in state suggest that domination is at times based only on naked power.

[o] This distinction may provide the major clue to the reconciliation of Machiavelli's *Discourses* with *The Prince*. The former is concerned with the preservation of civil society once it is established, whereas the latter is preoccupied with the founding of the state and the creation of authority.

than a catalogue of concepts and theories. We have therefore been led to consider social institutions and ideologies, economic developments and political structures, as well as religious values, in an effort to arrive at a more complete picture of Indian society and a realistic appraisal of Indian thought about man, his obligations to himself and his fellows, and particularly the authorities to which he submits himself. It has been a journey down a Ganges—its upper reaches the ancient heroic myth, the waters deepening as we reach the elaborate systems of the brahmans. Many tributaries join the sacred river; its surface becomes rough. We pass the great city of Pataliputra, and at length find ourselves in the broad marshland of Hinduism. The shore is indistinct and we are at times in danger of losing our bearings.

Now that this expedition is completed, a few concluding remarks may be useful in bringing together the major ideas that have appeared and reappeared along the way. Whether the people of ancient India were consistently guided by these principles is not our immediate concern. We are interested primarily in the ideals of conduct of king and subject and of the ordering of social relationships that were thought to be most worth attaining.

The brahmacharin ashrama was intended to instruct man in the discipline of his senses and to give him an awareness of the values that transcend worldly experience with its deceptions and material goals. It was not the preparation for a life devoted to social melioration. Nor was it an atmosphere to encourage the skeptical and analytical frame of mind. And yet because the spiritual ideal could be realized only after obligations had been met, and because these duties implied a social life that must be protected against the predatory and anarchical bent of human nature, the body of social speculation is not as slight as might be supposed. The forces operative in Indian social life produced institutional forms that have no exact counterpart in the West, but these forces were by no means unique in historical experience and we discover an appreciation of the role of economic factors and the general phenomenon of power. Religious belief lent a high color to social commentary, but this does not justify the argument of so many European observers that the Indian spirit was insensitive to the more prosaic requirements of human existence and provided no secular treatise comparable in any way to those produced in the West.

There is, as I have sought to indicate, a thorough rationale of society and the state, though religion often hinders the development of a systematic philosophy of government. The great bulk of social thought was meant not to challenge the existing order, but only to justify and explain. Whereas Western theory has been interlaced with utopian philosophies inspired by the wish to bring the kingdom of God to earth or by the wish for a more equitable distribution of the world's goods, the peculiar complex of Indian thought, with karma and samsara securing the values that legitimated institutions, impeded any thoroughgoing reconsideration of the bases of authority and obligation. Neither Buddhist thought nor

Mauryan administrative theory succeeded in establishing alternative norms capable of challenging Brahmanism.

Political speculation is essentially Aryan; by comparison the contribution of non-Aryan peoples to the corpus of political ideas is small. This theory is concerned almost exclusively with the monarchical form of government. Rarely do we find an attempt to evaluate the relative merits of kingdom and republic. The ancient theorists comprehended many of the elements that compose the state and are central to a definition of sovereignty. But we cannot assume that such a term as "rashtra" is the equivalent of the abstract idea of the state that we employ.

The state in early India was believed to be instrumental to the attainment of the spiritual goal. This ultimate purpose was itself so conceived as to presuppose an elite responsible for defining and interpreting the values that ordered the world and regulated even the actions of the king. This elite maintained its purity by remaining more or less apart from political life, which was tainted by the sin inherent in political and military roles. But the brahman might serve as the king's adviser and involve himself indirectly in governmental functions, for the state represented a concentration of power that could too easily become its own justification. This general aloofness of the priests and the jealous guarding of their own purity may help account for their toleration of the moral ambiguities that characterized the institutions that governed lesser men—institutions themselves dictated by the imperfection of the lower orders. It was Soma who was the *true* king of the brahmans.

The king's function was not simply negative. He must seek to translate the dharmic code into terms appropriate to the age. This relativism has its most dramatic expression in the powerful figure of the sinful Indra and the seemingly self-contradictory Krishna. The dharma of the individual, as the sacred texts reiterate, is linked with rajadharma: the king's own duties are the keystone of the system. But the king is compromised by the nature of this very duty; only by giving to the brahman and performing the sacrifice is he cleansed. As early as the period of the Upanishads the prosperity of the people implied moral as well as material welfare. In the *Chandogya Upanishad* a king remarks on the righteousness of his subjects and appears to take personal credit for the virtuous behavior that distinguishes his realm.[10] Jayaswal sees in this an early statement of the axiom that the king is the maker of his age, responsible for the moral condition of his subjects.[11] His task of preserving dharma committed him to maintaining the caste order, which was itself based on the moral authority and spiritual supremacy of the brahman. Though the king assumed a moral function, he was himself subject to the sacred tradition. And the spokesman for this sovereign tradition was the brahman.

In Hindu political speculation, duty occupies the central position that in European liberal thought belongs to conceptions of natural rights and freedom. The psychological sensationalism at the root of Locke's theory of individualism would not find much encouragement in a philosophical setting that limited the validity of sense experience and stressed the importance of escape from personality through the renunciation of desire and the fruits of action. The essential weakness in the Hindu theory of the state is its failure to provide any very searching analysis of the relation between government and the governed. One explanation for the infrequent reference to the rights of subjects is the fact that most of the political literature was composed expressly for the governing class. More important, the relation of the state to the stratified dharmic order pre-empted any consideration of human rights as the West understands the problem. The doctrine of transmigration and karma and the devaluation of mundane experience could result only in the subordination of the individual. Rights in this world were as nothing when measured against the requirements of eternal salvation, and freedom, which was conceived as the escape from the cycle of birth, death, and rebirth, could be attained only through the faithful discharge of duties. There was no sanguine faith in a natural identity of interests. Caste was the means for reconciling individual self-interest with broader social needs. Without the institutions of caste and state, human life would be like that of the animals of the jungle, the strong devouring the weak. In positing self-interest as the basic psychological fact, and in constructing authority as a negative restraint on antisocial expression, Hindu theory may be likened to several schools of Western political thought.

The egalitarian ideal, save possibly for Buddhist thought, never asserted itself in Indian thought as it did in the West. As in the case of civil rights, so also with the more specific rights of the citizen: the concept of "citizenship" had little meaning in Hindu society. For all practical purposes we are justified in saying that civil obligation rather than civil right formed the basis of the relation of state and subject. We must never look past the fact, however, that there always existed for the Hindu, as for the Western liberal, a criterion above the state by which its actions could be judged. It was not the idea of the sanctity of the individual personality or the association; it was sacred law and tradition.

Though not concerned with the rights of men, except the right to pursue that which is necessary to salvation, Hindu political thought does share with the natural rights theory the idea of contract and the belief that power must be limited. The contract theory is never elaborated beyond the most basic statement and the people are rarely party to the contract, but that it played a key role in Hindu polity cannot be denied. Authority was based on both function and status—the former finding its symbolic expression in the contractual exchange of allegiance for protection or in the differentiation of roles in the performance of the sacrifice, the latter in such images as the division of the primeval person of Purusha to form the various orders of society from the different parts of the body of this original man. This division of the organism suggests the close relation of status to function. Though the hymn does not stress this, the creation of the warrior from the arm of Purusha indicates as much about the function of the warrior as creation from the feet tells us about the status of the shudra. It is this intimate relation of status and function that keeps the theory conservative. Hindu thought assumes that there is a peculiar brahman mentality, a shudra mind, and so forth, and that the basic social group is composed of those of similar mental configuration. The caste system—the fundamental sociological context of Hindu polity—aimed at providing the individual with a milieu of like minds in which to fulfill the obligations of his social station. There is, in Brahmanical theory, the rationale of status in terms of character, and we are told that before the fall from grace all men were brahmans. The ethical life is dependent on knowledge of the Veda, and men whose energies are devoted exclusively to material pursuits have neither the opportunity nor the ability to pursue this sacred learning. Thus was the brahman intelligentsia able to establish itself in an almost impregnable position at the summit of the social hierarchy.

Still, the brahmans were themselves restricted in the creative use of their intellectual abilities. They were the interpreters of the sacred tradition; only indirectly did they exercise a legislative function. In certain important respects brahman theory recalls the political philosophy of Thomas Aquinas, although in relating the origin of political institutions to man's sinful nature it more closely resembles earlier medieval political ideas. For both St. Thomas and orthodox Indian thinkers, society is constructed on the fundamental differences in the practical talents of men. The political relationship is justified in terms of these differences—a *subjectio civilis* necessary for the attainment of the common good.[p]

In both theories the state was charged with maintaining security, promoting a minimum standard of morality, and protecting religion. The task of positive law, where it was recognized in brahman theory, was to realize in concrete terms the higher moral law. The sacred law of the brahmans, however, was not based on a universal ethic of the type we find in Christian thought, nor do we find the emphasis on the need to administer higher law in the interest of the common good that is a feature of Thomistic theory. The actions of the ruler were circumscribed by objective moral law. Because government existed to fulfill a trust, the deposition of a tyrant might be legitimate. As in the argument of Aquinas the spiritual goal of man is higher than his temporal ends. For this reason the spiritual sword, though coordinate with the secular, is the more exalted. Because man's purpose is ultimately spiritual, the temporal sphere of authority can never be completely independent of the representatives of religion.

The peculiar distribution of wealth, fighting power, and intellectual eminence obstructed the growth of the type of aristocracy common to many ancient polities. The power of the brahman class was due more to its control over culture than to its material position or its influence exercised through the ministries. To term the Hindu state a theocracy would be

---

[p] The two summas differ in that Brahmanism conceives of this subordination as crucial to the salvation of the individual.

to suggest its sectarian foundation on dogma and an identification of magistrate and priest. This was not the case, though a strong bond existed in theory between the brahman and kshatriya classes. Prosperity could result only if the two classes cooperated closely with one another. If the alliance should break, eternal confusion would be the result.

The great Mauryan empire of Chandragupta and Ashoka was reincarnated under the Guptas, and from time to time in the history of ancient India power was consolidated according to the grand design of Kautalya. At length the peninsula succumbed to the Sultanate, but Hindu culture survived in the apparently invincible institutions of caste and village. From the point of view of the modern world, the price of this strength was high. The tragedy of India is that it became a land where tragedy had become irrelevant. The depoliticizing of society through the penance ideology of caste subverted that most human of all urges, the wish for a better life in this world. The image of Utopia, the earthly kingdom of God, had no place in a culture resigned to an imperfect world. Aspiration and anticipation were relevant only to the future life of the soul. Thus was hope diverted.

Today the Indian state is as new as it was in Kautalya's time. And it is as old as all states must be in an age when sovereignty has proven an inadequate answer to the organizational requirements of security and peace. A solution as creative as that put forth in the *Arthashastra* is needed if the amoral tribalism of our century is not to end in the mutual destruction of peoples. At least in the struggle of the fishes, the image beloved of brahman theorists, the big fish survived. Now the big will be the first to go. But the political answer must be accompanied and reinforced by such truly radical programs as that of the Buddha, which would free the individual from the alienation that tortures the self and makes of freedom a mockery.

APPENDIX

LIST OF INDIC WORDS

CHRONOLOGICAL GUIDE

NOTES

BIBLIOGRAPHY

INDEX

APPENDIX

The *Mudrarakshasa*—the Web of Diplomacy[1]

The *Mudrārākṣasa* of Viśākhadatta belongs to the imperial Gupta era, but its subject is the technique of Mauryan diplomacy. We can accept it as throwing light on both periods, for it undoubtedly reads Gupta experience into a Mauryan context.

The central theme of the *Mudrarakshasa* is the Mauryan king's attempt to win over the chief minister of the deposed Nanda regime. Two masterminds, Chanakya (Kautalya) and Rakshasa, are pitted against one another. Kautalya has succeeded in installing the young Mauryan prince, Chandragupta, on the throne, but the structure of authority is still shaky. Stability evidently depends on harnessing the talents of Rakshasa (note the inclusion of his name in the play's title) to the service of Chandragupta Maurya. The schemes employed by Kautalya are elaborate, subtle, and amoral; they give a good idea of Mauryan-Gupta diplomatic intrigue. This purely political play is anything but politically pure. In its exclusive concern with politics, it differs from most Sanskrit dramas. The nuances of the more delicate sentiments of love find almost no place in the work. The plot is contrived and complex, but the dialectical development of the play is absorbing and the dialogue has a clarity and vigor befitting its theme. The ironic nature of the ultimate choice that confronts Rakshasa can be as readily appreciated today as it was in the day of the Gupta court. The *Mudrarakshasa* belongs to the category *nataka*; i.e., it fulfills a set of rigid structural requirements. For example, the major characters speak in classical Sanskrit, and the minor roles are expressed through Prakrit dialects.

In his introduction to the drama, M. R. Kale, the translator, sums up the important points in the plot's development: the acquisition of Rakshasa's ring by Chanakya; the forged letter; the imprisonment of Rakshasa's friend Chandanadasa (who has been sheltering the family of Rakshasa, the latter having fled the city); the faked rescue of Rakshasa's friend Shakatadasa from execution and the admission of Siddharthaka, Chanakya's spy, into the service of Rakshasa; the feigned quarrel between Chanakya and his prince; the arousing of suspicion in the mind of the Nanda prince, Malayaketu, against his minister Rakshasa, and the rupture

[1] Abridged from M. R. Kale (transl.), *The Mudrarakṣasa by Viśakhadatta,* Bombay, 1900.

of their relationship; the unjust murder of the five Mleccha (foreign) princes; Malayaketu's determination to wage war against Chandragupta; his defeat; the determination of Rakshasa to give himself up to the Mauryas in order to save his friend Chandanadasa; the report of the mysterious man in the grove about the imminent execution of Chandanadasa; and finally Rakshasa's reluctant consent to become Chandragupta Maurya's minister — with the consequent release of Chandanadasa (the perfect friend), the restoring of Malayaketu to his paternal territory, and the freeing of Chanakya for the life of an ascetic.

The play covers a year's time. The action does not begin until after the recital of a benediction and a contrivance that sets the stage for the intrigue to follow.

MANAGER : Enough of prolixity. I have been asked by the audience to present a new drama, 'Mudrarakshasa' by name, a composition by the poet Vishakhadatta, grandson of the tributary prince Vateśvaradatta and the son of Prithu, bearing the title of Maharaja. Surely, I too, who am now performing before an audience knowing the excellence of poetry, feel very great satisfaction. For,

Cultivation of seeds sown by even a foolish person when bestowed upon a good field bears fruit. . . .

I will therefore first go home, and having called my consort, will commence singing with the inmates of the house. . . . Holla, what do I see here? There seems to be a festival. . . .

Here is a woman fetching water; here is one pounding aromatic herbs; and here is another stringing together garlands. . . .

Well, I will call my wife and ask her.

O you, who are meritorious, who are an abode of expedients, who bring about the three objects of existence which are the cause of the stability of worldly life, . . . come here quickly.

ACTRESS (*entering*) : Here am I, my lord. May your honor favor me with your command.

MANAGER : Lady, let aside for a moment the entrusting-with-my-command. Tell me—has our family been favored by you by having invited venerable brahmans? Or have welcome guests come to our house, that there are these special preparations of meals?

ACTRESS : My lord, the worthy brahmans have been invited by me.

MANAGER : Tell me for what reason.

ACTRESS : Because they say the moon is to be eclipsed.

MANAGER : Lady, who says so?

ACTRESS : Such, indeed, is the talk among the townsfolk.

MANAGER : Lady, I have spent some labor on the science of astronomy with its 64 branches; therefore let your preparation of meals in honor of the worthy brahmans proceed; as for the eclipse of the moon, you are deceived by some one. For, see,

That well-known Ketu, the malignant planet, wishes perforce to attack the moon having the full orb; (VOICE *behind the curtain:* Who is he that, while I live, wishes to overpower Chandra?[2])—but the union (near) Budha [Mercury] saves him.

ACTRESS: But my lord, who is this that, being a denizen of the earth, desires to save the moon from the attack of the planet?

MANAGER: My lady, to tell you the truth, I too did not observe him. Well, being attentive again, I shall mark the manifestation of his voice. (VOICE *repeats*—That malignant planet . . .)

VOICE (*behind the curtains*): Ah! who is he that desires to attack Chandragupta while I am alive?

MANAGER: Ah, I see. It is Kautalya.

(ACTRESS *gesticulates fear.*)

MANAGER: This is that Kautalya of perverse intellect, by whom the race of the Nandas was, perforce, burnt up in the fire of his wrath. . . . He understands that there is to be an attack by the enemy on the moon-like Maurya who bears the same name [Chandra].

Let us therefore go away hence.

ACT I

CHANAKYA: . . . The nine Nandas have been eradicated like so many heart-diseases of the Earth; sovereignty has been made firm-footed in the case of Maurya like a lotus-plant in a lake; and the two-fold well-deserved fruit of the two things, anger and love, has been equally meted out with a careful mind to the foe and the friend.

Or rather, so long as Rakshasa has not been won over, how can the race of Nanda be said to be extirpated, or what stability has been given to the sovereignty of Chandragupta? (*Thinking.*) O! how unsurpassable is the excellence of devotion of Rakshasa to the house of Nanda! . . . Noble, very noble, oh minister Rakshasa; praiseworthy, O learned brahman; well done, oh you Brihaspati-like minister, well done! For,

These [ordinary] people serve their lord (so long as he is) not deprived of his sovereignty, for the sake of gain . . . but rarely are to be found those blessed persons of your type, who undertake the responsibility of duty out of disinterested devotion, remembering past favors, even after the utter destruction of their master.

. . . (I) am making an effort, as much as I can, to secure him. How is that? In the first place this (has been done). A scandal is caused to be circulated in the world that poor Parvataka, our extremely obliging friend, has been killed by Rakshasa by means of a poison-maid (thinking that this would do harm to Chanakya). . . . I have also employed emissaries in various disguises and conversant with various places, dresses, languages, manners and modes of dealing, with the desire of knowing the people that are attached to or disaffected towards our side or that of the

[2] Kale comments on this reference: "The sense understood by Chanakya is this— He of wicked resolve (Rakshasa), accompanied by Ketu (Malayaketu), wishes to attack with an army Chandra (-gupta), whose sovereignty is not fully established." *Chandra* is the word for moon.

enemy. . . . Thus then, nothing is wanting on our side. It is only Vrishala [Chandragupta], who, being a monarch entirely dependent on his minister, entrusts the responsibility of administering the kingdom to me, and always remains apathetic. . . .

(*Enter a spy.*)

SPY: . . . there are three persons in the city who have already conceived affection and a great regard for Rakshasa. . . . (one is) Jivasiddhi, by whom the poison-maid employed by Rakshasa was directed against king Parvateshvara.

CHANAKYA (*to himself*): This Jivasiddhi is but our spy. (*Aloud.*) Good fellow, who is the second man?

SPY: Your honor, the second man is a kayastha,[3] also a friend of Rakshasa, Sakatadasa by name.

CHANAKYA (*with a smile, to himself*): A kayastha is a matter of small moment. Yet it is not proper to neglect even a small enemy. . . .

SPY: The third man, the second heart as it were of the minister Rakshasa, is the chief of jewellers, Chandanadasa by name, and an inhabitant of Pushpapura, in whose house Rakshasa deposited his family and escaped from the town.

. . .

ACT II

(*Rakshasa's dwelling. Enter a snake-catcher.*)

SNAKE-CATCHER (*to himself*): . . . O, wonder! Seeing Chandragupta guided by the intellect of Chanakya, I consider the attempt of Rakshasa as futile; considering again (that) Malayaketu (is) aided by the counsel of Rakshasa, I look upon Chandragupta as almost deposed from his supreme power. For,

I consider the Royalty of king Maurya as stable, with her form tied down by the rope, in the form of the intellect of Kautalya; but that very Royalty I look upon as being snatched away by Rakshasa. . . .

The bewildered goddess of wealth is surely tired by moving backwards and forwards through indecision between these two eminent ministers strongly opposed to each other in this case, like a female elephant in a large forest between two wild elephants. . . .

(*Enter Rakshasa.*)

RAKSHASA (*looking towards the sky, with tears in his eyes*): O venerable lotus-throned goddess, you are quite incapable of appreciating merits. For,

Tell me why you, having discarded His Majesty Nanda, though a source of delight, have become attached to his enemy, the son of Maurya? Why, oh fickle one, did you not vanish forever at that time, like the line of ichor-water disappearing at the death of a scent-elephant? . . . Or rather (why should I blame you?); the mind of elderly ladies, which by

---

[3] A member of the caste of scribes.

nature is as fickle as the edge of a kasha flower, is averse to appreciate
the merits of men. . . .

(*On reading a poem of the snake-catcher, Rakshasa realizes that the
charmer is in fact one of his spies. The spy relates the many reverses the
Nandas have suffered.*)

VIRADHAGUPTA, the spy: Minister, he [a pro-Nanda physician] had
prepared a medicine mixed with powder of magical virtue for Chandragupta; but the villainous Chanakya happening to examine it, observed a
change of color in a gold plate, and said to Chandragupta—Vrishala, this
medicine is poisoned; you should not drink it.

RAKSHASA: He is a wily fellow indeed. What of the physician?

VIRADHAGUPTA: He was compelled to drink the same medicine, and
died.

. . .

RAKSHASA: . . . And what news of Bibhatsaka? . . .

VIRADHAGUPTA: Minister, . . . That wicked soul, the cursed Chanakya, entered the bed-chamber before Chandragupta's entry, when, the
very moment, casting a searching look about, he noticed a line of ants with
particles of food in their mouths issuing from some crevice in the wall,
whence concluding that there were men hidden in the interior of the house,
he ordered the bed-chamber to be set on fire. As it was burning, all those,
Bibhatsaka and others, with their eyes obstructed by smoke, could not find
the outlet through which they had previously arranged to make their exits,
and being enveloped in flames, perished.

. . .

RAKSHASA: Friend Viradhagupta, go on with the remainder of your
tale.

VIRADHAGUPTA: . . . This is what has come to light. . . . Chandragupta has got angry with Chanakya ever since Malayaketu's escape. Chanakya, of course, in his extreme arrogance does not bear this, and pains the
heart of Chandragupta with various acts of disobedience. . . .

RAKSHASA (*delighted*): Friend Viradhagupta, go again to Kusumapura in this very disguise as a snake-charmer. There lives a dear friend of
mine, Stanakalasha by name, disguised as a bard. Tell him in my name
that as Chanakya will be committing acts of disobedience, he should praise
Chandragupta with stanzas calculated to excite his jealousy. . . .

ACT III

(*Kusumapura. The chamberlain comments on Chandragupta.*)

CHAMBERLAIN: . . . Make haste, friends. His majesty Chandragupta
is at the gates. He,

Who being strong-minded, has resolved to bear aloft even in his prime
of youth that very yoke of the earth, which though heavy was for a long
time borne by his experienced and able father, who did not step amiss

even on rough paths on account of his firm limbs; he stumbles on account of his youthfulness, but bears it lightly.

(*Enter the king.*)

CHANDRAGUPTA (*to himself*): Sovereignty is, indeed, a source of great uneasiness to a king, who is intent on conforming to the duties of sovereigns. For,

. . . It is the advice of my esteemed minister that I should feign a quarrel with him and manage matters independently for some time. I accepted it with great difficulty as if it were a sin; . . . With my mind properly guided by his honor I am always independent. For,

In this world as long as a pupil acts in the right way, he experiences no check (from his preceptor); when, however, he strays from the proper path through infatuation, the preceptor becomes a goad to him; those good people therefore, who like to act according to instruction are always free from restraint; we for our part are averse to any independence beyond this.

. . .

(*Aloud to the chamberlain.*) How is it then that the festivities have not been commenced in Kusumapura?

Harlots accompanied by gay beaux skilled in free and clever talk do not grace the streets with their gaits slow on account of the weight of their plump hips; nor do the householders . . . partake, along with their consorts, in the desired festivities falling on the full-moon day.

CHAMBERLAIN: It is just this.

CHANDRAGUPTA: What is that?

CHAMBERLAIN: My lord, this. . . .

CHANDRAGUPTA: Speak clearly.

CHAMBERLAIN: The Kaumudi festival has been prohibited.

CHANDRAGUPTA: By whom?

CHAMBERLAIN: My lord, beyond this I am not able to say.

CHANDRAGUPTA: I hope the venerable Chanakya has not deprived the spectators of an exceedingly lovely sight.

CHAMBERLAIN: Sir, who else that loves life can transgress the command of Your Majesty?

(*Chandragupta exits, having ordered Chanakya brought before him.*)

. . .

CHAMBERLAIN: This is the palace Suganga. Your Honor may gently ascend.

CHANAKYA: O, Vrishala [Chandragupta] is seated on the throne. Very good, very good.

The throne wrested from the Nandas, who treated with scorn even Kubera,[4] has been occupied by Vrishala, the foremost among sovereigns; and it has thus been united with a worthy king. These good occurrences (brought about by me) produce a very great satisfaction in me.

---

[4] If they scorned even the god of wealth, the Nandas must have been exceedingly wealthy.

(*Approaches Vrishala.*) Victory to you, Vrishala.

CHANDRAGUPTA (*rising from his seat*): Venerable sir, Chandragupta bows to you. (*Falls at his feet.*)

CHANAKYA (*taking him by the hand*): Rise, child. . . . Vrishala, why did you summon me?

CHANDRAGUPTA: To bless myself with your honor's sight.

CHANAKYA (*with a smile*): No more compliments, please. Kings do not send for their officers without a purpose.

CHANDRAGUPTA: Sir, what good has your honor in view in forbidding the Kaumudi festival?

CHANAKYA (*with a smile*): You have then summoned me to administer a reproof?

CHANDRAGUPTA: God forbid, God forbid! No, not at all, only to make a respectful representation.

CHANAKYA: If so, the uncontrolled tastes of those who are to be respectfully treated ought by no means to be checked by a pupil.

CHANDRAGUPTA: It is so; there is no doubt. But your honor never does a thing without having some object in view. So there is scope for my question.

. . .

CHANAKYA: Vrishala, listen. In connection with this topic writers on politics mention three kinds of administration: (1) that dependent on the king, (2) dependent on the minister, (3) and dependent upon both. Now what have you, who are entirely dependent upon your minister, to do with enquiring into the reasons of a thing—since I who am the responsible officer will alone act in this matter?

(*Chandragupta turns away face in anger.*)

(VOICES *behind the curtains.*)

FIRST BARD: Whitening the sky with its ashen hue that surpasses the brightness of kasha flowers, counteracting the impression of the elephant-hide-like space dark with clouds by means of the streaming rays of the moon, bearing the bright moon-light like a white garland of skulls and displaying its swans like beauteous smiles, may the autumnal season, thus unusually accoutred, remove your trouble, like the body of Shiva. . . .

SECOND BARD: O best of kings, some universal sovereigns alone like you, who are for mysterious reasons created by the Creator the receptacle of pre-eminent valor, who, by their peculiar might, subdue kings having a large force of rut-shedding elephants, and who are distinguished by their sense of self-esteem and pride, do not put up with the disobedience of their command, just as the lords of beasts who for some reason are created by the Creator as the store-houses of strength, who by their fierce vigor conquer the rut-shedding leaders of elephant-herds, and whose dignity and haughtiness are distinctly manifested, do not bear the breaking of their jaws.

Moreover,

A lord does not become a lord by the wearing of ornaments, etc. He is said to be a lord, like you, whose order is not slighted by others.

CHANAKYA (*to himself*) : The first is a blessing describing the beauties of the autumnal season now set in, in the form of the praise of a specific deity. What the other is, I do not understand. (*After reflecting.*) Ah, I comprehend it now. It is the design of Rakshasa. You are detected, vile Rakshasa. Be sure Kautalya is wide awake.

CHANDRAGUPTA : Venerable Vaihinari [the chamberlain], let a hundred thousand gold coins be given to these bards.

CHAMBERLAIN : As your Majesty commands.

CHANAKYA (*angrily*) : Stop, Vaihinari, don't go. Vrishala, why this large expenditure for so paltry a thing?

CHANDRAGUPTA (*in a rage*) : Kingship is like bondage to me, when my course of action is thus checked in every case by your honor; it is not like kingship at all.

CHANAKYA : Vrishala, such evils are but the lot of those kings who do not apply themselves to their own duties. If you cannot bear them, apply yourself to your duties.

(*Chanakya tells the king that the prohibition of the festival was a deliberate defiance of the latter's order, and that—at this time—military exercises are more important than festivals. Then he tells Chandragupta of those who have gone over to Malayaketu.*)

. . .

CHANDRAGUPTA : If the causes of their discontent were known, why did not your honor promptly counteract them?

CHANAKYA : Vrishala, it was not possible to counteract.

CHANDRAGUPTA : Why, owing to want of skill or to some purposes in view?

CHANAKYA : How could there have been want of skill? There was a special purpose in view.

CHANDRAGUPTA : That purpose I want to hear now.

CHANAKYA : Hear it and bear it well in mind. With regard to the present matter (I have to observe that) there are two ways of dealing with discontented subjects, viz., favor or punishment. In the case of Bhadrabhata and Purushadatta who were dismissed from office, to show favor would mean to reinstate them. And if such people, who are careless of the discharge of duty on account of their addiction to vice, be restored to office, they would lead to destruction the whole body of horse and elephant, the main prop of the realm. . . . The other alternative, too, had to be given up. For after our recent acquisition of the realm of the Nandas, had we inflicted severe punishment upon the influential persons who were our adherents, we should have been distrusted by the subjects who are yet attached to the family of the Nandas. . . . The present is thus the time for exertion and not for festivities. . . .

CHANDRAGUPTA : Sir, I have much to ask in this matter.

CHANAKYA : Vrishala, ask without reserve. I too have much to explain.

CHANDRAGUPTA : Why did you allow Malayaketu, the cause of all this mischief, to escape?

CHANAKYA: In case he was not allowed to escape, there were two courses open—to punish him or to give him half the kingdom as promised. To have punished him would have given support to (the supposition) that the murder of Parvataka was an act of ingratitude perpetrated by us. On the other hand, had the promised half of the kingdom been given him, the only result of the assassination of Parvataka would have been the sin of ingratitude. For these reasons I suffered Malayaketu to escape.

CHANDRAGUPTA: This is your explanation in this case. Then again you neglected to take proper steps against Rakshasa who was living here. What has your honor to say to this?

CHANAKYA: . . . If, therefore, he had been allowed to remain in this very city, he would have indeed caused great internal trouble. Whereas, if he were removed from the city, and then he caused disaffection abroad, it would be possible to manage him. He was therefore pulled off even as he lived here, like a dart rankling in the heart, and removed to a distance.

CHANDRAGUPTA: Sir, why did you not capture him by force?

CHANAKYA: He is Rakshasa, mind you. Had we used violence against him, he would have destroyed many of our soldiers, or, found death himself—an unwelcome result in either case. See,

If being hard-pressed he were to meet with his end, then, O Vrishala, you would indeed lose so great a person as he is. . . . He must be won over with stratagems like an elephant of the forest.

CHANDRAGUPTA: We are unable to surpass your intelligence. But after all Rakshasa is more praiseworthy.

CHANAKYA (*in anger*): "Than you" I should supply. But it must not be so. O Vrishala, what has he done?

CHANDRAGUPTA: If you cannot know it yourself, then hear it from me. He, a magnanimous soul,

Dwelt in the city, which had been captured by us, as long as he liked, planting his foot on our neck, and forcibly offered resistance to the proclamation of victory made by our forces. . . .

. . .

CHANAKYA (*in anger*): Vrishala, you wish to lord it over me like a common servant.

My hand again runs to loosen the knot of hair though tied up.[5]

. . .

(*Checking his pretended anger.*) Vrishala, enough of bandying words. If you think Rakshasa is superior to me, give him this sword. (*Throws down the sword, comments to himself on the king's foolishness, exits.*)

CHANDRAGUPTA: Venerable Vaihinari, let it be proclaimed to the subjects that henceforward Chandragupta will rule independently of Chanakya.

CHAMBERLAIN (*to himself*): O, he calls him Chanakya, without any

[5] A threat to retire to the life of an ascetic.

epithet of respect, and not as revered Chanakya. Alas! Authority has been withdrawn from him. But His Majesty is not to blame in this matter. For, it is the fault of the minister himself if the king does wrong (or does not respect the minister). An elephant comes to be censured as a vicious animal through the carelessness of the driver. . . .

CHANDRAGUPTA (*to himself*) : My mind has, as it were, begun to enter the very cavity of the earth though I overstepped the limits of respectfulness by the command of his honor himself. Does not shame rend the hearts of those who wantonly slight their preceptors?

ACT IV

(*Rakshasa in conference with his aides. Eventually Malayaketu arrives to inquire after Rakshasa's headache—which will not leave until Nanda is restored.*)

MALAYAKETU : Sir, have you found out any weak point of the enemy?

RAKSHASA : Yes.

MALAYAKETU : Of what nature is it?

RAKSHASA : A ministerial one, what else? Chandragupta has fallen off from Chanakya.

MALAYAKETU : Sir, a weak point arising from the (loss of a) minister is no weak point.

RAKSHASA : A difficulty arising from a minister may be no difficulty in the case of other kings; but with Chandragupta it is so.

. . .

. . . The vile Chandragupta, however, is habitually dependent on his minister and is therefore like a blind man unfamiliar with the affairs of the world. How will he be able to resist us by himself?

The goddess of royalty stands with her legs rigidly placed on a king and on a minister when (both of them have) grown too powerful; being, as a woman, unable to sustain her weight she abandons one of them.

A king who entrusts everything to his minister, if drawn away from him, like a suckling child weaned from its mother's breast, will not be able to act even for a moment, his intellect not being unfolded on account of his inexperience of the affairs of the world.

MALAYAKETU (*aside*) : I am glad that I don't depend on a minister for the management of my affairs. (*Aloud.*) Although it is so, still when there are many reasons for commencing hostilities success is certain in the case of one who carefully tries to find out some misfortune of the enemy and then assails him. . . .

ACT V

(*Chanakya has arranged that the Nanda king should learn that it was Rakshasa that killed Malayaketu's father. The plot becomes exceedingly intricate and we are left with no doubts as to the competence and subtlety*) *of Kautalya. At the end of the act Malayaketu confronts Rakshasa with the condemning evidence.*)

MALAYAKETU (*pointing to the forged letter, and a box of ornaments*) : And what is this here?

RAKSHASA (*tearfully*) : The wanton play of fate. For,

It is the grand work of that fate, the frustrator of men's exertions, which, the accursed one, destroyed those kings who were the proper judges of men, and who, masters as they were, being grateful and of refined intellect, did not out of affection regard me as different from a son although there was the relation of servitude, which is subject to humiliation.

MALAYAKETU (*angrily*) : You will deny it, calling it the sport of fate and not of your greed! Unrighteous man!

O ungrateful one, having employed the (poison) maid, dangerous by the use of virulent poison absorbed by her, you formerly consigned my father, disposed to trust you, to the domain of history. And now coveting the post of (the enemy's) minister, you have commenced, in order to work my destruction, to sell me off to the enemy like a steak of flesh.

RAKSHASA (*aside*) : This is a pimple on a boil. (*Stops his ears; aloud.*) God forbid, God forbid! I never set the poison-maid against Parvateshvara.

MALAYAKETU : Who then killed my father?

RAKSHASA : Ask destiny.

MALAYAKETU (*angrily*) : I should ask destiny, and not Kshapanaka Jivasiddhi?

RAKSHASA (*aside*) : What? Jivasiddhi too a spy of Chanakya! Alas! The enemies have captured my very heart.

MALAYAKETU (*in a rage*) : Bhasuraka, give my order to Sekharasena thus:—The five princes, Chitravarman of Kuluta, Simhanada, king of Malaya, Pushkaraksha, the Kashmira king, Sushena, king of Sindhu, and Meghanada of Persia, having formed a close friendship with Rakshasa, wish to gain Chandragupta's favor by designing against our person. Of these the first three covet my territory; they should be taken to a deep pit and buried with earth; the other two who wish to have my elephants should be killed by means of an elephant. . . . (*to Rakshasa*) : Go. . . . And serve Chandragupta with all your heart. . . .

ACT VI

(*We learn that Chanakya has captured the Nanda forces. Rakshasa is in Pataliputra intent on rescuing his friend Chandanadasa. Chanakya has arranged for Rakshasa to hear that his loyal Chandanadasa is about to be executed.*)

ACT VII

(*Chandanadasa bids his wife and son farewell.*)

CHANDANADASA : Dear wife, return now with your son. It is not proper to follow me further.

WIFE (*weeping*): You leave, my dear, for the next world, not for a distant country.

CHANDANADASA: Dear wife, I die for a friend's sake, and not for a personal crime. Grieve not therefore. . . .

WIFE: I shall be blessed if I follow my lord's feet (in death).

. . .

(*Enter Rakshasa.*)

RAKSHASA: . . . Here am I, the man for whose sake this person, though worthy of veneration, has incurred thy enmity, he who, the glorious one, saving another at the cost of his own life in these evil times of the Kali age in which the tastes of the people are wicked, has rendered insignificant even the glory of Shibi, and who being pure in soul, has by his virtuous conduct eclipsed the course of conduct of the Buddhist saints.

. . .

(*Enter Chanakya.*)

CHANAKYA: Say, friend say,

Who bound with the skirt of his garment the fire red with the mass of its mighty flames? Who reduced the ever-moving wind to a state of stillness with snares? Who confined into a cage a lion with his mane still smelling of the rut-water of elephants? Who crossed by means of his arms the dreadful ocean, abounding in crocodiles and alligators?

EXECUTIONERS: By your honor whose intellect is adept in statecraft.

CHANAKYA: No, no, say not so. Say—by fate, the inveterate foe of the house of Nanda.

RAKSHASA (*aside*): This is the mean-minded—or rather noble-minded Kautalya.

The mine of all shastras, as the ocean is of jewels, with those merits we are not pleased, being simply jealous.

CHANAKYA (*looking at Rakshasa; joyfully, to himself*): Ah, here is the minister Rakshasa, by whom, the great-minded one,

The army of Vrishala and my own intelligence were seriously taxed for a long time with the heavy troubles of preparations, and of the devising of plans, which were the cause of protracted wakefulness. (*Removes his veil, approaches Rakshasa.*)

O minister Rakshasa, I, Vishnugupta, salute you.

RAKSHASA (*aside*): "Minister" is a humiliating epithet now. (*Aloud.*) Vishnugupta, please do not touch me, polluted by the touch (of an executioner, a chandala).

CHANAKYA: O minister Rakshasa, these are not chandalas. This one is a royal official named Siddharthaka whom you have already seen. This other here too is a servant of the king, Samiddharthaka by name. Poor Shakatadasa also was made to write that forged letter by me, he knowing nothing (about its nature). . . . Those (your) servants, Bhadrabhata and others, the letter written in that way, that Siddharthaka, those three sets of decoration, that your friend Bhadanta, the man you saw in the old garden, and the trouble of the merchant, all these, oh valiant one, were devices of mine through my desire for Vrishala's union with you.

(*Enter Chandragupta.*)

. . .

CHANDRAGUPTA (*approaching Chanakya*): Venerable sir, Chandragupta bows to you.

CHANAKYA: All your desires have been accomplished. Salute, therefore, his honor, your prime minister.

RAKSHASA (*aside*): He has established the relationship.

CHANDRAGUPTA (*approaching Rakshasa*): Sir, Chandragupta bows to you. . . .

Sir, just think—What have I not conquered in the world, when his honor and your honor are, as gurus, wide awake in the proper use of the six expedients?

RAKSHASA (*aside*): . . . In this world a minister, although dull-minded, is sure to rise to an exalted position when he has to serve a proper person who is ambitious, whereas a minister, though of unerring policy, falls in the manner of a tree on the bank of a river when he has to deal with an unworthy master.

. . .

CHANAKYA: . . . If then you really wish to save Chandanadasa's life, accept this weapon (the badge of ministerial office).

. . .

Unloose every tie except that of horses and elephants; having fulfilled my solemn declaration, I will now simply tie up my hair. . . .

INDIC WORD LIST

Pali and Sanskrit words that appear more than once in the text have been spelled phonetically to aid the reader in pronouncing them. The accepted classical spellings are listed below.

ahiṃsā	Dīgha Nikāya	mokṣa	saṃhitā
Ajātaśatru	Draupadī	Mudrārākṣasa	samrāṭ
Ājīvika	gaṇa	Muṇḍaka	saṃsāra
amātya	Gaṅgā (Ganges)	Nārada	Sānchī
Ānanda	Gītā	Nīlakaṇṭha	saṅgha
Āndhra	Gopāla	Nipāta	Śaṅkara
Anuśasanaparva	Gosāla	Nirvāna	Sāṅkhya
Āpastamba	grāma	niṣāda	sannyāsin
arājaka	grāmaṇī	nīti	Śāntiparva
Āraṇyaka	gṛhastha	Nītisāra	śāstra
Arthaśāstra	Gṛhya	Nītivakyāmṛta	Śatapatha
Āryan	guṇa	nivṛtti	Sātavāhana
Āryasūra	Harappā	Pāli	senāpati
Aśoka	Harṣa	Pañcāla	Siddhārtha
āśrama	Hemacandra	Pañcatantra	Śiva
Aśvaghoṣa	Himālaya	Pañcaviṃśa	śloka
aśvamedha	Hūṇas	Pāṇḍava	smṛti
Aśvins	Irān	Pāṇḍu	Śrauta
ātman	Jātaka	Pāṇḍya	śreṇi
avatāra	jāti	Pāṇini	śri
Bāṇa	jñāna	Panjāb	śruti
Bārhaspatya	Kālidāsa	Paraśurāma	śūdra
Baudhāyana	Kaliṅga	pariṣad	Śukranītisāra
Bhāgavata	kāma	Pārsīs	Śuṅga
Bharadvāja	Kāmandaka	Pārvatī	sūta
Bhīma	Kāmandakīya	Pāṭaliputra	sūtra
Bhīṣma	Kaniṣka	Patañjali	svadharma
Bimbisāra	Kaśmīr	pavṛtti	Śvetāśvatara
Bindusāra	Kaṭha	Piṭaka	Taittirīya
Brahmā [god]	Kātyāyana	Prajāpati	Tirukkuṟaḷ
brahmacārin	Kauśītaki	Prākrit	Tiruvaḷḷuvar
Brāhmaṇa	Kauṭalya	prakṛti	Upaniṣad
Bṛhadāraṇyaka	Kauṭalīya	Pṛthu	Uśanas
Bṛhadratha	kāyastha	Purāṇa	vairājya
Bṛhaspati	Kṛṣṇa (Krishna)	Puruṣasūkta	vaiśya
Buddhacarita	kṛta	Puṣyamitra	vājapeya
cakravartin	Kṣatra	rājā	Vālmīki
Cāṇakya	kṣatriya	rājanīti	vānaprastha
cāṇḍāla	Kumāra	rājanya	varṇa
Candragupta	Kuṣāṇa	rājaśāsana	varṇāśrama
Cālukya	liṅga	rājasūya	vārttā
Cāulukya	Mahābhārata	Rājput	Varuṇa
Cēra	mahāmantrin	rājya	Vasiṣṭha
Chāndogya	mahāmatta	Rāma	Vāyu
Cōḷa	mahārāja	Rāmāyaṇa	Vedānta
daṇḍa	Mahāvaṃsa	rāṣṭra	Veṇa
daṇḍanīti	Mahāvīra	Ṛgveda	vīra
Daṇḍin	Mahāyāna	ṛṣi	viś
dāsa	maṇḍala	ṛta	Viśākhadatta
Daśakumāracarita	Marāthā	sabhā	Viṣṇu
Devanāgarī	mātsyanyāya	śakti	Vṛtra
Dharmaśāstra	māyā	Śākya	Vyāsa
Dharmasūtra	Mīmāṃsā	samādhi	Yājñavalkya
Dhṛtarāṣṭra	Mitākṣara	Sāmaveda	Yudhiṣṭhira

CHRONOLOGICAL GUIDE

A chronological table showing main events in Indian history and literature from 2000 B.C. to A.D. 1000, and some non-Indian information for purposes of comparison, is given overleaf. Many of the dates are approximate, some conjectural.

CHRONOLOGICAL GUIDE

Date			
2000 B.C.		late phase of Harappa civilization; beginning of Aryan invasions	
1700	Hammurabi (?)		
1400	Aryan kings in Western Asia	second wave of Aryan invasions	earliest of *Rigveda* hymns
1100	Solomon; Homer (?)	Mahabharata war (?)	*Rigveda*
800		caste system emerges; Aryans in eastern Gangetic valley	later Vedas; Brahmanas and Upanishads
500	Solon, Thales; Pythagoras, Cyrus; Confucius (d. 479)	Buddha (c. 563–483); Ajatashatru, king of Magadha (490–458); Mahavira (d.c. 467); 1st Buddhist council (c. 480)	late Upanishadic age; *Dharma-sutras*
400	Plato (d. 347); Alexander (356–323)	Alexander's invasion (327–325); Chandragupta founds Mauryan dynasty (c. 324)	*Jatakas* and *Digha Nikaya*
300		reign of Ashoka (c. 270–232)	*Arthashastra* of Kautalya (probable period)
200	Ch'in conquests; Punic wars	end of Mauryan rule (c. 185); Greek kingdoms in Northwest	*Indica* of Arrian; *Bhagavad Gita*; *Maha-bharata* (extant)
100 B.C.	Caesar	end of Shunga dynasty (c. 71); Vikrama era (58)	

Date	World events	Indian events	Literature
	birth of Christ	Satavahana rule in Deccan Kushan power established in Indus valley (78)	
A.D. 100			
200	Antoninus (d. 180)	beginning of Mahayana Buddhism	*Yajnavalkya* and *Vishnu* smritis
300		beginning of Gupta dynasty (c. 320) Chandra Gupta II succeeds Samudra Gupta (c. 376) arrival of Fa-hsien (c. 405)	extant form of *Manusmriti* *Brihaspati* and *Narada* smritis *Kural*
400	Augustine (d. 430)	Huna invasions	Nitisara of Kamandaka *Panchatantra* Kalidasa (?)
500	fall of Rome	end of Gupta dynasty (c. 540) Harsha conquers North India (606–12) ; meets Huien Tsiang (643) first Chalukha dynasty	extant form of the puranas
600	Mohammed (d. 632)		*Mudrarakshasa* Dandin
700		Arab occupation of Sind (712) Buddhism enters Tibet	
800	Charlemagne (d. 814)		*Shukranitisara* Shankara (c. 788–820) Medhatithi's commentary on *Manu*
900		Chola revival	
1000			*Brihaspati Arthashastra* *Nitivakyamrita* of Somadeva

NOTES

Complete titles, authors' names, and publication data are given in the Bibliography.

CHAPTER 1

1. Fortes and Evans-Pritchard [125], pp. 20f. "Bonds of utilitarian interest between individuals and between groups are not so strong as the bonds implied in common attachment to mystical symbols." (*Ibid.*, p. 23.)

2. Karl Wittfogel [433].

3. *Vide* S. N. Eisenstadt, "The Study of Oriental Despotisms as Systems of Total Power," *The Journal of Asian Studies,* XVII (May 1958), pp. 435ff. "Today it seems to be accepted that the political institutions are one part of the social structure, and that they are necessarily dependent on other institutions for their own smooth functioning. They are dependent on them for various material resources, for their basic legitimation, and for support for various policies and activities." (*Ibid.*, p. 445.)

4. Karl Marx, Letter to Engels, London, 2 June 1853.

5. *Vide* Carlo Antoni, *From History to Sociology* (transl. Hayden White, Detroit, 1959), pp. 165f.

6. "Learning what a motive is belongs to learning the standards governing life in the society in which one lives; and that again belongs to the process of learning to live as a social being." (Winch [431], p. 83.)

7. On the subject of *Verstehen, vide* Parsons [318], pp. 484ff. Weber argued that *Verstehen* must be verified by empirical tests if it was to be regarded as having scientific validity. Cf. Winch [431], pp. 112ff.

8. "The one tendency that vitiates the study of ancient Indian institutions . . . is the attempt to concentrate on their purely political aspect as an independent and isolated phenomenon. Since primitive institutions hardly admit of any attempt at differentiation of functions, social and political, there can be no correct appraisal of their nature unless we examine their various aspects in interrelation with one another." (Sharma [389], p. 90.)

9. Nilakanta Sastri [303], pp. 97–98. Renou speaks in a similar context of "the political chimera of 'Dravidistan'" ([356], p. 125). For a brief review of ideological influences on Indian historiography, *vide* Sharma [389], chap. 1.

10. Weber [425], p. 147.

11. *Ibid.*, pp. 342ff.

12. W. Norman Brown [49], pp. 285f.

13. A. K. Sen [382], p. 58.

14. *Vide* B. K. Sarkar [377], p. 206.

15. Cf. *Kratylus,* 412c, on the derivation of the term "just."

16. *Bhagavad Gītā,* III, 35.

17. Anjaria [7], pp. 184f.

18. Edgerton [111], p. 151.

19. Ananda Coomaraswamy, quoting the *Arthashastra* on government ("The

whole of this science has to do with a victory over the powers of perception and action"), suggests that self-knowledge in every man is dependent on the ability to unite *sacerdotium* and *regnum*. Hence the duality has ethical as well as political connotations [70], pp. 88f. and *passim*).

20. *Manusmriti* VII, 18.

CHAPTER 2

1. *Vide* Renou [358], p. 10.

2. "Even when the sacrificer at times looked up to some supra-mundane fruits, his conceptions of them were mostly colored by his mundane needs and cravings." (Belvalkar and Ranade [27], p. 406.) *Vide* Chapter 4, Part 1, below.

3. *Rigveda* IX, 113.7ff. (*Vide* also VII, 88.5; X, 14.8, 15.7.)

4. *Rigveda* I, 32ff.

5. The fourth of the sacred Vedic texts, the *Atharvaveda*, is essentially a compilation of magical chants and practices. For an outstanding monograph on the *Atharvaveda*, *vide* Bloomfield [37].

6. Ernst Cassirer ([55], pp. 15f.) has commented, with reference to primitive forms of mythical thought, that "we are surprised to find to what a high degree the primitive mind feels the desire and need to discern and divide, to order and classify the elements of the environment. There is hardly anything that escapes its constant urge for classification. Not only is human society divided into diverse classes, tribes, clans which have different customs, different social duties. The same division appears everywhere in nature." On this exuberance of what he calls "the classifying instinct" *vide* Cassirer, "Die Begriffsform im mythischen Denken," *Studien der Bibliothek Warburg* (Leipzig, 1922), I.

7. H. and H. A. Frankfort, "Myth and Reality," in Frankfort *et al.* [127].

8. *Vide* Voegelin [419], pp. 16ff. On the reciprocal relationship of the social and the cosmic orders in ancient Greek belief, *vide* Werner Jaeger, *The Theology of the Early Greek Philosophers* (New York, 1947), p. 140.

9. *Shatapatha Brahmana* V, 3.3.12. (The Brahmanas, exegetical texts on the ritual, are discussed in Chapter 3.)

10. *Taittiriya Brahmana* II, 2.10.1.

11. Coomaraswamy [69], pp. 6–9.

12. *Vide,* for example, *Rigveda* I, 113.6, and VIII, 35.16–18. There are also scattered references in the *Rigveda* to the life-stages of *brahmacārin* (student), householder, and ascetic.

13. E.g., *Atharvaveda* III, 4.

14. Described in the *Aitareya Brahmana* VII, 19.

15. *Rigveda* X, 124.8.

16. Jayaswal [199], 2d ed., p. 15.

17. *Rigveda* X, 173.2f.

18. *Rigveda* IV, 42.8.

19. *Shatapatha Brahmana* XIII, 4.4.3; V, 4.3.4.

20. *Atharvaveda* VI, 87.1, 88.3. Jayaswal ([199], 2d ed., p. 194) translates the last line as ". . . for firmness the assembly here appoints you." Firmness is a distinctive quality of Indra.

21. *Atharvaveda* IV, 8.4.

22. *Vide* Ghoshal [143], "The Vedic Ceremonies of Royal and Imperial Consecration . . ."

23. *Rigveda* I, 25.13; *vide* also Macdonell and Keith [243], II, 213.

24. *Rigveda* I, 65.4; IV, 50.9.

25. Radcliffe-Brown's comments regarding the place of war and feud in primi-

tive African society are probably relevant to the tribal states of ancient India. "When such a war [of conquest] is successful it establishes one people as conquerors over another who are thus incorporated into a larger political society, sometimes in an inferior position as a subject people. But the institution of war may take a different form in which two communities stand in a permanent relation such that war between them is always a possibility and does from time to time occur, though neither seeks to conquer the other and absorb it as a conquered people in a larger political unity. In a political' system of which this is true, the occurrence or the possibility of war gives us the readiest means of defining the political structure." (Fortes and Evans-Pritchard [125], pp. xixf.)

26. *Rigveda* VIII, 4.9; IX, 92.6; X, 97.6, 166.4, 191.3.
27. Zimmer [437], pp. 172–77.
28. *Rigveda* X, 193.2–4.
29. *Rigveda* X, 71; VII, 1.4.
30. *Rigveda* I, 56.2, 159; *Atharvaveda* XVII, 1.15.
31. *Rigveda* V, 1.10; X, 173.6.
32. *Rigveda* X, 173f. *Vide* also *Atharvaveda* III, 3–5; VI, 86–88.
33. Hymn 22, Whitney transl.

CHAPTER 3

1. Parsons [316], pp. 375f.
2. The author has found an unpublished essay by Robert N. Bellah, "Some Suggestions for the Systematic Study of Religion" [26], particularly helpful in defining problems in the only partially explored area of the sociology of religion.
3. *Taittiriya Brahmana* I, 5.9.4. "We must do what the gods did in the beginning" (*Shatapatha Brahmana* VII, 2.1.4).
4. *Vide* Weber [425], p. 61.
5. Kosambi [218], p. 126.
6. *Ibid.*, p. 25.
7. Belvalkar and Ranade [27], pp. 28f.
8. *Shatapatha Brahmana* I, 4.11; *vide* Hume [187], p. 84. Cf. *Aitareya Brahmana* VII, 19: Prajapati created the sacrifice, and after its introduction the priestly and governing powers were created.
9. *Shatapatha Brahmana* IV, 1.4.1–4.
10. *Shatapatha Brahmana* I, 6.3.14; II, 4.4.10, 19; X, 4.1.5.
11. *Aitareya Brahmana* VIII, 1.4, 9.6; *Shatapatha Brahmana* V, 4.4.15; XII, 7.3.1; *Pañchavimsha Brahmana* XI, 1.2; and *Taittiriya Samhita* II, 6.2.5, indicate the supremacy of the brahman; *Pañchavimsha Brahmana* XIX, 1.4; *Taittiriya Samhita* II, 5.10.1; and *Shatapatha Brahmana* I, 3.2, and V, 4.2.7, suggest the superior position of the kshatriya class.
12. *Vide* Parsons [316], p. 165; Gerth and Mills [139], pp. 333ff.
13. *Aitareya Brahmana* VIII, 24.
14. *Shatapatha Brahmana* II, 2.2.6.
15. *Aitareya Brahmana* I, 14. The story appears also in *Shatapatha Brahmana* III, 4.2. *Vide* also *Aitareya Brahmana* VIII, 12.15, on the consecration of Indra.
16. *Shatapatha Brahmana* XII, 9.3. *Vide* also V, 4.2.8, where a ten-generation royal family is mentioned.
17. *Shatapatha Brahmana* III, 4.1.7.
18. Jayaswal [199], p. 118.
19. *Vide* Ingalls [191].
20. *Apastamba Dharmasutra* II, 4.9.11.

21. *Apastamba Dharmasutra* II, 10.27.18f.; *Vishnu Dharmasutra* III, 3; *Vashishtha* (*Vāśiṣṭha*) *Dharmasutra* XIX, 7f.
22. *Apastamba* II, 9.21–24; *Gautama* III, 3; *Vashishtha* VIII, 14–16.
23. *Rigveda* VII, 86.
24. *Chandogya Upanishad* III, 19.
25. Caillois [51], pp. 60f.
26. Wikander [429].
27. Caillois [51], pp. 65f.
28. *Maitri Upanishad* VI, 14.
29. Zimmer [441], p. 162.
30. *Mahabharata* III, 27.5ff.; XII (*Shantiparva*), 73 and 74.
31. *Vide*, especially, Dumézil [103]. The Agni-Indra combination probably represents the same principles. (Cf. *Shatapatha Brahmana* V, 3.5.32f.)
32. Dumézil [102], pp. 63f.
33. Dumézil [103], p. 49.
34. *Shatapatha Brahmana* II, 4.4.18; IV, 1.4.1ff.
35. Dumézil [100], p. 103.
36. Caillois [51], p. 98.
37. Dodds [98], p. 8.
38. Cornford [72], p. 16.
39. W. Norman Brown [49], p. 284.
40. Zimmer [441], p. 163.
41. *Bhagavad Gita* III, 35.
42. Dumézil [100], pp. 103f.
43. *Vide* Dumézil [103], pp. 82f.
44. Wikander [429].

CHAPTER 4

1. Cornford [72], p. 114.
2. Regarding expressive symbolism, *vide* Parsons [316], pp. 384ff.
3. *Vide* Caillois [51], p. 23.
4. Zimmer [441], pp. 66ff.
5. *Ibid.*, pp. 73f.; *yo evam veda* = "who knows thus."
6. *Vide* Dumont [104], pp. xiff.; Dumont emphasizes the link between the horse sacrifice and the solar cult, and the identification of Prajapati with the solar year.
7. *Mahabharata* XIV, 88.13f.
8. *Mahabharata* XIV, 89.41ff.
9. Caillois [51], pp. 120f.
10. Mauss [260], p. 4. (Mauss was a student of Durkheim and the Sanskritist Sylvain Lévi. He was among the first to recognize the importance of the gift in primitive and ancient societies.) Cf. the "Gamester's Lament," *Rigveda* X, 34. For the establishment of Yudhishthira's hegemony through the symbolic presentation of gifts to the "kings," *vide Mahabharata* XIV, 89.31f.
11. *Shatapatha Brahmana* XIV, 4.2.23ff.
12. Held [171].
13. *Shatapatha Brahmana* V, 4.3.1ff.
14. Sharma [389], p. 124; Sharma believes that the dice game and the cow raid are of Indian rather than Aryan origin.
15. *Rigveda* II, 27.12.
16. *Vide* Sharma [389], p. 122.
17. *Shantiparva* 26.25ff.

18. *Chandogya Upanishad* VII, 9.1; cf. *Maitri Upanishad* VI, 11.

19. *Taittiriya Upanishad* II, 2.

20. *Mahabharata* XIII, 63.5ff.

21. *Taittiriya Upanishad* II, 2; *Maitri Upanishad* VI, 12.

22. *Taittiriya Brahmana* II, 8.8.

23. *Brihadaranyaka Upanishad* V, 12: "Only by entering into a unity do these deities reach the highest state."

24. *Vide,* e.g., *Mahabharata* XIII, 63.32 and 63.41: "In the absence of food, the five elements that form the body cease to exist in unison. . . . Thus from food, the Sun and the god of wind and vital seed spring and act. All these are said to form one element or quantity, and it is from these that all creatures originate."

25. *Maitri Upanishad* VI, 37; cf. *Manu Dharmashastra* III, 76.

26. *Taittiriya Upanishad* III, 1.

27. Zimmer [441], pp. 347f.

28. *Mahabharata* XIII, 86.33.

29. *Mahabharata* XII, 8.34.

30. *Mahabharata* XIII, 59.5f.

31. *Mahabharata* XIII, 62.8.

32. *Mahabharata* XIII, 93.19, 61.5.

33. *Mahabharata* XIII, 60.10, 61.1, 61.9, and 61.15.

34. *Vashishtha Dharmasutra* XVII, 86.

35. Moret and Davy [280], pp. 102, 99.

36. Held [171], p. 203.

37. Huizinga [186], pp. 56f.

38. *Rigveda* III, 33.7; X, 61.13.

39. *Baudhayana Dharmasutra* I, 1.16.

40. Hubert and Mauss [185], p. 64 (and *passim*).

41. *Shatapatha Brahmana* I, 1.1.1ff.

42. "The Doctrine of Grace in the Religious Thought of India," in Campbell [54].

43. Zimmer [441], p. 338.

44. *Shatapatha Brahmana* V, 1.1.2; III, 2.2.4.

45. *Vide Aitareya Brahmana* VIII, 28.

46. *Rigveda* X, 8.5.

47. *Vide Maitri Upanishad* VI, 10.

48. Hubert and Mauss [185], p. 130. Some scholars believe that the link between shamanism and the traditional religion may be such narcotics as soma or ambrosia or kava (*vide* James [198], p. 236).

49. *Rigveda* VIII, 48.3.

50. *Shatapatha Brahmana* V, 4.2.3.

51. *Sumangala Vilāsinī* I, 245, cited in Sharma [389], p. 138.

52. *Atharvaveda* X, 7.32ff.

53. *Rigveda* X, 16.3.

54. *Chandogya Upanishad* IV, 4ff.

55. *Chandogya Upanishad* III, 18.2.

56. *Brihadaranyaka Upanishad* III, 2.13.

57. Zimmer [441], p. 341.

58. *Kena Upanishad* 14–28.

59. Cornford [72], p. 41.

60. Zimmer [441], p. 356.

61. Cornford [72], p. 108. This theory provides an insight into the nature and role of the "culture hero" or avatar—such as Krishna and Rama.

62. *Brihadaranyaka Upanishad* I, 4.10; cf. III, 4 and 7.

63. *Vide* J. H. Moulton, *Early Zoroastrianism* (London, 1913), p. 395. Cf. St. Paul: "I beseech you . . . that you present your bodies as a living sacrifice, holy, acceptable to God."

64. *Taittiriya Upanishad* III, 10.6.

65. Cornford [72], p. 181.

66. Hume [187], pp. 65f.

67. Zimmer [441], pp. 154f.

CHAPTER 5

1. Radhakrishnan [329], pp. 113f.; Gandhi, among others, has pointed out that the caste system is not actually based on inequality.

2. For the functional theory of stratification, *vide* Kingsley Davis and Wilbert Moore, "Some Principles of Stratification," in L. Wilson and W. L. Kolb (eds.), *Sociological Analysis* (New York, 1949), and Talcott Parsons, "A Revised Analytical Approach to the Theory of Social Stratification," in his *Essays in Sociological Theory* (rev. ed.; Glencoe, Ill., 1954). Cf. Dennis H. Wrong, "The Functional Theory of Stratification: Some Neglected Considerations," *American Sociological Review,* XXIV (1959).

3. Hopkins [184], p. 97.

4. *Atharvaveda* VI, 117; *Taittiriya Brahmana* VI, 3.10.5; *Shatapatha Brahmana* I, 7.2.1; II, 1.4.11; VI, 1.5.28, 4.4.3–13; XIV, 1.1.31; *Manusmriti* VI, 35.

5. For a reasonably charitable view of the relation of the state to the caste hierarchy, *vide* Altekar [6], pp. 49ff.

6. *Vide* Mees [264].

7. Bouglé [42], p. 4.

8. *Manusmriti* I, 87–98.

9. *Shukranitisara* IV, 3.22–23.

10. On social honor and Weber's distinction between status and class, *vide* Gerth and Mills [139], pp. 180ff.

11. Cox ([75], p. 103 and *passim*) warns against such a confusion.

12. Ghurye [148], p. 41.

13. Hutton [189], chap. 12.

14. *Ibid.*, p. 163.

15. Held [171], pp. 53f.

16. *Ibid.*, pp. 62f.

17. *Ibid.*, pp. 84ff.

18. *Ibid.*, pp. 121f.

19. *Vide* N. K. Dutt [107].

20. Nesfield [294].

21. Volume XV of the *Census of India*, 1911.

22. Dahlmann [79].

23. Hocart [176].

24. *Manusmriti* IV, 2ff; X, 82—but cf. the following verse, which counsels the brahman to "avoid agriculture, [as it] causes great pain [and] is dependent on other [creatures]." Gautama (X, 5f.) considered agriculture a legitimate occupation if the brahman did not do the work himself. Brahmans engaging in trade must not deal in certain goods.

25. *Rigveda* VII, 104.3; cf. *Manu* IV, 61.

26. Senart [385].

27. Held [171], p. 49.

28. Russell [371], I, 182.

29. Cox [75], p. 84; for a thorough critique of one of the more vulnerable theories, *vide* Cox's treatment of N. K. Dutt [107].

30. *Vide* Hocart [176], p. 20.

31. *Ibid.*, p. 29. On symbolic color, *vide* also Dumézil [102], pp. 25f.; J. G. Frazer, *The Golden Bough* (3d ed.; London, 1925), II, 59.

32. *Vishnu Dharmashastra* LVIII, 6–8.

33. Hocart [176], p. 16; Sanskritists might question this usage of karma.

34. *Shatapatha Brahmana* III, 2.1.11.

35. *Aitareya Brahmana* VII, 29; *Shatapatha Brahmana* I, 1.4.12; XI, 6.2.10.

36. *Shatapatha Brahmana* I, 1.1.6. *In re* the initiation, *vide Ashvalayana Grihyasutra* I, 19–22; *Apastamba Dharmasutra* I, 1.1.8ff.

37. *Vide* Held [171], pp. 181ff.

38. *Vide* Weber [425], p. 16.

39. *Ibid.*, pp. 11ff.

40. *Vide*, for example, Jackson [193], pp. 509ff.

41. D. H. H. Ingalls, review of D. D. Kosambi [218] in the *Journal of the American Oriental Society*, LXXVII (1957), 220ff.

42. Kosambi [218], p. 25.

43. *Shantiparva* 78.35ff.

44. *Shantiparva* 48.70. An Arab scholar of the eleventh century records that kingship originally resided in the brahman class, but that their inability to achieve practical objectives forced the brahmans to abdicate in favor of the kshatriyas.

45. *Vide*, e.g., *Apastamba Dharmasutra* II, 10.25.11 ("And in [the king's] realm no [brahman] should suffer hunger, sickness, cold or heat, be it through want or intentionally"), and II, 10.26.1.

46. *Brihadaranyaka Upanishad* I, 4.10ff.

47. Hocart [176], p. 50; the story is No. XXV in Pope's *Tamil Reader.*

48. *Rigveda* X, 124.8, 173; *Atharvaveda* III, 4.2.

49. Weber [425], pp. 49ff.

50. *Vide Mahabharata* I, 64.21f.

51. *Manu* VIII, 413.

52. *Manu* VIII, 414.

53. *Yajñavalkya* II, 182.

54. *Naradasmriti* V, 42f. Kosambi ([218], p. 93) points out that the ways in which one class of slaves in Mesopotamia could attain their freedom correspond precisely with what we find in the *Arthashastra* of Kautalya (III, 13). The other type of Mesopotamian slave, the *śirqūtu*, had become a caste and could not anticipate the possibility of manumission. *Vide* I. Mendelsohn, *Slavery in the Ancient Near East* (New York, 1949).

55. *Baudhayana Dharmasutra* I, 5.9.1.

56. *Manu* III, 110ff.

57. E.g., *Yajñavalkya* XIII, 361.

58. *Vide* "Caste" in *Encyclopedia of the Social Sciences.*

59. D. D. Kosambi, "The Basis of Ancient Indian History (1)," *Journal of the American Oriental Society*, LXXV No. 1 (1955), p. 35. The same writer, in his introduction to the *Subhāṣitaratnakoṣa* [220], remarks that "a class structure is maintained ultimately by force, but strong religious belief minimizes the need for violence in its maintenance." Cf. Riencourt [365], p. 97: "The caste system actually protected all those who would have been victimized in other societies; the weak became stronger through fraternal union within the group, and the individuals were thus sheltered and protected."

CHAPTER 6

1. Karl Jaspers, *The Origin and Goal of History* (New Haven, 1953).
2. Gerth and Mills [139], p. 325; for Weber's remarks on asceticism and mysticism, his distinction between the two types of prophecy and his discussion of the manner in which religions may come to terms with the world, *vide* [139], pp. 324–40. *Vide* also Parsons [318], pp. 563ff.
3. Belvalkar and Ranade [27], p. 84.
4. *Svetāśvatara Upanishad* V, 9.
5. *Shatapatha Brahmana* II, 3.3.8; X, 4.3.12.
6. *Brihadaranyaka Upanishad* VI, 2.16.
7. Dodds [98], chap. 2. Professor Dodds believes that the acceptance into Greek theogony of so monstrous a fantasy as the Kronos myth must be explained in terms of unconscious desires—in this case (of father castration) they are fairly obvious. In distinguishing the "shame culture" of the Homeric age from the "guilt culture" of the fifth century, Dodds acknowledges a debt to K. Latte, "Schuld u. Sünde i. d. gr. Religion," *Arch. f. Rel.*, XX (1920–21).
8. *Vide* Eliade [117], pp. 360f.
9. *Vide* the article on caste in the *Encyclopædia Britannica,* 14th ed.
10. Rhys Davids [360], p. 19.
11. *Jatakas* 158, 465, 536, 547.
12. E.g., *Sutta Nipāta* 685.
13. Ghoshal [143], pp. 398ff.
14. Weber [425], p. 225.
15. Kosambi [218], p. 158. This, he implies, was a major reason for the heterodox insistence on *ahiṃsā*, the injunction against killing.
16. *Vide* Zimmer [441], pp. 56ff.
17. Weber [425], chap. 6.
18. *Saṃyutta Nikāya* V, 421–23.
19. Freud [131], pp. 8, 13f.
20. Freud [130], pp. 24f.; note the long footnote in part VI, following Freud's discussion of the Platonic myth of the origin of the sexual instinct stated (via Aristophanes) in Plato's *Symposium.* He remarks on the similarity of the myth to the description of origin of the world from atman in the *Brihadaranyaka Upanishad* I, 4.1ff.
21. Cf. Coomaraswamy [69], p. 55.
22. *Ibid.,* pp. 67, 66.
23. Joseph Campbell, *The Hero with a Thousand Faces* (New York, 1949), p. 163.
24. Freud [131], p. 40.
25. The term has been used extensively by Sartre and his followers; *vide* "Key to Special Terminology," in [380], p. 629, and, for a discussion of an approach similar to that employed here, part II, chaps. 1 and 3 of that work.
26. Fingarette [124], p. 581.
27. *Dīgha Nikāya* III, pp. 84ff.
28. Kosambi [218], p. 162.
29. Marcuse [255], p. 31.
30. Merton [266], p. 128, "Social Structure and Anomie."
31. *Vide* Eliade [116], p. 98.
32. *Vide* H. J. Rose, *Religion in Greece and Rome* (New York: Harper Torchbook, 1959), pp. 94ff.

33. Dodds [98], p. 131.

34. Basham [24], p. 243.

35. Fick [122], pp. 18, 209. The inspiration for this idea may be the *Praśna Upanishad* VI, 5, or the *Muṇḍaka Upanishad* III, 2.8.

36. *Jatakas* IV, 399f.; but cf. IV, 224, and V, 98.

37. *Vide Digha-atthakatha* I. Dr. B. G. Gokhale writes [155] that the ideal king is a composite of *atthaññu, dhammaññu, mattaññu, kālaññu,* and *parisaññu.* "The Commentary explains these terms as knowledge of *hetus* (conditions, causal relationships, significance), of *paveṇidhamma* (traditional *dhamma,* norms, standards of behavior, life), of measure (*pamāṇa*) in punishment (*daṇḍa,* fines, chastisement) and taxation (*bali*), knowledge of the proper time for the enjoyment of personal pleasures, dispensing justice and carrying out tours of inspection (*rajjasukhānubhavana* . . .) and knowledge of proper treatment towards the various classes in society." (P. 162.)

38. E.g., *Jatakas* 490, 528.

39. *Jatakas* 51, 276, 282, 407, 422, 515, 521, 527.

40. *Buddhacarita* IX, 12ff.

41. Bellah [26], p. 19; "This relation will be close to that of the transference relation in psychotherapy."

42. *Vide* the relatively late *Ādipurāna* (III) of Jinasena.

43. *Nītivākyāmrita* 17, 180.

44. *Mahāvīracarita* 12, 59ff.

CHAPTER 7

1. Renou [358], p. 53.

2. *Rigveda* X, 114.5.

3. On the dual pressures of revitalized Sanskrit theology and Western secular ideas and technology in modern India, *vide* Srinivas [400], p. 481.

4. Radhakrishnan [329], p. 75.

5. Gandhi, *Harijan,* 23 March 1940, p. 55.

6. *Brihadaranyaka Upanishad* IV, 3.21.

7. *Vide* Eliade [117], pp. 254–73; *in re* Tantric Buddhism, *vide* Basham [24], pp. 279ff.

8. V. Raghavan [334], p. 346.

9. Aldous Huxley, "Knowledge and Understanding," in *Tomorrow and Tomorrow and Tomorrow* (New York, 1956). In the present study we have generally used knowledge in a broader sense than that employed here by Huxley for purposes of contrast.

10. Riencourt [365], pp. 114, 118.

11. *Kaṭha Upanishad* II, 5f.; *Muṇḍaka Upanishad* I, 2.8; *Brihadaranyaka Upanishad* III, 5; *Maitri Upanishad,* I, 3. For parallel passages in the *Gita, vide* Chapter 9.

12. *Brihadaranyaka Upanishad* IV, 5.7.

13. Eliade [117], p. xvi.

14. *Ibid.,* p. 360.

15. *The Bhagavadgītā* (London, 1948), p. 175.

16. *Vide* Hiriyanna [175], chap. 5. For a brief survey of the six great systems of Indian philosophy (of which Sankhya and Yoga are two), *vide* Joseph Campbell's appendix to Zimmer [441], pp. 605ff., and Basham [24], pp. 323ff. The yogic discipline is described in the *Svetāśvatara Upanishad* II, 8–13 (Hume's ed., p. 398).

17. Eliade [117], p. 361; Eliade believes that the absence of yogic mysticism from other Indo-European religions confirms the hypothesis that it was native to India.

18. *Ibid.,* pp. 339f.; *vide* also pp. 318–41.

19. W. Ruben, *Acta Orientalia,* XVII (1939), 164ff. On shamanism, *vide* Campbell [53], chap. 6.

20. Löwith [239], p. 4.

21. Riencourt [365], p. 107; cf. also Zaehner [436], p. 140.

22. A dizzying attempt to portray the vastness of time appears in the *Brahmavaivarta Purāṇa, Krishna-janma Khanda* 47.50ff.; it is paraphrased in Zimmer [440], p. 3. On the general subject of the temporal sense, *vide* Mircea Eliade, "Time and Eternity in Indian Thought," in Campbell [52]. For a comparison of Hindu and Buddhist conceptions of time, *vide* Coomaraswamy [71].

23. Eliade [117], p. 184.

24. Marcuse [255], p. 235.

25. Rousseau, *Rêveries,* Cinquième promenade, in Georges Poulet, *Studies in Human Time* (New York, Harper Torchbook, 1959), p. 172.

26. Strauss [404], p. 294.

27. "The Indian Theories of Redemption," in Campbell [54].

28. *Vide* Max Scheler, *Man's Place in Nature,* transl. by Hans Meyerhoff (Boston, 1961), pp. 35ff., for a discussion of the stages in which existence manifests itself.

CHAPTER 8

1. *Vide* Eliade [117], chap. 4.

2. Weber [425], pp. 181f. "The good" must be taken to mean those who keep the faith.

3. *Bhagavad Gita* IV, 20; XVIII, 11 and 48. *Vide* also Chapter 9 below.

4. Hopkins [182].

5. Dahlmann [80].

6. Holtzmann [180].

7. Held [171], p. 22.

8. *Ibid.,* pp. 296ff.

9. A. Ludwig, *Abh. K. Böhm. Ges. Wiss.* VI Folge Bnd. 12 (cited in Held [171], p. 5); Wikander [428]; *vide* Dumézil [102], pp. 75ff.

10. *Vide,* e.g., *Shantiparva* 14.

11. Huizinga [186], p. 52.

12. II Samuel 26.

13. *Vide* Hannah Arendt, "What Was Authority?" in Friedrich [133].

14. *Shantiparva* 59.13ff.

15. The *Shantiparva* invariably brings to mind the *Leviathan.* Prof. Ghoshal cautions against the comparison arguing that "the Hobbesian theory . . . is a complete philosophical system based on the methods of precise definition and relentless logical deduction," and therefore the *Mahabharata* cannot be compared with it. His critique of attempts to stress the similarity to Hobbes points up the subtle philosophic problems of social contract and the origin of the state that must be considered: *vide* Ghoshal [146], p. 288.

16. *Shantiparva* 68.52 and 68.59.

17. *Shantiparva* 67.16f.

18. *Shantiparva* 67.33.

19. *Shantiparva* 63.28.

20. *Shantiparva* 15.2 and 15.30.

21. *Shantiparva* 121.14ff.

22. *Shantiparva* 15; 78.41. Chapters 120 and 121 are also concerned with the subject of punishment, the foundation of social order.

23. *Shantiparva* 69.79.

24. *Shantiparva* 100.2ff.

25. *Shantiparva* 140.70; Varma [417] uses the phrase "dharma of distress" to describe this expediency.

26. *Ramayana* II, 118.19.

27. *Vide Shantiparva* 10.37; 15.53.

28. *Shantiparva* 15.20 and 15.49.

29. *Shantiparva* 10.18.

30. *Shantiparva* 10–14.

31. E.g., *Shantiparva* 69.23.

32. *Mahabharata* VI, 1.27; *Shantiparva* 96.1ff., 100.27ff.

33. *Mahabharata* V, 155.1ff.; VII, 25.58ff., 178.23ff.; *Ramayana* VI *passim.*

34. *Shantiparva* 15.49.

35. *Shantiparva* 34.32.

36. *Mahabharata* II, 69.15.

37. *Shantiparva* 94.1.

38. *Shantiparva* 100.6; 105.11ff.

39. *Shantiparva* 140.18.

40. *Shantiparva* 120.

41. *Shantiparva* 68.36ff.

42. *Shantiparva* 69.4.

43. *Shantiparva* 56.21 and 56.37ff.

44. *Shantiparva* 57.30f.

45. *Shantiparva* 59.103ff.

46. *Shantiparva* 59.108.

47. *Ramayana* II, 110.35ff.

48. *Shantiparva* 71.15ff.; cf. *ibid.*, 87.21 and 88.4f.

49. *Shantiparva* 87.35.

50. *Mahabharata* XIII, 112.19; "The king, O delighter of the Kurus, should take a sixth of the incomes of his subjects as tribute for performing the duties of their protection." (*Shantiparva* 69.25.)

51. *Shantiparva* 130.33ff.

52. *Shantiparva* 57.21; 130.4f.

53. *Shantiparva* 24.12.

54. *Shantiparva* 68.8–19.

55. *Mahabharata* XIII, 61.32ff.; cf, the milder *Shantiparva* 10.29, 90.39, and 93.3.

56. *Shantiparva* 57.43f.

57. *Mahabharata* III, 249.16.

58. *Shantiparva* 27.19f.

59. *Shantiparva* 65.

60. *Shantiparva* 83.2 and 83.7.

61. Hopkins [184], p. 151.

62. Jayaswal, [199], chap. 28.

63. *Shantiparva* 69.27ff.

64. *Shantiparva* 87.

65. *Shantiparva* 107.

66. *Shantiparva* 57.11.

CHAPTER 9

1. Hopkins [184], p. 182.

2. *Ibid.*, p. 63.

3. For indications of Vedic optimism and exuberance, *vide Rigveda* I, 104.8, 114.7f.; X, 14.8, 119.

4. *Vide* Held [171], p. 271.

5. *Ibid.*, pp. 172ff.

6. Cornford [72], p. 107.

7. *Mahabharata* VIII, 90.70; cf. VII, 169.31.

8. Hopkins [184], p. 69.

9. *Mahabharata* VIII, 93.55ff.; V, 131ff.

10. Zimmer [441], p. 74.

11. Hopkins [184], p. 315.

12. *Mahabharata* II, 47.36; VII, 135.1; VIII, 9.3.

13. *Shantiparva* 134.2f.

14. *Vide Rigveda* X, 119.2ff. for a vivid description of Indra as drunken braggart.

15. *Mahabharata* XII, 25; XIII, 6. Zimmer [441], pp. 98ff. provides a discussion of this dilemma.

16. *Odyssey*, 24.318; *Iliad*, 13.61.

17. Zimmer [441], p. 101.

18. *Bhagavad Gita* XVIII, 7.

19. *Bhagavad Gita* XVIII, 17.

20. *Bhagavad Gita* IX, 27.

21. *Bhagavad Gita* II, 62f.

22. *Bhagavad Gita* II, 47. Cf. III, 19; IV, 18f.; V, 2; XVIII, 2, 6.

23. *Bhagavad Gita* IX, 30–32, 36. But cf. III, 26: the ignorant, devoted to action (i.e., action which is not indifferent to the world), are not to be disturbed.

24. Radhakrishnan [327], p. 376.

25. Majumdar [251], II, p. 443.

26. *Bhagavad Gita* III, 22ff.

27. *Bhagavad Gita* V, 14; XVIII, 59.

28. *Bhagavad Gita* XI, 33.

29. *Institutes of the Christian Religion* III, 7.

30. *Arthashastra* VIII, 4 (p. 387).

31. *Mahabharata* XII, 134.5f.

32. *Bhagavad Gita* XVIII, 48.

33. *Arthashastra* I, 7 (p. 12). Of the trivarga, artha is thus the most important.

34. *Vide* Arendt, "What Was Authority?" in Friedrich [133].

35. Voegelin [419], pp. 39f.

36. Robert Michels, *Political Parties* (Glencoe, Ill., 1949).

37. These terms are borrowed from Alvin Gouldner who, in his *Patterns of Industrial Bureaucracy* (Glencoe, Ill., 1954), makes a distinction between two ideal types of organization that roughly coincide with the contrast suggested here.

38. Eliade [116], p. 155.

CHAPTER 10

1. Kosambi [218], p. 177.

2. Weber [425], pp. 86ff.

3. *Vide* Plutarch [321], chaps. 57–67.

4. Majumdar, "The Indika of Megasthenes," *Journal of the American Oriental Society,* LXXVIII (Oct. 1958), No. 4, pp. 273ff.

5. Mookerji, "Chandragupta and the Mauryan Empire," in Majumdar [251], II.

6. *Manusmriti* VII, 114 and 121; cf. *Shantiparva* 5.80, 87.3.

7. Rock Edict XIII.
8. *Vide* Thapar [407], p. 145.
9. Eggermont [113], pp. 69ff.
10. *Vide* Thapar [407], p. 3.
11. Rock Edict IV.
12. Rock Edict XII. *Vide* also Rock Edict VII: "King Priyadarshin, Beloved of the gods, wishes that all sects may dwell at all places, because they all desire self-restraint and purification of heart."
13. Rock Edict III.
14. *Vide* Kosambi [218], p. 225.
15. *Vide,* most recently, Albinski [4].
16. Weber [425], p. 86.
17. *Vide* Kosambi [218], p. 222.
18. *Arthashastra* III, 9f.
19. *Travels of Fa-hsien,* transl. H. A. Giles (Cambridge, 1923).
20. *Kamandakiya* XII.
21. *Vide Katyayanasmriti* 71ff.
22. *Kamandakiya* VI, 15.
23. *Naradasmriti* I, 2.
24. Quoted by Basham [23], p. 104.
25. Mahalingam, *South Indian Polity* (Madras, 1955), p. 9.
26. Nilakanta Sastri [299], p. 255.
27. Ramachandra Dikshitar [342], pp. 213f.
28. *Ibid.,* pp. 209ff.

CHAPTER 11

1. *Kamandakiya Nitisara* I, 2–6, translated by R. Shama Sastri.
2. DeBary [92], p. 237.
3. *Kautaliya Arthashastra,* edited and translated by R. Shama Sastri (Mysore, 1909). Page references are to the 1923 edition.
4. *Dasakumāracarita* II, 8.
5. *Shantiparva* 100.5.
6. *Mahabharata* IX, 61.28 and 61.38.
7. F. E. Pargiter, *The Purāna Text of the Dynasties of the Kali Age* (London, 1931), p. 26.
8. Rawlinson [353].
9. *Arthashastra* IX, 1 (p. 396).
10. Kane [208], p. 104. On the date of the *Arthashastra, vide* Keith [210], pp. 130–38; Jayaswal [199], Part I, Appendix C; Mookerji, Introduction to N. N. Law [233]; B. K. Sarkar [378], Book I (chap. 8); Kane [208], pp. 89ff.; Majumdar and Pusalker [251], II; Kalidas Nag [290], chap. 5; Kosambi [218], chap. 7 (section 4); Romila Thapar [407], Appendix I.
11. *Arthashastra* I, 7 (p. 12); cf. *Shantiparva* 128.48f.
12. Ajit Kumar Sen [383], p. 26. On the subject of acquisition, *vide* Derrett [93], pp. 66ff.
13. *Arthashastra* I, 3 (p. 7).
14. *Arthashastra* II, 24; III, 14 and 16; IV, 8; XIV, 3.
15. *Re* the saptanga concept of the state, *vide Arthashastra* VI, 1; *Manu* IX, 294; *Yajñavalkya* I, 353.
16. *Vide* also *Shukranitisara* I, 62.
17. *Vide* the discussion of Durkheim in Parsons [318], pp. 429ff.

18. *Ibid.,* p. 432.
19. *Arthashastra* I, 9 (p. 15).
20. Fick [122], p. 212.
21. On caste duties, *vide Arthashastra* I, 3 (p. 7).
22. *Arthashastra* I, 13 (p. 24).
23. *Vide* p. 137 (above), where it was argued that the compact is not popular in character.
24. *Arthashastra* VIII, 1 (pp. 377ff.). Bharadvaja proclaimed the crucial significance of the minister, Parashara stressed the major importance of the fortress, Vatavyadhi the ally, etc. *Vide* Rangaswami Aiyangar [350], p. 70.
25. Ghoshal [144], p. 84.
26. These constituents of sovereignty (svami, amatya, janapada, durga, kośa, bala, mitra) have been translated by Rangaswami Aiyangar (in a slightly different order) as "unity, as represented by a common ruler; a settled administration, as indicated by the existence of ministers; a definite system of revenue, forming the source of the treasure; an army, representing the strength [of the state]; a settled territory, occupied and held in adverse possession against the world, by means of forts, and independence of external control, as signified in the power to enter into alliances and freedom to make war and peace." For other translations of these terms, *vide* Ghoshal [144], p. 107, n.8; Sharma [389], pp. 14ff.
27. *Arthashastra* I, 19 (p. 41).
28. *Vide* especially *Arthashastra* III and IV. At least 340 categories of fines are enumerated.
29. *Arthashastra* III, 15 (p. 230).
30. *Shantiparva* 140.70ff.
31. *Shantiparva* 134.6f. *Vide* also, in the epic, *Adiparva* 142, *Sabhāparva* 32, *Vanaparva* 32 and 33.
32. *Shantiparva* 140. One student of ancient Indian diplomatic history hazards the suggestion that Kanika might be a thinly disguised version of Chanakya (Kautalya), whose theories may have been introduced into the epic. Nag [290], chap. 2.)
33. *Shantiparva* 15.49.
34. *Shantiparva* 140.47.
35. *Arthashastra* V, 2 (p. 296).
36. Weber [425], p. 146.
37. *Arthashastra* I, 4 (p. 9).
38. *Arthashastra* I, 6 (p. 11); cf. *Shantiparva* 5.34 (the king must first conquer his own soul).
39. *Arthashastra* VI, 1 (p. 311).
40. *Arthashastra* VI, 1.
41. *Arthashastra* VII, 5 (pp. 330f.).
42. Machiavelli, *Discourses on the First Ten Books of Titus Livius,* III, 5.
43. Machiavelli, *The Prince,* chap. 15.
44. Montesquieu, *The Spirit of the Laws,* VIII, 10.

CHAPTER 12

1. *Arthashastra* I, 19 (p. 39).
2. *Arthashastra* I, 5f. (pp. 9–12).
3. *Arthashastra* I, 17 (p. 34).
4. *Arthashastra* I, 10 (pp. 16ff.).
5. *Arthashastra* I, 19 (p. 40).
6. On the importance of the ministry to the king, *vide Arthashastra* I, 3; for

descriptions of the ideal minister, cf. *Shantiparva* 82ff., *Kamandakiya Nitisara* IV, 25–31, *Kural* 51.

7. *Arthashastra* I, 15 (p. 30).

8. *Arthashastra* I, 4 (pp. 8f.).

9. Cf. *Kamandakiya* VIII; *Manusmriti* VII, 154ff., 207; *Shukranitisara* IV, 1.39–43.

10. *Arthashastra* VII, 1 (p. 317). "Whosoever is inferior to another shall make peace with him; whoever is superior in power shall wage war; whoever thinks, 'No enemy can hurt me, nor am I strong enough to destroy my enemy,' shall observe neutrality; whoever is possessed of necessary means shall march against his enemy; whoever is devoid of necessary strength to defend himself shall seek the protection of another; whoever thinks that help is necessary to work out an end shall make peace with one and wage war with another. Such is the aspect of the six forms of policy."

11. *Arthashastra* IX, 2 (p. 401); cf. *Arthashastra* VI, 1. *Vide Manu* VIII, 348; *Kamandakiya* IV, 65f.; XV, 20. Megasthenes, however, says that the two lower classes were exempted from military service.

12. *Arthashastra* I, 16 (pp. 31ff.).

13. *Arthashastra* I, 12 (pp. 22f.).

14. *Arthashastra* III, 9 (p. 209).

15. *Arthashastra* II, 21 (pp. 132ff.).

16. *Arthashastra* IV, 3 (pp. 253ff.).

17. *Vide* Kosambi [218], pp. 147, 210f.

18. Ramachandra Dikshitar [338].

19. Formichi, Carlo, *Salo Populi* (Turin, 1908), quoted in B. K. Sarkar [378], Book II, pp. 188ff. (The *Arthashastra* of Kautalya had not yet been discovered.)

20. *Kamandakiya* XV, 1f.

21. *Kamandakiya* IV.

22. *Kamandakiya* I, 11.

23. *Kamandakiya* I, 37ff.

24. *Kamandakiya* II, 40.

25. *Kamandakiya* II, 37; VI, 7.

26. *Kamandakiya* II, 44.

27. *Kamandakiya* IX, 59.

28. *Kamandakiya* XVIII, 69.

29. *Kural*, chap. 76.

30. *Kural* 546. I.e., justice must be done.

31. *Kural* 543, 560.

32. *Kural*, chaps. 44 and 45.

33. *Manimēkhalai* VII, 5.12.

34. *Kural* 634, 654, 668, chap. 68.

35. *Kural*, chap. 69.

36. *Kural* 861.

37. *Kural* 471ff., 481ff., 491ff.

38. *Kural* 533.

39. *Brihaspati* VI, 7ff.

40. *Brihaspati* II, 55f.

41. *Brihaspati* I, 4f.

42. *Pañchatantra* I, 176.

43. *Pañchatantra* I, 116f.

44. *Nitivakyamrita*, Jainagranthamala ed., p. 256.

45. *Nitivakyamrita* XXX; cf. Hemachandra, *Laghvarhanniti* II, 1.19ff.
46. *Shukranitisara* VI, 1.92–102; cf. *Kamandakiya* II, 40–42.
47. Cf. *Shukranitisara* I, 21ff.
48. B. K. Sarkar (ed.), *The Sacred Books of the Hindus,* XXV, p. 29.
49. *Shukranitisara* III, 223; IV, 1171, 1247ff.; for the expedients of public policy, *vide* IV, 21–39.
50. *Shukranitisara* IV, 894ff.
51. *Shukranitisara* I, 62.
52. *Shukranitisara* I, 141–52.
53. *Shukranitisara* II, 5ff.
54. *Shukranitisara* IV, 1156ff.
55. *Shukranitisara* I, 277f.; IV, 109f.
56. *Shukranitisara* IV, 7.838f. This idea also appears in the Jaina political literature.
57. *Shukranitisara* I, 745.
58. *Shukranitisara* I, 187.
59. Ghoshal [144], p. 390.
60. *Shukranitisara* I, 382.
61. *Shukranitisara* II, 111f.
62. *Shukranitisara* I, 603–19.
63. *Shukranitisara* IV, 1.84.
64. *Shukranitisara* I, 357.
65. *Shukranitisara* IV, 2.222ff.
66. *Shukranitisara* I, 376ff.
67. *Shukranitisara* III, 32; IV, 250.
68. *Shukranitisara* IV, 5.92ff.

CHAPTER 13

1. *Manusmriti* VIII, 14f.
2. Kane [208], I, Appendix (Devanagari syllabary).
3. Maine [248], pp. 14f. *Vide* also his *Early Law and Custom* (London, 1914), pp. 7f.
4. Rangaswami Aiyangar [349], p. 13.
5. *Yajñavalkyasmriti* II, 21. Ghoshal ([144], pp. 161f.) states that this is the first instance in the smriti literature of the recognition of dharmashastra and arthashastra as the two sources of law.
6. On the date of the *Manusmriti, vide* Bühler, in *Sacred Books of the East,* XXV, Introduction, and, for a general survey of the problems of authorship and dating of the dharmashastra literature, *vide* Kane [208], I, pp. 79ff. and 135ff.
7. *Manusmriti* II, 6, 12; VIII, 3, 46; XIII, 3.
8. Altekar [5], pp. 38f.
9. *Manu* VII, 20ff.
10. *Manu* IX, 245.
11. Jayaswal [199], pp. 233ff.; *vide* Ghoshal's note [144], p. 173.
12. *Vide Manu* VII, 6f.; *Naradasmriti* XVII, 26ff. (In *Narada* XVIII, 31, divinity appears to be accepted.)
13. *Manu* IX, 303. "Like Indra bestowing the rain, the king bestows blessings on his kingdom; he absorbs taxes as the sun absorbs the moisture." Cf. *Mārkandeya Purāna* XXVII, 21ff.: the king is advised to assume the form of five deities.
14. *Shantiparva* 59.
15. *Manu* I, 31 and 87; cf. *Rigveda* X, 90.

16. *Manu* IX, 313ff.

17. *Yajñavalkya* II, 21; XIII, 343.

18. "Whatever a king does is right, that is a settled rule; because the protection of the world is entrusted to him, and on account of his majesty and benignity towards living creatures. As a husband though feeble must be constantly worshiped by his wives, in the same way a ruler though worthless must be constantly worshiped by his subjects." (*Narada* XVIII, 21f.) This extreme statement of the principle that the royal edict, regardless of its nature, is entitled to the same respect as the traditional forms of law is also found in the *Rājanītiprakāśa.*

19. *Manu* VIII, 4–7. The common law was thus classified: (1) nonpayment of debts, (2) pledge and deposit, (3) sale of property not owned, (4) partner relationships, (5) resumption of gifts, (6) failure to pay wages, (7) failure to carry out agreements, (8) rescinding of sale and purchase, (9) disputes with servants, (10) boundary questions, (11) assault, (12) defamation, (13) theft, (14) robbery, violence, (15) adultery, (16) duties of husband and wife, (17) division of inheritance, (18) gambling.

20. *Brihaspatismriti* X, 19ff.

21. *Brihaspati* VI, 5.

22. *Katyayanasmriti* 485.

23. *Manu* VIII, 163f.

24. *Brihaspati* VI, 2: "Punishment corresponding to the nature of the offense shall be ordained."

25. Hiuen Tsiang, *Si Yu-ki,* transl. S. Beal (London, 1883).

26. *Manu* VII, 2f. and 144; VIII, 307f.; *Yajñavalkya* I, 119.

27. *Manu* VII, 16–28.

28. *Manu* VII, 43f.; *Yajñavalkya* XIII, 309–11 (cf. *Arthashastra* I, 7).

29. *Manu* VII; *Yajñavalkya* XIII, 327–31 (cf. *Arthashastra* I, 19).

30. *Manu* VII, 27f. Cf. *Yajñavalkya* XIII, 341: "The fire arising from the heat of the suffering of the subjects does not cease without fully burning the family, fortune and life of the king."

31. *Katyayana* 4f.

32. *Manu* VII, 56f.

33. *Manu* VII, 146.

34. *Manu* XII, 110ff.

35. *Manu* VII, 122f.; *Yajñavalkya* XIII, 338.

36. *Manu* X, 118f.

37. *Manu* VII, 138.

38. *Manu* VII, 129.

39. *Manu* VII, 131f.; VIII, 398.

40. *Manu* VIII, 39; *vide* p. 214 note *h* above.

41. *Manu* VII, 114.

42. *Manu* IX, 294 (cf. *Vishnu Purana* III); in *Yajñavalkya* I, 353, jana (people) is used instead of Kautalya's janapada.

43. E.g., *Manu* VII, 170: "Whenever he [the king] thinks all the elements of the state very exalted, likewise himself very mighty, then let him make war."

44. *Manu* VII, 87ff.; IX, 323.

45. *Manu* VII, 198ff.

46. *Yajñavalkya* I, 346.

47. *Yajñavalkya* XIII, 352.

48. *Manu* VII, 63ff.

49. E.g., *Manu* VII, 180, 201ff.

50. *Vide* B. C. Mazumdar. "Origin and Character of the Purāṇa Literature,"

Sir Asutosh Mookerjee Silver Jubilee Volumes, III, part 2 (Calcutta, 1925), pp. 7ff.

51. *Markandeya Purana* 129.28ff. This reward is an old smriti principle, the fraction no doubt reflecting the traditional tax on the produce of the land. Cf. *Agni Purana* 223, 9f.; *Brihaddharma Purana* III, 3.10f.

52. *Agni Purana* 225.16ff.; *Matsya Purana* 215.47ff. and 218.2f.

CHAPTER 14

1. *Aitareya Brahmana* I, 14.23; VIII, 12ff.

2. *Shukranitisara* I, 375.

3. *Shantiparva* 67.19.

4. *Arthashastra* I, 13; *vide* also XIII, 1, where the king is advised to be seen by his more gullible subjects in the company of his own men disguised as gods.

5. *Naradasmriti* I, 1f.

6. E.g., *Vayu Purana* VIII, 31.41ff., 31.128, 31.142f.

7. *Sacred Books of the Buddhists* IV, 85ff.

8. *Mahabharata* XII, 59 and 68; *vide* p. 137 above.

9. Ihering, *Law as Means to an End* (New York, 1924), p. 190.

10. *Arthashastra* I, 11ff.; *Kamandakiya* I, 54f.; II, 42; XIII, 61; XIV, 67; *Manu* VII, 20–24, 47–51; *Shukranitisara* IV, 1.92–102.

11. *Manusmriti* II, 42; VII, 21ff.

12. *Arthashastra* I, 4.

13. *Rigveda* IV, 42.8.

14. *Shantiparva* 78.38ff.

15. *Shatapatha Brahmana* XIII, 4.4.3.

16. *Vide* Sharma [389], p. 180.

17. Friedrich [133], pp. 35f. "The reasoning involved is both 'instrumental' and 'valuational,' or to put it another way, it proceeds to argue both in terms of means and ends." (*Ibid.*, p. 42.)

18. Cf. *Manusmriti* V, 93f. and IV, 84ff.

19. Pillar Edict IV.

20. Rangaswami Aiyangar [348].

21. *Vide* R. W. and A. J. Carlyle, *A History of Medieval Political Theory in the West* (New York, 1903–16), Vol. I; and Chapter 3, Part 1 above.

22. Cf. Bracton, Folio 34.

23. However, cf. Jayaswal [199], pp. 345ff.

24. E.g., *Shantiparva* 71.10; *Naradasmriti* 18.48; *Shukranitisara* I, 188.

25. *Arthashastra* IV, 13.

26. *Naradasmriti* XVIII, 19ff.

27. *Arthashastra* I, 3.

28. Talcott Parsons, "Authority, Legitimation, and Political Action," in Friedrich [133], pp. 197ff.

29. Max Weber, *The Theory of Social and Economic Organization,* ed. and transl. Parsons and Henderson (New York, 1947), pp. 341ff.

CHAPTER 15

1. *Vide Arthashastra* II, 24; III, 9.

2. *Shantiparva* 88.4.

3. *Shantiparva* 87.27ff.

4. *Gautama Dharmasutra* X, 24.

5. *Shatapatha Brahmana* XIII, 7.1.15.

6. *Vide* Ghoshal [142].

7. Cited in Jayaswal [199], p. 345.

8. *Vide* particularly *Shantiparva* 103, 105.

9. "The Jackal's Foes," *Pañchatantra,* transl. Ayyar, p. 175; the *Pañchatantra* may have been written to popularize the study of diplomacy.

10. *Arthashastra* VII; *Manusmriti* VII, 154ff.; *Shukranitisara* IV, 1.39ff.; *Kamandakiya* VIII.

11. *Vide Manusmriti* VII, 201ff.; cf. IX, 251.

12. *Vide Manusmriti* VII, 87ff.; X, 119.

13. *Arthashastra* XII, 1; cf. VII, 15.

14. *Vide Arthashastra* VII, 1 (cf. XIII, 1); *Manusmriti* VII, 155ff.

15. On the humane conduct of hostilities, *vide Apastamba* II, 5.10f.; *Shantiparva* 100.27ff.; *Manusmriti* VII, 90; *Shukranitisara* IV, 7.379ff.

16. Weber [425], pp. 63–77.

17. *Vide* Mookerji [276].

18. *Vide* Turner [413], p. 378.

19. *Vide,* most recently, Burton Stein, "Economic Function of a Medieval South Indian Temple," *Journal of Asian Studies,* XIX, No. 2 (February, 1960).

20. *Shantiparva* 87.10; *Kautaliya* II, 36; *Manu* VII, 121.

21. *Vide* Weber [423], pp. 82f.

22. *Vide* Nilakanta Sastri [303], chaps. 3 and 4.

23. *Naradasmriti* X, 2. Narada holds further (I, 40) that "custom is powerful and overrules the sacred law."

24. Majumdar [250], pp. 28ff.

25. *Shukraniti* IV, 5.59f.

26. Majumdar [250], p. 68.

27. Kosambi [218], p. 221.

28. *Shantiparva* 81 and 107.

29. *Vide* Jayaswal [199], pp. 23ff.

30. Sharma [389], pp. 81ff.

31. *Vide ibid.,* p. 93.

32. Bhandarkar [30], p. 144.

33. *Vide* also the interpretations of Majumdar [250], pp. 221ff., and the survey essay by Ghoshal [143], chap. 11.

34. *Vide* Ghoshal [143], p. 363.

CHAPTER 16

1. *Vide* Marx, *Economic and Philosophic Manuscripts of 1844* (Moscow, n.d); Robert Tucker, *Philosophy and Myth in Karl Marx* (Cambridge, 1961), pp. 168f.; Michael Harrington, "Marx versus Marx," *New Politics,* I (1961); and cf. Herbert Marcuse, *Reason and Revolution* (New York, 1941), pp. 294f.

2. Rollo May, "The Significance of Symbols," in [261], p. 22.

3. Arendt [8], p. 16.

4. Julius Stone, *The Province and Function of Law* (Cambridge, Mass., 1950), p. 711.

5. Beni Prasad [323], p. 2.

6. Aurobindo Ghose [140], pp. 380ff.

7. *Vide* Fortes and Evans-Pritchard [125], pp. 9f.

8. Gerth and Mills [139], p. 328.

9. *Shatapatha Brahmana* V, 4.4.20ff.

10. *Chandogya Upanishad* V, 11.7.

11. Jayaswal [199], p. 219n.

BIBLIOGRAPHY

The Bibliography is organized in two alphabetical lists, Primary Sources and Secondary Sources, the latter preceded by a classified subject guide. The bracketed numbers used in the footnotes and Notes refer to the bracketed numbers in the Secondary Sources section, pp. 347–58.

PRIMARY SOURCES

Agni Purana
M. N. Dutt. "The Agni Purāṇa," *The Wealth of India,* Vol. VIII, parts 7–12.
Aitareya Brahmana
A. B. Keith. *Ṛg Veda Brāhmaṇas: Aitareya and Kausītaki Brāhmaṇas* (Harvard Oriental Series, Vol. XXV). Cambridge, Mass., 1920.
Alberuni (Muhammad ibn Ahmad, Abū al-Raihan, al-Bīrūnī)
E. C. Sachau. *Alberuni's India.* London, 1888.
Apastamba Dharmasutra
Georg Bühler. *Āpastamba Dharmasūtra* (Sacred Books of the East, Vol. II). Oxford, 1879.
Arrian (*vide* Megasthenes)
Arthashastra (*vide* Kautalya Arthashastra)
Aryasura
J. Speyer. *Jātakamālā.* London, 1895.
Ashoka, Edicts of
J. Bloch. *Les Inscriptions d'Asoka.* Paris, 1950.
Eugen Hultzsch. *Inscriptions of Aśoka.* London, 1925.
Radhakumud Mookerji. *Aśoka.* London, 1928.
Vincent Smith. *Aśoka.* Oxford, 1920.
Romila Thapar. *Aśoka and the Decline of the Mauryas.* London, 1961.
Ashvaghosha (Aśvaghoṣa)
E. H. Johnson. *Buddhacharita.* Calcutta, 1936.
Atharvaveda
M. Bloomfield. *The Hymns of the Atharva Veda* (Sacred Books of the East, Vol. XLII). Oxford, 1897.
W. D. Whitney. *The Atharva Veda* (Harvard Oriental Series, Vols. VII, VIII). Cambridge, Mass., 1905.
Bana, Harshacharita of
E. B. Cowell and F. W. Thomas. *The Harṣacarita of Baṇa.* London, 1897.
Barhaspatyasutra (*vide* Brihaspati Arthashastra)
Baudhayana Dharmasutra
Georg Bühler. *Baudhāyana Dharmasūtra* (Sacred Books of the East, Vol. XIV, part 2). Oxford, 1889.

Bhagavad Gita (*vide* Mahabharata)
Brahmanas (*vide* Aitareya, Pañchavimsha, Shatapatha, and Taittiriya Brahmanas)
Brihadaranyaka Upanishad (*vide* Upanishads)
Brihaspati Arthashastra
    F. W. Thomas. *Brihaspati Sūtra*. Lahore, 1921.
Brihaspati Dharmashastra
    J. Jolly. *Bṛhaspati Dharmaśastra* (Sacred Books of the East, Vol. XXXIII). Oxford, 1889.
    K. V. Rangaswami Aiyangar, *Bṛhaspati Smṛti* (Gaekwad Oriental Series). Baroda, 1941.
Buddhist Texts (*vide* also Aryasura, Ashvaghosha, Dhammapada, Digha Nikaya, Jatakas, Vinayas)
    E. B. Cowell, *et al. Buddhist Mahāyāna Sūtras* (Sacred Books of the East, Vol. XLIX). Oxford, 1894.
    Johannes Nobel. *Suvarṇaprabhāsasūtra*. Leiden, 1944.
    T. W. Rhys Davids. *The Questions of King Milinda* (Sacred Books of the East, Vols. XXXV, XXXVI). Oxford, 1890, 1894.
    E. J. Thomas. *Early Buddhist Scriptures*. London, 1935.
    H. C. Warren. *Buddhism in Translations* (Harvard Oriental Series, Vol. III). Cambridge, Mass., 1922.
Chandogya Upanishad (*vide* Upanishads)
Dandin (Daṇḍin)
    M. E. Kale. *Daśakumāracarita*. 3d ed., Bombay, 1926.
    Arthur Ryder. *The Ten Princes*. Chicago, 1927.
Dhammapada
    Eugene Burlingame. *Buddhist Legends* (Harvard Oriental Series, Vols. XXVIII-XXX). Cambridge, Mass., 1921.
    F. Max Müller. *Dhammapada* (Sacred Books of the East, Vol. X, part 1). Oxford, 1881.
    Sarvepalli Radhakrishnan. *The Dhammapada*. London, 1950.
Dharmashastras (*vide* also Brihaspati, Katyayana, Manu, Narada, Vishnu, and Yajñavalkya Dharmashastras)
    M. N. Dutt. *The Dharmaśastra Texts*. Calcutta, 1908–9.
Dharmasutras (*vide* Apastamba, Baudhayana, Gautama, and Vasishtha Dharmasutras)
Digha Nikaya (Dīgha Nikāya)
    T. W. Rhys Davids and J. E. Carpenter. *Dialogues of the Buddha*. London, 1899, 1900, 1921.
Fa-hsien
    H. A. Giles. *Travels of Fa-hsien*. Cambridge, 1932.
    James Legge. *A Record of Buddhistic Kingdoms*. Oxford, 1886.
Foreign Accounts (*vide* also Alberuni, Fa-hsien, Hiuen Tsiang, Megasthenes)
    J. W. McCrindle. *Ancient India as Described in Classical Literature*. Westminster, 1901.
    Nilakanta Sastri. *Foreign Notices of South India from Megasthenes to Ma Huan*. Madras, 1939.
Gautama Dharmasutra
    Georg Bühler. *Gautama Dharmasūtra* (Sacred Books of the East, Vol. II). Oxford, 1879.
Harshacharita (*vide* Bana)

Hemachandra

    H. N. Johnson. *Triṣaṣṭiśalākāpuruṣacarita.* Baroda, 1931.

Hiuen Tsiang

    S. Beal. *Si Yu-ki.* London, 1883. Also contains a translation of Fa-hsien's travels.

Inscriptions (*vide* also Ashoka)

    J. F. Fleet. *Inscriptions of the Early Gupta Kings* (Corpus Inscriptionum Indicarum, Vol. III). London, 1888.

    Robert Sewall. *Historical Inscriptions of Southern India.* Madras, 1932.

    D. C. Sircar. *Select Inscriptions Bearing on Indian History and Civilization.* Vol. I, Calcutta, 1942.

    Epigraphia Indica. 27 vols. Calcutta and Delhi, 1892–.

    South Indian Inscriptions. 13 vols. Madras, 1890–.

Jaina Texts (*vide* also Hemachandra, Somadeva)

    H. Jacobi. *Jaina Sūtras* (Sacred Books of the East, Vols. XXII, XLV). Oxford, 1884, 1895.

Jatakas

    E. B. Cowell. *Jatakas.* Cambridge, 1895–1913.

    T. W. Rhys Davids. *The Jataka.* London, 1877–96.

Kalidasa

    G. R. Nandargikar. *Raghuvaṁśam.* 3d ed., Bombay, 1897.

    M. Monier-Williams. *The Śakuntala.* London, 1894.

Kamandaka Nitisara

    M. N. Dutt. *Kāmandakīya Nītisāra.* Calcutta, 1896.

Katyayana Dharmashastra

    P. V. Kane. *Kātyāyanasmṛti.* Bombay, 1933.

Kautalya Arthashastra (Kautaliya)

    T. Ganapati Sastri, ed. *Arthaśastra of Kauṭilya.* Trivandrum, 1924–25.

    R. Shama Sastri. *Arthaśastra of Kauṭilya.* 2d ed., Mysore, 1923.

    J. J. Meyer. *Das Altindische Buch vom Welt- und Staatsleben: Das Arthaçastra des Kautilya.* Leipzig, 1926. Aus dem Sanskrit übersetzt und mit Einleitung und Anmerkungen versehen.

Kural (Tirukkural)

    V. V. S. Aiyar. *The Kural.* Tiruchirapalli, 1952.

    V. R. Ramachandra Dikshitar. *Tirukkural.* Madras, 1949.

    G. U. Pope. *The Sacred Kural.* London, 1886.

Mahabharata (and Bhagavad Gita)

    Swami Prabhavananda and C. Isherwood. *The Bhagavad Gita.* Hollywood, Calif., 1944.

    F. Edgerton. *The Bhagavad Gītā* (Harvard Oriental Series, Vols. XXXVIII, XXXIX). Cambridge, Mass., 1944.

    Sarvepalli Radhakrishnan. *The Bhagavadgītā.* London, 1948.

    M. N. Dutt. *A Prose Translation of the Mahābhārata.* Calcutta, 1895–1905.

    C. Rajagopalachari. *Mahabharata.* Bombay, 1951. (Abridged.)

    Protap Chandra Roy (or Ray). *Mahābhārata.* 2d ed., Calcutta, 1919–35.

    (Bhandarkar Oriental Research Institute critical ed. in progress, 1927–: Vols. XIII–XVI [Śāntiparvan] edited by S. K. Belvalkar.)

Maitri Upanishad (*vide* Upanishads)

Manu Dharmashastra

    Georg Bühler. *The Laws of Manu* (Sacred Books of the East, Vol. XXV). Oxford, 1886.

    A. C. Burnell. *The Ordinances of Manu.* London, 1884.

Manu Dharmashastra (*continued*)
   Ganganatha Jha. *Manubhāshya.* Calcutta, 1920–26. Commentary by Medhatithi.
Markandeya Purana
   F. E. Pargiter. *Mārkaṇḍeya Purāṇa.* Calcutta, 1904.
Matsya Purana
   B. D. Basu. *Mātsya Purāṇa.* Allahabad, 1916.
Megasthenes
   J. W. McCrindle. *Ancient India as Described by Megasthenes and Arrian.* London, 1877. Includes the *Indika* of Megasthenes [fragments] and part I of the *Indika* of Arrian.
Mudrarakshasa of Vishakhadatta
   M. R. Kale. *Mudrārākṣasa of Viśākhadatta.* Bombay, 1900.
Narada Dharmashastra
   J. Jolly. *Nārada Dharmaśāstra* (Sacred Books of the East, Vol. XXXIII). Oxford, 1889.
Pañchatantra
   A. S. P. Ayyar. *Pañcatantra.* Bombay, 1931.
   A. Williams. *Tales from the Pañcatantra.* Oxford, 1930.
Pañchavimsha Brahmana (Pañcaviṁśa)
   W. Caland. *The Brahmana of Twenty-five Chapters.* Calcutta, 1931.
Puranas (*vide* also Agni, Markandeya, Matsya, Vishnu Puranas)
   F. E. Pargiter. *The Purāṇa Text of the Dynasties of the Kali Age.* Oxford, 1913.
Ramayana
   R. Griffith. *Ramayana of Valmiki.* Benares, 1915.
Rigveda
   M. N. Dutt. *Rig Veda.* Calcutta, 1906.
   F. Geldner. *Der Rig-veda* (Harvard Oriental Series, Vols. XXXIII–XXXV). Cambridge, Mass., 1951.
   R. Griffith. *The Rig Veda.* 2d ed., Benares, 1896, 1897.
   F. Max Müller and H. Oldenberg. *Vedic Hymns* (Sacred Books of the East, Vols. XXXII, XLVI). Oxford, 1891, 1897.
   A. A. Macdonell. *Hymns of the Rigveda.* London, 1922.
Shantiparva (*vide* Mahabharata)
Shatapatha Brahmana
   Julius Eggeling. *Śatapatha Brāhmaṇa* (Sacred Books of the East, Vols. XII, XXVI, XLI, XLIII, XLIV). Oxford, 1882–1900.
Shrautasutras (Śrautasūtras)
   P.-E. Dumont. *L'Agnihotra.* Baltimore, 1939.
Shukranitisara
   B. K. Sarkar. *Sukranītisāra* (Sacred Books of the Hindus, Vol. XIII). Allahabad, 1914.
Shvetashvatara Upanishad (Śvetāśvatara) (*vide* Upanishads)
Smritis (*vide* Dharmashastras)
Somadeva
   C. H. Tawney. *The Ocean of Story* (Kathāsaritsāgara). London, 1925–28.
Taittiriya Brahmana
   N. Godbole. *Taittirīya Brahmāṇa* (Biblioteca Indica, not transl.). Poona, 1898.
Taittiriya Samhita (*vide* Yajurveda)
Taittiriya Upanishad (*vide* Upanishads)
Tirukkural (*vide* Kural)

Upanishads
  R. E. Hume. *The Thirteen Principal Upanishads.* 2d ed., London, 1931.
  F. Max Müller. *The Upanishads* (Sacred Books of the East, Vols. I, XV). Oxford, 1879, 1884.
  Swami Madhavananda. *The Bṛhadāraṇyaka Upaniṣad.* Almora, 1950.
  E. Senart. *Chāndogya Upaniṣad.* Paris, 1930.
Vasishtha Dharmasutra
  Georg Bühler. *Vasiṣṭha Dharmasūtra* (Sacred Books of the East, Vol. XIV, part 2). Oxford, 1882.
Vedas (*vide* also Atharvaveda, Rigveda, and Yajurveda)
  N. Macnicol *et al. Hindu Scriptures,* London, 1938.
Vinayas
  T. W. Rhys Davids and H. Oldenberg. *Vinaya Texts* (Sacred Books of the East, Vols. XIII, XVII, XX). Oxford, 1881–85.
  J. Jones. *Mahāvastu.* London, 1949, 1953.
Vishnu Dharmashastra
  J. Jolly. *The Institutes of Vishnu* (Sacred Books of the East, Vol. VII). Oxford, 1880.
Vishnu Purana
  H. H. Wilson. *Viṣṇu Purāṇa.* London, 1864–70.
Yajñavalkya Dharmashastra
  J. R. Gharpure. *Yajñavalkya Smṛti.* Bombay, 1936–44. (With Mitāksharā commentary.)
  S. C. Vidyarnava. *Yajñavalkya Smṛti* (Sacred Books of the Hindus, Vol. XXI). Allahabad, 1918.
Yajurveda
  A. B. Keith. *The Veda of the Black Yajus School entitled Taittirīya Saṁhitā* (Harvard Oriental Series, Vols. XVIII, XIX). Cambridge, Mass., 1914.
Yuan Chwang (*vide* Hiuen Tsiang)

SECONDARY SOURCES

The following is a classified guide to the secondary sources listed in this section.

GENERAL HISTORIES OF INDIAN CIVILIZATION
  Barnett [21], Basham [24], Bhandarkar [33], Garratt [136], Ghoshal [143], Grousset [161], Havell [168], Kosambi [218], Lévi [236], Majumdar [251], Masson-Oursel [259], Mookerji [275], Pargiter [315], Rapson [352], Renou [356], Riencourt [365], Smith [398], Weber [425], Wheeler [426]

PREHISTORY AND VEDIC PERIOD
  Brown [47], Childe [62], Das [81], Gordon [158], La Vallée Poussin [227], Law [228], Mackay [245], Marshall [257], Mehta [265], Piggott [320], Wheeler [427]

HISTORIES OF PHILOSOPHY AND RELIGION
  Basham [24], Belvalkar [27], Chatterjee [60], Dasgupta [84], Hiriyanna [175], Radhakrishnan [328, 330], Renou [358], Zimmer [441]

MYTH AND PSYCHE, ETC.
  Brown [46], Caillois [51], Campbell [53], Cornford [72], Davy [91], Dodds [98], Dumézil [101, 102, 103], Durkheim [105], Eliade [115, 116], Frankfort [127], Frazer [128], Freud [130, 132], Harrison [164], Held [171], Hubert [185], Huizinga

[186], James [197], Lévy-Bruhl [237], Linton [238], Malinowski [253], Mauss [260], May [261], Moret [280], Müller [287], Parsons [318], Rowland [370], Söderblom [399], Taylor [414], Voegelin [419], Zimmer [436, 440]

VEDIC AND BRAHMANIC RELIGION ; UPANISHADS
Bergaigne [28], Bloomfield [37, 38], Brown [48], Deussen [94], Geldner [137], Haug [167], Hillebrandt [174], Hume [187], Keith [213], Lévi [235], Macdonell [242], Majumdar [251–I], Monier-Williams [270], Oldenberg [308, 309], Radhakrishnan [331], Renou [357]

BUDDHISM AND JAINISM
Bagchi [12], Bareau [20], Basham [23], Conze [66], Coomaraswamy [67], Dutt [108], Eliot [118], Govinda [159], Guérinot [163], Keith [211], Lamotte [225], La Vallée Poussin [226], Oldenberg [307, 308], Rhys Davids [359, 360, 362], Thomas [408, 409], Varma [416], Weber [425]

HINDUISM
Avalon [11], Bhandarkar [34], Dasgupta [86], Edgerton [112], Eliade [117], Eliot [118], Garbe [135], Monier-Williams [270], Müller [288], Radhakrishnan [329], Raghavan [334], Weber [425]

LAW AND CUSTOM
Altekar [5], Banerjea [16], Davar [88], Dubois [100], Ghose [141], Ingalls [191], Jayaswal [201], Jha [203], Jolly [204, 205], Kane [208], Maine [248], Majumdar [251–II], Mayne [262], Mulla [284], Ramaswami Aiyer [345], Rice [363], Sen [384], Sen-Gupta [386, 387]. *Vide* also CASTE

CASTE
Blunt [39], Bouglé [42, 43], Cox [75], Dahlmann [79], Dutt [107], Fick [122], Ghurye [148], Held [171], Hocart [176], Hopkins [184], Hutton [189], Jackson [193], Ketkar [216], Mees [264], Motwani [282], Nesfield [294], Radhakrishnan [332], Risley [367], Russell [371], Senart [385], Sharma [391]

CORPORATIONS
Bhandarkar [30], Ghoshal [143], Jayaswal [199], Law [228], Majumdar [250], Mazumdar [263], Mookerji [276]

ECONOMICS AND DAILY LIFE
Banerji [15], Bose [40], Chakladar [56], Das [82], Derrett [93], Ghoshal [142], Maity [249], Raj [335], Rangaswami Aiyangar [346], Samaddar [374], Saran [375]

GENERAL STUDIES OF POLITICAL THOUGHT
Altekar [6], Anjaria [7], Bandyopadhyaya [13], Bhandarkar [30], Coomaraswamy [70], Ghoshal [144], Jayaswal [199], Kane [208], Kosambi [218], Law [231, 233], Nag [290], Nilakanta Sastri [304], Prasad [323], Ramaswami Aiyer [344], Rangaswami Aiyangar [349, 350], Sarkar [377], Sen [383], Sharma [389], Sinha [395], Varma [417]

GOVERNMENTAL INSTITUTIONS AND ADMINISTRATION
Altekar [6], Banerjea [17], Basu [25], Bhandarkar [31], Chakravarti [58], Das Gupta [83], Date [87], Ghoshal [145], Heesterman [170], Hillebrandt [173], Jayaswal [199], Kosambi [218], Law [232], Majumdar [251, 252], Nag [290], Nilakanta Sastri [299], Oppert [311], Panikkar [312], Prasad [322], Raj [335], Ramachandra Dikshitar [327, 343], Rapson [352], Rawlinson [353], Raychaudhuri [355], Saletore [371, 373], Sarkar [377], Sharma [389], Subba Rao [405], Venkateswara [418]

EPICS
Dahlmann [80], Dharma [96], Held [171], Holtzmann [180], Hopkins [182, 184], Jacobi [196], Radhakrishnan [327], Wikander [428]

MAURYA AND GUPTA POLITY
Banerji [18], Chattopadhyaya [61], Gopal [157], Majumdar [251–II, III], Mookerji [272, 273, 274], Nilakanta Sastri [296], Ramachandra Dikshitar [336, 339], Thapar [407], Timmer [411], Waddell [420], Watters [422]. *Vide* also ASHOKA ; KAUTALIYA

KAUTALIYA ARTHASHASTRA
Bandyopadhyaya [14], Breloer [44], Jacobi [195], Keith [210], Konow [217], Kosambi [221], Krishna Rao [222], Meyer [268], Mookerji [272], Nilakanta Sastri [302], Raghavan [333], Stein [403], Wilhelm [430]

ASHOKA
Albinski [4], Barua [22], Bhandarkar [29], Eggermont [113], Gokhale [154], Kern [215], McPhail [246], Mookerji [271], Nikam [295], Przyluski [326], Smith [397], Thapar [407]

SOUTH INDIA
Iyengar [192], Krishnaswamy Aiyangar [224], Mahalingam [247], Nilakanta Sastri [300, 301, 303], Ramachandra Dikshitar [342]

[1] Abul Fazl. *Ain-i-Akbari* (transl. H. Blochmann and H. S. Jarrett). Calcutta, 1873–94.

[2] Agrawala, V. S. *India as Known to Pāṇini.* Lucknow, 1953.
Aiyangar. (*Vide* [224], [346–351].)

[3] Akhilananda, Swami. *Hindu Psychology.* London, 1948.

[4] Albinski, H. S. "The Place of the Emperor Aśoka in Ancient Indian Political Thought," *Midwest Journal of Political Science,* II, No. 1.

[5] Altekar, A. S. *Sources of Hindu Dharma in Its Socio-Religious Aspects.* Sholapur, 1952.

[6] ———. *State and Government in Ancient India.* 3d ed., Benares, 1958 (1st ed., Benares, 1949).

[7] Anjaria, J. J. *The Nature and Grounds of Political Obligation in the Hindu State.* Calcutta, 1935.

[8] Arendt, Hannah. *The Human Condition.* Garden City, N.Y., Anchor paperback, 1959.

[9] *Aristotelian Society,* Supplementary Vol. XXXII (1958).

[10] Arokiaswami, M. "Some Political Philosophers of Ancient South India," *Journal of Indian History,* XXVIII.
Aurobindo. *Vide* [140].

[11] Avalon, Arthur (Sir John Woodroffe). *The Principles of Tantra.* 2 vols. London, 1914, 1916.

[12] Bagchi, Prabodhchandra. "Decline of Buddhism in India and Its Causes," in *Sir Asutosh Mookerjee Silver Jubilee Volumes,* III, part 2, Calcutta, 1925.

[13] Bandyopadhyaya, N. C. *Hindu Polity and Political Theory.* Calcutta, 1927, 1928.

[14] ———. *Kautilya.* Calcutta, 1927.
Bandyopadhyaya, P. *Vide* [15].

[15] Banerjea, Pramathenath. *A History of Indian Taxation.* London, 1930.

[16] ———. *International Law and Custom in Ancient India.* Calcutta, 1920.

[17] ———. *Public Administration in Ancient India.* London, 1916.

[18] Banerji, R. D. *The Age of the Imperial Guptas.* Benares, 1933.

[19] ———. *Prehistoric, Ancient and Hindu India.* Bombay, 1934.

[20] Bareau, André. *Les Premiers conciles bouddhiques.* Paris, 1955.

[21] Barnett, L. D. *Antiquities of India.* London, 1913.

[22] Barua, Beni Madhab. *Aśoka and His Inscriptions.* Calcutta, 1946.

[23] Basham, A. L. *History and Doctrines of the Ājīvikas.* London, 1951.

[24] ———. *The Wonder That Was India.* New York, 1954.

[25] Basu, Praphullachandra. *Indo-Aryan Polity.* London, 1925.

[26] Bellah, Robert N. "Some Suggestions for the Systematic Study of Religion" (unpublished manuscript, Dept. of Social Relations, Harvard University, 1955).

[27] Belvalkar, S. K., and R. D. Ranade. *History of Indian Philosophy.* Poona, 1927. Vol. II.

[28] Bergaigne, A. *La Religion védique.* Paris, 1878–83.

[29] Bhandarkar, D. R. *Aśoka.* Calcutta, 1925.

[30] ———. *Carmichael Lectures* (First Series, *Lectures on the Ancient History of India*). Calcutta, 1919.

[31] ———. *Some Aspects of Ancient Hindu Polity*. Madras, 1940.

[32] ———. *Some Aspects of Ancient Indian Culture*. Madras, 1940.

[33] Bhandarkar, R. G. *Early History of the Deccan*. Bombay, 1895.

[34] ———. *Vaishṇavism, Saivism and Minor Religious Sects*. Strassburg, 1913.

[35] Bhattacharya, S. *Select Asokan Epigraphs with Annotations*. Calcutta, 1952.

[36] Bloch, Jules. *L'Indo-aryen du Véda aux temps modernes*. Paris, 1934.

[37] Bloomfield, M. "The Artharvaveda," in G. Bühler, *Encyclopaedia*. Strassburg, 1899.

[38] ———. *The Religion of the Veda*. New York, 1908.

[39] Blunt, E. A. H. *The Caste System of Northern India*. London, 1931.

[40] Bose, Atindranath N. *Social and Rural Economy of Northern India*. 2 vols. Calcutta, 1942–45.

[41] Bottazzi, G. B. *Precursori di Niccolo Machiavelli in India ed in Grecia*. Pisa, 1914.

[42] Bouglé, Célestin. *Essais sur le régime des castes*. Paris, 1935.

[43] ———. "Note sur le droit et la caste en Inde." *L'Année sociologique*, X.

[44] Breloer, Bernhard. *Kauṭilyīa-studien*. Bonn, 1927–34.

[45] Brown, D. Mackenzie. *The White Umbrella*. Berkeley, 1953.

[46] Brown, Norman O. *Life Against Death*. Middletown, Conn., 1959.

[47] Brown, W. Norman. "The Beginnings of Civilization in India," Supplement to the *Journal of the American Oriental Society*, LIX (December 1939).

[48] ———. "The Creation Myth of the Rig Veda," *Journal of the American Oriental Society*, LXII (June 1942).

[49] ———. "Mythology of India," in Samuel Kramer, ed., *Mythologies of the Ancient World*. Garden City, N.Y., Anchor paperback, 1961.

[50] Burtt, E. A., ed. *The Teachings of the Compassionate Buddha*. New York, 1955.

[51] Caillois, Roger. *Man and the Sacred* (transl. M. Barash). Glencoe, Ill., 1959.

[52] Campbell, Joseph, ed. *Man and Time* (Eranos Papers). New York, 1957.

[53] Campbell, Joseph. *The Masks of God: Primitive Mythology*. New York, 1959.

[54] Campbell, Joseph, ed. *The Mysteries* (Eranos Papers). New York, 1955.

[55] Cassirer, Ernst. *The Myth of the State*. Garden City, N.Y., Anchor paperback, 1955.

[56] Chakladar, Haran. *Social Life in Ancient India*. Calcutta, 1929.

[57] Chakravarti, C. *A Study in Hindu Social Polity*. Calcutta, 1923.

[58] Chakravarti, P. C. *The Art of War in Ancient India*. Dacca, 1941.

[59] Chang-chun, Ho. "Fa-hsien's Pilgrimage to Buddhist Countries," *Chinese Literature*, 1956 (No. 3).

[60] Chatterjee, S. C., and D. M. Datta. *An Introduction to Indian Philosophy*. Calcutta, 1950.

[61] Chattopadhyaya, Sudhakar. *Early History of Northern India from the Fall of the Mauryas to the Death of Harsa, c. 200 B.C.–A.D. 650*. Calcutta, 1958.

[62] Childe, V. Gordon. *The Aryans*. London, 1926.

[63] ———. *New Light on the Most Ancient East*. London, 1935.

[64] Christensen, Arthur. *Les Types du premier homme et du premier roi dans l'histoire légendaire des Iraniens*. Uppsala, 1918.

[65] Contenau, Georges. *La Civilization des Hittites et des Mitanniens*. Paris, 1934.

[66] Conze, Edward. *Buddhism*. Oxford, 1951.

[67] Coomaraswamy, Ananda. *Buddha and the Gospel of Buddhism*. London, 1928.

[68] ———. "Hindu Theory of State and Social Compact," *Hindustan Review*, May–June 1918.
[69] ———. *Hinduism and Buddhism*. New York, n.d.
[70] ———. *Spiritual Authority and Temporal Power in the Indian Theory of Government*. New Haven, 1942.
[71] ———. *Time and Eternity*. Ascona, 1947.
[72] Cornford, F. M. *From Religion to Philosophy*. New York, Harper Torchbooks, 1957.
[73] Coulborn, Rushton, ed. *Feudalism in History*. Princeton, 1956.
[74] Courtillier, G. *Les Anciennes civilisations de l'Inde*. Paris, 1938.
[75] Cox, Oliver Cromwell. *Caste, Class, and Race*. New York, 1948.
[76] Crooke, William. *Things Indian*. London, 1906.
[77] *Cultural Heritage of India, The*. Calcutta, n.d.
[78] Cunningham, A. (ed. S. Majumdar). *The Ancient Geography of India*. Calcutta, 1924.
[79] Dahlmann, J. *Das Altindische Volkstum und seine Bedeutung für die Gesellschaftskunde*. Köln, 1899.
[80] ———. *Mahābhārata-Studien. Part I, Genesis des Mahābhārata*, Berlin, 1899.
[81] Das, A. C. *Rig Vedic India*. Calcutta, 1921.
[82] Das, S. K. *Economic History of Ancient India*. Calcutta, 1925.
[83] DasGupta, Ramaprasad. *Crime and Punishmnet in Ancient India*. Calcutta, 1930.
[84] Dasgupta, Surendra Nath. *A History of Indian Philosophy*. Calcutta, 1922–55.
[85] ———. *A History of Sanskrit Literature: Classical Period*. Calcutta, 1947.
[86] ———. *Yoga as Philosophy and Religion*. London, 1924.
[87] Date, G. T. *The Art of War in Ancient India*. London, 1929.
[88] Davar, R. S., and K. D. P. Madon. *General Principles of Indian Law*. Bombay, 1950.
[89] Davies, C. Collin. *An Historical Atlas of the Indian Peninsula*. London, 1953.
[90] Davis, Kingsley. *The Population of India and Pakistan*. Princeton, 1951.
[91] Davy, Georges. *La Foi jurée*. Paris, 1922.
[92] DeBary, W. T., *et al.*, eds. *Sources of Indian Tradition*. New York, 1958.
[93] Derrett, J. Duncan M. "The Right to Earn in Ancient India," *Journal of the Economic and Social History of the Orient*, I (August 1957).
[94] Deussen, Paul. *The Philosophy of the Upanishads* (transl. A. S. Geden). Edinburgh, 1906.
[95] Devasthali, G. V. *Introduction to the Study of Mudra-Rakśasa*. Bombay, 1948.
[96] Dharma, P. C. *The Ramyana Polity*. Madras, 1941.
[97] Diels, Hermann, ed. *Fragmente der Vorsokratiker*. Berlin, 1906.
Dikshitar. *Vide* [336–343].
[98] Dodds, E. R. *The Greeks and the Irrational*. Boston, Beacon paperback, 1957.
[99] Dowson, J. *A Classical Dictionary of Hindu Mythology*. London, 1950.
[100] Dubois, Abbé Jean Antoine. *Hindu Manners, Customs and Ceremonies* (transl. H. K. Beauchamp). *Oxford*, 1897.
[101] Dumézil, Georges. *Aspects de la fonction guerrière chez les Indo-Européens*. Paris, 1956.
[102] ———. *L'Idéologie tripartie des Indo-Européens*. Bruxelles, 1958.
[103] ———. *Mitra-Varuṇa*. Paris, 1940.
[104] Dumont, P.-E., *L'Aśvamedha*. Paris, 1927.
[105] Durkheim, Émile. *The Elementary Forms of the Religious Life* (transl. J. W. Swain). London, 1915.

[106] Dutt, N. K. *The Aryanisation of India.* Calcutta, 1925.

[107] ———. *Origin and Growth of Caste in India.* London, 1921.

[108] Dutt, Nalinaksha. *Early Monastic Buddhism.* Calcutta, 1941, 1945.

[109] Dutt, Sukumar. *Early Buddhist Monachism, 600 B.C.–100 B.C.* London, 1924.

[110] Dutta, B. N. *Studies in Indian Social Polity.* Calcutta, 1944.

[111] Edgerton, Franklin. "Dominant Ideas in the Formation of Indian Culture," *Journal of the American Oriental Society,* LXII (1942).

[112] ———. "The Meaning of Sāṇkhya and Yoga," *American Journal of Philology,* XLV.

[113] Eggermont, Pierre. *The Chronology of the Reign of Asoka Moriya.* Leiden, 1956.

[114] Eisenstadt, S. N. "Political Struggle in Bureaucratic Societies," *World Politics,* IX (October 1956).

[115] Eliade, Mircea. *Images and Symbols* (transl. P. Mairet). New York, 1961.

[116] ———. *The Myth of the Eternal Return* (transl. W. R. Trask). New York, 1954.

[117] ———. *Yoga: Immortality and Freedom* (transl. W. R. Trask). London, 1958.

[118] Eliot, Sir Charles. *Hinduism and Buddhism.* London, 1921.

[119] Elliot, Sir Henry M. *Studies in Indian History.* Calcutta, 1953, 1954.

[120] ———, and J. Dowson, eds. *The History of India as Told by Its Own Historians.* 8 vols., London, 1867–77.

[121] Farquhar, J. N. *A Primer of Hinduism.* Oxford, 1912.

[122] Fick, Richard. *The Social Organization in North-East India in Buddha's Time.* (transl. Maitra). Calcutta, 1920.

[123] Filliozat, J., and L. Renou. *L'Inde classique.* Paris, 1947.

[124] Fingarette, Herbert. "The Ego and Mystic Selflessness," *Psychoanalysis and Psychoanalytic Review,* XLV (1958). Reprinted in Maurice Stein, *et al.,* eds. *Identity and Anxiety.* Glencoe, Ill., 1960.

[125] Fortes, Meyer, and E. E. Evans-Pritchard, eds. *African Political Systems.* London, 1940.

[126] Frankfort, Henri. *Kingship and the Gods.* Chicago, 1948.

[127] ———, et al. *Before Philosophy.* Harmondsworth, Middlesex, England, Penguin paperback, 1949.

[128] Frazer, J. G. *The Golden Bough.* Part I, *The Magic Art and the Evolution of Kings,* New York, 1935.

[129] Frazer, R. W. *Indian Thought Past and Present.* London, 1915.

[130] Freud, Sigmund. *Beyond the Pleasure Principle.* New York, 1924.

[131] ———. *Civilization and Its Discontents.* London, 1930.

[132] ———. *Totem and Tabu.* New York, 1918.

[133] Friedrich, Carl J., ed. *Authority.* Cambridge, Mass., 1958.

[134] Fustel de Coulanges, Numa Denis. *The Ancient City* (transl. W. Small). Boston, 1874.

Ganganatha Jha. *Vide* [203].

[135] Garbe, Richard. *Sāṃkhya und Yoga.* Strassburg, 1896.

[136] Garratt, G. T., ed. *The Legacy of India.* Oxford, 1937.

[137] Geldner, K. F. *Vedische Studien.* Stuttgart, 1889.

[138] Gennep, Arnold van. *Rites of Passage* (transl. Vizedom and Caffee). Chicago, 1960.

[139] Gerth, Hans H., and C. W. Mills, eds. *From Max Weber.* New York, 1946.

[140] Ghose, Aurobindo. *The Foundations of Indian Culture.* New York, 1953.

[141] Ghose, Jogendra Chandra. *Principles of Hindu Law.* Calcutta, 1906.
[142] Ghoshal, U. N. *The Agrarian System in Ancient India.* Calcutta, 1930.
[143] ———. *Studies in Indian History and Culture.* Calcutta, 1957. Originally published as *The Beginnings of Indian Historiography and Other Essays* (Calcutta, 1944).
[144] ———. *A History of Indian Political Ideas.* Bombay, 1959. Originally published as *Hindu Political Theories* (Oxford, 1927).
[145] ———. *History of Hindu Public Life.* Calcutta, 1945.
[146] ———. "On Some Recent Interpretations of the Mahābhārata Theories of Kingship," *Indian Historical Quarterly,* XXXI (1955).
[147] ———. "The Relation of the Dharma Concept to the Social and Political Order in Brahmanical Canonical Thought," *Journal of the Bihar and Orissa Research Society,* XXXVIII.
[148] Ghurye, G. S. *Caste and Race in India.* New York, 1932.
[149] Gilbert, Allan H. *Machiavelli's Prince and Its Forerunners.* Durham, N.C., 1938.
[150] Gilbert, William H., *Caste in India* (a bibliography). Washington, 1948–.
[151] Glasenapp, Helmuth von. *Der Hinduismus; Religion und Gesellschaft im heutigen Indien.* München, 1922.
[152] Glotz, G. *La Solidarité de la famille en Grèce.* Paris, 1904.
[153] Gode, P. K. *Studies in Indian Literary History.* Bombay, 1953–.
[154] Gokhale, B. G. *Buddhism and Aśoka.* Baroda, 1949.
[155] ———. "Dhammiko Dhammaraja: A Study in Buddhist Constitutional Concepts," *Indica,* Silver Jubilee Commemorative Volume, 1953.
[156] Gonda, J. *Some Observations on the Relations between 'Gods' and 'Powers' in the Veda.* 's-Gravenhage, 1957.
[157] Gopal, M. H. *Mauryan Public Finance.* London, 1935.
[158] Gordon, D. H. *The Prehistoric Background of Indian Culture.* Bombay, 1958.
[159] Govinda, A. B. *The Psychological Attitude of Early Buddhist Philosophy.* Patna, 1937.
[160] Granet, Marcel. *La Pensée chinoise.* Paris, 1934.
[161] Grousset, René. *Les Civilisations de l'Orient.* Tome II, *L'Inde,* Paris, 1930.
[162] Guénon, René. *La Métaphysique orientale.* Paris, 1946.
[163] Guérinot, Armand. *La Religion djaina.* Paris, 1926.
[164] Harrison, Jane. *Themis.* Cambridge, 1912.
[165] Hastings, J., ed. *Encyclopaedia of Religion and Ethics.* Edinburgh, 1908–26.
[166] Hauer, J. W. *Der Vrātya. Untersuchungen über die nichtbrahmanische Kultgenossenschaften arischer Herkunft.* Stuttgart, 1927.
[167] Haug, Martin. *Brahma und die Brahmanen.* München, 1871.
[168] Havell, E. B. *The History of Aryan Rule in India.* London, 1918.
[169] Hearn, G., ed. *A Handbook to India, Pakistan, Burma and Ceylon.* London, 1952.
[170] Heesterman, J. C. *The Ancient Indian Royal Consecration.* The Hague, 1957.
[171] Held, G. J. *The Mahābhārata: An Ethnological Study.* London and Amsterdam, 1935.
[172] Herodotus. *History* (transl. Rawlinson). New York, 1947.
[173] Hillebrandt, Alfred. *Altindische Politik.* Jena, 1923.
[174] ———. *Vedische Mythologie.* 2d ed., Breslau, 1927, 1929.
[175] Hiriyanna, M. *The Essentials of Indian Philosophy.* London, 1949.
[176] Hocart, A. M. *Caste.* London, 1950.
[177] ———. *Kingship.* London, 1927.

[178] Hoebel, E. Adamson. *The Law of Primitive Man.* Cambridge, Mass., 1954.
[179] Hofinger, M. *Étude sur le concile de Vaisali.* Louvain, 1946.
[180] Holtzmann, Adolph. *Das Mahabharata.* Karlsruhe, 1845–47.
[181] Hopkins, E. W. "Epic Mythology," *Grundriss der Indo-arischen Philologie und Altertumskunde,* III, 1, B, Strassburg, 1915.
[182] ———. *The Great Epic of India.* New York, 1901.
[183] ———. *India Old and New.* New York, 1902.
[184] ———. "The Social and Military Position of the Ruling Caste in Ancient India," *Journal of the American Oriental Society,* XIII (1889).
[185] Hubert, H., and M. Mauss. "Essai sur la nature et la fonction du sacrifice," *L'Année sociologique,* II (1897–98).
[186] Huizinga, Johan. *Homo Ludens.* Boston, Beacon paperback, 1955.
[187] Hume, R. E., ed. Introduction to *The Thirteen Principal Upanishads.* 2d ed., London, 1931.
[188] Humphreys, Christmas. *Buddhism.* London, 1951.
[189] Hutton, J. H. *Caste in India.* Cambridge, 1946.
[190] *Imperial Gazetteer of India,* I, Oxford, 1907.
[191] Ingalls, D. H. H. "Authority and Law in Ancient India," Supplement to the *Journal of the American Oriental Society,* XXXI (1911).
[192] Iyengar, P. T. S. *History of the Tamils to A.D. 600.* Madras, 1929.
[193] Jackson, A. M. T. "Note on the History of the Caste System," *Journal and Proceedings of the Asiatic Society of Bengal,* III, No. 7 (1907).
[194] Jacobi, Hermann. "The Dates of the Philosophical Sūtras of the Brahmans," *Journal of the American Oriental Society,* XXXI (1911).
[195] ———. *Kultur- Sprach- und Literarhistorisches dus dem Kautiliya.* Berlin, 1911.
[196] ———. *Mahābhārata: Inhaltsangabe, Index und Konkordanz der Kalcuttaer und Bombayer Ausgaben.* Bonn, 1903.
[197] James, E. O. *Myths and Ritual in the Ancient Near East.* London, 1958.
[198] ———. *Origins of Sacrifice.* London, 1933.
[199] Jayaswal, K. P. *Hindu Polity.* 2d ed. (combined volume). Bangalore, 1943.
[200] ———. *History of India 150 A.D.–350 A.D.* Lahore, 1933.
[201] ———. *Manu and Yajñavalkya: A Comparison and a Contrast.* Calcutta, 1930.
[202] Jha. Balabhadra. "Village in Ancient India," *Journal of the Bihar Research Society,* XLI.
[203] Jha, Ganganatha. *Hindu Law in Its Sources.* Allahabad, 1930.
[204] Jolly, J. *Hindu Law and Custom* (transl. B. K. Ghosh). Calcutta, 1928.
[205] ———. *Outlines of an History of the Hindu Law of Partition, Inheritance, and Adoption.* Calcutta, 1885.
[206] Jones, Sir William. *Institutes of Hindu Law.* Calcutta, 1877.
[207] Jouvenel, Bertrand de. *Sovereignty.* Chicago, 1957.
[208] Kane, P. V. *History of Dharmaśastra.* Poona, 1930–1946.
[209] Katre, S. M., and D. K. Gode, eds. *A Volume of Studies in Indology.* Poona, 1941.
[210] Keith, Arthur Berriedale. "The Authenticity of the Kautiliya," *Journal of the Royal Asiatic Society,* January 1916.
[211] ———. *Buddhist Philosophy in India and Ceylon.* Oxford, 1923.
[212] ———. *A History of Sanskrit Literature.* Oxford, 1928.
[213] ———. *The Religion and Philosophy of the Veda, and Upanishads* (Harvard Oriental Series, Vols. XXXI, XXXII). Cambridge, Mass., 1925.
[214] ———. *The Sāṁkhya System.* New York, 1918.
[215] Kern, Fritz. *Aśoka: Kaiser und Missionar.* Bern, 1956.

[216] Ketkar, S. V. *History of Caste in India.* Ithaca, N.Y., 1909.

[217] Konow, S. *Kautalya Studies.* Oslo, 1945.

[218] Kosambi, D. D. *Introduction to the Study of Indian History.* Bombay, 1956.

[219] ———. "The Origin of the Brahmin Gotras," *Journal of the Bombay Branch of the Royal Asiatic Society,* XXVI.

[220] Kosambi, D. D., ed. Introduction to *Subhāṣitaratnakosa.* (Harvard Oriental Series, Vol. XLII). Cambridge, Mass., 1957.

[221] Kosambi, D. D. "The Text of the Arthaśastra," *Journal of the American Oriental Society,* LXXVIII (1958).

[222] Krishna Rao, M. V. *Studies in Kautilya.* Mysore, 1953.

[223] Krishnamachariar, M. *History of Classical Sanskrit Literature.* Madras, 1937.

[224] Krishnaswamy Aiyangar, S. *Evolution of Hindu Administrative Institutions in South India.* Madras, 1931.

Kumaraswami. *Vide* [67–71].

[225] Lamotte, Étienne. *Histoire du bouddhisme indien.* Tome I, *Des Origines à l'ère Sāka.* Louvain, 1958.

[226] La Vallée Poussin, Louis de. *Bouddhisme.* 3d ed., Paris, 1925.

[227] ———. *Indo-Européens et Indo-Iraniens.* Paris, 1936.

[228] Law, Bimala Churn. *Ancient Indian Tribes.* Lahore, 1926; Vol. II, London, 1934.

[229] ———. *A History of Pali Literature.* London, 1933.

[230] ———. *Some Kshatriya Tribes of Ancient India.* Calcutta, 1924.

[231] Law, Narendra Nath. *Aspects of Ancient Hindu Polity.* Oxford, 1921.

[232] ———. *Interstate Relations in Ancient India.* London, 1920.

[233] ———. *Studies in Ancient Hindu Polity.* London, 1914.

[234] ———. *Studies in Indian History and Culture.* London, 1925.

[235] Lévi, Sylvain. *La Doctrine du sacrifice dans les Brāhmanas.* Paris, 1898.

[236] ———. *L'Inde civilisatrice.* Paris, 1938.

[237] Lévy-Bruhl, L. *Les Fonctions mentales dans les sociétés inférieures.* Paris, 1910.

[238] Linton, Ralph. *The Tree of Culture.* New York, 1959.

[239] Löwith, Karl. *Meaning in History.* Chicago, 1949.

[240] Lyall, A. C. *Asiatic Studies: Religious and Social.* London, 1907.

[241] Macdonell, A. A. *A History of Sanskrit Literature.* London, 1917.

[242] ———. *Vedic Mythology.* Strassburg, 1897.

[243] Macdonell, A. A., and A. B. Keith. *Vedic Index.* London, 1912.

[244] McIllwain, Charles H. *The Growth of Political Thought in the West.* New York, 1932.

[245] Mackay, Ernest. *The Indus Civilization.* London, 1935.

[246] McPhail, J. M. *Aśoka.* Calcutta, 1926.

[247] Mahalingam, T. V. *South Indian Polity.* Madras, 1955.

[248] Maine, Sir Henry. *Ancient Law.* London, 1931.

[249] Maity, S. K. *Economic Life of Northern India in the Gupta Period A.D. 300–500.* Calcutta, 1958.

[250] Majumdar, R. C. *Corporate Life in Ancient India.* Calcutta, 1922.

[251] Majumdar, R. C., and A. D. Pusalker, eds. *The History and Culture of the Indian People.* Vol. I, *The Vedic Age,* London, 1951; Vol. II, *The Age of Imperial Unity,* Bombay, 1951; Vol. III, *The Classical Age,* Bombay, 1954.

[252] Majumdar, R. C., *et al. An Advanced History of India* (combined volume). London, 1952.

[253] Malinowski, B. *Myth in Primitive Psychology.* London, 1926.

[254] Mandelbaum, David G. "Materials for a Bibliography of the Ethnology of

India." Unpublished manuscript, Dept. of Anthropology, University of California, Berkeley, 1949.

[255] Marcuse, Herbert. *Eros and Civilization.* Boston, 1955.

[256] Marsh, Robert M. *The Mandarins: The Circulation of Elites in China.* Glencoe, Ill., 1961.

[257] Marshall, J. *Mohenjo-Daro and the Indus Civilization.* London, 1931.

[258] Martiis, Salvatore de. *Socialismo Antico.* Torino, 1880.

[259] Masson-Oursel, P., *et al. Ancient India and Indian Civilization* (transl. M. R. Dobie). London, 1934.

[260] Mauss, Marcel. *The Gift: Forms and Functions of Exchange in Archaic Societies* (transl. I. Cunnison). Glencoe, Ill., 1954.

[261] May, Rollo, ed. *Symbolism in Religion and Literature.* New York, 1960.

[262] Mayne, J. D. *A Treatise on Hindu Law and Usage.* Madras, 1892.

[263] Mazumdar, Haridas. "Hindu Group Concepts" (unpublished M. A. thesis, Northwestern University, 1926).

[264] Mees, Gualtherus H. *Dharma and Society.* The Hague, 1935.

[265] Mehta, R. N. *Pre-Buddhist India.* Bombay, 1939.

[266] Merton, Robert. *Social Theory and Social Structure.* Glencoe, Ill., 1949.

[267] Merton, Robert, *et al.,* eds., *Sociology Today.* New York, 1959.

[268] Meyer, Johann Jakob. *Über das Wesen der altindischen Rechtsschriften und ihr Verhältnis zu einander und zu Kauṭilya.* Leipzig, 1927.

[269] Mode, Heinz. *Indische Frühkulturen und ihre Beziehungen zum Westen.* Basel, 1944.

[270] Monier-Williams, Monier. *Brahmanism and Hinduism.* London, 1891.

[271] Mookerji, Radhakumud. *Aśoka.* London, 1928.

[272] ———. *Chandragupta Maurya and His Times.* Madras, 1943.

[273] ———. *The Gupta Empire.* Bombay, 1948.

[274] ———. *Harsha.* London, 1926.

[275] ———. *Hindu Civilisation.* London, 1936.

[276] ———. *Local Government in Ancient India.* Oxford, 1919.

[277] ———. *Men and Thought in Ancient India.* London, 1924.

[278] Moore, Barrington, Jr. *Political Power and Social Theory.* Cambridge, Mass., 1958.

[279] Moreland, W. H., and A. Chatterji. *A Short History of India.* London, 1936.

[280] Moret, A., and G. Davy. *From Tribe to Empire.* New York, 1926.

[281] Morgan, Kenneth W., ed. *The Religion of the Hindus.* New York, 1953.

[282] Motwani, K. *Manu: A Study in Hindu Social Theory.* Madras, 1937.

[283] Muir, John, ed. *Original Sanskrit Texts on the Origin and History of the People of India.* London, 1872–74.

[284] Mulla, D. F. *Principles of Hindu Law.* Bombay, 1912.

[285] Müller, F. Max. *History of Ancient Sanskrit Literature.* London, 1860.

[286] ———. *India: What Can It Teach Us?* New York, 1883.

[287] ———. *Selected Essays on Language, Mythology and Religion.* London, 1881.

[288] ———. *The Six Systems of Indian Philosophy.* New York, 1899.

[289] Murray, Gilbert. *Five Stages of Greek Religion.* Garden City, N.Y., Anchor paperback, n.d.

[290] Nag, Kalidas. *Les Théories diplomatiques de l'Inde ancienne et l'Arthacastra,* Paris, 1923.

[291] Naik, B. B. *Ideals of Ancient Hindu Politics.* Dharwar, 1932.

[292] Narain, A. K. *The Indo-Greeks.* Oxford, 1957.

[293] Nehru, Jawaharlal. *The Discovery of India.* London, 1946.

[294] Nesfield, J. C. *Brief View of the Caste System of the North-West Provinces and Oudh.* Allahabad, 1885.

[295] Nikam, K. A., and Richard McKeon. *The Edicts of Asoka.* Chicago, 1959.

[296] Nilakanta Sastri, K. A., ed. *Age of the Nandas and Mauryas.* Benares, 1952.

[297] Nilakanta Sastri, K. A. *The Colas.* Madras, 1935–37.

[298] ———. *Factors in Indian History.* Waltair, 1949.

[299] ———. *History of India.* Vol. I, *Ancient India*, Madras, 1953.

[300] ———. *A History of South India from Prehistoric Times to the Fall of Vijayanagar.* Madras, 1955.

[301] ———. *The Pandyan Kingdom from the Earliest Times to the Sixteenth Century.* London, 1929.

[302] ———. "The Place of Arthaśastra in the History of Indian Polity," *Annals of the Bhandarkar Research Institute,* XXVIII.

[303] ———. *Studies in Chola History and Administration.* Madras, 1932.

[304] ———. *The Theory of Pre-Muslim Indian Polity.* Madras, 1912.

[305] Northrop, F. S. C. *The Meeting of East and West.* New York, 1947.

[306] Oldenberg, Hermann. *Ancient India.* Chicago, 1898.

[307] ———. *Buddha: His Life, his Doctrine, his Order* (transl. W. Hoey). London, 1882.

[308] ———. *Die Lehre der Upanishaden und die Anfänge des Buddhismus.* Göttingen, 1915.

[309] ———. *Die Religion des Veda.* Berlin, 1894.

[310] Olmstead, A. T. *History of the Persian Empire.* Chicago, 1949.

[311] Oppert, Gustav. *On the Weapons, Army Organization, and Political Maxims of the Ancient Hindus.* Madras, 1880.

[312] Panikkar, K. M. *The Origin and Evolution of Kingship in India.* Baroda, 1938.

[313] Pant, Ramachandra. *Amatya: Royal Edict on the Principles of State Policy.* Madras, 1929.

[314] Paranavitana, S. "Two Royal Titles," *Journal of the Royal Asiatic Society,* 1936.

[315] Pargiter, F. E. *Ancient Indian Historical Tradition.* London, 1922.

[316] Parsons, Talcott. *The Social System.* Glencoe, Ill., 1951.

[317] ———. *Structure and Process in Modern Societies.* Glencoe, Ill., 1960.

[318] ———. *The Structure of Social Action.* 2d ed., Glencoe, Ill., 1949.

[319] Parsons, Talcott, *et al. Working Papers in the Theory of Action.* Glencoe, Ill., 1953.

[320] Piggott, Stuart. *Prehistoric India.* Harmondsworth, Middlesex, England, Penguin paperback, 1950.

[321] Plutarch's *Lives.* New York, Mentor paperback, 1950. (Abridged.)

[322] Prasad, Beni. *The State in Ancient India.* Allahabad, 1928.

[323] ———. *Theory of Government in Ancient India.* Allahabad, 1927.

[324] Prasad, Ishwari. *Medieval Indian History.* Allahabad, 1928.

[325] Prinsep, J. *Essays on Indian Antiquities.* London, 1858.

[326] Przyluski, J. *Légende de l'empereur Aśoka.* Paris, 1923.

[327] Radhakrishnan, Sarvepalli, ed. Introduction to *The Bhagavadgītā.* London, 1948.

[328] Radhakrishnan, Sarvepalli. *Eastern Religion and Western Thought.* London, 1939.

[329] ———. *The Hindu View of Life.* London, 1927.

[330] ———. *Indian Philosophy.* London, 1948.

[331] ———. *The Philosophy of the Upanishads.* London, 1924.

[332] ———. *Religion and Society.* London, 1947.

[333] Raghavan, V., *Kalidasa and Kautalya.* Nagpur, 1946.

[334] ———. "Some Leading Ideas of Hindu Thought," *The Vedanta Kesari,* XLI, No. 10 (February 1955).

[335] Raj, Dev. *L'Esclavage dans l'Inde ancienne d'après les textes palis et sanskrits.* Pondichéry, 1957.

[336] Ramachandra Dikshitar, V. R. *Gupta Polity.* Madras, 1952.

[337] ———. *Hindu Administrative Institutions.* Madras, 1929.

[338] ———. "Kāmandakīya Nītisāra," *Journal of Indian History,* XXVIII, part 1.

[339] ———. *The Mauryan Polity.* Madras, 1932.

[340] ———. "Notes on the Paura-Janapada," *Indian Historical Quarterly,* VI.

[341] ———. *Puranic Index.* Madras, 1952 [not completed].

[342] ———. *Studies in Tamil Literature and History.* London, 1930.

[343] ———. *War in Ancient India.* Madras, 1948.

[344] Ramaswami Aiyer, C. P. *Indian Political Theories.* Madras, 1937.

[345] ———. *The Philosophical Basis of Indian Legal and Social Systems.* Madras, 1949.

[346] Rangaswami Aiyangar, K. V. *Aspects of Ancient Indian Economic Thought.* Benares, 1934.

[347] ———. *Aspects of the Social and Political System of Manusmriti.* Lucknow, 1949.

[348] ———. *Indian Cameralism.* Madras, 1941.

[349] ———. *Rajadharma.* Madras, 1941.

[350] ———. *Some Aspects of Ancient Indian Polity.* Madras, 1935.

[351] ———. *Some Aspects of the Hindu View of Life According to Dharmaśastra.* Baroda, 1952.

[352] Rapson, Edward J., ed. *Cambridge History of India.* Vol. I, *Ancient India.* Cambridge, 1922.

[353] Rawlinson, H. G. *Intercourse Between India and the Western World.* Cambridge, 1916.

[354] Ray, H. C. "Position of the Brāhmaṇas in the Arthaśāstra," *Proceedings of the All-India Oriental Conference,* 1924.

[355] Raychaudhuri, H. C. *Political History of Ancient India.* Calcutta, 1938.

[356] Renou, Louis. *La Civilisation de l'Inde ancienne.* Paris, 1950.

[357] ———. *Études védiques et pāninéennes,* Tome I. Paris, 1955. (Publications de l'Institut de Civilisation Indienne, Série in 8°, fasc. 2.)

[358] ———. *Religions of Ancient India.* London, 1953.

[359] Rhys Davids, T. W. *Buddhism, Its History and Literature.* New York, 1896.

[360] ———. *Buddhist India.* New York, 1903.

[361] Rhys Davids, T. W., ed. *Dialogues of the Buddha.* London, 1910.

[362] Rhys Davids, T. W. *Early Buddhism.* London, 1908.

[363] Rice, Stanley. *Hindu Customs and Their Origins.* London, 1937.

[364] ———. "The Origins of Caste," *Asiatic Review,* XXV.

[365] Riencourt, Amaury de. *The Soul of India.* New York, 1960.

[366] Riepe, Dale. *The Naturalistic Tradition in Indian Thought.* Seattle, Wash., 1961.

[367] Risley, H. H. *The People of India.* Calcutta, 1908.

[368] Rohde, Erwin. *Psyche.* Freiburg, 1898.

[369] Rostovtzeff, M. I. *The Social and Economic History of the Hellenistic World.* Oxford, 1941.

[370] Rowland, Benjamin. *The Art and Architecture of India.* London, 1953.

[371] Russell, R. V. *The Tribes and Castes of the Central Provinces of India.* 4 vols., London, 1916.

[372] Saletore, Bhasker. *India's Diplomatic Relations with the East.* Bombay, 1960.

[373] ———. *India's Diplomatic Relations with the West.* Bombay, 1958.

[374] Samaddar, J. N. *Economic Conditions of Ancient India.* Calcutta, 1922.

[375] Saran, K. M. *Labor in Ancient India.* Bombay, 1957.

[376] Sarkar, Benoy Kumar. *Creative India.* Lahore, 1937.

[377] ———. *Political Institutions and Theories of the Hindus.* Leipzig, 1922.

[378] ———. *Positive Backgrounds of Hindu Sociology.* Book I (in revised edition), *Introduction to Hindu Positivism.* Allahabad, 1937; Book II, *Political,* Allahabad, 1921.

[379] Sarkar, S. C. *Some Aspects of the Earliest Social History of India.* London, 1928.

[380] Sartre, Jean-Paul. *Being and Nothingness.* New York, 1956.

Sastri. *Vide* [297–304], [388].

[381] Schwab, R. *La Renaissance orientale.* Paris, 1950.

[382] Sen, Ajit Kumar. *The Islamic State and Other Political Essays.* Calcutta, 1950.

[383] ———. *Studies in Hindu Political Thought.* Calcutta, 1926.

[384] Sen, P. N. *The General Principles of Hindu Jurisprudence.* Calcutta, 1918.

[385] Senart, Émile. *Caste in India* (transl. E. D. Ross). London, 1930.

[386] Sen-Gupta, N. C. *Evolution of Ancient Indian Law.* Calcutta, 1953.

[387] ———. *Sources of Law and Society in Ancient India.* Calcutta, 1914.

[388] Shama Sastri, R. *Evolution of Indian Polity.* Calcutta, 1920.

[389] Sharma, Ram Sharan. *Aspects of Political Ideas and Institutions in Ancient India.* Delhi, 1959.

[390] ———. "The Origins of Feudalism in India," *Journal of the Economic and Social History of the Orient,* I part 3.

[391] ———. *Śudras in Ancient India.* Delhi, 1958.

[392] Shastri, Jagdish Lal. *Political Thought in the Purāṇas.* Lahore, 1944.

[393] Sinha, B. P. "The Kautiliyan State," *Journal of the Bihar Research Society,* XL, No. 2.

[394] ———. "The King in the Kautiliyan State," *Journal of the Bihar Research Society,* XL, No. 3.

[395] Sinha, H. N. *Sovereignty in Ancient Indian Polity.* London, 1938.

[396] Smith, R. Morton. "On the Ancient Chronology of India," *Journal of the American Oriental Society,* LXXVII, 1957, Nos. 2, 4; LXXVIII, 1958, No. 3.

[397] Smith, Vincent. *Aśoka.* Oxford, 1920.

[398] ———. *The Early History of India from 600 B.C. to the Muhammadan Conquest.* Oxford, 1924.

[399] Söderblom, Nathan. *Das Werden des Gottesglaubens.* Leipzig, 1926.

[400] Srinivas, M. N., "A Note on Sanskritization and Westernization," *The Far Eastern Quarterly,* XV, No. 4.

[401] Srinivasa Murti, G., and A. N. Krishna Aiyangar. *Edicts of Aśoka.* Madras, 1950.

[402] Srinivasichari, C. S. "Some Phases of South Indian Polity," *Maharajah's College Magazine* (Vizianagaram), IV, No. 3.

[403] Stein, Otto. *Megasthenes und Kautilya.* Wien, 1921.

[404] Strauss, Leo. *Natural Right and History.* Chicago, 1953.

[405] Subba Rao, N. S. *Economic and Political Conditions in Ancient India as Described in the Jatakas.* Mysore, 1911.

[406] Tarn, W. W. *The Greeks in Bactria and India.* Cambridge, 1938.

[407] Thapar, Romila. *Aśoka and the Decline of the Mauryas.* London, 1961.

[408] Thomas, E. J. *History of Buddhist Thought.* London, 1933.

[409] ———. *The Life of Buddha as Legend and History.* New York, 1927.

[410] Thomas, Elbert D. *Chinese Political Thought.* New York, 1927.

[411] Timmer, B. C. J. *Megasthenes en de Indische Maatschappij.* Amsterdam, 1930.

[412] Tod, James. *Annals and Antiquities of Rajasthan.* Madras, 1873.

[413] Turner, Ralph. *The Great Cultural Traditions.* Vol. I, *The Ancient Cities,* New York, 1941.

[414] Tylor, Edward B. *Primitive Culture.* London, 1871.

[415] Underhill, Evelyn. *Mysticism.* New York, 1955.

[416] Varma, Vishwanath Prasad. "The Origins and Sociology of Buddhist Pessimism," *Journal of the Bihar Research Society,* XLIV.

[417] ———. "Studies in Hindu Political Thought and Its Metaphysical Foundations," *Journal of the Bihar Research Society,* XXXVIII, XXXIX.

[418] Venkateswara, S. V. *Indian Culture Through the Ages.* Vol. II, *Public Life and Political Institutions,* London, 1932.

[419] Voegelin, Eric. *Order and History.* Vol. I, *Israel and Revelation,* Baton Rouge, 1956.

[420] Waddell, L. A. *Report on the Excavations at Pataliputra.* Calcutta, 1903.

[421] Warmington, E. H. *Commerce Between the Roman Empire and India.* Cambridge, 1928.

[422] Watters, Thomas. *On Yuan Chwang's Travels in India.* London, 1904–5.

[423] Weber, Max. *The City* (transl. D. Martindale and G. Neuwirth). Glencoe, Ill., 1958.

[424] ———. *The Protestant Ethic and the Spirit of Capitalism* (transl. Talcott Parsons). New York, 1930.

[425] ———. *The Religion of India* (transl. H. Gerth and D. Martindale). Glencoe, Ill., 1958. Originally published in his *Gesammelte Aufsätze zur Religionsoziologie,* Band II, *Hinduismus und Buddhismus,* Tübingen, 1923. See also [139].

[426] Wheeler, R. E. M. *Early India and Pakistan to Ashoka.* New York, 1959.

[427] ———. *The Indus Civilization.* Cambridge, 1953.

[428] Wikander, Stig. "Pāṇḍava-sagan och Mahābhāratas mytiska förutsättningar," *Religion och Bibel,* VI (1947).

[429] ———. "Sur le fonds commun indo-iranien des épopées de la Perse et de l'Inde," *La Nouvelle Clio,* VII.

[430] Wilhelm, Friedrich. "Das Wirtschaftssystem des Kauṭalīya Arthaśāstra," *Journal of the Economic and Social History of the Orient,* II, part 3.

[431] Winch, Peter. *The Idea of a Social Science.* London, 1958.

[432] Winternitz, Maurice. *A History of Indian Literature* (transl. S. Ketkar). Calcutta, 1927–33.

[433] Wittfogel, K. *Oriental Despotism.* New Haven, 1957.

[434] Wolin, Sheldon. *Politics and Vision.* Boston, 1960.

[435] Wu, Kuo-cheng. *Ancient Chinese Political Theories.* Shanghai, 1928.

[436] Zaehner, R. C. *Mysticism, Sacred and Profane.* Oxford, 1957.

[437] Zimmer, Heinrich (d. 1910). *Altindisches Leben.* Berlin, 1879.

[438] Zimmer, Heinrich (d. 1943). *The Art of Indian Asia.* New York, 1955.

[439] ———. *The King and the Corpse.* 2d ed., New York, 1956.

[440] ———. *Myths and Symbols in Indian Art* (ed. J. Campbell). New York, 1946.

[441] ———. *Philosophies of India* (ed. J. Campbell). New York, 1951.

INDEX

Following certain entries are letters indicating these six categories: king or emperor (k); legendary hero, heroine, or king (h); teacher, author, or redactor (t); god, goddess, demon, or cosmic principle (g); religion, sect, or form of devotion or discipline (r); state, dynasty, or tribe (s). Page numbers in italics indicate chief sources.

METHODIST COLLEGE, FAYETTEVILLE N.C.

3 7110 0008 0363 9

915.4
D771k

Drekmeier, Charles

Kingship and community
in early India

WITHDRAWN

34117